Cambridge Studies in the History and Theory of Politics

EDITORS

Maurice Cowling   G. R. Elton
J. R. Pole

ENGLISH SOCIETY 1688–1832

ENGLISH SOCIETY
1688–1832

*Ideology, social structure and
political practice during the
ancien regime*

J. C. D. CLARK

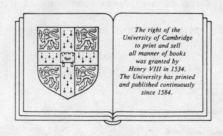

The right of the
University of Cambridge
to print and sell
all manner of books
was granted by
Henry VIII in 1534.
The University has printed
and published continuously
since 1584.

CAMBRIDGE UNIVERSITY PRESS

Cambridge
New York   New Rochelle
Melbourne   Sydney

Published by the Press Syndicate of the University of Cambridge
The Pitt Building, Trumpington Street, Cambridge CB2 1RP
32 East 57th Street, New York, NY, 10022, USA
10 Stamford Road, Oakleigh, Melbourne 3166, Australia

First published 1985
Reprinted 1986, 1988

Printed in Great Britain by the University Press, Cambridge

British Library cataloguing in publication data

Clark, J. C. D.
English society 1688–1832: ideology, social
structure and political practice during the ancien
regime. – (Cambridge studies in the history and
theory of politics)
1. Great Britain – Politics and government – 1689–1702
2. Great Britain – Politics and government –18th century
3. Great Britain – Politics and government – 1800–1837
I. Title
320.942 JN205

Library of Congress cataloguing in publication data

Clark, J. C. D.
English society, 1688–1832.
(Cambridge studies in the history and theory of
politics)
Includes bibliographical references.
1. Great Britain – Politics and government – 1689–1702.
2. Great Britain – Politics and government – 18th century.
3. Great Britain – Politics and government – 1800–1837.
4. Great Britain – Social conditions. I. Title.
II. Series
JN175.C58 1985   320.941   85-10995

ISBN 0 521 30922 0 hardcovers
ISBN 0 521 31383 X paperback

UP

...bad history often has a wider and longer currency than good history...

Sir Herbert Butterfield, *Cambridge Review*,
25 May 1957, p. 614.

The foremost task of honest history is to discredit and drive out its futile or dishonest varieties.

Sir Lewis Namier, *Avenues of History* (London, 1952), p. 6.

Contents

Preface	*page* ix	
Abbreviations	xi	
Note on Terminology	xiii	
Introduction	I	

I   REPRESENTATION AND OLIGARCHY IN ENGLAND FROM
THE REVOLUTION TO THE REFORM BILL: AN
HISTORIOGRAPHICAL SURVEY   8

    I. Preliminary   8
    II. The Psephological Argument   15
    III. The Party Argument   26
    IV. Conclusion   38

2   POLITICAL THEORY, PATRIARCHALISM AND CULTURAL
HEGEMONY: ENGLAND AS AN ARISTOCRATIC SOCIETY,
1688–1832   42

    I. Political Theory and Social Inference, Locke to Mill   42
    II. The Survival of Patriarchalism: or, Did the Industrial
Revolution Really Happen?   64
    III. The Social Theory of Elite Hegemony   93

3   THE SURVIVAL OF THE DYNASTIC IDIOM, 1688–1760: AN
ESSAY IN THE SOCIAL HISTORY OF IDEAS   119

    I. Preliminary   119
    II. Divine Right as a Political Strategy   121
    III. Divine Right as an Underground Loyalty   141
    IV. Allegiance, Religion and the Folk Culture   161
    V. The Transformation of Divine Right Ideology,
1745–1760   173
    VI. Conclusion: Law, Ideology, Allegiance   189

vii

4 THE SELF-IMAGE OF THE STATE: THE CASE FOR THE
   ESTABLISHMENT, 1760–1815   199
      I. Introduction   199
     II. The Royal Prerogative: Constitutional Controversy
         from Blackstone to Holland House   201
    III. Orthodox Anglican Political Theology, 1760–1793   216
    IV. The Political Theology of Methodism and
         Evangelicalism, 1760–1832   235
     V. Burke and the Anglican Defence of the State   247
    VI. Church-and-State: Anglicans versus Radicals,
         1789–1815   258

5 THE IDEOLOGICAL ORIGINS OF ENGLISH RADICALISM,
   1688–1800   277
      I. Introduction   277
     II. Deism, Arianism, Socinianism: the Official Reaction   279
    III. Heterodoxy, Convocation and Parliamentary
         Representation   289
    IV. The Impact of Heterodoxy, 1714–1754   299
     V. Radical Theory c. 1745–1765: Wilkes and the Revival
         of Socinianism in the Church of England   307
    VI. Dissent and its Aims, 1714–1775   315
   VII. Tom Paine and William Godwin   324
  VIII. Richard Price and Joseph Priestley   330
    IX. The Impact of Heterodoxy, 1772–1800   335
     X. Conclusion   346

6 THE END OF THE ANCIEN REGIME, 1800–1832   349
      I. The Ideology of the Old Society   349
     II. Business as Usual, 1800–1815   359
    III. Democracy, Demography, Dissent: the Erosion of the
         Old Society   366
    IV. The Defence of the Protestant Constitution, 1815–1827   383
     V. 'A Revolution Gradually Accomplished', 1827–1832   393
    VI. Consequences   408

Afterword   421

Index   425

Preface

In historical writing, we move from the particular to the general, and then back to the particular. Detailed research generates ideas which invite application over a wide field, and this in turn leads us back to particular studies to check and revise our general theories. In *The Dynamics of Change*, published in 1982, I undertook an examination in depth of a particular high-political crisis in England in the 1750s. My research suggested a solution to a technical problem which had been debated by political historians for several decades: what was the party structure which articulated English politics in the mid-eighteenth century, and, consequently, what dominant ideological issues can we infer from those tactical configurations? I believed that I could show, by an exhaustive narrative, how the traditional parties of Whig and Tory, dating from the 1690s, had been profoundly damaged in the crisis of 1754–7 in such a way as to bring about their inclusion under the aegis of the Pitt–Newcastle wartime coalition, so that, when the coalition broke up in the 1760s, the old party polarity was seen to have dissolved.

This seemed to me to be a thesis of wide implications; but the remorseless detail of *The Dynamics of Change* evidently obscured them. Some of the implications I had already outlined in an article in the *Historical Journal* in 1980, suggesting a new synoptic framework for the party-political history of 1688–1832. Nevertheless, the implications were clearly more evident to me than to my colleagues. This book explores far more widely the consequences of my initial study. Some of its suggestions are methodological, an attempt to identify instances of anachronism and teleology which are made to support the commonly-received historicist picture of eighteenth-century England. Others of its suggestions are substantive, especially on questions of political ideology, religion, psephology, social structure and cultural hegemony. My aim throughout has been to re-integrate religion into an historical vision which has been almost wholly positivist; to discard economic reductionism; to emphasise the importance of politics in social

ix

history; and to argue against the familiar picture of eighteenth-century England as the era of bourgeois individualism by showing the persistence of the ancien regime until 1828–32, and the autonomous importance of religion and politics in its final demise.

Historians who know a great deal about a carefully defined and chronologically limited subject tend to be very fierce (like the present author with his first book). They think, sometimes rightly, that they can make a useful approach to precision in answering the exact questions they have set themselves. The wider the canvas, the more diverse the themes, the more humble the historian. I have tried here to develop some new hypotheses, analyses and syntheses in many areas and over a wide time span: the larger part of that period which still languishes as the 'suppressed third' of English history since the Reformation, the period of the ancien regime between the Restoration in 1660 and the Reform Bill in 1832. Hardly ever have I had space for the sort of detailed documentation which the subjects demand and the perfectionist wishes to give: I am very conscious of how much more there is to be said on all the themes I deal with here. This book is offered as a breach of the historiographical peace, not as an obituary of its subject: as an attempt to stimulate a new debate, not as an attempt to bring an old debate to an end by a precise and definite statement.

Scholarship can hardly be undertaken alone, and I am grateful to all those with whom I have discussed the issues dealt with here. For their criticisms and suggestions I am particularly grateful to Professors Derek Beales, G. R. Elton, J. R. Pole, Edward Shils, Judith Shklar, John Shy and Gordon S. Wood, and to Drs P. F. Clarke, Eveline Cruickshanks, John Dinwiddy, Grayson Ditchfield, Eamon Duffy, Howard Erskine-Hill, John Morrill and John Walsh. In so desperately underpopulated an area of academic life, it is good to have such colleagues. None of them, of course, is necessarily in agreement with the arguments developed here. Professor Ian R. Christie stands in a class of his own as a wise and generous counsellor over many years, and readers may also trace in these pages the influence of my late friend Sir Herbert Butterfield. Dr W. E. K. Anderson and Dr V. A. C. Gatrell contributed more even than they intended; to my pupils at Eton and Cambridge, and my friends at Baldwin's Shore, I owe a special debt.

The research for this book was undertaken during my tenure of a Research Fellowship of the Leverhulme Trust. I gratefully acknowledge the support of that body, and, at other times, of the British Academy and of the Political Science Fund of the University of Cambridge.

September 1984

Abbreviations

AHR	*American Historical Review*
BIHR	*Bulletin of the Institute of Historical Research*
BJECS	*British Journal for Eighteenth Century Studies*
Bolingbroke, *Works*	*The Works of Lord Bolingbroke* (4 vols., London, 1844)
Burke, *Works*	*The Works of the Right Honourable Edmund Burke* (Nimmo edn, 12 vols., London, 1887)
Cannon, *Parliamentary Reform*	John Cannon, *Parliamentary Reform 1640–1832* (Cambridge, 1973)
Dickinson, *Liberty and Property*	H. T. Dickinson, *Liberty and Property. Political Ideology in Eighteenth-Century Britain* (London, 1977)
EcHR	*Economic History Review*
ECS	*Eighteenth Century Studies*
EHR	*English Historical Review*
HJ	*Historical Journal*
HLQ	*Huntington Library Quarterly*
Holdsworth	Sir William Holdsworth, *A History of English Law* (16 vols., London, 1903–66)
JBS	*Journal of British Studies*
JHI	*Journal of the History of Ideas*
JMH	*Journal of Modern History*
Kenyon, *Revolution Principles*	J. P. Kenyon, *Revolution Principles. The Politics of Party 1689–1720* (Cambridge, 1977)
Macaulay, *Works*	*The Works of Lord Macaulay* (Albany edn, 12 vols., London, 1898)
Nichols, *Literary Anecdotes*	John Nichols, *Literary Anecdotes of the Eighteenth Century* (9 vols., London, 1812)

P&P	*Past and Present*
Parl Debs	*The Parliamentary Debates from the Year 1803 to the Present Time* (ed. T. C. Hansard, London, 1812–)
Parl Hist	*The Parliamentary History of England, from the Earliest Period to the Year 1803* (ed. W. Cobbett, 36 vols., London, 1806–20)
Sedgwick	R. R. Sedgwick (ed.), *The History of Parliament. The House of Commons, 1715–1754* (2 vols., London, 1970)
Stephen, *English Thought*	Sir Leslie Stephen, *History of English Thought in the Eighteenth Century* (1876; ed. C. Brinton, 2 vols., London and New York, 1962)
TRHS	*Transactions of the Royal Historical Society*
WMQ	*William and Mary Quarterly*

Note on terminology

'Arian(ism)' and 'Socinian(ism)' were technical theological terms, and in the early part of the period covered the names were not admitted to by the proponents of these ideas; 'Unitarian' was brought into general use from the late 1760s as a euphemism, applied by Arians and Socinians to themselves, and denoting their identity as a group. 'Agnostic' is of Victorian origin; the eighteenth-century term for 'non-Christian' is 'infidel'. The word 'Orthodox', with a capital O, signifies the mainstream of the Church of England in succession to the High Church party of Anne's reign – Trinitarian, Arminian, apostolic, socially conservative. Without the capital, 'orthodox' carries a general, non-partisan meaning. Similarly, 'Evangelical' refers to a movement or group within the Church; 'evangelical' denotes a general attitude or position. The sense in which 'Whig' and 'Tory', 'Court' and 'Country' are used is explained in my article in the *Historical Journal* 23 (1980), 295–325. The reasons for the rejection of the later terminology of 'class', 'liberal(ism)', 'radical(ism)', 'bourgeois', 'Industrial Revolution' and their associated nexus of ideas are set out below. The term 'radical' is used in this book as a deliberate anachronism, in an attempt to identify phenomena which filled the place that 'radicalism' later filled; in future works one would wish to dispense with the word altogether in favour of an authentically ancien-regime terminology. The title of chapter 5 is a concession to current expectations: the text will be found to argue against the teleology which the title implies.

Introduction

This is a revisionist tract. It ventures to sound a note of dissent from the methodological conventions which I have come to realise are almost universally shared by a particular cohort of scholars who have worked in this field in recent decades, the heirs of the 'Whig interpretation of history'. Secondly, it begins the attempt to outline an alternative model of English society under the ancien regime, built now around the subjects which the received methodology has typically excluded from the agenda, or relegated to a minor place: religion and politics, the Church and the social elite of aristocracy and gentry. It would, however, have been premature to have tried to write a textbook, a comprehensive statement of a new position, giving due and balanced treatment to every subject that deserves inclusion. This study takes some early steps in that direction, working out certain arguments, pursuing certain themes, sketching in a new outline. It is a deliberately selective attempt to do certain specific things that appeared to be necessary at a particular moment in the evolution of the subject, a moment when it seemed possible to distance oneself from the characteristic historiography of the 1960s and view it critically as well as appreciatively, instead of operating unthinkingly in its idiom.

In recent decades the historiography of the period covered here, in particular, remained within the framework of assumptions and priorities established by writers like the Webbs, the Hammonds, R. H. Tawney, Harold Laski, Graham Wallas, G. D. H. Cole – authors who welded into a purposeful tradition many elements in ancien regime England which seemed to reach their culmination in the early- and mid-twentieth century State. If slickly packaged and marketed for the new campuses of the 1960s by another generation of historians, the structure of the argument was little changed. Yet as Attlee's England and the world view on which it was premised recedes from us, and especially after the change in mood of the late 1970s, it is easier to see the limiting effect of those assumptions and to begin to disengage ourselves from them. This book is only one of many contributions to that process.

1

In a work of this sort my indebtedness to others is inevitably great, and I trust I have acknowledged it fully in the references. These should, I hope, make clear my realisation of how much there is of interest and value in the works to which I address myself. Nevertheless, whatever may be original in this book arises less from an attempt to recapitulate or synthesise those works, than from a wish to adopt some different assumptions and to restructure a received argument. I hope one dissenting voice in a curiously unanimous profession will not provoke an outbreak of historical paranoia, and if I have used some books more than others as quarries for encapsulations of the positions with which I disagree, I trust their authors will merely believe that they have provided the best statements of the positions which I argue against.

It seemed particularly necessary to quote chapter and verse in this way, in order to identify with useful specificity the arguments which I consider to be no longer tenable. Sir Herbert Butterfield's classic *The Whig Interpretation of History* was highly generalised in its censures of errors of method, and he wrote no detailed substantive survey of the century he made his own; Sir Lewis Namier, whose critical powers might have destroyed his opponents rather than merely frightening most of them out of his territory, is said to have owed his chair at Manchester University to Trevelyan's patronage, and equally refrained from citing chapter and verse to identify the *obiter dicta* which his superb technical skills had, in fact, discredited.

A consequence of this reticence was the return of certain historical practices which, at an earlier date, seemed to have no future. In 1957, Sir Herbert Butterfield warned:

I am not sure that the professionalising of history has not resulted in the unconscious development of authoritarian prejudices among the professionals themselves; and it could happen that by 1984, if readers are not their own critics, a whole field of study might become the monopoly of a group and a party, all reviewing one another and standing shoulder to shoulder in order to stifle the discrepant idea, the new intellectual system, or the warning voice of the sceptic.[1]

Few such groups or parties existed when Butterfield wrote, and he devoted his attention almost wholly to the Namierites, who, perhaps, did not deserve it. By 1984, several new schools had emerged, any of which might repay the investigation of the sociologist. That is not the object of this book, however, which concerns itself with arguments and not with individuals. It is intended to sound a note of scepticism about certain assumptions, values and categories which are shared in common by most of the parties which at present divide the subject between them.

The importance of reviving a particular methodological perspective was not disguised even by its practitioners. One of the most intelligent statements

[1] Herbert Butterfield, *George III and the Historians* (London, 1957), p. 8.

of the 1960s world view declared the 'Whig interpretation' to be 'the only possible historical attitude: anything else involves the dangers of sentimental antiquarianism'. Consequently, this approach had a pre-defined agenda: 'We shall be looking for those elements of the new which are emerging.'[2] Scholars in this tradition did indeed write 'linear history', attending to the *origins* of a whole range of phenomena, so that the eighteenth century was made to seem important chiefly as a seed-bed for the nineteenth. The prevalence of linearity meant that – after the Namierites – almost no historians constructed their arguments around analyses of all that was being done or said in society at particular points, and the absence of cross-sectional studies drew attention away from what was typical: the survival of all previous patterns was systematically underemphasised.

If radicals and progressives were those who provided the blueprints for the future, conservatives were presumed to have engaged in debate, if at all, in terms devised by the radicals, and the result was a particular and loaded account of the evolution of 'radical' ideology.[3] In respect of parliamentary or other sorts of reform, the result was that 'it is generally held that there is little choice over the direction of change and that what is at stake is normally the pace of change'.[4] Such judgements are part of a long-standing tradition; as, notoriously, in Dicey's observation that

The efforts of obstructionists or reactionists come to nothing, the toryism of Eldon, the military rigidity of the Duke of Wellington, the intelligent conservatism of Peel, and at a later period the far less intelligent conservatism of Lord Palmerston, all appear, though the appearance is in some respects delusive, not in reality to delay for more than periods which are mere moments in the life of nations, the progress of change.[5]

Such views do not become more cogent for being 'generally held', however, and in adjacent periods those theories came under increasing attack from a new generation of scholars. By contrast the era between the Restoration and the Reform Bill was for long a backwater where such prejudices might flourish relatively undisturbed; indeed it probably became the preferred habitat of those holding such views.

Theirs was a profoundly positivist, and ultimately economic-reductionist, vision. '*Material life*', trumpeted one of its more successful international salesmen, 'is there at the root of everything', and it was certain now-familiar material developments which, after the eighteenth century, produced 'a violent breakthrough, revolution, total upheaval of the world'. The realm of the material provided 'rules'; man was 'locked in an economic

[2] Christopher Hill, *Reformation to Industrial Revolution* (1967; Harmondsworth, 1980), p. 20.
[3] The title of chapter 5 below is deliberately ironic.
[4] Cannon, *Parliamentary Reform*, p. 260.
[5] A. V. Dicey, *Lectures on the Relation between Law & Public Opinion in England During the Nineteenth Century* (1905; 2nd edn, London, 1924), pp. 209–10. The qualification was there for cosmetic reasons only.

condition'.[6] If it were the case that society evolved along rails ultimately
forged by an economic determinism, the historian's task would indeed be
simple. But these vague and pervasive assumptions about economic
reductionism were not strengthened by an unwillingness to examine them,
and the rise of a new cohort of scholars to whom such assumptions no longer
seemed self-evidently true meant that historians' fixations about organising
their accounts of social change in the eighteenth century around a fictitious
entity named the Industrial Revolution looked increasingly misguided.
Qualifying this polemical category, as recent scholarship in economic
history now permits us to do, might allow both a restatement of the
autonomy of people in the past, and an appreciation of the unity of the
English ancien regime as a thing-in-itself, not an anticipation of industrial
society. An examination of its self-image, its rationales and its links with
religion will allow us to see something also of the Establishment's strength,
and to understand the reasons for its survival until 1828–32.

Economic reductionism and a certain view of the role of the Industrial
Revolution harmonised with the belief that eighteenth-century English
society operated within a Lockeian consensus; that there was a 'rationalist
interlude' in English thought, so that society as a whole is aptly seen through
the categories of utilitarian psychology and contract theory. This study
continues the process of coming to terms with the idea that those assumptions
rest on the most insecure foundations. Consequently, it attempts to re-
integrate political ideology with the political theology appropriate to the
Church–State which prevailed in England until 1828–9.

Some historians would indeed feel an attack on their deepest values in
Butterfield's observations that progress was not 'a line of causation' but 'a
mental trick'; that 'History is not the study of origins; rather it is the
analysis of all the mediations by which the past was turned into our present.'
Nevertheless, it is suggested that a synoptic account of English society *can*
be derived from methodologies other than reductionist ones, and this book
is a small contribution to that development. If some historians wish to
ascribe a *necessary* general direction to the course of social and political
change, to impute a particular dynamic to those processes, one reply would
be to show how such expectations are not borne out for a particular (usually
political) episode. A sufficiently detailed study would reveal instead the
complexity and flux of human affairs, the subserviency of values to the
tactical conjunctures which give them expression, the large role of chance
and miscalculation as well as ambition as against purposeful endeavour or
anticipations of later alignments, and so forth. These familiar, salutary but
unwelcome morals are finally incompatible with large claims about events,
institutions and values reflecting an underlying logic of economic organi-

[6] Fernand Braudel, *Capitalism and Material Life 1400–1800* (1967; London, 1974), pp. x, xii,
xiv.

sation and class evolution; but historians committed to the second sort of history are unlikely to be eager to integrate into their work the implications of the first sort, however many specialised studies it gives rise to.[7] It seems better therefore to set out these conclusions in the form of a broad survey, despite the methodological objections it might incur.

A barrier to the earlier emergence of such a reinterpretation has undoubtedly been the close links between academic history and wider contemporary commitments and controversies. This was nothing new; nor was what Mr William Thomas acutely identified as the 'common process by which the polemics of one generation provide the historical categories for the next'.[8] The categories which made so much of the radical scholarship of the 1960s and 70s seem, to its admirers, new and exciting, too often had their origin in early-nineteenth-century social, political and religious polemic levelled against the institutions and values of the world before 1832. Indeed, by comparison with H. T. Buckle's *History of Civilization in England* (1857), some recent writings seem disappointingly derivative. This is not to suggest that the moderns read Buckle; on the contrary, they thought they were doing something fresh and revivifying. Rather, the similarities reveal the extent to which a certain sort of social polemic survived, unreconstructed, in English society and merely experienced a recrudescence in the 1960s.

Buckle constructed an eulogy of the 'progress' of the 'English intellect' via 'shaking off ancient superstitions', part of the retreat of 'the old theological spirit'. It had its origins in the reign of Charles II, and, of course, 1688 played a crucial role: 'It is, indeed, difficult to conceive the full amount of the impetus given to English civilisation by the expulsion of the House of Stuart.' As a result, the 'real interests of the nation began to be perceived, so soon as the superstitions were dispersed by which those interests had long been obscured'. The period dealt with here consequently played a central role: 'As the eighteenth century advanced, the great movement of liberation rapidly proceeded': the growth of schools, circulating libraries, provincial printing; the popularisation of science; literary periodicals; book clubs, debating societies, political articulacy among 'the industrious classes': all these things played the same part in Buckle's argument as they did in the 1960s model.[9]

There was a difference of emphasis: the 1960s model placed capitalism at the centre of the picture. According to one school of historians,

[7] This is not the case in other periods: detailed accounts of early-Stuart Parliaments, or of the letters and diaries of Victorian politicians, have provoked academic debates of the greatest intelligence and seriousness.

[8] W. E. S. Thomas, *The Philosophic Radicals. Nine Studies in Theory and Practice 1817–1841* (Oxford, 1979), p. 4.

[9] Buckle deserves reading in full, though the bitterness of his invective is shocking. It is sometimes difficult to see what, of importance, the 1960s added to his polemic against the ancien regime. Again, in Buckle, the 'spirit of inquiry' was choked off by reaction under George III, etc. etc.

'Economics made law', so that 'capitalist relations came to pervade all sectors of society' even by the sixteenth century; the Revolution of 1688 produced 'stable equilibrium', terminating 'monarchy in the traditional sense of the word', and hence 'Politics ceased to be ideological: the job of government was to increase the wealth of the country, and to furnish lucrative employment for the ruling families and their adherents.' Consequently, 1689 was 'the *annus mirabilis* of the rights of property', so that 'the fall of the absolute monarchy was the turning point in the evolution of capitalism'. 'Divine right was dead', and 'all roads led away from authority towards rationalism', an appropriate state of mind for a 'society of atomised individuals'. The 'heroic age' was over, both in politics and religion. Party labels lost their meaning: 'For all practical purposes England was a one-party state.' MPs were 'more interested in the spoils of office than in political principles... The system was suited to an age when no strong passions divided the political nation, but it made for inertia'. Both Church and State 'became impervious to reforming movements'. Walpole's era was one of 'spiritual desolation as men contemplated the barren mechanical universe of Newton, and the new dismal science of economics... Warmth and social solidarity were what was lacking in this atomised and individualized society.' Only the end of the eighteenth century broke this 'lethargy', with industrial take-off and 'the rise of true radicalism', so that 'principles were beginning to re-enter politics' with the revival of party in the 1780s, anticipations of 'working-class revolt', and the younger Pitt's 'new Toryism'.[10]

These points are worth listing at length partly because their author provided one of the most influential summaries of the 1960s model of ancien regime English society, and partly because the present author has come to dissent from every one of them. This book attempts to document some aspects of that dissent. It re-emphasises the similarities between England before 1832 and other European social systems of the ancien regime, and shows that the critique which English radicals levelled at their own society had strong parallels with the anticlericalism and theological heterodoxy of the intelligentsia of the European Enlightenment. It attempts to move beyond a preoccupation with the handful of figures in the traditional canon of political theorists; and it tries to give more weight to the behaviour and beliefs of the ordinary, the normal, the established.

The pattern of an ancien regime State could profitably be traced back to 1660; but that would be the subject of another book, and 1688 has some appropriateness as a starting point. The Revolution secured the hegemony

10 Hill, *Reformation to Industrial Revolution*, pp. 63, 89, 130, 143, 161, 173, 175 (quoting Lipson and Stone), 200, 206–7, 213–14, 218–19, 275–6, 279–80, 283–4. The influence of Penguin Books must have been immense in giving wide currency to such views in the works of Christopher Hill, E. J. Hobsbawm, J. H. Plumb, Lawrence Stone, E. P. Thompson, Raymond Williams, etc.

of the (Anglican) aristocracy and gentry against the threat perceived to be posed by a (Roman Catholic) monarchical bureaucracy: in that sense, 1688 only preserved what 1660 was supposed to have re-established, and establishment theorists consistently laboured to minimise the extent to which 1688 represented a fundamental discontinuity. Since, beating off Jacobite and radical challenges, they were largely successful in this attempt, the 'old society' until 1828–32 had three essential characteristics: it was Anglican, it was aristocratic, and it was monarchical. Gentlemen, the Church of England, and the Crown commanded an intellectual and social hegemony. In this respect as elsewhere, the present study suggests a return to an older interpretation. Where some modern commentators have never tired of emphasising the eighteenth century as the era of bourgeois individualism, earlier writers were more willing to recognise its dominant structure as that of an aristocratic society. Even Dicey suggested that 'in 1800 the government of England was essentially aristocratic...the social condition, the feelings and convictions of Englishmen in 1800, were even more aristocratic than were English political institutions'. And he recognised that this was true in a sense much more extensive than the strictly constitutional: aristocracy 'has for its intellectual or moral foundation the conviction that the inequalities or differences which distinguish one body of men from another are of essential and permanent importance'.[11] Such were the forces against which 'the new' directed its attack. In 1837 J.S. Mill defined 'philosophic radical': 'They were the men who traced the many evils of political life back to their root cause, "the aristocratic principle".'[12] How such a social order disintegrated is an underlying theme of this study.

Far from the 'old society' steadily declining in effectiveness, petering out in bumbling incompetence, a consideration of the cultural hegemony of the elite; of the political system of electoral management; and of the ideological defence of the State suggests the reverse. The ancien regime became steadily stronger in its own terms in the half century after the American revolution. Events therefore led to a decisive conflict with those elements in society which brought to the national arena fundamentally different terms of reference. The defeat of the 'old society', in and after the events of 1828–32, cannot be pronounced objectively more necessary or more inevitable than the outcome of any other battle; it was no more foreordained than Napoleon's defeat at Waterloo.

[11] Dicey, *Law & Opinion*, pp. 48, 50.   [12] Thomas, *Philosophic Radicals*, p. 2.

Representation and Oligarchy in England from the Revolution to the Reform Bill: an Historiographical Survey

I. PRELIMINARY

Sir Herbert Butterfield's last major statement on the eighteenth century, *George III and the Historians*, was published in 1957; Sir Lewis Namier died in 1960. Even at the second date it seemed possible that these two men, from their very different standpoints, had demolished the 'Whig interpretation of history'. In the field which that doctrine had first been devised to account for, the century and a half following the Glorious Revolution, the prevailing tone among historians had recently been cool, level, and sceptical of the autonomy of historical phenomena whose dynamic had traditionally been held to entail a 'Whig' perspective on events. This mood soon ceased to be typical. It was eroded by the rise of new enthusiasms and by the unrecognised intrusion of assumptions which these enthusiastic commitments made possible. The pursuit of new themes was held to be so self-evidently a function of a mushrooming academic community that their effects on the perspective in which the whole subject was viewed were either supposed to be justified *ipso facto*, or usually went unremarked. Often this was brought about by the neglect which enshrouded certain issues, and some of those issues will be explored in later chapters. This chapter focusses on the specific and technical questions of party politics and of psephology. Even here, by the early 1980s some of the effects might have been inferred from the concentration of recent scholarship on certain areas, leaving intervening topics and decades remarkably seldom explored. Political history was still too often written with reference to only a small time span, so that general assumptions about the direction and dynamic of social and political change were often allowed to remain unrevised by a need to integrate them into general theories. Namierite nominalism and a pervasive positivism were powerful disincentives which worked against the emergence of general explanatory schemes.

In the wider realms of economic and of social history, the themes dealt with continued to be highly selective; but though newly-fashionable themes were often different, the perspective which dictated their selection was essentially the same. The agenda was drawn up in the light of an economic-reductionist, 'Whig' theory of what mattered and of the direction in which events were held to be evolving. With this reinforcement, positivist assumptions dominated political history as much as they dominated social or economic history. Party was viewed not as conduct or ideology but as organisation. Reform was almost synonymous with the adjustment of the franchise to implement popular political opinions, naturally generated by material self-interest. Historians of reform wrote linear history. They attempted to trace themes: the progressive advocacy and achievement of things which were, in themselves, held to be constant, like representative democracy. This can only be made to seem plausible as an account of politics by an extreme and *a priori* selectivity about the themes to be examined;[1] and only a refusal to take politics seriously allowed this to pass unchallenged. Social history, too, was typically portrayed in material terms, and from the viewpoint of the radical urban artisan. Swamped by such assumptions, and largely excluded from the academic agenda, were such issues as the social, intellectual and political roles of the monarchy; of the aristocracy and gentry; of the armed forces; the law; the universities; and, above all, of religion. The Anglican Church in particular, its politics, its theology, its social theory, its relation to popular religion – all were dismissed from History syllabi in most universities, and with them went all forms of social history of a non-positivist kind.[2]

So marked a disregard of so much that was normal and central in Hanoverian England demands explanations of a very basic sort. It is often necessary to remind ourselves that the political values of eighteenth-century England were those appropriate to a society Christian, monarchical, aristocratic, rural, traditional and poor; but those of historians of the 1960s and 1970s were drawn from a society indifferent to religion; hostile alike to authority and to social rank; urban; 'plural'; and affluent. This in itself would have posed major problems of sympathetic insight in an attempt to cross such a divide. But, from the 1960s, an increasing number of historians ceased to make such an effort, and chose to believe that fresh historical insights were to be derived, rather, from a celebration of their own values

---

[1] The way in which this generates a 'Whig' perspective in even the most professional modern scholarship is well exemplified by Professor Cannon's justly acclaimed *Parliamentary Reform*. His 'enquiry' was 'limited' to what he defined as 'the two most important aspects of reform – namely changes in the franchise and changes in the distribution of seats' (p. xii). The sort of enquiry suggested here, by contrast, would seek to discover how these selected components of a system worked in different ways, and were conceived of in different ways, at different points in time; and how they related to the other components, which the 'Whig interpretation' might neglect.

[2] Cf. J. C. D. Clark, 'Eighteenth Century Social History', *HJ* 27 (1984), 773–88.

and a reliance on recent experience as a source of analytical categories and of analogies. Thus, for example, the opinion rapidly took hold, and was propagated as an article of faith, that it was actually more moral to study the social life of the common man than the thoughts and actions either of statesmen or of society's dominant elite. Among those who imbibed this assumption in the 1960s, it proved remarkably immune to revision: it was a value, not a result. As such, it issued in the 1960s and 70s in a great deal of social history, conceived as the material history of the 'working class'; though this will not be directly dealt with in this chapter, it is important that political history had become a minority interest by the 1980s, and that it was heavily influenced by other sorts of history adjacent to it.

Political, social and intellectual historians equally sought to justify their subjects in modern terms. This they evidently found not too difficult, and the justifications were often revealing. 'The eighteenth century in Europe, from its middle decades onward, was a time of spiritual turmoil, perhaps not too unlike the ferment we are now experiencing', wrote one in the early 1970s.[3] Few, for the eighteenth century, gave as explicit an acknowledgement of the force of an analogy with modern experience as Professor Lawrence Stone did for the seventeenth when he wrote of the effect of his witnessing 'les évènements de mai' in Paris in 1968, and of his active participation in the subsequent 'crisis' at Princeton University in protest against the Vietnam war, in teaching him about 'the nature and process of revolutions' as such.[4] These spectacles nevertheless prompted a temporary but widespread preoccupation with what one writer termed 'the évènements of the 1760s'.[5] This intrusion of modern reference into scholarship by a particular cohort of historians was curiously marked. Professor Kramnick, for example, sought to rescue the natural law tradition from the conservative prescriptions derived from it by some American scholars of the 1950s, demanding rhetorically of a fellow historian: 'Does he approve of the same appeal to higher natural law over the state's lower legislative and executive actions when made in his own day by Martin Luther King, Jr. in the *Letter from a Birmingham Jail*? Otis's appeal to higher law [in 1768] was repeated by draft-card burners and opponents of the Vietnam War in 1968.'[6] As Professor Maier warned, 'the current search for a "usable past" impels scholars toward historical subjects that resemble contemporary problems... many of those who faced the royal soldiers on King Street in Boston on March 5, 1770 were of the same age as those shot down at Kent State in the spring of 1970'. The present respectability of revolutionary violence and

---

[3] B. Semmel, *The Methodist Revolution* (New York, 1973; London, 1974), p. 6. Despite this reservation, I must record my indebtedness to much of the work discussed here.

[4] L. Stone, *The Causes of the English Revolution 1529–1642* (London, 1972), p. ix.

[5] J. Brewer, *Party Ideology and Popular Politics at the Accession of George III* (Cambridge, 1976), p. 268.

[6] I. Kramnick, *The Rage of Edmund Burke* (New York, 1977), p. 47.

a new estimate of the 'legitimacy of radical sources', Dr Maier recognised, had themselves re-emphasised a 'Whig' perspective on the American revolution, presented now as the apotheosis of a new radicalism.[7] One historian was disarmingly frank about it: 'But let me put the baldest face on my intention. In one sense the concern of the following chapters is ahistorical. I am less interested in eighteenth-century radicalism than in twentieth-century radicalism.'[8]

Perspectives of this sort were not unwelcome within the left-liberal sentiment and commitment which characterised western universities from the 1960s. Two decades of such responsiveness resulted once again in the wide prevalence, by the 1980s, of a conventionally progressive historiography of much of the period 1688–1832, some of which will be explored in a technical way in this chapter. Its prevalence was shielded, too, by the curious isolation of the subject in the universities; so that while similar conventional wisdoms were being challenged for the sixteenth century by Elton and others; for the seventeenth century by scholars such as Morrill, Russell and Skinner;[9] and for the nineteenth and twentieth centuries by Bentley, Cooke, Jones, Moore, Norman, Vincent and others; the eighteenth remained almost unscathed. Indeed, after the disruptions effected by the caustic realism of Sir Lewis Namier and the subtle doubts of Sir Herbert Butterfield had been smoothed away, a new generation of orthodoxies succeeded which carried a scarcely-hidden ideological cargo. The curious resistance of the period 1688–1832 to historiographical de-mythologisation was never explained. It seems increasingly likely, however, that its content is more basic to current concerns than the more immediately striking appositeness of some nineteenth-century industrial issues has encouraged us to suppose. The relevance is one which occurred to several Marxist historians;[10] but the perspective which a Marxist analysis induced often escaped their less theoretically articulate colleagues, since that perspective harmonised with their own assumptions. It escaped them not least since the chief characteristic of the 'Whig interpretation' is not that it is Whig in a party sense, as opposed to Tory,[11] but that it is moralistic, a virtue to which most scholars would lay claim. The 'Whig interpretation' focusses attention on those lines of development in the past which seem to culminate in present arrangements. This allows it, first, to justify present values (concerning those

---

[7] P. Maier, 'Revolutionary Violence and the Relevance of History', *Journal of Interdisciplinary History* 2 (1971–2), 119, 121.

[8] Staughton Lynd, *Intellectual Origins of American Radicalism* (London, 1969), p. vii.

[9] Cf. especially the work discussed by J. H. Hexter, 'Power Struggle, Parliament and Liberty in Early Stuart England', *JMH* 50 (1978), 1–50.

[10] For a recognition of this, which came to be a programmatic statement, *vide* E. P. Thompson, 'The Peculiarities of the English', in R. Miliband and J. Saville (eds.), *The Socialist Register 1965* (London, 1965), pp. 311–62.

[11] It is no paradox that there has never been a 'Tory interpretation of history'.

arrangements) by showing their historical rootedness, and, second, to read those values (once allegedly made tenable) back into the past to condemn the forces which are held to have inhibited the earlier emergence of modern practices. By being a theory of the direction of social change, it is enabled also to be a value system. As such, it harmonised perfectly with the changed academic mood of the 1960s and 70s, and the purposes of those who sought to bring it about. And since these were their purposes, it was sometimes necessary explicitly to deny them. Butterfield's *Whig Interpretation* was dismissed as 'an unsubstantial little pamphlet',[12] and the technical distortions produced by the present-mindedness which Butterfield identified again became respectable; even a scholar of such eminence as Professor Bailyn explained that he would pay little attention to the pamphleteers who argued against the American Revolution since 'the future lay not with them'.[13] Such a frank announcement of emancipation was unusual. The same effect was usually produced implicitly, and by the accumulating weight of research at certain points and on certain themes.

The channels into which this scholarship was directed can often be defined as ways of reacting against Namierism – a movement which Butterfield's criticisms had, paradoxically, done much to initiate. Four such broad channels in party-political history are evident in retrospect. One was the great volume of scholarship devoted to the reigns of William III and Anne, which was generally admitted to have disproved R. R. Walcott's attempt to read back Namier's multi-factional picture of the 1760s into those earlier decades. Once the party structure had been elucidated, too, it became possible effectively to relate to it the great outpouring of political argument and propaganda which those years witnessed.[14] Second, a body of mutually supporting work attempted to test the applicability of a party-based analysis of politics later in the century: for the Fox–North coalition;[15] for the Whig party in the late 1780s and early 1790s;[16] for the years after Waterloo.[17] Third, evidently encouraged by the success of some of these attempts, a similar party-analysis was read back into the 1760s by historians writing

---

[12] G. Stedman Jones, 'History: the Poverty of Empiricism', in R. Blackburn (ed.), *Ideology in Social Science* (London, 1972), p. 106.

[13] B. Bailyn, (ed.), *Pamphlets of the American Revolution 1750–1776* (Cambridge, Mass., 1965), vol. I, p. x. For a critique, *vide* Jack P. Greene, 'Political Mimesis: a Consideration of the Historical and Cultural Roots of Legislative Behaviour in the British Colonies in the Eighteenth Century', *AHR* 75 (1969), 337–67.

[14] Cf. especially Kenyon, *Revolution Principles* and Dickinson, *Liberty and Property*.

[15] J. Cannon, *The Fox–North Coalition. The Crisis of the Constitution, 1782–4* (Cambridge, 1969).

[16] D. E. Ginter, 'The Financing of the Whig Party Organization, 1783–1793', *AHR* 71 (1965–6), 421–40; *idem, Whig Organization in the General Election of 1790* (Berkeley, 1967); F. O'Gorman, *The Whig Party and the French Revolution* (London, 1967); L. G. Mitchell, *Charles James Fox and the Disintegration of the Whig Party 1782–1794* (Oxford, 1971).

[17] A. Mitchell, *The Whigs in Opposition 1815–1830* (Oxford, 1967); J. E. Cookson, *Lord Liverpool's Administration: the Crucial Years 1815–1822* (Edinburgh, 1975).

on, above all, the Rockingham Whigs.[18] Here, seemingly in the heart of
Namier's domain, was discovered a faction which allegedly behaved in
many of the ways usually expected of a 'party' in a Victorian sense. This
demonstration was generally accepted, though its implications for the wider
applicability of the Namierite model were not explored. J. H. Plumb, for
example, continued to claim that 'the parliamentary systems of the 1750s
and 1760s are indistinguishable',[19] a mistake whose consequences can
hardly be exaggerated. Still less was the cluster of scholarship on party at
the very end of the period extended into a general theory, and it squared
uneasily with Professor Gash's insistence on the great difference in politics
before and after 1832. So that, in general, this channel of scholarship, like
the two others, still had the character of a static, structural account. It failed
to generate a dynamic distinct from the 'Whig' one; and all three, however
excellent technically, were deliberately limited in chronological scope, and
tended not to raise deeper issues of perspective. But a fourth channel of
revisionist writing did, and for that reason will be focussed on here.

It took the form of an ingenious response to Namier's results – apparently
to accept them, but to take them as evidence for the mechanics of a 'Whig
oligarchy', 'single party government', which swiftly emerged after 1714 and
which gave British society stability at the price of corruption and inactivity.
Where Namier thought he was refuting a Victorian myth of an eighteenth-
century oligarchy sustained by ministerial bribery in the Commons, and
supposed he was revealing the widely-accepted social conventions which
informed a system of politics very different to that of modern representative
democracy, the new school reasserted the Victorian myth in a new form.
Namier's revelation of the local and central mechanisms of power was
interpreted as evidence for it; the distinction he wished to make was largely
disregarded.

It was possible (indeed it was made to seem proper) to disregard it because
the reassertion was not least a reassertion of an analysis of politics which
was drawn ultimately from a moral appraisal. Lecky's condemnation of a
lack of 'real earnestness in public life' consequent upon 'immense corrupt
influences' and 'an almost complete absence of a reforming spirit among
politicians'[20] led directly through Caroline Robbins's indignation at the
'notorious complacency and conservatism of politics in the reign of George
II'[21] to J. H. Plumb's lament that, as a result of the Whig oligarchy

---

[18] P. Langford, *The First Rockingham Administration 1765–1766* (Oxford, 1973); R. Hoffman,
The Marquis. A Study of Lord Rockingham 1730–1782 (New York, 1973); F. O'Gorman, *The
Rise of Party in England. The Rockingham Whigs 1760–82* (London, 1975); J. Brewer, *Party
Ideology* (Cambridge, 1976).

[19] J. H. Plumb, *New Light on the Tyrant George III* (Washington, 1978), p. 4.

[20] W. E. H. Lecky, *A History of England in the Eighteenth Century* (London, 1892), vol. II,
pp. 478–9.

[21] C. Robbins, *The Eighteenth Century Commonwealthman* (Cambridge, Mass., 1959), p. 271.

developed under George I, 'not until 1945 did England have a really radical government'.[22] One textbook on the period 1688–1815, published in 1965, reached its peroration by quoting Shelley's *Mask of Anarchy* as an appropriate critique and dismissal of ancien regime England. This tone of moral outrage at eighteenth-century society reached its height with a particular school.[23] In 1965 E.P. Thompson inveighed in the same way against Hanoverian government as 'a sophisticated system of brigandage', a 'parasitism' – not quite 'an aristocracy, conceived of as a ruling class' but a 'unique formation. Old Corruption.'[24] Moralising continued, for Mr Thompson, to yield his picture of the power structure: 'Old Corruption', he claimed, 'is a more serious term of political analysis than is often supposed.'[25] Those in sympathy with his approach often took up his analysis without its qualifications. W. A. Speck, for example, building to an extent on one such argument,[26] echoed Mr Thompson's thesis that the years 1790–1820 saw the 'making of the English working class' by positing the creation of the 'English ruling class' in the early decades of the eighteenth century.[27] The idea can be traced also to J. H. Plumb's widely acclaimed statement of the view that the early eighteenth century witnessed 'The triumph of the Venetian Oligarchy'.[28] As he formulated it, apart from its overt moral claims to credence, the thesis had two scholarly props. One was the innovative and important work done by Plumb, Speck and others on elections and pollbooks, revealing a vigorous electorate and frequent contests before 1714, and falling voting figures and fewer contests thereafter. The other was the claim that the Tory party died soon after 1715, extinguished by proscription, so that early Hanoverian England was an oligarchy both in the structural sense of being a one-party state, and in the substantive sense that, the rivalry between the Houses of Stuart and Hanover being discounted, politics was allegedly almost devoid of issues – it was, rather, about power and its perquisites, patronage and place. These two props to 'oligarchy theory' will now be examined in turn.

denunciation banishment

[22] J. H. Plumb, 'Political Man', in James L. Clifford (ed.), *Man versus Society in Eighteenth Century Britain* (Cambridge, 1968), p. 20.

[23] D. Hay, P. Linebaugh, E. P. Thompson (eds.), *Albion's Fatal Tree: Crime and Society in Eighteenth Century England* (London, 1975).

[24] Thompson, 'Peculiarities of the English', p. 323.

[25] *Idem*, 'Eighteenth-Century English Society: Class Struggle without Class?', *Social History* 3 (1978), 133–65.

[26] E. P. Thompson, *Whigs and Hunters* (London, 1975). The view of the Waltham Black Act of 1723 as an 'ideological index' to a Whig oligarchy's dominance, renewed regularly and unthinkingly by a subservient House of Commons, was seriously challenged by Sheila Lambert (ed.), *House of Commons Sessional Papers of the Eighteenth Century* (Wilmington, Delaware, 1975), vol. I, pp. 37–41.

[27] W. A. Speck, *Stability and Strife. England 1714–1760* (London, 1977), chapter 6. The theory was effectively refuted by Dr O'Gorman in *BJECS* 1 (1978), 213–16.

[28] J. H. Plumb, *The Growth of Political Stability in England 1675–1725* (London, 1967).

II. THE PSEPHOLOGICAL ARGUMENT

The argument from the behaviour of the electorate had several facets. Before 1715 its vigour and centrality to the alternating fortunes of the parties was advanced as evidence for a wide political literacy and popular involvement sustaining a massive output of pamphlets, broadsheets and ballads, often fuelling political disorder; after 1715, it was claimed, this vigorous culture was deliberately stifled by more efficient management of elections by the magnates; by the Septennial Act; by a repressive policy towards popular licence. The electoral argument ultimately rested on one about numbers. An initial estimate put the number of electors at the end of Anne's reign at 250,000; 'using Gregory King's figures for the total population, [this] gives a percentage of 4·7 who possessed the vote, whereas after the Reform Bill only 4·2 per cent did so'.[29] After 1715, it was argued, the electorate was deliberately shackled by minimising the number of contests and by successive Commons decisions in favour of narrow franchises,[30] culminating in the Last Determinations Act of 1729. Once shackled, 'the people' did not break free until the nineteenth century; so that Namier's picture of oligarchical, managerial politics could be accepted as an accurate account of that form of social dominance which survived until 1832 at least.[31]

The argument from numbers was generally accepted as convincing. It seemed the natural summation of the familiar picture of small, increasingly corrupt and controllable electorates in eighteenth-century boroughs. Yet these figures, as propounded by Professors Plumb and Cannon, contained a crucial flaw. They did not distinguish, in speaking of 'the electorate', between those actually voting and those entitled to vote.[32] Their figures were

[29] J. H. Plumb, 'The Growth of the Electorate in England from 1600 to 1715', *P&P* 45 (1969), 111. A similar approach was adopted by Cannon, *Parliamentary Reform*, pp. 40–3. Professor Holmes's figures were only slightly different: 4·6 per cent in 1715, falling to 2·63 per cent in 1831 and 4·7 per cent after the First Reform Act: G. Holmes, *The Electorate and the National Will in the First Age of Party* (Lancaster, 1976), p. 14.

[30] It is now scarcely possible to base an argument of the restriction of the franchise on Professor Habakkuk's picture of the declining small landowner and the rise of great estates, which has been seriously challenged at several points: H. J. Habbakuk, 'English Landownership, 1680–1740', *EcHR* 10 (1939–40), 2–17; cf. J. V. Beckett, 'English Landownership in the Later Seventeenth and Eighteenth Centuries: the Debate and the Problems', *ibid.* 30 (1977), 567–81.

[31] For one historian's explicit recognition, and acceptance, of this sort of link between political stability and a narrowing franchise, cf. Thompson, 'Eighteenth-Century English Society', p. 146 and *passim*.

[32] The same confusion was inherited by those who drew on Plumb's work: cf. Brewer, *Party Ideology*, pp. 6–7 (where falling numbers actually voting are taken to prove deliberate restriction by 'the forces of political constraint'), and John A. Phillips, 'Popular Politics in Unreformed England', *JMH* 52 (1980), 599–625. Cf. also Dr Phillips's *Electoral Behaviour in Unreformed England* (Princeton, 1982). The author discovered evidence for very high turnouts in certain (frequently contested and therefore perhaps untypical) boroughs (pp.

1716 Septennial Act — to extend duration of Parliament to 7 years (it was felt unsafe to risk a new election while country so unsettled c frequent Jacobite riots.

of those actually voting. They were, it was implied, a good guide to the total of those who 'possessed the vote'. But the identity was not proved; and the argument therefore hinged on the percentage turnout at the polls. This was difficult to establish, since, before the Reform Act of 1832, electoral registers were not drawn up in advance, with which the totals at the polls might be compared. Evidence nevertheless began to emerge which challenged the accepted picture. Professor Speck and his colleagues developed techniques of computer analysis and applied them to pollbooks for selected counties in the period 1701–15 with skill and to good effect.[33] They established that at this date most voters behaved as if they had conscious party loyalties; relatively few of them cast their two votes inconsistently in this respect. They discovered also that there was a large 'floating' vote, which changed its allegiance periodically; and that these county elections were not swayed by blocs of party loyalists voting consistently for their candidates in election after election, but by a large body of men who cast their votes on a few occasions, or on one occasion, only; 'the regular voters were outnumbered by the casual voters who turned out at only one election'. This, they confessed, was 'admittedly a puzzle'. Plumb, too, recognised it as a 'strange and important fact'.[34]

Dr Hirst, by contrast, took account of the two possible definitions of 'the electorate' in his research into early-seventeenth-century practice. He concluded that between 27 and 40 per cent of the adult male population were entitled to vote 'after the franchise decisions of the early months of the Long Parliament',[35] implying as much as 6·75 to 10 per cent of the population as a whole; and Plumb's earlier study had suggested a continuously growing electorate through that century. If so, one might infer that the figure in 1715 would be as high, if not higher, than Hirst's estimate, after many decades of growing totals at recorded polls, and bitter conflict between organised parties. Yet, however large the number of those who might have voted, Professor Holmes' research suggested remarkably low turnouts even among the gentry in the Suffolk and Hampshire elections of 1710, 39 and 30 per cent; under 18 per cent for a similar sample of West

86–90) and treated the question of turnout in all seats as unimportant for the unreformed system as a whole. Instead, Dr Phillips gave priority to a measurement of consistent voter participation where frequent contests allowed this to be measured, which gives a very different impression.

[33] W. A. Speck and W. A. Grey, 'Computer Analysis of Poll Books: an Initial Report', *BIHR* 43 (1970), 105–12; W. A. Speck, W. A. Grey and R. Hopkinson, 'Computer Analysis of Poll Books: a Further Report', *ibid.*, 48 (1975), 64–90.

[34] *Ibid.*, p. 86; Plumb, 'Growth of the Electorate', p. 113.

[35] Derek Hirst, *The Representative of the People? Voters and Voting in England under the Early Stuarts* (Cambridge, 1975), pp. 104–5. That early-seventeenth-century parliamentary determinations in favour of wider franchises were aimed at checking corruption and Court influence, not expressive of a democratic principle, is argued by R. L. Bushman, 'English Franchise Reform in the Seventeenth Century', *JBS* 3 (1963), 36–56.

Riding gentry in 1708; and the gentry, he suggested, were those most likely to cast their votes. Holmes rightly called these 'staggering figures'.[36] His examples may be extreme cases, though it is not easy to see why they should be. For simple practical reasons, too, it was easier to cast a vote in a borough than in a county election. One might therefore expect that the smaller the borough electorate, the larger the turnout as a percentage of those entitled to vote, and the more constant that percentage would be between elections. Yet, on the basis of current research, it would seem that this assumption is inappropriate for many boroughs,[37] and that the county figures are not aberrations.

Our surprise needs to be explained. In the late twentieth century we are accustomed to regular turnouts in general elections of nearly 80 per cent of those on the electoral register, and the question of turnout is not considered crucial to our definition of the system as 'democratic'. Speck's work raised the question whether it was proper to apply this assumption to the early eighteenth century.[38] Holmes' figures are 'staggering' in that, if remotely typical,[39] they demand a fundamental revision of our assumptions about the nature and working of the representative system. Historians were used to explaining consistently low figures in House of Commons' divisions as an aspect of the functioning of a one-party oligarchy and a Whig ideological consensus. But high turnover and low turnouts at the polls in addition is strong evidence against the existence of a large body of politically articulate men, seeking autonomously to defend their interests via the franchise and via their MPs once elected, and oppressed by being excluded from the polls. The familiar utilitarian, positivist interpretation wholly fails to do justice to the way in which the electoral structure of the ancien regime actually worked. We see, rather, a system with a similar formal structure to our own, but proceeding on very different assumptions and within a very different web of conventions.

The implications of Speck's discoveries were not worked out in these terms. He used his pollbook analysis, on the contrary, to adjudicate between a 'deference model' and a 'participatory model' of voting behaviour in

---

[36] Holmes, *Electorate*, p. 22. Yet, though Holmes was the first to draw attention to this crucial discrepancy between those voting and those entitled to vote, he did not place upon it the interpretation developed here. On the contrary, he attempted to accommodate the fact within the familiar scheme of explanation: 'far greater numbers', he inferred, 'were directly represented than has ever been appreciated'. Until 1722, he concluded, 'the representative system, for all its manifold faults, did by and large express the opinion of the electorate'; its role was described as one of 'dominance'; 'this rampaging electorate, for all but a few of the forty-three years from 1679 to 1722, controlled the political fortunes of the so-called governing classes': *ibid.*, pp. 4, 7.

[37] Plumb, 'Growth of the Electorate', p. 114; Holmes, *Electorate*, pp. 22–3.

[38] It is fair to say that he did not draw this conclusion from his evidence.

[39] Turnouts in general need not have been as very low as in Holmes' samples for the objections against 'oligarchy theory' developed here to hold good.

favour of the second. By the first was understood a claim that 'the majority of freeholders responded *not* to their own political inclinations when they voted, indeed they were not credited with any, *but* to pressures brought to bear upon them by their social superiors' (italics added). The second model claimed that freeholders were not, at the beginning of the eighteenth century, bound by 'the social and economic pressures which prevailed at the accession of George III', since 'the territorial magnates were not then, as they later became, united into a homogeneous ruling class' but were 'bitterly divided into two political parties...which appealed for support to the electorate below them'.[40] Floating voters and occasional voters were assumed to show an independent populace, persuaded and swayed first one way, then the other by the competing claims of political propaganda in broadsheets and ballads, pamphlets and newspapers. This assumption was not explicitly demonstrated, however, and the history of propaganda was not yet linked to the question of voter independence. The experience of other periods might lead one to expect that a large floating vote was more probably evidence against a high level of autonomous popular political involvement and commitment, and a measure of the problems which those very new phenomena, the Whig and Tory parties, had to face in their efforts to mobilise a still relatively uninformed electorate. More realistically, too, it might be suggested that a 'deference model' need not require that a magnate be able to manoeuvre his neighbours sharply from one side to another at will, but rather that there should be a long-term affinity in particular local communities;[41] but this was an aspect of the question which the initial work on pollbooks did not investigate.

This formulation of two alternative models was successfully challenged in 1979 by Dr Landau.[42] From a study of the Kent pollbooks of 1713 and 1715, she established that even the 'floating' and the 'occasional' voters at that point were far less responsive to political argument than the

---

[40] Speck, 'Further Report', p. 64.
[41] This Speck conceded: *ibid.*, p. 86. This would confirm Professor D. C. Moore's demonstration that villages voted nearly unanimously for one party or the other in early-nineteenth-century county elections, but is inconsistent with Plumb's observation that most villages in Suffolk in Anne's reign were divided on party lines. Cf. D. C. Moore, 'The Other Face of Reform', *Victorian Studies* 5 (1961–2), 7–34; *idem, The Politics of Deference* (Hassocks, 1976); Plumb, 'Growth of the Electorate', p. 113. It seems that much more pollbook analysis is needed, and over a longer time span, before a general pattern emerges. For the advantages of broad surveys, cf. John Morrill, 'Parliamentary Representation 1543–1974' in B. E. Harris (ed.), *A History of the County of Chester*, vol. II, (Oxford, 1979), pp. 98–166. Frank O'Gorman, 'Electoral Deference in "Unreformed" England: 1760–1832', *JMH* 56 (1984), 391–429, emphasises the complex nexus of mutual obligations and duties covered by the term 'deference': in no sense is it to be equated with 'obedience'.
[42] Norma Landau, 'Independence, Deference and Voter Participation: the Behaviour of the Electorate in Early-Eighteenth-Century Kent', *HJ* 22 (1979), 561–83. Dr Landau did not deal with the question of turnout, though her figures revealed that of 198 Kent JPs in 1713, only 111 voted, i.e. 56 per cent; 58 per cent in 1734; 64 per cent in 1754 (pp. 569, 579).

'participatory' model had suggested, and far more responsive to the pressures either of the local gentry, or of government agencies in urban areas; so that a composite model, which might be termed one of 'participatory deference', better described the voters' simultaneous involvement and susceptibility to the influence of their acknowledged superiors. If so, the early-eighteenth-century electorate cannot be contrasted in these respects with its successor in mid-century, as conceived by Namier. Local elites were equally important at both periods; it was these elites to which the parties and their propaganda chiefly addressed themselves, not to some independent electorate.[43]

Speck's results certainly suggested qualifications to the 'deference model' in his unduly rigid definition of it; but his definition of the 'participatory model' (a formulation of the assumptions on which many widely-accepted books had been written) was by far the more seriously damaged by the pollbook figures. For what did that model imply about political action? In what did voters participate, or think they were participating, by casting their votes? Undoubtedly, the electorate and some people outside it were politically articulate by the early eighteenth century; but this does not disprove the claim that the daily business of government was conducted at St James's and Westminster in terms which usually owed relatively little to a sense of popular pressure or wide accountability, and contemporaries did not generally suppose otherwise until the closing years of the ancien regime (if then). What is to be questioned is not the existence of a popular dimension but the place conventionally accorded to it in an overall map of society: the links between high and low politics, and the unquantifiable assumptions which surrounded the quantifiable activity of voting. In the last resort, under threat of rebellion, the Hanoverian regime rested in a very direct sense on its acceptability at large. Yet, aside from ultimate dynastic loyalties (explored in subsequent chapters), when the interconnections between politics at Westminster and in constituency elections are reconstituted, historians must not complain if they prove to be of a different sort, of a different strength, or of a different incidence to those which subsequent experience had led us to expect. Speck's work offered an example of the pioneering application of new techniques to ancient sources; but we must not assume that the pollbooks' apparent yielding to such conceptual tools means that the activity of voting was the same thing in the early eighteenth century as in the late twentieth, or that it was enmeshed in similar conventions. Some such assumption seems to have been introduced in the

---

[43] I differ from Dr Landau's important study only in her attempt to accommodate her findings to the old assumption that the reigns of George I and George II saw the 'substitution of non-party for party politics'. Dr Landau rightly denied that parliamentary parties depended on the existence of an 'independent' electorate; but we must press the argument further to reveal the parties, at different periods, creating their own electorate or allowing it to languish.

historiography of the 1970s, however. The work which led to the rediscovery and reinstatement of parliamentary political parties in the reigns of William and Anne was carried too far by its very success: it sometimes imported into modern accounts of the party system which emerged in those two decades assumptions appropriate only to later systems, if at all. Most simply, the number of those voting as a percentage of the total population was taken as an index of the degree to which the system approached 'democracy', with little regard to the other elements in a complex situation. In respect of the tactical conventions governing the relation of the parties at Westminster, the present author made an attempt to provide an alternative in 1980;[44] but further work is still necessary on voting, and on representation in relation to it.

In the absence of such a revision in the light of new data, an orthodoxy established itself and became entrenched in the textbooks. Plumb announced in 1969 that 'England was far more democratic between 1688 and 1715 than immediately after 1832' – and so, presumably, *very* much more democratic than in the period 1715–1832. Cannon duly quoted this judgement as 'compelling'.[45] It was a view exactly echoed by Speck: 'the electoral system was more representative in Anne's reign than it had ever been before, or was to be again until well into Victoria's',[46] and repeated by him seven years later: 'at George I's accession England was more "democratic" than it was to be again until well into Victoria's reign'.[47] In truth, the retrojection of modern categories was an unfortunate characteristic of two decades during which historians were eager to point to *The Modernity of the Eighteenth Century*.[48]

How, then, avoiding such a danger, is the growing electorate in both counties and boroughs in the years c. 1680–1715 to be accounted for? It seems likely that higher turnouts alone can explain the greater part of the very large increases in the numbers of those actually voting. The parties, in other words, created their electorate in these years (rather than vice versa), just as they were to do in the nineteenth century. Other causes operated: the natural growth of some towns; the artificial creation of votes in some boroughs by local managers. But it is difficult to believe that this can account for the scale of the increases recorded by Plumb in all sorts of constituencies, including counties. It seems, rather, that a new explanation

[44] J. C. D. Clark, 'A General Theory of Party, Opposition and Government, 1688–1832', *HJ* 23 (1980), 295–325.

[45] Plumb, 'Growth of the Electorate', p. 116; Cannon, *Parliamentary Reform*, p. 40.

[46] W. A. Speck, *Tory and Whig* (London, 1970), p. 17.

[47] *Idem, Stability and Strife*, p. 16. Following Professor Holmes, Professor Speck briefly noted the question of turnout, but similarly used the issue to argue that the system was *more democratic* than had been thought rather than to question the appropriateness of the notion of democracy itself.

[48] The title of a collection of essays edited by Louis T. Milic (Cleveland, 1971).

of these phenomena is necessary which takes account, in addition, of the priority of politics.

It would account, equally, for the period after 1715 largely in terms of falling turnouts. Election contests became more infrequent; but evidence has not been produced to show that contests were the result of the welling-up of an impulse from 'below', and that a decreasing number of contests was the result of a patrician attempt to frustrate a plebeian initiative. A falling number of contests after the Hanoverian accession is more remarkable in that the traditional occasions of conflict did not disappear. Normally, the old social divisions were still there: the same divisions, between the same people, and on the same issues. This continuity was important in improving politicians' efficiency at resolving contests before a poll, either by compromise or by the abandonment of a hopeless cause. It would be wrong to presume that, because there was no poll in a particular case, there was no political dimension to that election – that all was somnolence or repression. The politics were of a different sort, and contests were not a necessary part of the system. They were indeed the exception, not the rule. Growing identification of the English State as based on a Whig hegemony in the face of the Stuart challenge elevated the ideal of local unity of sentiment, still present from the sixteenth and seventeenth centuries, making it even more available as a justification for such arranged results. Yet the cry was not generally raised that electors were deprived of a right to participation by the absence of a contest. It is a modern assumption that there is, and ought to be, a contest in each constituency at each election in order that the system may function properly as a system of representative democracy: such a model can scarcely fit a world in which there are, as in 1701, only 89 contests for 243 English constituencies (40 counties and 203 boroughs); in 1774, 81; or in 1830, 83.[49] In Wales and Scotland, contests were less frequent still; in Ireland until 1768, the Dublin Parliament was dissolved only on the death of the monarch.

Major, though unremarked, problems vitiated any argument which treated the number of contests as a simple index of popular political involvement or participation. The total of contests remained relatively high even in the counties in the 1734 elections, though the received interpretation claimed that 'the faction-based oligarchy of the eighteenth century became firmly established in the 1720s'.[50] And the latter part of the century and the first three decades of the next witnessed a consistently low number of contests, despite the flowering of 'radicalism' and the growth of the newspaper press. The 1831 elections, in the middle of the Reform Bill crisis, saw only 75 contests for English county and borough seats. Even after 1832,

---

[49] The figures are derived from Cannon, *Parliamentary Reform*, pp. 278–89. I have omitted the two English University constituencies.
[50] Holmes, *Electorate*, p. 2.

the position was not immediately transformed: not until after 1910 were contests in almost all constituencies the norm.[51] So that here, as elsewhere in the historiography of the eighteenth century, weak arguments were shielded by being applied to a narrow time span only.

Scrutiny of the number of contests for county elections in isolation drew attention to the marked fall between the general elections of 1701–34 and those in the middle of the century, especially 1747–68. But an examination of the combined figure for polls in English counties and boroughs greatly weakens the force of this contrast; and, far more importantly, it reveals the consistently low number of polls, decade after decade – almost always nearer a third than a half of the total. The difference between polls in a third and in a half of possible cases seems not to entail any major transitions of principle. That it should have been such a low total is far more important than the observable fluctuations in the figures. Historians in the 1970s chose to look at the fluctuations; but the significance of the low totals was not confronted.[52]

Historians focussed on the counties, too, for another reason. They, it was suggested, were 'open' constituencies: their simple forty-shilling franchise and relatively large electorates made them an index of democratic opinion such as most boroughs could never be, and gave a special significance to the drop in the number of county contests after 1734. Yet, here again, the work of Professors Holmes, Gash and Moore showed this to be an untenable assumption. It was difficult and expensive for most of the voters to reach the single polling place in their county; usually they had to be paid to encourage or enable them to do so. In 1747, for example, Philip Yorke, one of the candidates for Cambridgeshire, reported to his father:

It was formerly the custom to treat all the electors, but the last time the entertainment was confined to the gentlemen, and the common freeholders had a largess given them to bear their expenses viz. a guinea to those that come out of the Isle [of Ely] and half a guinea to those of the County. It was paid to those entitled to it on their producing a ticket. Mr Shepard and Mr Jenyns both say they found it not only the cheapest method, but most liked by the people, because they put the best part of it in their pockets.[53]

To a large extent, the county turnout reflected the efforts and depth of pocket of the warring magnates – as it had done under Anne, and as it was

---

[51] T. Lloyd, 'Uncontested Seats in British General Elections, 1852–1910', *HJ* 8 (1965), 260–5; F. W. S. Craig, *British Political Facts 1885–1975* (London, 1976), p. 104; D. C. Moore, 'The Matter of the Missing Contests: Towards a Theory of the Mid-19th Century British Political System', *Albion* 6 (1974), 93–119; *idem, Politics of Deference*, pp. 281–99. Professor Moore's discussion of these issues is crucial; but it had apparently been overlooked by his English colleagues.

[52] E.g. John A. Phillips, 'The Structure of Electoral Politics in Unreformed England', *JBS* 19 (1979), 76–100. Dr Phillips offers the best presentation of this argument.

[53] Philip Yorke to Lord Hardwicke, 21st June 1747: P. C. Yorke, *The Life and Correspondence of Philip Yorke, Earl of Hardwicke* (3 vols, Cambridge, 1913), vol. II, p. 161.

to do well into the nineteenth century. Such considerations were still important even after 1832;[54] they can only have been yet more important in the eighteenth century. As a result of such pressures, Moore demonstrated, the counties, like the boroughs, were swayed by 'relatively small groups of men' long into Victoria's reign.[55]

In what sense, then, is eighteenth-century government describable as an 'oligarchy'? In a weak sense, government was clearly government by a few; but this is a truism, and it is far from clear that it was any less the case after 1832. The decline of the influence of local electoral elites since the introduction of the secret ballot in 1872 may actually have concentrated power at the centre, and in fewer hands. In the pages of many of the historians of the 1960s, however, 'oligarchy' is to be understood in a hard sense, and with overtones of class conflict. Beneath the ruling political group we are invited to see a democratic populace struggling to be 'free', and to use the 'representative system' to that end. By its use, claimed one, 'between 1688 and 1715 the voice of the electorate was able to make itself heard in many places'; thereafter, 'the individual' was 'excluded more and more from political activity' by 'the decline of party' and 'the growth of oligarchy'; but for the surviving vestigial role of the electorate, 'principles might have died a total death' as power was monopolised by self-interested managers.[56] It was this sense of 'oligarchy' which was actually made untenable by the pollbook research – the notion that the Hanoverian political regime deprived 'the people' of a 'right' which they understood as such, sought to exercise, had exercised in part before 1714, and were to recover as a result of finally successful pressure for franchise reform in the nineteenth century.

It apparently escaped most English historians writing on English electoral politics in the eighteenth century that historians of America in the same period had already arrived, by different routes, at a strikingly similar critique of the images of representative democracy which had been applied to colonial society. The earlier view of America, as Professor Bailyn summarised it, had owed much to an analogy based on the then-accepted view of eighteenth century England: in America, it ran, a provincial oligarchy had held power, in alliance with the royal executive, by 'restricting representation in the provincial assemblies, limiting the franchise, and invoking the restrictive power of the English state'; equally, it dominated economic life, 'engrossing landed estates and mercantile fortunes' and preserving them by the institutions of primogeniture and entail. This privileged, Old World hierarchy, it had been supposed, was then challenged and destroyed by the rise of a native democratic movement: its emergence

---

[54] Holmes, *Electorate*, pp. 18–21; N. Gash, *Politics in the Age of Peel* (London, 1953), p. 119.
[55] D. C. Moore, 'The Other Face of Reform', p. 17.
[56] Plumb, 'Growth of the Electorate', p. 116; 'Political Man', pp. 1, 8.

produced the Revolution and transformed a traditional society under the impact of radical doctrines and practices. But, as Bailyn correctly appreciated,

All arguments concerning politics during the prerevolutionary years have been affected by an exhaustive demonstration for one colony,[57] which might well be duplicated for others,[58] that the franchise, far from having been restricted in behalf of a borough-mongering aristocracy, was widely available for popular use. Indeed, it was more widespread than the desire to use it – a fact which in itself calls into question a whole range of traditional arguments and assumptions.

'Nowhere in eighteenth-century America', he concluded, challenging an earlier study, 'was there "democracy" – middle-class or otherwise – as we use the term.'[59]

Similar crucial insights were published simultaneously by Professor J. R. Pole, warning of the dangers of anachronism in supposing that colonial America was a democracy, or was struggling towards democracy in any modern sense. Historians, he claimed, had too often adopted 'a completely anachronistic note of apology for the insufficiency of democratic principles in early American institutions'. The principles on which colonial assemblies operated resembled, rather, those embodied by similar legislatures elsewhere. 'If this was democracy, it was a democracy that wore its cockade firmly pinned into its periwig.'[60] Rather, he suggested, it was a deferential society which survived until its destruction under the impact of Jacksonian democracy.[61] Professor Greene carried further this demonstration of the inappropriateness of a modern conception of eighteenth-century American society as having broken decisively with the values and traditions both of its seventeenth-century founders and of eighteenth-century England, and having, even before the Revolution, adopted a new set appropriate to 'democracy'. Colonial values, as well as colonial politics, were far more

---

[57] Robert E. Brown, *Middle-Class Democracy and the Revolution in Massachusetts, 1691–1780* (Ithaca, 1955); *idem, Virginia 1705–1786: Democracy or Aristocracy?* (East Lansing, 1964).

[58] It was demonstrated for other colonies in the works listed by Jack P. Greene, 'Changing Interpretations of Early American Politics', in R. A. Billington (ed.), *The Reinterpretation of Early American History* (San Marino, 1966), pp. 159, 179 n. 18.

[59] B. Bailyn, 'Political Experience and Enlightenment Ideas in Eighteenth-Century America', *AHR* 67 (1961–2), 339–51, at 340–2, 346. Bailyn seems to an extent to have changed his mind by 1965; cf. J. R. Pole's review of *Pamphlets of the American Revolution, HJ* 9 (1966) 229–54; Greene, 'Changing Interpretations', p. 183 n. 69.

[60] J. R. Pole, 'Historians and the Problem of Early American Democracy', *AHR* 67 (1961–2), 626–46, at 632, 639, 646. Much ground had been broken by R. N. Lokken, 'The Concept of Democracy in Colonial Political Thought', *WMQ* 3rd ser. 16 (1959), 568–80.

[61] A marked rise in turnouts seems good evidence for such a transition at this point: see W. N. Chambers and W. D. Burnham (eds.), *The American Party Systems: Stages of Political Development* (New York, 1967), pp. 11–12, cited in H. J. Hanham, *Elections and Party Management. Politics in the Time of Disraeli and Gladstone*, 2nd edn (Hassocks, 1978), p. xi.

indebted to the existence of elites and of English norms than had been thought.[62] In this insistence, especially, he was not alone.[63]

What was entailed by the ideas of representation and democracy in their eighteenth-century sense, if that sense was importantly different from the modern one, was explored by Richard Buel. 'Far from being the humble servant of his constituents, eighteenth-century thinkers tended to regard the representative as a quasi-magistrate to whose commands constituents owed presumptive obedience.' He was not a democratic agent, then, but a member of a ruling elite subject to an institutional sanction. 'What power the people did possess was not designed to facilitate the expression of their will in politics but to defend them from oppression.' Consequently, the American revolution itself stood in need of reinterpretation: 'For the colonial leadership independence was not a democratic movement which dissolved all the ligaments of subordination in colonial society and 'liberated' the people. It was much more the orderly transference of allegiance from one set of magistrates to a slightly different set who happened to be called the representatives of the people.'[64] As Greene summarised this research, even 'Revolutionary society...was essentially "a deferential society" that operated within an integrated structure of ideas fundamentally elitist in nature.'[65]

It is hardly conceivable that this was any less true of Hanoverian England. Yet the significance of the work of Pole, Bailyn, Greene, Buel and other scholars was seemingly unappreciated by English historians of the English electoral machine. The major flaw in the 'argument from numbers', the question of turnout, was not noticed until it was pointed out by Holmes in 1976, and, partly no doubt because of the interpretation he placed on it, its crucial importance was not appreciated even then. On the contrary, the assumption took root, and was held to be supported by exactly that pollbook

---

[62] Jack P. Greene, 'Search for Identity. An Interpretation of the Meaning of Selected Patterns of Social Response in Eighteenth-Century America', *Journal of Social History* 3 (1969–70), 189–220, *passim*; *idem*, 'An Uneasy Connection. An Analysis of the Preconditions of the American Revolution' in S. G. Kurtz and J. H. Hutson (eds.), *Essays on the American Revolution* (Chapel Hill, NC, 1973), pp. 50–2.

[63] Arthur M. Schlesinger, 'The Aristocracy in Colonial America', *Proceedings of the Massachusetts Historical Society* 74 (1962), 3–21; B. Bailyn, *The Ideological Origins of the American Revolution* (Cambridge, Mass., 1967), pp. 301–19.

[64] R. Buel, 'Democracy and the American Revolution: a Frame of Reference', *WMQ* 3rd ser. 21 (1964), 165–90 at 178, 179–80, 189. For a magisterial survey of colonial practice, see J. R. Pole, *Political Representation in England and the Origins of the American Republic* (London, 1966). I present a somewhat different interpretation of English practice from Professor Pole's, however.

[65] Jack P. Greene, 'Revolution, Confederation and Constitution, 1763–1787', in W. H. Cartwright and R. L. Watson (eds.), *The Reinterpretation of American History and Culture* (Washington, 1976), pp. 259–95 at p. 266; M. D. Kaplanoff, 'England, America and the American Revolution', *HJ* 21 (1978), 423–4.

research which had, in fact, rendered it untenable, that the parliamentary system of 1688–1832 was attempting to function in modern ways, and that the ways in which it did not do so were the symptoms of corruption which identified, which caught in a moral spotlight, the need for a particular sort of reform: the sort which arrived in 1832, 1867 and 1884. English historians, by contrast with their American colleagues, neglected the social and intellectual ascendancy of the aristocracy and of the aristocratic ethic within which politics was conducted. They were impressed, rather, by the two arguments which seemed increasingly to lend credence to 'oligarchy theory': the psephological argument, explored above, and a particular account of the pattern of eighteenth-century parliamentary parties – to which we must now turn.

III. THE PARTY ARGUMENT

Before 1714, it had been suggested by Plumb and others, an expanding and vital electorate had stimulated the formation of political parties and sharpened the party battle; after 1714 the frustration and limitation of this electorate promoted the fading and dissolution of party *qua* Whig and Tory and their replacement by a Court *v.* Country alignment. This argument may now be examined, secondly, from the other end: in respect of the claim that the Tory party was extinguished soon after 1715 and the Whig–Tory categorisation replaced by a Court–Country one in the two Houses of Parliament.

The party structure of the reigns of George I and George II continued, at Namier's death, to be a theme which attracted few historians. The most influential accounts were those of R. R. Walcott and J. B. Owen[66] – the first applying a Namierite analysis of parties to the reigns of William and Anne, the second to the 1740s. As such, they seemed to confirm each other, and were accepted into general studies.[67] From the mid-1960s, Walcott's work was to suffer almost unanimous criticism from scholars such as Bennett, Dickinson, Hill, Holmes, Horwitz, Kenyon, Jones, Plumb, Snyder and Speck, who successfully reinstated a Whig–Tory analysis as the dominant theme of the 1690s and 1700s. But, with near unanimity,[68] these historians strangely declined to carry their new party pattern beyond 1715. Dr Owen's analysis remained almost wholly unchallenged, and he was able to employ it with its full force for a textbook:[69] a work which made clear the intended

---

[66] R. R. Walcott, *English Politics in the Early Eighteenth Century* (Oxford, 1956); J. B. Owen, *The Rise of the Pelhams* (London, 1957).

[67] A. S. Foord, *His Majesty's Opposition 1714–1830* (Oxford, 1964).

[68] Dr B. W. Hill was an honourable exception in this respect.

[69] J. B. Owen, *The Eighteenth Century 1714–1815* (London, 1974).

applicability of his analysis to the parliamentary politics of the latter part of the century also. One of very few synoptic accounts of the earlier period stopped short without questioning Owen's structural picture directly.[70] As a result, historians in the 1970s were presented with a growing contrast between the party world which new research was uncovering before 1714, and the Namierite world which was held to prevail thereafter – a contrast which actually encouraged reception of the second analysis as one way of looking at the emerging 'Whig oligarchy' which these years were held to witness.

Despite the scarcity of modern research on the reign of George I, historians who had concentrated on an earlier period were eager to claim a major transition in or soon after 1715. Plumb, in 1967, had written of a *gradual process* as a result of which, 'By 1733...the two-party system was at an end, and Toryism as far as power politics at the centre was concerned had become quite irrelevant.' Soon these qualifications were dropped, and he wrote with more zest of a *precise event*: 'the total defeat of the Tory party in 1715 and its obliteration from the serious world of politics'. Holmes sharpened the chronology still further in arguing for 1716, not 1715, as the exact date of the 'suicide' of the Tory party.[71] Once enunciated with such authority, the doctrine was taken up by others, and used as a prop to a Court–Country analysis of the politics of 1714–60 even in works of otherwise admirable scholarship.[72]

The Court–Country analysis of parliamentary alignments seemed the obvious corollary of the 'oligarchy theory'. Equally, the latter seemed describable, as it was described by Plumb, as 'single party government'. By this was not meant (what the present author has since argued was the case) a system characterised by an institutional link between a single party and the ministry but not between party and opposition. Rather, the phrase seemed to refer to the pattern of post-colonial Africa or of communist eastern Europe, where one party might use its dominance to obliterate its rivals by force; and the vividness of the recent experience which lay behind this implied analogy distracted attention from the qualifications necessary if the concept was to be applied to eighteenth-century England.

Whig histories of parliamentary reform had, traditionally, begun in 1760. In order to trace the origins of trends which reached their apotheosis in 1832

---

[70] B. W. Hill, *The Growth of Parliamentary Parties 1689–1742* (London, 1976); but see his *British Parliamentary Parties 1742–1832* (London, 1985).

[71] Plumb, *Political Stability*, p. 172; *idem*, 'Political Man', pp. 5–6; G. Holmes, 'Harley, St John and the Death of the Tory Party' in Holmes (ed.), *Britain After the Glorious Revolution 1689–1714* (London, 1969), p. 235.

[72] H. T. Dickinson, *Bolingbroke* (London, 1970); *idem*, *Walpole and the Whig Supremacy* (London, 1973); *idem*, *Liberty and Property* (1977); J. P. Kenyon, *Revolution Principles* (1977); W. A. Speck, *Stability and Strife* (1977).

to the resistance offered to George III, those histories needed to establish
a contrast with the reigns of George I and George II:

The first half of the eighteenth century was a dead season: a time of material content
and political indifferentism. No sharp difference of principle marked off the
combatants from each other in the political arena, or divided them into clearly
defined and continuously hostile camps. No hotly contested measure of the first
public importance, no vital question of national policy, served to divide party from
party, to keep alive their mutual animosity, or to feed the fires of their divided
zeal...It was not until public opinion began to be more definitively formulated, it
was not until the machinery of political change was invented and developed, that
there was any hope of a serious measure of parliamentary reform.[73]

This constitutional perspective continued to generate a political analysis
into the 1970s. It issued in the extreme view that 'Few, if any, innovations
in government were made between 1720 and 1780',[74] derived from the more
sophisticated form it took in J. B. Owen's assumption that the pattern of
parties he discerned in the 1740s was true for the eighteenth century as a
whole.[75] The result was that while the political history of 1688–1715 and
1760–84 was increasingly seen in dynamic terms, in the light of the
development and manoeuvres of parliamentary parties, the politics of
1715–60 was still usually viewed in structural terms, through the static
analysis that seemed most appropriate to an oligarchy (so that here, as
elsewhere, conclusions and assumptions were for a time locked in a circular
argument). The effects of this limitation were most apparent in scholarly
discussions of party *qua* Whig and Tory; of the efficacy of patronage; and
of the content of political debate.

The Court–Country categorisation was initially drawn not from a
narrative of manoeuvres on the floor of the Commons, but from the
apparently successful analysis of MPs by type, both in Namier's initial work
and in the volumes of the *History of Parliament*.[76] As Dr Owen expressed it,
that typology was one of professional politicians; Court and Treasury party;
and Independents. Arranged as 'Ins' and 'Outs', they produced an illusion
of two parties in the Commons.[77] Discussion of this categorisation tended
to focus on the third class, the Independents: if it could be shown to be true
of them, it seemed to follow for the others also. Yet, until 1975, the debate
was distracted by being subsumed in a slightly different controversy

[73] G. S. Veitch, *The Genesis of Parliamentary Reform* (1913; ed. Ian R. Christie, London, 1965),
p. 23; cf. Cannon, *Parliamentary Reform*, chapter 2, 'Pudding Time'.
[74] J. H. Plumb, 'Reason and Unreason in the Eighteenth Century: the English Experience',
in J. H. Plumb and V. A. Dearing (eds.), *Some Aspects of Eighteenth Century England* (Los
Angeles, 1971), p. 8.
[75] J. B. Owen, *The Pattern of Politics in Eighteenth-Century England* (London, 1962).
[76] Sir Lewis Namier and John Brooke (eds.), *The History of Parliament. The House of Commons
1754–1790* (London, 1964).
[77] *The Eighteenth Century*, p. 106. Though it would be fair to call Dr Owen's analysis Namierite,
it was his own, and was not identical with that which Namier had sketched in 'Monarchy
and the Party System' (1952), in *Crossroads of Power* (London, 1962), p. 220.

between Plumb and Owen over the efficacy and force of patronage. Plumb had claimed that there had been some 200 Independent MPs in Harley's time, but that 'The spread of corruption and the growth of oligarchy steadily diminished this number until it reached about one hundred, a figure at which it remained for the rest of the eighteenth century.'[78] In 1967 the same author laid even greater stress on what he saw as the basic currency of eighteenth-century society: 'It was patronage that cemented the political system, held it together, and made it an almost impregnable citadel, impervious to defeat, indifferent to social change.'[79] Owen, in reply, vigorously defended the view of patronage he had advanced in *The Rise of the Pelhams*: that it was a necessary but not a sufficient condition of governments' survival; that it did not cement its recipients into a monolithic bloc; that the numbers of Independents were substantially higher than Plumb had suggested, and the importance of their political views much greater, in aligning the majority of them (until 1784) regularly against the ministry of the day.[80]

Dr Owen's replies to his critic effectively vindicated his interpretation of the significance of patronage. Politics, therefore, had to be seen as a real struggle, not an exercise in shadow-boxing. Yet, in a wider sense, this controversy was something of a red herring. The problem with the typology employed by John Owen, Sir Lewis Namier and John Brooke was not that it was invalid but that it had too general a validity – it could be applied with effect to any period of modern parliamentary history. As one historian of the nineteenth century wrote, 'In 1869 the Conservative party was still predominantly the Country party';[81] but we do not hesitate to describe politics at that date in party terms.[82] The validity of a sociological classification of MPs in a Namierite sense might be fully consistent with those MPs voting regularly in political parties, and doing so for ideological reasons which a structural analysis of the Commons would neither reveal nor disprove. This possibility was first explicitly raised by Dr Jarrett in 1975,[83] and

---

[78] J. H. Plumb, *Sir Robert Walpole. The Making of a Statesman* (London, 1956), p. 65.

[79] Plumb, *Political Stability*, p. 189. Such descriptions could more appropriately be applied to the workings of patronage in some areas of modern academic life.

[80] J. B. Owen, 'The Survival of Country Attitudes in the Eighteenth Century House of Commons', in J. S. Bromley and E. H. Kossman (eds.), *Britain and the Netherlands*, vol. IV (The Hague, 1971), pp. 42–69; *idem*, 'Political Patronage in Eighteenth Century England', in Paul Fritz (ed.), *The Triumph of Culture* (Toronto, 1972), pp. 369–87.

[81] James Cornford, 'The Transformation of Conservatism in the Late Nineteenth Century', *Victorian Studies* 7 (1963–4), 41.

[82] Moreover, party cross-voting was actually higher for much of the nineteenth century than is revealed by extant division lists for much of George II's reign (a point not grasped by Dr Speck, in John Cannon (ed.), *The Whig Ascendancy* (London, 1981), p. 61): cf. J. C. D. Clark, 'The Decline of Party, 1740–1760', *EHR* 93 (1978), 499–527, at 504–5.

[83] D. Jarrett, 'The Myth of "Patriotism" in Eighteenth Century English Politics', in J. S. Bromley and E. H. Kossman (eds.), *Britain and the Netherlands*, vol. v (The Hague, 1975), pp. 120–40.

by the present author in 1978.[84] As Jarrett observed, Dupplin's lists of the Commons elected in 1754 do not demonstrate the existence of a large bloc of independent country gentlemen: the same men are analysed in one list by type, in another under party labels.

More remarkable than the absence for so long of a direct critique of the Court–Country analysis of politics in 1715–60 was the actual propagation of this theory in the 1970s, and the neglect accorded to a definitive refutation of it at the beginning of that decade. The volumes of the *History of Parliament* covering 1715–54 had appeared in 1970.[85] Among the many points which were there advanced, and supported with massive documentation, were two relevant to the present argument: that the traditional parties of Whig and Tory retained their existence into the 1750s; and that the Tory party was heavily involved, at various times, with Jacobitism. The second of these claims quickly became controversial: it seemed extreme to those sharing, first, the widespread assumption that the survival of parties in general depended on organisation rather than on ideology, and, second, the related assumption that politics within the early-eighteenth-century oligarchy was largely devoid of issues and principles, and centred chiefly on a complex but uninteresting contest over the distribution of the material spoils of power.

The first argument, on the survival of party, was not necessarily dependent on the second, on the importance of Jacobitism, and the controversy over the second effectively disguised the fact that the first had been amply proved.[86] The authors of Sedgwick's volumes were able to show both a Whig and a Tory party manoeuvring and voting as such on the floor of the House, and the former at times dividing to give rise to a three-party pattern with the Whig oppositions of 1717–20, 1725–42, 1747–51 and 1754–6. Plumb's argument about Independents was thereby reversed: almost no MP escaped a party label from the reign of Anne to the death of George II; only after 1760 did the break-up of the old parties direct attention to an alternative, sociological, classification of Members. Yet the consequences of the *History of Parliament*'s work were not generally accepted within the academic community for at least a decade. Partly this was because of the initially unexplained contradiction between the party explanation employed in Sedgwick's volumes and the multi-factional pattern portrayed for the 1760s onward in Namier's,[87] but largely it seems that Sedgwick's results were neglected because they were correctly perceived

[84] Clark, 'Decline of Party'.
[85] Romney Sedgwick (ed.), *The History of Parliament. The House of Commons 1715–1754* (London, 1970).
[86] Cf., for example, Speck in *The Whig Ascendency*, p. 57.
[87] A contradiction which the present author attempted to reconcile in 1978: Clark, 'Decline of Party'.

to be inconsistent with the nexus of assumptions, values and commitments by that stage embodied in the 'oligarchy theory'.

Yet in the late 1970s and early 1980s the Court–Country analysis came under heavy shellfire; several accurate salvos left it in a sinking condition, and apparently about to share the fate of Walcott's theories.[88] New scholarship on party-politics in the reign of George II fully confirmed the Whig–Tory analysis advanced in Sedgwick's volumes of the *History of Parliament*. While these new results were slowly winning acceptance, however, other historians continued to employ the old assumptions of 'single party government' as an explanatory framework in their discussions of the content of politics – the issues, the beliefs, the propaganda. This constituted the third area in which the Court–Country misconception was influential. It helped to ensure that the discussion of political ideologies in the period c. 1714–60 continued to be conducted in resolutely secular terms, neglecting the central contribution of the clerical intelligentsia (a contribution which is explored in subsequent chapters here). Historians committed to the Court–Country analysis still insisted on the secularisation of politics under the first two Georges and on the virtual absence after 1720 of religious controversy; but this argument was based on a simple extrapolation of a structural picture of party-politics rather than on adequate studies of the full range of political argument (which would have demonstrated the contrary). It was inconclusive, therefore, to argue that because most of the issues which occasioned published Commons division lists were different in the period 1716–42 from those of Anne's reign, the previous alignment of Whig and Tory parties was replaced by a Court–Country one.[89] On the contrary, the issues of parliamentary conflict were often chosen by opposition Whigs as those most likely to *make* feasible their co-operation with Tories; their choice is evidence not for the previous existence of an ideological consensus, but for attempts to bring about a tactical alliance at Westminster made difficult by the lack of such a consensus. Court and Country have some use as descriptions of attitudes or dispositions; but the tactical units in Parliament and in the country at large were Whig and Tory. Furthermore, and crucially, as is argued in chapters 3 and 5 below, the ideological distinctions between Tories and opposition Whigs remained clear-cut and profound; and the element which above all explains their resolute independence of each other is the dynastic issue. Most recent historians were quite unwilling

[88] Professor D. A. Rubini had advanced a similar analysis in *Court and Country* (London, 1968). He was almost alone in seeking to defend this model for the earlier period: 'Party and the Augustan Constitution, 1694–1716: Politics and the Power of the Executive', *Albion* 10 (1978), 193–208.

[89] Speck, in *The Whig Ascendency*, pp. 59–61. A problem seems to be the belief that a party system must be a *two*-party system; that Whig schism, and the existence of a consistently-voting bloc of opposition Whigs, by refuting a Whig–Tory analysis, thereby establishes a Court–Country one. I dissent from both assumptions.

to take Jacobitism seriously, however.[90] If attended to at all, it appeared only as the idiom fortuitously taken by economically-motivated plebeian protest against 'social control'. The way in which Jacobitism was thus accommodated within 'oligarchy theory' was helpfully revealed: 'The fact is that Jacobitism became a cloak for political careerism. It was less feared than exploited to perpetuate Whig power. The losers were not only the Tory party...but the labouring poor, who faced a battery of sanctions against popular assembly and were vulnerable to the possible confusion of social protest with Jacobitism.'[91]

It was always possible to interpret Jacobitism as peripheral to Toryism. The coherence of party could be traced chiefly to organisation rather than to ideology; direct evidence for Jacobite complicity on the part of Tory MPs is often scanty; reports of Jacobite agents in England on their potential support are open to dismissal as largely wishful thinking. To sustain the 'oligarchy theory', to establish class conflict, it was necessary to dismiss a quite different idiom of allegiance and motivation; to minimise the ideological polarity which held Hanoverian England until the 1750s; and to blur the doctrinal identities of Whig and Tory until they came to seem no more than Court and Country parties, their doctrines merely expressions of material self-interest.[92] Having chosen to discount or reinterpret this type of political rhetoric, historians were then free to accept another sort at face value: as, for example, when Professor Dickinson endorsed the rhetoric of the Whig opposition to Walpole, denying (for tactical purposes) the continued survival of party *qua* Whig and Tory, as 'sophisticated and essentially accurate'.[93]

Here again, guidelines to a fully political treatment of the Tories were not lacking in the work of Dr Cruickshanks[94] and Dr Fritz;[95] but their work was not set at its true worth, because it was at odds with a received orthodoxy not only about the party structure, but about the nature of the forms of political motivation and 'social control' which were held responsible for the 'Venetian oligarchy'. In fact, their work provided a revision of both these things in establishing the existence of a real ideological divide between Tories and opposition Whigs.

The orthodoxy which checked the reception of Dr Cruickshanks' work,

[90] Cf. J. C. D. Clark, 'The Politics of the Excluded: Tories, Jacobites and Whig Patriots, 1715–1760', *Parliamentary History* 2 (1983), 209–22.

[91] N. Rogers, 'Popular Protest in Early Hanoverian London', *P&P* 79 (1978), 99.

[92] Speck, *Stability and Strife*, pp. 152, 162, 166.

[93] Dickinson, *Bolingbroke*, p. 196; Speck, *Stability and Strife*, p. 220.

[94] Especially the chapter on 'The Tories' in the Introduction to Sedgwick, *Commons; idem, Political Untouchables. The Tories and the '45* (London, 1979).

[95] 'Jacobitism and the English Government 1717–31', Cambridge PhD thesis 1967; 'The Anti-Jacobite Intelligence System of the English Ministers, 1715–45', *HJ* 16 (1973), 265–89; *The English Ministers and Jacobitism between the Rebellions of 1715 and 1745* (Toronto, 1975).

though developed principally for the reigns of George I and George II, proved influential on the historiography of the reign of George III also. The latter period needed a starting point, a contrast, a theory of origins. As Dr Brewer rightly saw, 'The key to understanding the peculiar development of Rockinghamite politics lies in the events and issues of the two preceding reigns.'[96] The problem came when a static theory had to be linked to a dynamic one of party development, radical ideology and extra-parliamentary pressure in the 1760s, for Brewer accepted from Plumb the picture of the years 1725–54 as 'the Indian summer of oligarchical politics', characterised by 'single party government',[97] in Plumb's sense, greatly understating the sharpness of organisational definition, and the doctrinal coherence, of the Old Corps. It was on this crucial issue of the nature of the transition between the political systems of the last years of George II and the early years of George III that the present author equally challenged Brewer and Owen in 1978.[98]

Professor Brewer had advanced a threefold division of eighteenth-century politics: 1675–1725 as witnessing 'the emergence of a stable political order'; 1725–54 as 'the halcyon days of oligarchical politics'; 1754–89 as the 'gradual disintegration and fragmentation...of a previously stable political order'. It was, in other words, an attempt to run Plumb's analysis in reverse. The monolithic establishment which Brewer imagined was under attack *for the first time* in the 1760s rested on four props: 'single party government'; the domination of the legislature by the executive; a 'sense of common identity' among 'the political class'; and 'the exclusion of a substantial part of the nation from the institutionalised political process'. The instability of the 1760s was explained as the result of challenges to each of them.[99]

Despite the merits of Professor Brewer's book, then, some of the phenomena of the 1760s were wrongly diagnosed, through incorrect views as to their origins, because of the misconceived picture of the reigns of George I and George II which was accepted as a starting point. Of the four props advanced, the fourth, the psephological argument, has been dealt with already. The first, concerning single-party government, is questioned above. The second was a misconception which derived from the first and which falls with it: it rested only on the Plumbian claim that 'patronage was the bedrock of politics, and the foundation stone of political stability,' already refuted by Owen. The third was a generalisation the function of which was to give point to a view of high-political tactics in the 1760s: that the ministerial instability of those years was due to 'an alliance, a union of monarch and those who were politically proscribed for so long', so offering

[96] J. Brewer, 'Rockingham, Burke and Whig Political Argument', *HJ* 18 (1975), 188.
[97] *Ibid.*   [98] Clark, 'Decline of Party'.
[99] J. Brewer, *Party Ideology and Popular Politics at the Accession of George III* (Cambridge, 1976), pp. 3–4.

an alternative to 'Whig aristocratic dominance': a 'new political alliance that would break Old Corps dominance'.[100]

This last claim had to be delicately framed in order to avoid Professor Christie's classic refutation of the view that the 1760s witnessed a 'new Toryism' in ministerial policy or the exercise of kingship,[101] a counterpart of his earlier demonstration that, despite the appearance in the Commons of a two-party alignment created by the American Revolution, the composition and dissolution of North's majorities gives no room for presuming the existence of a Tory *party* arrayed in his support.[102] Brewer's claim was framed, therefore, not by focussing on some royal reaction, but on the Rockingham Whigs, and on their 'assertion that a Whig/Tory struggle still existed – reconfigured...into an opposition/government rather than a government/opposition battle'.[103] Moreover, he avoided passing judgement on the appropriateness of the constitutional arguments he dealt with. His presentation of the Whig case against Bute thus seemed, by implication, to lend it credence.[104] And though this reconstruction of the political debates of the 1760s was in many ways valuable, it might be doubted whether any such exercise could properly be done without an accurate view of the realities which constitutional rhetoric attempted to appeal to, misrepresent or change for tactical advantage. Instead of a picture of the gradual disintegration of a political order in the years 1754–89 under the impact of growing political articulacy and popular extra-parliamentary action, in conjunction with a Rockinghamite Whig campaign against renascent ministerial Toryism and a royal bid for absolutism, a 'high-political' analysis might still support a different picture: a relatively rapid transition in the pattern of party-politics in the 1750s, a consequent period of ministerial instability in the 1760s, the establishment of a new formula for ministerial cohesion under Lord North, which was to remain effective until 1827, and the survival in its essentials of an aristocratic social and political order despite the evanescent phenomenon of John Wilkes.

The realities were indeed largely determined by the way in which the Rockinghams became 'a party by virtue of being an opposition, not an opposition by virtue of being a party'.[105] Earlier work had stressed the similarities between the Rockinghams and the other factions of the 1760s. Increasingly, this came to be questioned, first by Professors Christie and Cannon, and then in the detailed demonstrations of Dr Langford, Dr Hoffman and Dr O'Gorman. Other studies lent credence to a party analysis

---

[100] *Ibid.*, pp. 4–5, 10.
[101] Ian R. Christie, 'Was there a "New Toryism" in the Earlier Part of George III's Reign?', *JBS* 5 (1965–6), 60–76.
[102] Ian R. Christie, *The End of North's Ministry 1780–1782* (London, 1958).
[103] Brewer, *Party Ideology*, p. 15.
[104] *Ibid.*, p. 49; 'toryism' we find in the index, p. 381, 'revived under George III'.
[105] *Ibid.*, p. 60.

of later years by showing the continued existence of the Rockinghamite Whigs as the party of Charles James Fox and, in turn, of Grey. This work, together, seemed to erode both the possible interpretations of the last few decades of the eighteenth century. It seemed to leave little room for a Plumbian oligarchy. Equally, it impinged on the Namierite analysis, the applicability of which seemed earlier to have been confirmed for this period by, among others, D. G. Barnes.[106]

It had been correctly observed that the period 1790–1820 had seen 'checks and even retrogressions in the consolidation of parties'.[107] How those discontinuities might be synthesised was at that time unclear, and was not elucidated by the work on the Rockinghams in the 1760s. A solution might have been suggested by a wider frame of reference, for historians working on the emergent party systems of the 1830s and 40s had produced results which highlighted the differences between the pattern found before and after 1832. Those writing before that date had still been drawn to employ the anachronistic assumption that the existence of party indicated a party system (albeit one still emerging) and that a party system implied a *two*-party system. This was especially the case among historians who studied the Whigs, established their existence as a party, and inferred the existence of a Tory party as its counterpart.[108] As late as 1978, this issued in the claim that '*the* two-party system' emerged after 1807 and was in full operation by 1818.[109] Historians working chiefly on the period after 1832 had, however, insisted on the subsequent emergence of parties in a nineteenth-century sense, and of a marked contrast with the preceding decades.[110] Indications existed of similar conclusions to be drawn from the latter part of the eighteenth century (it was argued, for example, that the polarity of 1784–6 was temporary and did not mark the emergence of a two-party system);[111] but their implications were not linked with available work on the 1830s.

An unresolved problem therefore remained in the first three decades of the nineteenth century. What was the nature of the transition between the politics of the 1820s and 1830s, between the ancien regime and the seemingly familiar Victorian world? What was the role in that transition of the Reform Bill of 1832? Yet here lay an historiographical puzzle. If the Act was passed for the reasons for which Whig or neo-Whig historians had said that it was

---

[106] D. G. Barnes, *George III and William Pitt, 1783–1806* (Stanford, 1939).
[107] Ian R. Christie, *Myth and Reality in Late Eighteenth Century British Politics and Other Papers* (London, 1970), p. 14.
[108] A. D. Harvey, 'The Ministry of All the Talents: the Whigs in Office, February 1806 to March 1807', *HJ* 15 (1972), 647–8.
[109] *Idem*, 'The Third Party in British Politics, 1818–21', *BIHR* 51 (1978), 159. Italics added.
[110] N. Gash, *Reaction and Reconstruction in English Politics 1832–1852* (Oxford, 1965); D. Close, 'The Formation of a Two-Party Alignment in the House of Commons between 1832 and 1841', *EHR* 89 (1969), 257–77.
[111] P. Kelly, 'British Parliamentary Politics, 1784–1786', *HJ* 17 (1974), 733–53.

passed and said that it was necessary, why was it not passed much sooner? But if 'Old Corruption' functioned as they said it did, how could the Act have been passed at all? The answers, it seemed, would be 'high-political',[112] and the materials for such answers were to hand in work both on parliamentary parties and on psephology. The politics of the years from the early 1760s to the late 1820s, it became clear, could be regarded as in many respects bound by a constant set of conventions. The continuing power of the monarchy and the success of the non-party coalition ministries which it sustained meant that the dice were loaded against a Whig party-opposition. In the 1810s and 1820s the Whigs displayed a growing sense of frustration and helplessness, trapped, as they saw themselves, in a situation which offered them hardly any prospect of office. Their eventual response, Samson-like, was to pull down around their ears the late-eighteenth-century constitution. It was a gamble which paid handsome dividends: in the political world of early- and mid-Victorian England, the dice were loaded almost as heavily in favour of the Whigs as they had earlier been loaded against them.[113] And the crucial commitment of so many county Members to parliamentary reform in 1830–2 was then explained, not as their response to local democratic pressures, but as a reaction to the apostasy of Wellington's ministry, chiefly over Catholic Emancipation.[114]

No-one would deny the presence in English society in the half century to 1830 of urbanisation, population growth and industrial development; but there is no *objective sense* in which these things can be said to have made the electoral system inappropriate. What they did was to offer scope for tactical use to be made, within a high-political arena, of claims that it was. The fortuitous success of those claims does not prove their objective validity. As is argued in chapter 6 below, the first Reform Bill is not to be interpreted as the triumph of popular pressure and its democratic justification, the natural apotheosis of a reformist tradition revolving around the issue of the franchise. A rationale for such a measure had, of course, long been available within English political culture; but what made it the dominant public ideology was not that it was 'true', nor was it a democratic ideology which produced the Act. Rather, it was the passing of the Act which was held to have validated the ideology, and which entrenched it in the constitution as its chief and official rationale.

If constitutional history is demoted in this way, it is possible to see that the 1832 Act was as much of an aristocratic *coup* as the Glorious Revolution. In colonial America, as several scholars have shown, far from 'democracy' producing 'the Revolution', it was the Revolution which led on to

---

[112] The expression 'high politics' was apparently coined by Sir Herbert Butterfield: e.g. in *The Listener*, 18th May 1961, p. 875.
[113] Cf. Clark, 'General Theory', pp. 319–24.
[114] D. C. Moore, 'The Other Face of Reform'.

democracy.[115] It is tempting to make a similar remark about 1832. Yet this would be the oversimplification of an aphorism. What we observe in America, as in England in 1688 or 1832, is not the arrival of 'democracy' or 'constitutional monarchy' in an objective sense (whether wholly or in part), but the redefinition of that rationale of government which is officially endorsed and officially held to be exemplified by established political arrangements.[116]

In practical terms, Dr Owen had correctly written of the process by which, at some point after 1815, the politicians were to 'reach down and, through the medium of Party, absorb the independents' in the House of Commons.[117] Professor Beales, drawing on the work of Professors Aydelotte and Gash, sharpened the chronology: the process was given a powerful impetus during the debates on the Reform Bill, and was complete by 1835.[118] An exactly analogous process was revealed by the history of voting: the process by which, in and after the 1830s, the parties reached down to give the common man a party-political identity and allegiance distinct from his response to the influence of local magnates. By 1830, as Professor D. C. Moore's work showed, it was by no means clear that any movement in this direction had taken place in the counties. That was the achievement, rather, of the parties which emerged after 1832. For after each of the three nineteenth-century Reform Acts, the number of those eligible to vote was expanded not chiefly by the initiative of 'the excluded' themselves, whom some historians had portrayed as eager for participation, but through the labours of local party organisations in placing their supporters on the electoral registers which the 1832 Act created, and defending their supporters' titles against legal challenge: 'the parties established themselves as the custodians of the register', wrote one historian, to such effect that 'the parties virtually selected the voters'.[119]

---

[115] Cf. M. Jensen, 'Democracy and the American Revolution', *HLQ* 20 (1956–7), 321–41. Most American historians of England, by contrast, remained committed to a 'Whig' view of popular involvement.

[116] Such a process of redefinition is largely the subject, it seems, of Kenyon, *Revolution Principles*. We lack a similar study of the consequences of the Reform Bill.

[117] *The Eighteenth Century*, p. 293. Dr Owen's suggestion was a prescient one, for much research still remains to be done on the political history of 1800–30.

[118] D. E. D. Beales, 'Parliamentary Parties and the "Independent" Member, 1810–1860', in R. Robson (ed.), *Ideas and Institutions of Victorian Britain* (London, 1967), pp. 17, 12.

[119] P. F. Clarke, 'Electoral Sociology of Modern Britain', *History* 57 (1972), 33. See also J. A. Thomas, 'The System of Registration and the Development of Party Organisation, 1832–1870', *History* 35 (1950), 81–98; Gash, *Politics in the Age of Peel*, pp. 395, 412–17; Hanham, *Elections and Party Management*, pp. 399–403; N. Blewett, 'The Franchise in the United Kingdom 1885–1918', *P&P* 32 (1965), 27–56; J. Vincent, *The Formation of the Liberal Party 1857–1868* (London, 1966), pp. 84–96; F. B. Smith, *The Making of the Second Reform Bill* (Cambridge, 1966), pp. 6, 19–20, 42, 237–9; P. F. Clarke, *Lancashire and the New Liberalism* (Cambridge, 1971), pp. 103–29; D. C. Moore, *Politics of Deference*, pp. 300–24; J. Prest, *Politics in the Age of Cobden* (London, 1977) – accused by his reviewer of reducing politics to a 'registration game': *HJ* 21 (1978), 707.

Once selected, the post-1832 electorate as a whole began to behave in a markedly different way: it took on the voting patterns of the Dissenters. First, the level of split voting declined dramatically between the general elections of 1830 and 1835, most of the change apparently occurring, more specifically, between the polls of 1830 and 1832. Voters' allegiance between parties was now much more sharply defined. An individual would henceforth generally cast both his votes for candidates of the same party. Second, consistent partisanship increased markedly after 1832: an individual voting Liberal in one election was now very likely to vote Liberal in the next; a Conservative would very probably vote Conservative.[120] The era of the 'floating' and the 'occasional' voter was over. Party allegiances among the electorate were now well on the way to being as clear-cut and reliable as MPs' voting records in the Commons. Men were given every opportunity to align themselves, since the break-up of the ancien regime took place amid a spate of contests. General elections followed hard on each others' heels in 1826, 1830, 1831, 1832, 1835, 1837 and 1841: not since the 'first age of party' under William and Anne had there been so much activity at the polls. As between 1688 and 1714, so after 1826, the course taken by the party battle at Westminster meant that the parties politicised the nation and created an electorate in their own image.

IV. CONCLUSION

The widely-accepted account of the English ancien regime, then, was handicapped by a misconception about the pattern of parliamentary parties which was profoundly related, in turn, to a misconception about psephology and the functioning of the Commons as a system of representative democracy. The prevailing orthodoxies in both these respects were two sides of the same coin. That this coincidence shaped the interpretation of the period in many other ways passed unnoticed, not least because of the relative scarcity of textbooks on the period, and the reticence on general matters of those texts that *were* published (in the wake of Namierite nominalism, writing a textbook was for long considered a particularly hazardous undertaking). Trevelyan's *Two-Party System* retained its unacknowledged dominance, while the theoretical vacuousness of the subject in many respects drew in, *faute de mieux*, the Marxists.

In the absence of a new general theory, eighteenth-century history was given coherence by an older selection of organising categories – stability, oligarchy, the ruling class, the working class, 'Old Corruption'. It was probably a disinclination among historians to sacrifice the few explanatory

---

[120] John A. Phillips, 'The Many Faces of Reform: the Reform Bill and the Electorate', *Parliamentary History* 1 (1982), 115–35. Three boroughs were used as a sample: again, we need more research on the electorate in its full diversity.

categories that did seem available which helped to shield those categories almost wholly from explicit questioning.[121] Less attention, too, was given to the ideological dimension of politics as a whole than to selected issues on which a parliamentary furore was ignited; 'issues', instead of being interpreted politically and within a tactical framework, came to take on something of the autonomy once accorded to 'facts'. The reason why the framework was misunderstood was that politics was not taken seriously; the reason why politics was not taken seriously was that political events were judged in the light of an interpretative orthodoxy rather than being allowed to revise it.

This was as apparent in 1950, in Plumb's caricature of eighteenth-century government as a 'fantastic hybrid of mediaeval and Tudor institutions',[122] as it was in 1972 in Speck's suggestion that 'Judging by propaganda politics was a far more serious business in the late seventeenth century than it became in the mid eighteenth',[123] in 1973 when Cannon complained that 'complacency hardened into a national sclerosis' during 'Pudding time',[124] or in 1978 when Speck pronounced Walpole's opponents to be 'essentially reactionaries' because 'they never proposed the obvious solution, parliamentary reform'.[125]

This scarcity of general interpretations, and the use of moralistic categories, led to a lack of chronological discrimination in talk of, for example, the politics of '*the* eighteenth century', or of 'modern parties', 'real' parties, as existing only after 1832. This shaded, in turn, into what might be termed a definitional mode of enquiry in which an assumption was first reified and then searched for in the past. Much of the historiography of party in the years 1688–1832 was confused by the search for a single set of criteria which would allow 'the' phenomenon to be recognised among the diversity of the politics of a period which so often seemed just beyond the possibility of reconstruction in its necessary detail.[126] But the historian's task is not to initiate and refine *a priori* definitions of past phenomena; it is, on the contrary, to identify the ways in which, and the exact points at which, phenomena like parties *change* at different periods, and their appropriate descriptive criteria with them.

Recent scholarship typically has not favoured studies of this sort. As Professor Dickinson described it, most eighteenth-century history since

---

[121] Though cf. Joseph Lee's relatively undeferential analysis of the 'purely speculative', 'excessively elastic' and unsubstantiated nature of the assumptions concerning the social, intellectual, economic and political relations allegedly producing 'stability' in J. H. Plumb's sense, *The Times Literary Supplement*, 23rd January 1976, p. 90.

[122] *England in the Eighteenth Century* (Harmondsworth, 1950), p. 33.

[123] W. A. Speck, 'Political Propaganda in Augustan England', *TRHS* 5th ser. 22 (1972), p. 32.

[124] Cannon, *Parliamentary Reform*, p. 43.

[125] W. A. Speck, 'Politics' in Pat Rogers (ed.), *The Eighteenth Century* (London, 1978), p. 104.

[126] Cf. the discussion in *The Whig Ascendency*, pp. 190–2.

Namier had concerned itself either with political structures and organisations, whether high-political or extra-parliamentary; or with the disembodied study of politial ideas and issues. He rightly called, in addition, for studies of 'the mode of argument adopted' in debates about the latter.[127] Another possibility existed which the pursuit of these three might actually have obscured: the study of the strictly *political*, the *dynamic* aspect of general social arrangements. Ultimately, it is the dynamic which creates structures, gives reality to ideas, and sets a scale and a dimension for a mode of argument. Yet post-Namierite scholarship, which threw much light on ideas *per se* and on organisations *per se*, often neglected to focus directly on politics itself; so that even in the late 1970s the political *life* to which ideas and organisations are to be related remained, as it seemed to the present author, curiously obscure. Consequently, the assumed dynamic, the principle of social change, was still within the tradition of the 'Whig interpretation', whether related to accounts of popular unrest, economic growth, the shifting balance of classes, or a reforming impulse; the possibility of the existence of any forms of internal, high-political dynamic was overlooked or dismissed by those who wished to describe 'accounts of ministerial politicking in the hermetically sealed world of St James's' as merely 'staggeringly tedious'.[128]

One strong recommendation of the 'Whig interpretation', after all, and a reason for its long survival, was that it did contain a dynamic, a theory of the direction of the evolution of events and the cause of that direction; thanks to its nominalist implications, Namierite analysis, irrespective of its scholarly calibre, did not. If an alternative dynamic was to be sought in a study of politics, the appropriate method of enquiry might have been expected to be, chiefly, political narrative. No such expectation was current in the 1960s.[129] One writer explicitly voiced a widespread assumption that chronological narrative, being devoid of explanatory concepts, was the genre adopted by methodologically naive historians, victims of 'the empiricist delusion' – authors of the sort of history which, as Dr Stedman Jones subtly put it, had once 'provided a more or less coherent rationale of British capitalism' but which was now marked by 'conceptual archaism and reactionary apologetics' among professional historians.[130] By the end of the

[127] H. T. Dickinson, 'The Eighteenth Century Debate on the "Glorious Revolution"', *History* 61 (1976), 28.

[128] John Brewer, in *Social History* 4 (1979), 137. Cf.:

> Political historians are themselves responsible for that sense of tedium which has suffused their subject for the last ten years or so...they isolated their subject from social movements...The result was arid and self-destructive...the wearisome discipline of the old political history...as boring as Euclid or five-finger exercises to an indifferent schoolboy...the dessication and sterility of the last two decades.

> J. H. Plumb, 'The World Beyond Westminster', *New Statesman* 16th February 1973, pp. 234–5. It is necessary to defend 'high-political' history from this sort of unthinking dismissal if its potential for generating wide-ranging explanations is to be realised.

[129] Cf. the articles in the series 'New Ways in History', *The Times Literary Supplement*, 7th April, 28th July, 8th September 1966.

[130] G. Stedman Jones, 'History: the Poverty of Empiricism', *loc. cit.*, p. 100.

1970s, the tide was running strongly the other way. Lawrence Stone documented a growing interest in narrative on the part of several breeds of fashionable writers whose interests had occupied them elsewhere for over a decade. He may also have disclosed something of their evident pique, on returning to narrative, to find that its potential had meanwhile been exploited to good effect by what Stone stigmatised as the 'new British school of young antiquarian empiricists'.[131] But it is difficult to recognise under this label anything other than scholars in the classical mainstream of professional history; and for the reasons outlined here, it would be proper to presume that the antidote to the misconceptions identified above would lie in areas of historical enquiry which could sustain radically different methodologies.

An antidote was necessary. By the end of the 1970s, two decades of distinctively anti-Namierite writing seemed to leave the history of eighteenth-century England in a state of confusion, with implications pointing in different directions. The most likely ways out of the confusion seemed to be ones drawing on an available dynamic (any dynamic was better than none), whether via social history in the manner of E. P. Thompson or political history in the idiom of J. H. Plumb. Writing of this sort had caught and profited from the mood of the general intellectual culture within which it was embedded, just as Namier's history did not achieve wide currency until it seemed congruent with the conservatism of the 1950s in the work of such men as J. L. Austin, T. D. Weldon, and the 'end of ideology' theorists. A much more extensive survey than is attempted in this book would be necessary to account for the analogies and connections between these currents in a great range of intellectual disciplines contiguous with history – philosophy, psychology, economics and others. The object in this chapter has been merely to trace developments in a limited and technical aspect of historical writing and to point to a way of escape.

What course will the debate about parliamentary parties take? By the mid-1980s, there were several hopeful signs. Many writers were arguing that a certain intellectual consensus, which some dated from Attlee, others from Suez, was discredited and breaking up; and that this had wide consequences for historical scholarship. Secondly, the revisionism which had successfully toppled an orthodoxy in the field of early-Stuart parliamentary history now had an ally in the history of the Hanoverian era. If the old orthodoxy was still entrenched in eighteenth-century studies, its vulnerability was becoming daily more evident. Some of the criticisms which this orthodoxy seemed to invite are explored in this book.

---

[131] Lawrence Stone, 'The Revival of Narrative: Reflections on a New Old History', *P&P* 85 (1979), 20. The force of the word 'young' deserves attention.

2

Political Theory, Patriarchalism and Cultural Hegemony: England as an Aristocratic Society, 1688–1832

I. POLITICAL THEORY AND SOCIAL INFERENCE, LOCKE TO MILL

The main trend of popular and semi-scholarly writing on eighteenth-century England has been to portray it as essentially modern: a society of earthy, ambitious 'new men' fighting their way to the top; a world of thrusting entrepreneurs, eagerly adopting new methods in agriculture, commerce and industry; increasingly interested in empirical, scientific enquiry and the spread of rational knowledge; men zestfully engaged in the enjoyment of a new-found material well-being; commercialising leisure; resentful of traditional authority in Church or State; provincial men, Dissenters or sceptics in religion; hard realists in politics, thriving on the spoils of power, the mechanics of corruption and influence being the analogues of their commercial motivations; men with a strong streak of vulgarity, acknowledged and skilful social climbers; men who planned and realised England's industrial-democratic future.

Even recent historians have to a quite remarkable extent indulged in this sort of word-painting. In hard terms, it meant that they adopted the viewpoint of the radical provincial artisan of the 1830s and inflated it into an analysis of society as a whole. The elites which dominated ancien-regime England were therefore largely ignored. Paradoxically, the masses of men who so weakly failed to anticipate a nineteenth-century consciousness were equally the victims of a patronising neglect.[1] We still know remarkably little about the world view of the inarticulate millions – the unskilled; the illiterate; the really poor; those who thought they found dignity and meaning in their relations to things they did not create – their religion, their country, their rulers.

---

[1] For an indictment of the class bias introduced by the 'bourgeois' intelligentsia, cf. Harold Perkin, '"The Condescension of Posterity"': Middle-Class Intellectuals and the History of the Working Class', in *The Structured Crowd* (Brighton, 1980), pp. 168–85. The charge applies equally to the historiography of England's ancien regime.

Together with some historians' denigration of elites have always gone eulogies of those who allegedly heralded the future, whether an entrepreneurial future (as with Defoe) or an urban-radical future (as with Wilkes). Trevelyan said nothing new in claiming that 'The eighteenth century English, on the average, were an earnest, virile, original, unconventional, and energetic race' who 'practised self-help and individualism before the Victorians'.[2] In respect of the early Hanoverian years, it meant that 'Defoe, more than Swift, was the typical man of his day. Defoe the trader hailed the advent of the era of business prosperity... Defoe was one of the first who saw the old world through a pair of sharp modern eyes. His report... occupies the central point of our thought and vision.'[3] In part, this sort of analysis has rested on the use of dubious categories: 'national character', or personifications like 'the "average" English gentleman' and 'the "average" English working man'.[4] It seems almost cruel to despatch such helpless arguments, yet the task must be faced if they are to be deleted from even recent works aimed at a wide audience.[5] Nor is it a problem peculiar to this period, for the same arguments sustain a similar vision for other centuries, too.[6] If this caricature does contain any element of truth, it is not confined to the eighteenth century, and needs to be set in a different methodological framework. Taken literally, as an account of England 'in general', it hardly ranks above a parody; and this picture omits most of the features which made men of that time, in their various ways, different from us. It misses the religious dimension in which all moved, whether Anglican, Roman Catholic or Dissenter. And it misses those traditional, hierarchical, deferential forms which were neither antiquated, tenuous survivals nor mere veneers or superstructures on a reality which was 'basically' economic, but substantive and prevalent modes of thought and behaviour in a society dominated still by the common people, by the aristocracy, and by the relations between the two. For without an adequate weighting on these elements, the explanations of an historical orthodoxy have been unable to account for the persistence of Jacobitism into the eighteenth century, for the tardiness of parliamentary reform into the nineteenth, or for the survival

---

2 G. M. Trevelyan, 'The Age of Johnson', in A. S. Turberville (ed.), *Johnson's England* (2 vols., Oxford, 1933), vol. I, p. 1.

3 G. M. Trevelyan, *Illustrated English Social History*, vol. III: 'The Eighteenth Century' (Harmondsworth, 1964), pp. 17–18.

4 Expressions of E. P. Thompson, *The Making of the English Working Class* (Harmondsworth, 1968), pp. 257, 451.

5 The continued currency of the Trevelyan–Plumb tradition is all too evident in, for example, Roy Porter, *English Society in the Eighteenth Century* (Harmondsworth, 1982).

6 Cf. Keith Thomas's warning: 'Modern historians like to believe that the tough and self-reliant men of Stuart England, the pioneers of modern science and the founders of the British Empire, were too much like ourselves to be really worried' about portents, prodigies and the whole realm of folklore and the occult so ably reconstructed in Dr Thomas' *Religion and the Decline of Magic. Studies in Popular Beliefs in Sixteenth and Seventeenth Century England* (London, 1971); quotation, p. 91.

of aristocratic domination of English society despite all the vicissitudes of the years between the Restoration and the Reform Bill.

The subject of this and the following chapter, then, is not the triumph of 'the new' but the survival into the eighteenth century of certain elements of 'the old': a nexus of doctrines and practices which might be called, in its political aspect, the 'dynastic idiom'; in its social aspect, the 'aristocratic ethic'; in its structural aspect, 'patriarchalism'. It had its ramifications both in social history (where writers have denied it by asserting the centrality of Defoe) and in the realm of political thought (where historians have asserted against it the quick triumph of Lockeian empiricism and the swift demise of the doctrine of the divine right of kings). Both assertions were promoted by a particular form of argument, which must now be examined.

Political philosophers in the early modern period frequently deduced their accounts of political obligation and the origin of the State from a view of the nature of man, of human character and therefore of typical or essential motivation, as well as of divine purpose or ancient usage and custom. Historians of political thought are accordingly used to recovering the account of man which is implicit or explicit in these writers' works. Other historians equally recover an account of character: they are all too often dependent on a similar view of man for an organising category. The history of political thought and the history of society at large have therefore interlocked, and procedures in one area of enquiry have powerfully reinforced procedures in the other.

Not only have eighteenth-century politics been too often explained on the assumptions about human nature and conduct generated or seemingly confirmed by the reform polemics of 1832 and 1867; eighteenth century political thought has been reconstructed on a similar perspective. Historians' broadest unwritten assumption has been that the model of human nature which supplied political theorists' premises conformed to the model, reflecting social realities, whose eventual logic demanded the enfranchisement of the autonomous individual. As in the historiography of parliamentary reform, so in the historiography of political thought, a circular argument derived its conclusions from its premises, and used its results to validate its assumptions. At last, it seems possible to break free from this tradition. In their writing on certain individuals, a number of scholars have brilliantly shown the inadequacy of the conventional explanation in so far as it bore on Locke, Hume, Smith, Bentham and James Mill; but historians of eighteenth-century society as a whole have often been slow to see the implications of this work. This section presents a general reinterpretation of the writings of these five theorists in respect of the assumptions which writers like Veitch, Wallas, Laski and Trevelyan brought to bear on them – assumptions which, for lack of a synoptic critique, are still too widely current.

Historians who asked why a particular political philosopher posited his view of human character, then, often answered by saying that it was widely prevalent in his age. The temptation was strong to reinforce the circularity of the argument by treating the identity as proved and claiming, elsewhere, that because a philosopher made use of a characterisation of man, it must have been a generally accurate one at the time he wrote; that Locke, in particular, was important because he

...sensed at once, and all his readers sense it, that a political theory must correspond to something self-evident about ordinary men... He saw that neither Hobbes' Artificial Man nor Filmer's patriarchal state would ever be accepted on the common-sense grounds which really justify important beliefs. It was for these reasons, as well as because of the victory of the forces in society which Locke represented, that he has a far more important place in the texture of political society than either of the other two.[7]

Or, as Laski put it, more sweepingly, 'In the debate which followed [1688], his [Locke's] argument remained unanswered, for the sufficient reason that it had the common sense of the generation on his side.' With this sure foundation, Locke 'announced the advent of the modern system of parliamentary government; and from his time the debate has been rather of the conditions under which it is to work, than of the foundations upon which it is based'.

If so, it might indeed be true that in Locke 'we have the root of that utilitarianism which...is the real parent of all nineteenth-century change'.[8] But three objections can validly be made to this approach. First, that Locke *could not* have been defending 'the modern system of parliamentary government', for (as I have argued elsewhere) no such thing existed, even in outline, in essence, or in miniature when he wrote; and the system which did exist showed no linear urge to evolve into what it was later to become. Not even the most 'advanced' governments in early-eighteenth-century Europe fitted the nineteenth-century understanding of Locke's ideal: 'Representative government, in the Netherlands even more than in England, was based on respect for traditional rights rather than on any conception of popular sovereignty. The mere idea of majority rule was alien to a community which evolved its policies by a laborious process of compromise between local interests.'[9] A second objection is a textual one: such a meaning cannot be extracted from the *Two Treatises*. 'There is no reason to believe

---

[7] Peter Laslett (ed.), *Patriarcha and Other Political Works of Sir Robert Filmer* (Oxford, 1949), p. 42.

[8] H. J. Laski, *Political Thought in England from Locke to Bentham* (London, 1920), pp. 16, 29, 31, 66; cf. Stephen, *English Thought*, vol. II, p. 114: 'Locke expounded the principles of the Revolution of 1688, and his writings became the political Bible of the following century.'

[9] N. Hampson, *The Enlightenment* (Harmondsworth, 1968); cf. Laski, *op. cit.*, p. 31: 'the convenient simplicity of majority-rule solved, for [Locke], the vital political problems'.

that Locke ever enjoyed any authentic vision of a more libertarian and egalitarian political structure, still less social structure'; the liberal and the later Marxist picture of Locke as the herald of bourgeois society failed to survive Mr Dunn's analysis, despite the eloquent expression given to it in C. B. Macpherson's *The Political Theory of Possessive Individualism*.[10] The third objection to this view of Locke is that his political theory, whatever its logical implications, *did not* in fact function in this way (as a justification for representative democracy) in early-eighteenth-century England. It is now established that, under William III and Anne, Locke was scarcely cited even in defence of the Revolution itself,[11] let alone in defence of the forms of government which Victorians were to see the Revolution as intended to establish. The Tories, including the bulk of the intelligentsia, were almost unanimously unwilling to break decisively with doctrines of hereditary right and non-resistance to legitimate monarchs, which had been a distinguishing feature of the Church of England, whatever equivocations this might involve them in towards William, and whatever implied renunciations of the Revolution it led them to make under Anne. Among the Whigs, an extreme republican element did exist which invited monarchs after 1688 to acknowledge and affirm a wholly parliamentary title to the throne as the best answer to Stuart claims; but the monarchs did not comply, and that element represented only a small minority of the Whig party. Somers, Halifax and Sunderland formally disavowed this doctrine to the Electress Sophia in 1710.[12] Most Whigs evaded any description of 1688 as an act of rebellion and deposition, justified by violations of the Original Contract by James II and justifying the making of a new contract with William; equally unwilling to describe 1688 as a conquest, they laboured instead, though uneasily, to give credibility to the implausible idea of James II's abdication, and to the notion of the 'divine right of providence', to disguise *de facto* power.

The neglect of Locke might be puzzling if, as Mr Dunn rightly observes, his 'picture of social structure is one in which hierarchy is as unthinkingly accepted by most men as it is morally appropriate for it to be so'. It seems likely however that Locke was chiefly known not for his *Two Treatises of Government*, but for his technical work on epistemology, *An Essay Concerning Human Understanding* and for *A Letter on Toleration*; but these fell under suspicion for their theological implications. It was the *Essay* which John Byrom, then an undergraduate at Trinity College, Cambridge, was warned against reading by his Nonjuror father, Locke 'being (though a very learned

---

[10] John Dunn, *The Political Thought of John Locke* (Cambridge, 1969), pp. 123, 203–67.
[11] This account is chiefly based on Kenyon, *Revolution Principles*, and Martyn P. Thompson, 'The Reception of Locke's *Two Treatises of Government* 1690–1705', *Political Studies* 24 (1976), 184–91.
[12] Kenyon, *Revolution Principles*, pp. 147ff.

man) a Socinian or an atheist'.[13] At Oxford, Thomas Hearne bought and read Locke's *Essay* as an undergraduate but, he wrote in 1734,

...indeed I neither then nor ever since have had any good opinion of Locke, who, tho' a man of parts, was, however, a man of very bad principles. Mr Locke indeed hath been cry'd up and magnify'd by a set of men of republican principles, but orthodox and truly honest men have detected his errors and fallacies, and endeavoured what they could to obstruct his infection

though without preventing the *Essay*, as Hearne thought, being 'much read and studied at Cambridge and Dublin'.[14]

It seems likely that Locke's chief impact in eighteenth-century England was not to import contractarianism into politics, but Arianism into religion;[15] but this in itself raised formidable barriers against the acceptance of his political analysis. Even to the small extent to which Locke's political doctrines *were* used in the 1690s, it was, via the *First Treatise*, in an attack on the rationale of indefeasible monarchy rather than, via the *Second Treatise*, in a positive affirmation of an alternative, contractarian politics;[16] but the patriarchalist account of authority and the origins of the State was frequently reasserted, and used for a critique of Locke with devastating effect by a school of writers of whom Charles Leslie was not the last. In so far as the Whigs were willing to treat the Original Contract not merely as an explanatory device but as an historical event, expressing the entrenched, ancient, and continuing historical rights of 'the people', they were only committed to an ambiguity (exactly who was entitled to exercise those rights, and how often?) as serious as that which inhibited the Tories (who was the legitimate monarch?) – so opening up a gulf between ideal and reality which was to last as long as the Whig ascendancy itself.[17]

It has been aptly suggested that the Whigs' central political doctrine was not contract theory, with its egalitarian implications for the way in which government should be organised, but the right of resistance[18] – a right

---

[13] Edward Byrom to John Byrom, 16th Sept. 1709: R. Parkinson (ed.), *The Private Journals and Literary Remains of John Byrom* (2 vols. in 4 parts, Manchester, 1854–7), vol. I, part I, p. 6.

[14] P. Bliss (ed.), *Reliquiae Hearnianae*, 2nd edn (3 vols., London, 1869), vol. III, p. 162.

[15] Although Mr Dunn perceptively noticed 'the intimate dependence of an extremely high proportion of Locke's arguments for their very intelligibility, let alone plausibility, on a series of theological commitments' (*op. cit.*, p. xi), he did not remark on Locke's theological heterodoxy as the theoretical basis of his radicalism; for which, see chapter 5 below.

[16] But for the large areas of the patriarchalist case which Locke also embraced, cf. G. J. Schochet, 'The Family and the Origins of the State in Locke's Political Philosophy', in J. W. Yolton (ed.), *John Locke: Problems and Perspectives* (Cambridge, 1969), pp. 81–98, and Dunn, *Locke*, pp. 113ff, 152–3.

[17] Kenyon, *Revolution Principles*, pp. 200–1.

[18] Dickinson, *Liberty and Property*, p. 78; Dunn, *Locke*, p. 143: 'The role of the notion of consent is not to discriminate between governments which may be resisted and governments which should not be resisted. It is merely to explain why any government is in principle subject to just resistance, if it behaves wickedly'; cf. *idem*, 'Consent in the Political Theory of John

conceived as lying wholly outside the general run of politics, a forced
response to extreme provocation in exceptional circumstances; and circumstances, suggested orthodox Whigs, not now to be repeated. Locke's doctrine
of the right of rebellion was of great utility for the Whigs when formulated
in the 1680s, but equally inconvenient for them after 1714 when they were
defending their own regime against a succession of attempts to 'appeal to
Heaven'.[19] Sacheverell's trial proved to Whigs of Walpole's generation the
value of passive obedience to sovereigns for whom both an hereditary and
a parliamentary title could be claimed. It is hardly surprising that
'Revolution Principles', from Walpole's time to Newcastle's, were investigated as seldom, and defined as perfunctorily, as possible; and in no sense
used as the basis for fundamental deductions from human nature to political
representation.

If, as will be argued later, Locke was suspected as an advocate of
theological heterodoxy, not yet of democracy, it was in respect of the former
that his assumptions diverged most from those of his contemporaries. As we
shall see in chapter 5, Arianism was an argument *within* Christian theology,
though all the more bitter for engaging thus closely with the beliefs of the
orthodox majority. The view of political origins embodied in almost all
political theories, until Godwinian atheism at the end of the eighteenth
century, was some version of the Christian view. The state of nature, natural
rights, the social contract, patriarchal authority, monarchy could all be
related to their place in the divine scheme as Providential and historical
episodes and phenomena. Evidence to support or contest such theories had
therefore to be drawn either from English constitutional history, or, much
more powerfully, from scripture. The state of nature, divorced from Biblical
evidence, was a thin fiction compared to the closely-documented and subtly
argued cases which the clerical intelligentsia could propound. Locke was
neither a Biblical scholar nor a constitutional historian, and, as a result, was
largely outside the mainstream of debate. Even in William III's reign, in
the immediate aftermath of 1688, 'There is no comment, no mention, not
even a hint that churchmen were aware that John Locke had written two
treatises on government, supposed ever since to have been the prime Whig
defence of the Revolution.'[20]

As significant was the small currency given to Locke in the American
colonies. For it has been established that the *Two Treatises* hardly circulated

Locke', *HJ* 10 (1967), 154: 'Locke's theory of consent...is a theory of how individuals
come to be subject to political obligations and how legitimate political societies can arise.
It is not in any sense whatsoever a theory of how government should be organised.'

[19] F. J. McLynn, 'Jacobitism and the Classical British Empiricists', *BJECS* 4 (1981), 155–70,
for the failure of Locke, Berkeley and Hume to find 'a theory which would simultaneously
justify the revolution of 1688 but deny the legitimacy of any subsequent ones', or evade
the *a priori* arguments of absolute monarchy; cf. also G. P. Conroy, 'George Berkeley and
the Jacobite Heresy: Some Comments on Irish Augustan Politics', *Albion* 3 (1971), 82–91.

[20] G. M. Straka, *Anglican Reaction to the Revolution of 1688* (Madison, Wisconsin, 1962), p. 117
and *passim*.

there in the early eighteenth century; not until they were taken up and used in the controversies with Britain from the 1760s onward did they achieve prominence. Until then, it was a 'slackly ideological reading of the book which represented the characteristic English understanding of it': a slackness all the more remarkable if, as Mr Dunn has argued, its logical conclusion is 'a system of radical individualism, an individualism as radical in social terms as that of Hobbes and in its potential social implications considerably more subversive'.[21] Not even in America was Locke seized on as the herald of a bourgeois-democratic future. Yet we should beware of treating the American colonies as presciently modern in their outlook,[22] for among the forces making for the continuation of 'the old' at this point have been suggested both a culture-lag in relation to Europe and 'a conservative religious reaction against the growing claims of natural science'. The prevalent colonial vision of society was still deeply moulded by the hierarchical and naturalistic imagery of the 'chain of being', surrounded no longer with a 'web of occult relationships', as in the seventeenth century, but secularised, perhaps more potently, in a 'firmly ordered and structured' Whiggish mould as a law of nature.[23] American publishing in the reigns of the first two Georges echoes the themes explored in subsequent chapters of this book: religion, especially the dangers of Popery and the defence of Anglican Orthodoxy against Deism (Charles Leslie was republished in the colonies for that purpose); denials of the legitimacy of James III; controversies over the doctrines expressed in 30th January sermons; sermons on the deaths and accessions of monarchs; agitated reflections on Divine Providence in response to events like the London and Lisbon earthquakes. The works of Locke and the radical Whigs were not wholly absent; but they were not the ubiquitous symbols of a contractarian consensus.[24]

[21] John Dunn, 'The Politics of Locke in England and America in the Eighteenth Century' in Yolton (ed.), *John Locke*, pp. 45–80. Mr Dunn ascribed the neglect of the *Two Treatises* to their tedium and stylistic infelicities, but nevertheless argued that the book held a 'pre-eminent place as the official ideological defence of the revolution of 1688 during the succeeding seventy years', neglected because 'It was felt to contain principles of the most indubitable and parochial political orthodoxy' (pp. 54, 57). In the light of later research, especially that of Professor Kenyon, it is difficult to accept that *any* work occupied this canonical position up to 1760, let alone the *Two Treatises*.

[22] Cf. Dr Laslett's warnings: 'It would be easy in our own century to exaggerate the extent to which the new Englishmen of the American continent deliberately rejected the system of status established amongst the old Englishmen of Europe, for we are so interested in social differentiation, and so apt to seize upon every sign of social resentment or of disaffection'; 'the role of the gentry in the creation of America must have been an important one, if the analysis of English society presented here is at all accurate'. Peter Laslett, *The World We Have Lost*, 2nd edn (London, 1971), pp. 63–4.

[23] H. Leventhal, *In the Shadow of the Enlightenment. Occultism and Renaissance Science in Eighteenth-Century America* (New York, 1976), pp. 1, 190, 239, 259.

[24] American printing may be followed in a superb work, Charles Evans' *American Bibliography...1639...to...1820* (14 vols., Chicago, 1903–59). The lack of a similar short-title catalogue for eighteenth-century England has been a major reason for our failure to realise what is normal and central in that society's concerns.

Similar qualifications must also be made of the use to which Locke was put in early-eighteenth-century England: revered, if at all, as a Whig household god rather than deployed in real political battles. This was so partly because, of the various defences of the Revolution, the idea of an Original Contract quickly proved the most intellectually vulnerable; partly because the basic political issue – the title of the reigning monarch – could best be denied by appeal to the ideology of hereditary indefeasible right, and that ideology had to be resisted in terms of a rival dynastic title. The issue was decided practically, by the military defeat of the Jacobite challenge which articulated it: it was the defeat of the Jacobites which eventually exalted Locke, not 'Lockeianism' which defeated 'Jacobitism'. After that defeat, the question of legitimacy was suddenly a non-issue in British political thought; *de facto* and *de jure* merge after 1760, and for all except a minority of radicals (and their critics) the issue became the efficiency of government rather than its legitimacy. In Bentham the traditional preoccupation with legitimacy is absent. Bentham makes no distinction between a successful government and a legitimate one. Natural rights were useful, and were in the forefront of political argument, as long as legitimation and allegiance were open questions; but from the 1760s natural rights were an obsolete survival in the Providential utilitarianism which could provide commonplace assumptions even for a conservative and theocratic universe such as that of Paley.[25]

Neither utilitarianism nor contractarianism appropriately described the mental world of the first two Georges. These things were demoted to the level of truisms within the parameters set by the dominance of religion and dynastic legitimism. Taken literally, they were less persuasive. Bentham himself, born in 1748 into a Tory family in the City of London, claimed that he realised as a precocious adolescent that the Original Contract, offered by lawyers 'as a recipe of sovereign efficacy for reconciling the accidental necessity of resistance with the general duty of submission' was only a fiction. Rather, he later wrote,

The writings of the honest, but prejudiced, Earl of Clarendon...and the contagion of a monkish atmosphere; these, and other concurrent causes, had lifted my infant affections on the side of despotism. The Genius of the place I dwelt in, the authority of the state, the voice of the Church in her solemn offices; all these taught me to call Charles a Martyr, and his opponents rebels...I saw strong countenance lent

---

[25] H. V. S. Ogden, 'The State of Nature and the Decline of Lockian Political Theory in England, 1760–1800', *AHR* 46 (1940–1), 21–44, traced an increasingly historical view of the state of nature, especially from Rousseau's *Second Discourse* (1755), so weakening the natural rights school (which rested on a juristic conception of the state of nature and original contract), and provoking denials of an historical state of nature itself. It might be suggested that Ogden was unaware of the very widespread rejection of the historical accuracy of the original contract and the state of nature even from the 1690s.

in the sacred writings to monarchic government: and none to any other. I saw *passive obedience* deep stamped with the seal of the Christian Virtues of humility and self denial[26]

and he must have seen these things at Westminster School,[27] where he went in 1755, and at Queen's College, Oxford, as an undergraduate in 1760–3. Going up in the last months of George II's life, Bentham was excused on account of his extreme youth from taking the oaths of allegiance and abjuration; 'it relieved his mind from a state of very painful doubt', recorded Bowring. 'For kings, and especially the kings of England, he had felt unbounded reverence. "Loyalty and virtue", I have heard him say, "were then synonymous terms." '[28]

It was a world in which political legitimacy was bound up with questions of allegiance, conceived in personal and theological terms; and it was these issues to which political theorists continued to address themselves. The picture of David Hume as a proto-utilitarian, entertaining an atomistic and mechanical psychology, or as an emptily pragmatic Tory, familiar to readers of the older textbooks, has been similarly revised by modern scholarship.[29] If Hume is to be replaced in a European intellectual context, it is equally true that he generally rules no sharp dividing line between Scotland and England[30] in diagnosing the political ills of 'this island'. In 1739, in the *Treatise of Human Nature*, he wrote 'On the source of allegiance', 'On the measures of allegiance' and 'On the objects of allegiance' with a scrupulous anxiety reminiscent of Newman's *Grammar of Assent*. Hume's own position was that a man who examines the history of all governments

... will soon learn to treat very lightly all disputes concerning the rights of princes, and will be convinced, that a strict adherence to any general rules, and the rigid loyalty to particular persons and families, on which some people set so high a value, are virtues that hold less of reason, than of bigotry and superstition.

[26] Jeremy Bentham, *A Fragment on Government and An Introduction to the Principles of Morals and Legislation*, (ed. W. Harrison, Oxford, 1967), p. 50n.

[27] Westminster had a distinctly Tory, High Church tone. John Wesley's elder brother Samuel, a Jacobite sympathiser, was Usher there in 1714–33, appointed from Christ Church on the recommendation of Atterbury. Dr Robert Freind, Headmaster 1711–33, shared these opinions, and the school flourished in his time (Eton languished under the Whig regime imposed by Sir Robert Walpole: its fortunes did not revive until the reign of George III). It seems that Westminster School began ostentatiously to cultivate the Hanoverians from c. 1727; but the idiom in which this was done changed little. Bentham's attendance at Westminster was hardly surprising; his paternal grandfather was, as he wrote, 'a Jacobite', and his father was 'bred up in the same principles' until he 'transferred his adherence from the Stuarts to the Guelphs'. Bentham stressed to his disciple and literary executor John Bowring the considerable extent of Jacobite affiliation in the London of his boyhood: Bowring (ed.), *The Works of Jeremy Bentham* (London, 1843), vol. x, pp. 2–3.

[28] Bentham, *Works*, vol. x, pp. 36, 43.

[29] In particular, Duncan Forbes, *Hume's Philosophical Politics* (Cambridge, 1975).

[30] With one exception, quickly retracted: *ibid.*, p. 94.

Nevertheless, he realised that his contemporaries thought differently:

...were you to ask the far greatest part of the nation, whether they had ever consented to the authority of their rulers, or promised to obey them, they would be inclined to think very strangely of you; and would certainly reply, that the affair depended not on their consent, but that they were born to such an obedience. In consequence of this opinion, we frequently see them imagine such persons to be their natural rulers, as are at that time deprived of all power and authority, and whom no man, however foolish, would voluntarily choose; and this merely because they are in that line, which ruled before, and in that degree of it, which used to succeed; though perhaps in so distant a period, that scarce any man alive could ever have given any promise of obedience...we do not commonly esteem our allegiance to be derived from our consent or promise...Where no promise is given, a man looks not on his faith as broken in private matters, upon account of rebellion; but keeps those two duties of honour and allegiance perfectly distinct and separate. As the uniting of them was thought by these philosophers a very subtle invention, this is a convincing proof, that 'tis not a true one; since no man can either give a promise, or be restrained by its sanction and obligation unknown to himself.

Only an explicit promise, Hume insisted, created an obligation. But far from being a 'subtle invention', it might be argued that the persistence of Jacobitism among those who had had no opportunity to take the oaths to James II shows the link between honour and allegiance to have been a popularly comprehensible attitude. Hume's 'science of man', far from showing him to be always and everywhere the same, revealed some crucial differences; and differences which found the most marked political expression.[31]

It was widely accepted, Hume believed, that everyone allowed a right to resist tyrants; "'Tis certain, therefore, that in all our notions of morals we never entertain such an absurdity as that of passive obedience.' Against this, it might be objected that the Whigs' use of a similar doctrine, effectively abrogating the right of resistance to Hanoverian sovereigns, created the problem rather than solved it. No amount of stigmatising divine right and passive obedience could disguise the fact that both sides largely shared similar attitudes to monarchy, and were divided not so much about the attitudes themselves as about their application. Hume appreciated how irreconcilable a division this created in admitting that 'a century is scarce sufficient to establish any new government, or remove all scruples in the minds of the subjects concerning it'. Consequently, he realised that contract theory was only a party dogma, not yet a generally accepted orthodoxy: it 'has become the foundation of our fashionable system of politics, and is in a manner the creed of a party amongst us', the Whigs; though Hume identified himself with that party,[32] he admitted the very limited acceptance

---

[31] *Ibid.*, pp. 102–21.

[32] Hume's political allegiance has caused endless confusion. It is correctly diagnosed by Forbes, *op. cit.*; James Coniff, 'Hume on Political Parties: the Case for Hume as Whig', *ECS* 12(1978–9), 150–73; and V. G. Wexler, *David Hume and the 'History of England'* (Philadelphia, 1979).

of the doctrine at the same time as he demonstrated its falsity. The duty of allegiance, rather, 'quickly takes root of itself, and has an original obligation and authority, independent of all contracts'.[33]

Hume discussed the process of legitimation more fully in the *Essays*:

When a new government is established, by whatever means, the people are commonly dissatisfied with it, and pay obedience more from fear and necessity, than from any idea of allegiance or of moral obligation. The prince is watchful and jealous, and must carefully guard against every beginning or appearance of insurrection. Time, by degrees, removes all these difficulties, and accustoms the nation to regard, as their lawful or natural princes, that family, which, at first, they considered as usurpers or foreign conquerors. In order to found this opinion, they have no recourse to any notion of voluntary consent or promise, which, they know, never was, in this case, either expected or demanded. The original establishment was formed by violence, and submitted to from necessity. The subsequent administration is also supported by power, and acquiesced in by the people, not as a matter of choice, but of obligation. They imagine not that their consent gives the prince a title: But they willingly consent, because they think, that, from long possession, he has acquired a title, independent of choice or inclination.[34]

This was the ideal, the process of reconciliation for which Hume hoped. The reality was still different.

The house of Lancaster ruled in this island about sixty years; yet the partizans of the white rose seemed daily to multiply in England. The present establishment has taken place during a still longer period. Have all views of right in another family been utterly extinguished; even though scarce any man now alive had arrived at years of discretion, when it was expelled, or could have consented to its dominion, or have promised it allegiance? A sufficient indication surely of the general sentiment of mankind on this head.[35]

If resistance to the new dynasty was so obdurate, a closer analysis of the process that 'time, by degrees' should bring about was called for. Hume had really described the process of reconciliation rather than discovered its causes. This was so since that process was explicitly not to be understood in Lockeian contractarian terms:

...nothing is a clearer proof, that a theory of this kind is erroneous, than to find, that it leads to paradoxes, repugnant to the common sentiments of mankind, and to the practice and opinion of all nations and all ages. The doctrine, which founds all lawful government on an *original contract*, or consent of the people, is plainly of this kind; nor has the most noted of its partizans, in prosecution of it, scrupled to affirm, *that absolute monarchy is inconsistent with civil society, and so can be no form of civil government at all*; and *that the supreme power in a state cannot take from any man, by taxes and impositions, any part of his property, without his own consent or that of his representatives*. What authority any moral reasoning can have, which leads into opinions so wide of the general practice of mankind, in every place but this single kingdom, is easy to determine.

---

[33] David Hume, *A Treatise of Human Nature*, eds. L. A. Selby-Bigge and P. H. Nidditch, 2nd edn (Oxford, 1978), pp. 542, 548–9, 552, 557, 562.
[34] David Hume, *Essays Moral, Political and Literary*, eds. T. H. Green and T. H. Grose (2 vols., London, 1875), vol. I, pp. 450–1.   [35] *Ibid.*, p. 454.

The only passage I meet with in antiquity, where the obligation of obedience to government is ascribed to a promise, is in Plato's *Crito*: where Socrates refuses to escape from prison, because he had tacitly promised to obey the laws. Thus he builds a *Tory* consequence of passive obedience, on a *Whig* foundation of the original contract.[36]

But a very similar demand for obedience was in fact made by the Hanoverian monarchs and the Whig ascendancy. Contract theory was important for them only in so far as it provided a formal answer to the dynastic question. Hume's qualification, 'in every place but this single kingdom', was unnecessary, and is contradicted by the whole trend of his argument, frequently repeated, both in the *Treatise* and in the *Essays*. If the champions of contract theory, he claimed, would only 'look abroad into the world', they would find no such practice.

On the contrary, we find, every where, princes, who claim their subjects as their property, and assert their independent right of sovereignty, from conquest or succession. We find also, every where, subjects, who acknowledge this right in their prince, and suppose themselves born under obligations of obedience to a certain sovereign, as much as under the ties of reverence and duty to certain parents. These connexions are always conceived to be equally independent of our consent, in Persia and China; in France and Spain; and even in Holland and England, wherever the doctrines above-mentioned [i.e. Whig contractarianism] have not been carefully inculcated. Obedience or subjection becomes so familiar, that most men never make any enquiry about its origin or cause, more than about the principle of gravity, resistance, or the universal laws of nature. Or if curiosity ever move them; as soon as they learn, that they themselves and their ancestors have, for several ages, or from time immemorial, been subject to such a form of government or such a family; they immediately acquiesce, and acknowledge their obligation to allegiance. Were you to preach, in most parts of the world, that political connexions are founded altogether on voluntary consent or a mutual promise, the magistrate would soon imprison you, as seditious, for loosening the ties of obedience; if your friends did not before shut you up as delirious, for advancing such absurdities. It is strange, that an act of the mind, which every individual is supposed to have formed, after he came to the use of reason too, otherwise it could have no authority; that this act, I say, should be so much unknown to all of them, that, over the face of the whole earth, there scarcely remain any traces or memory of it.[37]

How was reconciliation possible, if not by a reliance on time somehow to soften antagonisms – an ideal which showed little sign of realisation? The problem was the existence of two extreme cases, each of which had an element of truth on its side:

The one party, by tracing up government to the Deity, endeavour to render it so sacred and inviolate, that it must be little less than sacrilege, however tyrannical it may become, to touch or invade it, in the smallest article. The other party, by founding government altogether on the consent of the people, suppose that there

---

[36] *Ibid.*, p. 460. The 'most noted of its partizans' was, of course, Locke.
[37] *Ibid.*, pp. 446–7.

is a kind of original contract, by which the subjects have tacitly reserved the power of resisting their sovereign, whenever they find themselves aggrieved by that authority, and which they have, for certain purposes, voluntarily entrusted him.[38]

The solution, suggested Hume, lay in a recognition of the truth of both sides. All governments must have been formed by association, implying a contract in a loose sense. But there was obviously no explicit and exact agreement which could regulate future governments.[39] Similarly, government is a divine institution in a weak sense which applied to all its agents, not merely to monarchy: 'A constable, therefore, no less than a king, acts by divine commission, and possesses an indefeasible right.'[40] As a theoretical answer to the problem, this seems evasive. As a practical answer, it is a prescient anticipation of the form which reconciliation was in fact to take in the uncontractarian, monarchical, confessional State that was late-eighteenth-century England. But it was political tactics, not political moralising, which was to bring it about. Lockeian contractarianism was not in fact a good account of how eighteenth-century Englishmen acted to shape and change their society, and failed in fact to provide a solution to their problems.

Hume has been quoted at length both because of his centrality in respect of these problems, and because of the accuracy of his premonitions. Almost equally important in both respects was Adam Smith,[41] whose account of social and political authority is consistent in these ways with Hume's. Smith, too, rejected the Original Contract. His picture of social relations was not one characterised by the dominance of a cash nexus or by the impersonal, calculated and limited obligations of commerce. Though the extent and importance of trade was scarcely a secret to him, Smith was not a prophet of liberal individualism, employing 'a psychology basic to the radical bourgeois vision of man.'[42] His mind was formed in the Oxford of the 1740s, an intellectual matrix still capable of producing unabashed Stuart loyalists. In Smith's account of social evolution, the culturally-based phenomenon of deference *succeeded* the primitive utilitarian relations of material dependence. Monarchs and peers no longer supported hordes of feudal retainers. Nevertheless, a commercial society was perfectly consistent with aristocratic hegemony:

When we consider the condition of the great, in those delusive colours in which the imagination is apt to paint it, it seems to be almost the abstract idea of a perfect and happy state. It is the very state which, in all our waking dreams and idle reveries, we had sketched out to ourselves as the final object of all our desires. We feel,

---

[38] *Ibid.*, p. 443.   [39] *Ibid.*, p. 445.
[40] *Ibid.*, p. 444.
[41] Adam Smith (1723–90). Balliol College, Oxford, 1740–6; Professor of Logic at Glasgow, 1751; of Moral Philosophy, 1752. The importance of freeing Smith from the perspectives imposed on his work by its later relevance to nineteenth-century economic liberalism is well stressed by Donald Winch, *Adam Smith's Politics* (Cambridge, 1978).
[42] Isaac Kramnick's phrase, quoted Winch, *op. cit.*, p. 181.

therefore, a peculiar sympathy with the situation of those who are in it...Every calamity that befalls them, every injury that is done them, excites in the breast of the spectator ten times more compassion and resentment than he would have felt, had the same things happened to other men. It is the misfortune of kings only which affords the proper subjects for tragedy...

Upon this disposition of mankind, to go along with all the passions of the rich and powerful, is founded the distinction of ranks, and the order of society. Our obsequiousness to our superiors more frequently arises from our admiration for the advantages of their situation, than from any private expectations of benefit from their good-will. Their benefits can extend but to a few; but their fortunes interest almost every body. We are eager to assist them in completing a system of happiness that approaches so near to perfection; and we desire to serve them for their own sake, without any other recompense but the vanity or the honour of obliging them.

Neither is our deference to their inclinations founded chiefly, or altogether, upon a regard to the utility of such submission, and to the order of society, which is best supported by it. Even when the order of society seems to require that we should oppose them, we can hardly bring ourselves to do it. That kings are the servants of the people, to be obeyed, resisted, deposed, or punished, as the public conveniency may require, is the doctrine of reason and philosophy; but it is not the doctrine of nature. Nature would teach us to submit to them, for their own sake, to tremble and bow down before their exalted station, to regard their smile as a reward sufficient to compensate any services, and to dread their displeasure, though no other evil was to follow from it, as the severest of all mortifications.[43]

The tone of admiration for traditional elites is unmistakable beneath the simple reporting, and it should be set against Smith's suspicion of the manufacturer's and the merchant's propensity to defraud the public. Economic progress, in Smith's account, comes not through an exaltation of their values but through an impersonal process, harnessing the greed of mere tradesmen.

Smith's analysis, then, neither pictures a simple pattern of evolution from status to contract, nor provides an economic theory which is a direct translation of the notion of an Original Contract.[44] Indeed it seems likely that contract theory, in England, achieved only limited and ambiguous acceptance as part of the creed of one party – a minority party among the intelligentsia – until the disappearance of the Jacobite option in the 1750s elevated the doctrine to the status of a revered but only distantly relevant orthodoxy. Whig extremists' loud insistence, under George I, on the triumph of Whig principles is to be read as evidence of their incomplete success. American colonists, in taking up the doctrine from the 1760s, were more archaic than modern. And if, after Locke's *Essay*, it became impossible for some philosophers to speak of innate ideas, emphasis may merely have shifted to divine revelation and to custom as sanctions for the hierarchical structure of a confessional state.

Within such a social order, political theorists who were later to be simply

---

[43] Adam Smith, *The Theory of Moral Sentiments* (1759); 4th edn (London, 1774), pp. 87-9.
[44] For substantiation of these points cf. Winch, *Adam Smith's Politics*, *passim*.

labelled 'contractarian' or 'utilitarian' continued to treat the importance of families as a self-evident truth, or to elaborate variations on that theme. The object was to explain why Authority was inherent, not accountable. Hume, who rejected familial authority as the historical origin of political authority,[45] nevertheless explained 'why all governments are at first monarchical' in terms of war and military necessities, not an Original Contract: 'Camps are the true mothers of cities.' Armies imply a unified command. 'And this reason I take to be more natural, than *the common one* derived from patriarchal government, or the authority of a father, which is said first to take place in one family, and to accustom the members of it to the government of a single person.' Hence hardly any governments are not 'primarily founded on usurpation and rebellion'.[46] With a less ruthless moral, this was the account of the origins of the State which was proclaimed by Paley[47] and widely propagated by his writings, the alternative possibilities comfortably comprehended in a single formula:

Government, at first, was either patriarchal or military: that of a parent over his family, or of a commander over his fellow-warriors... Paternal authority, and the order of domestic life, supplied the foundation of *civil government*... A family contains the rudiments of an empire. The authority of one over many, and the disposition to govern and be governed, are in this way identical to the very nature, and coeval no doubt with the existence, of the human species.[48]

Paley combined an extreme paternalist case with a justification for hereditary monarchy which was entirely utilitarian and prudential. The refutation of contract theory is as sweeping as Bentham's: 'Wherefore, rejecting the intervention of a compact, as unfounded in its principle, and dangerous in the application, we assign for the only ground of the subject's obligation, the will of God, as collected from expediency.' But in his justification of hereditary succession – that, to men in general, no rule of succession 'presents itself so obvious, certain, and intelligible, as consanguinity of birth'[49] – Paley is not reflecting the view of man apparently presented in Bentham or James Mill. The career open to talents rests on a radically different view of man, and his place in the social order.

It begins to seem, then, that while Locke was paid deference as a philosopher who had written in favour of the Revolution, almost *all* lay philosophers in the eighteenth century chose to argue against him, including Shaftesbury, Bolingbroke,[50] Hutcheson, Hume, Bentham and (if he falls into

[45] Forbes, *Hume's Philosophical Politics*, p. 75.

[46] Hume, *Treatise*, pp. 540–1, 556. Italics added.

[47] William Paley (1743–1805); Fellow and Tutor of Christ's College, Cambridge, 1766–76; Archdeacon of Carlisle, 1782–d.

[48] *Moral and Political Philosophy* (1785) in *The Works of William Paley DD* (5 vols., London, 1845), vol. II, p. 314.

[49] *Ibid.*, pp. 317, 325, 333ff.

[50] Cf. Isaac Kramnick, 'An Augustan Reply to Locke: Bolingbroke on Natural Law and the Origin of Government', *Political Science Quarterly* 82 (1967), 571–94.

this category) Burke. More important still, the majority of political theorists were clergymen. To Lockeian epistemology the Church quickly found an answer in the writings of Bishop George Berkeley, whose doctrines 'sought to inspire stronger convictions of the spirituality, omnipresence, providence, omniscience, and infinite power and goodness of God', and which were directed to the support of passive obedience.[51] Berkeley was only one contributor to an explicitly conservative strand of argument defending traditional Anglican social theory, whether by Nonjurors or by, for example, William Sherlock, Bishop Blackall, or the late-eighteenth-century prelates whose work is examined in chapter 4 below. It 'remained throughout the century the dominant teaching of the Anglican church and by far the most widely believed theory of political obligation in the population at large'.[52] If the 'great bulk' of this criticism is a rejection of Locke's account of the state of nature, it is ultimately also a rejection of Locke's account of the nature of human motivation.

The attacks on the historical plausibility of the contract theory, while not for the most part criticisms of the precise theory which Locke had enunciated, undoubtedly devastated the entire conventional Whig political theory of the succeeding [i.e. eighteenth] century. And the image of the social order which they advanced to refute Locke was undoubtedly the image held as an item of religious faith and moral belief by the majority of their contemporaries.[53]

Anglicans replied to abstract theories of contract or natural rights with a view of man which was ultimately religious, and premised on Pauline, Trinitarian theology. As with Locke, it was theological heterodoxy which turned contract theory into a virulently revolutionary creed. Revolutionary violence, insisted Burke in 1790, perverted man's moral character; the fault lay with 'those who profess principles of extremes... This sort of people are so taken up with their theories about the rights of man, that they have totally forgot his nature.'[54] But if the 'Enlightened' attack on Orthodox, established religion succeeded in France and had little to overcome in America, in England it was countered by the clerical intelligentsia with a large degree of success. English 'radicalism' was contained. Locke was, in the 1770s and 80s, relevant to the purposes of American colonists; at many points he was important for French theorists; but throughout the century, he was largely irrelevant to English political disputes. As Chateaubriand found, to his surprise: 'De 1792 à 1800, j'ai rarement entendu citer Locke en Angleterre: son système, disait-on, était vielli, et il passait pour faible en *idéologie*... Les ouvrages des politiques anglais ont peu d'intérêt général. Les

---

[51] C. J. Abbey, *The English Church and its Bishops 1700–1800* (2 vols., London, 1887), vol. II, pp. 332, 343.

[52] Dunn, 'Locke', pp. 60–2.

[53] *Ibid.*, p. 63. That contract theory *was* the conventional Whig position is qualified in chapter 3 below.

[54] Burke, *Reflections* in *Works*, vol. III, p. 316.

questions générales y sont rarement touchées: ces ouvrages ne s'occupent guère que des vérités particulières à la constitution des peuples britanniques.'[55]

But what of Bentham and James Mill? Do they not provide evidence of the existence, towards the end of our period, of modern man in Trevelyan's sense? Admittedly, the ground of debate has shifted. No sooner had an ex-Tory and convert like Blackstone acceded to Whig contract theory than Bentham, the scion of a Jacobite family, shot it down as a polite fiction. Subsequently, after Hume's and Bentham's demolitions, '...attempts to explain the origin of the social order in terms of rationally controlled purpose had been largely abandoned. The Benthamites for the most part ignored the question. It was enough to demonstrate the advantages offered by the social order, and to assume that the perception of these advantages played a major part in maintaining it.'[56] Ignoring the question of the historical origin of the State only focussed attention instead on the sort of contemporary human personality which would validate Bentham's prescriptions and make his blueprints workable.

Bentham's world has rightly been described as a 'two dimensional' one which 'contains few mysteries'. His account of human nature seems to rest on two linked propositions. The 'logic of the will' suggests that 'every man throughout the duration of his life is perpetually seeking to advance his own personal welfare, and that this is his only preoccupation'; the 'principle of utility' reveals that 'the sole basis of moral behaviour is the promotion of the greatest happiness of all men'. Consequently, the will of the majority became the infallible guide to correct political goals. It justified Bentham's lack of interest in 'suicide, philosophy, history, literature or painting; he advocates only one path of escape from suffering: namely, premeditated action'. Premeditated calculation justified the elimination of 'customary, spontaneous and emotional actions from human affairs'. The identity of different pleasures, their summability, implied the equality and autonomy of their recipients: the moral arithmetic produces a rational society.

The rational society is truly democratic and egalitarian in one sense at least: namely, that all right[s] to independent rule stemming from the claim to superior education, breeding, skill and ability are inadmissible. It was Bentham's intention, and this is the measure of his radicalism, to abolish every kind of aristocratic distinction between those who govern and those who are governed.

Family loyalties, codes of honour, the prerogative of blue blood, the demands of patriotism surrender before the moral arithmetic.[57]

---

[55] François-René de Chateaubriand, *Essai sur la Littérature Anglaise* (2 vols., Paris, 1836), vol. II, pp. 293–4.

[56] J. W. Burrow, *Evolution and Society* (Cambridge, 1970), p. 103.

[57] D. J. Manning, *The Mind of Jeremy Bentham* (London, 1968), pp. 30, 33–4, 37, 63, 74. Dr Manning's book is essentially an Oakeshottian critique of Bentham.

Whatever its polemical effectiveness, it is hardly necessary to point out that this characterisation, if taken empirically, is wildly implausible. The most obvious objections are, in this context, the most telling. The English were noted for a morbid proneness to suicide.[58] Philosophy flourished both with the utilitarians themselves and in the Scottish school. Gibbon and Macaulay wrote in Bentham's lifetime. It would be unnecessary to list the figures who adorned literature and the arts in his day. His theory is reduced to a truism if it comprehends in its formulae charitable activity, Methodism, the Evangelical movement, or the abolition of the slave trade. The aristo-cratic code of honour was not laid aside; nor, on the other hand, did the Crown and the aristocracy despoil the nation. Bentham himself (not sur-prisingly in view of his background) admitted as much in acknowledging the force of custom.

In spite of his proposition that men can only be moved by an appeal to their self-interest, he saw that, amongst the ignorant multitude, it was irrational sentiment that disposed men to obey, and that until a popular belief in the utility of representative assemblies, majority decisions and rational administration was substituted for the popular belief in the authority of custom and consent, nothing could be done to persuade people to support his campaign for reform. In view of this, he committed himself to a programme of political education.

The latter part of his life is a graphic record of the frustration of his aspirations by, as he saw it, malevolent forces; for him,

At the root of most political evil is custom, that dark shroud with which sinister interest has so long cloaked its true design. 'Ah!' sighed Bentham, 'when will the yoke of custom – custom, the blind tyrant of which other tyrants make their slave – ah! when will that misery-perpetuating yoke be shaken off? – When will Reason be seated on her Throne?'[59]

Rather, as recent scholars are agreed, Bentham's 'logic of the will' is 'not a psychology but a system of definitions'[60] designed to re-structure arguments about human conduct in terms of the moral system to which their author was already committed – utilitarianism. That is to say: what appear in Bentham's pages to be simple empirical characterisations of mankind are in fact the definitions of a formal argument from which Bentham *obviously* realised that reality diverged. Nevertheless, if the utilitarians' message was to be sold to a wide public, this gap between ideal and reality had to be denied, or blamed on the corruption of a ruling elite. The difference was consequently fudged, and utilitarianism demanded that men acted up to

---

[58] Cf. S. E. Sprott, *The English Debate on Suicide from Donne to Hume* (La Salle, Illinois, 1961).
[59] Manning, *Bentham*, pp. 37, 59, citing Bentham's *Plan of Parliamentary Reform* (1817), p. cxcviii.
[60] Burrow, *Evolution and Society*, p. 37.

the standard of rationality which all were supposed to share.[61] Yet if Bentham's doctrine of man is ultimately prescriptive, it ceases at once to be evidence for its general accuracy in his day. More probably, it merely indicates that he 'just could not bring himself to ponder the infinite complexity and diversity in men and circumstances'.[62]

The second caution against reading back Bentham's assumptions (if they are taken as such) about character as evidence of fact is the very slow, grudging and hesitant reception given to his doctrines. As one historian observed, 'The utilitarians, properly so called, were always a minority. Their theories were not flattering to mankind and were therefore repeatedly attacked.'[63] Dicey postponed the predominance of 'Benthamism or Individualism' to the years 1825–70.[64] Many students of Bentham are agreed in dating his acceptance, his growing credibility and influence, to the 1820s. This prompted one historian to identify a crucial link with the emerging language of 'class' in those decades. The Benthamites, 'a group of thoroughly emancipated and disillusioned intellectuals who up to now had been more often laughed at than read', began to be taken seriously when they echoed a social reality: 'Ricardo's *Principles of Political Economy* (1817) and James Mill's *Essay on Government* (1820) did for the middle class what Cobbett's *Address* did for the working class: they gave expression to the emergent fact of class antagonism'[65] in the 1810s and 20s. If Bentham's and Mill's seeming attempts to reflect human nature were not immediately plausible, they needed some other important development to give some men reasons for saying that they *were* plausible.

The third criticism that must be made of the success of the utilitarians' attempt (or seeming attempt) to deduce political prescriptions from an account of human nature arrived at by introspection is that, with Mill, the argument was pressed too far. James Mill's *Essay on Government*, too, took the form of 'a set of deductions from certain essential attributes of mankind', describing a society in which political difficulties 'are those raised by the unchanging factor of human egotism, not by historically conditioned manners, habits, morals and modes of thought'.[66] As Mill claimed, 'the very

---

[61] There remained an ambiguity in Bentham's work between *is* and *ought*, e.g.: 'There is, or rather there ought to be, a *logic* of the *will*'; 'Nature has placed mankind under the governance of two sovereign masters, *pain* and *pleasure*. It is for them alone to point out what we ought to do, as well as to determine what we shall do': Harrison (ed.), *Introduction to the Principles*, pp. 123, 125. For the ambiguous status of the felicific calculus, cf. Professor Harrison's Introduction, p. xxxiii.

[62] Manning, *Bentham*, p. 73.

[63] J. Plamenatz, *The English Utilitarians*, 2nd edn (Oxford, 1966), p. 45.

[64] A. V. Dicey, *Lectures on the Relation between Law & Public Opinion in England during the Nineteenth Century*, 2nd edn (London, 1924), pp. 126–210.

[65] Harold Perkin, *The Origins of Modern English Society 1780–1880* (London, 1969), pp. 28, 214–15.   [66] Burrow, *Evolution and Society*, pp. 24, 27.

principle of human nature upon which the necessity of government is founded' is 'the propensity of one man to possess himself of the objects of desire at the cost of another'. Moreover, 'It is...not true, that there is in the mind of a king, or in the minds of an aristocracy, any point of saturation with the objects of desire.' Consequently, 'if powers are put into the hands of a comparatively small number, called an aristocracy, powers which make them stronger than the rest of the community, they will take from the rest of the community as much as they please of the objects of desire'.[67] Though a time-honoured device of political theorists, the argument was recognised to be absurd when pushed to such lengths; and the weapon broke in the utilitarians' hands. That it did so was the central theme of Macaulay's three brilliant demolitions of James Mill in the *Edinburgh Review*:[68]

Our object at present is, not so much to attack or defend any particular system of polity, as to expose the vices of a kind of reasoning utterly unfit for moral and political discussions; of a kind of reasoning which may so readily be turned to purposes of falsehood that it ought to receive no quarter, even when by accident it may be employed on the side of truth.

Our objection to the essay of Mr Mill is fundamental. We believe that it is utterly impossible to deduce the science of government from the principles of human nature.[69]

Far from being everywhere the same, human nature was endlessly various.[70]

Macaulay had a second objection which was equally telling. Not only could a political system not be deduced from the principles of human nature; Mill's deduction, too, was faulty. Just as Locke's doctrines were built on a contradiction (the *Two Treatises'* use of natural law assuming access to 'innate ideas', the *Essay* denying their existence), so, as Macaulay saw, James Mill employed two contradictory sets of assumptions about human nature. One set, belonging to rational individualism, assumed that the individual pursued 'pleasure and the relief of pain as *ends*' and 'wealth and power' as the chief means; and that there was 'no limit' to his appetite for those things. Aristocratic dominance was therefore to be condemned. The other set of assumptions, directed to an alternative goal of class hegemony, suggested that if the 'middle rank' gained an ascendancy it would not despoil the nation, but exercise its power responsibly, as a trust; that the common people would gratefully look up to the middle class for leadership,

[67] James Mill, *An Essay on Government* (1820, ed. E. Barker, Cambridge, 1937), pp. 12, 20, 23.

[68] 'Mill on Government', March 1829; 'Westminster Reviewer's Defence of Mill', June 1829; 'Utilitarian Theory of Government', October 1829, in *Works*, vol. VII, pp. 327–449.

[69] *Ibid.*, pp. 364–5.

[70] That the similarity of human nature *was* Bentham's position is evidenced by the interpretation which Leslie Stephen and J. W. Burrow, among others, have placed on Bentham's essay *Of the Influence of Time and Place in Matters of Legislation*: 'the real assumption is that all such circumstances are superficial, and can be controlled and altered indefinitely by the legislator': Burrow, *Evolution and Society*, pp. 37–42.

advice and assistance. It is open to the reader to choose whichever set of assumptions he wishes; one historian at least has emphasised that 'Mill's argument was premised upon the existence of a vertically structured and hierarchically organised society.'[71]

Bentham displayed the same logical flaw in writing to Daniel O'Connell in 1828, identifying his target as 'cold, selfish, priest-ridden, lawyer-ridden, lord-ridden, squire-ridden, soldier-ridden England'.[72] He could hardly complain, on his assumptions, that it was selfish; his real complaint was that it was aristocratic and Christian. Similarly, only the wide acceptance of the themes in Mill's hatred of the ancien regime could make the argument of his *Essay on Government* seem plausible. Yet, clearly, Mill wished to retain as many assumptions of the 'old society' as suited his case for middle-class hegemony in the new. Class stratification need not imply class antagonism. But, as Macaulay pointed out, if Mill's claims of trusteeship for the 'middle rank' were valid, 'his whole system falls to the ground':[73] men need not be infinitely acquisitive. In fact, they need not have similar motivations at all.

Once this intellectual weapon had broken, it became even more evident in retrospect that it had always been deeply flawed. From that point, therefore, types of social analysis gathered strength which were based on ideas of organic unity, evolution, and the historical uniqueness and individuality of different periods and nations:

Men's purposes were not essentially one but many and diverse. The social order was maintained not primarily by men's rational appreciation of the advantages they derived from it, nor simply by coercion, but by the influence of habits and customs, many of them, particularly in the earlier stages of society, apparently irrational. Moreover, men appeared to obey these customs, not for the true reason that they helped maintain social order, but for reasons which often seemed entirely fanciful, or for no reason at all.

This insight is the central core of the emerging sociology of the nineteenth century.[74]

It begins to be evident, therefore, why the handful of political theorists traditionally attended to by historians are peculiarly unreliable guides to a general understanding of eighteenth-century society. Certainly the uses which historians have made of these authors to chart the advance of modernity have rested on some basic misunderstandings as well as on the elision of certain polemical contradictions in the authors themselves. How far can we characterise a nation or a period? It seems better that we should

[71] D. C. Moore, 'Political Morality in Mid-Nineteenth Century England: Concepts, Norms, Violations', *Victorian Studies* 13 (1969), 11; *idem, The Politics of Deference* (Hassocks, 1976), 416–7; cf. W. E. S. Thomas, *Philosophic Radicals*, pp. 140–5.
[72] Bentham, *Works*, vol. x, p. 595.
[73] Macaulay, *Works*, vol. vii, p. 363.
[74] Burrow, *Evolution and Society*, p. 104; cf. pp. 41ff, 66ff, 102ff.

reify - To convert mentally to a
thing , To materialise

avoid using 'character' in this reified sense at all. If human conduct
continued to be massively diversified by regional and social variation,
reifications of it all too probably reflect a polemical purpose, whether
contemporary or modern. The language of 'character', like the language
of 'class', does not involve an objective description; rather, such language
functions as the propaganda of certain sectional interests. If Bentham's and
Mill's images of man were used to effect in an attack on the aristocracy,
this process reflects chiefly the growing success of men claiming to 'stand
for' the middle class within the national public arena. Their success was
a *political* one, as Professor Perkin observed: 'not only the ruling class but
every other represents its interest as the common interest, and universalizes
its own ideal. It is not so much that the ruling class imposes its ideal upon
the rest, but that the class which manages to impose its ideal upon the rest
becomes the ruling class'.[75] The mythical triumph of Lockeian individualism
was explained by some historians as the reflection of the rise of a middle
class. If, as is argued here, this cannot be *inferred* from the course taken by
eighteenth-century political thought in the received canon,the question of
dominant class ideals must be confronted directly. It will be argued below
that it was an aristocratic ideal which commanded an intellectual hegemony
before the first Reform Bill.

II. THE SURVIVAL OF PATRIARCHALISM; OR, DID THE INDUSTRIAL REVOLUTION REALLY HAPPEN?

Historians have written much about the Industrial Revolution as the great
divide between a 'world we have lost' and the modern world: where the
French Revolution brought to an end the ancien regime in France, the
Industrial Revolution is supposed to have terminated traditional society in
England. It was, as Fabian and Marxist economic historians in particular
insisted, '*a fundamental social change.* It transformed the lives of men beyond
recognition. Or, to be more exact, in its initial stages it destroyed their old
ways of living and left them free to discover or make for themselves new
ones, if they could and knew how.'[76] There is no doubt that a certain sort
of historians' rhetoric has grown up around the subject, and the advance
of industrial society is still more often *celebrated* than critically *assessed* (this
is even true of Marxist historians: the rise of capitalist industry, whatever
the human cost, at least validates their analysis).

In the light of the material presented in this book, it is possible to begin
to look critically at the notion of an 'Industrial Revolution' in late-

[75] Perkin, *English Society*, p. 271.
[76] E. J. Hobsbawm, *Industry and Empire* (Harmondsworth, 1969), p. 80; cf. p. 13: 'The
Industrial Revolution marks the most fundamental transformation of human life in the
history of the world recorded in written documents.'

eighteenth-century England from the standpoint, adopted here, of the social historian. He finds an important ally in the 'new' economic history, which has subjected to a destructive scepticism many traditional assumptions about causation, chronology and exploitation.[77] The very term 'Industrial Revolution'[78] is a nineteenth-century invention which vastly exaggerates eighteenth-century Englishmen's perceptions of the changes they were living through. Even today, the metaphor encourages many to regard the process as a relatively sudden event, occurring 'some time in the 1780s'[79] – as sudden as a political revolution (but for the French Revolution, it might be suggested, the idea of an industrial revolution would never have existed).[80] Many writers have succumbed to the temptation to treat the phenomena of industrial advance as the measure of society's transformation, so that the regularly doubling figures for coal and iron output, and the rocketing increase in cotton production, are made to seem indices of the predominance of a wholly new society after c. 1780. It is important to emphasise that they were nothing of the sort. The urban-industrial society of the twentieth century is indeed profoundly different from the old; but transitions so profound were slow, partial, belated, complex and irregular. It is by no means clear that the sort of material changes witnessed by the vast majority before 1832 were enough in themselves to necessitate or effect immediate and basic *transformations* of outlook and belief: only the slow passage of generations did that.

Most sectors of the economy witnessed substantial growth before 1832, but only cotton increased exponentially. Not until the 1830s and 40s, when the railway and the steamship arrived, did the output of iron and coal surge ahead. Not until then did mass-production and powered machine tools spread to many industries. Meanwhile the economy was dominated by its traditional sectors and by traditional technologies, slowly evolving. In 1832 Britain was still essentially horse-drawn and sail-driven. Estimates put the number of steam engines in use in Britain in 1800 at 1,200 with a horsepower

[77] Roderick Floud and Donald McCloskey (eds.), *The Economic History of Britain since 1700. I. 1700–1860* (Cambridge, 1981) provides a superb synopsis of this work. It might be objected that the editors have quite incongruously appended the 'old' social history (pp. 253–75) to the 'new' economic history.

[78] It may be that the invariable use of capital letters is a clue to the extent to which historians have reified some much-cherished assumptions.

[79] E. J. Hobsbawm, *The Age of Revolution. Europe 1789–1848* (London, 1962), p. 28: 'To call this process the Industrial Revolution is both logical and in line with a well-established tradition, though there was at one time a fashion among conservative historians – perhaps due to a certain shyness in the presence of incendiary concepts – to deny its existence', etc. etc.

[80] The term 'industrial revolution' was evidently coined in France in the 1820s, given academic currency by, for example, Blanqui in the 1830s, translated into German by Marx and Engels in the 1840s, and popularised in English by Arnold Toynbee's book of 1884; among such writers it has *always* served the polemical purposes which, quite plainly, it still serves. For the history of the expression, Sir George Clark, *The Idea of the Industrial Revolution* (Glasgow, 1953).

of approximately 20,000; in 1824, perhaps 5,000 engines with a combined horsepower of only 100,000 (early engines lacked power). Even in 1838, the Factory Inspectors' Returns recorded only 74,000 h.p. derived from steam engines in textiles, where most steam power was concentrated. All these figures were still dwarfed by the major source of motive power, the horse: a modern estimate of the British horse population in 1800 sets it at 1,287,000. Professor Musson warns:

It is not generally appreciated that in 1800 steam power was still in its infancy, that in the vast majority of manufactures there had been little or no power-driven mechanization, and that where such mechanization had occurred water power was still much more widespread and important than steam. And after 1800, the 'triumph of the factory system' took place much more slowly than has generally been realized; water-wheels long continued to be built and used, while most manufacturing operations remained largely unmechanized until after 1870.[81]

Calculations of the relative contributions of different sectors of the economy to the total increase in national productivity point to the predominance, even up to 1860, of all those many miscellaneous sectors, including agriculture, which remain when the more famous sources of growth (textiles, iron, transport) are deducted.[82] The picture is one of relatively rapid transformation in a few spectacular areas whose aggregate contribution was small, against much slower (though eventually significant) increases in sectors generating a much larger share of national income. Quantifying these things allows us both to scale down the rhetoric surrounding technological innovation in certain spheres, and to appreciate that the 'Industrial Revolution' meant, as yet, minor changes of degree for the great majority of men, not massive changes of kind.

A great debate has raged around the 'standard of living question': that is, whether the real income of labourers rose or fell in the early stage of industrialisation. This question, though important, has distracted attention from other aspects of the work experience and, indeed, from the extent to which labourers' perceptions of hierarchy and authority were hardly altered. Whatever happened to real wages, technology and working conditions changed little for the great majority, whether in agriculture, transport, shipping, mining, building; for domestic servants, tailors, shoemakers, and labourers and craftsmen in a thousand specialised trades from printing to furniture making.[83] Urban growth did not necessarily mean

---

[81] F. M. L. Thompson, 'Nineteenth-Century Horse Sense', *EcHR* 2nd ser., 29 (1976), 60–81, at 80; A. E. Musson, 'Industrial Motive Power in the United Kingdom, 1800–1870' *ibid.*, 415–39 at 416, 422–4.

[82] McCloskey, Table 6.2, in Floud and McCloskey, *The Economic History of Britain since 1700*, vol. I, p. 114.

[83] 'In 1861, at the end of the customary dating of the industrial revolution, only about 30 per cent of the labour force was employed in activities that had been radically transformed in technique since 1780': McCloskey, *ibid.*, vol. I, p. 109. Shipping and mining are included in this figure; but had the work-experience of their labour forces beeen changed as greatly as the technologies employed?

large-scale units of industrial production. Sheffield and Birmingham were still conglomerations of small workshops; large mills were still the exception even in cotton, and the assembly-line came later. Factories came into existence only towards the end of the eighteenth century: as yet their numbers were few. Even coal mines were typically of modest size: a workforce of forty has been suggested as a typical figure.[84] For most workers, the unit of production was the workshop. Such relations of production as workshops witnessed, hierarchical and personal, were capable of being idealised in traditional ways. In 1795 John Aiken, describing even textile industries in the Manchester area, praised the traditional pattern of small masters each employing a few journeymen and working alongside them: such a system was 'highly favourable to the paternal, filial, and fraternal happiness – and to the cultivation of good moral and civil habits – the sources of public tranquillity'.[85] For such reasons, 'Perception of a separate labour interest distinct from and opposed to that of capital was not widespread enough to talk of a conscious working class in any formed or remotely homogeneous sense.'[86]

Before joint-stock companies, the normal units of economic as well as political continuity were families. In the first, 'heroic', stage of industrialisation, even the entrepreneur was aptly labelled a 'master' (the age of the capitalist financier came later). 'The iron-masters might, like the Crawshays of Cyfartha, demand – and often receive – political loyalty from "their" men which recalls the relation between squires and the farming population rather than between industrial employers and their operatives.'[87] The social structure in which Methodism most thrived was still hierarchical, as in the domestic outwork system which early economic growth greatly expanded,[88] and Methodist organisation mirrored this; collectivism as much as individualism was a child of the new age. If the personal presence of the employer was common in manufacturing and trade, the institution of service was ubiquitous. In the countryside, it included in its nexus not only domestic servants but a whole range of specialised farm workers: 'Between one-third and one-half of hired labour in early modern agriculture was supplied by servants in husbandry, and most early modern youths in rural England were servants in husbandry'[89] – all under the same rule as wives and children. Service, the common experience of most of the landless rural population between childhood and marriage, shaped the patriarchal

[84] J. Rule, *The Experience of Labour in Eighteenth Century Industry* (London, 1981), pp. 30–1.

[85] J. Aiken, *A Description of the Country from Thirty to Forty Miles round Manchester* (London, 1795), p. 573, quoted Rule, *op. cit.*, p. 38.

[86] Rule, *op. cit.*, p. 209.

[87] Hobsbawm, *Industry and Empire*, p. 57.

[88] A. D. Gilbert, *Religion and Society in Industrial England. Church, Chapel and Social Change, 1740–1914* (London, 1976), p. 114.

[89] A. Kussmaul, *Servants in Husbandry in Early Modern England* (Cambridge, 1981), p. 4 and *passim*.

perceptions of generation after generation until the institution declined in the early nineteenth century, the decline beginning, in the late eighteenth century, in the south and east. Not until then did the greater efficiency of wage labour, and newly-affluent, increasingly gentrified farmers' reluctance to eat with their labourers, combine to weaken the institution of service itself.[90]

If the position of the cottager and small freeholder was progressively eroded by enclosure in some areas, this may even have tended to increase the numbers of living-in servants, for the effect of more efficient agriculture was to increase, not reduce, the demand for labour. The rural population grew, as did the average number of surviving children per household. For many such reasons, the 'agricultural revolution' did not at once destroy the communal values and sentiments long embedded in folk custom, whether or not it reduced the standard of living of the new day-labourers. When those men substantially increased in numbers, even they seemingly emerged as a group feeling a common interest in the defence of as much of the old order as could be saved. 'Capitalist agriculture was established by the eighteenth century, but the social transformation was not complete until the second half of the nineteenth', observed one researcher. Finally, it was the labourers who preserved the attitudes of a hierarchical rather than a class society:

...while the objective conditions of their lives were those of a working class, subjectively they were reluctant to abandon traditional values, and preserved a communal outlook in a class society. If being determines consciousness, it does not do so instantaneously. The decisive period of change came late for the labourers, in the second and third quarters of the nineteenth century.[91]

The relations of tenant farmer and landlord were presumably more hierarchical than the relations of greater and lesser yeomen freeholders. The conversion of the rural poor into wage labourers pure and simple can only have increased their subordination to their rural employer, whether freeholder or tenant. The increasing affluence and consequent gentrification of the rural clergy similarly distanced them from their parishoners, and lengthened the social scale in many villages. Again, the post-1760 alliance of old Whig and old Tory contributed powerfully to fuse patricians into a homogeneous elite, presenting plebeians with a far more united front. It might therefore be argued that rural society became *more* hierarchical in many areas as the eighteenth century progressed: the essential components of patriarchalism were strengthened, not weakened (though Merrie England was shown up more often as the creation of nostalgia).

[90] Except, paradoxically, in industrial counties, where rival manufacturing employment kept up farm labourers' wages and led farmers to seek an assured workforce by retaining the institution of living-in servants.

[91] James Obelkevitch, *Religion and Rural Society: South Lindsey 1825–1875* (Oxford, 1976), pp. 23–6, 61.

Many of the patriarchal characteristics of social structure, so well described for seventeenth-century England,[92] can thus be traced throughout much of the eighteenth also. If the household remained the normal unit of production in farming, cottage industries, and craft occupations, the slow rise of daily wage labour did not at once break this emotional mould. What opened a social gulf in the nineteenth century was not only, it has been suggested, the capitalists' accumulation of wealth as such, but, as importantly, 'the transformation of the family life of everyone which industrialism brought with it'; industry turning 'the people who worked into a mass of undifferentiated equals',[93] the atomised individuals of classical political economy. If so, a major qualification to such a view is that until late in the nineteenth century, only a small minority of the population worked in new industries. The initial impact of economic growth was not to subvert rural society and produce a massive migration of population to an alternative (and different) urban culture, but to sustain proportionately almost equal population growth, especially in manufacturing regions, in both town and countryside, and to stimulate steady growth in the many towns of the old society as well as mushroom growth in the few towns of the new.

Before 1832, the major changes were demographic and geographical: the shifting balance of a growing population mostly moved it into new units, especially small towns and industrial villages, which were typically susceptible not to Jacobin-atheist democracy but to Dissent;[94] and as will be argued in chapter 6, it was Dissent which did more than anything to break down the old order. By contrast the fully urbanised society of the late nineteenth century, living in great cities and conurbations, was susceptible neither to Anglican nor to Dissenting missionary endeavour: only that society came to organise itself around universal suffrage, and to regard religion with widespread secular indifference.

Yet although demographic and geographical change were important, they should not be simply grouped under a blanket category of 'urbanisation'. If Dissent was insufficient of itself to break down the old order, it is equally true that no homogeneous urban phenomenon, whether defined in terms of *mentalité* or mere numbers, swamped English society in the period covered here. Towns were growing in the eighteenth century, enough to invite comment, but not enough to transform the daily lives of more than a minority. Setting aside London, towns of over 5,000 inhabitants accounted for only some 5·29 per cent of the total population of England and Wales in 1700; by 1801 this had grown substantially, but still amounted to only

---

[92] Peter Laslett, *The World We Have Lost Further Explored* (London, 1983), and Dr Laslett's work there summarised.

[93] *Ibid.*, p. 18. But does 'modern man' conform to the political economists' model? An implication of this book is that the contrast between the old society and the new has sometimes been exaggerated.

[94] Cf. Gilbert, *Religion and Society*, pp. 110–15.

16·24 per cent. London, though prodigious in size even in 1700, only kept pace with expansion in the countryside: 11·1 per cent of the total population of England and Wales in 1700, it had slipped marginally to 10·7 per cent in 1801.[95] These gross figures conceal, of course, a steady stream of migration from country to town (above all, to London) and a lesser reverse flow from town to country. At all levels, English society was in a sense amphibious:[96] if distinctively rural and urban mentalities existed at the extremes, there was a large area between them which partook of both, but most strongly of the country. France, with its score of substantial provincial capitals like Bordeaux, Toulouse, Aix en Provence, Strasbourg, Nantes, Rennes, Rheims, Lyons, Marseilles, Dijon, had evolved a specialised *bourgeois* culture (significantly, the word had no real English equivalent except 'City', meaning City of London).[97] England, Wales, Ireland and Scotland, more backward societies, had not. If all strata of society were geographically mobile to an extent, the English elite especially (again unlike the French) prided itself on its rural roots. The key English word is 'county', meaning 'county gentry'. The relative balance of country and town, still in 1800 heavily weighted towards the first, would lead one to expect that the dual culture remained heavily influenced by the values of rural society: and that was indeed the case.

The deference to the landed elite of the mercantile or professional 'bourgeoisie' is not wholly to be measured by the extent to which the latter invested in land, or were recruited from the younger sons of the aristocracy and gentry, important though these might be. It is possible that both have been over-emphasised as necessary conditions of the elite's strength, and that both were declining in the eighteenth century, especially (or perhaps chiefly) in London.[98] Marxist historians would anyway wish to read the symbiosis of land and trade as evidence of the permeation of the gentry by commercial values; others will appreciate the self-sustaining strength of the traditional elite, its relative independence of transfusions of new money, and the resistance of the aristocratic code to redefinition in order to accommodate social mobility. If there was less movement between the occupational ranks of patricians and bourgeoisie as the century progressed, the non-Marxist

[95] Figures calculated from P. J. Corfield, *The Impact of English Towns 1700–1800* (Oxford, 1982), p. 8, Table 1. Dr Corfield prefers to take places over 2,500 inhabitants as 'towns'; even this does not greatly alter the pattern.

[96] Professor Wrigley has estimated that one English adult in six lived in London at some stage in their lives in the early eighteenth century: 'A Simple Model of London's Importance in Changing English Society and Economy 1650–1750', in P. Abrams and E. A. Wrigley (eds.), *Towns in Societies* (Cambridge, 1978), p. 221.

[97] Instead, the English created a 'suburban' culture (similarly, it had no French equivalent and was uneasily naturalised as *suburbain*) – but this indicated an English rejection of the town, an attempt to escape back to a tamed, domesticated countryside. To the Frenchman, a suburb is, disparagingly, a *faubourg* – a *faux bourg*.

[98] Cf. Nicholas Rogers, 'Money, Land and Lineage: the Big Bourgeoisie of Hanoverian London', *Social History* 4 (1979), 437–54.

case is only strengthened. Yet this lack of occupational mobility among men was in sharp contrast to marriage patterns: if few daughters of top businessmen married into the aristocracy, many married into gentry families, and many big businessmen married the daughters of the gentry.[99] If the landed and mercantile elites were specialised and distanced by function, they were still united in deferring to a common code of manners and values: that of the traditional elite. New men were accepted; but on terms set by the aristocracy and gentry. As the century progressed, an increasingly sophisticated system of trade, credit and transport meant that the successful merchant or lawyer could participate in the experience of landed gentility by buying a house in the country without an estate attached, leaving the bulk of his fortune in more remunerative investments. The mercantile, financial and professional elite, like the landed elite, increasingly became 'amphibious' between town and country, money and status: the emerging social divide was a cultural one, between the patrician landowner, banker, lawyer, clergyman or merchant on one hand and the plebeian tradesman and manufacturer on the other, not a Marxist one between an aristocracy and a bourgeoisie, and the challenge to the ancien regime, when it came, was from culturally defined groups, not from economically defined classes. 'Class' was more a consequence than a cause of that regime's collapse.

If economic growth as yet did little to the political, cultural and even demographic balance between town and country, it seems to have been equally slow significantly to alter the distribution of income within the social hierarchy. Already highly unequal, it showed no unambiguous trend to greater equality in the period 1688–1832 in response to the 'rise' of any 'middle class'. It cannot be argued on the basis of data currently available that the hierarchical nature of the 'old society', as measured by income, was eroded by new wealth flowing into the hands of plebeians (though wealth undoubtedly did flow into such hands). Members of the expanding traditional elite were also major beneficiaries of economic growth, and much evidence is now available on the ways in which the aristocracy, gentry and even clergy participated in and profited from agricultural improvement, urban development, mining and canal building.[100] A pioneering study suggested that, by 1800, this process had seemingly left the balance of income within society approximately where it was in 1688: in broad terms, the whole economy had become more affluent, the different strata moving up together.[101] In the light of more recent research, it is possible to refine this

---

[99] Rogers, *loc. cit.*, pp. 444–5. I adopt a different argument to that of Dr Rogers.

[100] Cf. J. T. Ward and R. G. Wilson (eds.), *Land and Industry: the Landed Estate and the Industrial Revolution* (Newton Abbot, 1971); J. R. Ward, *The Finance of Canal Building in Eighteenth Century England* (Oxford, 1974); M. W. McCahill, 'Peers, Patronage and the Industrial Revolution', *JBS* 16 (1976), 84–107.

[101] L. Soltow, 'Long-Run Changes in British Income Inequality', *EcHR* 2nd ser. 21 (1968), 17–29.

picture. If the top 5 per cent of income-earners advanced their share marginally between Gregory King's survey in 1688 and Joseph Massie's in 1759, this was balanced by a small increase on the part of the lowest 40 per cent. These plebeian gains in percentage share were wiped out by the time of Patrick Colquhoun's estimates for 1801–3; the years from 1759 to 1801–3 saw a strengthening of the position of the top 10 per cent; and this was followed by a marked and decisive increase in the share of the top 10 per cent, and especially of the top 5 per cent, between 1801–3 and Dudley Baxter's survey in 1867. Using the important revisions of King's and Colquhoun's figures provided by Professors Lindert and Williamson, where the top 1·41 per cent of families, the traditional elite, commanded 16·19 per cent of national income in 1688, the same categories (aristocracy, gentry, bishops) constituted 1·24 per cent of families in 1801–3, with an estimated 13·87 per cent of national income. But the gross totals alone, revealing a slight relative decline, conceal an important development: the rise of a new elite within the rest of the population. King's revised figures for 1688 suggest only some 5,264 families of merchants with incomes of £280 p.a. and over, which sum he took as the minimum for the 19,626 families of the old elite (aggregate annual incomes of £2,105,600 for the merchants, £8,813,300 for the elite). Colquhoun's revised figures, by contrast, indicate 42,800 families from the commercial, industrial and civil office-holding categories with incomes equal to or higher than the £700 p.a. he adopted as the threshold figure for 'gentlemen': 42,800 families with an aggregate income of £37,810,000 p.a. against the traditional elite's 27,203 families commanding £27,545,000 p.a. out of a total of 2,193,114 families.[102]

In terms of absolute income figures rather than percentage shares, the upper echelons of the traditional elite preserved their preponderance to 1800 and beyond: the average income of a peer was several times that of a great merchant, who in turn commanded several times the income of a flourishing manufacturer. In terms of property rather than income, the position of the landowners was still one of dominance. But a new group had come into being which could begin to match the bottom rungs, and sometimes the middle rungs, on the ladder of traditional income. Would the individuals of this new group still seek to assimilate, subscribing or deferring to the values of the old elite, or would they come to regard themselves as a 'class' with a separate identity and interest? Would their choices differ? The answers were to be political, and until the 1820s most signs pointed to 'assimilation'. If entrepreneurs derived encouragement from their growing wealth and held

---

[102] P. H. Lindert and J. G. Williamson, 'Revising England's Social Tables 1688–1812', *Explorations in Economic History* 19 (1982), 385–408, and 'Reinterpreting Britain's Social Tables, 1688–1913', *ibid.* 20 (1983), 94–109, 329–30. My use of figures of those above a threshold of course greatly simplifies the problem of comparing the wealth and size of social groups.

their values to have been vindicated, few of them drew a 'class' conclusion. Meanwhile an equally powerful process of moral reinforcement bolstered the cultural and ideological pre-eminence of the aristocracy and gentry. In either case, economic growth did not yet promote a broad, democratic equality: its first effect was to strengthen the aristocracy and to create a new, and highly unequal, set of mercantile and manufacturing elites.[103]

The implications of this for the received account of social dynamics within the ancien regime deserve consideration. It has been traditional in British historiography to trace industrial growth and technological innovation to the sturdy virtues of bourgeois individualism, and especially to the individualism of Protestant-democratic England.[104] Such a theory dovetails naturally with the 'rise of the middle class'. The picture is less persuasive if, as Lindert and Williamson have argued, the percentage share of national income drawn by the top 40 per cent to 90 per cent strata of the population was steadily falling between 1759 and 1867. Moreover, the example of Japan in our own time refutes the necessity of any such connection, for Japan has demonstrated the possible industrial dynamism of a highly deferential society, indeed a society which has only recently masked the values and practices of a divine-right monarchy. It is perhaps possible in the changed climate of the 1980s to re-emphasise the extent to which England's commercial and industrial achievement in the eighteenth and nineteenth centuries rested not only on success in war, averting revolution and eliminating French competition, but also on the virtues of loyalty, diligence, discipline, subordination and obedience in the work-place, whether factory, mine or office (indeed the British economy was eventually overtaken by others which practised these virtues to a higher degree). But such practices had already been elevated to the status of social ideals within the Anglican-aristocratic nexus; and it was the military elite, not the nation of shopkeepers, which won the wars. The values of nineteenth-century industrial society owed far more to the values of the ancien regime than the Victorians were prepared to admit.

Insular historians, too, have explained England's 'Industrial Revolution'

---

[103] Cf. Perkin, *English Society*, pp. 17–23, 135–6, for his discussion of the estimates of Gregory King, 1688, and Patrick Colquhoun, 1803. Did the Stuart sympathiser Gregory King, the admirer of a much older order, underestimate the income and numbers of the 'middle ranks'? Did the Benthamite critic of the aristocracy, Patrick Colquhoun, exaggerate them? We need more research on these intractable problems, but see G. Holmes, 'Gregory King and the Social Structure of Pre-Industrial England', *TRHS* 5th ser. 27 (1977), 41–68; P. Mathias, 'The Social Structure in the Eighteenth Century: a Calculation by Joseph Massie' in Mathias, *The Transformation of England* (London, 1979), 171–89; L. D. Schwarz, 'Income Distribution and Social Structure in London in the Late Eighteenth Century', *EcHR* 32 (1979), 250–9; J. D. Marshall, 'Agrarian Wealth and Social Structure in Pre-Industrial Cumbria', *ibid.* 33 (1980), 503–21.

[104] Importantly, Christopher Hill, *Reformation to Industrial Revolution* (1967; Harmondsworth, 1980), pp. 27, 40, 66, 117, 182, 196, 207 etc.

as a special case, claiming (in an argument of formidable circularity) that England *alone* had the necessary mix of natural resources, skills, entrepreneurship and social structure. A less xenophobic perspective would reveal the sophisticated technologies and powerfully advancing industrial output of many other ancien regime states, especially France, which in the next century went on to as advanced an industrialisation as England.[105] The loaded question 'Why was England so special?' has encouraged us to adopt a teleology of economic growth, and to give immense emphasis to those respects in which England *was* different; this emphasis has naturally coloured our limited vision of all those other respects in which England was similar to its major European rivals. The question might be better put: 'Why were continental states *delayed* in their economic development?' Thus expressed, our attention is directed inexorably back to the impact of revolution and war, which inhibited, disrupted, and sometimes devastated, large areas of the continental European economy in the quarter-century after 1789 (only occasionally do we sense a silent presence, just over the mental horizon of most economic historians – the Royal Navy).

Where the Fabian or Marxist, committed to a view of the priority of heavy industry and the centrality of capital formation as a motor of change, necessarily sees an 'Industrial Revolution', the social historian sees many things as well as a personified Industry which changed the old society; and he sees a series of irregular changes, some fast, the majority slow. In respect of the quantifiable, it took many decades to build up the material infrastructure of an urban, capitalist, industrial economy. Not much of it was in place by 1832. The revolution which did more than anything to terminate the traditional society is to be sought elsewhere, in the realm of attitudes, ideas, beliefs, and ultimately in the confrontation of politics and religion. It is the subject of chapter 6.

What are the implications if the social relations generally supposed to underlie the nexus of beliefs and practices covered by the term 'patriarchalism' were not simply swept aside by new forces? A qualification must first be offered to the model of patriarchalism which has won general acceptance in recent years. The more important reason why the authority of the father was held to be like the authority of the State was not that the family was the literal origin of the State (though this continued to be argued) but that both family and State were regarded as divine institutions. Consequently the essence of patriarchalism was hierarchy and divinely appointed, inherent authority, not the lineal descent of the monarch from Adam, fatherly care as a gloss on collectivism, or the degree of kindliness

[105] Cf. N. F. R. Crafts, 'Industrial Revolution in England and France: Some Thoughts on the Question, "Why was England First?"', *EcHR* 30 (1977), 429–41.

we might fancy we can measure in social relations.[106] After 1688, explicit acknowledgements to Filmer became politically difficult. Nevertheless, the structure of men's ideas remained little changed. Families, too, were still important in English social structure. And there was a contrary development: the contractarian case was quickly shot down, and theorists soon fell back on the familial explanation as the more historically realistic account of the origin of the State. This linked naturally with the continued dominance of the Church: its message on the divine institution of civil authority retained its intellectual hegemony until the dismantling of the confessional State.

The familial characteristics of daily relationships cannot, of course, be measured. Yet it is possible to see that familial metaphors continued to be used, if less frequently than in the seventeenth century. Bolingbroke's *Patriot King* enjoyed a considerable vogue throughout the reign of George III, and, as we shall see, William IV will be found quoting it during the Reform Bill crisis, at the point of the monarchy's effective demise. Social pundits could produce the idea with effortless blandness, like Soame Jenyns in 1757: 'The Universe resembles a large and well-regulated Family, in which all the officers and servants, and even the domestic animals, are subservient to each other in a proper subordination; each enjoys the privileges and perquisites peculiar to his place, and at the same time contributes by that just subordination, to the magnificence and happiness of the whole.'[107] On a local level, too, a Berkshire vicar could write in 1795: 'For it is manifest that our laws consider all the inhabitants of a parish as forming one large family, the higher and richer part of which is bound to provide employment and subsistence for the lower and labouring part.'[108] To point to a gap between ideal and reality is to imply that we can quantify the shortfall; yet at all times, ideals and realities are generically different. The credibility of social imagery is only partly a utilitarian matter.

Even Bentham could be moved to recognise the predominant idiom taken by social relations in his own day, in endorsing Filmer:

Filmer's origin of government is exemplified everywhere: Locke's scheme of government has not ever, to the knowledge of any body, been exemplified any where.

[106] I dissent here from Mr E. P. Thompson's formulation of the model, which he calls 'paternalism': 'the term cannot rid itself of normative implications: it suggests human warmth, in a mutually assenting relationship...some sense of emotional cosiness': 'Eighteenth-Century English Society: Class Struggle Without Class?', *Social History* 3 (1978), 136. As will be evident later, I believe that neither the humane nor the voluntary elements, though doubtless present to an unquantifiable degree, are *essential* to the model here discussed. A model which relies on 'emotional cosiness' or justice-as-fairness is likely to be applicable to no period, as Mr Thompson merely succeeds in proving.

[107] *A Free Inquiry into the Nature and Origin of Evil* (London, 1757), quoted Dunn, 'Locke', p. 65.

[108] Rev. David Davies, *The Case of the Labourers in Husbandry* (London, 1795), p. 28, quoted Laslett, *The World We Have Lost Further Explored*, p. 149.

In every family there is government, in every family there is subjection, and subjection of the most absolute kind: the father, sovereign, the mother and the young, subjects. According to Locke's scheme, men knew nothing at all of governments till they met together to make one. Locke had speculated so deeply, and reasoned so ingeniously, as to have forgot that he was not of age when he came into the world...

Under the authority of the father, and his assistant and prime-minister the mother, every human creature is enured to subjection, is trained up into a habit of subjection. But, the habit once formed, nothing is easier than to transfer it from one object to another. Without the previous establishment of domestic government, blood only, and probably a long course of it, could have formed political government.

Filmer had failed to prove divine right, insisted the secularised Bentham; but he *had* proved 'the physical impossibility of the system of absolute equality and independence, by showing that subjection and not independence is the natural state of man'.[109] This was slightly unfair on Locke: in some places he accepted a large part of the patriarchalist case. Nevertheless, for much of the eighteenth century, many people, and especially churchmen, saw instead in Locke a radical case potentially so extreme as to make them wish to attack Locke's logical contractarian weaknesses, not use his common-sense, patriarchal, authoritarian strengths.

If hierarchy and natural (not contractual, accountable) authority were the two essential features of English patriarchalism, then all the rest (analogies with families and fatherly care) was sentimental trimming and political rhetoric.[110] The extended family has for centuries been no part of the English experience: patriarchalism operated as metaphor. Yet we should remember that sentiment has been able to turn many sorts of social reality into powerful and effective ideals in different eras – especially where religion frequently, and common human decency briefly, intruded. But the hardest thing in dealing with patriarchalism is to discard sentimental approval or censure as sources of analytical categories. It is particularly difficult since hierarchy and natural authority were still found in families, and families were economically powerful. Not only did behaviour not transform itself in response to a material imperative before 1832, but even the citizens born into later industrial society fell short in many ways of the expectations of their self-appointed theorists, whether liberal-bourgeois capitalists or

---

[109] Elie Halévy, *La Formation du Radicalisme Philosophique* (3 vols., Paris, 1901–4), vol. I, Appendix III, printing Bentham's mss 'Locke, Rousseau and Filmer's Systems'. Bentham's critique of Locke might be compared with that of Joseph de Maistre in *Soirées de Saint-Pétersbourg*, noted in E. D. Watt, '"Locked In": De Maistre's Critique of French Lockeianism', *JHI* 32 (1971), 129–32.

[110] It might be doubted whether ramshackle Tudor legislation on prices, wages and apprenticeship constituted an effective paternalist system, and whether the repeal of that legislation in the late eighteenth century amounted to an abandonment of paternalism. Nor was it fatherly care that workers demanded, but restrictive practices and artificial prices. The old poor law was the real measure of the elite's care for the helpless: and this was a casualty of the new regime after the Reform Bill.

socialists and radicals. Some men continued, at times, 'irrationally' to prefer war, or strikes, to profitable commerce and employment; to defer to monarchs and gentlemen rather than to expropriate them; to fail to picture themselves as members of a 'working class'; and to entertain a religious faith. Only the secret ballot conceals the full extent of the 'irrationality' of the modern elector.

If a certain sort of social polemic that was part of the 'old' economic history is discarded, what are the consequences for our picture of personal relations in eighteenth-century England, and for the longer validity of the ideas about patriarchalism, hierarchy and authority which certain scholars have revealed for the seventeenth century? If even modern man is somewhat less than 'modern', a study of the general patterns of belief, opinion, behaviour, disposition, attitude and manner in eighteenth-century England shows how little they were *revolutionised*. Such a study is necessarily an account of diversity and continuity, seen 'from below'; seen 'from above', it is an account of the continued cultural dominance of Anglican and aristocratic ideals and norms. Together with hierarchical patterns in labour, religion and politics went a body of theory which focussed on society's elite. What we shall term the 'aristocratic ideal' included both an account of the elite's inner logic, and a set of ideals about how society at large should orient itself towards that elite. They must be looked for in a variety of places. Historians who turned to political thought in an attempt to document the advent of the self-reliant Victorian individual in Defoe's England were helped in that attempt by giving attention only to the level of 'high theory' concerning chiefly the hypothetical origin of the State, and often, even at that level, to the work of a very limited number of major figures. A wider perspective would have revealed not only the small number of champions of Lockeian individualism, but the persistence for long into the eighteenth century of attitudes relating to the title of existing social structures which had much in common with seventeenth-century patriarchalism.

The most broadly-based, detailed and objective evidence for this is the pattern of electoral behaviour disclosed, for certain counties as late as the 1840s, in the work of Professor D. C. Moore, and discussed in chapter 1 above. In the light of that work, we now know that 'voters must be considered less as atomised individuals singularly vulnerable to bribery than as members of a family community...it is already clear that voting was a familial and hereditary affair', influenced also by the occupation of the voter,[111] which gave him an additional group allegiance and identity. At a national level, political connection and affiliation before 1832 still took the form of personal allegiance and loyalty, whether with ministerial

---

[111] F. O'Gorman, 'Fifty Years After Namier: the Eighteenth Century in British Historical Writing', *The Eighteenth Century* 20 (1979), 113.

meritocrats – 'Mr Pitt's friends' – or Whig patricians – 'the friends of Mr Fox'. It was more than a verbal convention. Behind the form of words lay an infinite variety of social relationships, and attitudes recognising, justifying or idealising them, which can aptly be labelled 'patriarchal' or 'deferential' in the sense in which seventeenth- and nineteenth-century historians respectively have usually employed those terms.[112] It is legitimate thus to extend patriarchalism forward, and deference back, to discover both the transitions and the more important continuities between them;[113] for it is clearly inadequate to suppose that patriarchalism aptly applied in the late seventeenth century and deference in the early nineteenth, but that bourgeois individualism is the only acceptable category in the intervening period.

If 1688 was momentous in this respect, it was by demonstrating in the aftermath of the Revolution that the totality of patriarchalism did not depend on the intellectual viability or political usefulness of doctrines of indefeasible kingship, and long outlasted them. England nevertheless remained a monarchical state in more than name. If we can at last discard denunciations of Stuart 'tyranny', we can be equally cautious of parodies of forelock-tugging yokels, elevated into models of deferential behaviour.[114] Deference meant not mere servility; it involved sympathetic involvement, expectations of reciprocity, common outlook, identification of interest and sheer coercion in the name of a social ideal far more than weak submission. What patriarchalism did depend on was the vitality of an ideology of order which meshed with the practicalities of achieving civil stability in early-modern England, and the prevalence and viability of a hierarchical picture of society, upheld as a proto-class ideal, but which could also be claimed to correspond to very many social relationships formed by power, wealth

---

[112] 'Paternal' is here avoided: it carries, by now, too heavy a connotation of idealistic approval to be used neutrally. But an argument could be sustained that early-nineteenth-century paternalist ideologues were original chiefly in applying still-current patriarchalist ideals, for the first time, to social welfare issues, the 'condition of England question'. It would be wrong to deduce from the doctrines of Robert Southey, S. T. Coleridge, Thomas Sadler, Richard Oastler and others that they expressed a reaction; that 'There was in the early eighteenth century a calculating commercial spirit abroad, as there was a lax and easygoing indifference to paternal duties...The attitude of many in the governing classes, though by no means all of them, was selfish, demanding, and parsimonious...Even before Adam Smith they were bent on the creation of a laissez faire society': D. Roberts, *Paternalism in Early Victorian England* (London, 1979), p. 20. Dr Roberts' study is in other respects a valuable reminder of the survival of the hierarchical vision.

[113] We lack such a study of the hierarchical world view underlying eighteenth-century English politics. Not without value is B. N. Schilling, *Conservative England and the Case against Voltaire* (New York, 1950), which, however, still employs the crudest Whig approach to the question of parliamentary reform.

[114] Some historians create absurd parodies of 'deference', then present us with a great discovery in showing that they do not fit, e.g. 'common people did not jump to attention by reflex at orders barked directly from above (for instance from Anglican pulpits)': Porter, *English Society*, p. 173. But whoever said they did?

and faith. And these two preconditions for the survival of patriarchal ideals can be documented throughout the eighteenth century.[115]

The 'ideology of order' has best been described for an earlier period.[116] It involved stress on the correspondence between hierarchy in the divine sphere and the hierarchy of creation, including human government, and in the other direction an anthropomorphic analogy between a man's natural body and the body politic – the monarch being the head, the labourers lesser members. The argument from correspondence thus showed the naturalness of unified authority at the same time as it justified it morally. Order within creation was the result of a just harmony of ranks and a due arrangement of them. 'Law and order' meant the social subordination of the illiterate more than the atomised individual's observance of the details of legislation. It was not unique to Europe: the strength of this outlook in early-eighteenth-century America, too, has begun to be noted.[117] If in England at that point this world view, as an explicit doctrine, was especially associated with the Tory party, the currency of Toryism even in the largest urban constituencies and among the innovative, 'rising' bourgeoisie must be remembered,[118] as well as the strong aristocratic element among the Whigs, from the Cavendishes and Russells to the Rockinghams and Hollands. The metamorphosis of Toryism in and after and 1750s made the doctrine as much of a common property as the disposition of mind. Yet

Even after the decline of the political theory of order as a coherent ideology certain aspects of it continued to be very persuasive. The emphasis on the absolute personal sovereignty of the king died away but not that on the naturalness and superiority of monarchy. Nor was it so easy to set aside the doctrine of the organic nature of society with its hierarchy of unequal men. Similarly, the insistence on the maintenance of the *status quo* reflected an abiding interest. And despite the great changes wrought by the advance of natural knowledge, the cogency of correspondence arguments continued to be heeded. In fact, many of these views became strands in the development of both the Romantic movement and the philosophy of modern conservatism. They were also a major source of those other modern doctrines which have been based on the organic theory of the state.[119]

[115] The argument here and in subsequent chapters is at variance with the suggestion that 'by 1750 almost all other *common-sense influences* were against [Filmer]...The reason of course was the triumph of Whig principles and of Whig institutions, *the growth of rationalism* and the steady expansion of *urban, commercial and bourgeois culture*. Retreating perpetually before them were the political institutions and *political prejudices* of European patriarchalism.' Laslett (ed.) *Patriarcha*, Introduction, p. 41. Italics added.

[116] W. H. Greenleaf, *Order, Empiricism and Politics. Two Traditions of English Political Thought 1500–1700* (Oxford, 1964).

[117] Leventhal, *In the Shadow of the Enlightenment*, pp. 239–42 and *passim*.

[118] For the strength of metropolitan Toryism, cf. Nicholas Rogers, 'Resistance to Oligarchy: The City Opposition to Walpole and his Successors, 1725–47' in J. Stevenson (ed.), *London in the Age of Reform* (Oxford, 1977), pp. 1–29; for the involvement of Tories with industrial growth, cf. Philip Jenkins, *The Making of a Ruling Class. The Glamorgan Gentry 1640–1790* (Cambridge, 1983), pp. xxii, 57–72. For Hume's awareness of Jacobite commitment among the 'middling rank' cf. Forbes, *Hume's Philosophical Politics*, p. 94.

[119] Greenleaf, *Order, Empiricism and Politics*, p. 263.

It would be wrong to exaggerate the decline of these seventeenth-century idioms, and many are explored in subsequent chapters here. Pope's *Essay on Man* of 1733, for example, echoed the 'great chain of being':

> So from the first eternal ORDER ran,
> And creature link'd to creature, man to man

and gave a patriarchal account of the origins of monarchy:

> The same which in a Sire the Sons obey'd,
> A Prince the Father of a People made.

Many of the central themes of the seventeenth-century ideology of order can, of course, be found in Burke, including the crucial one, that the social hierarchy was a divine institution; and the survival of the confessional State until 1828 might be thought to have given immediate credibility to his claims that 'Our political system is placed in a just correspondence and symmetry with the order of the world.' Such imagery was no longer typical when Burke wrote, though (as we shall see) the structure of the argument within an Anglican politico-theology was remarkably similar. Yet if the forms of argument which had lent support to the confessional State in its earlier manifestations underwent changes, the new forms which they took sustained very similar ends. The 'argument from correspondence' faded into the background but was replaced, chiefly, by the curiously-similar 'argument from design', classically in Paley's *Natural Theology* (1802): from a watch we infer a watchmaker, and so on through the whole natural realm, including the State and political affairs. The proper (and divinely ordained) function of things (including political institutions) could thus still be inferred from their actual functions: a doctrine of powerfully conservative implications, and one which was used by Paley and most of his contemporaries to conserve the established constitution in Church and State. 'Law and order' meant, to them, its successful defence.

The second precondition of patriarchalism and deference was the form taken by the typical descriptions of social relations in a society both Christian and not yet subscribing to a class-analysis: the relationships of

...master and servant, teacher and student, employer and worker, landlord and tenant, clergyman and congregant, and magistrate and subject – were all understood as identical to the relationship of father and children. This patriarchalism was not just the characteristic understanding of social status that was shared by those who commented on the family and its implications...it was supported by an official and regularly taught ideology that corresponded to, justified and rationalized life as it was actually experienced by the illiterate and inarticulate masses of seventeenth-century Englishmen.[120]

[120] G. J. Schochet, *Patriarchalism in Political Thought. The Authoritarian Family and Political Speculation and Attitudes Especially in Seventeenth-Century England* (Oxford, 1975), p. 66.

A recent student of patriarchalism, approaching it from a seventeenth-century viewpoint, concluded that it experienced a 'rapid decline after 1690' as a 'viable political ideology', and that those writers who did expound the doctrine in the eighteenth century 'were all curiously out of place'. The argument 'from familial status to political obligation', Dr Schochet suggested, was made impossible because of the 'collapse' of two attitudes: 'first, the appeal to origins to discover the nature of political authority' and 'second, the identification of all status relationships with one another and specifically the social and familial with the political. They were replaced by *a rational outlook* and a distinction between state and society.'[121]

As has been suggested above, the appeal to origins remained unavoidable in any social philosophy which could command wide acceptance in a Christian society; speculation about the state of nature, and man's conduct in it as either a subordinate or a freely contracting individual, inevitably had force at least as long as the Creation and Fall were conceived literally as recent and datable historical episodes.[122] It is true that ministerial Whigs, in low-level discussion for practical political purposes, were often content to avoid the issue of contract by extolling the Revolution settlement as creating a mixed and balanced constitution, securing individual liberty and other desirable goals by its efficient working; so that assent to it could be described as merely pragmatic.[123] But this was only a prudential tactic in a world in which political allegiances, and high-level political theory, were very different. Bentham and James Mill, similarly, sought to halt the inconvenient search for origins with an ahistorical argument about human character as a starting point; but they were untypical, and when this intellectual device was discredited, it only stimulated the search for the historical origins of the State in the work of a wide range of nineteenth-century academic disciplines.[124]

The alleged collapse of the analogy between all status relationships and familial relationships is also to be qualified. If the metaphor was less often used, the hierarchical nature of the relationships was not thereby abolished; in many cases it was even strengthened. Nor did secular contractarianism replace theories of the divine origin of the State. It seems likely that what were less often heard in the eighteenth century were not patriarchalist accounts of the State as a whole (which Paley, Burke and others regarded as viable) but appeals from familial authority to what Whigs designated as slavish doctrines of indefeasible monarchy; and that the main reason for the

---

[121] *Ibid.*, pp. 223–4, 273–4. Italics added.
[122] Following Archbishop Ussher, the Creation was conventionally dated 4004 B.C.; Adam and Eve were created on Friday, 28th October. The Fall followed soon afterwards; Cain was born in 4003. John Blair, *The Chronology and History of the World, from the Creation to the Year of Christ 1753* (London, 1754, and subsequent editions).
[123] Cf. Dickinson, *Liberty and Property*, pp. 142–8.
[124] Cf. Burrow, *Evolution and Society, passim.*

change was not the perceived refutation of the argument from correspondence or the arrival of individualism and 'modern society', transforming actual patriarchal relationships, but the course taken by political polemic in response to events: the fact that the Hanoverian monarchy itself, through its Whig party mouthpieces, officially discountenanced those doctrines of indefeasible kingship, the wider intellectual consequences of which could, in the first half of the century, have been sustained, and which might, in the aftermath of a Stuart restoration, have been successfully and credibly revived.[125] What changed, then, was less the patriarchal doctrine itself than its application.

Meanwhile, even Whigs (as will be argued more fully in chapters 3 and 4) shared much of their opponents' case: the more limited patriarchalism which had preceded Filmer 'provided an essential argument for the *Whig* and *anti*-Jacobite theorists of 1688 and after'.[126] And although Whigs like Dean Tucker or Edmund Burke took pains to *renounce* Filmer, it was to no effect: the hierarchical, confessional State which they supported could only be defended with arguments which radicals found indistinguishable from Filmer's. It was a nice irony; but it accurately reflected Locke's demotion to the status of the prophet of a small group of the theologically heterodox, not the architect of a secular, contractarian consensus as some had hoped.

Patriarchal doctrine, then, was sustained after 1688 not so much by the polemical needs of a dynastic regime as by the continued domination of society by the Anglican Church on one hand, and, on the other, by the aristocracy and gentry. If (as will be argued in section III) traditional society was dominated by a *culturally* defined elite of gentlemen, it is necessary to set against this the fact that gentlemen did not occur in isolation, but in families. To an extent, wealth could offset birth. Both wealth and birth mattered in the old society; but wealth could only outweigh birth within the ranks of those already known to be gentlemen.

Most property, of course, was still landed property, and it is easy to account for eighteenth-century preoccupations with primogeniture and

---

[125] Neglect of the priority of politics, and the still-widespread affinity with Trevelyan's approach, may be seen in Dr Schochet's argument (*Patriarchalism*, p. 275, cf. p. 268):

> We can sense in Locke's use of consent an attempt to free man from tradition and to establish an immediacy for his activities and life. One was not required to become a member of the commonwealth of his father but had the right to seek a civil society more to his liking. An implication of this doctrine is that the ends served by a government might become outmoded with the passage of time; what answered the father's needs might be inadequate for the son's. Behind this type of reasoning was the 'individualism' born of the Protestant Reformation. The discriminate, self-contained, and personally responsible being that Protestant man was becoming was surely entitled to affect if not control his own life.

Dr Schochet's study is a valuable one; but the perspective on the eighteenth century which it is made to support cannot be accepted.

[126] Schochet, *Patriarchalism*, p. 139.

entail. The complexity and importance of the laws regulating the inheritance of land was mirrored by the rules of succession designed to ensure the unbroken descent of titles of nobility, despite demographic vicissitude. Such provisions culminated in the ruling House itself, and the history of England over previous centuries was conventionally organised on a framework of the dynastic lineage (and sometimes counter-claims) of kings.[127] The suggestion has been made that the very idea of the hereditary descent of the crown had been worked out and strengthened in the middle ages not least because 'the feudal land law, resting on the territorial character of kingship, assimilated the descent of the crown to the descent of an estate in fee simple'.[128] The 'symbolic provision of permanence' was a prime function of the royal family in a secular sense, as it was of the Church in a spiritual.[129]

Beneath this symbolism, 'England was an association between the heads of…families', for children, servants and other dependent individuals such as paupers were subsumed or 'caught up…into the personalities of their fathers and masters'. According to Gregory King's definitions, more than half the population was 'dependent'; and from his remaining half must also be subtracted women and children.[130] The survival of this assumption, fully shared by, for example, Locke's contemporary James Tyrrell,[131] can be gauged from the ease with which even James Mill, in his *Essay on Government*, excluded women from the franchise: 'One thing is pretty clear, that all those individuals whose interests are involved in those of other individuals, may be struck off without inconvenience… In this light women may be regarded, the interest of almost all of whom is involved either in that of their fathers, or in that of their husbands.' To which Macaulay pertinently replied that, on the same grounds, the interests of the people could be said to be 'involved in' that of the sovereign.[132] It was a telling reply since, it has been suggested, James Mill did indeed share a large part of the 'corporate and hierarchical assumptions'[133] of the old society. His famous eulogy of the middle class (p. 92 below) was not an argument for restricting the franchise to them: Mill's advocacy of universal suffrage rested on an assumption that the masses were legitimately and beneficially influenced, advised and directed by their natural leaders. His position was radical in that it was coupled with a claim that the aristocracy, gentry and Anglican clergy were not those natural rulers, but represented an irrelevance and an abuse.

Among the most valuable attempts to integrate political theory and social history have been those of recent historians who have written on the

---

[127] Cf. T. D. Kendrick, *British Antiquity* (London, 1950), for the fanciful but still-current genealogies of the English stretching back to Brutus or even to Japhet, son of Noah.

[128] Sir William Anson, *The Law and Custom of the Constitution*, vol. II: 'The Crown', part I, 4th edn (ed. A. B. Keith, Oxford, 1935), p. 261; cf. Dunn, *Locke*, p. 122.

[129] Laslett, *The World We Have Lost Further Explored*, p. 9.

[130] *Ibid.*, pp. 19–20, 31.   [131] Quoted *ibid.*, pp. 221–2.

[132] Macaulay, *Works*, vol. VII, pp. 353–4.   [133] Moore, 'Political Morality', p. 14.

institution of the family. Professor Stone, in particular, has argued ably for a transition between 'distance, deference and patriarchy' in domestic relations and 'affective individualism'. The cult of individual autonomy, the introspective nuclear family, the loving care of children, are all now dated to the years after 1660 and, in particular, after 1688, and linked to the advance of Enlightened attitudes in a whole range of areas.[134] A similar model has even been applied to America, and adduced as a cause of the American Revolution.

By the middle of the eighteenth century family relations had been fundamentally reconsidered in both England and America. An older patriarchal family authority was giving way to a new parental ideal characterised by a more affectionate and equalitarian relationship with children...Parents who embraced the new child-bearing felt a deep moral commitment to prepare their children for a life of rational independence and moral self-sufficiency.

These attitudes allegedly provided an important source of 'antipatriarchal rhetoric and ideology' during the American revolution, attacking a political theory which had become 'almost vestigial' even when formulated by Filmer. The agent of change was, we are to believe, the widespread reading and acceptance of Locke's *Some Thoughts Concerning Education*:

Locke's educational theory redefined the nature of parental authority in very much the way that the Revolution of 1688, which replaced an absolute monarchy with a constitutional one, redefined the rights and duties of the crown. The revolution Locke enthusiastically defended in his political writing declared there was 'no king in being'. The authority of William III was legislatively not divinely created and thus was not sovereign in the manner of an agent of God on earth.[135]

Yet although historians have rightly pointed to a change in manner and literary style among a part of the articulate and educated middle ranks, a growing emphasis on benevolence and a decline of cruelty and brutality among a wider circle, much of the force of this argument derives from the obsolete assumptions that Lockeian philosophy swept the board in the 1690s, providing a widely-accepted refutation of patriarchal arguments and signalling the swift disintegration of the doctrine of the divine right of kings; that Deism and indifference swept aside traditional piety and paved the way for a consumer society, pursuing pleasure rather that heedful of moral injunctions.[136] Although some eighteenth-century Englishmen can be found

[134] Lawrence Stone, *The Family, Sex and Marriage in England 1500–1800* (Harmondsworth, 1979).

[135] J. Fliegelman, *Prodigals and Pilgrims. The American Revolution Against Patriarchal Authority 1750–1800* (Cambridge, 1983), pp. 1, 4, 13.

[136] E.g. Stone, *The Family*, pp. 158–60, 164–9, 178. There is an acute methodological problem in work of this sort: 'This material needs to be treated with the same critical scrutiny which the historian gives to documents in political history', Professor Stone rightly insists (p. 25); 'an exchange of love letters needs to be handled with exactly the same sceptical caution as an exchange of diplomatic notes'. But the problem seems to be that Professor Stone has linked his account of the family to the model of political history derived from Christopher Hill, J. H. Plumb *et al.*, now no longer tenable.

who appear to match at least some of these assumptions, their *general* invalidity is the central argument of this book.

If the Revolution of 1688 gave rise to a certain amount of libertarian rhetoric, it was quickly contradicted by political realities and hardly intended even by its authors to apply to their families: as the disillusioned feminist Mary Astell complained in 1706,

If absolute sovereignty be not necessary in a State, how comes it to be so in a family?... Is it not then partial in men to the last degree to contend for and practise that arbitrary dominion in their families which they abhor and exclaim against in the State?... If all men are born free, how is it that all women are born slaves?[137]

But Mary Wollstonecraft still found it necessary to say the same things in the 1790s, admitting: ''till society is very differently constituted, parents, I fear, will still insist on being obeyed, because they will be obeyed, and constantly endeavour to settle that power on a Divine right which will not bear the investigation of reason'.[138] Although much interesting evidence about changing moods and manners within the family has been uncovered, the large extent to which political, social and domestic life retained an authoritarian, hierarchical structure for all but a handful of the 'Enlightened' may have been obscured;[139] and the application of familiar 'Whig' accounts of the triumph of Lockeian contractarianism to the sphere of family relations may reflect an aspect of the experience of the liberal intelligentsia in the 1960s more than in the 1690s (the influence of Locke *On Education* is not to be equated with that of Dr Spock).

An important qualification to the changes of familial mood diagnosed by Professor Stone is that they scarcely extended to one important category within the family circle: domestic servants. This seems evident even though their role and status were chiefly defined by their employers. Their station was entered upon contractually; but it was a contract in which the servant was held temporarily to have relinquished his freedom. The master undertook extensive obligations; but the servant's whole time and energy was then at his disposal. The state of submission

...necessarily arises from the nature of servitude; for the very condition of that compact is, that one man shall submit his will and actions to the discretion and direction of another: and therefore a servant is supposed to have no will of his own, where his master is concerned; but to submit himself intirely to the will of his master, and to obey all his lawful commands.[140]

---

[137] Quoted Stone, *The Family*, p. 165.

[138] Mary Wollstonecraft, *A Vindication of the Rights of Woman* (1792; ed. C. W. Hagelman, New York, 1967), p. 235; cf. p. 78: 'The *divine right* of husbands, like the divine right of kings, may, it is to be hoped, in this enlightened age, be contested without danger.'

[139] For a critique of Professor Stone's account cf. Laslett, *The World We Have Lost Further Explored*, pp. 119–21, 328–9 nn. 12, 13, and work there cited.

[140] [Patrick Delany], *Twenty Sermons upon Social Duties and their Opposite Vices* (London, 1750), p. 182, quoted in J. J. Hecht, *The Domestic Servant Class in Eighteenth-Century England* (London, 1956), p. 73.

It is therefore as relevant for the history of the family that the servant was considered to be part of it. Legally, as Adam Smith told his lecture audience, 'There are 3 different relations in which the members of a family may stand to one another. They may be either in the relation of husband and wife; or of father and son; or of master and servant.'[141] What reinforced the analogy to the point of literal similitude was that the master, having an authority over his servants alike in scope and character to his authority over his children, was entitled to administer physical punishment to both: as Guy Miège wrote in 1703, 'As for stubborn and unruly servants, the law of England gives masters and mistresses power to correct them; and resistance in a servant is punished with severe penalty.'[142]

So common was the master–servant relationship that it could be used as an ideal, a model of the necessary structure of social order. Paley wrote:

The labour of the world is carried on by *service*, that is, by one man's working under another man's direction. I take it for granted, that this is the best way of conducting business, because all nations and ages have adopted it. Consequently service is the relation which, of all others, affects the greatest number of individuals, and in the most sensible manner... a continuance of this connection is frequently the foundation of so much mutual kindness and attachment, that very few friendships are more cordial or more sincere; that it leaves oftentimes nothing in servitude, except the name; nor any distinction, but what one party is as much pleased with, and sometimes also, as proud of, as the other.[143]

Paley drew no distinction between domestic servants and commercial and industrial employees: all could still be embraced within the same social nexus, and covered by the same social ideal (if the culturally-dominant employer wished). Nor was the institution an anachronism, declining in a new age: in point of numbers, service was even expanding. Unequal economic growth reinforced the spending power of aristocracy, gentry, merchant, manufacturer: some of the new wealth was spent on domestic servants, whose numbers increased faster than the population as a whole – 600,000 in 1801, 1,300,000 in 1851.[144] What was different was that, by then, the phenomenon of service had been subsumed by the categories of class.

Until the evolution of class, hierarchical subordination was scarcely dissolved even by the spread of popular education, for both its champions and its opponents accepted 'a pattern of society whose values were symbolised by the terms rank, station, duty and decorum'.[145] Until the early

[141] Adam Smith, *Lectures on Jurisprudence* (eds. R. L. Meek, D. D. Raphael and P. G. Stein, Oxford, 1978), p. 141.

[142] [Guy Miège], *The New State of England under our Sovereign Queen Anne* (London, 1703), part 2, p. 288, quoted Hecht, *Domestic Servant*, p. 79.

[143] William Paley, *Reasons for Contentment; Addressed to the Labouring Part of the British Public* (London, 1793), pp. 13–14.

[144] P. Deane and W. A. Cole, *British Economic Growth 1688–1959* (Cambridge, 1967), p. 143.

[145] V. E. Neuburg, *Popular Education in Eighteenth Century England* (London, 1971), p. 2.

nineteenth century, even those sufficiently articulate to escape from such a world, and to write about their escape, would cast their self-awareness within the ancient idiom of the spiritual, not the working class, autobiography.[146] As late as the mid-nineteenth century, it has been suggested, 'it would appear that the class [of rural labourers] as a whole had to some extent internalised in its self-image the scorn and contempt felt for it by the upper classes':[147] this was the unpleasant side of the intellectual hegemony of a rival class ideal.

Whether early-modern societies were unitary or plural, whether men's professed public values and motives were essentially similar or self-righteously various depended, first and foremost, on religion. The salient fact for the social historian of eighteenth-century England is that Christian belief is initially almost universal, a belief calling attention to the history of a chosen nation conceived as a family or group of families, with a Holy Family as its culmination; a faith whose established Church taught obedience, humility and reverence to superiors with unanimity and consistency down the decades. A Christian faith and moral code was a common possession of all social strata: the realm of the communal, of what were later to be designated 'public goods', was largely the realm of religion. Government, war, allegiance, law, capital punishment and the social hierarchy would be ultimately unintelligible to an historian of early-modern England who was unaware of the last three Articles of Religion of its established Church. Allied with Christian symbolism, familial status was another of the symbolic elements which, in so poor a society, enabled 'a minority to live for all the rest',[148] turning much of social life into a vicarious identification with the elite and working against the emergence of a simple antagonism between rich and poor. Even in 1820, a clergyman declared:

The peculiar excellence of that admirable structure of society established in this country consists not, as we all know, in equality of rights and privileges; which, under the free and varied exertions of the human powers would be neither practicable nor desirable; but in that singular coherence and adaptation of its several parts, by which many classes and ranks of men, rising in orderly gradation, and melting as it were into each other, through the lightest shades of difference – united by a common interest, and cemented by Christian charity, – compose together one solid, well compacted, and harmonious whole – presenting a scheme as beautiful in theory, as it is valuable in practice, and productive of a far greater sum of utility and happiness, than is attainable under any other form.[149]

---

[146] David Vincent, *Bread, Knowledge and Freedom. A Study of Nineteenth-Century Working Class Autobiography* (London, 1981).

[147] Obelkevitch, *Religion and Rural Society*, p. 99.

[148] Laslett, *The World We Have Lost Further Explored*, p. 52.

[149] Rev. William Otter, *Reasons for Continuing the Education of the Poor at the Present Crisis: A Sermon, Preached...16th of March, 1820* (Shrewsbury, 1820), pp. 8–9.

On a local level, the personal morality which the Church taught and enforced, whether directly or via the JP, was closely linked to the economic survival or wellbeing of the community to Malthus and beyond.[150]

In this society, social subordination and political obedience were founded on tradition. Therefore critical examination of the reasons why some were better placed than others was unlikely to come about. This submissive cast of mind is almost universal in the statements made by individuals about themselves...A further reason why...society...must be presumed to have been acquiescent in its usual tendency is that the phrase stable poverty does on the whole seem to be a fair description of most of its area. It is a commonplace of observation that stable poverty means resignation to the situation as it is.[151]

To gentry hegemony, suggests Mr E. P. Thompson, there was no real alternative 'until the 1790s': 'The crowd, at its most advanced, can rarely transcend the libertarian rhetoric of the radical Whig tradition; the poets cannot transcend the sensibility of the humane and generous paternalist. The furious anonymous letters which spring up from society's lower depths blaspheme against the gentry's hegemony but offer no strategy to replace it.' Even the 'potential members' of a middle class were 'content to submit to a condition of abject dependency...consenting adults in their own corruption' for most of the century.[152] Discarding Mr Thompson's characteristic denigration of the ancien regime will help us to trace the ascendancy of the aristocratic ideal for even a little longer still. Certainly, it seems too modest of Dr Laslett to advance 1700–10 as the 'final decade of the old world' on the grounds of the absence at that point of enclosures.[153] If little changed in English society in his senses between the reigns of Elizabeth I and Anne, it is difficult to see that much changed, in those senses, before the very end of the eighteenth century in most areas. As is argued below, it is difficult to agree that Wilkesite radicalism in the 1760s may 'rightly be heralded as a sign of an altered relationship between the common man and his gentleman superior, in which quiescent political ignorance had begun to give way to demands for a share in the national political life'.[154] Far more radical doctrines and traditions of action, extending even to insurrection, had long survived in the mental world of the old order, without refuting

---

[150] The idea that the illegitimacy rate is an index to the effectiveness of the Church's moral control or to the wider cohesion of a traditional, repressive social order (e.g. in Stone, *The Family*, pp. 382–404) does not survive the analysis in Laslett, *The World We Have Lost Further Explored*, pp. 153–81. Illegitimacy varied almost exactly with general fertility rates. Moreover, the differentials between counties in respect of illegitimacy rates were often little changed over decades or even centuries (pp. 167–8), another example of profound continuities scarcely affected by industrialisation.

[151] Laslett, *op. cit.*, pp. 213ff.

[152] Thompson, 'Eighteenth-Century English Society', pp. 142, 162–3. One must admire Mr Thompson's conjuring skill in producing the rabbit of class conflict from the eighteenth-century hat; the less gifted historian will be content to wait until the 1830s.

[153] Laslett, *op. cit.*, p. 60.   [154] *Ibid.*, p. 238.

'the patriarchal explanation of social rank'. As is shown in chapter 5, those radical doctrines, even in the eighteenth century, were not rooted in contractarian individualism. At a parish level, it would be wrong to see a necessary contradiction between a contractarian and a patriarchal nexus. Patriarchal relations could be entered into contractually; and it has been aptly denied that 'ordinary Englishmen' understood the contractarian tradition 'in terms of the factors that the twentieth century attributes to the contract device in political theory: limits on authority and the source for personal rights and claims. The contract seems to have been used more as a formal explanation of how people entered relationships than as a definition of the nature and content of those stations.'[155] In any case, the great age of contractarian individualism in political thought was not the eighteenth century (when such doctrines were subjected to devastating criticism) but the seventeenth; and the prevalence, in seventeenth-century society, of patriarchal relationships which would make those contractarian theories only tenuously relatable to social practice is scarcely in question.

What destroyed the ancien regime in England, it will be argued later, was not chiefly the widespread adoption of a democratic world view, but the advance of Dissent, Roman Catholicism and religious indifference. Non-Anglicans grew from about $\frac{1}{2}$ million out of 7 million in England and Wales in 1770 to slightly over half the churchgoing population at the 1851 religious census; and over half the population did not then attend church at all. The confessional State had been partly undermined by 1828 not by its intellectual invalidity or some new awakening to it but by the erosion of the numerical position of the Church of England. This became apparent very late; the Oxford movement was a response not long delayed. But in the light of what has already been said of the non-reception of Lockeian doctrines, and the distortions embodied in the late-nineteenth-century interpretation of Bentham and James Mill, we may fully endorse Dr Laslett's observation on the 'world we have lost':

It may begin to look odd that any one was ever bold enough to escape at all, impossible that ideas of individual rights, of the accountability of superiors, of contract as the basis of government could ever have occurred to the men of seventeenth-century England... There can be no doubt of the contrast between what some men sometimes said about the rights of individuals and what those rights actually were.[156]

It was a contrast which lasted as long as the old society itself. Even in 1802, Cobbett wrote: 'When, from the top of any high hill, one looks round the

---

[155] Schochet, *Patriarchalism*, p. 82.
[156] Laslett, *The World We Have Lost Further Explored*, p. 219. In the light of the arguments developed in his book, the profound congruity between the demographic work of the Cambridge Group for the History of Population and Social Structure and the psephological work of Professor D. C. Moore and others need not be stressed.

country, and sees the multitude of regularly distributed spires, one not only ceases to wonder that order and religion are maintained, but one is astonished that any such thing as disaffection or irreligion should prevail.'[157] Cobbett was, perhaps, ill-informed about the course of events in these respects during the previous century. How disaffection and irreligion emerged and advanced within the 'old society' is the theme of chapter 5.

Nevertheless, it is suggested in chapter 6 that the accumulating forces hostile to the old order were as yet insufficient to destroy it; that its destruction in 1828–32 was political, not inevitable. What was lost at that point, however, was not merely a constitutional arrangement, but the intellectual ascendancy of a world view, the cultural hegemony of the old elite. Nor was this the result of the triumph of 'individualism'. Dicey's identification of the mid-nineteenth century as 'The Period of Benthamism or Individualism' has encouraged us to see those two terms as synonymous; an eighteenth-century perspective would yield a different result, as it does with Adam Smith. It might explain Bentham's reliance on the State, and on the coercive role of Authority in all situations, as a secular translation of the Tory-Anglican social ethic of the 1740s into which he was born. It may ultimately prove to be the case that the mythical tradition of English individualism has been taken so much for granted that its origins have been wrongly diagnosed, and its incidence greatly exaggerated. Perhaps, at all times, it is little more than an 'infantile disorder' of the intelligentsia.

It is not easy to reconcile the ideals of individualism with many men's acceptance of class ideals and practices in the nineteenth century. No such problem arose under the ancien regime, however. The idea of class (and it is only an idea) failed to establish itself in the public arena during the intellectual ascendancy of the confessional State. After 1828–32, however, the widespread acceptance of a class analysis, and of a view that classes were economically determined, was remarkably rapid. Until near its close, the old society by contrast witnessed no clash between competing class ideals, and no apprehensive attention to the shifting balance between economic strata. The old society had only one class, if that word may be used as a deliberate anachronism: gentlemen (let us call them patricians). The vast majority of patricians were, almost necessarily, members (active or nominal) of the Church of England. Religion provided for Anglicans a nationwide definition of unity, and, for non-Anglicans, the definition of their inferior status. Non-gentlemen (let us call them plebeians) constituted the vast majority of Englishmen and included every diversity of outlook, accent, education, occupation and location. Gentlemen by contrast attended to a unified ideal which, after 1832, was to be translated into a class ideal. We need not suppose that the class structure of Victorian England, as

---

[157] Cobbett to Windham, 27th May 1802; quoted in G. F. A. Best, 'Church and State in English Politics 1800–1833' (Cambridge PhD thesis, 1955).

contemporaries perceived it, was determined by the economic structure of society. The idea of class merely provided the perspective in which economic matters were viewed, a perspective drawn from a group loyalty prior to industrial capitalism being carried over and applied in a new age.[158] What made it (subjectively) a new age was not the quantifiable but the narratable, the events of 1828–32. Marxists and others would wish to see the survival of the idea of a gentleman as an anachronism. Yet patricians sustained, in the old society, the intellectual model of group cohesion, loyalty and status which was to be the pattern for the form which *all* classes took in the new society.

'Class' was not a fact, but a way of describing facts; it did not objectively come into being, but was slowly and partially adopted as a terminology. From the 1820s into the Victorian era, the middle ranks, most conscious of the adjacent group ideals of the elite, led the trend to define social phenomena in class terms. Industrial labourers, farm labourers, even skilled workers lagged behind: radicalism among the masses from the 1790s was an intellectual contagion, not a response to an autonomous economic definition.[159] The chronological priority of the elite had a consequence which was observable as long as class-based society survived: it was the elite which henceforth formed the most class-like class, the most cohesive, the most self-aware, the most sharply defined. The middle class never quite reached these standards, and was always divided by its diversities and its affinities with groups above and below it. The working class was not only the last to picture itself as such; it was also the least unanimous in its subscription to the idea of class, the most diverse, the least capable of grasping and acting on a theory, the most stolidly conservative in its habits. The working class as such posed little threat to the old order before 1832. What the 1820s did witness was, importantly, the rise of the ideologues of a middle class.

Until then, the Christian hierarchical ideal had absorbed the middle ranks, placing a traditional interpretation on the facts of their new affluence. As a commentator wrote in *Blackwood's Edinburgh Magazine* even in 1824:

In most other countries, society presents hardly anything but a void between an ignorant labouring population, and a needy and profligate nobility...but with us the space between the ploughman and the peer, is crammed with circle after circle, fitted in the most admirable manner for sitting upon each other, for connecting the former with the latter, and for rendering the whole perfect in cohesion, strength and beauty.[160]

---

[158] On this subject I am indebted to, though often in disagreement with, Professor Harold Perkin's brilliant discussion in *The Origins of Modern English Society*, chapter 6, 'The Birth of Class'.

[159] Cf. chapters 5 and 6 below. In the case of machine breakers or farm labourers in the unindustrialised south and east, disturbances were the unideological response not to industry but to the failure of distressed counties to benefit from industry.

[160] Quoted in Harold Perkin, 'The Social Causes of the Industrial Revolution' in *The Structured Crowd*, p. 32.

Apart from the crude xenophobia, it was an accurate perception of a long-familiar rationale. Already however it was being challenged by a theory which invited the middle orders to see themselves as a homogeneous group, defined over against the elite.

James Mill's *Essay on Government* famously apostrophised the 'middle rank':

Another proposition may be stated, with a perfect confidence of the concurrence of all those men who have attentively considered the formation of opinions in the great body of society, or, indeed, the principles of human nature in general. It is, that the opinions of that class of the people, who are below the middle rank, are formed, and their minds are directed by that intelligent, that virtuous rank, who come the most immediately in contact with them, who are in the constant habit of intimate communication with them, to whom they fly for advice and assistance in all their numerous difficulties, upon whom they feel an immediate and daily dependence, in health and in sickness, in infancy and in old age; to whom their children look up as models for their imitation, whose opinions they hear daily repeated, and account it their honour to adopt. There can be no doubt that the middle rank, which gives to science, to art, and to legislation itself, their most distinguished ornaments, the chief source of all that has exalted and refined human nature, is that portion of the community of which, if the basis of representation were ever so far extended, the opinion would ultimately decide. Of the people beneath them, a vast majority would be sure to be guided by their advice and example.[161]

Historians from other social classes might well dismiss this as merely preposterous. Yet Mill was advancing the claims of the 'middle rank' by describing it in exactly the terms in which the aristocracy and gentry had described themselves time out of mind. The middle class identified itself as a *class* by adopting the model of the pre-existing elite. They adopted a definition that was cultural, not economic. In 1832 an objective criterion was added to this rationale, a definition as clear as the elite's distinction between gentlemen and others. The Reform Act's £10 borough householder franchise for the first time provided an objective, nationwide standard, ruling a sharp line through traditional gradations. That many below this line doubtless felt their exclusion unjust only served to make the issue more sensitive; it was more important that a national standard had been set than that some might think it inaccurate. In this sense too, class was a consequence rather than a cause of parliamentary reform.

Before 1828–32, the ideal of the gentleman exercised an intellectual ascendancy. Both patricians and the majority of plebeians subscribed to it. The main challenge came not from plebeians as such but from non-Anglicans as such. In general, Anglican plebeians would have wished to become gentlemen if they could. As eighteenth-century society became increasingly affluent, more and more of them tried to do so, many successfully. Assimilation was the keynote. In the early nineteenth century this changed

---

[161] Quoted Dicey, *Law & Public Opinion*, p. 187; cf. Macaulay, *Works*, vol. VII, p. 363.

totally. Pundits arose designating themselves 'middle class' who vilified the values and manners of gentlemen; other pundits, claiming to speak for the 'working class', in turn denounced all the classes above them. The events of 1828–32 were the victory which the new analysts needed; they claimed it as a symbolic victory. All religions were now equal in the eyes of the State, they maintained (vestiges of Anglican exclusiveness were therefore even more to be excoriated). If utilitarian criteria were the appropriate ones, all groups must justify their existence in those terms. The class war had begun: that is, the phenomena of conflict and resentment between individuals, present in all societies, were henceforth assimilated to the intellectual categories of class warfare.

Although attention is drawn in this book to the importance of politics and religion, and to the events of 1828–32, between the quantifiable aspects of the old and the new societies no sharp line is to be drawn. In respect of the issues discussed here, however, it is possible to say that the important transitions occurred in and after the 1830s. In March 1833, Wellington told a friend

> ...that he thought the operation of the Reform Bill though it would probably be slow, was nevertheless sure. The old aristocratical interest has great stamina, and will hold together a long while, but seeing how it has yielded before this shock when in its entire strength, what is it to do in a succession of shocks, each of which will give fresh powers to the democracy?[162]

III. THE SOCIAL THEORY OF ELITE HEGEMONY

In 1790, Burke wrote: 'Nothing is more certain than that our manners, our civilisation, and all the good things which are connected with manners and with civilisation, have, in this European world of ours, depended for ages upon two principles, and were, indeed, the result of both combined: I mean the spirit of a gentleman, and the spirit of religion.'[163] Traditional society looked, above all, to two ideals: the ideal of a Christian, and the ideal of a gentleman. Were they compatible? Theorists laboured to reconcile them, and to a large extent they were mutually reinforcing. The Christian ideal, above all, validated the model of a homogeneous, hierarchical society, a unitary and confessional State. Rank, order and degree had their place within the Providential dispensation; religion and charity, condescension and deference, the idealised agents of patriarchalism, would integrate each small gradation in the social order. Much of this was underwritten by the ideal of the gentleman: order, degree and subordination were all given a concrete location in respect of a particular social group. These two ideals

---

[162] L. J. Jennings (ed.), *The Correspondence and Diaries of the Late Right Honourable John Wilson Croker*, 2nd edn (3 vols., London, 1885), vol. II, pp. 207–8.
[163] Burke, *Reflections on the Revolution in France*, in *Works*, vol. III, p. 335.

appealed for credence to a society whose realities – families, landowners, Anglicans, masters, kings – partly echoed both. But there was, ultimately, a contradiction between the ideals which pulled them apart. On the social level, the elite ideal threatened to cut across the homogeneous hierarchy, each gradation shading into the other, ruling a firm and definite line between those who were and those who were not gentlemen.

The contradiction was evident on a personal level also. Could one be both a gentleman and a Christian? It was a problem for moralists throughout the period of the ancien regime. In general, Christian moralists did their best to answer 'yes'; they were almost compelled to try to embrace both of society's dominant ideals. The practice of duelling, however, was the acid test, and provided evidence for some pessimists to conclude that in the last resort gentlemen would place their own code before Christian injunctions to charity, humility and forgiveness (there was nothing special about gentlemen in this respect: all subsequent classes gave a similar priority to their class ideals). The problem had a political reflection: to what extent would lay politicians support the Church? To many Anglicans in the 1690s, the Revolution and the Toleration Act heralded the destruction of everything they most valued. Yet the Church proved remarkably resilient, Anglicanism fighting off most of a succession of radical attacks. This came to an end in 1828–9, when sufficient gentlemen could be found in Parliament who were willing to sacrifice the Church in the name of expediency or of secular ideals. Retribution was swift: with great suddenness for so unquantifiable a change, the hegemony of gentlemen in English society disintegrated. In the 1830s, a class society was born in which gentlemen were only one group among many fighting for survival. The remarkable rearguard action which they fought in the nineteenth century, and in some areas even into the twentieth, is a theme for other historians.

The object here is to emphasise that one central characteristic which disqualifies English society under the ancien regime from consideration as modern, whether as practice or as ideal, was the survival of the aristocratic ethic. The credibility of a hierarchical image of society, and the force of the patriarchal ideologies of order derived from it, obviously reflected the continuing existence of a lofty social hierarchy whose most conspicuous exemplars were the aristocracy and gentry. Added to the hierarchical ideology of order was a body of doctrines and assumptions which justified the ascendancy of a *particular* group, articulating a cultural hegemony which did not meet with significant defeats until 1832 and 1846. The elite's ideal could claim a divine justification for gentility independent of divine-right monarchy,[164] and the strength of the old elite's hold on society proved, in

---

[164] R. B. Schlatter, *The Social Ideas of Religious Leaders 1660–1688* (Oxford, 1940), esp. pp. 106–23, focusses on divine sanctions for inequalities of wealth; much more could be said on the rationales for nobility as such.

fact, to be largely independent of the theoretical and practical strength of Stuart kingship. The aristocratic ideal invites separate consideration. Its vitality and power in the eighteenth century is of immense importance. Yet, remarkably, it has received no full-scale treatment by modern scholars.[165] The charge is often heard that historians have been accustomed thoughtlessly to view society 'from the top down'. In reality, this has almost never been done; and the accusation has inhibited the attempt. Few writers have investigated the aristocratic viewpoint as such, and fewer still have tried to depict the *inwardness* of that social and political code.[166] When the aristocracy is dealt with, it is only too often with the outsider's tone of surprise or resentment; and the component of aristocratic supremacy usually dwelt on – the economic structures of their dominance – could more profitably be explained as a symptom than a cause. Historians have, as a profession, carried their own class-perspectives back into the ancien regime with a near-unanimity which has hindered them from recapturing the world views of peer and peasant alike.

French historiography has paid greater attention to these issues: aristocratic cultural hegemony has been a leading theme, and historians' investigations of the nobility have been marked by a greater willingness to see it in its own terms.[167] English historians have typically echoed their eighteenth-century countrymen's pride in English liberties compared to French, and celebrated the alleged advance of bourgeois values on this side of the Channel. Yet if we attend to the issues excluded from the agenda of economic historians, it is possible to see that England and France had more in common than either's patriotism was willing to concede. Both were ancien regime societies, and the analogies are an important corrective to the insular, Fabian historiography of England. Both societies were dominated by a ruling group which justified its power by reference to similar patrician ideals. Both monarchies were held by their defenders to be absolute, but not arbitrary: in France, as in England, the crown was limited not so much by

---

[165] Honourable exceptions are the brief discussions in Hampson, *The Enlightenment*, pp. 68–71; Perkin, *English Society*, pp. 237–52; J. P. Jenkins, 'A Social and Political History of the Glamorgan Gentry c. 1650–1770' (Cambridge PhD thesis, 1978), chapter 6; and D. T. Andrew's article, cited below, n. 237. Two studies in a less rigorous idiom, but not without some value, are A. Ponsonby, *The Decline of Aristocracy* (London, 1912) and O. F. Christie, *The Transition from Aristocracy 1832–1867* (London, 1927). The most stimulating treatment of these themes is by a sociologist: Norbert Elias, *The Court Society* (Oxford, 1983).

[166] For one valuable example of a particular institution used as a point of access into a code and a set of social relationships, cf. D. Itzkowitz, *Peculiar Privilege. A Social History of English Foxhunting 1753–1885* (Hassocks, 1977). But the hunt was an institution which reached maturity only in the nineteenth century.

[167] Cf. G. Chaussinand-Nogaret, *La Noblesse au XVIIIe Siècle. De la Féodalité aux Lumières* (Paris, 1976), esp. pp. 93–117; F. Bluche, *La vie quotidienne de la noblesse française au XVIIIe siècle* (Paris, 1973); P. Goubert, *The Ancien Régime. French Society 1600–1750* (1969; London, 1973), esp. pp. 153–202; J. Levron, 'Louis XIV's Courtiers' in R. Hatton (ed.), *Louis XIV and Absolutism* (London, 1976), pp. 130–53.

a democratic, contractarian sanction as by the counter-claims of aristocratic privilege ultimately derived from the largely independent basis of noble status. Such issues gave rise to a considerable literature of controversy in France, the rivalry between *noblesse de robe* and *noblesse d'épée* being closely bound up with the position of the monarchy itself.[168] The royalist case was that 'Nobility is defined as a quality which the sovereign power imprints upon private persons in order to place them and their descendants above other citizens'[169]: that is, that the monarch could so honour anyone he chose. *In France* Its antithesis was the nobility's conviction, as one of them put it in 1839, that 'La noblesse...tient au sang':[170] that is, that their status was independent and indefeasible. The alternatives were explored in such classics as G. de la Roque's *Traité de la Noblesse* (Paris, 1678), which argued a biological case; Comte Henri de Boulainvilliers's *Essai sur la noblesse de France* (Paris, 1732), which put forward an historical justification for his class, or Claude François Menestrier's *Les diverses espèces de la noblesse et les manières d'en dresser les preuves* (Paris, 1683).[171]

French aristocrats' disagreements on the subject of their origin did not, however, destroy the vitality of the social ideals they held in common. It may even have encouraged emulation in that respect, appropriating monarchical hauteur for their own purposes. Was the aristocratic ethic losing its hold in eighteenth-century France? Arthur Young's impression was that French monarchical deference had dissolved only on the eve of the Revolution.[172] Earlier travellers seem to have been in little doubt of its strength. They had typically emphasised, of the French nobility, the universality of their 'passive obedience and non-resistance to the will and injunctions of the Court'. Moreover, it was reported (though perhaps with a little wishful thinking) that

Nobleness of blood, in France, is an invincible protection from the insults and slight of the vulgar, who are early taught to reverence their superiors without measure; and to act, on all occasions, with the most boundless deference and condescension in whatever relates to them.

---

[168] F. L. Ford, *Robe and Sword. The Regrouping of the French Aristocracy after Louis XIV* (Cambridge, Mass., 1953).

[169] Pierre Guyot, *Répertoire Universel et Raisonné de Jurisprudence* (Paris, 1784–5), vol. XII, p. 65; quoted *ibid.*, p. 23.

[170] C. B. A. Behrens, *The Ancien Régime* (London, 1967), p. 78. For earlier English debates cf. J. P. Cooper, 'Ideas of Gentility in Early Modern England', in Cooper, *Land, Men and Beliefs* (London, 1983), 43–77.

[171] Cf. Chaussinand-Nogaret, *La Noblesse* and *idem* (ed.), *Une histoire des élites 1700–1848* (Paris, 1975); J. Q. C. Mackrell, *The Attack on 'Feudalism' in Eighteenth Century France* (London, 1973).

[172] Arthur Young, *Travels During the Years 1787, 1788 and 1789. Undertaken More Particularly with a View of Ascertaining the Cultivation, Wealth, Resources, and National Prosperity, of the Kingdom of France* (2 vols., Bury St Edmunds, 1792), vol. I, p. 10.

The nobility, in turn, were said to defer to the king:

A Frenchman's method of establishing his country's title to superior merit, is by expatiating on the grandor [sic] of his monarch; his uncontrollable dominion, his irresistible will; to obey and submit to which, in its most extensive latitude, is not less his pleasure than his glory.

An Englishman, on the contrary, cites his own liberty; the certainty of his possessions; his defiance of tyranny...

The principal argument adduced by the French in disputes of this nature, in support of their countrymen's superior worth, is their inviolable attachment and fidelity to the persons of their kings, and the unabated reverence they have always preserved, even for such as were not guiltless of transgressing the bounds of mildness and moderation in their government.[173]

The Comte d'Allonville in 1788 chose to highlight his country's code by drawing a similar contrast: 'L'auteur voit en chaque société un principe moteur, le patriotisme chez les Romains, la religion en Espagne, le mercantilisme en Angleterre. Celui de la France est plus noble et plus éclairé: c'est le principe de l'honneur, espèce de religion nationale... patriotisme des monarchies.'[174] Was the Revolution the result of a massive rejection of such values? Against Arthur Young's impressions must be set the evidence of peasant grievances contained in the *cahiers de doléances* in 1789. Even at that point, they do not reveal a rejection of the monarchy; 'the king and kingship inspire loyalty and love'. The nobility and seigneurs (who were not distinguished) were objects of hatred for their financial exactions and petty local tyrannies; but it does not seem that the aristocratic code and ethic was held up to attack as such.[175]

Many, perhaps most, Englishmen analysed the French Revolution largely in terms of a breakdown of religious, not aristocratic, sanctions and norms. In 1791 Burke denied, on the basis of his recent stay in France, that the Revolution was the product of 'any dread of arbitrary power that lay heavy on the minds of the people'. Some 'persons of rank' had such opinions, but not all.

As to the lower orders, and those little above them, in whose name the present powers domineer, they were far from discovering any sort of dissatisfaction with the power and prerogatives of the crown. That vain people were rather proud of them: they rather despised the English for not having a monarch possessed of such high and perfect authority.

The common people were tricked into 'their present spirit of levelling'.

Neither did that people despise or hate or fear their nobility: on the contrary, they valued themselves on the generous qualities which distinguished the chiefs of their nation.[176]

---

[173] [J. Andrews], *An Account of the Character and Manners of the French* (2 vols., London, 1770), vol. I, pp. 124, 126–7, 262–4.   [174] Quoted Bluche, *La vie quotidienne de la noblesse*, p. 25.
[175] Goubert, *The Ancien Régime*, pp. 10–12.
[176] *An Appeal from the New to the Old Whigs*, in *Works*, vol. IV, pp. 107–8.

The fate of the French elite made men realise how central it had been, and how similar the English pattern was. It had been traditional, of course, for observers to dwell on the differences: the relative lack of deference spontaneously paid to Englishmen of rank; the comparatively little 'respect and submission' which the English nobility claimed from their inferiors; the contrasting lack of polish in English manners. One traveller ascribed this to a political cause: on the continent,

Every subject in a monarchy trembles on account of the most trifling circumstance. The most indifferent action, a single word, sometimes even a supposition, are sufficient to deprive the miserable wretch of his subsistence; nay, it often costs him his fortune, sometimes his life. Upon the least of these events the welfare and existence of a family depend: they, therefore, affect an uncommon refinement in manners; and from thence it appears, that the most ridiculous prejudices often regulate the laws of that phantom to which they give the name of honour.[177]

Englishmen, too, were struck by the elaborate courtesy of speech and compliment in France, and the greater formality of dress.[178] French observers were less admiring of the absurd English custom of dressing informally, like their servants: 'indeed there is great room to fear, that persons, who deviate so far from their own condition, have imbibed the manners of those, whom they make it their glory to resemble...is it not ridiculous in a peer of the realm to appear cast in the same mould with a brewer?'[179]

There is much similar, though highly subjective, evidence that London high-society manners were less uniform, less of a formalised and self-sustaining code, than those of Paris. But it would be wrong to use such claims that English society was *less* deferential than the French as evidence that English society was *not* deferential, and that a bluff, blunt, common-sensical ideal type had triumphed on this side of the Channel whose egalitarian manners matched his Lockeian philosophy and his Deistic religion. It depended, of course, on one's standards. To American colonial visitors, London society seemed insufferably formal; and what some commentators wished, for their own reasons, to represent as egalitarian manners among the people at large, reflecting a sturdy independence of spirit, seemed to most people, in a less political light, to be merely the gross behaviour of an unpolished nation.[180]

In 1790 the aristocratic ethic was famously apostrophised by Burke, who saw under attack in France, as a result of the Revolution,

...that generous loyalty to rank and sex, that proud submission, that dignified obedience, that subordination of the heart, which kept alive, even in servitude itself,

[177] J. W. von Archenholz, *A Picture of England* (Dublin, 1790), pp. 4, 24, 27.
[178] [Andrews], *Account*, vol. I, pp. 64, 138–41.
[179] Abbé Le Blanc, *Letters on the English and French Nations* (2 vols., London, 1747), vol. I, p. 19.
[180] Cf. Dickinson, *Liberty and Property*, p. 152. Travel literature, and the description of national manners, had a definite political relevance – a theme yet to be explored.

the spirit of an exalted freedom! The unbought grace of life, the cheap defence of nations, the nurse of manly sentiment and heroic enterprize, is gone! It is gone, that sensibility of principle, that chastity of honour, which felt a stain like a wound, which inspired courage whilst it mitigated ferocity, which ennobled whatever it touched, and under which vice itself lost half its evil by losing all its grossness!

'Nobility is a graceful ornament to the civil order', he continued. 'It is the Corinthian capital of polished society.'[181] He obviously believed in England, now, as its securest refuge. These remarks are familiar to generations of students (if only because they appear in a work which has become part of the received canon of political theory); but the inner structure of the ideal, or how it imposed itself on society, have not been the subject of enquiry. Burke's eulogy is admired or rejected, but seldom analysed.

A subject of such international scope might, however, warrant investigation. As Goldsmith saw in 1759: 'The polite of every country seem to have but one character. A gentleman of Sweden differs but little, except in trifles, from one of every other country.'[182] Even America had its powerful gentry elite:

Scorn of the lower classes, distrust of those who sought to play upon the emotions of the masses, and fear that the 'mechanics and country clowns' would come to take a place in society rightfully belonging only to 'the people of property, of best sense and character': these were motives influencing the final position of many members of the colonial aristocracy.[183]

Because such phenomena were open to description in more than one way, we should remember Professor Palmer's suggestion of the effect of the comparatively relaxed tone of English society, and of social mobility from the gentry into the peerage:

The result was to strengthen the aristocracy, and to deprive the truly common people of an effectual leadership. Precisely because it had avoided the crude dualism of *noblesse* and *roture*, England was of all countries the most successfully aristocratic. If the idea of equality seemed in England especially shocking and nonsensical it was because what some called inequality, and others a due subordination of ranks and orders, was seen not merely as social necessity, but as an adornment of civilised society, interesting and warmly attractive in itself.[184]

It is an observation which echoes Montesquieu's:

Si le faste et la splendeur qui environnent les rois font une partie de leur puissance, la modestie et la simplicité des manières font la force des nobles aristocratiques.

[181] *Reflections on the Revolution in France* in *Works*, vol. III, pp. 331–2, 416.
[182] Quoted in A. Smythe-Palmer, *The Ideal of a Gentleman* (London, 1909), p. 266.
[183] L. W. Labaree, *Conservatism in Early American History* (London, 1948), p. 116; cf. A. Guttman, *The Conservative Tradition in America* (New York, 1967); R. Lora, *Conservative Minds in America* (Chicago, 1971); Louis B. Wright, *Tradition and the Founding Fathers* (Charlottesville, Va. 1975); W. H. Nelson, *The American Tory* (Oxford, 1961).
[184] R. R. Palmer, *The Age of the Democratic Revolution* (2 vols., Princeton, 1959–64), vol. II, p. 464.

Quand ils n'affectent aucune distinction, quand ils se confondent avec le peuple, quand ils sont vêtus comme lui, quand ils lui font partager leurs plaisirs, il oublie sa faiblesse. Chaque gouvernement a sa nature et son principe. Il ne faut donc pas que l'aristocratie prenne la nature et le principe de la monarchie.[185]

Tocqueville, in turn, noticed the way in which the aristocratic mood and ideal had permeated English society, whereas in France the same group had become progressively isolated.[186] And despite the splendour of the French nobility and the sophistication of its self-justifications, it was relatively powerless as a body: it was, rather, the English peerage which had an institutionalised share in the political process via the House of Lords, and an even more important informal share through its stake in the Commons.

Despite the differences in idiom and mood between the English elite and its French paradigm, it is necessary to emphasise the large degree to which an aristocratic ideal and an aristocratic code existed equally in England, survived, adapted itself, and flourished.[187] It succeeded in doing so not least because it was not a force to be set over against the Enlightenment, an obsolete survival in the way of the advance of modern ideas. Most elements in Enlightenment thought were produced for, if not by, the ruling elites; in France, most *philosophes* sought to assimilate themselves to the aristocracy if they could: 'Voltaire – who incessantly cultivated courtiers, tried to become one himself, and at last managed to buy his way into the nobility – thought that the Enlightenment should begin with the *grands*: once it had captured society's commanding heights, it could concern itself with the masses – but it should take care to prevent them from learning to read.'[188]

One scholar has drawn attention to the importance of the 'restatement of the *thèse nobiliaire*' in Montesquieu, Fénelon, Saint-Simon, and Boulainvilliers.[189] Montesquieu's contribution was crucial, for, in reconciling the traditions of *noblesse de robe* and *noblesse d'épée* to produce a theory of kingship limited by aristocratic claims, he formulated the classic statement and defence of the aristocratic code which united the two elements in the French nobility. The strength of that code, he suggested, was in itself a constitutional check: 'Dans les États monarchiques et modérés la puissance est bornée par ce qui en est le ressort; je veux dire l'honneur, qui règne, comme un monarque, sur le prince et sur le peuple. On n'ira point lui alléguer les lois de la religion; un courtisan se croirait ridicule: on lui

---

[185] Montesquieu, *De l'Esprit des Lois* (ed. R. Derathé, 2 vols.; Paris, 1973), vol. I, pp. 58–9.

[186] D. Spring, 'An Outsider's View: Alexis de Tocqueville on Aristocratic Society and Politics in 19th Century England', *Albion* 12 (1980), 122–31.

[187] To a French scholar, it can seem that 'England has never destroyed her ancien regime'. Goubert, *The Ancien Régime*, p. xv. Perhaps not; but English historians have come very close.

[188] R. Darnton, 'The High Enlightenment and the Low-Life of Literature in Pre-Revolutionary France', *P&P* 51 (1971), 90.

[189] Ford, *Robe and Sword*, pp. 222–45; cf. N. O. Keohane, *Philosophy and the State in France. The Renaissance to the Enlightenment* (Princeton, 1980), 346–50.

alléguera sans cesse celles de l'honneur.' Those laws entailed '*qu'il faut mettre dans les vertus une certaine noblesse, dans les moeurs une certaine franchise, dans les manières une certaine politesse*', since, within aristocratic society, 'On n'y juge pas les actions des hommes comme bonnes, mais comme belles; comme justes, mais comme grandes; comme raisonnables, mais comme extra-ordinaires.' The code 'permet la ruse lorsqu'elle est jointe à l'idée de la grandeur de l'esprit ou de la grandeur des affaires, comme dans la politique, dont les finesses ne l'offensent pas'; but 'Il n'y a rien que l'honneur prescrive plus à la noblesse que de servir le prince à la guerre.' Consequently, the chief laws of honour were

...qu'il nous est bien permis de faire cas de notre fortune, mais qu'il nous est souverainement défendu d'en faire aucun de notre vie.

La seconde est que, lorsque nous avons été une fois placés dans un rang, nous ne devons rien faire ni souffrir qui fasse voir que nous nous tenons inférieurs à ce rang même.

La troisième, que les choses que l'honneur défend sont plus rigoureusement défendues, lorsque les lois ne concourent point à les proscrire; et que celles qu'il exige sont plus fortement exigées, lorsque les lois ne les demandent pas.

It was not necessarily virtue which supported this code: 'Elle naît de l'envie de se distinguer. C'est par orgueil que nous sommes polis: nous nous sentons flattés d'avoir des manières qui prouvent que nous ne sommes pas dans la bassesse, et que nous n'avons pas vécu avec cette sorte de gens que l'on a abandonnés dans tous les âges.' It was virtue of a sort; it was also a counter-code. In either case it was all-pervasive: 'l'honneur, se mêlant partout, entre dans toutes les façons de penser et toutes les manières de sentir, et dirige même les principes'.[190]

De l'Esprit des Lois, published in 1748, 'became the nobleman's Bible all over Europe'.[191] The counterpart to this theoretical treatise was an English practical manual, Chesterfield's *Letters to His Son* – an immediate success when published posthumously in 1774. Most of the letters date from c. 1747–51, and echo Montesquieu's ideal in demanding 'engaging, insinuating, shining manners; a distinguished politeness, an almost irresistible address; a superior gracefulness in all you say and do'.[192] This pursuit of a 'superior gracefulness' has often been remarked in unconnected studies of the trappings of eighteenth-century high life, whether in manners, speech, clothes, architecture, furniture, landscape gardening. These scattered instances are best understood as reflections of a principle.[193] Without

---

[190] Montesquieu, *De L'Esprit des Lois*, pp. 35–9.

[191] Behrens, *Ancien Régime*, p. 78.

[192] Chesterfield to Philip Stanhope, 19th April 1749: B. Dobrée (ed.), *The Letters of Philip Dormer Stanhope, 4th Earl of Chesterfield* (London, 1932), vol. IV, p. 1330.

[193] The cultural force of the world of absolute monarchs is well captured, though in a relaxed idiom, in H. D. Molesworth, *The Princes* (London, 1969).

idealising it, it is possible to say that the aristocratic code existed both as ideal and as reality; as a code, and as a set of practices. As Adam Smith described the nobleman:

> ...he acts, upon the most indifferent occasions, with that freedom and elevation which the thought of this [that he is always noticed] naturally inspires. His air, his manner, his deportment, all mark that elegant and graceful sense of his own superiority, which those who are born to inferior stations can hardly ever arrive at: these are the arts by which he proposes to make mankind more easily submit to his authority, and to govern their inclinations according to his own pleasure: and in this he is seldom disappointed. These arts, supported by rank and preheminence, are, upon ordinary occasions, sufficient to govern the world.[194]

Whether as ideal or reality, the inwardness of the aristocratic code is still largely to be explored. The history of manners, a crucial component of cultural hegemony, has been written within the now-familiar perspective, as an explanation of how reprehensible eighteenth-century coarseness or absurd formality were justly reformed to produce the standards of Victorian England.[195] Georgian schools, similarly, are almost invariably held up as examples of declining, somnolent institutions in which neglect, corruption and the irrelevance of their studies cried out for utilitarian reappraisal.[196] The considerable industry which they demanded of their pupils, and the academic levels which they attained, have largely gone unregarded. Beyond the narrowly scholarly, too, the great schools, Eton and Westminster pre-eminent among them, were playing a distinct social role: preparing their charges to take their place within an aristocratic world of values, by an acquaintance with the patrician ideals of classical civilisation and the practical skills of oratory.[197] In that function, it might be argued, they served their society effectively: classical 'virtue' did indeed become a key component in the rationale for aristocratic 'deference' (democrats have always attacked a classical education).

The close liaison of classical values and aristocratic codes was quickly

---

[194] Adam Smith, *Theory of Moral Sentiments*, p. 91.

[195] E.g. Dorothy George, 'Manners' in Turberville (ed.) *Johnson's England*, vol. 1, pp. 336–60; M. J. Quinlan, *Victorian Prelude. A History of English Manners 1700–1830* (New York, 1941). More sympathetic, but less scholarly and still didactic is Harold Nicholson, *Good Behaviour: Being a Study of Certain Types of Civility* (London, 1955). Better, though superficial, is J. Wildeblood and P. Brinson, *The Polite World. A Guide to English Manners and Deportment from the Thirteenth to the Nineteenth Century* (London, 1965). Once again, Norbert Elias, *The Civilising Process. The History of Manners* (1939; Oxford, 1982), will astonish mere historians.

[196] Nowhere does the 'Whig interpretation' seem more self-evidently true to some historians than when they write on the history of English public schools.

[197] Cf. R. M. Ogilvie, *Latin and Greek. A History of the Influence of the Classics on English Life from 1600 to 1918* (London, 1964); G. C. Brauer, *The Education of a Gentleman. Theories of Gentlemanly Education in England, 1660–1775* (New York, 1959).

evident. Dr John Nicholl, Headmaster of Westminster 1733–53, was admired because he

> ...had the art of making his scholars gentlemen;[198] for there is a court of honour in that school to whose unwritten laws every member of our community was amenable and which to transgress by any act of meanness that exposed the offender to public contempt, was a degree of punishment, compared to which the being sentenced to the rod would have been considered as an acquittal or reprieve.[199]

More important than the content of formal instruction was a process complete by the mid-eighteenth century, 'the virtual conquest of the public schools by those who attended them':[200] the emergence of an autonomous culture which reflected, in miniature but more intensely, the values of the families whose sons carved their names on the panelling in ever deeper letters as the decades went by. The *esprit de corps*, the worship of tradition, and the impatience of any authority outside that of the ruling elite, produced a set of ideals which was internalised with remarkable unanimity.

This autonomous culture promoted, too, a characteristic of the English elite which distinguished it more and more from its continental counterparts: the equality of all gentlemen.[201] England increasingly possessed a unified, not a stratified, patrician corps. It expressed the solidarity not of a caste or of an economically-defined class but, principally, of a culturally-defined elite. Nowhere else in Europe was school education so important to the structure of the elite's code. It was a nineteenth-century Lord Willoughby de Broke who said: 'As is the attitude of the average Englishman to someone who is not an Englishman, so is the attitude of all Etonians to someone who is not an Etonian.'[202] This only began to be true towards the end of the Georgian era, as Eton assumed Westminster's former pre-eminence; but, throughout, it neatly expresses the sense of distance which separated gentlemen from those who were not gentlemen. Gentlemen owed allegiance to a different code.

From that position of strength they dictated taste, manners and morals. The cultural tone of eighteenth-century England was set by an elite composed of the highest nobility, the wealthiest gentry and their satellites. Variously styled the Ton, the Great, the Polite, the Beau Monde, the World of Fashion, and, simply, the World, this small group constituted the fount of norms and values. No level of the social structure escaped the impact of its scheme of life, its modes of behaviour.[203]

---

[198] That is, in the eighteenth-century sense. The great expansion of the Victorian schools, embodying Dr Arnold's essentially middle-class adaptation of the ancien regime's ideal of a gentleman, was chronologically and conceptually a distinct development.

[199] Richard Cumberland, quoted in L. E. Tanner, *Westminster School* (London, 1934), p. 26.

[200] The best account is Edward C. Mack, *Public Schools and British Opinion 1780 to 1860* (London, 1938); cf. pp. 34ff.

[201] Cf. M. V. Wallbank, 'Eighteenth Century Public Schools and the Education of the Governing Elite', *History of Education* 8 (1979), 1–19.

[202] Quoted in O. F. Christie, *Transition from Aristocracy*, p. 41.

[203] Hecht, *Domestic Servant*, p. 200.

It was an influence which operated via cultural emulation in situations in which no process of coercion from above was conceivable. Domestic servants formed an important link in this chain of emulation since, as it was suggested in 1760, 'the servant who is near the person of a nobleman, or a gentleman...derives an importance from it which renders him respectable'.[204] The century is full of remarks on 'The insolence...so much complained of among noblemen's servants': 'a consciousness of the dignity of the noble personage they serve...naturally make[s] them arrogant and proud'.[205] Such behaviour could be sustained only in a world receptive to the manners of the great. In 1763, the press remarked: 'The present rage of imitating the manners of high-life hath spread itself so far among the gentlefolks of lower-life, that in a few years we shall probably have no common people at all.'[206] Observers of society 'from the top down' drew a lesson from this process with remarkable unanimity. 'The most ignorant naturally *look up* for example: the common people will be what their *superiors* are.'[207] Hannah More, in her best-selling *Thoughts on the Importance of the Manners of the Great to General Society* (1788) was unequivocal : ' *Their* example is the fountain from whence the vulgar draw their habits, actions and characters.'[208] Henry Fielding had been no less sure: the bad habits of the elite were 'as infectious by example, as the plague itself by contact.' Luxury and emulation were the problem. 'Thus while the nobleman will emulate the grandeur of a prince, and the gentleman will aspire to the proper state of the nobleman, the tradesman steps from behind his counter into the vacant place of the gentleman. Nor doth the confusion end here; it reaches the very dregs of the people.'[209]

It is difficult to find a quantifiable index of such things. There was deference and emulation; there was insubordination and disrespect. Despite the latter, however, the elite remained convinced of the importance of its own leadership of society both culturally and politically; it elaborated an ideology to justify and defend that state of affairs; the ideology was not effectively challenged on the level of theory; and the elite behaved as if it was true.

If the elite was progressively expanded at the end of the century, especially by Pitt's peerage creations, it is not clear that it was thereby diluted in its adherence to its code. Although social mobility took place in

[204] [Jonas Hanway], *Eight Letters to His Grace — Duke of —, on the Custom of Vails-Giving* (London, 1760), p. 59: Hecht, *op. cit.*, p. 180.

[205] *Court Miscellany* 3 (London, 1767), 413: Hecht, *op. cit.*, p. 180.

[206] *British Magazine* 4 (1763), 417: Hecht, *op. cit.*, p. 204.

[207] Jonas Hanway, *Virtue in Humble Life* (2 vols., London 1774), vol. I, p. xx; Hecht, *op. cit.*, p. 204.

[208] Hannah More, *Works*, vol. XI, p. 57; Hecht, *op. cit.*, p. 204.

[209] Henry Fielding, *An Enquiry Into the Causes of the Late Increase of Robbers, &c* (London, 1751) in W. E. Henley (ed.), *The Complete Works of Henry Fielding, Esq* (16 vols., New York, 1967), vol. XIII, pp. 21–2.

the eighteenth century, the theoretical pattern of the aristocratic code did not make many concessions to it. Mobility was chiefly seen as an experience of the lower and middle orders within their own ranks, or of picaresque adventure and capricious fortune. Not until near the close of the ancien regime does the book of etiquette appear, in the Victorian idiom, as a detailed practical guide to good manners for those initially ignorant of them.[210] Until then, it seems that no body of theory and counsel existed in print to sanction and smooth the 'rise' of any 'middle class'. Defoe himself conceded that 'the born gentleman' and 'the bred gentleman' were 'two sorts or classes of men', obviously different; the first was distinguished by 'an invisible influence of the blood.' Though he argued against 'mere pride and arrogance founded upon birth and the pretended prerogative of blood', contending that gentility ought to go with 'learning, education, virtue and good manners', even he had to respect his society's leading ideal in attempting to establish his own: 'I am far from intending to lessen or dishonour the gentleman I am speaking of: I allow him to be the glory of the creation, the exalted head of the whole race, that demands honour and distinction from the rest of the world.' Defoe's *Complete English Gentleman*, written in 1728-9, was his fullest and most objective statement on the subject; but it remained unpublished at his death,[211] and the 'bred gentleman' remained without an adequate defence.

Was mobility into (or out of) the ranks of patricians increasing? We need more research before the question can be answered. But it seems possible to say that the literature of gentility made no allowance for widespread, natural and honourable mobility up the social hierarchy. The assumptions were better expressed in the conveniently-explicit title of an anonymous satirical pamphlet of 1737:

The Man of Manners: or, Plebeian Polish'd. Being Plain and Familiar Rules for a Modest and Genteel Behaviour, on Most of the Ordinary Occasions of Life.
Whereby the Many Vanities, Weaknesses and Impertinences Incident to Human Nature, (which Expose Persons to Contempt and Ridicule) May be Easily Avoided.
Written Chiefly for the Use and Benefit of Persons of Mean Births and Education, who have Unaccountably Plung'd Themselves into Wealth and Power.

Delusions of rising social status, its author claimed, were even dangerous (pp. 54-5):

It has produced very mischievous consequences, when persons of great rank have condescended to converse, and shew tokens of familiarity to mean illiterate men: the mechanicks who reside about the Liberty of Westminster, are for ever boasting of what friendship this or that great man has for them, what particular marks of

---

[210] J. E. Mason, *Gentlefolk in the Making. Studies in the History of English Courtesy Literature and Related Topics from 1531 to 1774* (Philadelphia, 1935), p. 292.
[211] Daniel Defoe, *The Complete English Gentleman* (ed. K. D. Bülbring, London, 1890), pp. 3, 16, 18, 20-1, 29.

esteem they have been distinguished by; and how acceptable they are at all times
to them, intimating thereby their own great merit and abilities. I have known
tradesmen actually ruined by receiving orders and instructions in the way of their
business, from a nobleman's mouth: They have gone quite mad upon it, and run
into such excessive vanities, and fooleries, as have quite undone their families.

Not even Adam Smith, whose views were formed in the pre-industrial 1740s,
offered comfort to those eager for social advancement: 'Politeness is so much
the virtue of the great, that it will do little honour to any body but
themselves. The coxcomb, who imitates their manner, and affects to be
eminent by the superior propriety of his behaviour, is rewarded with a
double share of contempt for his folly and presumption.'[212]

The English literature of gentility does seem to be restricted in volume
and scope in this era, especially in the early eighteenth century. Chesterfield's
Letters to His Son were written as private letters and were published only after
the author's death, by his son's widow, for financial gain. Their success
revealed a new market, but not one previously explored by English authors
to any extent. Earlier texts had fallen within the idiom either of Renaissance
'books of civility' – especially Sir Thomas Hoby's translation of Castiglione's
Book of the Courtier (1561), Henry Peacham's *Compleat Gentleman* (1622) and
Richard Braithwaite's *English Gentleman* (1630) – a tradition exhausted by
the end of the seventeenth century – or within the idiom of devotional
literature, addressed to persons of rank and quality; texts which sought to
promote Christianity by reconciling it with the aristocratic code, and by
arguing that 'True honour, though it be a different principle from religion,
is that which produces the same effects.'[213]

This was not always the case in practice. The pleasures of the elite did
not, typically, excite the admiration of the professional moraliser. But the
practices and pastimes, amusements, vices and malaises stemming from the
aristocratic code struck observers as having a common thread. One censor
diagnosed as typical the three social evils of duelling, gaming and suicide:
'these are crimes so great in themselves, so intimately connected with each
other, and such increasing evils (particularly the two latter) as to require
every nerve to be strained in reprobating their practice'.[214] Readers of the
Gentleman's Magazine for 1787 could ponder a piece entitled 'The Origin of
Gaming, and Her Two Children Duelling and Suicide. An Allegory.' The

[212] Smith, *Theory of Moral Sentiments*, pp. 92–3. His reading does not argue an exclusively
materialist or utilitarian taste: he owned, for example, copies of Boulainvilliers's *Essai sur
la Noblesse de France*, Filmer's *Patriarcha*, and the Jacobite Thomas Carte's *A General History
of England*: J. Bonar (ed.), *A Catalogue of the Library of Adam Smith* (London, 1932).

[213] *The Gentleman's Library: Containing Rules for Conduct in all Parts of Life*, 5th edn (London,
1760), p. 84; cf. [R. Allestree], *The Gentleman's Calling* (London, 1660 and many subsequent
edns).

[214] Charles Moore, *A Full Inquiry into the Subject of Suicide. To Which Are Added (As Being Closely
Connected With The Subject) Two Treatises On Duelling And Gaming* (2 vols., London 1790),
vol. I, Introduction, n.p.

technical formality of the aristocratic ethic was indeed echoed in the elaborate rules of card games.[215] A feature of that society was its addiction to gambling for high stakes, its exaltation of recklessness and careless sacrifice echoing the virtues of the battlefield.[216] And the point could be made the other way round: 'War is the Faro table of governments', wrote Tom Paine censoriously.[217]

Gaming was more than an occasional practice; it could become, said its critics, a defining characteristic of a way of life. As such, it attracted the denunciations of churchmen throughout the period, seemingly with little effect (some of the most spectacular examples come towards the close of the ancien regime). *The Connoisseur* complained in 1754

...that gaming is now become rather the business than the amusement of our persons of quality; and that they are more concerned about the transactions of the two clubs at *White's*, than the proceedings of both houses of parliament. Thus it happens, that estates are now almost as frequently made over by whist and hazard, as by deeds and settlements; and the chariots of many of our nobility may be said (like Count *Basset's* in the play) 'to roll upon the four aces'.

This love of gaming has taken such entire possession of their ideas, that it infects their common conversation. The management of a dispute was formerly attempted by reason and argument; but the new way of adjusting all difference in opinion is by the sword or a wager: so that the only genteel method of dissenting is to risk a thousand pounds, or take your chance of being run through the body. The strange custom of deciding every thing by a wager is so universal, that if (in imitation of *Swift*) any body was to publish a specimen of *Polite Conversation*, instead of old sayings and trite repartees, he would in all probability fill his dialogues with little more than bet after bet, and now or then a calculation of the odds.[218]

Humorous exaggeration nevertheless identified a widespread custom. It was a mania which touched all sections of the ruling elite; none more so at the end of the century than the aristocratic Whigs in the circle of Charles James Fox, in whose high play it might not be fanciful to see a lofty gesture of defiance at the prudent, bureaucratic virtues which they imagined were increasingly imposing themselves on those drawn into the orbit of government. Brooks's, the Whig club, quickly became notorious: 'At Brookes's, for nearly half a century, the play was of a more gambling character than at White's. Faro and Macao were indulged in to an extent which enabled a man to win or lose a considerable fortune in one night.'[219] Faro and Macao were games of chance, not skill.

[215] The tone of this world may be recaptured from [C. Cotton], *The Compleat Gamester* (London, 1674), and T. Lucas, *Memoirs of the Lives...of the Most Famous Gamesters* (London, 1714), reprinted in C. H. Hartmann (ed.), *Games and Gamesters of the Restoration* (London, 1930) and Andrew Steinmetz, *The Gaming Table: its Votaries and Victims* (2 vols., London, 1870).

[216] I owe this suggestion to Ford, *Robe and Sword*, p. 212. On the psychology of gaming, though for a later period, cf. Henry Blyth, *Hell and Hazard* (London, 1969).

[217] Thomas Paine, *Rights of Man* (ed. H. Collins, Harmondsworth, 1969), p. 191.

[218] Quoted in Percy Colson, *White's 1693–1950* (London, 1951), p. 100.

[219] *The Reminiscences and Recollections of Captain Gronow* (2 vols., London, 1892), vol. I, p. 56.

All ranks in society, of course, gambled; but it was more difficult for the lower orders. Common gaming houses (though they existed) were illegal in early Hanoverian London, and the legal obstacles were strengthened by the Acts of 12 Geo II c 28 and 18 Geo II c 34. Moreover, those laws were often put in execution. For the aristocracy, serious gaming had traditionally centred on the Court, where it had been regulated by an officer of the Lord Steward's department of the Royal Household, the Groom Porter. The office was abolished in, it seems, 1772, but gambling had already been discouraged by George III.[220] It soon found other venues. The great London clubs of the eighteenth century were even more an expression of an aristocratic sense of caste, and of a gambling mania, than of a desire for political organisation.[221] As expressions of the aristocratic ethic, these institutions are of peculiar importance; but, with a few exceptions,[222] they have failed to capture the imagination of the academic historian.[223] Only the outlines can yet be sketched. But it seems likely that White's (founded in 1693) had reached its peak as a place of high play by the last decade of George II's reign,[224] presumably largely superseding the Court. It was this extensive and growing market which the new clubs, founded in and after the 1760s, attempted to capture – in the case of Brooks's (1764) with considerable success. Goostree's (1773), the younger Pitt's club, ran it close for a time; and Almack's Assembly Rooms, an instant success in 1781, catered for gaming by both sexes.[225] The Cocoa Tree, famous as a Tory headquarters in the first half of the century, survived as a gaming club in the second half.[226]

These clubs were small, and socially exclusive,[227] the vast, and commercially lucrative, Crockford's (1827), belongs to a new age, like the Carlton and the Reform.[228] Before that, gaming was engaged in not least as an appropriate expression of the aristocratic ethic, and much of the

[220] J. Ashton, *The History of Gambling in England* (London, 1898), pp. 48–9.

[221] When, in 1762, Shelburne's friends founded a club (later famous as Boodle's) for political purposes, they had to include a rule explicitly limiting the amount that could be lost there at any one time in gaming. Roger Fulford, *Boodle's 1762–1962* (privately printed, London, 1962), pp. 8–9, 14. Boodle's soon ceased to be political.

[222] An honourable exception is R. J. Allen, *The Clubs of Augustan London* (Cambridge, Mass., 1933); but it scarcely extends beyond Anne's reign.

[223] 'Socialists, like women, are not, on the whole, clubbable': Anthony Lejeune, *The Gentlemen's Clubs of London* (London, 1979), p. 14.

[224] [W. B. Boulton], *The History of White's* (privately printed, 2 vols., London, 1892) vol. i, pp. 94, 125–6.

[225] J. Timbs, *Clubs and Club Life in London* (London, 1872), pp. 71–3; H. S. Eeles and Earl Spencer, *Brooks's 1764–1964* (London, 1964).

[226] Cf. Walpole to Mann, 6th Feb. 1780: *The Letters of Horace Walpole* (ed. Mrs Paget Toynbee, 16 vols., Oxford, 1903–5), vol. xi, p. 124; Ashton, *History of Gambling*, p. 86.

[227] The membership lists are accessible: of Almack's in Timbs, *Clubs*, p. 72; of White's in [Boulton], *History of White's*, vol. ii; of Brooks's in [V. A. Williamson], *Memorials of Brooks's* (privately printed, London, 1907), pp. 3ff.

[228] Cf. A. L. Humphreys, *Crockfords* (London, 1953).

anecdotal history of London clubs records either gambling triumphs and disasters, or the problems raised by the delicate issue of blackballing unsuitable candidates. The very prevalence of the code of honour in such a world, a code carefully tended and explicitly shared by all, meant that such issues were highly sensitive. Where every insult was, or soon became, public, a public vindication of honour was forced on the offended party: 'Custom has made it a maxim, that we must defend what we call our honour: for to suffer under the imputation of cowardice, is worse than being buried alive.'[229] Even Wilberforce recognised duelling as a practice which, 'whilst it powerfully supports, mainly rests on, that excessive over-valuation of character, which teaches that worldly credit is to be preserved at *any* rate, and disgrace at *any* rate to be avoided'.[230] It included both parties: though only one were insulted, both men were obliged to fight: 'If...a gentleman evade a *justifiable* call, he thus necessarily puts himself without the pale of honour, and a notification of the fact to honourable society produces his expulsion from it.'[231]

Duelling is for the eighteenth century what trials for witchcraft are for the seventeenth: inconvenient and anachronistic survivals to many historians, but ones which, when examined seriously, demand a revision of some of our basic assumptions about the period. For duelling is the best index to, and proof of, the survival and power of the aristocratic ideal as a code separate from, and ultimately superior to, the injunctions of law and religion. Each duel was a deliberate act of rebellion against both, and a gesture of contempt towards the prudent, rational, calculating values which plebeians might be thought necessarily to hold.[232] It seemed to express the atavistic insight that 'without shedding of blood is no remission'. As such, duelling had attracted the condemnation of religious writers throughout the century. Not all of them were outspoken. Wilberforce complained:

To read indeed the writings of certain Christian moralists and to observe how little they seem disposed to call it in question, except where it raves in the conqueror, one should be almost tempted to suspect, that, considering it as a principle of such potency and prevalence, as that they must despair of bringing it into just subjection, they were intent only on complimenting it into good humour (like those barbarian nations which worship the evil spirit through fear) ; or rather, that they were making a sort of composition with an enemy they could not master, and were willing, on condition of its giving up the trade of war, to suffer it to rule undisturbed, and rage at pleasure.[233]

[229] *The Gentleman's Library*, p. 90.
[230] William Wilberforce, *A Practical View of the Prevailing Religious System of Professed Christians, in the Higher and Middle Classes in this Country, Contrasted with Real Christianity* (London, 1797), p. 219.
[231] *The British Code of Duel: a Reference to the Laws of Honour and the Charactc. of a Gentleman* (London, 1824), p. 53.
[232] J. G. Millingen, *The History of Duelling* (2 vols., London, 1841) provides a casebook in which the detailed circumstances of many encounters can be traced.
[233] Wilberforce, *Practical View*, pp. 223–4.

The standard work on the morality of suicide, duelling and gaming at the end of the century was frankly despondent about the possibility of doing anything:

It is a disagreeable and discouraging task, to undertake the investigation and exposure of a custom of such fashionable and honourable report, as that of 'duelling' is esteemed to be... Indeed a moral writer, who wishes to be guided in all his researches by maxims of truth and reason alone, must be prepared to encounter neglect, if not ridicule and contempt, whilst he is opposing opinions and customs established in the circles of polite association, though militating against the principles of humanity and virtue. A respectful deference is certainly due to the sentiments and manners of those, who move in the superior walks of life. Their liberal education, exalted connexions, and enlarged mode of living, must furnish them with opportunities of improvement and knowledge, far beyond what can fall to the lot of those in a more private station. This respect however is to be distinct from a slavish submission, inasmuch as a still greater deference is to be paid to the decisions of 'truth'.[234]

It was a weak protest, but one which realistically recognised the viability of the elite's hegemony. Paley, by contrast, adopted an extreme position in claiming: 'If unauthorised laws of honour be allowed to create exceptions to divine prohibitions, there is an end of all morality, as founded in the will of the Deity.'[235] But this was clearly not the case: the two codes co-existed, side by side. To a large extent they reinforced each other.

Early-eighteenth-century critics sought mainly to redefine the idea of honour, so that duelling would no longer be a part of it: 'The notion of honour is certainly to be taken from the laws and government, and not from any private set of people, how valuable soever in other respects.'[236] But from the 1770s, a different wave of criticism began which attacked duelling as part of an attack on the code of honour itself: 'it explained the genesis and historical function of the code of honour and strove to replace its view of society with a more rational and modern one'.[237] Despite both these channels of criticism, duelling continued unabated;[238] subjective impressions suggest it even increased in frequency before the demise of the custom in the decade or so after 1832.[239] 'Duels, like suicide, bear a fashionably

234 Charles Moore, *A Full Inquiry*, vol. II, p. 218.
235 Paley, *Moral and Political Philosophy* in *Works*, vol. II, p. 177.
236 *The Gentleman's Library*, p. 91.
237 D. T. Andrew, 'The Code of Honour and its Critics: the Opposition to Duelling in England, 1700–1850', *Social History* 5 (1980), pp. 417, 420.
238 Reliable statistics are not available; but *The Times* of 4th Jan. 1791 reported 33 duels, and of 12th March 1792 69 duels, in the preceding 12 months: Andrew, 'Code of honour', p. 410. The 56 volumes of the *Gentleman's Magazine* for 1731–86 are reported to mention only 36 duels: J. D. Aylward, 'Duelling in the XVIII Century', *Notes and Queries* 189 (1945), pp. 31–4, 46–8, 70–3, at 32; this seems to be only a very small percentage of those actually fought.
239 Cf. Captain Gronow, *Reminiscences*, vol. I, pp. 104–15 for duelling by the British army of occupation in France after 1815; R. Baldick, *The Duel. A History of Duelling* (London, 1965); A. F. Sieveking, 'Duelling and Militarism', *TRHS* 3rd ser. 11 (1917), 165–84.

contagious character', wrote an historian of the first practice in the years of its demise.[240] Until then, the self-confidence of its champions was seemingly undiminished. One would-be reformer, evidently echoing Charles Moore, lamented even in 1822:

A moral writer, wishing to trace his way by the paths of reason and truth, must prepare himself to meet with ridicule, scorn, and contempt, if he opposes opinions and customs militating against the principles of religion, virtue, and humanity, or to question the sentiments of those whose rank gives them an influence over, and forms the tone of manners in those immediately inferior.[241]

Meanwhile, the practice found its defenders willing to meet the critics on their own ground. One author counselled caution before a conflict, and an attempt to settle disputes by negotiation, but nevertheless claimed:

To expect...that any law, now existing, or hereafter to be made, can abolish duelling, is quite chimerical...It is a principle inherent in the breast of man, when he is aggrieved, to seek redress in the most summary way, regardless of personal danger; and in many cases the offence may be of such an aggravating and insupportable nature, that no redress which the law may give, can compensate the injury.[242]

A handbook to the detailed procedure to be observed was even less apologetic: 'even in this legislating age, with a powerful religious party in Parliament, there is still certainly *no positive law against duel*'. Duels were fought under their own law, the law of honour:

...honour is a principle generated by virtue, as demonstrated in useful and agreeable services to a community; and from appreciation of which arose those exterior distinctions to which it gives name, for the purpose of their preservation to posterity...Hence the influence under which the duel still prevails against every discouragement, and will in all probability continue to prevail till the dissolution of the present society.[243]

It was a prophetic observation.

If the Church condemned duelling, the law meanwhile condoned it. The survivor of a fight which occurred at the time of the quarrel faced a charge of manslaughter; if convicted, he could (on one occasion) 'plead clergy' and so secure his release, paying his gaoler's fees. The plea of clergy was abolished in 1827; but it had never been possible to raise it as a defence in a case of murder, which was the charge, if death resulted, where a formal duel was arranged at another time and place,[244] In that case, duellists and

---

[240] Millingen, *History of Duelling*, vol. II, p. 90.
[241] *The Duellist, or a Cursory Review of the Rise, Progress and Practice of Duelling* (London, 1822), pp. 1–2.
[242] A. Bosquett, *The Young Man of Honour's Vade-Mecum, Being a Salutary Treatise on Duelling* (London, [1817]), pp. 16–17.
[243] *The British Code of Duel*, pp. 3–4, 6–7.
[244] For the law on the subject, cf. Aylward, 'Duelling' and J. F. Stephen, *A History of the Criminal Law of England* (3 vols., London, 1883), vol. I, pp. 461–8; vol. III, pp. 99–102.

seconds depended on the jury for an acquittal. This they felt entitled to expect: as their handbook promised them, 'if the conflict take place, and one falls, and the survivors are tried for murder, the jurors virtually recognise the laws of honour, and, if these have been fulfilled, pronounce acquittal'.[245] This was admitted also by the abolitionists. In 1773 Granville Sharp, the anti-slavery campaigner, argued

> That the indulgence allowed by the Courts to voluntary manslaughter in rencounters, and in sudden affrays and duels, is indiscriminate, and without foundation in law:
>
> And that impunity in such cases of voluntary manslaughter is one of the principal causes of the continuance and present increase of the base and disgraceful practice of duelling.[246]

As the *Edinburgh Review* observed in 1814, 'No instance is known of the law being executed against any person for being engaged in a duel, fought in what is called a *fair* manner'[247] – that is, according to the code. It was not only the judiciary which recognised and condoned the social pressures which forced men to fight;[248] juries too, with a fine regard for 'cultural hegemony', respected the values of their social superiors even at the moment when they had the power, by a secret vote, without fear of reprisal, decisively to undermine them.

Two bodies of quantifiable evidence reveal the unwillingness of the great body of men in the 'old society' to act in class terms: the behaviour of the electorate, and the behaviour of juries. Electors in almost all seats, for almost all of the eighteenth century, failed to divide on class lines in their support of pro- and anti-administration candidates. Jurymen, too, generally continued to convict men who infringed the property rights of the elite and refused to convict duellists. Such deference extended even to those below the age of majority. On 18th November 1791, two Cambridge undergraduates had 'a violent dispute' in public. A challenge was issued on the 21st; they fought a correct, set-piece duel with pistols on Newmarket Heath on the 23rd. The challenger was hit, and died of his wound on the 25th.

> A Coroner's inquest was held upon the body and the verdict was, 'Wilful murder against the surviving principal (by name), and two persons unknown.'
>
> At the Lent Assizes held at Bury for the county of Suffolk, the bill of indictment preferred against the principal by the friends of the deceased, was thrown out by the grand jury. The principal was then arraigned upon the Coroner's inquest, when his counsel objected to it as informal, upon the ground that it did not state in which of the two parishes of Newmarket the fact happened, which was a degree of certainty

---

[245] *The British Code of Duel*, pp. 4–5.

[246] Granville Sharp, *A Tract on Duelling: Wherein The Opinions of Some of the Most Celebrated Writers on Crown Law are Examined and Corrected* (London, 1773; 2nd edn, 1790), p. iii.

[247] Quoted Andrew, 'Code of Honour', p. 412. Millingen, *History of Duelling*, vol. II, p. 84 cites 172 duels in the reign of George III, resulting in 69 deaths; 18 trials; 7 convictions for manslaughter; 3 convictions for murder, of whom 2 were executed.

[248] Cf. the words of Mr Baron Eyre in 1783, quoted in Aylward, 'Duelling', p. 72.

required by the law: the court held this objection to be valid, and directed the jury to acquit the prisoner.

The inquisition did not mention the seconds by their names, and there being no prosecution against them, they were not arraigned.[249]

A Fellow of Trinity preached a moralising sermon on the episode before the University, rehearsing again the familiar arguments against the practice, and referring his hearers to that standard source, the two bulky quarto volumes of Charles Moore's *A Full Inquiry*.

Though they would have found there a moral condemnation, they would also have discovered that events had gone very much as Moore (himself lately a Fellow of Trinity) had predicted. Duelling was forbidden, he had written, by the familiar law against murder:

Yet how little are these wholesome statutes regarded! Challenges are forwarded and accepted, and the names of all the parties proclaimed at length in the public prints without disguise, or shame, or censure. The combat itself is pursued and its proceedings made public in defiance of all decency and law. If one party fall, the survivor either absconds for a time without much enquiry made after him or puts himself on his trial; where the whole business seems to turn (as if these were the days of chivalry) on the 'mode' of that fighting, which produced death, whether it were 'fair and honourable' rather than on the 'absolute illegality of the fight itself'; which circumstance alone (viz. its being an illegal action) would in other cases be sufficient to condemn the culprit. But this point is generally pretty well secured before the defaulter appears to stand his trial; and then either a total acquittal ensues, or the statute of manslaughter is egregiously perverted to protect the duellist – a statute which was certainly never designed to countenance murder, but to express a peculiar abhorrence of it, by assigning a degree of punishment even to its accidental commission.[250]

Undergraduates, though under the age of majority, were still gentlemen.

A feature of the code of honour was that, although regular acquittals show it to have been respected by the common people, it was not available to them: their conflicts were mere affrays, punishable at law. In 1688, the Crown was (as contemporaries largely supposed) deprived of a dispensing power. But the power itself was not eliminated: rather, in this one symbolic respect, it devolved upon the patrician elite. An earlier moralist had warned of the danger of the lower orders adopting the same dispensing power towards inconvenient laws: 'If all subjects should take the same liberty as these dangerous duellists, we should have wild work? If the under sort of people should take the hint, and practice upon it in the instance of property?'[251] Plainly, however, they did not think themselves entitled to behave, in this key respect, like gentlemen.

[249] Thomas Jones, *A Sermon upon Duelling, preached before the University of Cambridge, on Sunday, Dec. 11, 1791* (Cambridge, 1792), Preface, pp. i–ii.
[250] Moore, *A Full Inquiry*, vol. II, pp. 248–9.
[251] *The Gentleman's Library*, p. 92.

The small-sword was an article of everyday wear for all gentlemen until the last two decades of the eighteenth century: that gentlemen normally went armed is an important defining characteristic of membership of the elite. The sword, too, was an object of display, of conspicuous consumption: it was an affirmation of status. Its use was a difficult and aristocratic skill, slowly acquired. Like horsemanship, that other point on which the gentleman prided himself, swordsmanship was taught by professionals: the *maîtres d'armes* enjoyed considerable social standing and were responsible for an extensive and sophisticated literature on their art.[252] From the mid-1740s, however, pistols largely replaced swords as the common duelling weapon. One effect of this was to make the practice more widely available: any tyro could fire a pistol, and the advantages which skill and experience in swordsmanship conferred were considerably reduced. Did this democratise or dilute the duel's elite status? It is not clear, from evidence now available, that it did.

The evidence suggests that duelling became more frequent at the end of the century;[253] the pistol duel probably acted rather to promote the idea of the equality of all gentlemen, the homogeneity of gentry and aristocracy, a process in any case under way as the Squire Westerns were smoothed and polished by the progress of 'improvement'. The numbers of those wishing to behave as gentlemen doubtless increased;[254] but the earliest beneficiaries of growing commercial and professional prosperity typically still subscribed to the values of the patrician elite. The moralists' critique of duelling seems not to have triggered a middle class reaction against it. Even politicians were not deterred from an encounter by the inevitable publicity,[255] and the

---

[252] The classic manual in late-eighteenth-century England was Domenico Angelo, *L'École des Armes* (London, 1763), superseding the works of Sir William Hope (1664–1729) and the French classic, Labat's *Art en fait d'Armes* (Toulouse, 1697; trans. A. Mahon, Dublin, 1734, London, 1735). Domenico Angelo (1717–1802) founded the greatest of all English fencing academies in 1763, after being appointed riding and fencing master to the royal children by the Dowager Princess of Wales in 1759 (he also ran a branch of his academy at Eton). The culture of an armed ruling elite can be investigated in J. D. Aylward, *The House of Angelo. A Dynasty of Swordsmen* (London, 1953) and *idem*, *The English Master of Arms* (London, 1956).

[253] It may have been the increasing frequency of duels which prompted attempts to codify the rules regulating contests: cf. the Irish code, drawn up at the Clonmel Summer Assizes of 1777 in Baldick, *The Duel*, pp. 34–6; the French code, in Millingen, *History of Duelling*, vol. I, pp. 274–93.

[254] Cf. Jenkins, 'Glamorgan Gentry', vol. II, p. 350. Duellists at Cardiff in 1790 included industrialists and surgeons; 'The gentry ethos had spread to a very wide section of society.' The effect on the generally-recognised boundaries of gentility of the social changes of the late eighteenth century would repay further study.

[255] Distinguished duellists included Thomas, 1st Earl of Wharton; Sir Henry Hobart, MP (died in a duel, 1698); Lord Hervey v. William Pulteney, 1731; John Wilkes v. Samuel Martin, 1763; Lord George Germain v. George Johnstone, 1770; Lord Townshend v. Earl of Bellamont, 1773; C. J. Fox v. Mr Adam, 1779; Earl of Shelburne v. Col. Fullarton, 1780; HRH the Duke of York v. Col. Lennox, 1789; William Pitt v. George Tierney, 1798; Sir Francis Burdett v. Mr Paull, 1807; Lord Castlereagh v. George Canning, 1809;

number of Prime Ministers who fought seems actually to have increased towards the end of the century, such contests often being provoked by political manoeuvres or verbal exchanges at Westminster. No damage was done to their political careers:[256] evidence, again, not only of the enclosed nature of the code but of its acceptance in the political community. Archdeacon Paley began his classic *Moral and Political Philosophy* by recognising that men were governed by three codes: 'The Law of Honour'; 'The Law of the Land'; and 'The Scriptures' – in that order.

The Law of Honour is a system of rules constructed by people of fashion, and calculated to facilitate their intercourse with one another; and for no other purpose...this law only prescribes and regulates the duties *betwixt equals*; omitting such as relate to the Supreme Being, as well as those which we owe to our inferiors. For which reason, profaneness, neglect of public worship or private devotion, cruelty to servants, rigorous treatment of tenants or other dependents, want of charity to the poor, injuries done to tradesmen by insolvency or delay of payment, with numberless examples of the same kind, are accounted no breaches of honour; because a man is not a less agreeable companion for these vices, nor the worse to deal with, in those concerns which are usually transacted between one gentleman and another.[257]

And yet the practice of duelling, which had existed time out of mind in spite of the disapproval of the Church and of 'advanced' opinion, and which was so closely bound up with a deeply-rooted social code, declined with remarkable suddenness in the late 1830s and 1840s, and was extinct by the 1850s.[258] The story of its demise is a problem which has only begun to attract attention. It is important, however, not least because it suggests a quite different model of reform to that which is generally applied to the end of the ancien regime. The traditional model represents the old society as bumbling, incompetent, and increasingly ineffective, its vigour dissipated by blatant anachronisms and abuses. Reforming proposals were a set of obvious responses to self-evident shortcomings: enunciated in one decade by advanced thinkers, taken up in a following decade by others, organised

---

O'Connell *v.* D'Esterre, 1815; Duke of Bedford *v.* Duke of Buckingham, 1822; Duke of Wellington *v.* Earl of Winchelsea, 1829. Even the Irish radicals were involved, either as principals or seconds: Wolfe Tone, Napper Tandy, William Drennan, Hamilton Rowan, Arthur O'Connor, Thomas Emmett, Bagenal Harvey, Matthew Dowling: cf. R. B. McDowell, *Ireland in the Age of Imperialism and Revolution 1760–1801* (Oxford, 1979), pp. 48–9.

[256] Though criticism began to be voiced. The pro-ministerial *Blackwood's Edinburgh Magazine* was critical of Wellington for hazarding his life in 1829. But, of course, Wellington had just betrayed his party by embracing Catholic Emancipation: *Blackwood's* echoed this disillusion.

[257] *Works*, vol. II, pp. 1–2.

[258] Cf. T. H. Ford, 'The Trial of Lord Cardigan', *History* 60 (1975), 44–58. On the continent, it survived longer. A. Grisier, *Les Armes et le Duel*, 3rd edn (Paris, 1864), is a practical manual to a still-current practice. In Germany, the incidence of duelling 1870–95 reveals a striking difference of social composition between a *bürgerlich* navy and an aristocratic army: Jonathan Steinberg, 'The Kaiser's Navy and German Society', *P&P* 28 (1964), 102–10.

into a campaign by an extra-parliamentary pressure group, plans of reform were eventually imposed on a weak establishment by 'pressure from without'.

Duelling, however, suggests a very different process, and an alternative model which will be applied more widely in chapter 6 below. The practice had been denounced for decades even by the established intelligentsia without much effect. The elite of the old society vindicated its characteristic practice; and, far from declining into ineffectiveness, the elite increased its hold over English society with time. The picture is, on the contrary, one of increasing strength and self-confidence followed by a sudden collapse from within in the 1830s. Hitherto-ineffectual moralists then claimed the credit and placed an interpretation on the outcome.

Part of this hypothesis was anticipated by an anonymous author of the 1930s: the decline of duelling was not an example of humanitarian sentiment successfully brought to bear by a reforming association of the familiar Victorian variety, he argued; it was no 'story of persistent propaganda triumphing at last over dogged resistance'. Rather, duelling became unnecessary: effective laws of libel and slander, and police forces, removed the need to resort to force to protect one's honour.[259] A more recent historian has suggested that the decline of the institution reflects a wider development:

An outcome of the long struggle against duelling was the emergence of a body of thinking, which, while at first identifying itself merely negatively, that is, against duelling, came to a new vision of society based on reasonableness, Christianity and commerce, in which duelling ceased to be practiced simply because it appeared incongruous and foolish...To the old-fashioned sort of gentleman, the man of honour, they opposed a new type of gentleman, the good citizen...[the critics attacked] an entire vision of society, of privilege and of civility, and in the process formulated a new ideal of a society bound together by the equal subordination of individuals to law and to the market place.[260]

If a new set of social ideals was elevated in the 1830s, however, it does not follow that it was their advance which destroyed the patrician hegemony of the old society. It will be argued in chapter 6 that the political events of 1828–32 represented a decisive practical and intellectual defeat for the old order in the widest sense; and that that defeat was not rendered inevitable by the scale of the forces hostile to the establishment. Those events, then, constituted a defeat for a social order; and, relatively quickly, many of its characteristic beliefs and practices became untenable.

It has been suggested that we can trace the embodiment of different groups' ideals in social practices, and therefore approximately date them;

---

[259] 'Bedford', 'The Disappearance of the Duel from English Life', *Contemporary Review*, 156 (1939), 217–24.
[260] Andrew, 'Code of Honour', pp. 411, 430, 434.

in this sense, taking one characteristic practice as an index, it is possible to talk of an aristocratic cultural hegemony in an eighteenth-century form until the decade following the Reform Bill.[261] Its long survival is a paradox for those historians who have dated the bourgeois ethic from Locke and Defoe, and attributed the advance of that ethic not least to its inherent rationality. The evidence points instead to a strengthening of the elite's group ideal at the end of the century, an 'aristocratic resurgence';[262] but it does not follow that it had earlier been in decline.[263] 'Advance' would be a better term than 'resurgence', though the forms taken by aristocratic dominance obviously changed. One such manifestation was conspicuous: England's growing militarisation, promoting an essentially aristocratic code of honour and service, heroism and sacrifice. As Charles Moore recognised in 1790, the practice of duelling owed its vitality not least to its currency in the army:

From the ideas of military men on the subject of personal affronts all other ranks of gentlemen will adopt theirs; and though it is not so clear, why military notions of honour should ever have been introduced into the habits of civil life, yet having once found their way from the camp into a social and peaceful intercourse, in the army alone must a reform originate.[264]

It was indeed the case that a change in the army's Articles of War in 1844 both effectively halted what remained of the custom among military officers, and powerfully influenced its demise in civilian life.[265]

This prestige attaching to the officer corps was relatively recent when Moore wrote in 1790. In the reigns of the first two Georges, at least half the nation had regarded standing armies and Hanoverian militarism with scarcely-concealed aversion. Zealous Jacobites tried to cut the army to the bone in the hope of paving the way to a restoration (in the 1740s, it almost worked). But from the 1760s, this schism was healed. From the mid 1770s, Britain was committed to an era of almost continuous warfare, ending only at Waterloo, which greatly expanded military establishments at the same time as it professionalised them and put them on a more permanent basis, in a way which even the efforts of the Seven Years' War had only anticipated.[266] Social historians, anxious to trace 'progress', have generally

---

[261] For a fuller study of the conflict between class ideals, cf. Perkin, *English Society*, pp. 218–339.

[262] Cf. N. Ravitch, 'The Social Origins of French and English Bishops in the Eighteenth Century', *HJ* 8 (1965), 309–25; *idem, Sword and Mitre. Government and Episcopate in France and England in the Age of Aristocracy* (The Hague, 1966). For a critical examination of the thesis, W. Doyle, 'Was there an Aristocratic Reaction in Pre-Revolutionary France?', *P&P* 57 (1972), 97–122.

[263] I cannot agree with this implication of Paul Lucas, 'A Collective Biography of Students and Barristers of Lincoln's Inn, 1680–1804: a Study in the "Aristocratic Resurgence" of the Eighteenth Century', *JMH* 46 (1974), 227–61, though in other respects the study is most valuable.

[264] Moore, *Full Inquiry*, vol. II, p. 281.   [265] Andrew, 'Code of Honour', p. 432.

[266] Aspects of the military code are studied in A. N. Gilbert, 'Law and Honour among Eighteenth-Century British Army Officers', *HJ* 19 (1976), 75–87.

neglected the effect of the negative and destructive elements in national life, especially the social impact of war.[267] Yet while France eliminated a *noblesse d'épée* after 1789, England acquired one.[268] The younger Pitt's peerage creations, often of admirals and generals, recognised as well as endorsed and forwarded an already-existing development. He built on a firm base; for between the 'aristocratic survival' of the first half of the century and the 'aristocratic resurgence' of the second half, there was no room for Trevelyan's bourgeois modernity.

[267] Exceptions are Clive Emsley, *British Society and the French Wars 1793–1815* (London, 1979) and Geoffrey Best, *War and Society in Revolutionary Europe 1770–1870* (Leicester, 1982).

[268] Similar effects can be traced to the wars of William III and Anne. But their impact was temporary and modest by comparison with the conflicts of the late eighteenth century.

3

The Survival of the Dynastic Idiom, 1688–1760: an Essay in the Social History of Ideas

I. PRELIMINARY

If what some have regarded as the social preconditions for the credibility of monarchical or legitimist doctrines were not swept away in the early eighteenth century, it is necessary to ask what became of the doctrines themselves. The conventional view has undoubtedly been that they were rapidly extinguished: 1688 was followed by 'a settlement which nearly all Englishmen accepted'.[1] With the Revolution, 'the dogma of Divine Right disappeared for ever from English politics'.[2] Alternatively, 1714 was proposed as the date of its demise, but for identical reasons.

Clergymen rivalled each other in preaching the doctrine of unconditional submission till the Church and King quarrelled, and none but a few Jacobites could adhere to the old creed. The Hanoverian dynasty was too obviously endowed with no divine sanctity. George I was clearly not the representative of God Almighty; and the disappearance with Queen Anne of the quaint superstition of touching for the evil marked the extinction of the last fragments of the belief in the special sanctity of kings.[3]

Whichever date was chosen, historians attended to the doctrine rather as truth than as political rhetoric: its extinction was to be expected not least because it was untrue; it was absurd.[4] And they found it impossible not to dismiss a theory which they judged irrational:

...the conduct of James II made it impossible for the average man and even for the average Churchman to swallow the Gospel of Divine Right. [Rather, the nation] proceeded with the leisurely construction of our constitutional liberties. The Revolution Settlement was the triumph of common sense. The last of the Die-hards

[1] Caroline Robbins, *The Eighteenth Century Commonwealthman*, (Cambridge, Mass., 1959), p. 5.
[2] Laski, *Political Thought in England from Locke to Bentham*, p. 7. Nothing replaced it; there was a 'relative barrenness of abstract ideas' until Hume and Bentham.
[3] Stephen, *English Thought*, vol. II, pp. 111–12.
[4] Cf. the verdicts of Vaughan, Pollock, Sabine, Figgis, Zagorin, Allen and others noted in Greenleaf, *Order, Empiricism and Politics*, pp. 6–7, and still current in the work of such influential historians as Christopher Hill and Lawrence Stone.

were brushed aside because the modern Englishman is practical, prosaic, and empirical, inclined to compromise, caring nothing for mysticism and little for logic, but testing the value of institutions and principles by their fruits alone.[5]

If such an argument and such a characterisation of 'the English' are illegitimate, it becomes necessary to take divine right seriously once more if we are properly to account for its gradual demise. For the paradox entailed by the old interpretation was the astonishing suddenness and completeness of the doctrine's alleged disappearance:'With the fall of James II it was overthrown, completely and for ever. Few changes in religious thought were more decisive in character...essentially the overthrow of divine right supplies the most striking example of a dramatic change that can be found anywhere in the history of English thought.'[6] Seen simply as an account of the triumph of truth, this is immediately implausible. Historical phenomena seldom stop dead in their tracks, especially ideologies as widespread and powerful as this. There is indeed a problem of transition, but in order to solve it we must first confront the problem of survival. Lord John Russell, as a reformer of the 1820s, found it easy at that distance to admit that the Revolution had been a 'violation of all the rules of legitimacy'; but it was, he smugly insisted, 'the triumph of the enlightened few over the bigotry of millions'.[7] We now know that the Revolution was an episode which few men had foreseen, planned or sought in the form which it eventually took. But a corollary of this is that the attitudes and dispositions of those millions were not instantly dissipated. To trace their metamorphosis, divine right will be examined in three aspects: as a political strategy; as a doctrine of wide incidence, but which (in one of its forms) became unavailable for use in

---

[5] G. P. Gooch, Introduction to L. M. Hawkins, *Allegiance in Church and State. The Problem of the Nonjurors in the English Revolution* (London, 1928), p. viii. Even in the 1980s, it was still possible to read that the Declaration of Rights was 'informed by a long-term libertarian political philosophy' so that 'The events of the revolution and the terms of the Bill of Rights destroyed the essential ingredients of the ancient regime: the theory of divine right monarchy, the idea of the direct hereditary succession, the prerogatives of the king over law, the military, taxation, and judicial procedures that were to the detriment of the individual': L. G. Schwoerer, *The Declaration of Rights, 1689* (Baltimore, 1981), p. 291.

[6] G. R. Cragg, *From Puritanism to the Age of Reason. A Study of Changes in Religious Thought in the Church of England 1660 to 1700* (Cambridge, 1950), pp. 157, 184; cf. *idem, Reason and Authority in the Eighteenth Century* (Cambridge, 1964): 'when James II rashly put the theory' of divine right 'to the test, it collapsed, completely and irrevocably. The vacuum thus created was filled by John Locke'; Locke 'worthily served his day' until 'for the first time, his assumptions about man and society were boldly challenged' by Burke at the time of the French Revolution (pp. 182, 275). For an essentially similar chronology, cf. James Daly, *Sir Robert Filmer and English Political Thought* (Toronto, 1979): 'The story does not quite end with Locke'; but Nonjuror writers 'ably defended what was nonetheless a cause that was dying if not already dead. With that suddenness which occasionally changes a whole intellectual landscape overnight, a political crisis had rendered a large body of political thinking embarrassing if not irrelevant, even to its former following' (p. 11).

[7] Lord John Russell, *An Essay on the History of the English Government and Constitution, from the Reign of Henry VII to the present time*, 2nd edn (London, 1823), p. 212.

public debate after 1714; and as a cultural survival, caught up with the social function of religion, in the slow-moving, backward-looking world of popular and rural attitudes.

II. DIVINE RIGHT AS A POLITICAL STRATEGY

What gave the doctrine of the divine right of kings a continued relevance to the practice of government into the eighteenth century was that England remained an hereditary monarchy in a Europe which was overwhelmingly monarchical. As late as 1775, a libertarian Swiss had to acknowledge that

In almost all the states of Europe, the will of the prince holds the place of law; and custom has so confounded the matter of right with the matter of fact, that their lawyers generally represent the legislative authority as essentially attached to the character of the king; and the plenitude of his power seems to them necessarily to flow from the very definition of his title.[8]

Even a Dissenting clergyman, in 1760, conceding that 'there is no power but of God' but quoting Bishop Sherlock to prove that God had not ordained any particular form of government, was forced to admit: 'tho' 'tis indeed very amazing, how absolute monarchy has become, not here and there prevalent, but almost every where, and universally so'.[9] In the Catholic monarchies especially, sovereigns could appeal for a divine sanction both to an institution of formidable international authority, and to bodies of national theory. Bossuet and Richelieu retained their currency in France long after Filmer ceased to be openly resorted to in England,[10] partly because they were used by and on behalf of an unbroken political regime.[11]

[8] J. L. de Lolme, *The Constitution of England; or, An Account of the English Government* (1775; new edn, London, 1807), pp. 60–1. This he conceded despite his claim that in 1688, in England,

> ...it was finally determined that nations are not the property of kings. The principles of passive obedience, the divine and indefeasible right of kings, – in a word, the whole scaffolding of false and superstitious notions, by which the royal authority had till then been supported, fell to the ground; and in the room of it were substituted the more solid and durable foundations of the love of order, and a sense of the necessity of civil government among mankind.

[9] Samuel Morton Savage, *The Duty of Subjects to Honour the King, Consider'd and Enforc'd. In a Sermon Preach'd on Occasion of his Present Majesty's Accession* (London, 1760), p. 26.

[10] It might be suggested that seventeenth-century French theorists were read longer partly because French changed less than English, as a language, between 1600 and 1800.

[11] R. Hatton, *Europe in the Age of Louis XIV* (London, 1969), pp. 67–73, 78–9; Keohane, *Philosophy and the State in France*, pp. 244–61, 346–50. Professor Walzer's valuable study, *Regicide and Revolution. Speeches at the Trial of Louis XVI* (Cambridge, 1974), relies heavily on mediaeval rather than eighteenth-century legal and constitutional history in outlining the position of absolute monarchy; and I cannot accept the argument that divine right kingship as such died with the executions of Charles I and Louis XVI, so that William III and the Hanoverians owed nothing to that nexus of ideas (pp. 5, 19): 'The erosion of royalist ideology', as Professor Walzer points out, 'still awaits its historian' (p. 88).

Monarchs in western Europe were held by their defenders to be absolute, not arbitrary: absolute as against men, but under God and the law. They occupied a point of delicate balance within a sophisticated theory.[12] Appropriately, the theory could serve many up-to-date purposes, whether to advance a national cause in international power-politics,[13] to promote bureaucratic centralism, to defend the monarchy against aristocratic resurgence, or – as in Austria or France – to distance the national Church from Papal control.[14] At the end of the century, the conventional German defence of princely absolutism still 'consisted of a simple reaffirmation of the old theory of the divine right of princes...however intellectually "uninteresting" [it] is of great historical importance'.[15] The same doctrine was current in the Austria of Maria Theresa[16] and Joseph II, who equally sought to isolate the Roman Catholic Church in their country from Rome's oversight. In Austria especially, it had more uses than the merely defensive; in the Europe of the first half of the eighteenth century, it has been suggested, 'The main force of change was the determination of the ruler and his advisers to introduce more effective forms of government...To justify the abrogation of practices sanctioned by prescription, rulers invoked their Divine Right to absolute power, which made them accountable to God alone.'[17] The doctrine achieved prominence once again in the work of the continental opponents of the French Revolution. The Abbé Barruel's *Le patriote véridique* (1789) combined divine right with the paternalist thesis; both can be found, most famously, in the theocratic politics of Joseph de

[12] For the problems of defining 'absolutism', cf. the works discussed by John Morrill, 'French Absolutism as Limited Monarchy', *HJ* 21 (1978), 961–72. Historians now have no excuse for 'using "absolute" and "arbitrary" quite interchangeably' as a way of 'simplifying everything': James Daly, 'The Idea of Absolute Monarchy in Seventeenth-Century England', *HJ* 21 (1978), 248.

[13] Louis XIV's acceptance of the will of Charles II of Spain in 1700, and recognition of James III after James II's death in 1701 (in contravention of the terms of the Treaty of Ryswick) may be viewed as imprudent results of an overriding commitment to a doctrine of legitimacy, or as strategic ploys, or both.

[14] The links between English and Scottish Jacobites and Nonjurors, especially those in exile, and Gallicans among French clergy in the 1720s are noted by P. F. Anson, *Underground Catholicism in Scotland 1622–1878* (Montrose, 1970), p. 134; cf. R. Clark, *Strangers & Sojourners at Port Royal. Being an Account of the Connections between the British Isles and the Jansenists of France and Holland* (Cambridge, 1932), pp. 138, 160–86, 230–55. Nonjurors of the circle of Hickes and Leslie had earlier tried to bring about a reconciliation between the Anglican and Gallican churches, partly, it has been suggested, as a basis for restoring James II as an Anglican sovereign without his renouncing his religion: G. Every, *The High Church Party 1688–1718* (London, 1956), p. 70.

[15] K. Epstein, *The Genesis of German Conservatism* (Princeton, 1966), pp. 265–76. We lack a synoptic study of the intellectual rationales of monarchies in eighteenth-century Europe as a whole – the *un*enlightened despots. Historians have preferred to record the triumph of revolutionary thought, rather than to reconstruct the case which established governments used in their defence.

[16] Epstein, *German Conservatism*, pp. 402, 462.

[17] Hampson, *The Enlightenment*, p. 66.

Maistre (1753–1821) and Louis de Bonald (1754–1840). It has been proposed as paradoxical that 'the great counter-revolutionary doctrines published from 1789 to 1804 did not begin to be widely known until after the victory of the counter-revolution in 1814', when such writers became 'the oracles of the restored monarchies'.[18] Yet it was the case of these doctrines, as of all political theories, that they were given their currency not only by the strength of their pretensions to truth, but by being used in practical political situations.[19]

We are now familiar with the situation in England in the 1670s and 80s which led to the resuscitation of Sir Robert Filmer's writings of forty years earlier;[20] the political predicament of James I need not be stressed as an explanation for his own recourse to such theories. Political exigencies continued to demand dynastic defences of the ruler's title throughout the reigns of William III, Anne, and the first two Georges, for as long as the practical security of the dynasty was in doubt. Considerations of expedience also came into play in the doctrines' acceptance. Immediately before the Civil War, passive obedience derived from a divine title had seemingly not been widely insisted on; after it, 'all who had suffered through the war entertained no doubt but that obedience to the most oppressive of regular authorities would lead to less misery than would resistance'.[21] The revolutions of 1688–9 and 1714–15 were interpreted by the Whigs as providential exceptions; granted the just titles of William III and George I, non-resistance could still be demanded on their behalf on both utilitarian and politico-theological grounds. Most of the clergy continued to preach the doctrines of divine right and passive obedience throughout the reigns of William III and Anne, and beyond, whether from Whig commitment or in hope of better times. Abednego Seller's influential *History of Passive Obedience since the Reformation* (1689–90), for example, was designed to show that the theories 'were not innovations of clever Stuart policy, but had been basic tenets of the Church from its beginnings, designed to counter the claimed deposing power of the Pope and the pretended right of popular deposition'.[22] The Whig regime attempted to steer between these two extremes. Jacobites denied that the Whigs did indeed conform to this shared doctrine: James II had, they insisted, been deposed, but *de facto*, not *de jure*. By the time of Sacheverell's trial, the issues had been explicitly worked out

---

[18] J. Godechot, *The Counter-Revolution: Doctrine and Action 1789–1804* (1961; trans. London, 1972), pp. 41ff, 84–102, 385; cf. B. Menczer, *Catholic Political Thought 1789–1848* (London, 1952).

[19] One reason for the neglect of ancien regime ideologies has probably been the very bad press which Roman Catholicism has traditionally received within the Anglo-Saxon historiographical tradition.

[20] Laslett (ed.), *Patriarcha*, Introduction.

[21] J. N. Figgis, *The Divine Right of Kings*, 2nd edn (Cambridge, 1914), p. 143.

[22] G. M. Straka, *Anglican Reaction to the Revolution of 1688* (Madison, Wisconsin, 1962), p. 27.

to the point where a Hanoverian group emerged among the Tory clergy – men who 'pretended to reconcile the doctrine of non-resistance and passive obedience with the principles on which the Revolution was founded and by which the deposing of kings was justified', as the Jacobite George Lockhart mocked.[23] What was most at issue was not the doctrine itself, but its application.

A modification of the political function of divine right theory had become evident in the decade after c. 1678, when it ceased to be chiefly a defence of a royal conception of the role of the monarchy in government and became primarily a defence of an attempt to recast the theocratic basis of the State around Roman Catholicism. This inconvenient element became a distant danger after 1688. From articulating a practical and innovatory programme, the doctrine became an affirmation of allegiance and Anglican religious identity, as well as the most theoretically effective way of challenging a Whig ascendancy. Paradoxically, therefore, far from suffering steady decline, divine indefeasible hereditary right actually won adherents after 1688 and 1714,[24] and Whigs were drawn to defend the titles of *de facto* sovereigns in similar terms – by arguing the hereditary claims of William III, Anne and George I, or by the doctrine of the 'divine right of providence', identifying God as 'the great disposer of Crowns'. Providence was still 'the age's leading concept of natural and historical causation'. It was invoked to explain both events in the natural world, from harvests and sickness to earthquakes, and events in the life of man. Incidents like the minor earthquake of 1692 allowed commentators to draw the two closely together;[25] and the Revolution of 1688 took its place beside other episodes in English history – the Armada, the Gunpowder Plot, the Restoration – which were celebrated as obvious interventions of the Deity in advancing the interests of Protestant England. The Hanoverian accession in due course was hailed by some as just such a national deliverance. Almost all churchmen joined in endorsing and preaching the notion of Providence, to the point where the victory of William III, significantly landing at Torbay on that fraught anniversary, 5th November, could be argued by Whigs to show as direct a divine commission and mandate as anything James II could claim.[26]

[23] Quoted in G. S. Holmes, *The Trial of Dr Sacheverell* (London, 1973), pp. 271–2.

[24] One such convert was, remarkably, Thomas Hearne, who became a leading Jacobite intellectual. In 1731, to his disgust, someone published one of his youthful essays, evidently written in 1700 and discovered now among the papers of his late patron, Francis Cherry. It was entitled *A Vindication of Those who Take the Oath of Allegiance, to His Present Majesty from Perjurie, Injustice, and Disloyaltie...Wherein is Evidently Shewed that the COMMON GOOD of a Nation is What is Primarily and Principally Respected in an Oath, and Therefore When the Oath is Inconsistent with that, the Persons who have Taken it, are Absolved from it. In a Letter to a Non-Juror.* Anything further removed from his later views can hardly be imagined.

[25] E.g. [Robert Fleming], *A Discourse of Earthquakes; as they are Supernatural and Premonitory Signs to a Nation...* (London, 1693).

[26] Straka, *Anglican Reaction*, chapter 6, pp. 65–79.

Some men agreed that the obligation of Christian obedience extended to *de facto* powers, and said so. Many however did not draw this inference. Jacobites subscribed to four linked doctrines: the divine institution and status of monarchy; the descent of the title to the crown by indefeasible hereditary right; the accountability of kings to God alone, not to subjects possessing a right of deposition; and the unequivocal scriptural injunction of non-resistance and passive obedience, even towards monarchs of whom subjects might disapprove.[27] To a Jacobite, these four principles had a necessary unity. Ministerial Whigs denied this: they openly rejected the second and third, but sought to salvage the rest. Yet they greatly weakened their claim of royal accountability by minimising the popular role, except in giving a token endorsement of Whig rectitude. Whig equivocation about 'the people' was matched, after 1689, by a Tory problem.

Divine right posed problems for all who used the idea. For Tories it meant a conflict of loyalties between its theological guarantor, the Anglican Church, and its practical implication, a Papist dynasty. Because they chose the first at the expense of the second, or because a choice had been made for them, did not mean that the second was divested of its appeal. It remained a credible political option. The suggestion that by 1714 'most Tories' has salvaged the 'ideology of order' which defended 'their privileged position' by transferring 'their unconditional loyalty and their notion of divine ordination' to the composite sovereign of the King-in-Parliament, so abandoning the idea of personal, *jure divino* monarchy,[28] overlooks the large extent to which many Tories' professed allegiance to their *de facto* monarchs after 1688 remained ambiguous and equivocal, not easily tested, and not capable of summary in an acceptable constitutional formula.

It was neither obvious nor inevitable that divine right should be discountenanced either by William III or by George I. The history of the succession to the English throne since the Conquest had been, to say the least, erratic. A break in continuity, even if admitted, *need* not have made the doctrine intellectually unavailable. Though other writers could be found who argued thus, it could be maintained that nowhere does Filmer himself 'actually say that Charles Stuart was the literal father of all the English in virtue of his unique relationship with Adam or Noah'.[29] Rather,

...the essence of Filmer's theory of political obligation was not that all present kings were the true and direct heirs of Adam's power, not that they were the literal and natural fathers of their people, but...that they must be considered to wield a power *like* that of Adam and the patriarchs and to be in a position in relation to their people *like* that of the father of a family. That is to say, the crux of the matter was not an historical argument at all, but an analogy or correspondence between the

---

[27] *Ibid.*, pp. 8off. Scriptural authorities for these views included Romans 13:1–8; I Peter 2:13–14; Proverbs 8:15 and 24:21; Matthew 22:21; Titus 3:1.

[28] Dickinson, *Liberty and Property*, pp. 28, 42, 46, 164 etc.

[29] Laslett (ed.), *Patriarcha*, p. 37.

king of a people and the father of a family and between the authority of each. In this way the basis of Filmer's political thought may be seen fundamentally as a version of the political theory of order[30]

– whose survival in other forms has already been noted. Filmer's leading critics, especially John Locke, James Tyrrell, Thomas Hunt and Algernon Sidney, though arguing against the direct lineal title of Stuart kings, all

...recognised the close relationship between familial and political authority at some historical point. Although they generally attempted to maintain a normative distinction between the family and the state, these writers embraced the anthropological theory and agreed that the familial association was the progenitor of the political order.[31]

It cannot be said that William III or George I and II wholly refused to avail themselves of the most powerful (and, at that time, the only convincing) justification for monarchy. Though the full doctrine of *indefeasible* right as taught by the Church of England between 1660 and 1688 was not deployed in their favour, nevertheless the doctrine of 'divine right by Providence' was; it, equally, had wide-ranging and almost identical implications for the proper behaviour of subjects. Humility, reverence, submission and obedience to social superiors continued to be the message of the pulpit[32] and of 'the most widely read of all contemporary manuals of devotion',[33] *The Whole Duty of Man*.[34] Composed during the Protectorate and first published in 1658, it was understandably reticent about explicitly extending these principles to *any* rulers. This reticence was one reason which prompted the appearance of *The New Whole Duty of Man* (1744, and many subsequent editions). This work announced its superiority to the former, and its relevance to the modern age: the 1658 text had addressed itself chiefly to moral duties; what was needed now, it claimed, was a doctrinal defence of the faith against atheists and Deists.

Yet this modern theoretical work dealt with kingship in terms both traditional and extravagant. The (Hanoverian) king was 'the civil parent', and the seventeenth-century implications of that status were invoked in his

---

[30] Greenleaf, *Order, Empiricism and Politics*, pp. 86–7; cf. Schochet, *Patriarchalism*, p. 197. I differ on this point from the argument of Daly, *Filmer*, pp. 67–8.

[31] Schochet, *Patriarchalism*, p. 200; cf. p. 259: 'Locke's reconstruction of the historical origins of the state was not vastly different from the position of Sir Robert Filmer, for Locke acknowledged that government had, in all probability, begun in the family and that the first ruler was a patriarchal monarch.'

[32] At Sacheverell's trial, the defence submitted in evidence assertions of the doctrine of non-resistance made by three archbishops and eleven bishops since 1688: Holmes, *Trial of Dr Sacheverell*, pp. 186, 190–2; Kenyon, *Revolution Principles*, p. 75.

[33] Cragg, *From Puritanism to the Age of Reason*, pp. 162–76. Great currency was also enjoyed by that other High Church classic, Pearson *On the Creed* (1659, *et seq.*).

[34] In 1688, Wake cited the book to prove that the Church of England's doctrine of non-resistance applied to *de facto* monarchs: Norman Sykes, *William Wake Archbishop of Canterbury 1657–1737* (Cambridge, 1957), vol. I, p. 47.

favour. The familiar Biblical texts commanding obedience were para-
phrased, as if truisms:

Therefore, seeing that sovereigns are God's vicegerents, and do reign by his
authority, they have also a right to be honoured and reverenced by their subjects;
because they bear God's character, and do shine with the rays of his majesty: and
consequently, it is an affront to God's own majesty, for subjects to condemn and
vilify their sovereigns, to expose their faults, and uncover their nakedness, and
lampoon and libel their persons and actions: therefore never speak evil of the ruler
of thy people.

Because 'sovereigns are ordained of God', they have a right to their subjects'
assistance; 'And moreover, they have a right to be obeyed in all things,
wherein they not interfere with the commands of God.' The king, too, was
the fountain of authority, from whence all power descends upon lower
magistrates': all lesser officials therefore

...have a right to be honoured and reverenced, and obeyed by the people, according
to the degree and extent of their authority and power: because wherever it is placed,
authority is a sacred thing, as being a ray and image of the divine majesty, and such
as may justly claim honour and reverence from all men; and whoever condemns
the lowest degree of it, offers an affront to the highest; for he that resisteth the power
resisteth the ordinance of God.

The authority of all magistrates, as derived from the king's, demands men's
'reverence & obedience by a right *that cannot be dispensed with*'.[35] If the main
Anglican devotional manuals argued in this way, it is not surprising that
Nonjuror manuals were indistinguishable from them; if anything, they were
merely more reluctant to discuss political duties at all.[36]

Divine right itself was not renounced as a title, because hereditary right
was not discarded. It was retained, alongside the 'divine right of Providence',
until the two fused in George III's reign. William III was always aware of
his Stuart lineage. His mother was Charles I's daughter Mary; he married
in 1677 the daughter of the Duke of York, later James II.[37] William both
stood in line to the succession himself, and was the husband of the
heir-presumptive until the birth of the future James III; until then, Charles
II and James II (in common with Louis XIV) had been 'implacably
opposed' to any attempt to alter the succession away from William.[38]
Though it was Parliament which recognised William as king, it did not

[35] *The New Whole Duty of Man...Authorised by the King's Most Excellent MAJESTY*, 12th edn
(London, 1754), pp. 187–90. Italics added.
[36] This applies especially to the Nonjuror Nathaniel Spinckes' collection, *The True Church of
England-Man's Companion in the Closet: or, a Complete Manual of Private Devotions...Collected
from the Writings of Archbishop Laud, Bishop Andrews, Bishop Kenn, Dr Hickes, Mr Kettlewell,
Mr Spinckes and Other Eminent Divines of the Church of England* (London, 1721). It reached
a seventh edition by 1736, and was 'frequently quoted as a leading manual of devotion
until the beginning of the nineteenth century': H. Broxap, *The Later Non-Jurors* (Cambridge, 1924), pp. 14–15.
[37] For the family links, cf. P. Geyl, *Orange and Stuart 1641–72* (London, 1969).
[38] E. Gregg, *Queen Anne* (London, 1980), p. 32.

appoint him, and he did not acknowledge a merely elective title to the throne. Some politicians undoubtedly wished to make William's title purely contractual; some explicitly did not; most thought it impossible to do so. All these views may be found expressed in the debates of the Convention Parliament.[39] But it was after only a short discussion that the Commons, on 28th January 1689, produced their grammatically ambiguous resolution

That King James the Second, having endeavoured to subvert the Constitution of this Kingdom, by breaking the Original Contract between King and People; and, by the Advice of Jesuits, and other wicked Persons, having violated the fundamental Laws; and having withdrawn himself out of the Kingdom; has abdicated the Government; and that the Throne is thereby vacant.[40]

James's fictional abdication might have been produced by his flight alone – whether enforced or voluntary.[41] Even so the Lords, almost evenly divided, dissented from the wording; arguing, in a conference of the two Houses, that the concept of 'abdication' was unknown in English law; that it implied a voluntary act, which hardly fitted James's case; and that a declaration that the throne was vacant implied that the Crown 'was thereby become elective; to which they cannot agree'. Those arguments also commanded widespread support in the Commons, which was split 151 to 282 in a division on 5th February 1689 to insist on its version.[42]

As discussion increasingly focussed on the issue of 'abdication' as a convenient legal fiction to avoid the question of deposition, the extremists' idea that James II had been dismissed for breaking an original contract became increasingly unavailable for political purposes. Whether he had 'abdicated' or 'deserted' the throne, however, if the throne were not vacant, Mary might succeed if James, Prince of Wales were excluded by doubts cast on his birth; and the joint sovereignty of William and Mary was a compromise to avoid a clear answer to this problem.[43] Nor was any election

---

[39] The debates may be traced in G. L. Cherry, 'The Role of the Convention Parliament (1688–9) in Parliamentary Supremacy', *JHI* 17 (1956), 390–406; R. J. Frankle, 'The Formulation of the Declaration of Rights', *HJ* 17 (1974), 265–79; H. Horwitz, 'Parliament and the Glorious Revolution', *BIHR* 47 (1974), 36–52; Kenyon, *Revolution Principles* (1977); Eveline Cruickshanks, John Ferris, David Hayton, 'The House of Commons Vote on the Transfer of the Crown, 5 February 1689', *BIHR* 52 (1979), 37–47; Schwoerer, *Declaration of Rights*; Eveline Cruickshanks, David Hayton, Clyve Jones, 'Divisions in the House of Lords on the Transfer of the Crown and Other Issues, 1689–94: Ten New Lists', *BIHR* 53 (1980), 56–87; T. P. Slaughter, '"Abdicate" and "Contract" in the Glorious Revolution', *HJ* 24 (1981), 323–37. I differ from the implication of Dr Slaughter, in his otherwise perceptive study, that the Revolution settlement can be said to have had a single meaning. [40] *Commons Journal*, vol. x, p. 14.

[41] Kenyon, *Revolution Principles*, pp. 10–11. The Commons' representatives put a stronger construction on the words in their meeting with the Lords' representatives on 4th February: Slaughter, '"Abdicate" and "Contract"', p. 331.

[42] Cruickshanks, 'Commons Vote' and 'Divisions in the House of Lords'.

[43] Even if 'abdicated' could widely be understood to mean 'deposed', as Dr Slaughter contends, it was not equally widely supposed to follow that the throne was then to be disposed of by contract.

or contract necessarily involved in the presentation to William and Mary of the Crown and the Declaration of Rights on 13th February, though some Whigs undoubtedly wished events to carry this implication. The document itself remarkably made no mention of a contract. It merely rehearsed the ancient rights which were held to be embodied in existing law,[44] and announced that the members of the Convention Parliament, 'Having...an entire confidence' that William 'will perfect the deliverance so far advanced by him and will still preserve them from the violation of their rights which they have here asserted and from all other attempts upon their religion rights and liberties', declared William and Mary sovereigns. William's reply accepted 'what you have offered' (whether the statement of existing rights or the Crown in addition was not made explicit), not mentioning the Declaration and giving only the most generalised assurance 'to preserve your religion laws and liberties'.[45] The final outcome was therefore completely ambiguous, doubtless deliberately so, and in the intellectual climate of the age it quickly failed to offer a lasting or secure basis for a contractarian understanding of kingship among any but ultra-Whig theorists: 'in a very real sense, the Bill of Rights was the victory of Church theory, for the alternative to the contract, the abdication, made no mention of the origins of government and kingship, which could still be assumed to be of divine right, requiring a continued obedience and nonresistance to the new monarch.'[46] This culminating attempt to embody the seventeenth-century understanding of an original contract in the constitution broke down in the theoretical controversies and political realities of the following two decades.

The 'ardent Anglican who believed in Charles's and James's right could do no less than allow William his divine right to rule;'[47] if he granted William a right at all, it would almost necessarily be a divine right. Political considerations, especially his need for Whig support, prevented William III using that doctrine in only one of its two forms. But it was still available in its fuller version, and Anne evidently had little reluctance in reviving it.[48] As Princess Anne, she had formally notified the Convention Parliament on 6th February 1689 that she would waive her superior hereditary claim to the throne during William's lifetime,[49] and again endorsed his title following

---

[44] Cf. Frankle, 'Formulation', p. 278.

[45] Schwoerer, *Declaration of Rights*, pp. 295–8. Dr Schwoerer (p. 26) nevertheless wished to argue that the offer of the crown *was* conditional; but her evidence points rather to the failure of radical Whigs to achieve that result in any strong sense.

[46] Straka, *Anglican Reaction*, pp. 35–6.

[47] G. Straka, 'The Final Phase of Divine Right Theory in England, 1688–1702', *EHR* 77 (1962), 638–58, at 639.

[48] Anne had occasional doubts, at least about the prudence of using the doctrine politically: Dickinson, *Liberty and Property*, p. 40. But its prevalence, and Anne's general attitude towards it, are not in doubt: cf. Kenyon, *Revolution Principles*, pp. 83–101, 128–69.

[49] H. Horwitz, *Revolution Politicks* (Cambridge, 1968), p. 80; *idem*, 'Parliament and the Glorious Revolution', p. 46; Gregg, *Queen Anne*, p. 71.

Queen Mary's death in 1694. It seems possible that after the death of her own son and last surviving child, the Duke of Gloucester, in 1700, Anne led the Stuart court at St Germain to believe that James, Prince of Wales (1688–1766) would be restored in due course if her own accession after William's death were not threatened.[50] Divine-right monarchy was a clear principle; but its application in practice left room for negotiation.

After 1714, things became more simple. In 1745, a Whig stigmatised his Jacobite enemies: 'The principle that distinguishes their side of the question, is, "the *hereditary indefeasible right of princes* to the government of mankind; a right unalienable from their persons and families, by any abuse of power, or exercise of tyranny".' This changed little, and Whigs continued to react against it with particular bitterness as obscurantist and superstitious: 'will it follow, that because a man has a property in his goods or his lands, that therefore a prince has a personal right and inherent property in the persons, liberties and lives of his fellow creatures; or that he can derive them to himself, and transmit them to his posterity by the same tenure?' Jacobite doctrine, claimed the same author, amounted to arguing 'that since men were never intended to be equal, they were therefore never intended to be free'.[51]

The strength of lineal indefeasible right was its appeal to a principle which even mainstream Whigs shared: 'That government is of a divine original, or, which is the same, is indispensably necessary for the preservation of society, is readily granted, and upon the least consideration unprejudiced reason will assent to it.'[52] Most Whigs accepted the principle but denied the application. But the moral distinction between legitimate authority and usurped power was an easily intelligible one and continued to be a principle of Stuart apologists. In 1750, one explained Romans 13 in this sense:

The construction of the word powers, has been sadly tortured by ill-designing men, but the true meaning is, and can be no other than that submission should be made to such persons, who have authority and a moral capacity to inforce obedience; for if power meant mere force, then this absurdity would follow, that every successful violence would be the power of God, and then consequently the Devil, and usurpers upon the constitution, and robbers on the highway, who have all of them doubtless some power, must be submitted to as the ordinance of God, which as it would be horrid to affirm, so it would confound the common received notions of right and wrong, and encourage all sorts of rapine and injustice.[53]

---

[50] *Ibid.*, pp. 103, 121–2.

[51] *The Spirit and Principles of the Whigs and Jacobites Compared. Being the Substance of a Discourse Delivered to an Audience of Gentlemen at Edinburgh, December 22, 1745* (London, 1746), pp. 23, 31.

[52] *Hereditary Right not Indefeasible: or, Some Arguments, Founded upon the Unalterable Laws of Society and Government, Proving that the Right Claimed by the Jacobites, Can Never Belong to Any Prince or Succession of Princes* (London, 1747), p. 13.

[53] *A Letter from a Gentleman in Town, to His Friend in the Country, Recommending the Necessity of Frugality* (London, 1750), pp. 20–1.

Latterly, it was observed

> There are a set of mongrel Jacobites risen up of late, who pretend, that they don't go the length of asserting divine indefeasible right, and only contend, that the Crown by our constitution is hereditary; who say, it is not *divinely*, but *constitutionally* indefeasible: And, according to this scheme, tho' they pretend to admit the justice of the revolution, yet they blame its continuance.[54]

Even the legal mind did not reject a religious sanction, however. The author of *The Divine and Hereditary Right of the English Monarchy Enquired into and Explained. By a Gentleman Late of the Temple* (London, 1749) summed up his case in ten propositions:

1. There must be an absolute unlimited and uncontroulable power lodged somewhere in every government. 2. It is not lawful to resist such a supreme power on any pretence whatsoever. 3. The laws of every country must be the rule of the subject's obedience. 4. Particular forms of government may be altered by the consent of all interested in them. 5. Monarchy is the best sort of government. 6. Hereditary monarchy is the best sort of monarchy. 7. The monarchy of England has long been hereditary. 8. The hereditary monarchy of England was irresistible. 9. The monarchy of England is still hereditary. 10. The monarchical government of England has a divine right.

In law, 'Every man may renounce his own right.' This affected equally a claim of indefeasible right either for the people or the sovereign. But was James II legally deprived? Was the Convention a lawful Parliament? The clear implication of the argument was that it was not. At least, suggested the author, subscribers to this doctrine were more likely to 'pay an handsome regard to the House of Hanover' than freethinking, semi-republican opposition Whigs.[55] It was a shrewd hit.

Whigs were forced, into the 1740s, to continue to argue against the exponents of indefeasible hereditary right on the latters' own ground[56] – whether the divine institution of kingship in scripture, with Saul, David and Samuel; or the confused and debatable succession to the crowns of England and Scotland. The Hanoverians' hold on power was in doubt until after the '45. Some Whig radicals defended the dynasty with arguments purely contractarian, describing kings as appointed by, and accountable to, the

---

[54] *The Spirit and Principles of the Whigs and Jacobites Compared*, p. 38.

[55] As reported in *The Mitre and Crown*, vol. 1, pp. 489, 509–20, 557–72, 605–19.

[56] See also: *The Right of the House of Stewart to the Crown of Scotland Consider'd* (Edinburgh, 1746); George Logan, *A Treatise on Government* (Edinburgh, 1746); Thomas Ruddiman, *An Answer to the Rev. Mr George Logan's Late Treatise on Government* (Edinburgh, 1747); *An Essay upon Liberty and Independency* (London, 1747); J. Owen, *Jacobite and Nonjuring Principles Freely Examined* (Manchester, 1747); *King's Right by Divine Law Conditional* (?Edinburgh, ?1747); George Logan, *A Second Treatise on Government* (Edinburgh, 1747); William Webster, *A Vindication of his Majesty's Title to the Crown* (London, 1747); Thomas Ruddiman, *A Dissertation Concerning the Competition for the Crown of Scotland* (Edinburgh, 1748); Sir T. Leman, *An Historical Deduction of Politics* (London 1748); George Logan, *The Doctrine of the Jure-Divino-Ship of Hereditary Indefeasible Monarchy Enquired Into and Exploded* (Edinburgh, 1749); [Caleb Fleming], *A Fund Raising for the Italian Gentleman* (London, 1750).

nation. But ministerial Whigs, and the monarchs themselves, were reluctant to stress such a claim. They could not begin confidently or credibly to boast that they derived their title from the free consent of 'the people' until the habit of allegiance to them had taken root of itself in the manner Hume anticipated and described. Tories continued to believe, under George I and George II, that an uncorrupt general election would give their party a parliamentary majority, even with the existing electoral system. This was a realistic belief: the Tories probably secured a majority of the votes cast at every general election between 1702 and 1741, with the exception of 1715 (approximately equal) and 1708. It was widely held that a plebiscite would have refuted any Hanoverian contractarian claim to the throne, as Samuel Johnson bluntly observed. Even ministerial spokesmen sometimes admitted as much. In the Commons on 29th January 1740, Henry Pelham opposed Samuel Sandys' Place Bill, evidently with the words: 'We know, Sir, how numerous the disaffected still are in this kingdom...I am afraid that, if this Bill should pass into a law, we might have a majority of Jacobites, instead of placemen in this House.' And on 28th April 1742, Walpole's henchman Thomas Winnington said:

There are still many gentlemen of figure and fortune amongst us, who openly profess their attachment to the Pretender: there is a sort of enthusiastical spirit of disaffection that still prevails among the vulgar: and, I am afraid, there is by far too great a number of men of all ranks and conditions, who now seem to be true friends to the Protestant succession, that would declare themselves otherwise, if they thought they could do so without running any great or unequal risk. These considerations shall always make me jealous of the Jacobite party's getting any opportunity to rebel.[57]

Lord George Murray, the outstanding Jacobite general, echoed this verdict almost exactly. In 1755 he wrote of his opinion that if Prince Charles Edward had been properly supported by France at the outset of the '45,

...his R.H. could not have failed of success. I had at that time opportunities of knowing the sentiments and way of thinking of most people in Great Britain. Many, very many, wished well to the royal cause. Great numbers would have looked on, and would have turned to the side that had success. And for those who for their own interest were zealous for the Hanoverian government, they would easily have been mastered, if, as I have said, his R.H. had been supplied from the beginning with a proper force.[58]

Consequently, the Hanoverians were obliged to counter the Stuarts' dynastic claims with a dynastic title of their own, weak though it was. George I deliberately confronted the republican element present in English

---

[57] *Parl Hist*, vol. XI, cols. 350–1; vol XII, col. 615. He was in a position to know: he came from a Jacobite family, and deserted the Tories only in 1729: Sedgwick, vol. II, pp. 550–1.
[58] Lord George Murray to Mr Edgar, 22nd Sept. 1755: James Brown, *A History of the Highlands and of the Highland Clans* (Glasgow, 1838), vol. IV, p. 128. Note the assumption of the leadership of the elite in Murray's implausible use of 'most people'.

Whiggism in announcing even in 1710 that he would come to Britain 'as a ruler by "hereditary right", that right having been made extinct "only for the Catholic members of the House of Stuart". This declaration was meant to scotch any Whig interpretation that parliament had given him the kingdom. At the same time it was also intended to convince the Tories that he was no usurper.'[59] Intermediary claimants had merely disqualified themselves by their religion. Daniel Waterland, the most formidable orthodox Anglican theologian of his day and a Whig in politics, announced in 1723: 'Does the royal family, as formerly, still want restoring? But who knows not that his Majesty now reigning (and long may he reign) is a branch of the same royal stock with him whose restoration we are now celebrating; and but one remove farther distant, in the course of natural descent, from the same royal progenitor.'[60] Eventually this was taken further still. In 1743 George Ballantyne expounded an ingenious hypothesis about English mediaeval history:

> ...there was no branch of the royal family of Henry the Second, for the true hereditary right to descend to, upon the death of the Princess Elenor, and the forfeiture of King John, but the Princess Maud [Matilda], eldest daughter of King Henry the Second, mother of the first royal blood of England, in the ancestors of King George...all King John's children were born in unlawful wedlock; and therefore could have no title to inherit the true hereditary right.

George I derived his title from Matilda: he thus enjoyed a parliamentary title, and the only hereditary title.[61]

Jacobites pointed out how tenuous the Hanoverian hereditary claim was: George I was fifty-eighth in line of succession in 1714. Nevertheless, the

---

[59] R. Hatton, *George I Elector and King* (London, 1978), p. 119. The degree to which discontinuities can be retrospectively wished away is remarkably shown in Michael MacDonagh, *The English King* (London, 1929), p. 63 (italics added): George I

> ...was *really* as much a Stuart in blood as his immediate predecessor on the Throne, Queen Anne...Anne was the granddaughter, and George was the great grandson, of the first of the Stuart kings, James I. George I and Chevalier St George were cousins of the Blood Royal, *the only difference* between them in their common descent from a common ancestor being that the Pretender was in the direct male line from James I, and King George I was in a collateral female line through James's daughter Elizabeth, who married the Elector Palatine of the Rhine...Accordingly, though the succession to the Throne was changed at the Revolution of 1688, the association of the Stuart blood with it was preserved, and also, of course, the Tudor, Plantagenet, Norman, and Saxon blood. The story of the ancestry of the Royal Family provides wonderfully impressive evidence of the enduring fabric of this realm, of the continuity of its national life, under its truly national Throne, from far-off ages to the present day.

[60] 'A Sermon preached at the Cathedral Church of St Paul...On Wednesday, May 29, 1723. Being the Anniversary Day of Thanksgiving for the Restoration', in W. Van Mildert (ed.), *The Works of the Rev. Daniel Waterland, DD* (10 vols., Oxford 1823–8), vol. VIII, p. 461.

[61] George Ballantyne, *A Vindication of the Hereditary Right of His Present Majesty, King George II to the Crown of Great Britain, &c...Being a full Answer to All the Arguments of the Nonjurors* (London, 1743), p. 10. It was this argument which was later seized on by John Wesley (see chapter 4).

King's Speech to his first Parliament began: 'My Lords, and Gentlemen; This being the first opportunity that I have had of meeting my people in parliament, since it pleased Almighty God, of his good Providence, to call me to the throne of my ancestors...'.[62] Even the Deist and Whig extremist John Toland wrote: 'Never before did Britain possess a king endued with so many glorious qualities; as true piety, fortitude, temperance, prudence, justice, knowledge, industry, frugality, and every other virtue...The Whigs admire King George almost to adoration.'[63] His title was, in fact, defended in two quite contradictory ways.

The official rationale, inherited from previous regimes, was therefore not renounced but toned down. The process was reflected in successive editions of John Chamberlayne's best-selling and semi-official handbook, *Magnae Britanniae Notitia: or, the Present State of Great Britain*. The edition of 1708 was explicit:

Of monarchies, some are despotical, where the subjects, like slaves, are at the arbitrary power and will of their sovereign, as the Turks and other Asiatick nations; others political or paternal, where the subjects, like children under a father, are governed by equal and just laws, consented and sworn unto by the King; as is done by all Christian princes at their coronations.

The kingdom of England is an hereditary paternal monarchy, governed by one supreme independent head, according to the known laws and customs of the constitution.

The English is such a monarchy, as that, by the necessary concurrence of the Lords and Commons in the making and repealing all Statutes or Acts of Parliament, it hath the main advantages of an aristocracy, and of a democracy, and yet free from the disadvantages and evils of either.[64]

Essentially the same form of words survived the Revolution, the Bill of Rights, the Act of Settlement and the accession of George I, and was still reprinted in full in the twenty-fourth edition of 1716. Only the twenty-fifth edition of 1718 saw a major modification, omitting the first paragraph and proceeding:

The kingdom of England is an hereditary limited monarchy, governed by one supreme independent head, according to the known laws and customs of the kingdom.

It is a monarchy free from all interregnum, and with it from many mischiefs whereunto elective kingdoms are subject.

It is such a monarchy, as that, by the necessary concurrence of the Lords and Commons in the making and repealing all Statutes or Acts of Parliament, it hath

---

[62] *Parl Hist*, vol. VII, col. 42.

[63] John Toland, *Memorial to a Minister of State on the Accession of King George I* quoted in C. J. Abbey and J. H. Overton, *The English Church in the Eighteenth Century*, (2 vols., London, 1878), vol. I, p. 98.

[64] Chamberlayne, *Magnae Britanniae Notitia*, p. 52. It thus repeated almost word for word its predecessor of Charles II's reign, Edward Chamberlayne's *Angliae Notitia: or, the Present State of England*. There are slight differences of tone: the 3rd edn (London, 1669, pp. 101–3) has, para. 1, 'subjects, like servants...Turks and Barbarians'; para. 2 'independent and indeposable head'; para. 3 'the necessary subordinate concurrence'.

the main advantages of an aristocracy, and of a democracy, and yet free from the disadvantages and evils of either.

It is such a monarchy as, by most admirable temperament, affords very much to the industry, liberty, and happiness of the subject, and reserves enough for the majesty and prerogative of any king that will own his people as subjects, not as slaves.[65]

And in this form, denying the elective basis of the monarchy, asserting, in effect, the doctrine that 'the king never dies', it remained until the final, thirty-eighth edition of 1755. Yet even this edition went on at once to say, in the words of the 1708 text: '*Rex Angliae est persona mixta cum sacerdote*, say our lawyers: he is as it were[66] a priest as well as a king'; at his coronation 'he is anointed with oil as the priests were at first, and afterwards the Kings of Israel, to intimate that his person is sacred and spiritual'.[67] In 1714, similarly, James Paterson's *Pietas Londiniensis* had explained that St James' Chapel was outside episcopal jurisdiction, because under the sovereign's personal jurisdiction: 'Our king is a priest as well as a king; he is *primogenitus Ecclesiae*.'[68]

The doctrine of the 'mixed person' of the sovereign was an ancient one in English law, traceable back to Lyndewode or beyond. A modern scholar has claimed that the 'whole service' of coronation 'revolves' around the rite of unction, not the oaths or the symbolic election of the monarch:

Nothing that goes before, and nothing which follows, can approach the anointing in significance. Without it the king cannot receive the royal ornaments, without it, in a word, he is not king... The object of the unction is the reception of the sevenfold gifts of the Holy Ghost which are sacramentally conferred by the anointing. Grosseteste says as much in his letter to Henry III, and it finds support in the new text of the *Electorum fortitudo* which was introduced in 1689. It is curious that in 1689 this mediaeval idea should have been so forcibly expressed.

The new form of service introduced in that year, to repair James II's Papist emendations of the historic rite in 1685, actually strengthened the analogy with the consecration of a bishop.[69]

Kingship was widely held to have been limited or confined after the Revolution; but only in a much weaker sense is it possible to say that its essential nature was thought to have been changed, within its newly

---

[65] *Ibid.*, pp. 37–8. The editions are numbered consecutively with *Angliae Notitia*.

[66] The phrase 'as it were' first appears in the 18th edn of *Angliae Notitia*, 1694; it is absent in the 17th (1692) and previous editions. The qualification is nowhere stressed; though it might be crucial, the argument proceeds as if it had not been inserted.

[67] The element is played down in P. E. Schramm, *A History of the English Coronation* (Oxford, 1937); but Professor Schramm focussed almost wholly on the mediaeval period, and stressed the contrasts rather than the continuities with later practice.

[68] Quoted Abbey, *English Church and its Bishops*, vol. II, p. 103.

[69] L. G. Wickham Legg, *English Coronation Records* (London, 1901), pp. xvi–xix, xxxiv; Arthur Taylor, *The Glory of Regality: an Historical Treatise of the Anointing and Crowning of the Kings and Queens of England* (London, 1820), pp. 347ff; J. Brooke-Little, *Royal Ceremonies of State* (London, 1980), p. 41.

restricted sphere. That it *had* been changed was, of course, both an extreme Whig and a Jacobite position. But, as has been seen, the extreme Whig case was officially disavowed, and even the Jacobite challenge could be expressed as an argument that the Hanoverians were at fault in that they made a false claim to right – divine right. One man's authority, argued Charles Leslie, cannot, of itself, be superior to another's. 'Therefore, Government among men cannot be derived from mere human authority. This is so very obvious that all Governments whatever, of whatsoever sort, and among all nations and religions, do pretend to a Divine Right.'[70] Consequently, it seemed possible to some that the clergy, having adapted *jure divino* doctrines to support the Hanoverian regime, might adapt them back again in the wake of another restoration. Prince Charles Edward said as much during the '45:

> I remember Dr Wagstaff (with whom I wish I had conversed more frequently, for he always told me the truth) once said to me, that I must not judge of the English clergy by the bishops, who were not promoted for their piety and learning, but for very different talents, viz., for writing pamphlets, for being active at elections, and voting as the ministry directed them. After I've won another battle, they'll write for me and answer their own letters.[71]

He correctly appreciated the priority of politics in such matters. For political reasons, England under the Hanoverians, until 1828–9, was almost as much of a monarchical, confessional State as it had been under the Stuarts. What was chiefly viewed with alarm in eighteenth-century England was the threat of the extension of a Papist monarchy's claims into the life of the individual, not the nature of the Hanoverian monarchy's title in a Protestant, Anglican, political theology.

The nature of the Church establishment was therefore of considerable importance, and the conventional caricature of it as somnolent, corrupt, and unthinkingly subservient to the civil power is particularly distorting. Even Low Churchmen of the eighteenth century sought, as their ideal,[72] not a subordination of the sacred to the secular but a purposeful identity, a close connection between Church and State which would take as its motto George Lawson's words: 'Politics are from God; not only allowing and approving governments, but commanding them, for the better manifestation of His own glory, and men's greater good, temporal and spiritual. Hence it is evident that politics, both civil and ecclesiastical, belong unto theology; and

[70] Charles Leslie, *The Rehearsal*, vol. 1, p. 53; Hawkins, *Allegiance*, p. 133.
[71] Prince Charles Edward to James III, 21st Sept. 1745: A. C. Ewald, *The Life and Times of Prince Charles Edward* (London, 1875), vol. 1, pp. 218–19. Thomas Wagstaffe (1692–1770), son of Nonjuror Dr Thomas W. (d. 1712). Nonjuror: ordained deacon 1718, priest 1719 in that congregation. Scholar. At Rome from c. 1738–d. Anglican chaplain to James III and Prince Charles Edward.
[72] The Nonjuror position is usually assessed as an ideal; Low Church 'Erastianism' as a practice. The comparison is unfair.

are but a branch of the same.'[73] Under the first two Georges, just such an alliance was sustained between the Whig political establishment and the bishops. It was a formidable combination: in the face of an assertive Anglicanism, the number of Dissenters and of Roman Catholics in England was each roughly halved in the years c. 1690–1740. At the latter date, 'while the Church was far from being the universally patronised monopoly envisaged in traditional Establishment theory, its wealth, its influence and authority remained immense. In much of England Anglicanism and society remained virtually coterminous.'[74] Its increasing power was aided in the early eighteenth century by a growing alliance between squire and parson, generating 'a new version of establishment theory, emphasising the social affinities of clergy and laity, tending to glorify their interconnexions and mutual dependence'.[75] This was a reason for Tory reconciliation to the regime, urged one commentator: 'at what period of time, since the Reformation, was the national Established Church of England...in a state more prosperous than in the year 1750?...Are not the numbers of Protestant Dissenters from the Church communion daily diminishing?'[76] The establishment was safe in Whig hands, men urged; and their argument was not without its effect.

Social and doctrinal primacy was allegedly won at the price of political subordination; but, significantly, the alliance was cemented not by Hoadly but by Walpole's ally Gibson,[77] 'a prelate whom the satirists pilloried as the spiritual descendant of Archbishop Laud, and the most dangerous enemy of the civil constitution since his execution...the apostle of the divine right of the hierarchy and of the independence of the spiritual society...he was implacable in his hostility to all preachers of false doctrine'.[78] What happened to the High Church party after 1714? A large section of it took the oaths, accommodated itself to the new regime, and pursued very similar

---

[73] Abbey, *English Church and its Bishops*, vol. II, p. 105. The most sympathetic treatment of the Church–Whig alliance is G. V. Bennett, *White Kennett 1660–1728 Bishop of Peterborough* (London, 1957); cf. Ravitch, *Sword and Mitre*, pp. 102–17.

[74] A. D. Gilbert, *Religion and Society in Industrial England. Church, Chapel and Social Change, 1740–1914* (London, 1976), pp. 12, 16–17.

[75] *Ibid.*, p. 13; G. F. A. Best, *Temporal Pillars* (Cambridge, 1964), p. 61, though Professor Best insisted that 'the laity still were ultimately in control'. A statistical survey is now available in D. R. Hirschberg, 'The Government and Church Patronage in England, 1660–1760', *JBS* 20 (1980–1), 109–39.

[76] *A Letter to the Oxford Tories. By an Englishman* (London, 1750), p. 16.

[77] Edmund Gibson (1669–1748). Sizar of Queen's College, Oxford. BA 1691. Anglo-Saxon scholar; noticed by Bp Tenison. Fellow of Queen's; chaplain to Tenison as Bp of London; livings. Engaged in Convocation controversy, culminating in *Synodus Anglicana* (1702). 1713 published *Codex Juris Ecclesiae Anglicanae*. Bp of Lincoln 1716, on Wake's recommendation; 1720–d. Bp of London. Passed over for Canterbury, 1737; refused it, 1747, on grounds of age.

[78] Norman Sykes, *Edmund Gibson* (London, 1926), pp. 119, 182.

ends under a new label; and it took control of more and more senior posts.[79] The ascendancy of radical Whig churchmen after 1714 was brief, and has been exaggerated. After he had called down the wrath of Orthodox divines in the Bangorian controversy, Hoadly's influence was checked. With the new reign, he was largely irrelevant: George II detested him.[80] It was not Hoadly but High Churchmen who most shaped what became Orthodox Anglicanism in the early Hanoverian era.

With Potter and Gibson, that party took into the Church–Whig alliance a particular theory. Gibson's *Codex* of 1713 claimed

> ...that the Spiritual Body was independent of and equal to the Temporal, that the Temporal Courts ought to be restrained from interference with the Ecclesiastical, that the clergy were the proper judges of the degree of assistance which the Church required from the State, and of the means by which that support should be rendered, and that the suppression of vice was the proper function of the Spirituality not of the laity.

The *Codex* thus 'became the symbol of aspiration to ecclesiastical tyranny'. Despite the fact that it contained a section on the laws of succession which was explicitly Hanoverian, Gibson thought it prudent not to publish a further treatise arguing that ecclesiastical canons were binding on laymen.[81] Despite their later Whiggery, Hearne believed that both Wake and Gibson had been of Nonjuring sympathies in 1689, and that Gibson delayed taking the oaths, until 'preferment' persuaded him. It was a charge which continued to be made of Gibson into the 1730s:[82] men remembered that prelates' obedience was not automatic.

Gibson's successor in Whig ministerial councils was John Potter.[83] Whiston was alarmed to see Potter take a 'high and pontifical state upon him' after his elevation to Canterbury in 1737: it was a reminder that he had earlier written a work 'against the Erastians, or for the ecclesiastical authority, as distinct from the state',[84] which had won the approval of the Nonjuror Robert Nelson.[85] This was not surprising: Potter's *Discourse* had

---

[79] Cf. Richard Sharp, 'New Perspectives on the High Church Tradition: Historical Background 1730–1780', in Geoffrey Rowell (ed.), *Tradition Renewed* (London, 1986), pp. 4–23.

[80] John, Lord Hervey, *Some Materials Towards Memoirs of the Reign of King George II* (ed. Romney Sedgwick, 3 vols., London 1931), vol. II, pp. 395, 398–9, 498–500.

[81] Sykes, *Gibson*, pp. 69–71.

[82] *Ibid.*, pp. 8–9.

[83] John Potter (?1674–1747). Wakefield Grammar School; servitor of University College, Oxford. BA 1692. Deacon 1698, priest 1699. Fellow of Lincoln 1694. Living 1697. 1704 domestic chaplain to Tenison, Bp London. 1707 Regius Professor of Divinity, Oxford, on Duke of Marlborough's interest. Bp of Oxford, 1715; Abp of Canterbury, 1737.

[84] *Memoirs of the Life and Writings of Mr William Whiston...Written by Himself* (London, 1749), p. 359. Whiston claimed that he was consulted by Queen Caroline about Potter's appointment, and that he, Whiston, later regretted it.

[85] C. F. Secretan, *Memoirs of the Life and Times of the Pious Robert Nelson* (London, 1860), p. 226. John Potter, *A Discourse of Church–Government: Wherein the Rights of the Church and the Supremacy of Christian Princes, are Vindicated and Adjusted* (London, 1707; 3rd edn, 1724).

much in common with Nonjuror theology, and 'asserted an exclusive spiritual authority in the Church descended from the Apostles through the bishops'.[86] Yet, remarkably, he equivocated at the accession of a Lutheran monarch in 1714, and his coronation sermon for George I accepted by implication the validity of the sovereign's baptism. What most distinguished High Churchmen like Potter and Gibson was their willingness to compromise on the dynasty if everything else, the place of the Church in English society, could be saved. This applied also, for example, to Thomas Sherlock.[87] Lord Hervey wrote that Bishop Sherlock 'was hated by the Tories for ceasing to be a Jacobite, and not loved by the Whigs because Jacobitism was the only Tory principle he had renounced'.[88] But part of the quip may be doubted, for Sherlock emerged as the acknowledged leader of the Tory clergy,[89] and his co-operation with Whig ministries from the 1740s spelled no dilution of Church claims.

The strength and assertiveness of the Church within the Church–Whig alliance has often been underestimated. But it was an alliance which many were led to support because, as Gibson observed, the State, not the Church, was the weaker partner: 'there is far greater probability that the Tories will be able to destroy our present establishment in the State than that the Dissenters will be able to destroy our establishment in the Church'.[90] This did not necessarily call for a devaluation of all spiritual claims. One reaction to Nonjuror disaffection after 1714 was undoubtedly Hoadleian minimalism; another, more important and far more typical, was the assertion of a firm identity between a Whig Church and a Whig State, a policy whose man of action was Gibson and whose ideologue was William Warburton. The latter is often taken for an archetypal Erastian; but he did not suppose himself to be defending a subservient position. As he outlined the possibilities:

The Papist makes the State a creature of the Church; the Erastian makes the Church a creature of the State: the Presbyterian would regulate the exercise of the State's power on Church ideas; the Free-thinker, the Church, by reasons of State; and, to complete the farce, the Quaker abolishes the very being of a Church; and the Socinian suppresses the office of the civil magistrate.

[86] John Findon, 'The Nonjurors and the Church of England 1689–1716' (Oxford D.Phil. thesis, 1978), p. 182.

[87] Thomas Sherlock (1678–1761). Son of William S., Dean of St Paul's. Eton; St Catharine's Hall, Camb., 1693. Near contemporary and rival of Hoadly. BA 1697; Fellow 1698; ordained 1701. Master of the Temple 1704 in succession to his father. 1711 chaplain to Queen Anne. Master of St Catharine's 1714–19; Vice Chancellor 1714; suspected of Jacobitism. Dean of Chichester 1715; Canon of Norwich 1719; wrote in Bangorian controversy. His *Vindication of the Corporation and Test Acts* (1718) led to loss of royal chaplaincy. Bp of Bangor 1728; Bp of Salisbury 1734; Bp of London 1748–d.

[88] Hervey, *Memoirs*, vol. 1, p. 89.

[89] Cf. E. Carpenter, *Thomas Sherlock 1678–1761* (London, 1936).

[90] Gibson to Nicholson, 3rd Dec. 1717: Sykes, *Wake*, vol. 11, p. 119.

Warburton recognised 'two parties, into which we are divided, in this matter'; that 'the one defends a Test on such reasonings as destroy a toleration, and the other opposes it on such as conclude equally against the very essence and being of a national religion'.[91] The Jacobites and Freethinkers constituted the two extremes, he claimed. Warburton's achievement was to devise a formula which commanded wide assent. It proved however to be a treaty of peace which different Anglican groups might subscribe to without abandoning their characteristic beliefs, as Warburton indignantly realised:

I had the honour to be told by the heads of one party, that they allowed my *principles* [footnote: Bishop Hoadly]; and by the heads of the other, that they espoused my *conclusion* [footnote: Bishop Sherlock]; which however amounted only to this, that the one was for liberty however they would choose to employ it; and the other for power, however they would come at it.[92]

Yet both High Churchmen and Hoadleians could use the arguments of the *Alliance* against Dissenters and Freethinkers. It defended the Establishment 'upon principles which republicans themselves cannot easily deny', as Bishop Horsley later pointed out.[93]

That this was so meant that the party left in possession was not Hoadleian, not Erastian, but Orthodox Anglican. Warburton's *Alliance* thus had much in common with Potter's *Discourse*, an explicitly anti-Erastian work:

Scarce any thing in religion has been more mistaken, than the nature and extent of that power, which our blessed Saviour established in his Church. Some have not only excluded the civil magistrates of Christian states from having any concernment in the exercise of this power, and exempted all persons invested with it from the civil courts of justice; but have raised their supreme governor of the Church [the Pope] to a supremacy, even in civil affairs, over the chief magistrate; insomuch, that he has pretended on some occasions to absolve subjects from their allegiance to their lawful princes. And others [Freethinkers] have run so far into contrary mistakes, as either to derive all spiritual power wholly from the civil magistrate, or to allow it to be exercised by all Christians without distinction. The first of these opinions manifestly tends to create divisions in the state; and to excite subjects to rebel against their civil governors: The latter do both plainly strike at the foundation of all the power, which Christ hath left in his Church; and wherever they are put in practice, not only the external order and discipline, but even the sacraments of the Church must be destroyed, and its whole constitution quite dissolved.[94]

---

[91] [W. Warburton], *The Alliance between Church and State, or, the Necessity and Equity of an Established Religion and a Test-Law Demonstrated, From the Essence and End of Civil Society, upon the Fundamental Principles of the Law of Nature and Nations* (London, 1736), pp. 2, 20, 48–9.

[92] Dedication to Books IV–VI of *The Divine Legation of Moses* to Lord Mansfield, 2nd Feb. 1765, in *The Works of the Right Reverend William Warburton, Lord Bishop of Gloucester* (7 vols., London, 1788), vol. II, p. 269.

[93] S. Horsley, *A Review of the Case of the Protestant Dissenters* (London, 1787), Preface.

[94] J. Potter, *A Discourse of Church–Government* (London, 1707), pp. 1–2.

Yet the *Alliance* was greeted as an academic argument, not a description of contemporary practice.[95] The Nonjuror position at that point sought to separate Church from State in order to shield the former from Whig contamination; and the deep cleavage of opinion in the nation after 1714 perhaps encouraged Warburton to present his case as an argument for an alliance between two bodies which are initially, and thus fictionally, conceived as separate. By the end of the century, in contrast, the disappearance of this schism allowed Burke, like Hooker, or Sacheverell in 1702, to talk of Church and State once more as two aspects of a single national community.[96] But, in their time, Warburton's arguments served their purpose; so that, as the Archbishop of Canterbury could assure the Lord Chancellor in 1748, 'philosophy, Christianity and policy are all against changes' in the Establishment.[97] Warburton's *Alliance* breathes such a 'confident optimism concerning the correspondence between the establishment of England and the eternal order of the universe'[98] that doctrines of indefeasible kingship were perhaps unnecessary as intermediaries between the two. It remained the case, however, that the divine right of kings 'in its philosophical aspect is merely the form given by circumstances to a doctrine of sovereignty';[99] and such a doctrine was as essential to Hanoverian England as it had earlier been under the Stuarts. This fact was not directly dependent on the sincerity of individual belief. One pamphleteer wrote: 'I take active Jacobitism, that is only founded on personal discontent or personal ambition, to be worse and more dangerous, than that speculative sort which owes its birth to principle or education.'[100] Nevertheless, the second variety deserves attention also, and to it we now turn.

III. DIVINE RIGHT AS AN UNDERGROUND LOYALTY

The divine, hereditary, indefeasible right of kings may be considered as a doctrine which, however widely held up to 1714, it was dangerous publicly

---

[95] Warburton later complained that the *Alliance*, 'though framed upon a model before our eyes, was considered as an utopian refinement'. R. W. Greaves, 'The Working of the Alliance. A Comment on Warburton', in G. V. Bennett and J. D. Walsh (eds.), *Essays in Modern English Church History in Memory of Norman Sykes* (London, 1966), p. 167; which offers a different interpretation to that advanced here.

[96] Cf. Abbey, *The English Church and its Bishops*, vol. II, pp. 114–16, 120–2; Best, *Temporal Pillars*, pp. 71–4; Holmes, *Trial of Dr Sacheverell*, p. 51 for the Doctor's description of the secular and spiritual powers as 'twisted and interwoven into the very being and principles of each other'. Cf. also Kenyon, *Revolution Principles*, p. 86.

[97] Thomas Herring to Lord Hardwicke, quoted in Norman Sykes, *Church and State in England in the XVIIIth Century* (Cambridge, 1934), p. 284.

[98] *Ibid.*

[99] Figgis, *Divine Right*, p. 246.

[100] *Three Letters to the Whigs. Occasion'd by the Letter to the Tories*, 3rd edn (London, 1748), p. 7.

to avow thereafter. As a chief of the pro-Stuart clan Macgregor wrote at the time of the '45,

The many sanguinary penal laws since the Revolution, whereby the crime of Jacobitism is rendered more horribly dreadful in its consequences than murder, witchcraft or even open deism or atheism...has brought such a habit and spirit of dissimulation on them, that a Jacobite can never be discovered by his words. It must be his actions that decypher him.[101]

One result was a great flowering of secret societies with elaborate rituals and, in the general absence of more purposive activity, much conviviality – especially on the Stuart anniversaries.[102] As one Whig don recognised, observing the social life of Oxford undergraduates: 'good cheer, especially good liquor, is the very life and support of Jacobitism in this kingdom'.[103] Bolingbroke recognised the idiom, though minimising the survival of the thing, in claiming that the 'Jacobite Tories...continue steady to engagements which most of them wish in their hearts they had never taken; and suffer for principles, in support of which not one of them would venture further, than talking the treason that claret inspires.'[104] Jacobite assertions became possible, if not behind locked doors, only in anonymous publications, covertly printed and distributed, or under a disguise of metaphor, allegory and ambiguity. But for that reason, a world of symbolism was created far richer than that, for example, which later grew up around the figure of Wilkes.[105]

One reason for the survival of Jacobites' and Nonjurors' allegiance was their ignorance of their falling numerical strength – a sheer lack of statistics. Hearne wrote even in 1730: 'I have been told for certain that, at the court at London, the non-jurors are esteemed to be the honestest part of the nation, and that even Caroline says so herself. I am also certainly informed that

---

[101] Quoted in Cruickshanks, *Political Untouchables*, p. 45.

[102] The Welsh 'Cycle of the White Rose', 'Club of 27' and 'Society of Sea Serjeants' (of which Sir John Philipps was President in 1754) fall into this category, as does the London-based 'Honourable Board of Loyal Brotherhood' or Cambridge's 'The Family'. Cf. P. D. G. Thomas, 'Jacobitism in Wales', *Welsh History Review* 1 (1962), 279–300; Francis Jones, 'The Society of Sea Serjeants', *Transactions of the Honourable Society of Cymmrodorion* (1967), 57–91; J. P. Jenkins, 'Jacobites and Freemasons in Eighteenth-Century Wales', *Welsh History Review* 9 (1979), 391–406.

[103] Edward Bentham, *A Letter to a Fellow of a College* (London, 1749), p. 53. The more formally organised of such clubs created an art form, in the engraved glasses which expressed their political allegiance.

[104] Bolingbroke, *The Idea of a Patriot King* (1749), in *Works*, vol. II, p. 411. Claret was a Tory taste, almost an affirmation of allegiance, discriminated against by successive Whig governments through preferential duties on Portuguese wines: Edmund Penning-Rowsell, *The Wines of Bordeaux*, 4th edn (London, 1979), pp. 101, 132. That was one reason, quipped the Jacobite antiquary the Rev. William Cole, why Jacobitism would never appeal to the parsimonious family of Lord Hardwicke, 'if claret is their liquor, very little of so expensive a wine ever appearing at their wretched table'. Yorke, *Hardwicke*, vol. II, p. 566.

[105] It awaits its historian; meanwhile, unexpectedly, G. R. Francis, *Old English Drinking Glasses. Their Chronology and Sequence* (London, 1926), chapter 16, offers a useful starting point.

the non-juring Church of England gains ground in London every day.'[106] This was unlikely. But the point most at issue is not the number of those who can in some simple way be labelled Jacobite, but the common currency of discourse which almost all shared, which allowed Jacobite and Tory to shade equivocally into each other, and which allowed men to change sides.

When it was safe to express them, therefore, Jacobite doctrines might resurface. With Prince Charles Edward's army bearing down on Manchester during the '45, a local Whig wrote: 'Some marks of joy and hope very evidently show themselves, and the topics of absolute monarchy and hereditary right (which were always grateful) are now more resumed than before among us. These you will think show the inclinations of people, and perhaps their intentions, if opportunity favours.'[107] Even in 1747, one controversialist defended his decision to publish an attack on traditional doctrines: 'though the Rebellion be crushed, the seeds and principles thereof, are yet alive in the minds of too many, and will, if ever an opportunity offer, discover themselves in disturbing this nation and government'.[108] The extent of Stuart sympathy at a local level has scarcely yet been investigated by historians, though some legends survived into the early nineteenth century to be recorded by antiquarians: aged servants recalled conspiracies at Ancoats Hall, near Manchester, in 1744, or armed men in Cornbury Park, in Oxfordshire, waiting for the '45 to take a favourable turn.[109] No mere addition of such stories will give us an index of the extent of Jacobite sentiment and potential commitment, for there was a deeper reason than prudential concealment why divine right doctrine might 'go underground' and survive there. It had never sought to be, even when it had served a practical purpose, a self-interested commitment alone: it was a doctrine which might involve a quasi-religious act of allegiance which could not easily be dispensed with, any more than could a religious faith or an obligation of personal honour.[110] Appropriately, therefore, it was not conversion and persuasion so much as the passing of a generation of senior figures which coincided with the exhaustion of Jacobitism and the dissolution of the Tory party in the 1750s.

One zealous Whig, who wished to argue that 'a very great part' of those

---

[106] P. Bliss (ed.), *Reliquiae Hearnianae*, 2nd edn (3 vols., London, 1869), vol. III, p. 62. Local evidence reveals the initial growth and remarkable tenacity of Nonjuring allegiance, e.g. Richard Sharp, '100 Years of a Lost Cause: Nonjuring Principles in Newcastle from the Revolution to the Death of Prince Charles Edward Stuart', *Archaeologia Aeliana*, 5th ser. 8 (1980), 35–55.

[107] Quoted in S. W. Baskerville, 'The Management of the Tory Interest in Lancashire and Cheshire, 1714–47' (Oxford D.Phil. thesis, 1976), p. 308.

[108] *Hereditary Right not Indefeasible* (1747), p. iii.

[109] Sir Oswald Mosley, Bt, *Family Memoirs* (privately printed, 1849), p. 45; W. H. Hutton (ed.), *Burford Papers* (London, 1905), p. 113; Cruickshanks, *Political Untouchables*, pp. 88–91.

[110] Professor Kenyon has even suggested that John Kettlewell and Charles Leslie treated the oath of allegiance to James II as 'quasi-sacramental': *Revolution Principles*, p. 21.

who rebelled in 1715 were 'the vicious, the wicked, the profligate, and profane; men extremely ignorant, and destitute of all the principles of religion and virtue', nevertheless added: 'Yet I must confess there was a great number amongst them of a different stamp, persons who did really act upon principle, who believed in their consciences, that the Pretender was the only rightful heir to the Crown, and in consequence of such a persuasion concluded that he had a legal right to their aid and assistance.'[111] The very sense in which the Hanoverian monarchy did not regard itself as merely elective meant that to use divine right ideas to attack the regime struck at the heart of its claims to power. It is clear that such sentiments were widespread and popular at the time of Sacheverell's trial in 1710;[112] but the '15, the Atterbury plot, and an effective witch-hunt against the disaffected counselled prudence. Repression failed to extinguish rooted belief, however, and it survived as the major idiom in which fundamental theoretical challenges to the Whig regime were phrased.

Until the 1750s, periods of Jacobite unrest produced a minor rash of prosecutions across the country of indiscreet (or inebriated) loyalists for uttering 'seditious words'. These were only small fry. More effective action was taken against Tory ideologues. In February 1717, for his pamphlet *The Case of Schism in the Church of England Truly Stated*, published anonymously the previous year, the Rev. Lawrence Howell was condemned to three years' imprisonment, to pay a fine of £500, and to be whipped: he died in gaol in 1720. Matthias Earbery fled the country in 1717 to escape prosecution for seditious libel after the publication of his *The History of the Clemency of our English Monarchs*; a sentence of outlawry kept him abroad until December 1725. Charles Leslie, too, became an enforced exile in 1711, following James III from St Germain to Bar-le-Duc and then to Rome; only when dying was he able to return to his native Ireland in 1721. Thomas Carte fled to France in 1722 and was only able to return in 1728 through the intervention of Queen Caroline. In 1719 an eighteen year old printer, John Matthews, was seized for producing a Jacobite pamphlet, *Vox Populi, Vox Dei*, and, refusing to reveal the author, was hanged.[113]

The State Papers Domestic for the reigns of the first two Georges are littered with prosecutions of Jacobite publicists, a story of ideological resilience in adversity that has yet to be fully investigated.[114] The extent of

---

[111] *A Blow at the Root* (London, 1749), p. v.
[112] Holmes, *Trial of Dr Sacheverell*. Professor Holmes points to a 'resuscitation' of the doctrines of non-resistance and passive obedience in c. 1704–5 (p. 33); but this need not imply their earlier demise. Pamphleteering attention to controversial topics in early-eighteenth-century England usually came in bursts, not in a steady stream.
[113] R. J. Goulden, '"Vox Populi, Vox Dei". Charles Delafaye's Paperchase', *The Book Collector* 28 (1979), 368–90.
[114] Cf. meanwhile, P. Chapman, 'Jacobite Political Argument in England 1714–1766' (Cambridge Ph.D. thesis, 1983).

the Tory–Jacobite component among the intelligentsia has consequently been underestimated. As a rule of thumb, one might take the list of London printers produced by the printer Samuel Negus in 1724, identifying as 'known to be well affected to King George', 34; Nonjurors, 3; 'said to be High Flyers', 34; Roman Catholics, 4. Of 3 daily newspapers, 1 was Hanoverian, 2 were High Flyers; of 6 weeklies, 3 were High Flyers, 3 loyal to George I.[115] This Jacobite press was the object of sustained ministerial harassment over several decades. George Flint, editor of *Robin's Last Shift*, only cheated the hangman by escaping from Newgate in 1717 dressed as a woman (he reached France and entered James III's service). The forfeiture of sureties for good behaviour closed Carte's *The Freeholder's Journal* (1722–3) and the Duke of Wharton's organ *The True Briton* (1723–4).[116] One journal in particular, however, proved much more long-lived.

Between 1716 and 1728, when he fled to France, Nathaniel Mist was evidently in trouble with the law on at least fourteen occasions;[117] only buoyant sales and an eager market allowed him and other like-minded journalists to be so resilient. A series of short-lived titles succeeded one another alongside Mist's seemingly unstoppable enterprises: *The Weekly Journal; or, Saturday's-Post* (1717–25), continued as *Mist's Weekly Journal* (1725–8) and as *Fog's Weekly Journal* until finally extinguished by the government in 1737. It was in *Fog's* of 17th January 1736, for example, that Chesterfield published his satirical essay, arguing that an army of waxwork dummies would be cheaper, and just as useful; 'Let nobody put the Jacobite upon me, and say, that I am paving the way for the pretender, by disbanding this army. That argument is worn threadbare; besides, let those take the Jacobite to themselves, who would exchange the affections of the people for the fallacious security of an unpopular standing army.'[118] The tradition continued with *Common Sense or the Englishman's Journal* (1737–43), launched at the direct suggestion of James III 'as a paper which he could use for his own purposes, but which would not be overtly Jacobitical' – the journal in which Dr William King published an article on 28th May 1737 recommending a new government for a kingdom thinly disguised as 'Corsica' – a divine right monarchy.[119] Even after the '45, the flag was kept

---

[115] Nichols, *Literary Anecdotes*, vol. 1, pp. 288–312. Cf. L. Hanson, *Government and the Press 1695–1763* (Oxford, 1936), pp. 64–5 for the *London Journal*'s fears of Papist infiltration of the press in 1720.

[116] Hanson, *Government and the Press*, pp. 65–6. *The Freeholder's Journal* boasted a circulation of 8,000: *ibid*. Mist's papers quickly reached perhaps 10,000: Chapman, 'Jacobite Political Argument', p. 182.

[117] F. S. Siebert, *Freedom of the Press in England 1476–1776* (Urbana, Ill., 1952), pp. 373, 382; Chapman, *loc. cit*., p. 181. Mist was in exile from 1728 to 1736.

[118] M. Maty (ed.), *Miscellaneous Works of...Chesterfield* (London, 1777), vol. 1, part 1, p. 7. His other pieces in *Fog's* follow.

[119] D. Greenwood, *William King. Tory and Jacobite* (Oxford, 1969), pp. 77–8.

flying by the *London Evening Post*, *The Mitre and Crown* (1748–50) and *The True Briton* (1751–3). The provinces too were served by journals many of which have been observed to have a 'marked Jacobite leaning'.[120]

It was possible for Whig governments in the 1720s to suppress a popular culture of printed ballads and broadsheets. They were only partially successful in muzzling the Jacobite press, and least successful in silencing or refuting Stuart ideologues. Legitimist 'high theory' enjoyed the longest run, for it rested on massive foundations, and appealed to principles which both Whigs and Tories largely held in common. This was true with respect to the 'State point'; it was also true with respect to the 'Church point'. Nonjurors were not a particular type of churchman, but men who were hindered by scruple in the application of doctrines widely shared.[121] The years to 1714 saw a great outpouring of Nonjuror and Jacobite polemic from a second generation of able combatants including Thomas Brett, Henry Dodwell, Matthias Earbery, Henry Gandy, Samuel Grascome, George Harbin, Luke Milbourne, Henry Sacheverell, Nathaniel Spinckes, and, above all, the prolific Charles Leslie. The third generation, though few in number, was able to boast the contribution of William Law. Both generations built on the intellectual foundations laid at and shortly after the Revolution by such controversialists as Jeremy Collier,[122] George Hickes, Robert Jenkin, Thomas Ken, John Kettlewell, and Thomas Wagstaffe.[123] 'Non-juror' was not, of course, synonymous with 'Jacobite'. Some men were the first without being the second, and many more were the second without being the first. But the degree of identity increased with time, as the ranks were thinned of those who had taken an oath of allegiance to James II. The death in 1710 of Bishop Lloyd, the last of the bishops deprived at the Revolution, encouraged further desertions from the Nonjurors, but clarified the reasons for remaining in that communion. By the 1740s, the links between the Nonjuring hierarchy and the Stuart court at Rome were in good repair, especially via the historian Thomas Carte.[124] Even those Nonjurors like Dodwell who rejoined the Church of England after Lloyd's death may often have represented another injection of Jacobites into the parent body.[125]

Nonjuror writings have usually been neglected as ephemera, like the political pamphlets of the 1760s, buzzing noisily for a few hours before sinking into oblivion. In fact, many of their politico-theological works were

---

[120] Rupert C. Jarvis, *Collected Papers on the Jacobite Risings* (Manchester, 1971–2), vol. II, p. 6.

[121] I adopt here the argument of John Findon, 'The Nonjurors' (1978).

[122] Cf. J. Hopes, 'Politics and Morality in the Writings of Jeremy Collier', *Literature and History* 8 (1978), 159–74.

[123] T. Lathbury, *A History of the Nonjurors* (London, 1845); J. H. Overton, *The Life and Opinions of the Rev. William Law* (London, 1881); R. J. Leslie, *Life and Writings of Charles Leslie* (London, 1885); J. H. Overton, *The Nonjurors* (London, 1902); Broxap, *Later Non-Jurors*; Hawkins, *Allegiance*.

[124] Broxap, *Later Non-Jurors*, pp. 1, 218, 226–7.

[125] Every, *High Church Party*, pp. 127–8.

as physically substantial as they were powerful and complex in their argument. They found permanent places in the libraries of universities and colleges, clergymen and gentlemen. George Horne, evidently while an undergraduate in the late 1740s, was led to Nonjuror theology by discovering the 1721 collected edition of Charles Leslie's works on the shelves of the Rev. Sir John Dolben, Bt, Vicar of Finedon, Northants.[126] Even at a much later date, the last English Jacobite theorist, the antiquary Joseph Ritson,[127] was introduced to divine right political ideology when as a young man he walked to Edinburgh in 1774 from his native Newcastle and bought there the works of Thomas Ruddiman,[128] the foremost Scottish Jacobite intellectual of the 1740s, who had served his cause by a long-running polemical battle with Whig opponents in that decade on the not-irrelevant question whether the right to the crown of Scotland had, before the Union, descended by indefeasible hereditary succession. The year 1750 even saw the reprint, in a six-volume collected edition, of Charles Leslie's periodical *The Rehearsal*, that great compendium of arguments against Deists, Whigs and contractarians.

The political application of the Nonjuror case was intensely difficult to make explicit after 1714, and it is not suggested that the Jacobites won a propaganda war. On the contrary, the Whigs won it; but the terms in which the controversy was conducted reflected the shape given to the conflict by the Jacobite challenge. Nonjuror theological and devotional works, however, were under no such ban. They were frequently reprinted[129] in the first half of the century, some into the second half, and some reissued at the time of the Oxford movement; it was not least via their theological works that the

---

[126] William Jones, 'Memoirs of the Life and Writings of Dr Horne', in *The Works of the Right Reverend George Horne, DD*, 2nd edn (6 vols., London, 1818), vol. i, p. 64.

[127] B. H. Bronson, *Joseph Ritson Scholar-at-Arms* (2 vols., Berkeley, California, 1938). In 1778 Ritson published a set of tables of the descent of the English crown, arguing for an indefeasible hereditary title until 1688, when 'the constitution appears to have suffered so violent and total a change, that the very nature of things should seem to have been perverted along with it, and reduced to the original chaos': vol. i, pp. 57ff.

[128] Douglas Duncan, *Thomas Ruddiman. A Study in Scottish Scholarship of the Early Eighteenth Century* (Edinburgh, 1965).

[129] George Hickes, *A Gentleman Instructed in the Conduct of a Virtuous and Happy Life* (1709, 16, 27, 32, 55); Nathaniel Spinckes, *The Sick Man Visited* (1712; 6th edn, 1775); Robert Jenkin, *The Reasonableness and Certainty of the Christian Religion* (1708, 6th edn, 1734); Charles Leslie, theological works (1721, 1832), *A Short and Easie Method with the Deists* (1698; 9th edn, 1745), *A Short and Easie Method with the Jews* (1715, 26, 37, 55, 58), *The Truth of Christianity Demonstrated* (1711; 6th edn, 1726); John Kettlewell, *The Measures of Christian Obedience* (1681; 6th edn, 1714), *An Help and Exhortation to Worthy Communicating* (1683; 10th edn, 1737); Thomas Ken, *The Retired Christian* (8th edn, 1769); William Law, *Three Letters to the Bishop of Bangor* (1st letter, 1717; collection, 10th edn, 1757), *The Case of Reason, or Natural Religion Fairly Stated* (1731; 3rd edn, 1757), *A Demonstration of the Errors...* (1737; 4th edn, 1757), *A Serious Call to a Devout and Holy Life* (1729; 6th edn, 1753, many subsequently); and especially Robert Nelson, *A Companion to the Festivals and Fasts of the Church of England* (1704; at least 28 edns by 1800), which has been called 'a complete popular manual of Anglican theology': Secretan, *Nelson*, p. 167.

Nonjurors' continuing influence was exercised, defending, paradoxically, that Church from which they were separated, both in the grand, set-piece controversies of the age and in devotional practice, adding an important weight to the scale to counterbalance the State in Gibson's Church–Whig alliance. The viability of the late-eighteenth-century confessional regime depended on the intellectual defeat, as contemporaries largely supposed, of the Deists by c. 1750; and in their defeat, the Nonjurors played a large part.

Nevertheless, their political writings, too, remained in the hands of the political classes after 1714, and the issues they so ably formulated remained on the public agenda. A leading characteristic of the political scene from the accession of George I to the 1750s was how little the issues changed; and once the theoretical positions had been worked out, as they had by the end of Anne's reign, the events of the next four decades called rather for their tactical application than for their theoretical re-examination. Controversy took a more practical form, as accepted principles were applied to the record of successive Whig governments; but the idiom changed little. Principled reaffirmations and denials therefore continued, though the moral could seldom be safely drawn on one side. The question of touching for the King's Evil continued to be a subject of controversy, part medical, part political, into the 1750s. A complaint was made in 1747 of the 'continued prevalence' of such beliefs.[130] Forward-looking journals like the *Monthly Review*, founded in 1749, were zealous in sniffing out seditious doctrines. It quickly condemned as 'inflammatory' Zachary Pearce's sermon to the House of Lords on 30th January 1749, and praised a pamphlet attacking it.[131] The Rev. Thomas Fothergill's sermon before the University of Oxford on the same anniversary in 1753 called forth a cautionary anecdote:

> The first and greatest advantage which Mr Fothergil tells us we can propose to ourselves, from the due celebration of this anniversary, with public fasting and humiliation, 'is restoration to the divine favour'; which, it seems, we have lost all title to, on the score of good King Charles's violent death.
>
> At a noted reading coffee-house in the City, where this learned sermon was bought for the use of the subscribers, a certain critic made some exception to this passage, imagining he perceived an error of the press in it, which misrepresented the author's meaning. Persuaded, however, that he had hit upon the true reading, he boldly erased the word *favour*, and wrote FAMILY; which he judged would render the passage more agreeable to the general tenor of the discourse. Whether or not this emendation really expresses the sense of the author better than the word expunged, we shall not pretend to determine; but are informed that many zealous citizens, who,

---

[130] Figgis, *Divine Right*, p. 173.
[131] *A Letter to the Bishop of Bangor, Occasioned by His Lordship's Sermon before the House of Lords, January 30, 1749*, By Phileleutheros Eboracensis (London, 1749). *Monthly Review*, November 1749, p. 36.

like Simeon of old, are waiting for the consolation of Israel, have since devoutly perused the copy so corrected, with great comfort to themselves, and no less admiration of the preacher.[132]

A pamphlet in reply to Fothergill's sermon was duly puffed: 'The author ridicules Mr Fothergill, as a reviver of the exploded doctrine of passive obedience, etc.'[133] When an explicit defence of the hereditary principle in government appeared in 1749,[134] the *Monthly Review* warned its readers of the work's true meaning: 'This author proceeds on the old principles of passive obedience, and non-resistance; and is a fast friend to the House of Stuart.'[135] And when a polemical work justifying Charles I was published in 1758,[136] the *Review* dismissed it with a sneer: 'We shall only observe, that this writer is a champion worthy of the cause he espouses: and that such subjects deserve to live under the government of such kings.'[137]

The possible intellectual foundations of government were no less apparent in the colonies. In 1750 in Boston, Massachusetts, the Congregational Minister Jonathan Mayhew, defiant Arian and proto-revolutionary, preached a sermon on Romans 13:1–8, in which, with 'painstaking care', he

...analysed every Biblical injunction in order to prove that Christian doctrine recommended obedience only to magistrates who were politically 'good' and that resistance to politically 'bad' magistrates could not be considered rebellion by any laws of God or man... The remarkable thing about this unusually long sermon is that Mayhew should have put so much serious thought into tearing down, one by one, the scriptural supports of nonresistance, thereby admitting his awareness of the danger which such doctrines held for contemporary colonial thought.[138]

Mayhew still took seriously the full doctrine of *jure divino* kingship, though he exaggerated the practical danger as part of his campaign to resist the establishment of an Anglican episcopate in the colonies. But when Filmer

---

[132] *The Reasonableness and Uses of Commemorating King Charles's Martyrdom. A Sermon Preached before the University of Oxford, at St Mary's, on Tuesday, Jan 30. 1753.* By Thomas Fothergill (Oxford, 1753). *Monthly Review*, April 1753, pp. 319–20.

[133] *A Letter to the Rev. Thomas Fothergill, MA relating to His Sermon...* (London, 1753). *Monthly Review*, June 1753, p. 471.

[134] *The Divine and Hereditary Right of the English Monarchy, Enquired into and Explained, in and under Several Propositions; Partly Collected from Lord B[olingbroke], and Others; Partly from the Laws of Nature, the Laws of the Land, and the Law of God. By a Gentleman, late of the Temple* (London, 1749).

[135] *Monthly Review*, August 1749, p. 315.

[136] *A Melius Inquirendum into the Character of the Royal Martyr King Charles I* [By John Lindsay] (London, 1758).

[137] *Monthly Review*, May 1758, p. 496.

[138] H. W. Randall, 'The Rise and Fall of a Martyrology: Sermons on Charles I', *HLQ* 10 (1946–7), 164–5. Jonathan Mayhew, *A Discourse Concerning Unlimited Submission and Non-Resistance to the Higher Powers: with Some Reflections on the Resistance Made to King Charles I. And on the Anniversary of His Death: in which the Mysterious Doctrine of that Prince's Saintship and Martyrdom is Unriddled* (Boston, Mass., 1750); C. Rossiter, 'The Life and Mind of Jonathan Mayhew', *WMQ* 3rd ser. 7 (1950), 531–58.

surfaced again in America, in the arguments of the Maryland loyalist the Rev. Jonathan Boucher, this element was missing: Filmer's ideas on the 'sacredness of kings' are called 'extravagant notions', but they were, Boucher said, incidental to the argument: rather,

The leading idea, or principle, of Sir Robert Filmer's Patriarcha is, that government is not of human, but divine origin; and that the government of a family is the basis, or pattern, of all other government. And this principle, notwithstanding Mr Locke's answer, is still (in the opinion of the author of these sermons) unrefuted, and still true.[139]

It is between these two occasions (not in 1688 or 1714) that a profound change must be located if sense is to be made of it.

Contemporary English Whigs, for polemical impact, frequently coupled the doctrines of divine right and passive obedience as the defining conditions of tyrannical personal rule. Jacobite principles have too often been reconstructed from the condemnations of their Whig enemies. This has had the effect of concealing the similarity of the sense in which divine right was claimed for the Whig monarchy, and of portraying Stuart doctrines as excuses for slavery. Whatever the reality of James II's government, in respect of ideals 'passive obedience' was not a more slavish sort of obedience, but a theory of non-obedience to wrongfully used power. Whigs after 1714, having defined their regime as the perfect and indispensable embodiment of English liberties, could demand towards it an obedience which was, paradoxically, more complete than the Stuarts could expect; and with an increasingly effective state machine, could enforce it far more efficiently. There is a sense in which early Hanoverian England was among the most effectively totalitarian of European states at that time, and a parallel sense in which its intellectual hegemony shielded it from that charge with a defence which only Jacobites could pierce.

They could deploy against the Hanoverians both the Whig contractarian case itself, and, more importantly, a religious theory of political obligation. Whigs continued to respond to both, until the 1750s, with a violence which itself offers a gauge of their persuasiveness. For a marked feature of the ideology of indefeasible divine right was its continued ability to appeal both to the intelligentsia and to the young. Voltaire was recruited to write in favour of Prince Charles Edward's rising in 1745 without any sense being generated that he was supporting an anachronistic cause.[140] A Fellow of Oriel, addressing his advice on political propriety to the Oxford under-

---

[139] Quoted in Daly, *Filmer*, p. 169. Boucher emerges as almost an American Burke in M. D. Clark, 'Jonathan Boucher: The Mirror of Reaction', *HLQ* 33 (1969), 19–32; cf. A. Y. Zimmer and A. H. Kelly, 'Jonathan Boucher, Constitutional Conservative', *Journal of American History*, 58 (1972), 897–922.

[140] L. Bongie, 'Voltaire's English, High Treason and a Manifesto for Bonnie Prince Charles', *Studies on Voltaire*, 171 (1977), 7–29; F. J. McLynn, 'Voltaire and the Jacobite Rising of 1745', *ibid.*, 185 (1980), 7–20.

graduate of 1748, assumed him to have adopted the traditional doctrine entire: while considering yourself a patriot and a friend of English liberties, the Whig demanded,

...do you not at the same time consider yourself as the rightful subject and vassall of one whose only claim to your subjection is his being the lineal descendant of a person formerly invested with royal power? – One who has never exercised that which is the only rational foundation of civil power, the giving protection to yourself or your parents; and who can have no right to your service and obedience, unless you were really born in a state of more abject slavery than was ever yet felt in any part of the world, and are at this time the absolute property of a foreign master; because his supposed ancestors at some former time had a dominion over yours; a dominion you think, unalienable and indefeasible, how arbitrarily and oppressively soever they may have behaved?[141]

The following year the same author expressed his incredulity at Jacobite millenarianism: could one really imagine

...that all political evils must necessarily cease upon the introduction of another Royal Family? What mighty charm is likely to operate on this occasion, that will so certainly dispel at once the wickedness and follies of men, and correct the common accidents to which human affairs are liable by the very condition of nature? – As well might we hope (and perhaps some poet will promise so much) that the golden age will once more be restored.[142]

Whigs continued to treat such doctrines as a threat through the 1740s; the idiom broke down only in the following decade.[143]

The 'rage of party', similarly, did not die away in 1714. Party distinctions, on the contrary, permeated every aspect of life. Hearne noted in 1731 that the Royal Society 'sinks every day in its credit both at home and abroad', partly because 'this Society is now as much tinged with party principles as any public body, and Whig and Tory are terms better known than the naturalist, mathematician, or antiquary'.[144] This applied elsewhere in academic life. One Whig argued in 1749 that the rebellion of 1715 was 'entirely occasioned by the wicked principles taught in our universities and schools', and that the same doctrines were still taught there.[145] Some such suspicions had attached to Eton, which flourished under the Head Mastership of High Churchman Andrew Snape (1711–20) – who, like Sherlock, enjoyed the distinction of being struck off the list of chaplains to

---

[141] Edward Bentham, *A Letter to a Young Gentleman of Oxford* (Oxford, 1748), p. 12. Among Bentham's pupils at Oriel may have been Thomas Nowell (see below). If so, this advice was not conspicuously successful.

[142] Edward Bentham, *A Letter to a Fellow of a College* (London, 1749), p. 34.

[143] Its currency at constituency level in 1754 is clear from R. J. Robson, *The Oxfordshire Election of 1754* (Oxford, 1949); its currency in the fiction of the 1740s and 50s, especially Fielding, Smollett and Richardson, is explored in J. T. Boulton, 'Arbitrary Power: An Eighteenth Century Obsession', *Studies in Burke and His Time* 9 (1968), 905–26.

[144] Bliss (ed.), *Reliquiae Hearnianae*, vol. III, p. 71.

[145] *A Blow at the Root*, pp. vi–vii, xv.

George I. Robert Walpole, an Etonian himself, took care to bring the place under his control, and secured the appointment of a politically acceptable Head Master and Provost. At Winchester the rumours were even stronger, the Grand Jury of Hampshire presenting the College on 6th March 1717 for 'their known disaffection and corruption of manners': a purge of senior posts followed in 1724.[146]

As a political language, the dynastic idiom was kept alive not least because of its currency among the educated classes. We lack studies of the intellectual culture of Oxford and Cambridge in the early eighteenth century:[147] but much of the torpor which seems evident in retrospect reflects only the irrelevance of the preoccupations of the late-scholastic mind to subsequent problems. The reading of John Wesley, while an Oxford don in the 1720s and 30s, was very largely concerned with patristic learning and the works of the Caroline divines. Although he was prepared to read authors with whom he profoundly disagreed – Samuel Clarke, William Wollaston, John Locke – his main emphasis was on the Fathers. 'The majority of contemporary works on theology that came his way were by writers in the tradition of the Nonjurors and High Churchmen. His favourite authors in his Oxford period...were men like John Norris, Bishop Bull...Beveridge, Sprat, Atterbury, Sharp, Smalridge, George Hickes, John Kettlewell, Charles Leslie, Richard Fiddes, Robert Nelson, Bishop Ken and John Rogers.' Titles included, in 1725, Hickes' *The Constitution of the Catholic Church and the Nature and Consequences of Schism* (1716) and John Jackson's *The Duty of Subjects towards their Governors* (1723); in 1726–7, works relating to Atterbury's controversy with Hoadly; in 1730, Bishop Berkeley's *Of Passive Obedience* and the High Church Henry Stebbing's tracts against Hoadly; in 1732, John Norris' *The Charge of Schism Continu'd* (1691); in 1733, Kettlewell's *Measures of Christian Obedience*, 6th edn (1714) and William Higden's *A View of the English Constitution, with respect to the Sovereign Authority of the Prince, and the Allegiance of the Subject* (1709).[148]

In Cambridge, a reform of 1731 revived the practice of requiring undergraduates to engage in public disputations during the Lent term. This prompted Thomas Johnson to compile a handbook of suggested questions, with lists of sources *pro* and *con*.[149] Though a Whig fellow of Daniel Waterland's Magdalene, Johnson faithfully listed, for example, anti-

---

[146] H. C. Maxwell Lyte, *A History of Eton College 1440–1875* (London, 1877), pp. 285–94, 303–4; A. F. Leach, *A History of Winchester College* (London, 1899), pp. 370–2. For Westminster, see chapter 2 above.

[147] Though cf. C. Wordsworth, *Scholae Academicae: Some Account of the Studies at the English Universities in the Eighteenth Century* (Cambridge, 1877); R. J. White, *Dr Bentley* (London, 1965); R. T. Holtby, *Daniel Waterland* (Carlisle, 1966); Greenwood, *William King*.

[148] V. H. H. Green, *The Young Mr Wesley* (London, 1961), pp. 28–9, 274–7, 306ff. For Wesley's politics, see chapter 4.

[149] T. Johnson, *Quaestiones Philosophicae In justi Systematis Ordinem Dispositae* (Cambridge, 1732; further edns 1735, 1741).

Lockeian sources arguing for the reality of innate ideas; to the question 'Utrum existat lex naturae?' Hobbes was cited in the negative, and in the affirmative to 'Utrum status naturae sit status belli?' The question 'Utrum omnes homines sint natura aequales?' listed, against, Filmer's *Patriarcha*, Andrew Ramsay's *Essay*[150] and George Harbin's monumental *The Hereditary Right of the Crown of England Asserted* (1713), an answer to Higden's *View*. And to the problem 'Utrum status civilis, vel imperium civile, oriatur ex pactis?'the alternative to Locke and Hoadly was presented as the patriarchalist case of Filmer and Charles Leslie's *On the Origin of Civil Government*.[151] Johnson's Whig bias was plain; but he recognised the existence of an alternative ideology.[152] It was not only the subject of academic disputation: it was imparted to the young through all the machinery of Oxbridge conviviality. Dons mixed easily with undergraduates of sufficient social standing, especially if noblemen or gentleman-commoners, as is recalled by an account of the 'extreamly elegant' dinner party given by the youthful Marquess of Carnarvon in his rooms in Balliol to a group of friends, and Tory dons, of a particular political persuasion.[153]

Conflicting loyalties within the two universities can be amply documented from their political divisions. The bitterness of political warfare at Oxford has even been advanced as a main cause of falling academic standards through its distortion of the appointment of fellows, professors and heads of houses. The struggle for control of both universities was a continuing preoccupation of successive Whig ministries; their achievement was, at most, partial. The foundation of Regius chairs of history at Oxford and Cambridge by George I 'owed much to the almost Fabian illusion of Whig intellectuals that Tory principles could not survive an historical education'.[154] Clearly, however, they did. Fellowships were freeholds. Whig and Tory interests, once entrenched, were formidably difficult to dislodge; and tenure meant a licence to propagate doctrine. Some societies were

---

[150] *An Essay upon Civil Government. Wherein is Set Forth, the Necessity, Origins, Rights, Boundaries and Different Forms of Sovereignty. With Observations on the Ancient Governments of Rome and England: According to the Principles of the Late Archbishop of Cambray* [Fénelon] (London, 1732).

[151] Also cited on similar questions were Jeremy Taylor's *Ductor Dubitantium* (1660 and subsequent edns, inc. 1725) and the published version of Sacheverell's trial. Johnson, *Quaestiones* (2nd edn, pp. 190–6). A marked feature of the lists is the prominence of the European natural law school – Grotius and Pufendorf – compared with the English contractarians – Milton, Sidney, Locke, Tyrrell, Hoadly.

[152] Johnson's undergraduate manual made its way to Cambridge, Massachusetts, and was used into the 1760s as a prompt for Harvard MA disputations: M. Myers, 'A Source for Eighteenth-Century Harvard Masters' Questions', *WMQ* 38 (1981), 261–7. The questions on natural rights themes seem not to have aroused interest there (p. 267). Jonathan Mayhew graduated from Harvard in 1744.

[153] Greenwood, *William King*, p. 23: diary of Erasmus Philipps, 9th April 1721. Dr King was present; so was Henry Fox, later converted to Whiggery.

[154] W. R. Ward, *Georgian Oxford. University Politics in the Eighteenth Century* (Oxford, 1958), p. 132.

divided, like Jesus College, Oxford, which in 1759 had two tutors, one Whig, one Tory. Thomas Jones, arriving as an undergraduate in that year, recorded: 'I was to be entered upon the principles of the Revolution of 1688':[155] others, presumably, were not. Oxford's Chancellor from 1715 was the Duke of Ormonde's successor and brother the Earl of Arran, irremovable until his death in 1758. He 'saw to it that no Whig head of house was nominated as vice-chancellor'.[156] Under the umbrella of freehold, and propagated by patronage, a Jacobite culture survived.[157] 'Towards which of the contending parties in our national disputes the general bias of this place hath been supposed to lie', admitted one don, 'I need not mention.'[158]

It was not an irrelevant observation: even into the 1740s and 50s, almost all the leaders of the Tory party at Westminister and in the country had emerged from the intellectual matrix of legitimist, divine right Oxford. It provided a very obvious, and vulnerable, target. In the Commons on 27th November 1754, William Pitt replied to the claim that there were no Jacobites left in the kingdom by citing the treasonable songs with which a party of carousing undergraduates had, he said, replied to his own party's loyal tune during a visit to the university the previous summer. Prints of the Young Pretender, Pitt said, were openly on sale in the streets of Oxford.[159] This had already been complained of in the pamphlet press: undergraduates, it had been claimed, decorated their rooms with them.[160] Just such a print hung, long unchallenged, in the Bachelors' Common Room of Corpus Christi College in the early 1750s until the London *Evening Advertiser* printed the story on 10th December 1754. The fellows were obliged to publish a careful excuse, but only after the offending object had already been burnt by a Whig undergraduate.[161]

[155] J. N. L. Baker, *Jesus College, Oxford 1571–1971* (Oxford, 1971), p. 43.
[156] V. H. H. Green, *A History of Oxford University* (London, 1974), p. 99.
[157] The Jacobite Duke of Beaufort extended his patronage network by endowing in 1745 an exhibition at Oriel College for sons of 'loyal' families; one of its first holders, in 1747, was Thomas Nowell (see below). Jacobite MP Sir John Philipps founded a similar award at Pembroke College. Jenkins, 'Glamorgan Gentry', vol. 1, p. 279; G. C. Richards and C. L. Shadwell, *The Provosts and Fellows of Oriel College Oxford* (Oxford, 1922), p. 140.
[158] Bentham, *Letter to a Fellow*, p. 59.
[159] Horace Walpole, *Memoirs of the Reign of King George the Second* (London, 1846), vol. 1, p. 413. Pitt was an undergraduate at Trinity, 1726–7, narrowly succeeding Henry Fox, who was at Christ Church 1721–4. Fox stood in his first election as a Tory, flirted with the Cocoa Tree in London, and at that time 'says he dares not commit his politics to paper'. Among Pitt's contemporaries was William Murray (Christ Church, 1723–7), who beat Pitt for a University prize. In the Long Vacation of his second year, Murray, in Paris, sent money and a written promise of loyalty to James III via one of his Secretaries of State, John Hay, Murray's brother-in-law. William's brother James Murray was another of James III's Secretaries. Lord Ilchester, *Henry Fox, First Lord Holland* (London, 1920), vol. 1 p., p. 23; Sedgwick, vol. 1, pp. 283, 285.
[160] Bentham, *Letter to a Fellow*, p. 52.
[161] The BAs who had earlier voted to replace the print after an undergraduate had slashed a previous copy in 1753 were duly punished (one of their tasks was to translate Archbishop Potter's coronation sermon for George II); 'The President also made complaint to the Vice

These incidents, slight in themselves, are evidence for the continued vitality of a certain political culture, and of the intelligibility of an ideology which this symbolism represented. Sometimes it was thinly veiled in a learned language, as with Dr William King's[162] famous invocation at the opening of the Radcliffe Camera in 1749: 'REDEAT nobis Astrea nostra...REDEAT simul magnus ille Genius Britanniae...REDEAT, efficiatque, ut revirescat respublica, revocetur fides, firmetur pax... REDEAT, efficiatque, cum nihil hoc conventu cernere est illustrius... REDEAT, efficiatque, ut in omne aevum alma haec floreat Academia.'[163] Dr King forbade its translation,[164] so leaving the sense ambiguous: the third person singular could be rendered as *it* or *him*. It was left to another to produce the explicitly Jacobite English text: 'Restore and prosper him'.[165] Those present hardly needed it. As Benjamin Kennicott, a Whig don, wrote, King had 'entered a strong caveat against being misunderstood or misrepresented; but 'tis probable most of those who understood his language very readily apprehended his meaning...If these were some of his expressions, 'tis certain they couldn't be understood in many different senses.'[166] Similar views were expressed more bluntly in the words of defiance with which an undergraduate from Dr King's own college had accosted a Whig don during a riot on 23rd February 1748, the birthday of Prince Henry Stuart: 'I am a man, who dare say, God bless K—g James the Third; and tell you, my name is Dawes of St Mary Hall. I am a man of an independent fortune, and therefore afraid of no man.'[167] That this should be such an offensive remark is more significant than any speculation about how many of his contemporaries shared his sentiments, since there is sufficient evidence that a substantial part of the university did.

Such undergraduate outbursts were news in London and taken seriously

Chancellor against the print-shop where this picture was sold, who promised to take all reasonable care that no such prints should for the future be sold there.' Minute Book, Corpus Christi College, Oxford, 11th Dec. 1754. I owe this reference to Dr Philip Pattenden.

[162] William King (1685–1763), Principal of St Mary Hall 1719–d. Engaged in controversy with Edward Bentham and Richard Blacow; delivered pro-Jacobite Latin orations at the ceremonies to confer honorary degrees on Jacobite Tories, the Duke of Hamilton (aet. 18), Lord Lichfield (aet. 26) and Lord Orrery in 1743, and at the installation of the Jacobite Earl of Westmorland as Chancellor of the University in 1759, after the Earl of Arran's death. (The young Jeremy Bentham was taken to Oxford to witness the event.)

[163] *Oratio in Theatro Sheldoniano Habita Idibus Aprilibus, MDCCXLIX. Die dedicationis Bibliothecae Radclivianae* (Oxford, [1749]). Among those present was the young George Horne (see below, chapter 4).

[164] Greenwood, *William King*, pp. 199–200.

[165] *A Translation of a Late Celebrated Oration. Occasioned by a Lible, Entitled, Remarks on Doctor K—g's Speech* (London, 1750).

[166] 'The Opening of the Radcliffe Library in 1749', *Bodleian Quarterly Record* 1 (1914–16), 170. Tory dignitaries and academics were cheered by a crowd of undergraduates as they left the Sheldonian; the Rector of Exeter College, a Whig, was hissed.

[167] Richard Blacow, *A Letter to William King, LLD* (London, 1755), pp. 11ff.

at Whitehall.[168] The government had a vested interest in what was being thought and taught at the only two English universities. Ministerial plans for a politically-inspired 'reform' of both were floated in 1719, and of Oxford in 1749.[169] A similar recalcitrance was expressed electorally. Oxford University continued to return two Tory MPs until the old guidelines were seen to be erased in 1768.[170] At Cambridge the battle was more even. The Nonjurors had been far more numerous there in the 1690s,[171] but the Whig interest was also strong. A Jesus freshman in 1705 complained that his undergraduate contemporaries were 'up to the ears in division about High Church and Low Church, Whig and Tory'.[172] The issues at stake were not only intelligible to them, but entered into their studies. Over their heads was conducted a political struggle for control of six parliamentary seats, two each for county, city and university. One of the county seats fell to the Whigs in 1724, the other in 1727, but the city was solidly Tory until both seats were lost in 1741. The university consistently returned two Tories until its representation fell irreversibly to the Whigs in 1727 through the royal creation of a flood of honorary doctors.[173] But the Tory interest, represented locally by the Cottons of Madingley and (until 1740) the Harleys of Wimpole, was not extinguished.

Within the university, a Tory interest remained. It was strong enough to elect Dr Lambert, Master of the Nonjuror stronghold St John's, to the Vice Chancellorship in 1729 in preference to Mawson, Master of Whig Corpus, and there were further contests in 1733 and 1734. The Duke of Newcastle's hold on the university advanced only slowly. His succession to the Chancellorship after the Duke of Somerset's death in December 1748 was jeopardised by the threatened candidacy of Frederick, Prince of Wales, in alliance with the Tory dons: it reflected an alliance at Westminster provoked not least by the apparent imminence of a ministerial purge of Tory Oxford.[174] Some heads of houses remained unequivocally Tory, like Roger

---

[168] When Dr Purnell, the Vice Chancellor, avoided action, Blacow appealed to the Duke of Newcastle. Three undergraduates – Luxmore and Whitmore of Balliol and Dawes of St Mary Hall – were arrested, taken to London, and tried in the Court of King's Bench in November 1748. Two of them were sentenced to two years' imprisonment.

[169] Sedgwick, vol. 1, pp. 306–7. The 1719 measure was one prong of a campaign involving also the Peerage Bill, and a repeal of the Septennial Act – so making the Westminster Parliament as permanent as its Dublin equivalent. All were abandoned in the face of disquiet in Whig quarters.

[170] Ward, *Georgian Oxford*, p. 236.   [171] Overton, *The Nonjurors*, pp. 186ff.

[172] The University was disturbed at the beginning of his second year when a Mr Tudway was accused by a Dr Plumtree of 'some scandalous and Toriacall reflections on the Queen, was degraded and expelled the University by the Vice Chancellor and the Heads. Most of the Tory or rather Iacobite party blame their proceedings very much as too rigorous upon him but the Whigs say just the contrary': Wordsworth, *Scholae Academicae*, pp. 291, 298.

[173] Sedgwick, vol. 1, pp. 200–1. No such royal prerogative applied at Oxford.

[174] Sedgwick, vol. 1, p. 307; D. A. Winstanley, *The University of Cambridge in the Eighteenth Century* (Cambridge, 1922), pp. 38–47. George II intervened to forbid the Prince of Wales to stand.

Long, Master of Pembroke 1733–70. Others, without necessarily discarding their attitudes, adapted themselves to the Whig regime. The Jacobite antiquary William Cole wrote of Sir Thomas Gooch, Master of Caius 1716–54, that

Dr Gooch and Dr Conyers Middleton had been great friends, were both of a party, and both changed it: yet it is my real belief that both their hearts were with their old friends…They had made an opposition till they saw the utter impossibility of doing any good by it, and seeing that the full tide and stream of preferment was against them, they did wisely swim with the stream.[175]

In the case of Gooch, who evidently abandoned the Tory cause at the 1727 election, the decision was rewarded by the bishoprics of Bristol (1737), Norwich (1738) and Ely (1748). He was not alone: his brother-in-law Bishop Sherlock, suspected of Jacobitism as Master of St Catharine's Hall after 1714 and like Gooch deprived of his royal chaplaincy under George I, left Gooch's son £150,000 at his death in 1761.[176]

By the 1760s, this polarised world had passed away. When Hardwicke died in 1763, the contest for his place of High Steward (recognised as heir-apparent to the Chancellorship) was fought as an internal battle between Whigs.[177] The old world left few survivals in the new. Its echo may be caught in the senior dining club in the university, largely confined to heads of houses, significantly named The Family.[178] The reference, of course, is to one family in particular:

> God Bliss the Prince of Wales
> The true-born Prince of Wales
> Sent us by thee
> Grant us one favour more
> The King for to restore
> As Thou hast done before
> *The Familie*[179]

– an appropriate reminder of the patriarchal ideal. Nor is the echo of the National Anthem coincidental. Thomas Arne, who gave the anthem its immense currency when he arranged it as a Hanoverian patriotic song for

---

[175] Quoted in John Venn, *Biographical History of Gonville and Caius College* (Cambridge, 1901), vol. III, p. 117. I owe this reference to Professor Christopher Brooke.
[176] *Ibid.*, pp. 115ff.
[177] Winstanley, *Cambridge*, pp. 55–138.
[178] S. C. Roberts, *The Family* (Cambridge, 1963). The society is careful to toast 'The Family' only after the servants have left the room. Whether that ancient undergraduate dining club, the True Blue, has a similar Jacobite origin is not clear. For a song of that title, dated 1737, cf. Milton Percival (ed.), *Political Ballads illustrating the Administration of Sir Robert Walpole* (Oxford, 1916), p. 107; for a Jacobite addition, Thomas, 'Jacobitism in Wales', pp. 289–90; cf. J. Hogg, *The Jacobite Relics of Scotland* (2 vols., Edinburgh, 1819), vol. I, p. 148; for the the song inscribed on a Jacobite drinking glass of c. 1750, J. Bles, *Rare English Glasses of the XVII & XVIII Centuries* (London, 1924), p. 128.
[179] Roberts, *The Family*, p. 3.

the London stage in September 1745, believed 'that it was a received opinion that it was written for the Catholic Chapel of James II'.[180]

An important genre in which such sentiments could be expressed was the tradition of State sermons preached on 5th November; on Restoration Day, 29th May; and, especially, on the anniversary of Charles I's execution, 30th January. It was a genre legitimated, and indeed required, by specific provision: not until 1859 were the forms for the three services removed from the Book of Common Prayer.[181] Hanoverian sovereigns, until 1760, affirmed their rightful place in monarchial genealogy by observing the anniversary of Charles I's martyrdom. Even George II regularly attended church on that day, in mourning; and people attended court in mourning. This ceased with George III, despite his piety: the dynasty was secure.[182]

By convention, preachers on these occasions addressed the sovereign, at the Chapel Royal; the House of Lords in Westminster Abbey and the House of Commons in St Margaret's, if Parliament was sitting; the Lord Mayor, Corporation and citizens of London in St Paul's; the two universities; both Houses of Convocation, if sitting; town corporations throughout the country; and every parish church saw a small-scale version of these great displays. By command of the Lords and Commons, their preachers' sermons were regularly published, as were others', and reached a wide audience. They were occasions for the regular and solemn reiteration of traditional doctrine on traditional themes. Even by c. 1670–88, State sermons had become vehicles for political instruction, the occasions when, above all, *jure divino* doctrines were worked out, and warnings given against the seditious theories of 'such men as Knox, Buchanan, Fenner, Cartwright, Goodman, Milton, Baxter and Calamy' rather than emotional eulogies of Charles I himself. In this cooler idiom, the sermons continued throughout the eighteenth century to be important occasions for the restatement of the thesis of the divine institution of government and the sacred quality of authority,

---

[180] W. H. Cummins, *God Save the King. The Origin and History of the Music and Words of the National Anthem* (London, 1902), p. 35. Alternative texts of the Jacobite version are printed in Hogg, *Jacobite Relics*, vol. II, pp. 50–2; cf. Bles, *English Glasses*, p. 91; Francis, *Old English Drinking Glasses*, p. 167. It had also circulated, to different words, as a Hanoverian drinking song: Hogg, *op. cit.*, vol. II, p. 466.

[181] The forms of service for 5th November, 30th January and 29th May are printed in W. Keeling, *Liturgiae Britannicae, or the Several Editions of the Book of Common Prayer... Arranged to Show Their Respective Variations* (London, 1842). Unfortunately Keeling does not include the 'service of healing'. Mid-nineteenth-century clergy could be profoundly disturbed by the implications of touching for the King's Evil, and felt obliged to disown it: 'the Church is in no way responsible for the service in question, or for the practice. Though printed with the Book of Common Prayer, yet the form was of no authority whatever': T. Lathbury, *A History of the Convocation of the Church of England*, 2nd edn (London, 1853), p. 439. But however embarrassing for the Victorians, the wholehearted involvement of the seventeenth- and early-eighteenth-century Church is not in question.

[182] A. Francis Steuart (ed.), *The Last Journals of Horace Walpole during the Reign of George III* (London, 1910), vol. I, p. 40.

and one important means by which kingship was still hedged with the aura of divinity.[183]

The occasion was made use of by all *de facto* sovereigns. As John Sharp hardly needed to remind the Lords in 1700: 'You all know what kind of argument this day calls for: for by the design of keeping it, the business that the preacher hath to do, is to press obedience and subjection to the government we live under, and to preach against faction and rebellion.' Did this not mean siding with a party? Sharp was ready with a denial: it was factious only to seek to overturn the established government. The clergyman 'sets himself against all parties: And so he ought to do; for his business is, to be on the side of the government as it is by law established'. The Archbishop set out the doctrine of Christian allegiance as he understood it:

And this is that doctrine of passive obedience which of late hath had so ill a sound among many of us: But I dare say, for no other reason, but because it may have been by some misrepresented: For wherever it is rightly understood, it can give offence to none, but to such as are really disaffected to the government, and do desire alterations.

Romans 13:1–2 defended William III: 'so long as this text stands in our Bibles, the doctrine of non-resistance, or passive obedience, must be of obligation to all Christians'.[184] Jacobites were naturally indignant at this flagrant and shameless misapplication, as they saw it, of traditional teaching. They had a remedy, however. Denunciations of rebellion to lawful monarchs might be made in such a way, without naming names, as to make it clear that it was not William III or George I who was being defended. Political sermons on 30th January consequently continued to be occasions for controversy long into the century.

The Tory the Rev. Luke Milbourne made a particular use of his preaching on that occasion in the City church of St Ethelburga, and published them both year by year, and in a collected edition as *The Royal Martyr Lamented* in 1720. The London Congregationalist minister Thomas Bradbury made a similar use of State sermons on the other side. Dr Sacheverell's sermon on 30th January 1715 was inconveniently taken down in shorthand and published by an enemy, further to discredit him. In 1730, John Taylor's 31st January sermon before the University of Cambridge caught the attention of the Nonjuror John Byrom: 'as for the matter it was said to be Tory', he noted.[185] John Wesley similarly recognised Dr Owen's sermon before Oxford University in 1726 and Dr George Coningsby's in 1727: the

---

[183] Randall, 'Sermons on Charles I', pp. 136, 147–52, 154–8, B. S. Stewart, 'The Cult of the Royal Martyr', *Church History* 38 (1969), 175–87.

[184] John Sharp, Archbishop of York, 'The Duty of Subjection to the Higher Powers. Preach'd...the 30th of January, 1699/1700', in *The Works of the Most Reverend Dr John Sharp* (7 vols., London, 1749), vol. ii, pp. 42–3, 50, 59–60.

[185] Byrom, *Journal*, vol. i, part 2, p. 420.

latter, Hearne also saw as a direct attack on George II and the Revolution.[186] If Tories were heartened by such sentiments, Whig radicals were incensed. One, in 1750, used the arguments of 1720s anticlericalism to denounce this whole genre of sermons, citing *The Independent Whig*.[187] George Coade, a merchant at Exeter, was provoked to a similar review of the English constitution. Evidently a Dissenter, he defended his coreligionists: 'Upon their principles, Sir, stands the parliamentary succession of the Crown of these realms, in the present reigning family.' But the case against which he argued so bitterly was the full 'doctrine of passive obedience, the absolute, indefeasible, and hereditary right of succession to he crown'. He coupled his rejection of a traditional polity with a repudiation of transubstantiation, the Athanasian creed, 'and many other things I could mention' as 'truly mysterious and unintelligible'. His partisanship was plain: the tract was dedicated to Hoadly.[188] Many published sermons provoked heated politico-theological controversy throughout the reigns of the first two Georges;[189] the furore caused by Dr Nowell's sermon before the Commons on 30th January 1772 was an echo of strife which had only recently died away.

Nevertheless, the sermons continued; the American and French revolutions reinvigorated them, as pronouncements against insurrection and declarations of the specifically Christian character of political obligation. Dynastic doctrines themselves remained highly sensitive until the 1750s. In 1747 the Jacobite historian Thomas Carte published the first volume of his *History of England*, dedicated to the Duke of Beaufort and other patrons, Oxford colleges and City Companies. Lord Egmont had earlier anticipated that 'there is reason to believe that his history will be wrote to support the doctrine of indefeasible hereditary right, in order to serve the Pretender'.[190] The first volume caught the public's attention by recording as fact a successful case of touching for the King's Evil in 1716, performed, it was implied, by James III at Avignon.

---

[186] Green, *Wesley*, p. 79; Hearne, *Collectanea*, vol. ix, pp. 263–8.

[187] *A Discourse on Government and Religion, Calculated for the Meridian of the Thirtieth of January. By an Indépendent.* (London, [1750]).

[188] George Coade, *A Letter to a Clergyman, Relating to His Sermon on the 30th of January: Being a Compleat Answer to All the Sermons that Ever Have Been, or Ever Shall Be, Preached, in the Like Strain, on that Anniversary* (London, 1746; 3rd edn, Belfast, 1747), pp. 50–1, 59.

[189] A list of State sermons 1714–60 which provoked hostile exchanges includes Dr Bentley's before the University of Cambridge, 1715; Dr Andrew Snape's, before the Commons, 1717; William Bradshaw, Bishop of Bristol's, before the Lords, Samuel Croxall's before the Commons, and Dr Joseph Trapp's and Dr Middleton's before the Lord Mayor, 1730; Francis Hare, Bishop of Chichester's, before the Lords, 1732; Dr Berryman's and Mr Chamres', before the Lord Mayor, 1733; Nathaniel Collier's, before the Commons, 1743; Zachary Pearce, Bishop of Bangor's, before the Lords, 1749; Dr Thomas Pickering's, before the Lord Mayor, 1750; Thomas Fothergill's, before the University of Oxford, 1753.

[190] Historical Manuscripts Commission *Egmont Diary*, vol. iii, p. 312 (18th Jan. 1745/6). Egmont had been importuned into promising to subscribe, but now excused himself from doing so.

It is upon this rite of unction, used in the coronation of our kings, that our common lawyers have founded their notion of a king's being a *persona mixta*, as if he was half a spiritual and half a temporal person; though the same might be as well said of every Christian baptised or confirmed according to the Roman ritual, which prescribes unction in those offices. It is upon this precarious footing, that some of them have injudiciously put the jurisication of the crown in ecclesiastical matters; though it be an incident to royalty, and inherently vested in all sovereigns, who have not made a cession of their prerogative in that respect. It is to this unction likewise, Sir John Fortescue and others ascribe the gift of healing the scrophulous humour called the *king's evil*, exercised by some European princes, anointed at their coronations, and succeeding lineally to their crowns by proximity of blood, hath been generally attributed. But whatever is to be said in favour of its being appropriated to the eldest descendant of the first branch of the royal line of the kings of France and England etc., I have myself seen a very remarkable instance of such a case, which could not possibly be ascribed to the regal unction.[191]

The outcry was immediate: such an event, if true, must be a divine refutation of Hanoverian legitimacy. Carte defended himself in the press obliquely, claiming that he had only reported the opinions of others, that many doctors had written in defence of the healing power, and that he included the case 'to show it was erroneously ascribed to the unction', that is, that it had taken place before the monarch in question had been crowned and anointed.[192] But this could be interpreted as making the claim in an even stronger form; and the Corporation of London was obliged to cancel its subsidy to Carte's project.[193] The wording had been ambiguous. As Carte explained himself, 'the person touching is not named, and what is said of him agrees to more than one person'. Louis XV of France, born in 1710, was not crowned until 1722; James III was never crowned.

How convincing was the Hanoverians' title? *De facto*, their regime was impregnable after 1745; *de jure*, a doubt remained even in their own minds. In 1828 John Wilson Croker recorded an anecdote of George III's daughter Princess Augusta (1768–1840): that she 'said lately to a private friend, "I was ashamed to hear myself called Princess Augusta, and never could persuade myself that I was so, as long as any of the Stuart family were alive; but after the death of Cardinal York [in 1807], I felt myself to be really Princess Augusta."'[194]

IV. ALLEGIANCE, RELIGION AND THE FOLK CULTURE

Sensible Whigs were indignant that charismatic Stuart monarchy retained so much of its fascination: 'These enthusiasts will talk with great seriousness

[191] T. Carte, *A General History of England*, vol. 1 (London, 1747), p. 291.
[192] The controversy in the *General Evening Post* which followed Carte's first volume can be followed in Whiston, *Memoirs*, pp. 432ff and Nichols, *Literary Anecdotes*, vol. 11, pp. 495ff.
[193] It later restored it: *ex inf.* Dr Eveline Cruickshanks.
[194] L. J. Jennings (ed.), *The Croker Papers. The Correspondence and Diaries of the Late Right Honourable John Wilson Croker*, 2nd edn (London, 1885), vol. 1, p. 406.

too, of something they call dignity of aspect, and majesty of presence, that shows the birth of a prince, and bespeaks his divine title to sway a sceptre.' There was a rational explanation, Whigs insisted:

Nothing one would think, were more easy than to suppose that the port and demeanour of majesty, said to be so striking in what they call natural-born princes, has only been the effect of fancies constantly infused into them from their earliest education; and their being perpetually buoyed up by their flattering attendants, with the senseless notions of the royal blood that flows in their veins, and of those rights to dominion which nothing can bereave them of: for thus an impression of some natural superiority over the rest of mankind, grows apace in their minds, whence an air of grandeur and loftiness comes of course to be insensibly assumed; which to that fond wonder at things uncommon (a kind of native superstition in the minds of men) inflamed as it is by the artifice of priests, may easily be supposed to take that appearance of a greatness and majesty, which is at once presumed the divine signature of indelible royalty.[195]

Credible or not, such an explanation was found necessary in the 1740s. The third aspect of the divine right of kings is the way in which it survived, embedded in the popular consciousness, in that great grey area where folklore and popular religion joined. The State festivals of 5th November and 29th May (though not, of course, the fast of 30th January) were widely celebrated and struck deep roots.[196] But the practice of touching for the King's Evil was the crucial index of the persistence of a non-secular image of monarchy. It was important not only as the most extreme claim which could be made for a political institution, but also because of its very great frequency under the Stuarts and its continued resonance in popular custom.

Not only the memories survived but in many cases the individuals also. In 1728 the Jacobite intellectual Thomas Hearne met a man who had been touched, and, as he supposed, cured by Charles II as long ago as 1660; he 'hath constantly wore the piece of gold about his neck that he received of the King, and he had it on yesterday when I met him', wrote Hearne.[197] Between the Restoration and his death, Charles II exercised his thauma-turgical powers on between 105,000 and 106,000 of his subjects at a cost of £49,000 in gold 'touch pieces' alone:[198] it was a significant item of royal expenditure. It seems likely that *most* of the humble folk who met Charles II did so in this most moving context of the monarchy's semi-magical claims. In view of the numbers involved, it is both understandable and important that although William III and George I refused to touch, they were asked to do so. It cannot have been immediately apparent to all that a break in the succession had occurred of a kind which altered the essential nature of

[195] *The Spirit and Principles of the Whigs and Jacobites Compared* (London, 1746), pp. 32–4.
[196] T. F. Thiselton Dyer, *British Popular Customs* (London, 1876), pp. 301–7, 410–15.
[197] Bliss (ed.), *Reliquiae Hearnianae*, vol. III, p. 12.
[198] H. Farquhar, 'Royal Charities', *The British Numismatic Journal* 13 (1917), 133.

kingship, and which deprived sovereigns of the aptly-so-named *Charisma Basilicon*.[199] One early historian recorded:

We have been informed, by an ancient nonjurant still alive, that a gentleman of England having applied to King George the First, soon after his accession, to have his son touched, and being peevishly desired to go over to the Pretender, actually obeyed the command, and was so well pleased with the result of the experiment, that he became and continued ever after a firm believer in the *jus divinum*, and a staunch friend of the exiled family.[200]

Chesterfield believed that

The idle story of the Pretender's having been introduced in a warming-pan into the Queen's bed, though as destitute of all probability as of all foundation, has been much more prejudicial to the cause of Jacobitism than all that Mr Locke and others have written to show the unreasonableness and absurdity of the doctrines of indefeasible hereditary right and unlimited passive obedience.[201]

The 'warming pan myth' was an absurd fiction;[202] but it was one which people, including Queen Anne, were driven to entertain as the best way of countering James III's overwhelmingly strong claim to the throne.

At most, this tactic could only insinuate a doubt. Although, at the time of the Sacheverell trial, a few Whigs were willing to dispense with the myth in order to emphasise what they claimed was the parliamentary title of sovereigns,[203] William, and the Hanoverians, were compelled to some extent to fight the Stuarts on their own ground, the doctrine of *jure divino* monarchy with all that it implied. They fought there at a major disadvantage. It seems that William III, George I and George II preferred to avoid explicit public disavowals of the divine gift of healing, however sceptical they might be personally.[204] The forms of service for that ceremony continued to be included, unused though not proscribed, in some editions of the Prayer Book even after 1714 – in some English editions until 1732, in a Latin edition until 1759.[205] Both French and English monarchies traced the gift to the same

[199] The title of a tract by the King's surgeon John Browne (London, 1684).
[200] R. Chambers, *History of the Rebellion in Scotland in 1745, 1746* (2 vols., Edinburgh, 1828), vol. I, p. 183. The story cannot be checked; but that it should have been current is in itself indicative. It is claimed that 'a few Welshmen were still resorting to Rome to be cured of the King's Evil by the royal touch, as late as 1737': Jenkins, 'Glamorgan Gentry', vol. I, p. 251.
[201] Chesterfield to Philip Stanhope, 7th Feb. 1749: B. Dobrée (ed.), *The Letters of Philip Dormer Stanhope, 4th Earl of Chesterfield* (London, 1932), vol. IV, p. 1304. But earlier in the decade, Chesterfield had been playing a double game, maintaining his links with the Stuart court: Cruickshanks, *Political Untouchables*, pp. 27–8, 45, 47, 74, 95.
[202] For the political significance of the 'Protestant plot to discredit the birth', cf. Gregg, *Queen Anne*, pp. 52–8, 62–3.
[203] Gregg, *Queen Anne*, p. 297.
[204] William III's refusal to touch inconveniently became news in the *Gazette de France*: M. Bloch, *The Royal Touch. Sacred Monarchy and Scrofula in England and France* (1923; trans. London, 1973), p. 119.
[205] H. Farquhar, 'Royal Charities', *The British Numismatic Journal* 15 (1918–20), 154–5.

source, King Edward the Confessor; and the Church of England had been
heavily involved in endorsing the claim and the practice. Even James II
had been willing to exercise the prerogative of healing in association with
Anglican clergy, at least at the beginning of his reign.[206] William Whiston,
Newton's successor as Lucasian professor of mathematics at Cambridge, was
strangely uncertain whether William, Mary or the first two Georges had
exercised that gift or not; 'while yet I suppose they might have done it with
the like success as our former kings', that is, no success at all. The Arian
Whiston was a sceptic, but still found it necessary to argue that even if the
gift were genuine, there was nothing in scripture to prove the title of its
owner to a throne.[207] But this was an unusual position: for most people, the
inference of a just title was easy and obvious.

Debate was therefore about the efficacy of the thaumaturgical power, not
its political significance. Many claims of its successful exercise were published
in Anne's reign by members of the medical profession.[208] The gold 'touch
pieces' distributed at the services continued to be handed down among the
people,[209] with supposedly magical properties in curing illness. As late as
1838, in the Shetlands, even ordinary coins bearing Charles I's head were
used as medical remedies.[210] It seems that this is one instance where the
'Established Church and its rites... seem to have had a practical power and
utility even for those who could not or would not subscribe to its formal
creed.'[211] Though the subject of English popular religion at this period needs
more study,[212] it seems that 'the English labouring people perceived
themselves and their environment within the framework of a pre-scientific
culture... The vision of reality that was commonly held posited the
existence of a material reality and a spiritual (or supernatural) reality, and

[206] Bloch, *Royal Touch*, p. 220.

[207] Whiston, *Memoirs*, pp. 442–3. He later added: 'N.B. I have been very lately informed, that
King William was prevailed upon once to touch for the King's Evil: *Praying to God to heal
the patient, and grant him more wisdom at the same time*; which implied he had no great faith
in the operation. Yet was the patient cured notwithstanding' (p. 653). This is to be read
as a claim that the sufferer recovered for other reasons, not that the royal gift was effective
independent of its owner's belief in it. Macaulay (*Works*, vol. IV, p. 247) misunderstood.

[208] Raymond Crawfurd, *The King's Evil* (Oxford, 1911), p. 145.

[209] *Ibid.*, p. 153.

[210] M. R. Toynbee, 'Charles I and the King's Evil', *Folk-Lore* 61 (1950), 1–14. A similar and
widespread belief attached to silver given in the offertory at Holy Communion: cf.
J. E. Vaux, *Church Folk Lore*, 2nd edn (London, 1902), pp. 394–5, giving an example of
such a belief by a Primitive Methodist.

[211] A. Smith, *The Established Church and Popular Religion 1750–1850* (London, 1971), p. 21.

[212] For the continent cf. Owen Chadwick, *The Popes and European Revolution* (Oxford, 1981),
pp. 3–95; O. H. Hufton, *Europe: Privilege and Protest 1730–1789* (Brighton, 1980), p. 187:

> ...everything we know about popular religion in the eighteenth century, anywhere in
> Europe, underscores its total revulsion from anything savouring of the Jansenist ethic.
> Vivid, immediate, semi-pagan, the religion of the masses wallowed in the accretions of
> baroque images, fête days, processions and cared nothing for better instruction, more
> exigent morality and a religion pared down to its purest essentials.

the latter was assumed to have a large and continuous impact on the operation of the former.'[213]

The supernatural attributes of seventeenth-century kingship found credence within a world view which gave countenance, also, to the possibility of similar interventions of the Deity to effect miraculous cures at the hands of Christian laity. The *cause célèbre* of the 1660s was provided by Valentine Greatrakes (1628–83), the Irish Protestant squire whose thaumaturgical cures, even of sufferers whom Charles II had touched for the King's Evil in vain, provoked controversy and deep interest among English churchmen and scientists.[214] Such beliefs did not come to an end with the departure of the Stuart dynasty. The mass credulity which had met Greatrakes both in Ireland and England was repeated in 1748–9 in the case of Bridget Bostock, a domestic servant of about sixty-four years of age and a pious Anglican, who drew crowds to her Cheshire cottage by acts of healing through a form of touching and prayer which, as before, echoed the royal ceremony. The interest of John Byrom, the Nonjuror and Jacobite, was aroused.[215] From Brecknockshire, Sir John Price, Bt, of Buckland, presumably informed by the *Gentleman's Magazine*, even wrote to ask Bridget Bostock to exert her powers and raise his late wife from the dead.[216] The decisive shift in attitudes in relation to science and its claims against religion, or what Professor MacDonald has called 'therapeutic eclecticism', evidently came not in the decade following 1688 but between about 1740 and 1750.[217]

Doctrines of divine right, whether indefeasible or providential, thus appealed quite appositely both to such a nexus of beliefs, and to 'the people's desire to lead quiet, safe lives in timeless resignation to the ways of kings and courts'.[218] Too little weight is often given to the immense continuity, the vast inertia, of popular and rural sentiment, especially in the case of England. Not least has this reflected the polemical denigration, within the 'Whig interpretation', of the Church as somehow at once both somnolent or ineffectual, and the advance guard of modern rationalism. Studies at parish level might offer a corrective; one of them, at least, has argued that far from being 'feeble, inert and corrupt', the Church was 'intimately involved in the life of the people'.[219] France has been better served; we now

[213] R. W. Malcolmson, *Life and Labour in England 1700–1800* (London, 1981), p. 83. It may be suggested that Dr Thomas's choice of c. 1700 as a terminal date for his widely-acclaimed study *Religion and the Decline of Magic* indicates more the drying up of certain of his chosen sources (p. ix) than the arrival of 'modern man'; there is room for further research on the persistence into the eighteenth century of many of the beliefs and attitudes he describes.

[214] Eamon Duffy, 'Valentine Greatrakes, the Irish Stroker: Miracle, Science and Orthodoxy in Restoration England', in K. Robbins (ed.), *Studies in Church History* 17 (1981), 251–73.

[215] Byrom, *Journal*, vol II, part 2, pp. 459ff. Byrom drew a parallel with Greatrakes.

[216] Press reports on the case are reprinted in W. H. Chaloner (ed.), *Bridget Bostock* (Crewe, [1948]).

[217] Cf. Lester S. King, *The Philosophy of Medicine. The Early Eighteenth Century* (Cambridge, Mass., 1978), p. vii.   [218] Straka, 'Final Phase of Divine Right Theory', p. 649.

[219] A. Warne, *Church and Society in Eighteenth-Century Devon* (Newton Abbot, 1969), p. 9.

See historiography notes ↓

know how shallowly the Enlightenment penetrated, leaving untouched a scarcely-changing popular culture with its own cheap literature of almanacs and chap-books: legends, lives of the saints, popular devotion or folk tales, which were capable of embracing the 'aristocratic ideal' but which were not expressive of the least critical sophistication or secular scepticism in political outlook.[220]

In England, John Clare described the reading matter of a typical cottage at the end of the century as consisting of a Bible, an almanac, *The Whole Duty of Man*, and a few chapbooks.[221] His subjective impression was confirmed by a survey conducted by the Central Society of Education in 5 Norfolk parishes, published in 1839. Only 6 out of 66 families were without books; 'In three of the remaining sixty there was only a hymn book; the rest were provided with Bible, Testament and Prayer-Book, generally with two and sometimes with all three; but there does not appear to have been any other description of book in any one of the cottages.'[222] Similar results emerged from surveys at that period in Kent, Essex and Herefordshire:

There might be a few chap-books, the odd volume of travel and exploration, a few old newspapers and journals, but on the whole secular works were comparatively rare. Instead the tiny libraries were largely composed of works connected with the Protestant religion. There would normally be a Bible and perhaps a Prayer Book, a haphazard collection of religious commentaries and sometimes one of the classic works of religious imagination, particularly *Pilgrim's Progress* and *Paradise Lost*.[223]

The situation had changed little since the eighteenth century.

In both France and England, new developments served mainly, at first, to widen the gap 'between the educated classes and the lower strata of the rural population',[224] rather than to 'modernise' the attitudes of the mass of the people. The symbolism of kingship in France, despite the greater renown there of the Enlightenment, recognised this continuity;[225] the rationales for absolute monarchy worked out under Louis XIV remained in force. The coronation of Louis XVI in 1775 was an event of great popular emotional significance, and slight changes in the ceremony were the subject of constitutional controversy.[226] That monarch made only a gesture to

---

[220] R. Mandrou, *De la culture populaire au XVIIᵉ et XVIIIᵉ siècles* (Paris, 1964), esp. pp. 146–63. For England, cf. J. Ashton, *Chap Books of the Eighteenth Century* (London, 1882); V. E. Neuburg, *Chapbooks. A Bibliography* (London, 1964); B. S. Capp, *Astrology and the Popular Press: English Almanacs 1500–1800* (London, 1979).

[221] V. E. Neuberg, *Popular Education in Eighteenth Century England* (London, 1971), p. 94.

[222] Quoted in David Vincent, *Bread, Knowledge and Freedom. A Study of Nineteenth-Century Working Class Autobiography* (London, 1981), p. 110.

[223] *Ibid.*, p. 110.

[224] Thomas, *Religion and the Decline of Magic*, p. 666; cf. H. Chisick, *The Limits of Reform in the Enlightenment* (Princeton, 1981).

[225] For an anthropological study of monarchy, and the deep roots of its semi-magical attributes, cf. A. M. Hocart, *Kingship* (London, 1927).

[226] K. M. Baker, 'French Political Thought at the Accession of Louis XVI', *JMH* 50 (1978), 279–303.

Enlightened opinion in altering the formula, in touching for the Evil, from *Dieu te guérit* to the conditional *Dieu te guérisse.*[227] There was undoubtedly a growing scepticism among French intellectuals about the high doctrine of kingship. As with all changes of mood among small groups, it may have been relatively sudden, and that acute observer Chesterfield may have been correct in sensing, in the early 1750s, that the 'change of the temper and genius of the French people with regard to their government is astonishing'; 'I foresee, that before the end of this century, the trade of both king and priest will not be half so good a one as it has been.'[228] But we must not ante-date this change, difficult though it is to date a change in mood, nor exaggerate the depth of its penetration into French society. Even after the French Revolution, the monarchical ideal was still considered important, if only as a shibboleth; as part of the affirmation of his just title, Charles X touched for the evil at his coronation in 1824.[229] Here as elsewhere, the example and the practice of the most prestigious monarchy in Europe gave a credibility to these ideologies which no arguments alone could have done.

Historians of nineteenth-century England have sometimes written as if a dramatic personal monarchy, projected to a mass public with a skilful use of symbolism and ceremonial, was a Victorian invention. Yet no English monarch from Charles II to George IV – whose coronation cost a staggering £238,238 – neglected to state his case in rituals which carried a heavy religious and political charge, and, at least until the mid-eighteenth century, in a world where 'all phenomena are understood as transparent to some spiritual or historical analogue'.[230] The violent thunderstorm at the end of Charles II's coronation was the subject of much anxious speculation. The mishaps and ominous portents at James II's coronation were, even much later, discussed by the Nonjuror Dr George Hickes: 'I put no great stress upon these omens, but I cannot despise them; most of them, I believe, come by chance, but some from superior intellectual agents, especially those which regard the fate of kings and nations.'[231] If the occasional mishap had significance for opponents, a successful spectacle and public ritual were even more the occasion for the regime's self-affirmation: not merely a personal apotheosis, but a demonstration of the monarchy's roots in religion, aristocracy, and (a factor here synthesised inextricably with the others)

---

[227] It is not even certain that he did so. For a suggestion that Louis XIV also used the conditional form cf. Nichols, *Literary Anecdotes*, vol. II, p. 499.

[228] Cf. Chesterfield to Huntington, 25th Nov. 1751, and to Philip Stanhope, 13th April 1752: Dobrée (ed.), *Letters of Chesterfield*, vol. V, 1793, 1857.

[229] Crawfurd, *King's Evil*, pp. 159–60.

[230] G. Reedy, 'Mystical Politics: the Imagery of Charles II's Coronation', in P. J. Korshin (ed.), *Studies in Change and Revolution. Aspects of English Intellectual History 1640–1800* (London, 1972), p. 20.

[231] Dr Hickes to Dr Charlett, 23rd Jan. 1710/11: W. Jones, *Crowns & Coronations: A History of Regalia* (London, 1883), p. 317. At George III's coronation, the largest diamond fell from his crown: an ominous warning (p. 322).

popular acclamation. The literature of coronations and of the monarchy's self-projection in the eighteenth century has only begun to be studied.[232] But it was extensive, and its form implies a belief that not only the formal, constitutional and contractual elements of the occasion, but also the symbolic and religious, were attended to in the political nation at large.[233]

How far did this awareness extend beyond the politically literate? Much more research is needed before we can answer that question, if it can ever be answered, and before we can gauge or date the politico-religious effects of any process of secularisation in popular and rural mentalities. On a local level, regional culture did change in eighteenth-century England under the impact of growing wealth and better communications. One bookseller, writing in 1792, placed the change firmly at the end of the period:

...the sale of books in general has increased prodigously within the last twenty years... The poorer sort of farmers, and even the poor country people in general, who before the period spent their winter evenings in relating stories of witches, ghosts, hobgoblins, &c, now shorten the winter nights by hearing their sons and daughters read tales, romances, &c, and on entering their houses, you may see Tom Jones, Roderic Random, and other entertaining books stuck up on their bacon racks.[234]

Statistical surveys show the danger of relying on such subjective impressions without careful qualification.

In taking 'educated opinion' as a yardstick, we must remember that it was neither widely prevalent, nor necessarily similar to opinion of other

---

[232] Cf. also G. S. Rousseau, '"This Grand and Sacred Solemnity": Of Coronations, Republics and Poetry', *BJECS* 5 (1982), 1–19.

[233] Royal houses were matters of interest, e.g. Henry Rimius, *Memoirs of the House of Brunswick* (London, 1750); *Successions and Characters of the Kings... Who Have Reigned since the Christian Era* (London, 1751); ceremonies were regularly and fully reported, e.g.: *An Exact Account of the Form and Ceremony of His Majesty's Coronation* (London, 1714); *The Whole Ceremony of the Coronation of... King George* (Dublin, 1715); *An Account of the Ceremonies Observed at the Coronation of the Kings and Queens of England* (London, [1727]); *The Form of the Proceeding to the Royal Coronation of their Majesties King George II and Queen Caroline* (London, 1727); *An Account of the Ceremonies Observed at the Coronation of... George III... To which is Added, an Account of the Ceremonies Observed at the Coronation of King James II... King George II* (London, 1761); *An Account of the Ceremonies Observed in the Coronations of the Kings and Queens of England* (London, 1761). Coronation sermons were published, and reached a wide audience. Prints depicted the ceremonies themselves. Continental parallels could be drawn from such works as Nicolas Menin, *An Historical and Chronological Treatise of the Anointing and Coronation of the Kings and Queens of France* (London, 1723) and *The Form, Order and Ceremonies of Coronations...* (London, 1727), works adapted and republished in 1775. The constitutional issues were publicised and considered from, for example, *The Sacred and Solemn Oath to be Taken by... King George* (London, [1714]), to works which summed up the tradition, like T. C. Banks, *An Historical and Critical Enquiry into the Nature of the Kingly Office* (London, 1812) and Arthur Taylor, *The Glory of Regality: an Historical Treatise of the Anointing and Crowning of the Kings and Queens of England* (London, 1820). For the controversies over George IV's coronation oath and Catholic Emancipation, see chapter 6 below.

[234] James Lackington, *Memoirs of the Forty Five First Years of the Life of James Lackington*, 13th (sic) edn (London, 1810), p. 257, quoted in R. Porter and M. Teich (eds.), *The Enlightenment in National Context* (Cambridge, 1981), p. 13. Lackington was a self-made man; social mobility may have coloured his judgement.

sorts. It seems clear, for example, that the educated classes ceased to believe in the reality of witchcraft in the early eighteenth century, and that the repeal of the Witchcraft Act in 1736 reflects this scepticism.[235] Their disbelief did not at once extend to the population at large. One writer in 1718 listed some twenty-four works published since 1660 and taking the subject seriously: 'These books and narratives are in tradesmen's shops, and farmers' houses, and are read with great eagerness, and are continually leavening the minds of the youth, who delight in such subjects.'[236] Many of these books must have remained in circulation. On the continent, the reality of witchcraft continued to be the subject of academic debate throughout the first half of the century.[237] In England, the issues involved were evidently important enough to be discussed by the radical Whig writers, John Trenchard and Thomas Gordon, in three successive issues of *Cato's Letters*; even they admitted, though condemning, that 'the popular impressions and fears of spirits, apparitions, and witches... more or less afflict and terrify the greatest part of the world'.[238] Their interest in the subject was not in the quaint survival of an unimportant belief, or in a source of injustice to individuals. As John Wesley later wrote: 'While I live I will bear the most public testimony I can to the reality of witchcraft. Your denial of this springs originally from the Deists; and simple Christians lick their spittle. I heartily set them at open defiance.'[239]

It was not the 'advance of science' which eroded popular belief in religious therapeutics or in witchcraft in the early eighteenth century, but the course taken by political events, and by controversy within the governing elite, which made the expression of those beliefs impossible.[240] After the 1720s, serious and scholarly studies of witchcraft largely ceased, dealt a serious blow by Francis Hutchinson's book of 1718.[241] But the

[235] Thomas, *Religion and the Decline of Magic*, pp. 570–81.

[236] P. J. Guskin, 'The Context of Witchcraft: The Case of Jane Wenham (1712)', *ECS* 15 (1981–2), 57.

[237] H. C. Lea, *Materials toward a History of Witchcraft* (3 vols., Philadelphia, 1939), vol. III, pp. 1380–464.

[238] *Cato's Letters*, 3rd edn (4 vols., London, 1733), vol. III, pp. 90–118 (19th May–2nd June 1722), p. 90.

[239] John Wesley to Thomas Tattershall, 13th Nov. 1785: J. Telford (ed.), *The Letters of the Rev. John Wesley, AM* (8 vols., London, 1931), vol. VII, p. 300.

[240] I adopt here the argument of Michael MacDonald, 'Religion, Social Change, and Psychological Healing in England, 1600–1800', in W. J. Sheils (ed.), *Studies in Church History* 19 (1982), 101–25.

[241] Cf. John Beaumont, *An Historical, Physiological and Theological Treatise of Spirits, Apparitions, Witchcrafts and Other Magical Practices* (London, 1705); Joseph Glanvill, *Saducismus Triumphatus: or Full and Plain Evidence Concerning Witches and Apparitions* (London, 1681; 4th edn, 1726); [R. Boulton], *Compleat History of Magick, Sorcery and Witchcraft* (2 vols., London, 1715); Francis Hutchinson, *An Historical Essay Concerning Witchcraft, with Observations... Tending to Confute the Vulgar Errors about that Point* (London, 1718, 2nd edn, 1720); R. Boulton, *The Possibility and Reality of Magick, Sorcery, and Witchcraft, Demonstrated... in Answer to Dr Hutchinson's Historical Essay* (London, 1722); Daniel Defoe, *A System of Magick* (London, 1727).

popular literature continued, in cheap and sensational tracts like *An Authentick and Complete History of Witches and Apparitions. Shewing the Reality of their Existence in Upwards of Twenty-Five Curious and Uncommon Relations* (London, 1759), *The History of Apparitions, Ghosts, Spirits or Spectres; Consisting of Variety of Remarkable Stories of Apparitions, Attested by People of Undoubted Veracity. By a Clergyman* (London, 1762), or *The History of Witches, Ghosts and Highland Seers: Containing Many Wonderful Well-attested Relations of Supernatural Appearances* (Berwick, [?1800]). In the early nineteenth century, romantics and antiquarians had their fancy caught by this aspect of Highland life;[242] but such patterns of belief had always been there, largely out of sight of the rational bourgeois, on both sides of the Border.

It was such attitudes in Hertfordshire in 1751, for example, which allowed one Colley to raise a mob against a certain Ruth Osborne on suspicion of her being a witch. Ruth Osborne died as a result of the treatment she received. Colley was duly tried for the crime and hanged, after delivering a speech from the gallows abjuring belief in witchcraft as a regrettable and outdated superstition.[243] But Colley was of humble origins; the speech bears the marks of having been written by a social superior, probably a clergyman. Yet at Colley's execution, according to the *Gentleman's Magazine*, 'many thousands stood at a distance to see him go, grumbling and muttering that it was a hard case to hang a man for destroying an old wicked woman that had done so much damage by her witchcraft'.[244] And this in the high noon of the Enlightenment, in the socially 'advanced' Home Counties. Nor was it an isolated instance. The persecution of women by their neighbours on suspicion of witchcraft, or similar manifestations of that belief, is recorded for Suffolk (1744, 1752, 1792, 1795, 1825, 1890), Buckinghamshire (1759, 1770), Leicestershire (1760, 1766), Kent (1762), Northamptonshire (1785), Huntingdonshire (1807, 1815), Dorset (1845), Cambridgeshire (1908). There seems little doubt that a systematic search would reveal many more cases.[245] And the incidents differed little from their seventeenth-century patterns: 'scoring' and 'swimming' suspected witches, and weighing

242 E.g. *A Collection of Rare and Curious Tracts on Witchcraft and the Second Sight; with an Original Essay on Witchcraft* (Edinburgh, 1820); Sir Walter Scott, *Letters on Demonology and Witchcraft, Addressed to J. G. Lockhart, Esq.* (London, 1830).

243 *The Remarkable Confession and Last Dying Words of Thomas Colley, Executed on Saturday, August 24th 1751...for the Cruel Murder of Ruth Osborne* (London, [1751]).

244 W. B. Carnochan, 'Witch Hunting and Belief in 1751: the Case of Thomas Colley and Ruth Osborne', *Journal of Social History* 4 (1971), 389–403.

245 Clifford Morsley (ed.), *News from the English Countryside 1750–1850* (London, 1979), pp. 15–22, 71, 176–7, 299; C. J. Billson (ed.), *County Folk-Lore. Printed Extracts, No 3. Leicestershire & Rutland* (London, 1895), pp. 46, 50; C. F. Tebbutt, *Huntingdonshire Folklore* (np, 1952), pp. 32–3, 47–8; Lady E. C. Gurdon (ed.), *County Folk-Lore. Printed Extracts, No 2. Suffolk* (London, 1893), pp. 185–6, 191, 193; T. F. Thiselton Dyer, *Church-Lore Gleanings* (London, 1891), p. 307; *Gentleman's Magazine* 29 (1759), 93; 55 (1785), 658; Thomas Somerville, *My Own Life and Times 1741–1814* (Edinburgh, 1861), p. 366; James Obelkevitch, *Religion and Rural Society: South Lindsey 1825–1875* (Oxford, 1976), p. 283.

against the Church Bible, were all current, if not as frequent. Officially, 'The last execution for witchcraft in England occurred in 1684, in America 1692, in Scotland 1727, in France 1745, and in Germany 1775.'[246] Unofficial action went on rather longer. Even Ruth Osborne's murder was not the last of its kind in the United Kingdom: there is an instance of a young woman of twenty-seven being burnt as a witch in Clonmel in 1894.[247]

Though not 'typical' in the sense of being everyday occurrences, gruesome incidents like these allow us to see below the surface of the everyday, the commonplace and the mundane to the great mass of fundamental prejudice which was scarcely touched by the Olympian doubt of the mandarins of advanced opinion. They were reminders to contemporaries, also. Another incident which operated in the same way was the reaction in London to the Lisbon earthquake of November 1755. Following the alarm caused by two slight tremors in England in February and March 1750, news of Lisbon's destruction produced a mass panic; religious and eschatological fervour revealed a popular world view in which the supernatural and the natural were seldom far apart.[248] Sherlock's pastoral letter of 1750, which appealed to such a sense of Providence as an avenging agent of 'divine justice' set a publishing record. It is supposed to have sold 100,000 copies in a month[249] – a figure equalled, before Hannah More's tracts, only by Dr Sacheverell's famous sermon.[250] In such a mental world it did not seem absurd that Monmouth should touch for the King's Evil during his rebellion in 1685,[251] that James III should do so in Scotland in 1716,[252] or Prince Charles Edward during the '45:[253] it was a badge of

---

[246] J. B. Russell, *A History of Witchcraft* (London, 1980), p. 122.

[247] As the Lord Lieutenant explained to Queen Victoria:

> In this case the unhappy victim was supposed, at any rate by some of those concerned, to have been carried off by the faeries, while a spirit took possession of her mortal frame. It was supposed that this could be expelled by fire, and hence the burning to which the poor woman was subjected. Afterwards the whole party assembled for several nights at an ancient rath or camp, prepared to see her riding on a white horse, in the belief that if the reins were cut with a black-handled knife, she would return to them in her proper form. (J. Pope-Hennessy, *Lord Crewe 1858–1945* (London, 1955), pp. 44–5.)

[248] T. D. Kendrick, *The Lisbon Earthquake* (London, 1956), pp. 142–64.

[249] 'A Letter from the Lord Bishop of London to the Clergy and People of London and Westminster, on Occasion of the Earthquakes in 1750', in T. S. Hughes (ed.), *The Works of Bishop Sherlock* (5 vols., London, 1830), vol. IV, pp. 302–11; Nichols, *Literary Anecdotes*, vol. III, p. 213.

[250] Holmes, *Trial of Dr Sacheverell*, p. 75. The number of 'earthquake sermons' in the wake of the tremors was very large; their message was similar.

[251] 'In Somersetshire, 'tis confidently reported, that some were cured of the king's-evil, by the touch of the Duke of Monmouth': John Aubrey, *Miscellanies* in *Three Prose Works*, ed. J. Buchanan-Brown (Fontwell, 1972), p. 80.

[252] Farquhar, 'Royal Charities', *British Numismatic Journal* 15 (1918–20), 166.

[253] Chambers, *Rebellion in Scotland*, vol. I, p. 183. Charles III continued to do so, in Italy, into the 1780s: Crawfurd, *King's Evil*, pp. 157–8. In 1794 the English Jacobin Thelwall praised the French for overthrowing the superstition: Goodwin, *Friends of Liberty*, p. 319.

legitimacy which the Jacobite would assert and the Whig indignantly denounce, but neither could ignore.

The events of the '45 have invited historians to give more attention to these matters in Scotland. There, the advance of evangelical Presbyterianism against disestablished Episcopalianism[254] and Roman Catholicism was slow indeed; and the points at issue were as much political as religious. 'Each of the contestants in that prolonged conflict possessed a political loyalty which was, in effect, an integral part of his religious faith. It was scarcely possible to think of a Jacobite Evangelical, or of a Whig Episcopalian or Roman Catholic.'[255] Nor should we conceive of this as the survival of an outdated past. 'So far from being rooted in the immemorial culture of an anachronistic Celtic past, the Highland aristocracy which came out for the Pretender in 1715 was conspicuously anglicised and indeed rather cosmopolitan.' They rose because, on the contrary, 'they shared the mental world of their social counterparts in the Lowlands'.[256] As has been argued, the social structure in Scotland which gave location and substance to such attitudes remained intact after the '15; it was, if anything, strengthened in the three succeeding decades.[257] Jacobitism therefore survived until the '45 as a 'quasi-mystical political religion'. James III's declaration of December 1743, intended to be distributed after a landing, appropriately expressed the 'usual Jacobite mysticism about the magic effects of the restoration of a rightful prince'. And the justifications which active Jacobites advanced, both during the '45 and at their subsequent executions, dwelt above all on the issue of indefeasible hereditary right: a commitment they were bound to uphold by what Dr Archibald Cameron called, before his execution in 1753, 'the principles of Christian loyalty'.[258]

Against the whole Whig complex of beliefs and attitudes, summed up in the phrase 'Liberty and Property', could be set in the first half of the century a rival complex whose slogan could well be 'Loyalty and Honesty'. The existence of such an idiom has encouraged a recent historian to suggest that, had a French invasion force won a military victory in 1744–5, 'there was every likelihood of widespread Tory support for, and even more widespread

254 Nonjuring Episcopalians were more important in Scotland, and, surviving into the 1780s, developed links with English Orthodox churchmen after Charles III's death: cf. F. C. Mather, 'Church, Parliament and Penal Laws: Some Anglo-Scottish Interactions in the Eighteenth Century', *EHR* 92 (1977), 540–72.
255 J. Macinnes, *The Evangelical Movement in the Highlands of Scotland 1688 to 1800* (Aberdeen, 1951), p. 79. Some estimates have suggested a steady increase in the numbers of Roman Catholics in the Highlands c. 1688–1750: Anson, *Underground Catholicism*, pp. 152–3. If so, it would be all the more remarkable in running counter to the downward trend in England.
256 Bruce Lenman, *The Jacobite Risings in Britain 1689–1746* (London, 1980), pp. 146, 149.
257 *Ibid.*, pp. 175–6, 223: the survival of Jacobitism 1725–39 'was not based on hope of an impending successful rebellion, for hope there was none. Rather it was the product of deep-seated intellectual attitudes and social structures which...continued to exist and indeed develop in their own way'.
258 *Ibid.*, pp. 24–7, 239.

general acquiescence in, the overthrow of an unpopular minority Whig regime and its foreign dynasty'.[259] William Pitt agreed: speaking of the rebels in the Commons four years after the event, he is reported as saying: 'if they had obtained a victory, and made themselves masters of London, I question much if the spirit of the populace would not have soon taken a very different turn'.[260]

In the far more backward peasant society of eighteenth-century Russia, political opposition at local level *typically* crystallised around a pretender to the throne: specific economic grievances were not enough in themselves to justify or trigger resistance to monarchial legitimacy. An individual was needed, deliberately playing a charismatic role, usually in alliance with the more articulate disaffection of sections of the rural clergy, especially those associated with 'Old Belief'.[261] Illiteracy, ignorance and regional isolation created conditions which allowed many such bids for power. In Britain, by contrast, there could be no doubt about *who* was the claimant after 1689, and the choice was perceived as a simple one between dynastic alternatives. If the British situation differed vastly in degree from the Russian, the differences of kind were less great.

V. THE TRANSFORMATION OF DIVINE RIGHT IDEOLOGY, 1745-1760

Military realities, above all, helped keep alive the Stuart dynastic ideology as a possible political option: and the realities were that a French invasion had every prospect of success in 1744, and a marginal chance as late as 1759.[262] The combination of a credible military threat to the Hanoverian dynasty, and the way in which the possibility of a change of dynasty gave an edge to political ideologies which focussed on the dynastic element, meant that the situation was as different as could be from that described by Figgis: that after the Act of Settlement, 'the Divine Right of Kings is the expression of regretful aspirations, and in no sense of actual fact. From a practical force it has become a romantic sentiment... The feeling which keeps it alive is partly artistic partly sentimental... a mere romantic pose... the inevitable

---

[259] *Ibid.*, p. 238.

[260] 21st April 1749: *Parl Hist*, vol. XIV, col. 506.

[261] Cf. P. Longworth, 'The Pretender Phenomenon in Eighteenth-Century Russia', *P&P* 66 (1975), 61–83.

[262] Cruickshanks, *Political Untouchables*; F. J. McLynn, *France and the Jacobite Rising of 1745* (Edinburgh, 1980). A full study of the diplomatic context of the invasion attempt of 1759 is expected from Professor Claude Nordmann; meanwhile, see his article 'Choiseul and the Last Jacobite Attempt of 1759' in Eveline Cruickshanks (ed.), *Ideology and Conspiracy: Aspects of Jacobitism 1689–1759* (Edinburgh, 1982), pp. 201–17. There was a profound contrast with the situation in 1779: when a joint Franco-Spanish fleet gained a temporary superiority in the Channel, French plans did not aim at a change of dynasty. Piers Mackesy, *The War for America 1775–1783* (London, 1964), pp. 279–97.

feeling, that touches all dying causes with a sunset charm.'[263] The process by which this doctrine, and the ideological polarity which it engendered in England, was metamorphosed into something else in the decades following the '45 has never been studied. But it seems possible that patriarchalism played a larger part in English than in French divine right theories, so that, in England, the 'indefeasible' element in that world view could more easily fall into disuse without endangering the whole. The full doctrine of divine *indefeasible* hereditary right was placed beyond hope of retrieval by the military failure of the '45; it became obvious to all by 1760 that it could never be implemented. But the emotional and theological dispositions which had given it force remained. They found outlets, it may be suggested, in four ways.

The first was a pathway which had been opened up quickly after 1688 and had been the official and eagerly-adopted orthodoxy of the majority of Whigs since that date. For them, indefeasible divine right was largely replaced by Providential divine right.[264] The successful outcome of a socially stable revolution in 1688 was repeatedly ascribed, by Whigs, to the hand of God in human affairs; the Whig ascendancy after 1714 concealed the fact, awkwardly evident in the 1690s, that the doctrine could equally be used in defence of *any* established power.[265] Soon, however, this Whig immunity wore off, and contractarian doctrines were used against them. After the '45, wrote one observer, the 'enemies of the present establishment' no longer rested their case on the traditional doctrines of Stuart absolutism alone: without abandoning those arguments,

...they are now become as loud as any of their neighbours in putting in their claim to that liberty, which was established by the Revolution, and argue thus; 'If the Revolution brought about by King William III was justifiable, why may not the people seek their redress of grievance on any other occasion, by the same or similar methods?'...The people therefore are exhorted to do justice to themselves, and to assert their right to dissolve a government, that is no longer exercised in a manner agreeable to their desires, nor placed in such hands as they can confide in...This is the plausible appearance under which the modern Jacobite hath of late chosen to represent his cause.[266]

It was one of the routes by which the conflict between Whig monarchical traditionalism and Tory monarchical traditionalism gave rise to a new radical idiom.

[263] Figgis, *Divine Right*, pp. 167–70.
[264] Cf. esp. Straka, *Anglican Reaction* and 'The Final Phase of Divine Right Theory in England, 1688–1702'. The present study does not bear out 1702 as a terminal date, if intended to define a process whereby 'In the course of the eighteenth century providential right as a justification for the Revolution was to fall before the law of nature in politics as enunciated by Locke': *EHR*, p. 658.
[265] Kenyon, *Revolution Principles*, pp. 24–6. I cannot agree with Professor Kenyon's verdict (pp. 26, 29) that the doctrine was 'finally discredited' in the controversy immediately following William Sherlock's *The Case of the Allegiance Due to Soveraign Powers* (London, 1691).   [266] Bentham, *Letter to a Fellow*, pp. 7–8.

Elements of the divine right of Providence, justifying the deposition of some kings, may be found even in Filmer,[267] and explain the doctrine's wide acceptability in the years following a revolution which both Whigs and Tories had combined to make. Tories could therefore use the argument for their own purposes. Even Francis Atterbury, the Jacobite conspirator of the 1720s, employed the doctrine in preaching before the Commons in 1701 a sermon which carried the strong implication that divine Providence, having changed the government once, might do so again.[268] In Anne's reign, divine right was less clearly defined as Providential; as in Archbishop Sharp's[269] coronation sermon, what were typically stressed were the patriarchal implications which could be derived from it,[270] whether literal or metaphorical he did not insist, and many were willing to revive in Anne's favour the divine right appropriate to a Stuart sovereign.

Even an extreme Whig like Bishop Burnet had been willing in 1691 to describe princes as 'God's deputies and vicegerents here on earth', so that 'The outward respect paid them, carries a proportion to that character of divinity which is on them, and that supposes an imitation of the divine perfections in them'[271] It was not a great step, in point of tone, to the full-blooded doctrines which flourished under Anne, heralded by William Binckes' famous sermon on 30th January 1702, comparing Charles I to Christ and exalting monarchical divinity to a degree which provoked both outcry and imitation.[272] After 1714, 'Providence' became more exclusively the property of the Whig establishment, as events played into their hands. William Talbot, Bishop of Oxford, who preached George I's coronation sermon, argued 'How wonderfully the providence of God has appeared in bringing about this great event, his Majesty's peaceable accession to the throne of these kingdoms.' George I was likened to William III, who, 'by many wonderful providences', had been 'the happy instrument in [God's] hands, of delivering us from popish tyranny and arbitrary power...of settling us again upon the old foundation of our envy'd legal establishment

---

[267] Dickinson, *Liberty and Property*, p. 35.

[268] 'The Wisdom of Providence Manifested in the Revolutions of Government. A Sermon Preach'd before the Honourable House of Commons...May the 29th, 1701' in F. Atterbury, *Sermons and Discourses On Several Subjects and Occasions* (2 vols., London, 1723), vol. I, p. 243.

[269] John Sharp (1645–1714). Born Bradford, son of a tradesman. Christ's College Camb. 1660–; BA 1663. Ordained 1667. Chaplain in household of Sir Heneage Finch until 1676. Livings. Dean of Norwich 1681; chaplain to James II 1686; Dean of Canterbury 1689; 1690 offered a vacated see, but declined during lives of deprived bishops; 1691–d Archbishop of York. Patron of Beveridge and Potter.

[270] Its text was Isaiah 49:23: 'Kings shall be thy nursing fathers, and their Queens thy nursing mothers.'

[271] Gilbert Burnet, *A Sermon Preached at White-Hall, On the 26th of Novemb 1691* (London, 1691), p. 2.

[272] W. Binckes, *A Sermon Preach'd on January the 30th 1701/2...Before...the Lower House of Convocation* (London, 1702); cf. *Animadversions on the Two Last 30th of January Sermons* (London, 1702); *An Explanation of Some Passages in Dr Binckes's Sermon* (London, 1702).

in Church and State'. And to the first of the Hanoverians was applied the text, 'Blessed be he that cometh in the name of the Lord.'[273]

A consciousness that they were on the winning side led great numbers of Whigs blithely to overlook the Hobbesian implications of the doctrine of Divine Providence in applying it to their regime. Scripture, announced one preacher, commands obedience to governments; 'But yet God has left it to every nation and people, as their fundamental right, to be governed in such a manner, by such persons, and such laws (provided they be not inconsistent with his own) as they may judge to be best for them in their particular circumstances.' This became a truism. If the succession had obviously been broken, 'popular choice' and the 'divine right of Providence' were crucial as the fictions which together provided an appearance of continuity. 'God does sometimes more eminently over-rule and determine the succession to regal dignity', he argued.

As for the right which has been wont to be claimed by virtue of primogeniture, and which has been asserted to be absolutely indefeasible, we find that God himself did not please to regard it, when he preferred Jacob to Esau, Judah to Reuben; Saul, who descended from Benjamin, the youngest of Jacob's sons; and David and Solomon, to others their brethren superior in age.[274]

The same episodes of Biblical genealogy were being used by a preacher in the American colonies in 1727 as evidence of a divine disproof of the doctrine of indefeasible hereditary succession. God advanced David to the throne by 'a wonderful chain of various providential changes' – usefully analogous to that which had occurred in England.[275]

In England itself, Whigs had held that Protestantism was under direct threat; God, by His Providence in installing George I, declared the Bishop of Lincoln, 'has thereby given the utmost strength, and confirmation, to the limitation of the succession in the Protestant line; upon which the whole security of our religion, laws, and liberties, depends'. If that were assured, Whig prelates did not labour to secularise the Whig monarchy. 'The inspired writers warrant us to say of kings, that they are Gods: and we may thus far, without flattery, ascribe that character to them, that they do not only derive their power from God, but ought to exercise it after the same

---

[273] William Talbot, Bishop of Oxford, *A Sermon Preach'd at the Coronation of King George in the Abbey-Church of Westminster, October the 20th, 1714* (London, 1714), pp. 11, 14, 30. William Talbot (?1659–1730), Dean of Worcester, succeeding the deprived George Hickes, 1691; Bishop of Oxford, 1699; Bishop of Salisbury, 1715; patron of Thomas Secker; Bishop of Durham 1721–d.

[274] Samuel Rosewell, *The King's True Divine Right. The Flourishing of His Crown: And the Shame of His Enemies. A Sermon Preach'd upon Occasion of His Majesty's Coronation* (London, 1714), pp. 5–8.

[275] Thomas Prince, *A Sermon on the Sorrowful Occasion of the Death of His Late Majesty King George of Blessed Memory, And the Happy Accession Of His Present Majesty King George II to the Throne* (Boston, Mass. 1727), p. 8.

manner',[276] declared Wake: as far as the Whigs were concerned, the Church's whole doctrine of obedience to higher powers, and non-resistance, hitherto perhaps misguided in the case of popish sovereigns, was now to be enlisted in defence of George I, who could be relied on to exercise his powers in defence of Whig ideals.[277] This was already a familiar claim by Williamite Whigs. As William Sherlock had argued in his sermon before the Commons on 30th January 1692, 'those who believed the doctrine of non-resistance and passive obedience to be a good doctrine before [the Revolution] may think so still, and be never the less friends to the present government'.[278] Jacobites were, of course, outraged; but the Whigs' partly successful attempts to steal their opponents' arguments continued unabated – it was essential that they should do so.

By the accession of George II, a Protestant prince with a Protestant heir already living, there is a definite note of triumphalism in Whig statements of the doctrine of divine right by Providence. Potter was almost effusive in his coronation sermon for that monarch. Princes are 'of divine appointment', he announced unequivocally; the 'evident and undeniable footsteps of the superintendency of divine providence' in the 'late glorious Revolution' sufficiently demonstrated it. The events of 1688 were used to justify those of 1714, and both were described in similar terms:

God is not only affirmed to have made Solomon king, but his royal throne is called the throne of God, and he is said to be *King for the Lord his God*, that is, in the stead, or place of God. Solomon therefore, and consequently all other princes in their respective dominions, are here described as the vice-gerents of God...Thus therefore every sovereign prince, that is, every one invested with royal, or supreme authority, is *seated on God's throne*, and is *King for the Lord his God*.

If one of the purposes of the doctrine of Providential divine right was the provision of apparent continuity, it was all too successful. George II was hailed as 'a prince lineally descended from a long race of great progenitors, who for many ages have happily swayed the same august sceptre, which, through the gracious disposal of providence, is now delivered into his sacred hands'. Divine appointment, plus this hereditary title, seemed to call for something like total obedience:

Next after God, and chiefly on his account, our gratitude is due to him, who by divine appointment is the minister of so many great and invaluable blessings to us; which must appear, as well in our entire submission to his authority, as in the reverence we pay to his sacred person: *Whosoever resisteth, resisteth the ordinance of God,*

---

[276] William Wake, Bishop of Lincoln, *A Sermon Preached Before the King in St James's Chapel, Upon the First of August 1715: Being the First Anniversary Return of His Majesty's Inauguration* (London, 1715), pp. 6, 9.

[277] *Ibid.*, pp. 19–20. Cf. John Potter, Bishop of Oxford, *A Sermon Preach'd Before the Honble House of Lords, On the First Day of August, 1715. Being the Day on which His Majesty Began His Happy Reign* (London, 1715), pp. 16–18.

[278] Randall, 'Sermons on Charles I', p. 153.

and shall therefore *receive to himself damnation.* Where *resisting* implies not only that violent opposition by force of arms, which in the construction of human laws is rebellion; but all that repining and murmuring, that contradiction and averseness of what kind soever, which is inconsistent with the hearty and cheerful *subjection to the higher powers* in this, and other places of scripture enjoined. Let us then be *subject* in the fullest sense of this expression, and that, not only through the fear of wrath, but from a principle of conscience towards God, and of sincere love to our Prince.[279]

Handel's Coronation Anthems gave resounding and triumphant expression to the texts of that service: 'Zadok the priest, and Nathan the prophet, anointed Solomon king'; and, in 'My Heart is Inditing', 'Kings shall be thy nursing fathers, and their queens thy nursing mothers.' The anthems became widely popular, frequently performed at concerts and festivals, and borrowed by the composer for use in his later oratorios *Esther, Deborah* and *Athalia.*[280] Their doctrines were public property.

A Whig was indignant, addressing Potter: 'My Lord, The doctrine delivered by your lordship in your coronation sermon, seems to me an infringement in some particulars, of the scheme of our glorious Act of Settlement (which is the foundation of the present government).' The accession of the House of Hanover proved 'the absurdity of the patriarchal scheme, which can never more be embraced in these kingdoms, till the Act of Settlement is repealed'. Potter's doctrine was 'running full into the old exploded scheme of Jure Divino, and resolves itself into a plain question, If no earthly potentate must presume to judge of the good or bad administration of rulers, by what plea is that revolution defendible which is so fresh in our memories?'[281] But it was to no effect: Hoadly's day was over.

In no sense did Whig orthodoxy describe a secularised monarchy in a materialist universe. Indeed, it is far from clear that belief in a directing Providence, ordering English history through a subtle but continuous intervention in day-to-day human actions, is not more 'superstitious' than the theory of indefeasible right[282] – a theory which recognised that God might stand aside to allow even princes humanly to err. Under kingship by indefeasible right, too, the Church had paradoxically been less important, reduced almost to a department of state. Under kingship by Divine

---

[279] 'A Sermon Preach'd at the Coronation of King George II and Queen Caroline in the Abbey-Church of Westminster, October 11 1727' in *The Theological Works of the most Reverend Dr John Potter late Lord Archbishop of Canterbury* (3 vols., Oxford, 1753), vol. I, pp. 246–9, 255, 257–8.

[280] For such works as both defences of orthodox religion against the Deist attack, and analogies between England's fortunes and those of the nation of Israel under divine guidance, cf. Ruth Smith, 'Intellectual Contexts of Handel's English Oratorios', in C. Hogwood and R. Luckett (eds.), *Music in Eighteenth-Century England* (Cambridge, 1982), pp. 115–33.

[281] *Hoadly and Potter Compared. Being Remarks upon some Passages in the Sermon Preached at their Majesties Coronation* (London, 1728), pp. 4–5, 8.

[282] Cf. the objection of Pierre Allix in Kenyon, *Revolution Principles*, p. 26.

Providential right, it became in the reigns of the first two Georges the co-equal oracle of Providence, and the indispensable sanction of civil power. In one way, 1688 and 1714 weakened the spiritual ambience of everyday politics; in another way, they strengthened it. 'The character of majesty has something sacred in it', repeated even a Dissenting preacher at the accession of George III.[283] Thus described, the ideology of Hanoverian kingship was sufficiently convincing to win seemingly authentic converts. John Wesley professed himself convinced in the 1730s that his Anglican principles of Christian-monarchical obedience did apply to George II; and it has been suggested that the decline of Welsh Jacobitism even before 1745 is closely related to the rise of Methodism, the doctrines and emotional dispositions which produced Stuart allegiance finding a new, but closely related, channel.[284]

The second outlet for divine right attitudes was provided by a doctrine which was even more clearly the property of a particular political grouping. In the 1740s and 50s, dissident Whigs attempting to build a parliamentary opposition around Leicester House and in alliance with the Tories, embraced the idea, given classic expression by the ex-Jacobite Bolingbroke, of the Patriot King.[285] It was an ideal which exploited the aura which men wished to ascribe to kingship; it had the right emotional resonance (thought its inventors) to appeal to the Tories; and it articulated the conveniently unspecific aspiration that a charismatic prince's accession would somehow bring about national regeneration or healing – as it were, at a touch.[286]

The same sentiments were a principal theme of the men of letters whom Frederick and his allies, especially George Lyttelton, encouraged, and often pensioned:[287] in poems such as James Thomson's *Liberty* (1735–6), dedicated to Frederick as one in whom 'the noblest dispositions of the prince and of the patriot united', and Richard Glover's *Leonidas* (1737); or in plays like Henry Brooke's *Gustavus Vasa* (1738), David Mallett's *Mustapha* (1739), Thomson's *Edward and Eleonora* (1739) or Mallett and Thomson's joint masque *Alfred* (1740), acted before Prince Frederick at Cliveden (George III

---

[283] Savage, *The Duty of Subjects*, p. 4.
[284] H. M. Vaughan, 'Welsh Jacobitism', *Transactions of the Honourable Society of Cymmrodorion* (1920–1), 11–36.
[285] Henry St John, Viscount Bolingbroke, *The Idea of a Patriot King*: written c. 1738 and circulated privately; first published London, 1749; reprinted in David Mallett's edition of Bolingbroke's works, 1754, and subsequent eighteenth-century editions. Here cited from the 1844 *Works*.
[286] It thereby echoed the millenarian hopes of many Jacobites, evident, for example, in the speeches before execution of some of the prisoners of the '45: H. Paton (ed.), *The Lyon in Mourning* (3 vols., Edinburgh, 1895), vol. I, p. 46.
[287] M. H. Cable, 'The Idea of a Patriot King in the Propaganda of the Opposition to Walpole, 1735–1739', *Philological Quarterly* 18 (1939), 119–30; R. J. Phillimore, *Memoirs and Correspondence of George, Lord Lyttelton* (2 vols., London, 1845), *passim*; J. Loftis, *The Politics of Drama in Augustan England* (Oxford, 1963), pp. 118–53; B. A. Goldgar, *Walpole and the Wits. The Relation of Politics to Literature, 1722–1742* (Lincoln, Nebraska, 1976), pp. 134–85.

in time named one of his sons Alfred). *Gustavus Vasa* and *Edward and Eleonora* went so far that they were suppressed under the Licensing Act of 1737, the first plays so honoured. The classic theatrical eulogy of liberty was still Addison's *Cato*; Frederick used a performance of it in 1737 for a personal political demonstration whose success must have confirmed to him the potential of such a bid for popularity.[288] The young Prince George was duly initiated into this imagery when he took the lead in a private production of the same play in 1749, acted by Prince Frederick's children (together with the future Lord North).[289]

The classic political statement of these attitudes was, of course, Bolingbroke's *The Idea of a Patriot King*. It claimed to offer an account of 'the duties of a king to his country; of those kings particularly who are appointed by the people, for I know of none who are anointed by God to rule in limited monarchies'. The theory appealed to Whigs (especially to Whig radicals) with an explicit and reiterated disavowal of indefeasible divine right: 'Nothing can be more absurd, in pure speculation, than an hereditary right in any mortal to govern other men: and yet, in practice, nothing can be more absurd than to have a king to choose at every vacancy of the throne.'[290] Yet even when a new royal family has been installed by human choice, and the crown then descends by hereditary succession, the last of the line holds the throne by the same title as the first. 'I mention this the rather, because I have an imperfect remembrance, that some scribbler was employed, or employed himself, to assert the hereditary right of the present family.'[291] The dignity of kings descends via their office, not their persons: 'majesty is not an inherent, but a reflected light'.[292] The present-day Jacobite is a rebel not only to the existing king, but also (in a sense which was not true, claimed Bolingbroke, during the conflict between York and Lancaster) to the constitution:

The law of his country has settled the right of succession in a new family. He resists this law, and asserts, on his own private authority, not only a right in contradiction to it, but a right extinguished by it...it is urged, that no power on earth could alter the constitution in this respect, nor extinguish a right to the crown inherent in the Stuart family, and derived from a superior, that is, from a divine, authority. This kind of plea for refusing submission to the laws of the land, if it was admitted, would serve any purpose as well as that for which it is brought.[293]

It might not be fanciful to see in such an argument one beginning of that idealisation of the law which was to characterise late-eighteenth-century conservatives, and to receive its classic formulation from the ex-Tory Sir William Blackstone.

[288] Hervey, *Memoirs*, vol. III, p. 839.
[289] John Brooke, *King George III* (London, 1972), pp. 22–3.
[290] Bolingbroke, *Works*, vol. II, p. 372, 380.
[291] *Ibid.*, p. 392. Irony. This was constitutional orthodoxy.
[292] *Ibid.*, p. 380.   [293] *Ibid.*, p. 409.

Yet having renounced the *indefeasible* right of kings, Bolingbroke at once went on to endow his imagined sovereign with every other idealised quality and dignity of a charismatic prince. 'I esteem monarchy above every other form of government', he announced, 'and hereditary monarchy above elective... the character and government of a Patriot King can be established on no other [principles], if their office and their right are not always held divine, and their persons always sacred.'[294] This is so, since the particular laws of nations are sanctioned by the general laws of God:

It follows, therefore, that he who breaks the laws of his country resists the ordinance of God, that is, the law of his nature. God has instituted neither monarchy, nor aristocracy, nor democracy, nor mixed government: but though he has instituted no particular form of government among men, yet by the general laws of his kingdom he exacts our obedience to the laws of those communities, to which each of us is attached by birth, or to which we may be attached by a subsequent and lawful engagement.

English society has lawfully instituted monarchy: the title of kings is, initially, a human title.

But the principles we have laid down do not stop here. A divine right in kings is to be deduced evidently from them: a divine right to govern well, and conformably to the constitution at the head of which they are placed... The office of kings is, then, of right divine, and their persons are to be reputed sacred.[295]

Every State contains an 'absolute, unlimited, and uncontrollable' sovereign power, but this need not be lodged in the monarch alone: 'with reverence be it spoken, God is a monarch, yet not an arbitrary but a limited monarch, limited by the rule which infinite wisdom prescribes to infinite power'.[296] But apart from eulogies of the perfection of the British constitution, which the Patriot King was to restore, uphold, and rule by, Bolingbroke supplied no information on the checks to be applied to the human sovereign whose title had been thus divinely endorsed. Crucially, the work contains no discussion of natural rights, which the subject might plead against the sovereign; without which, the disavowal of *indefeasible* right might be relatively unimportant.

The heart of the book is an entirely unspecific panegyric on the quality of patriotic kingship. Its two central characteristics were unity and regeneration.

Instead of abetting the divisions of his people, he will endeavour to unite them, and to be himself the centre of their union: instead of putting himself at the head of one party in order to govern his people, he will put himself at the head of his people in order to govern, or more properly to subdue, all parties.

Such an ideal inevitably found expression in the patriarchal images which had once seemed natural to English monarchy before the rise of party

[294] *Ibid.*, p. 378.   [295] *Ibid.*, p. 379.
[296] *Ibid.*, p. 382.

government: 'The true image of a free people, governed by a Patriot King, is that of a patriarchal family, where the head and all the members are united by one common interest, and animated by one common spirit.'[297] Such unity was the precondition for national regeneration:

A Patriot King is the most powerful of all reformers; for he is himself a sort of standing miracle, so rarely seen and so little understood, that the sure effects of his appearance will be admiration and love in every honest breast, confusion and terror to every guilty conscience, but submission and resignation in all. A new people will seem to arise with a new king. Innumerable metamorphoses, like those which poets feign, will happen in the very deed: and, while men are conscious that they are the same individuals, the difference of their sentiments will almost persuade them that they are changed into different beings.[298]

As a political programme, this apparently terminated with the death of Frederick in 1751. Yet attention soon shifted instead to the education of Prince George. Although the contemporary myth (and the historiographical misconception) that he was covertly indoctrinated with Jacobite principles has been properly denied, historians have overlooked the extent to which he was the heir of Whig doctrines of kingship which were generically similar to Jacobite ones and which had been modified, if anything, by an explicit and politically significant compromise with theories of indefeasible hereditary divine right.

The Idea of a Patriot King has often been found wanting by political scientists who read it as a literal programme or blueprint for an active and dominating personal monarchy, held out by Bolingbroke as a sufficient solution to England's practical problems. The contention here, on the contrary, is that no very precise programme was intended to be derived from its endless generalisations (apart from the replacement of the Old Corps ministers at Frederick's accession); that its practical purpose was, rather, the provision of an ideology sufficiently lofty and generalised to promote the unity of Whig and Tory elements in the Leicester House opposition.[299] In May 1749, the Nonjuror John Byrom was told 'that the Prince F[rederick] met Lord Lichfield in the park, and asked him if he had read Lord Bolingbroke's late book about a patriot King? and his lordship answering that he had, the Prince told him, Well, my lord, I shall be that patriot King.'[300]

In 1747 a similar tactic was employed in bidding for Tory support by

---

[297] *Ibid.*, pp. 401–2. [298] *Ibid.*, pp. 396–7.

[299] I dissent here from part of the interpretation of Quentin Skinner, 'The Principles and Practice of Opposition: the Case of Bolingbroke versus Walpole', in N. McKendrick (ed.), *Historical Perspectives* (London, 1974), pp. 93–128. Professor Skinner reconstructed Bolingbroke's ideas in the light of a political 'context' challenged in chapter 1 above, and of a view of 'Commonwealth' ideology questioned in chapter 5 below.

[300] Byrom, *Journal*, vol. II, part 2, p. 492. George, 3rd Earl of Lichfield (1718–72). Tory leader; Jacobite; among those working for a Tory alliance with Leicester House after 1747.

Frederick's ex-ally George Lyttelton, now a Lord of the Treasury in the Pelhams' ministry. In an anonymous pamphlet of that year he assumed the character of a non-Jacobite Tory in order to exhort that party to an alliance with ministerial Whigs. 'My aim is to incite you, not to change your principles, but to adhere steadfastly to them', he declared. Tories, he assured them, were often wrongly suspected of Jacobitism, 'some only for maintaining the old doctrine of the duty of passive obedience (so evidently due either to all established governments or to none)'. Tories should therefore take particular care to seem loyal, or people would not believe that George II,

...to whom we behave so undutifully can be the king we mean when we talk of passive obedience and non-resistance. The world will do us the honour to believe us consistent with ourselves; which the supposition of Jacobitism makes us, and nothing else can. But if we show ourselves honestly consistent by making our actions agree with the principles we profess and with our oaths, there is nothing which we may not expect from the favour of the crown.

He therefore recommended political co-operation

...as well as profess our old principles, to let the world see (by our reverence to the person of the King, by supporting his government, by discountenancing the saucy democratical spirit of sedition and by a religious observance of the laws according to the obligation of our oaths and allegiance) that we are true Tories, and not disguised and perjured Jacobites.

This would, Lyttelton claimed, entail no doctrinal sacrifice:

...in this comprehension no rigid, narrow terms of communion will be exacted, but on the contrary the right hand of fellowship frankly given you, that all this may be accomplished without your departing from the practice of any one Tory principle, that you will be met at least half way.[301]

Were the Tories convinced? Both Prince Frederick and the ministry were angling for their goodwill, if not their active co-operation. Until Frederick's death, it was Leicester House which seemed likely to capture the Tory party; then the Duke of Newcastle lulled it into quiescence; finally, from 1756, it aligned itself with the opposition forming around Frederick's son, Prince George. Both options seemed credible, but there were problems. Lyttelton's disguise was soon seen through.[302] On the other side, the most perceptive review of the *Patriot King* appeared in the Tory journal, *The Mitre and Crown*. Its author saw 'some great truths, and others as great errors' in Bolingbroke's tract, but on the whole judged it vacuous and utopian. Its denial of divine right in both monarchy and priesthood offended Anglican sensibilities. The reviewer soon put his finger on Bolingbroke's 1720s anticlericalism, and saw its consequences for the popular appointment of kings. He replied with a

[301] [George Lyttelton], *A Letter to the Tories* (London, 1747), pp. 9–10, 13, 15, 22.
[302] *Three Letters to the Whigs. Occasion'd by the Letter to the Tories* (London, 1748).

series of articles summarising the doctrines expressed in his own work, *The Divine and Hereditary Right of the English Monarchy Enquired into and Explained* (1749), and contrasting them with the tenets of the *Patriot King*.[303] Bolingbroke's most famous tract almost succeeded in its purpose, but its flaws and compromises became all too clear when judged beside genuine legitimist doctrine. An alliance between Leicester House and the Tories still needed much work to bring about.

The tactical problems which beset the opposition between 1747 and 1760 meant that these hopes achieved no easy or immediate realisation. But as a description of the ideological transformations that eventually came about, Bolingbroke's fudged synthesis has a striking appositeness; it anticipates in many ways the later mood of Leicester House and the sense of mission which contemporaries realised was being translated into action after 1760.[304] The revival of an opposition from 1755–6, including, with all the familiar reluctance and frictions, both Whigs and Tories, and the tactical effect of the wartime coalition after 1757, provided hard political reasons very similar to those previously faced by Prince Frederick's opposition for hailing the new reign in 1760 in these diffusely idealistic terms. The refurbished doctrine of kingship, with George III's Anglican piety, was the ideal which allowed the Tories to declare themselves reconciled to the dynasty.

The third sort of transmutation which the divine indefeasible hereditary right of kings underwent was in large part the result of its fusing with the official orthodoxy, Providential divine right. Both had been political doctrines focussed on the specific and narrow questions of dynastic title to the throne. When, with the accession of George III, that question was generally agreed to be settled, those doctrines could broaden into something else: a theory of the structure of society. Divine right had been, among its other uses, 'the form in which was expressed the sense of the need of some bond of moral sentiment and conscience other than the belief in its utility, to attach men to any government'.[305] The association with the regime after 1760 of the divine right ideal in the diffuse form anticipated earlier, promoted this generalised tendency to sanctify the whole political and social order. From such reinforcements, the intellectual vitality of the idea of the confessional state actually received a boost in the late eighteenth century[306] – a theme explored in chapter 4 below. So strong were the intellectual pressures against conceiving of the State as a mere human artifact, to be judged therefore in utilitarian terms, that even neo-Harringtonians were

---

[303] *The Mitre and Crown*, 1749: June, pp. 479–89; July, pp. 509–20; August, pp. 557–73; September, pp. 605–19.

[304] What allowed this programme to be seemingly implemented was the quite unrelated and separate development of the break-up of the traditional party system. In no very strong sense was George III a theorist, imposing an inappropriate dogma on a recalcitrant reality.

[305] Figgis, *Divine Right*, p. 254.

[306] Cf. E. R. Norman, *Church and Society in England, 1770–1970* (Oxford, 1976), pp. 15–70.

influenced. One, writing in 1750 with the object of strengthening 'that particular frame of orders and subordinations, of which a government is composed', did so by demonstrating that the State was not a 'mere artificial form' but an 'actual natural system arising by the vigour of natural principles from that balance of property, which is founded in the site and circumstances of each people and their country'.[307]

There was, perhaps, a fourth channel taken after 1760 by the attitudes which had predisposed men to accept divine-right doctrines. If opposition Whiggery was one heir of these dispositions in the 1740s and 50s via its use of the symbol of the Patriot King, its association with the Tories in those decades and the exile into opposition in the early 1760s of a considerable part of the Whig bloc may have contributed a certain strand to radical arguments, evident from 1760 onwards. It was a result which had been anticipated by the Nonjuror Samuel Grascome:

It is flat nonsense to talk of any supreme governor [as] if he be only a trustee or commissioner of the peoples; and every man will pride himself as no less than a petty king while those who are supposed to be only intrusted with the government are accountable to him and the rest of the original kinglings.[308]

After the disappearance of the preoccupation with the rivalry of Hanover and Stuart, this aspect of the question became prominent. For Paine's claim that the individual has an inherent right to 'liberty' was of just the same metaphysical standing as the claim that the monarch had an inherent right to 'authority'. The indefeasible, hereditary right of the sovereign was not abandoned by late-eighteenth-century radicals, but atomised into a possession of all individuals: what Paine hailed as the 'indefeasible hereditary Rights of Man'.[309] Such theories had long been in existence, though pushed into the background by the realities of patriarchalism and dynastic power-politics: 'Sidney's notion, that the sovereignty of the people is inalienable, as being a grant from God, which neither human ordinance nor the people's own consent may alienate, is every whit as much a theory of Divine Right as the views of Mainwaring or Sacheverell.'[310] After 1760 the effective end of the dynastic rivalry inevitably brought these theories to the forefront, and gave them relevance as effective weapons in the hands of individuals against an establishment whose defenders, for their part, increasingly sought to grace it with a similar diffused sense of divine sanction. Just as divine right had its consequences for both sides at the

---

[307] *A Treatise on Government: Being a Review of the Doctrine of an Original Contract* (London, 1750), pp. 7, 9.

[308] S. Grascome, *Schism Triumphant* (1707), cited in Hawkins, *Allegiance*, pp. 87–8.

[309] T. Paine, *Rights of Man* (1791–2; ed. H. Collins, Harmondsworth, 1971), p. 184.

[310] Figgis, *Divine Right*, p. 178. For Locke's reintroduction of 'innate' categories in the form of natural rights to property in the *Second Treatise*, cf. McLynn, 'Jacobitism and the Classical British Empiricists', p. 156.

beginning of the eighteenth century, its legacies descended to both radicals and conservatives at the end of it.

These sorts of transition have been expressed in abstract terms. Many could be traced concretely in a single life. Samuel Johnson was aged fifty-one at the accession of George III; his mind had been formed in an older tradition. His father, as Boswell wrote, was 'a zealous high-churchman and royalist, and retained his attachment to the unfortunate House of Stuart, though he reconciled himself, by casuistical arguments of expediency and necessity, to take the oaths imposed by the prevailing power' in order to hold office as a local magistrate. As a child, Johnson, on the advice of a Lichfield doctor, was touched for the scrofula by Queen Anne. He was at Pembroke College, Oxford, during the mastership of Dr Panting, whom Johnson admired as 'a fine Jacobite fellow'. In 1739 he published, as almost his first political piece, a pamphlet attacking both Walpole and the Hanoverian succession, *Marmor Norfolciense* (it was reprinted by a personal enemy in 1775, as evidence of inconsistency).[311] We know little of Johnson's life before 1760, but there is some circumstantial evidence. His London church was St Clement Dane's, in the Strand. In 1721 the church was in the news, complimented for its handsome new picture of Charles I. By 1725 a new altarpiece caused another outcry: an angel was supposed to be a portrait of Clementina Sobieska, James III's wife. Crowds came to see it; Gibson, Bishop of London, was approached, and it had to be removed. Later, it was probably in this church that Prince Charles Edward was received into the Church of England during his clandestine visit in 1750. Opposite St Clement Dane's stood a favourite haunt of Johnson, the Crown and Anchor Tavern. Here met the Oak Society, a Jacobite club dating from c. 1740, which 'ordered the engraving and striking of a medal for its members in 1750, when another rising was in contemplation, and when Prince Charles secretly visited London and attended one of the Society's meetings'.[312]

Johnson's whereabouts during 1745 and 1746 are unknown, and have defied generations of enquirers to discover. Boswell recorded, however, that Johnson owned a musket, sword and belt. In 1777, he called the rebellion of '45 'a noble attempt'. He was a friend of the Jacobite Dr William King, Principal of St Mary Hall, who was the first to bring Johnson news of his honorary Oxford MA. At the table of King's successor, Dr Nowell,[313] Johnson drank the toast of 'Church and King' with 'true Tory cordiality'. Nowell's censure by the Commons, added Boswell, was the effect of 'that

---

[311] In D. J. Greene (ed.), *The Yale Edition of the Works of Samuel Johnson*, vol. x: 'Political Writings' (New Haven, 1977), pp. 19–51.

[312] Grant Francis, *Romance of the White Rose* (London, 1933), p. 237; J. Wickham Legg, *English Church Life from the Restoration to the Tractarian Movement* (London, 1914), pp. 130–1.

[313] For whom, see below.

turbulence and faction which disgraced a part of the present reign...Dr Nowell will ever have the honour which is due to a lofty friend of our monarchical constitution.' Johnson was an admirer of Charles Leslie, to whom he paid tribute as 'a reasoner who was not to be reasoned against'. Johnson showed a clear understanding of the theological dimension of the issues involved when he said, though in jest:

A Jacobite, Sir, believes in the divine right of kings. He that believes in the divine right of kings believes in a Divinity. A Jacobite believes in the divine right of Bishops. He that believes in the divine right of Bishops believes in the divine authority of the Christian religion. Therefore, Sir, a Jacobite is neither an Atheist nor a Deist. That cannot be said of a Whig; for *Whiggism is a negation of all principle*.

In typical Nonjuror and Jacobite fashion, Johnson's politics implied a view of the social order: 'When the right of the king is not reverenced, there will not be reverence for those appointed by the king.' Boswell may have been an acceptable companion partly because he shared these opinions exactly. He first met Johnson in May 1763; but in January that year Boswell had revealed to a 'loyal' Scots family his own belief that the Stuarts were unjustly 'driven from the throne'; 'That by the many changes and popular confusions the minds of the people were confused and thrown loose from ties of loyalty, so that public spirit and national principle were in a great measure destroyed.'[314] Even in 1777, when drawn into a violent argument with a Whig, Johnson could be provoked to affirm that

...if England were fairly polled, the present king would be sent away to-night, and his adherents hanged tomorrow...Sir, the state of the country is this: the people knowing it to be agreed on all hands that this king has not the hereditary right to the crown, and there being no hope that he who has it can be restored, have grown cold and indifferent upon the subject of loyalty, and have no warm attachment to any king. They would not, therefore, risk any thing to restore the exiled family. They would not give twenty shillings a piece to bring it about. But, if a mere vote could do it, there would be twenty to one; at least, there would be a very great majority of voices for it...Dr Taylor [his Whig antagonist] admitted, that if the question as to hereditary right were to be tried by a poll of the people of England, to be sure the abstract doctrine would be given in favour of the family of Stuart; but he said, the conduct of that family, which occasioned their expulsion, was so fresh in the minds of the people, that they would not vote for a restoration.

Johnson's psephology, at that date, may be questioned; but it was a common opinion before 1760. Equally notable is the alleged freshness of these issues. Politically articulate Englishmen were still articulate about a received canon of events and of English sovereigns, beginning with Charles II and James II. Johnson had strong views about succeeding monarchs. William III he thought 'one of the most worthless scoundrels that ever existed'. George I,

---

[314] It was 'a bold and rash way of talking', he thought: F. A. Pottle (ed.), *Boswell's London Journal 1762–3* (Harmondsworth, 1966), p. 171.

he despised; George II he loathed, as 'unrelenting and barbarous'. But in July 1762, Johnson accepted a pension from the new king, at the hands of Lord Bute.

Bute acted after prompting in a letter from an anonymous Cambridge petitioner, now identified as Richard Farmer, Fellow and later Master of Emmanuel College, one of the last bastions of Cambridge Toryism. The petitioner pointed out: 'I am told that his political principles make him incapable of being in any place of trust, by incapacitating him from qualifying himself for any such office. But a pension my Lord requires no such performances' – Johnson would not have to take the oaths of allegiance and abjuration (these he had never subscribed: by leaving Oxford before graduating, he had avoided them. His later, honorary, degrees did not require the oaths).

If it be objected that his political principles render him an unfit object of His Majesty's favour, I would only say that he is to be the more pitied on this account, and that it may sometimes happen that our opinions, however erroneous, are not always in our power. Add to this that a disregard to this would be a further prosecution of his Majesty's noble plan, the total abolition of all party distinctions.[315]

Political enemies were less willing to admit that that plan had succeeded. In the Commons on 16th February 1774, Charles James Fox produced an article by 'A South Briton' which had appeared in the press that day, denouncing the Revolution and the regime which owed its existence to that event. Fox demanded that the author be brought to justice. Thomas Townshend was moved to sarcasm: why punish 'A South Briton' when so many 'more pernicious' writings had been allowed in the present reign? On the contrary, 'the revilers of the Revolution, and of the principles of the Revolution, have been applauded, revered, and even pensioned': Dr Shebbeare and Dr Johnson.[316] The charge was not wholly groundless.

Johnson was not, in fact, as 'cold and indifferent' after 1760 as his Jacobite theories ought to have made him. In praising George III, after his interview with his sovereign in 1767, Johnson compared him with Louis XIV or Charles II. The latter he called, in 1775, 'the best king we have had from his time till the reign of his present Majesty, except James the Second, who was a very good king, but unhappily believed that it was necessary for the salvation of his subjects that they should be Roman Catholicks'. And in 1773:

It should seem that the family at present on the throne has now established as good a right as the former family, by the long consent of the people; and that to disturb

---

[315] —— to Bute, 15th Nov. 1761, in M. Waingrow (ed.), *The Correspondence and Other Papers of James Boswell Relating to the Making of the Life of Johnson* (London, 1969), pp. 512–5. The attribution is made in B. H. Davis, 'The Anonymous Letter Proposing Johnson's Pension', *Transactions of the Johnson Society* (December 1981), pp. 35–9. I owe these references to Dr Howard Erskine-Hill.   [316] *Parl Hist*, vol. XVII, cols. 1054–8.

this right might be considered as culpable. At the same time I own, that it is a very difficult question, when considered with respect to the house of Stuart. To oblige people to take oaths as to the disputed right, is wrong. I know not whether I could take them: but I do not blame those who do.[317]

After 1760, the whole disposition in favour of order, rank and subordination, which Johnson classically represents, found a single and undivided object of loyalty. And the impact upon the intelligentsia was profound. Many of the leading figures of the mid-eighteenth century, in a wide range of disciplines, pose problems for modern interpreters for the same reason. Born and educated in one political universe, they survived into another, labouring to adapt their now-anachronistic ideas, or to re-express them in a new form. It is a process which can be traced in Wesley, Hume, Blackstone, Adam Smith, Gibbon, Bentham and Burke; but the experience of Dr Johnson provides the key.

VI. CONCLUSION: LAW, IDEOLOGY, ALLEGIANCE

The historical study, over long periods, of such themes as party, democracy or class is, by now, too heavily influenced by forward-looking perspectives. To avoid them, one might ask questions of a slightly different sort: what was the nature of political allegiance in early-eighteenth-century England? What was involved in the act of assent, and the continued disposition of loyalty? What sorts of language were available to men to describe and justify their motivation? What sorts of objects did those professed motives make credible? How did political options imposed from abroad shape the form of domestic political activity?

Implied answers to such questions have been attempted in this and the preceding chapter through consideration of the proper bearing of the work of political theorists on historical explanation; of the survival of patri-archalism; of the success and tenacity of the aristocratic code; and of the wider social function of doctrines of kingship. The received Whig view is related also to the psephological assumptions criticised in chapter 1. Those assumptions present eighteenth-century men as increasingly well-informed about their society. Men calculated rationally, it is suggested; they pursued their material self-interest, and used or attempted to use the House of Commons – however imperfect it was – as a system of 'representative democracy' to forward such ends. Contract theory was the appropriate abstract reflection of this actual mode of conduct. It led naturally to Bentham. As in his vision of English society, political allegiance is claimed as a prudential, temporary, calculated, secular, impersonal exercise in

---

[317] *Boswell's Life of Johnson* (Oxford Standard Authors edn, Oxford, 1965), pp. 28, 32, 53, 103–5, 107, 198–9, 305, 384, 515, 610–11, 840–1, 845, 1195, 1287, 1294, 1311.

self-interest and limited liability; the politics of a society in which Jacobitism *must have* stood no chance because it 'had nothing to offer for most people'.[318]

Too much of this analysis has ultimately derived from nineteenth-century polemic, especially that type of polemical category engendered by utilitarianism and by the debates over parliamentary reform in 1832, 1867 and 1884. The terms of at least the second and third of those bills were drafted and fought over on the assumption that classes as such pursued their self-interest; that it would be conceived, and could be expressed, in material and numerical terms. The electoral system came to be treated as a machine recording and giving effect to this felicific calculus: as the means whereby power was seized by one class or other and used for its own ends. Historians of nineteenth-century franchise reform were then faced with the problem of why such forces, if correctly diagnosed, failed to produce the expected results. The classic answer had to be, not that the assumptions were wrong, but that it was residual corruption which prevented the working class from being politically effective after 1832 and 1867.[319]

Much history of eighteenth-century society is still at that stage in its diagnosis of 'political stability', of the 'Whig oligarchy', or of resistance to the 'making of the English working class'. An alternative view is possible, for the examination of political allegiance as such bears closely on the assumptions about typical motivation (or English 'character') on which Whig theories of the electorate are premised. Lockeian contractarianism itself was brought to bear at this point in the argument in an attempt to refute the 'interpretation of allegiance as a purely natural relationship'[320] – the interpretation held by James I, Filmer and later theorists of monarchy. Did society in fact behave in Lockeian ways? The question is accessible not least via the law of nationality, for allegiance and nationality were synonymous. From the thirteenth century, 'it is the duty of allegiance, owed by the subject to the crown, which differentiates the subject from the alien'.[321] Locke's hypothetical State is legitimated by consent, either express (e.g. by oaths) or tacit (e.g. by residence). The second, to be realistic, must imply a right of emigration. In fact, English law largely corresponded to Filmer's picture. As 'summed up, restated and adapted' in *Calvin's Case* in 1609, it placed the chief emphasis, as Holdsworth pointed out, on 'the conception of allegiance as a personal bond between the king and his subjects'. The judges maintained that 'the duty of allegiance, and consequently the status of a subject, were attached, not to the corporate, but to the natural capacity of the king'. In the words of Lord Ellesmere:

The bond of allegiance...is vinculum fidei; it bindeth the soul and conscience of every subject severally and respectively, to be faithful and obedient to the king: and

[318] H. T. Dickinson, in Cannon (ed.), *The Whig Ascendency*, p. 186.
[319] Charles Seymour, quoted in Clarke, 'Electoral Sociology of Modern Britain', p. 36.
[320] Dunn, *Political Thought of John Locke*, pp. 136, 145.   [321] Holdsworth, vol. IX, p. 72.

as a soul or conscience cannot be framed by policy; so faith and allegiance cannot be framed by policy, nor put in a politic body. An oath must be sworn by a natural body; homage and fealty must be done by a natural body, a politic body cannot do it.

Paine's doctrine was revolutionary in contending that an oath of allegiance has to be to a nation; that it cannot be sworn to an individual.[322] It was particularly ironic therefore that when Americans in Paris sought to release Paine from imprisonment in 1794, when he was in fear of execution, their application was refused on the grounds that Paine had been born in England – that he was an English national.[323]

From *Calvin's Case*, it is quite clear in English law that 'the status of a subject was indelible'. As late as 1812, it was the doctrine which was used to justify the impressment into the Royal Navy of British-born seamen serving on American ships, despite their claim to be naturalised Americans. Not until the Naturalisation Act of 1870 was a procedure for renouncing British nationality laid down.[324] In the case of one of the prisoners of the '45, Aeneas Macdonald, whose defence was that he was a subject of the King of France, but who failed to prove his birth in that country, the court held in 1747 that 'It is not in the power of any private subject to shake off his allegiance, and to transfer it to a foreign prince. Nor is it in the power of any foreign prince by naturalizing or employing a subject of Great Britain to dissolve the bond of allegiance between that subject and the crown.' – This, despite the defence's claim that 'the doctrine of natural allegiance' was 'a slavish principle, not likely to prevail in these times; especially as it seemed to derogate from the principles of the Revolution'.[325]

Although some Englishmen generally had a practical freedom to emigrate, they had no legal right to do so; so that an English subject was not, in law, free to refuse acts which Locke would call ones of tacit assent. And, in fact, throughout the seventeenth and eighteenth centuries, oaths played a major role as tests of allegiance – not because some men might not break them, or lie in taking them, but because they were central to contemporaries' understanding of the political bond. The Jesuit doctrine of equivocation was therefore regarded with horror; for, as Sir Walter Raleigh had said, oaths defend 'the life of man, the estates of men, the faith of subjects to kings, of servants to their masters, of vassals to their lords, of wives to their husbands, and of children to their parents, and...all trials of right'.[326] The patriarchal,

[322] Paine, *Rights of Man*, p. 228.
[323] T. Paine, *The Age of Reason* (ed. M. D. Conway, New York, 1896), p. 86.
[324] Holdsworth, vol. IX, pp. 72, 81–2, 84, 87, 90–1.
[325] T. B. Howell (ed.), *A Complete Collection of State Trials*, vol. XVIII (London, 1813), cols. 858–9.
[326] Quoted in C. Hill, *Society and Puritanism in Pre-Revolutionary England* (1964; Panther edn, 1969),p. 383. The present argument is at variance with Dr Hill's suggestion that oaths lost their force in 'the new Hobbist society' of the late seventeenth century as 'the assumptions of the self-interest society' took over: 'The supernatural sanction backing the oath of

hierarchical, confessional state found its legal language not in rights, but in writs;[327] its political language not in secret ballots, but in personal oaths. It is not, therefore, an exaggeration to say that the letter and the reality of the English law of allegiance flatly contradicted Locke's theory at a central point. This objection, and the discrepancy between theory and practice, occurred forcibly to Hume:

> Should it be said, that, by living under the domain of a prince, which one might leave, every individual has given a *tacit* consent to his authority, and promised him obedience; it may be answered, that such an implied consent can only have place, where a man imagines, that the matter depends on his choice. But where he thinks (as all mankind do who are born under established governments) that by his birth he owes allegiance to a certain prince or certain form of government; it would be absurd to infer a consent or choice, which he expressly, in this case, renounces and disclaims.
>
> Can we seriously say, that a poor peasant or artizan has a free choice to leave his country, when he knows no foreign language or manners, and lives from day to day, by the small wages which he acquires? We may as well assert, that a man, by remaining in a vessel, freely consents to the dominion of the master; though he was carried on board while asleep, and must leap into the ocean, and perish, the moment he leaves her.[328]

It is exactly because men did not behave politically as Locke's theory, to be viable, assumed they must, that Locke's currency in the later eighteenth century did not imply a rejection of the law, but a partial and partly mistaken understanding of Locke. Not only was Locke misunderstood, then, but the extent of the reception of Lockeian contractarianism after 1688 has been exaggerated. As has been seen, High Church doctrines, patriarchal attitudes and a stress on the personal nature of government were all in full flower in the reign of Anne. In 1714, that world view was not refuted and discarded. It was, rather, divided between the adherents of the royal houses of Hanover and Stuart. From Whig England, George I and George II inherited not a little of the deference accorded their Stuart predecessors. The weakness of the early Hanoverian monarchs vis-a-vis their Whig ministers

loyalty and the judicial oath – God the supreme overlord – was succeeded in capitalist society by the discovery that it paid a man to make his word his bond because of the rise in social importance of credit, reputation, respectability', so that the Nonjurors' argument was 'the final *reductio ad absurdum* of the traditional position' (*op. cit.*, chapter 11, 'From Oaths to Interest', *passim*). Cf. Mr Dunn's reply (*Locke*, p. 141 n. 4):

> It is a matter of some interest that the arch bourgeois Locke should fail so dimly to follow the historicist line of [Dr Hill's] chapter in substituting rational interest for religious taboo as a basis for the sanction of oaths, indeed that he should suppose the bonds of society to be dissolved by the very adoption of atheism as a theory.

[327] Cf. F. W. Maitland, *The Forms of Action at Common Law* (Cambridge, 1968, ed. A. H. Chaytor and W. J. Whittaker). Until the nineteenth-century reforms, Maitland's principle holds good: 'the forms of action are given, the causes of action must be deduced therefrom' (p. 5). Political historians must draw the moral.

[328] Hume, 'Of the Original Contract', in *Essays*, vol I, p. 451.

has been overstated;[329] Whig dependence on the Hanoverian dynasty actually committed them to a form of royalism. The two dynasties became, of course, political badges. The identification of the reigning house with England's fortunes against a foreign military threat fused – contingently – three elements: Whig, Hanoverian, Protestant. So, equally, for the Tories, consistent and honourable conduct came to revolve around the dynastic issue, and the ambiguities, equivocations and disloyalties it imposed on them.[330]

It was because both sides shared so many elements of their world view that Bishop Butler's words were so often quoted: 'Civil liberty, the liberty of a community, is a severe and restrained thing; implies in the notion of it, authority, settled subordinations, subjection, and obedience; and is altogether as much hurt by too little of this kind, as by too much of it.'[331] Whigs as late as Burke reiterated this insistence on *settled* subordinations. Their argument that the points at issue had been irrevocably decided was generically similar to the Jacobite argument. As a Whig don addressed a hypothetical undergraduate in 1748: 'The law hath already precluded your enquiry, and determined where your allegiance is due: under that law you were born; – it hath hitherto afforded you protection; to it therefore, by all the ties of nature and gratitude, is your duty pre-engaged.'[332]

This is not to adjudicate on the sincerity of professions of political principle. It is rather to point to what is prevalent in the principles to which men appealed. Many there were, of course, whose sincerity and consistency the historian would not wish to urge. Self-interested calculation may be thought inseparable from any profession of principled action. It is exactly this mediation between theory and reality that makes politics central, not contingent. Politics, before the 1750s, permitted a variety of alignments and re-alignments within the terms of dynastic ideology. For that reason, in calling an early-eighteenth-century Englishman a Jacobite, we should not expect conformity to the pattern of a William Shippen, openly, frankly (and therefore harmlessly) committed to the Stuarts, just as, in speaking of men as Whigs, we should not always think of Hardwicke and Newcastle, whose whole careers were bound up with the dynasty, without also remembering those major figures who had been prudent enough to take out an insurance policy at St Germain. The priority of the dynastic issue did not guarantee

---

[329] As is shrewdly demonstrated by J. B. Owen, 'George II Reconsidered', in Anne Whiteman (ed.), *Statesmen, Scholars and Merchants* (Oxford, 1973), pp. 113–34.

[330] For a perceptive and scholarly investigation of this, cf. especially Howard Erskine-Hill, *The Social Milieu of Alexander Pope* (London, 1975); *idem*, 'Alexander Pope: The Political Poet in His Time', *ECS* 15 (1981–2), 123–48; *idem*, 'Literature and the Jacobite Cause: Was There a Rhetoric of Jacobitism?', in Cruickshanks (ed.), *Ideology and Conspiracy*, pp. 49–69.

[331] Butler's 30th January sermon before the House of Lords in 1741, in S. Hallifax (ed.), *The Works of . . . Joseph Butler* (2 vols., Oxford, 1820), vol. II, p. 347.

[332] Bentham, *Letter to a Young Gentleman*, p. 7.

unequivocal loyalty, and the existence of such reservations as late as the 1740s bears out the insight of a pamphleteer of 1710: 'These distinctions of Whig and Tory do properly belong to the second class, or inferior rank of men; for persons of the first rank, who either by their birth or abilities are entitled to govern others, do not really list themselves in those parties, but only put themselves at the head of either of them.'[333]

This priority of a certain type of political issue from the time of the Exclusion Crisis gave political allegiance a principle of continuity and a noble ideal which the final extinction of the Jacobite option in the 1750s was sometimes thought to have destroyed. Its evident absence in the squalid factious conflicts of the 1760s led one observer to complain: 'When the nation was split into two parties Whigs and Tories, there was a principle of honour which connected their friends, and which disappeared the moment they separated themselves into distinct factions.'[334] When, in this newly unstable world of shifting alliances and destructive manoeuvre, George III was drawn to play a more active role in the search for viable and acceptable administrations, he aroused fears and hopes of attempting to reassert a pre-1688 idiom of kingship. Those fears are not evidence for the reality of any such attempt (as we now know, there was no royal conspiracy against liberty in the 1760s), but they are evidence for the survival up to that point of such a political language as an intelligible and powerful one.

Nevertheless, 1760 marked a break in two respects. The uniting of old Whig and old Tory allowed the monarchy to be progressively hedged with a certain divinity, but as a diffused sense of reverence which also embraced the whole social order, not as the sharply-focussed spotlight which early-eighteenth-century dynastic conflict had made it. For Paley, who explicitly rejected contract theory and embraced both patriarchalism and hereditary monarchy, the divine right of kings was not to be understood as endorsing 'the most exalted and superstitious ideas of the royal character'. St Paul's doctrines commanding obedience, he claimed, apply equally to all forms of government, not just absolute hereditary monarchs. And God commands obedience to all lesser officials for the same reason:

The divine right of *kings* is, like the divine right of other magistrates, the law of the land, or even actual and quiet possession of their office; – a right ratified, we humbly presume, by the Divine approbation, so long as obedience to their authority appears, to be necessary or conducive to the common welfare. Princes are ordained of God by virtue only of that general decree by which he assents, and adds the sanction of his will, to every law of society which promotes his own purpose – the communication of human happiness.[335]

---

[333] Quoted in Kenyon, *Revolution Principles*, p. 104.

[334] Sir George Colebrooke, *Retrospection: or, Reminiscences Addressed to My Son Henry Thomas Colebrooke Esq* (2 vols., privately printed, London, 1898), vol. I, p. 70.

[335] Paley, *Moral and Political Philosophy* in *Works*, vol. II, p. 347.

In this form the attitude was in full repair until the destruction of the confessional state in 1828–32.

The second sense in which 1760 marked an important break, with respect to political allegiance, was that the political morality which had provided a principle of coherence for the two traditional parties was now regarded as obsolete. The parties themselves dissolved into the factions of the 1760s. Efforts to conserve or re-create group unity, from that decade, concerned themselves not chiefly with programmes or the mechanics of party organisations, but, ultimately, with a *soi-disant* virtuous crusade against alleged ministerial conspiracy, and a defence of the morality of a certain sort of political conduct: '*Party Allegiance*' as J. W. Croker later hailed it – 'a great moral and political discovery'.[336] Like many great discoveries, it was in a sense a re-discovery; but there can be little doubt about the importance of the part played in it by Burke and the Rockingham Whigs. In respect of the nature of allegiance, therefore, a choice between dynasties translated itself after 1760 into a choice between parties: the political options acted, if only gradually, to depersonalise the nature of the commitment itself.

The contrast in these respects between political activity after 1832 and before 1760 is immense. Added to the dynastic issue, the attempted identity of Church and State in the early eighteenth century – two bodies with the same head, composed of the same individuals, professing the same moral goals – cast the ideal of political obedience (however far the reality fell short) in terms of Christian humility; phrased political loyalty in terms of the consistency of religious faith and each man's loyalty to a sovereign Deity; and commended political participation – vicarious identification with a distant monarch – by analogy with the receipt of grace. Where Benthamism assumed justification by works, politics, cast in the idiom of the aristocratic ideal, assumed justification by political faith. Englishmen were aware of England's special status in Europe as a religious experiment for a century and a half before they began to be aware of her special position as a constitutional experiment after 1688. The religious element in this sense of nationality bulked large even into the Victorian era. Victorian writers correctly sensed it. But they were inclined to read it in terms of the middle-class evangelical churchmanship of their own day. Later rejections of that religious stance have obscured the insight, though an imperfect insight, which that position expressed: that the form and fortunes of English religion profoundly influenced the nature of English political activity and allegiance. It did so, as we can now see, not in a nineteenth-century way, but in a manner appropriate to the Church of Leslie, Sacheverell, Atterbury, Berkeley, Gibson, Butler, Law, Warburton, Sherlock and Potter.

The object should already have become evident of the attempt which has been made to trace the themes of patriarchalism and deference, of the

[336] [J. W. Croker], review of Phillimore, *Lyttelton* in *The Quarterly Review* 78 (1846), 258.

divinity of kings or the State, of the aristocratic code, beyond 1760 and in some respects until 1832. For the problem with the question of Jacobitism in England in the reigns of George I and George II is not that it cannot be made plausible, but that, if examined seriously, it at once becomes too plausible. The social and intellectual preconditions for the credibility of that form of political allegiance are either valid for many decades after the strategic threat of a Stuart restoration is patently extinct, or are transformed only as a consequence of that extinction. The solution to the paradox, of course, is that the decline of Jacobitism is chiefly to be explained not in terms of the prior exhaustion of its necessary preconditions, but in terms of the political and military events of the 1740s and 50s. Whig and neo-Whig historians have been too used to being on the winning side: they give infinitely too little importance to the outcome of battles.

Jacobitism is a problem not least because it was a movement which failed, an alternative which was not taken. Despite Sir Herbert Butterfield's warnings, many still have difficulty in taking such options seriously; in endorsing the reality of the alternatives which they represented; in judging the narrowness of the margin by which they missed success; and, consequently, in interpreting everything else in the light of those possibilities. For the real challenge to the conventional historical wisdom of the 1960s and 70s is not that the Tory party survived into the eighteenth century. That, in itself, might be explained in the mechanical terms of party organisation and ambition for office and its spoils on the part of an essentially loyal opposition (flavoured, perhaps, with a dash of proto-radicalism). By far the more disturbing contention is that the survival of the Tory party had to do also, and importantly, with the persistence of Jacobitism, and that it was able to persist because political allegiance itself was conceived of in those decades as a different thing from what it was later to become. The roots of allegiance were not presumed to reside in class, party organisation or oligarchic self-interest. Political loyalties were describable, and were frequently described, as hereditary, personal, emotional, uncalculating, and even quasi-religious, bound up with faith as much as with feelings of nationalism, in a society in which these things were given reality on a personal scale. Kettlewell spoke for more than the Nonjurors in denying that allegiance is 'only a tribute for protection'. Allegiance is 'the band, which ties not one stranger to another, who may look on with mere indifference, as idle spectators; but the members to the head'.[337]

What is at issue, then, is the survival into the eighteenth century of certain elements of 'the old' which made possible a number of defining characteristics of political life. The continued domination of national politics by the aristocracy, and of local politics by the gentry. The reality,

---

[337] [John Kettlewell], *The Duty of Allegiance Settled upon its True Grounds, According to Scripture, Reason, and the Opinion of the Church* (London, 1691), pp. 4, 9.

via the intellectual hegemony of nobility, gentry and clergy, of a widely-received understanding of a hierarchic and confessional State, claiming a divine sanction. The early function of an English consciousness, through the personification of the State in the ruling family, long in advance of nineteenth-century nationalism. The casting of political attitudes within a personal mould, creating the possibility of expressing political choices in terms of dynastic allegiance. The strong links between dynastic allegiance and religious affiliation. And the English invention of political parties, in their different forms, given coherence not chiefly or initially by the party machines or platforms appropriate to a representative democracy, but by a principle of conduct drawing on this idiom of dynastic allegiance and aristocratic honour.

Though political forms were in flux in the eighteenth century, the attitudes and predispositions discussed in this chapter changed little in the time of Locke and Defoe. 'English individualism' is best understood not as something which emerged with the disintegration of a supposedly feudal economy in the seventeenth century, but as something appropriate to the structure of English society for many centuries before that.[338] Yet, in general, where the most recent historians of the seventeenth century have been anxious to emphasise the differences of the mental world within which their characters moved, writers on the eighteenth century have usually tried to emphasise the modernity of that age, and to express its differences from us largely in material and quantitative terms. It has been exhibited as the recent modernity of a state struggling to throw off 'the trappings of feudal society'.[339] Its provincial towns, like London, were 'full of opportunity for men of tough temperament, endless vigour, and resource'; 'English industrialists and merchants were aggressive, inventive, and fully alive to a sense of their own future and greatness', boasting 'that sense of independence and decisive judgement which made England capable of democracy long before the reform of her oligarchic institutions'. 'The age of Walpole was rough, coarse, brutal; a world for the muscular and the aggressive and the cunning', enjoying its 'prosperity and opportunity, which bred a boundless self-confidence', to such effect that, with Pitt's resignation in 1761, 'the day of the bourgeois radical dawned'.[340]

It was, we are told, a false dawn. In the provincial towns, which 'felt tradition to be inimical to their interests', there was 'a seedbed in which

---

[338] For a denial that mediaeval and early-modern England was a 'peasant society' in the classical sense, cf. Alan Macfarlane, *The Origins of English Individualism* (Oxford, 1978). For a contrary view that it was eighteenth-century enclosures which 'witnessed the near-elimination of the peasantry as a class', cf. J. H. Plumb, 'Political Man', in J. L. Clifford (ed.), *Man versus Society in Eighteenth Century Britain* (Cambridge, 1968), p. 8.

[339] J. H. Plumb, *The First Four Georges* (London, 1956), p. 143.

[340] J. H. Plumb, *England in the Eighteenth Century* (Harmondsworth, 1982), pp. 17, 24-5, 32-3, 115.

critical attitudes could grow, in which the acres of ignorance and superstition could be steadily narrowed. So startling were the results of science and technology... that one might have expected a quick victory and the growth of a society in Britain addicted to education, knowledge, experiment, and the scientific attitude.' But 'It was not to be': traditionalism, and therefore irrationalism, reimposed itself.[341] In the light of the arguments advanced above, it might be possible to progress beyond a blank map of early-modern social history, whole areas labelled merely 'acres of ignorance and super-stition'. Rather than deducing the course or the structures of English politics from judgements of this sort, it would be better to confront the question directly: when did the political parties of early-eighteenth-century England break down? I have attempted an answer elsewhere.[342]

[341] J. H. Plumb, 'Reason and Unreason in the Eighteenth Century: the English Experience', in J. H. Plumb and V. A. Dearing (eds.), *Some Aspects of Eighteenth-Century England* (Los Angeles, 1971), pp. 19–20 and *passim*.

[342] Clark, 'A General Theory of Party, Opposition and Government, 1688–1832', (1980); *The Dynamics of Change* (1982).

4

The Self-Image of the State: the Case for the Establishment, 1760–1815

I. INTRODUCTION

It was mainly the issues of allegiance and sovereignty, not representation and reform, which the American crisis raised and which dominated British politics in the 1770s and early 1780s. Largely the same issues, focussing on the monarchy and the Church, were inescapably at the head of the agenda from the French Revolution until 1815. Such issues sustained an ideological consensus of great unity and strength. By contrast, the American problem (and, still more, the French Revolution) revealed the 'intellectual bankruptcy of the mainstream Whig tradition'.[1] It was bankrupt not merely, however, because the ministries of Lord North and William Pitt could defend their policies with arguments which were as Whig in their origins as the arguments of Rockingham and Fox. It was bankrupt chiefly because the radical elements of the Whig tradition which the Rockingham Whigs chose to emphasise and others chose to develop were regarded as intellectually weak compared to the conservative elements of the same tradition, meshing as the latter did with an Anglican political theology of even greater power.

That political theology, and its relation to the law, has been largely neglected by historians. No single book has been devoted to it. As a result, the frustration of the radical impetus has often been made to seem either the result of 'mindless authoritarianism', material greed, and corrupt manoeuvre, or the paradoxically large consequence of the relatively small and often half-hearted body of constitutional theory which grew up to defend the unreformed electoral system. The suggestion has been aptly made[2] that the radicals of the 1790s were defeated not principally by

---

[1] Paul Langford, 'Old Whigs, Old Tories, and the American Revolution', *The Journal of Imperial and Commonwealth History* 8 (1980), 120. The Rockinghams' claim to be the heirs of the *mainstream* should not go unquestioned.

[2] By Professor Dickinson, *Liberty and Property*, chapter 8.

'reaction' but by the 'force of their opponents' arguments' and the conservative consensus which those arguments made possible. Yet we still know all too little about the Establishment viewpoint, not just in the 1790s, but throughout the period from the accession of George III to the Reform Bill. By focussing almost exclusively on secular figures, historians have left the Establishment with puzzlingly few advocates.

Historians preoccupied with the supposed importance of Locke as the prophet of bourgeois capitalist values have assumed, too, that the defence of private property and therefore of a privileged social elite was the central function both of the legislature and of Establishment political theory in the Lockeian idiom.[3] It was, no doubt, one function; but by identifying it as the *central* function, historians have encouraged each other to disregard the force and the autonomy of those ties, obligations and commitments which distinguished political and social theory, and to a large degree political and social practice, before 1832. By disregarding the Church, by ignoring its political theology, many writers have given us no basis for understanding the position of strength which the Anglican-aristocratic regime occupied until 1828–32.

This chapter attempts to outline the main theoretical elements in the conservative Whig ideology which provided the intellectual structure of the British Establishment into the early nineteenth century. It suggests that the conservative position was neither unthinking nor amoral – that it possessed a sophisticated body of theory with the widest religious dimensions. Thus identified, it becomes clear that the conservative case was not suddenly contrived in response to a radical challenge after 1789. Nor did it then return to the doctrine of divine right: it had never left it. The conservative repudiation of a right of resistance under George III was fully prefigured in the orthodox Whigs' refusal to concede any right of resistance to the first two Georges in practice, even if they allowed a distant right in theory. The conservative case owed its form to being the living and vital descendant of Orthodox Whig theory as it existed in the reign of George II, adapted to a new political situation.

The political theology identified here represented the State's high-level ideology concerning its origins, authority and sphere of action. On a lower level, its specific governmental institutions could be defended with a variety of arguments, whether asserting the wisdom of an ancient constitution, the mutual balance of King, Lords and Commons, or more recently the ability of 'interests' (land, commerce, the professions) to secure parliamentary representation through the existing structure of seats and franchises.[4] The place of the elite in the social hierarchy had its own theory, briefly explored

---

[3] This is the position adopted in Dickinson, *Liberty and Property*.
[4] Classically discussed by J. R. Pole, *Political Representation in England and the Origins of the American Republic* (London, 1966), pp. 442–99.

in chapter 2. Each of these defences, equally, could be challenged on its own level: were landowners the proper members of the elite, or James Mill's middle ranks? Did trade, or manufacture, receive the representation due to its growing importance as an 'interest'? Was the suffrage itself a form of property? Yet, as is argued in chapters 5 and 6, none of these debates was sufficient in itself to produce the convulsion of 1828–32. In order to understand the strategies of those who sought to undermine the old order, we must first trace its theoretical structure in the formulations given to it by its defenders.

II. THE ROYAL PREROGATIVE: CONSTITUTIONAL CONTROVERSY FROM BLACKSTONE TO HOLLAND HOUSE

In chapter 3 it was shown that the official rationale for the *de facto* regimes in England, after 1688 and indeed throughout the reign of George II, was a politico-theological one. This was true in grass-roots discourse also. As Dr William King had put it, 'We are convinced by daily experience, that it is impossible to converse with any Englishmen, of whatsoever sect or party, unless religion and politics make a part of the entertainment.'[5] Nothing occurred in 1760 to break this intellectual mould. With the final eclipse of the Jacobite threat in the 1750s, the need to defend the regime in dynastic terms was, for the moment, removed: the major challenge had evaporated. But the official rationale for George III's monarchy remained unaltered, and was, if anything, given a note of quiet assurance both by a practical victory over the Stuart danger, which could then be interpreted as a just ideological victory, and by the confluence after 1760 of two strands of monarchical legitimism.

The Establishment orthodoxy may be traced both in the Church, and in the law. The law was perhaps the most direct channel through which such doctrines were conveyed to the new king. Lord Bute, in charge of Prince George's education after 1755, read in manuscript the Oxford lectures of William Blackstone, and taught his royal pupil doctrines which Bute himself was doubtless predisposed to believe. George III inherited a polemically Tory attitude to English history since 1714, as his instructor's papers reveal.[6] The Hanoverian succession had been the work of both parties, it ran, but the Whigs had quickly monopolised George I's favour and needlessly proscribed their opponents. Tory desperation, and the factious tyranny of the Whigs, provoked the '15 and the '45. Far from being educated in Jacobite principles, Prince George seems not to have been made aware of a cogent and powerful Tory–Jacobite case against his dynasty's title. Rather,

[5] [William King], *The Dreamer* (London, 1754), p. xvi.
[6] Cf. the document attributed to Bute in J. L. McKelvey, *George III and Lord Bute. The Leicester House Years* (Durham, N.C., 1973) p. 85.

he was presented with the Tory gambit[7] which attributed the failure of hopes for 'a coalited, that is a national' party in 1727 to the Whigs' success in maintaining their selfish, factious and unjustified monopoly of royal favour under George II. Consequently, it was essential that the new king should rise above party at his accession, breaking the Whig stranglehold; and this could only be done by the independent and vigorous exercise of the royal prerogative. The key to Blackstone's view of the law, as to Bute's of the constitution, was a renewed emphasis on the prerogative as the justification for the removal of Whig ministers of the seniority, stature and distinction of Newcastle, Hardwicke and Pitt.

Blackstone was not the only lawyer giving expression to such sentiments. In 1764 appeared an anonymous study of the laws concerning the royal prerogative, entitled *Droit le Roy*. Its eulogy of prerogative echoes the importance which a newly-united society attached to its principle of unity:

...on this law (which exalts our king so much above his subjects) depends that due subordination which constitutes the political beauty, harmony and strength of every well governed state, and without which no state whatever can long endure without rushing into anarchy and confusion.

On the basis of a codification of the law, the author continued:

Having thus sufficiently proved out of our books, that the power of the kings of England is an exempt, absolute, supreme and independent authority, acknowledging no superior, but God almighty, not to be divided, communicated nor transferred to any person whatsoever, without previous assent and consent of the nation in parliament assembled. I proceed to show the reader in the next place, that George the third, our now gracious sovereign lord and king, is the lawful and undoubted heir of the blood royal of this realm, as appears by the pedigree following: and consequently his most excellent majesty, has the same absolute, sovereign and regal power over the subjects of this nation, that his royal predecessors, the kings and queens of England, have heretofore claimed and enjoyed.

These were obviously extensive: for, since 'this realm admits of no inter regnum', James II having abdicated, 'the vacated crown, devolved on his eldest daughter Mary, as the nearest Protestant heir, and in her right on her husband William Prince of Orange'.

The author was unequivocal in his disqualification of a Popish sovereign, and in identifying the Hanoverian monarchy as quintessentially a Protestant one. The problem was that George III's title, thus solidly established, seemed to fill the whole constitutional stage. To the objection that 'the legislative power is not solely in the King, but in him and the two houses of Parliament', so that the Lords and Commons were 'partners of the sovereignty', turning 'the monarchy of England, into a tripartite and

---

[7] Remarkably, some historians still mistake this disingenuous tactic for a disinterested and accurate analysis.

co-ordinate government, which others call a mixt monarchy', the author replied

...that to the two houses of Parliament, belongs a right of privilege, for the making of laws, by yielding their consent; but that they have a co-ordinate, co-equal, co-rival and collateral power with the sovereignty of royalty, all able jurists, and true politicians utterly deny; for the houses are called together by the royal authority, not to be dictators but counsellors; not to be partners in the legislature, but petitioners.[8]

Thus the most strictly Protestant State, the most scrupulous attention to constitutional legalities, and the most explicit disavowals of 'Popery and arbitrary power', were to be made compatible with the most extensive conceptions of kingship.

Droit le Roy was published immediately after the furore over General Warrants, which had been used in an attempt to identify such parliamentary lawyers as Fletcher Norton, Philip Webb, Dr George Hay and Alexander Wedderburn as agents of a new absolutism. The opposition therefore seized another opportunity to blacken a position which, they implied, the ministry had adopted. Horace Walpole described the volume:

This pestilent treatise was a collection from old statutes and obsolete customs of the darkest and most arbitrary ages of whatever tended, or had tended, to show and uphold the prerogative of the Crown. The fulsome flattery and servility of ancient lawyers in every reign were amassed together, and shoved upon the world as the standing law of England; no retrospect had to all the immunities obtained since by the Civil War, by the Revolution, and by various other struggles of Parliaments with the Crown...Without metaphor, such a compilation proved that prerogative must have been the object of the Court before such gross adulation could dare to step forth in the face of both Houses of Parliament.[9]

George, Lord Lyttelton, who had seen his best days as an opposition Whig in the 1730s and 40s, and had committed himself to the view that 'the prerogative of the King is no more sacred than the liberty of the subject,'[10] now 'moved for a censure of the book as Jacobitical, and violating the Bill of Rights and the Revolution'.[11] This was ironic, since the text was explicitly and forthrightly the reverse; but in face of such a charge, the tactful course was for the ministry not to oppose it, and to allow through a formal motion that the book be burnt, like the *North Briton*.

The author, Timothy Brecknock,[12] was the forerunner. He drew the fire

[8] [Timothy Brecknock], *Droit le Roy. Or a Digest of the Rights and Prerogatives of the Imperial Crown of Great-Britain. By a Member of the Society of Lincoln's-Inn* (London, 1764), pp. ix, 20, 25, 32.

[9] Horace Walpole, *Memoirs of the Reign of King George the Third* (ed. G. F. Russell Barker, London, 1894), vol. I, pp. 304–5.

[10] George, Lord Lyttelton, *Considerations upon the Present State of our Affairs at Home and Abroad* (1739) in G. E. Ayscough (ed.), *The Works of George Lord Lyttelton* (London, 1774), p. 78.

[11] Walpole, *George III*, vol. I, pp. 305.

[12] By 1784, a Mr Brecknock was in receipt of money from the Secret Service fund: Aspinall, *Later Correspondence of George III*, vol. I, p. 118.

of the opposition, and aroused charges of reviving an anachronism. Yet it was not dissimilar in form, though different in tone, to doctrine which was soon to be accepted as orthodoxy in Blackstone, and which once again shocked radicals in the polemical use made of it by John Reeves in the 1790s.

It was William Blackstone[13] who provided the most acceptable statement of the case which the early-eighteenth-century Tory intelligentsia used,[14] in the field of law, as their justification for a reconciliation with the dynasty after 1760.[15] The wide currency of Blackstone's *Commentaries* was owed to their being acclaimed not only by Whigs but by those from a very different background, like the ex-Jacobite Lord Mansfield;[16] nor is it a coincidence that the sons of country gentlemen and of clergymen, especially Oxford graduates, returned in large numbers to the Bar after the accession of George III.[17] It was, perhaps, this confluence of praise which led later radicals to represent Blackstone, a Court lawyer, as merely a complacent apologist for all existing institutions. In fact, a considerable number of points of law attracted his restrained censure,[18] and several elements of the early-eighteenth-century Tory critique of the Whig regime carried over into Blackstone's appraisal of the law as it actually stood after 1760.

One such element was his muted reiteration of traditional Tory indignation at Walpolian manipulation of the electoral machine. Blackstone had been heavily involved on the Tory side in the bitterly partisan Oxfordshire contest of 1754, and it was rather the gentleness of his suggestion in 1765 which was remarkable: 'if any alteration might be wished or suggested in the present frame of parliaments, it should be in favour of a more complete representation of the people'.[19]

A second area in which an element borrowed from earlier Tory arguments is discernible was in his treatment of the royal prerogative. In typically Whig

---

[13] Sir William Blackstone (1723–80). Charterhouse; Pembroke Coll., Oxford 1738; Fellow of All Souls 1744; called to Bar 1746; Vinerian Professor 1758–66; MP 1761–70; Solicitor General to the Queen 1763–70; knighted 1770; justice of Common pleas 1770 – d.

[14] Holdsworth, vol. x, p. 420 erroneously supposed Blackstone regarded politics 'from the point of view of a Revolution Whig'.

[15] Blackstone delivered the Oxford lectures on which his *Commentaries* were based as a private lecturer from 1753 to 1758, and as Vinerian Professor from 1758 to 1766. Much in the *Commentaries* may therefore be evidence for the progressive reconciliation of many Tories to the dynasty even in the last ten years of George II's reign.

[16] J. Holliday, *The Life of William Late Earl of Mansfield* (London, 1797), pp. 89–90. Murray pressed Blackstone on Newcastle in 1752 for the Regius Chair of Civil Law, but Blackstone's Tory politics prevented his success.

[17] Paul Lucas, 'A Collective Biography of the Students and Barristers of Lincoln's Inn, 1680–1804: A Study in the "Aristocratic Resurgence" of the Eighteenth Century', *JMH* 46 (1974), 227–61, points also to a growing 'alliance' of clergy and lawyers in the later eighteenth century, part of the consolidation of elites into a unified, conservative upper class.

[18] Holdsworth, vol. xii, p. 728.

[19] William Blackstone, *Commentaries on the Laws of England* (4 vols., Oxford, 1765–9), vol. i, p. 166.

fashion Blackstone recounted with approval the checks and restrictions on the power of the Crown during the previous century, especially by the Revolution Settlement, so that 'we may perhaps be led to think, that the ballance is enclined pretty strongly to the popular scale, and that the executive magistrate has neither independence nor power enough left, to form that check upon the Lords and Commons, which the founders of our constitution intended'. On the contrary, Blackstone insisted, the royal influence had increased in many other ways: the augmentation of the hereditary revenue, the growth in the numbers of officials (customs and excise officers), the growth of the national debt, a standing army, 'will amply make amends for the loss of external prerogative'.

Upon the whole therefore I think it is clear, that, whatever may have become of the *nominal*, the *real* power of the crown has not been too far weakened by any transactions in the last century. Much is indeed given up; but much is also acquired. The stern commands of prerogative have yielded to the milder voice of influence; the slavish and exploded doctrine of non-resistance has given way to a military establishment by law; and to the disuse of parliaments has succeeded a parliamentary trust of an immense perpetual revenue.[20]

Blackstone's solution, and a justification of his injunction to reverence, loyalty and obedience, was nothing more intellectually complex than an eulogy of George III, 'a sovereign, who, in all those public acts that have personally proceeded from himself, hath manifested the highest veneration for the free constitution of Britain; hath already in more than one instance remarkably strengthened its outworks; and will therefore never harbour a thought, or adopt a persuasion, in any the remotest degree detrimental to public liberty.'[21]

Blackstone had insisted that 'The idea and practice of this political or civil liberty flourish in their highest vigour in these kingdoms, where it falls little short of perfection';[22] but radicals might well be alarmed by his synoptic account of the considerable extent of the prerogative, and his enthusiastic tone when discussing it. The crown was held by a right which, though not indefeasible, was emphatically hereditary, not elective. Those, insisted Blackstone, were the only two alternatives. Therefore, though he rejected a title '*jure divino*', he could still advance the doctrine that 'the king never dies'. English history since King Egbert was reviewed to substantiate the anti-Jacobite position that 'the doctrine of divine right' was 'wild and absurd'. Yet, having discarded it, Blackstone argued forcefully against any notion that the king was elective and therefore 'accountable' to the people,

---

[20] Holdsworth, vol. XII, p. 729 aptly compares this to Burke's *Present Discontents* (1770): 'the power of the Crown, almost dead and rotten as Prerogative, has grown up anew, with much more strength, and far less odium, under the name of Influence'.

[21] Blackstone, *Commentaries*, vol. I, pp. 322–6.

[22] *Ibid.*, vol. I, pp. 122–3.

as Charles I had been told by his judges. Consequently, he was forced to the familiar Whig account of the Revolution:

The true ground and principle, upon which that memorable event proceeded, was an entirely new case in politics, which had never before happened in our history; the abdication of the reigning monarch, and the vacancy of the throne thereupon. It was not a defeazance of the right of succession, and a new limitation of the crown, by the king and both houses of parliament: it was the act of the nation alone, upon an apprehension that there was no king in being

– as the resolution of both Houses in February 1688/9 showed (above, p. 128). Consequently, Blackstone refused to justify the Revolution

from its justice, moderation, and expedience: because that might imply a right of dissenting or revolting from it, in case we should think it unjust, oppressive, or inexpedient. Whereas, our ancestors having most indisputably a competent jurisdiction to decide this great and important question, and having in fact decided it, it is now become our duty at this distance of time to acquiesce in their determination; being born under that establishment which was built upon this foundation, and obliged by every tie, religious as well as civil, to maintain it.

The English State, as much as the English church, was now a *via media*:

The extremes, between which it steers, are each of them equally destructive of those ends for which societies were formed and are kept on foot. Where the magistrate, upon every succession, is elected by the people, and may by the express provision of the laws be deposed (if not punished) by his subjects, this may sound like the perfection of liberty, and look well enough when delineated on paper; but in practice will ever be productive of tumult, contention, and anarchy. And, on the other hand, divine indefeasible hereditary right, when coupled with the doctrine of unlimited passive obedience, is surely of all constitutions the most thoroughly slavish and dreadful. But when such an hereditary right, as our laws have created and vested in the royal stock, is closely interwoven with those liberties, which, we have seen in a former chapter, are equally the inheritance of the subject; this union will form a constitution, in theory the most beautiful of any, in practice the most approved, and, I trust, in duration the most permanent. It was the duty of an expounder of our laws to lay this constitution before the student in its true and genuine light: it is the duty of every good Englishman to understand, to revere, to defend it.[23]

In this way, ex-Tories came to accept the Whig redefinition of 'passive obedience'. From being a dignified and Christian theory of non-obedience, it was misrepresented as a slavish and unmanly theory of total obedience. Tories were able therefore to disavow it and yet, at the same time, to demand an obedience towards the regime of George III which excluded a right of resistance and which called for obedience for conscience' sake, as a Christian duty. Disavowing the name, men were able to retain the substance:

After what has been premised in this chapter, I shall not (I trust) be considered as an advocate for arbitrary power, when I lay it down as a principle, that in the exertion of lawful prerogative, the king is and ought to be absolute; that is, so far absolute, that there is no legal authority that can either delay or resist him.

[23] *Ibid.*, vol. I, pp. 184–211.

Only in the most extraordinary circumstances of oppression or tyranny, as in 1688, was deviation from this rule permissible. But such circumstances were entirely outside the ordinary course of events, and they could not be defined in advance. Consequently, they should not be discussed at all: 'it becomes us to be silent'.[24] Early-eighteenth-century Whigs had a more open and explicit defence of the Hanoverian dynasty's title. When Whig and Tory fused in 1760, the whole subject of the right of resistance was swept under the carpet.

The third chief respect in which Blackstone echoed early-eighteenth-century Toryism was in his firm defence of the Church. The *Commentaries* mirror High Church doctrine in their attitude to the legal standing of Dissent. Two Dissenting ministers, Joseph Priestley[25] and Philip Furneaux,[26] seized on the fourth volume of the *Commentaries* when it was published in 1769, objecting to the doctrines of chapter 4, 'Of Offences against God and Religion'. Set out in full, these were numerous, and the penalties often severe. They began with apostasy, which, in response to 'the most horrid doctrines subversive of all religion' propagated in the aftermath of the Revolution of 1688, was reaffirmed to be a crime by the Act of 9 & 10 W. III c 32. The offences continued with heresy; and anti-Trinitarian doctrines were punishable under the same statute. Reviling the ordinances of the Church was abominated by several statutes. Rightly, said Blackstone:

Nor can their continuance to this time be thought too severe and intolerant; when we consider, that they are levelled at an offence, to which men cannot now be prompted by any laudable motive; not even by a mistaken zeal for reformation: since from political reasons...it would now be extremely unadvisable to make any alterations in the service of the Church;

so that 'the virulent declamations of peevish or opinionated men' could only be intended 'to disturb the consciences, and poison the minds of the people'. This led him to Nonconformity. Those who absented themselves from the Church of England's worship and 'through total irreligion' attended no other, were still subject to many penalties. Those who worshipped elsewhere, 'through a mistaken or perverse zeal', whether Papists or Protestant Dissenters, were 'equally schismatics', but 'indulgence' had been extended to some of them:

The penalties are all of them suspended by the statute of 1 W & M st 2 c 18 commonly called the Toleration Act; which exempts all Dissenters (except Papists, and such as deny the Trinity) from all penal laws relating to religion, provided they

---

[24] *Ibid.*, vol. 1, pp. 238, 243.

[25] J. Priestley, *Remarks on Some Paragraphs in the Fourth Volume of Dr Blackstone's Commentaries... Relating to the Dissenters* (London, 1769).

[26] P. Furneaux, *Letters to the Honourable Mr Justice Blackstone, Concerning His Exposition of the Act of Toleration, and Some Positions Relative to Religious Liberty, In His Celebrated Commentaries on the Laws of England* (London, 1770). 'The truth is', he admitted, 'the legal state of religious liberty in these kingdoms is very little understood.' (p. iv).

take the oaths of allegiance and supremacy, and subscribe the declaration against Popery, and repair to some congregation registered in the bishop's court or at the sessions, the doors whereof must be always open: and dissenting teachers are also to subscribe the thirty nine articles, except those relating to church government and infant baptism.

The Test and Corporation Acts seemed to follow from this principle.[27] A mere suspension of penalties was very far from the *right* to toleration which Dissenters maintained they possessed, whether by natural law or by Mansfield's judgement in *The Corporation of London v. Evans* (1767);[28] and although Blackstone altered the wording of a subsequent edition, he did not abandon his position that nonconformity as such was a crime.[29]

In the light of Blackstone's implicit rejection of the Lockeian concept of the Church as a voluntary society, it is all the more remarkable that Blackstone's synthesis of Tory and Whig should include a rejection of the contractarian account of the origin of the State, but an acceptance of a contractarian understanding of its present functioning:

The only true and natural foundations of society are the wants and fears of individuals. Not that we can believe, with some theoretical writers, that there ever was a time when there was no such thing as society; and that, from the impulse of reason, and through a sense of their wants and weaknesses, individuals met together in a large plain, entered into an original contract, and chose the tallest man present to be their governor. This notion, of an actually existing unconnected state of nature, is too wild to be seriously admitted; and besides it is plainly contradictory to the revealed accounts of the primitive origin of mankind, and their preservation two thousand years afterwards [i.e. by Noah]; both which were effected by the means of single families...But though society had not its formal beginning from any convention of individuals, actuated by their wants and their fears; yet it is the *sense* of their weakness and imperfection that *keeps* mankind together; that demonstrates the necessity of this union; and that therefore is the solid and natural foundation, as well as the cement, of society. And this is what we mean by the original contract of society; which, though perhaps in no instance it has ever been formally expressed at the first institution of a state, yet in nature and reason must always be understood and implied, in the very act of associating together.

The protection extended by the State to the citizen created reciprocal duties; 'And these reciprocal duties are what, I apprehend, were meant by the Convention [Parliament] in 1688, when they declared that King James had broken the *original contract* between king and people.'

[27] Blackstone, *Commentaries*, vol. IV, pp. 41–65.
[28] Mansfield had said: 'Bare non-conformity is no sin by the common law; and all positive laws inflicting any pains or penalties for non-conformity to the established rites and modes, are repealed by that Act of Toleration; and dissenters are thereby exempted from all ecclesiastical censures': Holdsworth, vol. XII, p. 714. Mansfield's position was not to be fully accepted until 1828–9.
[29] That the Toleration Act 'was neither in purpose nor in fact a declaration that the rights of political citizenship were independent of the character of the citizen's religious practices' was the doctrine set out in *Church & State. Report of the Archbishops' Commission on the Relations Between Church and State* (2 vols., London, 1935), vol. I, p. 16.

But however, as the terms of that original contract were in some measure disputed, being alleged to exist principally in theory, and to be only deducible by reason and the rules of natural law; in which deduction different understandings might very considerably differ; it was, after the Revolution, judged proper to declare these duties expressly; and to reduce that contract to a plain certainty. So that, whatever doubts might be formerly raised by weak and scrupulous minds about the existence of such an original contract, they must now entirely cease; especially with regard to every prince, who has reigned since the year 1688.[30]

Again Blackstone's desire to treat the subject as settled and to stifle discussion is evident. It was the reverse of successful; because his case was an amalgam of different elements, it contained patent contradictions. These were seized on by Jeremy Bentham, ironically himself from a Tory background, who had attended Blackstone's lectures at Oxford, and who published *A Fragment on Government* in 1776 as a direct attack on the *Commentaries*. The social contract was a 'chimera' which 'had been effectually demolished by Mr Hume': sometimes Blackstone used it, sometimes he rejected it. Bentham had merely dispensed with it: 'I bid adieu to the original contract: and I left it to those to amuse themselves with this rattle, who could think they needed it.' What was remarkable about Bentham's case was that in rejecting this Whig device, he rejected also the whole Tory case, now built on it, that a new contract in 1688 had made allegiance thereafter non-contractual. The individual, insisted Bentham, was not bound by his ancestor's promises.[31]

The principle of utility commended itself not least because the alternative was patently self-contradictory. Yet Blackstone's contradictions were more the reflection of a social and political compromise than of intellectual inadequacy; and the ambiguities of his argument have continued to interest legal historians.

The philosophical part of Blackstone's work is confused and obscure. While accepting the theory of natural law in the sense in which Grotius had understood it, he sometimes seems to make some approach to the doctrines which deny or alter this superior and immutable law...We can read in the first chapters of the *Commentaries* the doctrines of Grotius: he has copied them word for word from Burlamaqui. The theory of Locke, which derives law from the social contract, and that of Hobbes which has for its object the denial of natural right, do not induce him to abandon the doctrines of Grotius, though they had long divided English political thinkers into hostile camps.[32]

The currency of theories is not destroyed by their inner contradictions. Blackstone, not Bentham, was appealed to as the official expositor of

---

[30] Blackstone, *Commentaries*, vol. I, pp. 47–8, 226.

[31] Jeremy Bentham, *A Fragment on Government. Being an Examination of What is Delivered, on the Subject of Government in General, in the Introduction to Sir William Blackstone's Commentaries* (London, 1776; ed. W. Harrison, Oxford, 1948), pp. 49, 51, 56.

[32] E. D. Glasson, *Histoire du Droit et des institutions...de l'Angleterre*, quoted Holdsworth, vol. XII, p. 73; cf. W. Harrison, *loc. cit.* p. xxv.

late-eighteenth-century constitutional law. And the central thread running through political conflicts from the reign of George III to that of William IV was not (as had been the case from William III to George II) the nature of the dynastic title, but the exercise of the royal prerogative.

Opposition thinkers consequently devoted considerable attention to the matter. Successive political episodes in George III's reign only added to the paranoid Whig legend, invented in the 1760s, of their exclusion by the illegitimate exercise of a royal veto. Lord John Russell wrote in 1821:

We have seen... that the influence of the Crown has increased to an alarming extent, and that the recurrence of periods of popular ferment, instead of checking this influence as it was wont to do in old times is made the occasion of passing new laws, clipping away something every time from the established liberties of the nation.

Moreover, there had been a change of mood in a monarchical direction:

During a long period of the late reign, comprising more than half its extended duration, no attempts were wanting to inflame the public mind, daily and hourly, against the rebellious subjects of our own king, and against a neighbouring nation, which deposed and executed its sovereign. It is impossible but that these invectives must have had their effect, and it can create surprise in no-one that a country so excited, so taught, and so inflamed, and that too by one of the most eloquent writers, and one of the most eloquent speakers whom England has produced, should become at last extremely alive to every supposed misdemeanour against prerogative, and completely dull and insensible to any violation of constitutional rights.

The Stuart threat, while it survived, meant that 'the king was obliged to make up in good government what he wanted in legitimate right'. But this threat had disappeared, and the king's advisers

... have accordingly revived, in a less odious form, the doctrine of passive submission, and they have carried along with them that immense rabble, who think 'the people are born with a saddle on their backs, and the king with a whip and spurs to ride them'.[33]

The complaint was taken up in more precise terms by Holland House's tame atheist, John Allen.[34] His *Inquiry into the Rise and Growth of the Royal Prerogative in England* was hailed by the *Edinburgh Review* on its appearance in 1830 as 'beyond all comparison the most important book upon constitutional antiquities and law that has appeared for many years':

... we hold the light which this book throws upon the early history of our constitution to be of the greatest importance. It shows us that, whatever the slavish propensities of priests or lawyers may have affected to believe, absolute power never was of right, and by law, naturalized in England; that freedom never was an exotic or a stranger, but the birthright and inheritance of Englishmen; that the presumption where no

[33] Lord John Russell, *An Essay on the History of the English Government and Constitution, from the Reign of Henry VII to the present time* (London, 1821; 2nd edn, 1823), pp. 433–8, 455.
[34] John Allen (1771–1843). Son of bankrupt; MD Edinburgh; failed in practice. Zealous for political reform in Scotland; became attached to Holland House, 1806; a paid retainer.

law or usage appears is always in favour of liberty, and against royal prerogative; that it is in no case for the subject to show his title to be free, but for the monarch to prove his right to oppress.[35]

Allen addressed himself to Blackstone as a summary of constitutional orthodoxy as it stood as late as 1830: there is no suggestion that anything essential had changed since the latter's death. From Blackstone he drew a series of paradoxes. The constitution was said to be founded in reason, argued Allen, yet 'the law of England attributes to the king absolute perfection, absolute immortality, and legal ubiquity'. Men 'may have been told, that the royal prerogative in England is limited: but, when they consult the sages of the law, they will be assured, that the legal authority of the King of England is absolute and irresistible, that he is the minister and substitute of the Deity; that all are under him while he is under none but God'. Those who had had 'the benefit of a liberal education' would assume the State had been instituted 'to obtain security for persons and property'; but the law taught that 'all jurisdiction emanates from the crown'.

Allen continued this contrast through all the king's prerogatives. Nor did they add up to a merely secular body, a 'corporation sole' in the legal expression: there was

...something higher, more mysterious, and more remote from reality, in the conception which the law of England forms of the king, than enters into the notion of a corporation sole. The ideal king of the law represents the power and majesty of the whole community. His *fiat* makes laws. His sentence condemns. His judgements give property, and take it away. He is the state. It is true, that in the exercise of these powers, the real king, to whom they are necessarily entrusted, is advised, directed, and controlled by others. But in the contemplation of law the sovereignty and undivided power of the state are in the king.

Moreover, allegiance to this absolute sovereign was both involuntary and indelible: a duty 'held to be perpetual and indefeasible by any act of the subject, due from all men born in the king's dominions immediately on their birth, and incapable of being forfeited, cancelled, or altered by any change of time, place, or circumstances, or by any power short of the legislature'. There 'cannot be a doubt', concluded Allen, 'that such is the constitution of England, as laid down most strongly and emphatically in the works of lawyers, and in the homilies of churchmen'. His book was an attempt to counter this historically, showing the very different origins of monarchy and the only limited acceptance of Blackstone's presentation of its current rationale. 'My object is to show in what manner the reasonings of lawyers and established maxims of constitutional law with respect to the real king have been warped and perverted by considerations drawn from his ideal prerogative'.

[35] *Edinburgh Review*, 103 (Oct. 1830), quoted in Allen, *Inquiry*, 2nd edn (London, 1849), pp. xxxi, lxiv.

After many a struggle between liberty and prerogative, the result has been in England that the real power of the king has been limited and defined by constitutional law and usage, but that the old attributes are still ascribed to him in law books; that an incongruous mixture of real and imaginary qualities has been formed, which has been called the union of his natural with his mystic or politic capacity; and that many privileges and peculiarities have been assigned to him in his natural person for reasons derived from his ideal or politic character.[36]

It was by opening up this distinction that the Whigs of 1830 sought to justify the limitation of royal prerogative. Allen, as an atheist, was sensitive to the extent to which the monarchy was still depicted, in orthodox formulations, in non-secular terms. For it was churchmen, not lawyers, politicians or a secular intelligentsia who kept in being the most eloquent and sophisticated body of generally-received political theory in the years up to 1832. That this was so meant that the traditional issues continued, occasionally, to find echoes within the House of Commons, and to be made the vehicles for new purposes.

In January 1763 Lord Strange attempted to have the House sit to do business on 30th January, and found himself involved in a division which he lost by 103 to 36. Henry Fox 'was of the majority, who, very few years before, had been for putting an end to that Jacobite holiday – a clear indication of the principles of the new Court', commented Horace Walpole, sourly. 'Lord Strange causing that part of the Act of Parliament, which ordains observance of the day, to be read, and affirming that the words, *Neither Parliament nor People can judge the King*, were contrary to the constitution; Fox denied it, and maintained that the constitution had always held that language.'[37] On 6th February 1772, the 'Feathers Tavern' petition was presented to the Commons, demanding the abolition of the requirement that Anglican clergy subscribe the Thirty-Nine Articles; it was rejected by 217 to 71. The forces of 'enlightened' opinion sought an opportunity for revenge. Only a few days before, Dr Thomas Nowell,[38] Lord North's choice in 1771 as Regius Professor of Modern History at Oxford and Dr King's successor as Principal of St Mary Hall, had preached the sermon on 30th January before the House of Commons – or rather, before four Members and the Speaker, the total attendance. The following day, the House voted its thanks, and ordered the sermon to be printed, as was customary. When seen in print, it was too much for one Newcastle Whig, Boyle Walsingham, though he had difficulty on 25th February in pointing

[36] John Allen, *Inquiry into the Rise and Growth of the Royal Prerogative in England* (London, 1830) pp. 1–10, 22, 27, 50, 54ff, 83, 86.

[37] Walpole, *George III*, vol. 1, pp. 190–1; Clark, *Dynamics of Change*, p. 141.

[38] Thomas Nowell (1730–1801) Oriel, 1746–; Fellow 1753–64; Principal, St Mary Hall, 1764 – d; Regius Professor of Modern History 1771 – d. Wrote in support of the expulsion of six Methodist undergraduates from St Edmund Hall, 1768, in the controversy which followed.

out exactly which passages were unacceptable. Another of the late Duke's friends, Thomas Townshend, sustained the attack: it was, he claimed, a throwback to Charles I's preachers, Mainwaring, Sibthorp and Montague, 'who preached then the same doctrines which Dr Nowell has now revived'.

Was the charge justified? In the passages Townshend indicated, Nowell had argued only that the rebels against Charles I had been impelled by their levelling principles: 'ambition, envy, and malice...the genuine offspring of depraved nature, shooting up in every age and nation from that root of bitterness, which interwove itself into the human constitution at the fall of man'. The Rebellion was an attack not only on a secular ruler, but on a providential social order:

When men consider themselves placed in their several subordinate stations, not by mere chance, or by any compact or agreement of their own framing, but by the will of Him who is the fountain of government, the supreme Lord of heaven and earth; when they consider that all authority, dominion, and power, are his prerogative, and derived from him to those, whom his Providence has delegated to be his representatives upon earth; chearful duty, and willing obedience, will be the natural result of such reflections.

Charles' government was not a despotic royal tyranny, continued Nowell. The rebels had no real grievances: their conduct 'was more deeply laid in the principles of the times, in the factious zeal, and turbulent spirit of men devoted to enthusiasm, frenzy, and madness'. And, finally, that Nowell's hearers 'behold the bright resemblance of those princely virtues, which adorned the royal martyr, now shining forth in the person of our gracious sovereign', George III.

Sir Roger Newdigate, in Nowell's defence, claimed that he had preached only what many others had preached, including Bishop Fleetwood. This was strictly true: Whig churchmen had hailed George I and George II in similar terms. But not only had Whigs out of office changed their tune; the old doctrine was also given a specific application both to the Feathers Tavern agitation and the 'Present Discontents' when Nowell warned that the events of the 1640s should 'put us on our guard against the attempts of men, who have artfully *revived* those disputes in the Church, and clamours in the State, which once terminated in the ruin of these kingdoms'.[39] The ministry was embarrassed: the ground was difficult to fight on, and the House voted to delete its vote of thanks from the Journals.[40]

This did not end the matter. A Chathamite carried it into public controversy, to justify 'the secession of every honest man from the councils of his majesty', and to vilify those who remained. 'When the leaders of the church, and the favourite preachers of the court begin to hold forth the

[39] Thomas Nowell, *A Sermon Preached before the Honourable House of Commons, at St Margaret's, Westminster, on Thursday, January XXX, 1772* (London, 1772), pp. 6, 10, 15, 19, 23.

[40] *Parl Hist,* vol. XVII, cols. 312–21. On 2nd March the House voted by 125 to 97 against abolishing the observance of 30th January.

antiquated doctrines of non-resistance and passive obedience', he argued, 'it is time for this nation to take the alarm.' Nowell had preached 'the indefeasible right of princes'; and the ministers, 'Being in diametrical opposition to their constituents...know that the permanence of that authority, at which they aim, depends upon a general belief, that religion requires an unreserved submission to the powers that *are*.' The anonymous author, seemingly bitter at loss of office, stigmatised 'the Brunswick line' with deserting 'the favourites of the people'; attempted to pin a 'Tory' label on the ministry; and gave content to that identity by recalling the Stuart doctrine of monarchy in its fullest extent.[41]

In a literal sense, these three contentions were invalid; but they caricatured real developments. Nowell was neither alone, nor eccentric, in his doctrine. His tone had been roundly oratorical; but a cooler, more scholarly, more closely-argued account of Orthodox doctrine emerged almost simultaneously from Cambridge.[42] Dr John Gordon explicitly disavowed 'the exploded doctrine of Government being founded in parental authority', and acclaimed the British constitution as the perfect *via media* between 'prerogative' and 'licentiousness'. Nevertheless, he went on to expound 'the sober politics of the Bible' in ways which ascribed great substance to the patriarchal ideal. The doctrine that 'all men are naturally equal' was openly disavowed: 'There is scarce more difference between us and other animals, than there is between man and man.' 'It is another favourite maxim with some, that all power is derived from the people. It is well, if they do not also tell us, that parental authority is derived from the children.' Most citizens were, and 'must ever in a great degree be...mere children; and pay of course a due submission to the authority of their political Fathers'. Contract theory was a nonsense; but false doctrines, and self-interested agitators, had succeeded in making many Englishmen dissatisfied with the best of governments. Positive laws would be of no effect without 'a spirit of subordination, a principle of reverence *for* and confidence *in* those, to whom the execution of the laws is entrusted', especially the king, whose person 'should be considered as the living body of the laws'.

Gordon's doctrine was not an antique survival, an academic exercise. It had a specific target in the social developments of the 1760s. Prosperity, literacy and the long enjoyment of liberty were (he thought) beginning to weaken the bonds of subordination, making men 'like wayward children too much indulged';

...since clubs of the lowest artificers have been formed to dispute and decide upon the most abstruse questions in religion and government, the meanest mechanic now

[41] *Critical Remarks on Dr Nowel's Sermon...* (London, [1772]), pp. 3–5, 7.

[42] John Gordon, *The Causes and Consequences of Evil Speaking against Government, Considered in a Sermon, Preached before the University of Cambridge...on the King's Accession, Oct. 25, 1771* (Cambridge, 1771). It was noticed by the author of the *Critical Remarks*: another indication of the currency of political sermons.

thinks himself fully qualified to supply the ministers, either of God or the King, with *his* superior information. . . . Formerly, when principles of a dangerous tendency were confined to books and pamphlets; they, in general, fell into the hands of such only, as were in some sort qualified to judge of their contents, and by that means to withstand their dangerous effects: but now every common mechanic at his house of call is sure to find a daily or weekly collection of news and essays lying ready for his perusal; and he has the benefit of drinking (for his usual club) poison to the mind as well as to the body. Swoln with a proper dose of such incentives he goes home a fit instrument for the future purposes of any incendiary, that will have the courage to call him into action; and in the mean time lives a sullen, discontented, insolent, untractable citizen.[43]

The theorists of Orthodox politics lacked the demotic skills of 1760s agitators; their response to the 'Present Discontents' was to return to, re-emphasise and repair the doctrine of monarchical legitimacy as a social ideal.[44] Aimed henceforth against radical insubordination rather than, as hitherto, against a dynastic challenge, the doctrine pointed forwards to early-nineteenth-century paternalism.

Distant echoes of the Stuart bogey remained, though not with sufficient force to attach a 'Tory' identity to successive Whig coalition ministries, or to deflect them from their policies. In 1773 Sir John Dalrymple published the second volume of his *Memoirs of Great Britain and Ireland*. Not only did it excuse the conduct of the last Stuart kings and speak scathingly of William III; it produced evidence which revealed the Whig heroes Lord William Russell and Algernon Sidney as in receipt of money from Louis XIV with the object of establishing a republic. Horace Walpole, languishing in obscurity, wrote bitterly that Dalrymple 'had been a hearty Jacobite; pretended to be converted; then paid his court where he found his old principles were no longer a disrecommendation at Court; and affected to admire King William; while the great object of his work was to depreciate and calumniate all the friends of the Revolution'.[45]

In June 1774 the Quebec Bill passed the Commons, allegedly placing many Protestants in that province under a Roman Catholic jurisdiction. Horace Walpole's objection remarkably anticipated a point made by Tom Paine in *Rights of Man*: 'James II lost his crown for such enormities: the prince that wears it to the prejudice of that family is authorized by a free Parliament to do what James was expelled for doing!'[46] The American Congress took up the charge, contending that the constitution itself prevented Parliament from establishing Popery – though at the same time

---

[43] Gordon, *op. cit.*, pp. 3, 5–7, 9–13.

[44] Cf. also Robert Lowth, Bishop of Oxford, *A Sermon Preached before the Lords Spiritual and Temporal in the Abbey-Church, Westminster; on Friday, January 30, 1767* (London, 1767), p. 19 and *passim*.

[45] Horace Walpole, *Last Journals*, vol. I, pp. 271–2.

[46] *Ibid.* vol. I, p. 357. The opposition's outcry travestied the terms of the Act, which embodied a careful compromise between English and French communities.

trying to incite French Canadians to join them in rebellion, as Dr Johnson tartly observed.[47]

Colonial policy could sometimes make the underlying aim of a government more explicit than could domestic policy. After American independence, Pitt's ministry took up the problem of promoting a social structure in Canada which would prevent a similar insurrection there. To do so, it returned to the earlier, abortive, plans to establish an Anglican episcopate in the American colonies. Leaving French Canada intact, the Anglican Church was to be introduced into Upper Canada, and endowed by means of clergy reserves. The first bishop was appointed, to Nova Scotia, in 1788, and plans for Anglican clerical education pressed ahead. The object was 'to produce a plant which could withstand the blasts of French Catholicism on the one hand and American radical dissent on the other'. The growth of a landed aristocracy was to be promoted, given a stake in the government via an hereditary (later changed to an elective) upper house, and social stability provided by the traditional English alliance of squire and parson, peer and bishop. The Canada Act of 1791, embodying these provisions, was the answer of Pitt and Grenville not only to the American but, now also, to the French revolutionary constitution; it was an affirmation of their commitment to an Anglican, aristocratic establishment at home, then so powerfully challenged. Appropriately, it was in the debates on the Canada Act that Burke broke with Fox over events in France.[48]

III. ORTHODOX ANGLICAN POLITICAL THEOLOGY, 1760–1793

If colonial policy could sometimes be expressed in terms of religious commitments, this was even more true of events at home. At the outset, George III's position was strengthened by the acclamations not only of Tory and Whig Anglicans, but of Protestant Dissenters. Despite Deist and Arian tendencies within their ranks on the part of a minority, the Dissenters in general had been effusively and noisily loyal under William III and the first two Georges, recognising in those sovereigns a none-too-secure barrier against 'Popery and arbitrary power'. George III was therefore hailed on his accession, by many Dissenters, as the apotheosis of a Whig tradition of Protestant monarchy. One of them, typically, congratulated his age 'that the slavish doctrine of passive obedience, and non-resistance to the will of tyrants, is thoroughly exploded amongst us, and that generous sentiments of liberty every where prevail'. The classic texts, he insisted, enjoined obedience only to 'good' kings: Romans 13; Titus 3:1; I Timothy 2:1–2.

---

[47] Dr Johnson, *Taxation no Tyranny*, in *Political Writings*, pp. 438–9.
[48] John Ehrman, *The Younger Pitt: The Years of Acclaim* (London, 1969), pp. 366–71. It was not a success: 'the squires and the parsons failed to take root'; but it survived until the Durham Report in 1839.

Sherlock's *Discourses* were quoted to show that Christianity 'stands "clear of all disputes about the rights of princes and subjects, which must be left to be decided by the principles of Equity, and the constitution of every country"'. The origin of power from God, 'as Bishop Sherlock well observes, "does not prove it unbounded, nor determine its extent"'. Such complacency had its dangers. The preacher had already committed himself to say: 'Such is the dignity and importance of the office of supreme magistrates, that they are sometimes styled Gods in scripture; as they are appointed of God, and derive an authority from him, which bears a resemblance to his own.'[49] Two generations of orthodox Dissenters' adulation of Hanoverian kings carried over to a new sovereign; it took a decade for Dissenters, released now by the extinction of the Jacobite threat, and impelled by the consequences of advancing Socinianism within their ranks, to move to a position of radical disaffection.

Robert Hay Drummond, Bishop of Salisbury (soon to be translated to York) echoed the destruction of Jacobitism in preaching George III's coronation sermon. The ancient texts, commanding allegiance under penalty of damnation, were no longer stressed; the title of the dynasty, the hereditary principle, was no longer defended. Prominence was, instead, given to the scriptural commission 'to do judgement and justice' in promoting religion and political virtue; and 'the colour, the vigour, the consistency of public conduct rest chiefly upon the prince himself'. 'He bears the weight of government, that his subjects may live easy under it: he avails himself of the prerogative, and resists the dangers of his exalted station, that he may be a living law to them'; and the culminating appeal:

May the sacred oath, which our sovereign takes at the altar of the king of kings, ever recur to his mind, as the genuine intentions of his own heart! May the homage, which we pay him in all truth and faithfulness, be bound upon our hearts and minds with the ties of duty, gratitude and love! and from us, may unfeigned loyalty spread itself through all ranks, give a right temper to the conduct of all his subjects, and establish his kingdom![50]

Few sovereigns have begun their reigns with such a sense of mission so clearly articulated for them by circumstances, or so tied to the Coronation Oath – an obligation which George III never could, and never wished to, escape.

Yet we cannot relate political theory to the Christian religion as if the latter was in every respect an unchallenged or unchanging body of doctrine. One of the major problems for the upholders of an ideology of theological politics in the early eighteenth century was to defend the intellectual

---

[49] Samuel Morton Savage, *The Duty of Subjects to Honour the King, Consider'd and Enforc'd, In a Sermon Preach'd on Occasion of his Present Majesty's Accession* (London, 1760), pp. 4, 14–15, 26.

[50] Robert Hay Drummond, *A Sermon Preached at the Coronation of King George III and Queen Charlotte...* (London, 1761), pp. 6, 8, 11, 16, 20.

* Socinians – sect who denied the divinity of Christ

viability of the idea of Providence, an active divine sanction for particular governments, against the interpretation which Arians, Socinians and Deists wished to place on Newtonian physics: that God, like a watchmaker, having created the universe, stood back to allow it to run according to its unvarying natural laws. Man, if living in a self-sufficient world, would be free to treat the State as a machine and to use or remodel it at will for his purely secular purposes. One response to this was the anti-Newtonian physics of John Hutchinson (1674–1737), who sought to derive an alternative system from a re-examination of the Hebrew scriptures; reasserting revealed, as against natural, religion; reconciling a self-sufficient universe, acting by second causes, with divine power and superintendence.[51]

Some Hebrew scholars, like Thomas Sharp, treated this as somewhat fanciful. But Hutchinson's theories were taken up with enthusiasm by a group of intellectuals in the Oxford of the 1750s who were neither Hebraists nor physicists, but men profoundly concerned with the defence of theological politics and Orthodox theology, and aware of the dependence of the first on the second. As William Jones[52] 'of Nayland' wrote in 1799, in retrospect:

When we are describing Hutchinsonians, it would be unjust to forget, that they are true churchmen and loyalists; steady in the fellowship of the apostles, and faithful to the monarchy under which they live. This, however, is not from what they find in Hutchinson, though it *is* to be found in him; but from what he has taught them to find, by taking their principles from scripture.[53]

Hutchinson had been mainly concerned to develop a physico-theology; but traditional High Church political and social preferences were present in his works also, documented from scripture: the divine appointment of kings, 'typologically representative of Christ', claiming a similarly absolute power, and in alliance with a priesthood similarly sanctioned; the complete dependence of man on God, the impossibility of self-sufficiency for man in the civil sphere, and the necessity of dependence and social subordination; the centrality of revelation, tradition, and the Church as the repository of both.[54]

---

[51] A. J. Kuhn, 'Glory or Gravity: Hutchinson vs. Newton', *JHI* 22 (1961), 303–22; C. B. Wilde, 'Hutchinsonianism, Natural Philosophy and Religious Controversy in Eighteenth Century Britain', *History of Science* 18 (1980), 1–24; *idem*, 'Matter and Spirit as Natural Symbols in Eighteenth-Century British Natural Philosophy', *British Journal for the History of Science* 15 (1982), 99–131.

[52] William Jones (1726–1800). Charterhouse and University Coll., Oxford; BA 1749; curacies; FRS 1775; perpetual curacy of Nayland, his subsequent residence, 1777. Prolific author.

[53] William Jones, Preface, to Jones (ed.), *The Works of the Right Reverend George Horne, DD late Bishop of Norwich*, 2nd edn (6 vols., London, 1818), vol. I, p. xxvii.

[54] Wilde, 'Hutchinsonianism', p. 10; 'Matter and Spirit', pp. 123–5. Smollett had noted that Methodist preachers 'bitterly inveighed against Newton as an ignorant pretender who had presumed to set up his own ridiculous chimeras in opposition to the sacred philosophy of the Pentateuch': quoted in B. Semmel, *The Methodist Revolution* (London, 1974), p. 20.

These elements, secondary in Hutchinson's writings, were emphasised by his followers in Oxford. An Oxford Whig, the Hebraist Benjamin Kennicott, attacking the Hutchinsonians, claimed that they, 'under the pretence of glorifying revelation, insult and trample upon reason'; but his main fire was reserved for their politics, and in particular for the Rev. Nathan Wetherell's sermon on 30th January 1755. The preacher was 'truly wonderful in the double character of politician and divine', objected Kennicott.

...it was indeed surprising (tho' we were in expectation of the marvellous) to hear the preacher maintain the justly-exploded doctrine of absolute passive obedience, and this in terms so extremely gross, as even to have out-Filmer'd Filmer: to maintain it to be the indispensable duty of all Christian subjects, under the worst of tyrants, to bow down in the dust or upon the block; and patiently to permit him to ravish from them religion, liberty, property, and life itself – and, at last, to tell the congregation, that no man could vindicate resistance in any case whatsoever, without giving up all regard for the Bible, and all pretension to common sense!

How were these principles, he challenged, consistent with loyalty to George II, 'so eminently the father of his people?' 'And if the Stuart family, which now claims these kingdoms upon this preacher's principles, claims them rightfully; does not every British subject act wrongfully, in not attempting another restoration?' But resistance was surely inconsistent with the preacher's doctrine? Where Wetherell's principles led, challenged Kennicott, was either to the Stuarts, or to absolute obedience to *any* regime: 'absolute obedience to the powers that be; to the supreme power, that is, at any time, and by any means, established? If so; can there be such a thing as usurpation? At least, must not every usurper of government, as being the power that is, be obeyed absolutely?'[55]

All this was very alarming to a Whig of the old school. In fact, during George II's reign, the Hutchinsonians practised passive obedience towards a regime which, as George Horne believed, blocked their promotion. In 1760, that barrier was removed. High Churchmen, with Hutchinsonians prominent among them, went on to provide a sophisticated, scholarly, official ideology for the English monarchical, aristocratic and Anglican regime which so successfully fought off all ideological and most practical challenges until 1828.

One side to that enterprise was the reassertion of Trinitarian orthodoxy; the classic work was William Jones's *The Catholic Doctrine of a Trinity* (Oxford, 1756; at least twelve editions by 1830). Jones drew explicitly on the

[55] [Benjamin Kennicott], *A Word to the Hutchinsonians: Or Remarks on Three Extraordinary Sermons Lately Preached before the University of Oxford, By The Reverend Dr Patten, The Reverend Mr Wetherall, and The Reverend Mr Horne* (London, 1756), pp. 7, 15–17. Thomas Patten (1714–90) was a Fellow of Corpus and a member of Wesley's Holy Club. Nathan Wetherell (1727–1807), lately of Lincoln, was a Fellow of University College, where he was Master 1764–1807. For George Horne, see below, n. 60.

theological works of Charles Leslie, and Leslie's increasing currency in the later eighteenth century seems to have evoked no awareness of his political disaffection to an earlier Hanoverian. William Jones' *An Essay on the Church*, stressing the apostolical succession as the source of its authority, similarly drew on the Nonjuror William Law's crushing polemic in reply to Hoadly, the *Three Letters to the Bishop of Bangor*. Locke's *Reasonableness of Christianity* was gently dismissed: 'it is too apparent, that Mr Locke's ideas of the Christian priesthood and sacraments, were exceedingly low'. Morality was not a substitute for doctrine;[56] and the consequences of supposing that it was, were explored in *Reflexions on the Growth of Heathenism among Modern Christians* (1776). Samuel Hallifax, apart from his political sermons, was responsible for bringing back into the arena Butler's *Analogy*: his standard edition of 1788 was reprinted in 1791, 1802, 1809, 1817, 1820 and long into the next century. Even Richard Watson, weak though he was on the issue of subscription, defended revealed religion as such against the 'religion of humanity'.[57] The Rev. John Whitaker intervened effectively with his weighty and difficult *The Origin of Arianism Disclosed* (London, 1791). William Paley, by contrast, provided an account of Anglicanism which was as easily accessible as it was widely current. *A View of the Evidences of Christianity* (London, 1794) had reached over twenty-eight editions by 1831. The most formidable scholarly defence of doctrinal Orthodoxy was provided by Dr Samuel Horsley in his duel with Joseph Priestley.[58] Horsley was widely held to have demonstrated 'the impossibility of taking any middle ground between Trinitarianism – in other words, the Catholic faith – and Unitarianism pure and simple'. Church historians have hailed him as 'the strongest writer in defence of the Catholic faith since the days of Butler, Waterland and Law...his reputation was immense'.[59]

The second aspect of the enterprise was the provision of an explicitly political theory for a new age. There was a distinct sense that, in this process, an older position was being revived and adapted. Prominent among such

---

[56] William Jones, *An Essay on the Church* (Gloucester, 1787), pp. 33, 69, 76. Also cited with approval was J. Boswell, *The Case of the Royal Martyr Considered with Candour* (London, 1758).

[57] Cf. Richard Watson, *An Apology for Christianity in a Series of Letters Addressed to Edward Gibbon, Esq.* (Cambridge, 1776; 6th edn, 1797); *A Defence of Revealed Religion, in Two Sermons Preached in the Cathedral Church of Llandaff* (London, 1795); *An Apology for the Bible, in a Series of Letters Addressed to T. Paine, Author of...the Age of Reason, Part the Second* (London, 1796; 10 edns by 1820).

[58] Samuel Horsley, *Letters from the Archdeacon of St Albans in Reply to Dr Priestley* (London, 1784); *Remarks on Dr Priestley's Second Letter to the Archdeacon of St Albans* (London, 1786); *Tracts in Controversy with Dr Priestley* (Gloucester, 1789; 3rd edn, 1812); *A Review of the Case of the Protestant Dissenters* (London, 1790; reprinted in *The Churchman Armed*, 1814); *An Apology for the Liturgy and Clergy of the Church of England* (London, 1790).

[59] J. H. Overton and F. Relton, *The English Church from the Accession of George I to the End of the Eighteenth Century* (London, 1906), pp. 254–7.

theorists, both in time and calibre, was the Oxford divine, George Horne.[60] His friend William Jones wrote:

The sight of Mr Leslie's two theological folios prepared Mr Horne for the reading of such of his political works as should afterwards fall in his way: and it was not long before he met with a periodical paper, under the title of *The Rehearsals*, which the author had published in the time of Queen Anne, when the infidels and dissenters were most busy; and had conceived strong hopes (as they said themselves) of destroying the established church. This paper boldly encountered all their arguments, dissected Sidney and Locke, confuted the republican principles, and exposed all the designs of the party...This singular work, then lately reprinted in six volumes (1750), fell into the hands of Mr Horne at Oxford, and was examined with equal curiosity and attention. According to his own account, he had profited greatly by the reading of it; and the work which gave to one man of genius and discernment so much satisfaction, must have had its effect on many others; insomuch that it is highly probable, the loyalty found amongst us at this day [1799], and by which the nation has of late been so happily preserved, may have grown up from some of the seeds then sown by Mr Leslie: and I have some authority for what I say.[61]

Horne drew on John Hutchinson, Charles Leslie, George Hickes and William Law for a modern and effective synthesis.[62] Oxford was the perfect platform for a series of Discourses, preached as learned sermons before the university, and published both individually and in collected editions.[63] His wartime Discourse on Restoration Day, 29th May 1760, set the tone, enjoining men to act to 'convince the world of this great and important truth, that the Christian is the loyal subject, and the churchman the true patriot'.[64] His 30th January sermon at St Mary's in 1761 appeared as Discourse XXVIII, 'The Christian King'. It was a round assertion of the propriety of comparisons 'between our Lord and the royal martyr': all men were called to an imitation of Christ, 'particularly in the article of suffering patiently'. The sermon of William Warburton, Bishop of Gloucester, before the House of Lords the previous year was excoriated: if anything could exceed the 'enormity' of Charles I's murder, 'it must be a supposition, were such a supposition possible, that this noble attachment to the church should be sneered at by a churchman of that high order for whose preservation he resisted even unto blood': 'It was not through church bigotry or pious prejudice that he was firmly attached to her constitution, but from a full

---

[60] George Horne (1730–92). Son of clergyman. University College, Oxford 1746–; Fellow of Magdalen 1750–; President 1768–; chaplain-in-ordinary to George III 1771–81; Dean of Canterbury 1781; Bishop of Norwich 1790. For his interest in Charles Leslie's writings, cf. Broxap, *Later Non-Jurors*, pp. 295–7; for his admiration of the Jansenists, Clark, *Strangers & Sojourners at Port Royal*, pp. 256, 262, 266.

[61] Horne, *Works*, vol. I, pp. 65–6.

[62] *Ibid.*, vol. I, pp. 62, 67.

[63] George Horne, *Discourses on Several Subjects and Occasions* (4 vols., Oxford, 1787; reprinted 1793, 1799, 1803, 1824, 1827 etc.).

[64] Horne, *Works*, vol. III, p. 136.

and thorough conviction of its rectitude and conformity to the apostolical model.' What remains, concluded Horne, 'but that while we detest, and use our utmost endeavours to eradicate out of the minds of men those diabolical principles of resistance to government in church and state, which brought his sacred head to the block, we testify our regard for his precious memory by an imitation of his godlike virtues'.[65]

Warburton was attacked more for his tone than for a doctrine; but the use of the sovereign as the focus and standard of civic and religious virtue called for an account of the institution of the State in non-contractarian terms. This Horne provided, his Assize sermon of 2nd March 1769 becoming Discourse xxiv, 'The Origin of Civil Government'. Warburton and Locke, again, are brushed aside. The idea that, as government emerged from the state of nature, 'the civil magistrate was called in as an ally to religion' was inadequate, since the state of nature knew neither magistrate nor priest. Nor could men escape from that state by a contract: Warburtonian assumptions about human nature would prevent him from surrendering himself to civil or religious authority. If 'the free consent of every individual is necessary to be obtained for the institution of civil government', it was hardly likely to be achieved.[66] And why should the free individual agree to be bound by majority decisions? 'It is indeed sometimes asserted, that "no man can submit himself to the absolute will of another":[67] in which case he cannot submit himself to any government whatsoever', since every government must be absolute.

His farther reason (why no man can submit himself to the arbitrary power of another) is, that no man can give what he hath not, viz. a power over his own life. How then came any government possessed of a power of life and death? Divine right surely must come in here: what else can give to another that power over my life, which I have not in myself?[68]

These anti-Lockeian arguments would have been familiar. What gave them new force was the relevance of the alternative, theocratic, case: 'For, without the interposition of some power superior to human, a system of civil polity calculated to answer, in any degree, the end of its institution, can neither be framed nor supported.' 'If the right of government be not inherent in the persons of governors, there can be no such thing as government upon earth.'[69] Could it be imagined that God, with such a noble purpose in view for man, should have created him in a condition of

---

[65] Horne, *Works*, vol. III, pp. 398, 401, 406, 408, 411–13, 421. He cited Clarendon, Carte, Hume, and the *Eikon Basilike*.

[66] Locke, *Two Treatises*, Bk II, ch. 8, s. 95. As Horne pointed out, Locke concedes, s. 98, that it is 'next impossible ever to be had': *Some Considerations on Mr Locke's Scheme of Deriving Government from an Original Compact* in *The Scholar Armed* (2 vols., 1795), vol. II, pp. 289–97.

[67] Locke, *Two Treatises*, Bk II, ch. 11, s. 135.

[68] Horne, *Some Considerations*, p. 290.   [69] *Ibid.*, p. 293.

barbarism and disorder? 'Did God indeed, at the beginning, bring into being, at the same time, a number of creatures independent of each other, and turn them uninstructed into the woods, to settle a civil polity by compact among themselves? We know he did not.' Christians, unlike Greek or Roman theorists, had an authentic record of these events in scriptural history. It showed that

...he who is the God of peace and order, provided for the establishment and continuation of these blessings among mankind, by ordaining, first in the case of Adam, and then again in that of Noah, that the human race should spring from one common parent.

Unless, therefore, some other origination of mankind be discovered, all equality and independence are at an end. The state of nature was a state of subordination; since, from the beginning some were born subject to others; and the power of the father, by whatever name it be called, must have been supreme at the first, when there was none superior to it...

The creation of one pair, the institution of marriage, and the relations flowing from it, do so evidently show subordination at the beginning to have been natural, and not founded on compact between peers, that two of the ablest advocates for a different hypothesis have, in fact, reduced the supposed compact at last to a *probable* or *tacit* consent of the children to be governed by their father. So that we may fairly look upon this point to be given up.

States were collections of families; the history of tribes or empires could equally be explained in those terms.[70]

Aristocracy and democracy were 'illegitimate forms of government' arising, though via compact, only among those who had 'broken off from their allegiance to their natural rulers'. That hardly applied to England, 'a regular and well constituted monarchy'. Christian subordination was its basic rule, solemn occasions like Assize sermons reminding men 'that there is an intimate connexion between religion and government; that the latter flowed originally from the same divine source with the former, and was, at the beginning, the ordinance of that Most High'; so that the civil magistrate, at the present day, was, in the words of Romans 13, 'the minister of God to us for good'. In rejecting Locke and Warburton, Horne appealed to Hooker: 'To fathers within their private families, nature hath given a supreme power':[71] existing governments were built up by conquest, or degenerated into a primitive and disorganised state (which was not the state of nature) through moral and political failings. Contract was an irrelevance.

---

[70] *Ibid.*, pp. 295–6:

Mr Locke's great argument against the patriarchal scheme proceeds on a supposition, that its patrons held an *universal monarchy in a right line from Adam*, and desires to be shewn who that monarch now is. But this God never intended. Adam was ruler in his own family; but if a colony went off to a distance under one of his sons, *he* was ruler *there*, and so on; which is sufficient to shew there could be no independent state of nature from the beginning.

[71] Discourse XXIV, 'The Origin of Civil Government', *Works*, vol. II, pp. 434–49.

The ecclesiastical tradition of theorising on the origin of the State, which Horne classically represented, reached its apogee in response to the French Revolution. In 1795 the Rev. John Whitaker,[72] who had earlier distinguished himself as a critic of Arianism, published *The Real Origin of Government*, deriving the State from revelation, not natural religion. In the familiar manner, reminiscent of Horne and the Nonjurors, Locke's weak arguments about the institution of government by contract in a state of nature were destroyed. Whitaker sought to show that since government could not have been founded on contract, it could not 'be founded on the will of man'; only 'anti-scriptural theorists of government' contended otherwise. On Locke's principles, the consent of every individual would be necessary both at the outset, and for the whole time of a government's continuance; but Locke admits this is 'next impossible to be had'; if a man cannot subject himself to the arbitrary power of another, he cannot subject himself to any government; individuals cannot depute to government a power over life and death; and so on. Consequently, 'No government can ever be founded but upon the institution of HIM, who formed man for government, and then framed government for man.' Secular theories of government were the invention of 'the children of Heathenism':

Ignorant of the true origin of man, as well as of the true nature of God, they fancied in their blindness to facts; that mankind were born originally in a large society together, when *we* know they were only a single pair; that all *those* were equal in nature and appointment, when *we* know one even of the two to have been made the superior of the other; and that government was therefore the posterior refinement of man, when *we* know it was the original institution of God. But how much more must we be amazed, at all these theories being adopted by Christians, and the darkness of heathenism courted in preference to the light of revelation!

Christians know that 'Man comes into the world, man has always come, in the obedience of a child to a parent, in the submission of a subject to a sovereign.' A positive prescription could be deduced from that fact: God did not institute 'government' in the abstract, but a particular government.

The same power which the father of a family possessed, the king of a nation retained of course. This power in the father, when he had no civil authority over him, was supreme in itself; and Adam must of necessity have been, at once the father and the king of his children... Monarchy therefore is the primary, the natural, the divine form of government for man. All history accordingly records it, to have been the original form. Nor was that deviation from it, that illegitimate and spurious mode of polity, a Commonwealth, ever obtruded upon the world till a late era; till man began to bewilder himself in the mazes of his own imagination about government, and wildly fancy he could improve upon the very models of God himself.[73]

[72] John Whitaker (1735–1808). Son of an innkeeper in Manchester. Brasenose College, Oxford 1752–; Corpus Christi College 1753–; Fellow 1763. Ordained 1760. Friend of Johnson and Gibbon. Rector of Ruan Lanyhorn, Cornwall, 1777–d.
[73] Rev. John Whitaker, *The Real Origin of Government* (London, 1795), pp. 1–27.

In the 1760s, this message was a positive one; after the American war, Horne's tone became defensive. In 1788:

We have a church, and we have a king; and we must pray for the prosperity of the last, if we wish to retain the first. The levelling principle of the age extends throughout. A republic, the darling idol of many amongst us, would probably, as the taste now inclines, come attended by a religion without bishop, priest, or deacon; without service or sacraments; without a Saviour to justify or a Spirit to sanctify; in short, a classical religion without adoration.

Horne raised the spectre of civil war and insurrection, not seen since the Restoration, if the levelling principles of the 1640s 'be adopted and disseminated among us'. These were not more explicitly defined than that 'the governed' would be 'taught to esteem themselves superior to their governors': the crucial link was, rather, that between Church and State. Horne was even prepared to concede that, although 'All power is originally and essentially in God, [and] from him it descends to man', each state's constitution was a human ordinance. Government must be submitted to once legally instituted, according to the state's constitution.[74]

By the same anniversary the following year, after George III's 'madness' and his recovery, and the outbreak of the French Revolution, Horne was willing to be even more indeterminate about the form of government if he could salvage the principle of subordination and obedience. The constitution was even, now, in traditional Whig fashion, described as a tripartite one, each part a check upon the others. The principle was

... that the law of God enjoins obedience to every government settled according to the constitution of the country in which it subsists; and that, even though the governor should be elected by the people; as in lesser matters, a man is free to choose that master into whose service he will enter; but when he is once entered, the Scriptures press upon him from thenceforth the several duties which a servant owes to his master.

This was necessary, since 'in the present state of human nature, it may be said of too many of our own species, as it is said of some other creatures in the book of Psalms, "Their mouths must be held with bit and bridle, lest they fall upon thee."' Horne continued the quotation from I Peter 2, after the classic verse 13, to the end of the chapter: an explicit command to accept even wrongful suffering. 'You will say, the doctrine is unreasonable, and of tyranny there can be no end, if it be unlawful to resist it.' He had three answers. First, if subjects were allowed a deposing power, 'who is to be judge when there is a sufficient reason for exerting such power?' In Horne's scheme, a right to resist became at once a power to depose the prince. Second, rebellion was worse than occasionally-erring government: 'more

---

[74] Discourse XXXII 'The Duty of Praying for Governors', preached in Canterbury Cathedral on the anniversary of George III's accession, 25th October 1788: *Works*, vol. II, pp. 563–4, 568–9, 571.

mischief will be done by the people, thus let loose, in a month, than would have been done by the governor in half a century'. Third, subjects should rely on God's Providence to correct the occasional inconveniences of 'the principle of obedience'. But theoretical appraisals were scarcely to the point: 'Happy are we of this nation (did we but know our own happiness!) in possessing a constitution so framed by the wisdom of ages, as almost to preclude the necessity of nice questions and disputes upon this topic.'[75] For the structure and working of the British constitution, its checks and balances, its precise provisions for liberty, did not preoccupy Horne. Rather, the constitution and the monarchy could be eulogised because they carried a divine sanction, because (following Hooker) they were a Church-State. Consequently, Clement, Ignatius and Cyprian could take their place with Robert Nelson's *Festivals and Fasts*, with William Jones' *Essay on the Church* and with Burke as defenders of a Christian political establishment.[76]

It was a position associated with the most powerful scholarship of the day. Robert Lowth,[77] the Hebraist and academic opponent of the self-taught William Warburton, enunciated the same doctrine:

That civil government cannot subsist without regard to the will of God, or, in other words, without the sanctions of religion, is manifest from the universal experience and practice of mankind... human laws can never inforce an obedience adequate to their purpose, unless it be grafted upon a prior principle of obedience to the laws of God...The will of God being the first principle and foundation of civil government; from the same principle the obligation of obedience to legal authority, and reverence to governors, as the ministers of God, immediately arises.[78]

From Oxford, the most vocal associate of Horne was his undergraduate contemporary William Jones. He engaged in a campaign over five decades in opposition to the forces, as he saw them, of heterodoxy and radicalism, ranging from his *Catholic Doctrine of a Trinity* (1756) to *A Letter to the Church of England* (1798) and *Considerations on the Religious Worship of the Heathen* (1799).[79] In 1776 he republished, as a work of contemporary relevance, and without disclosing its author, an extract from the Nonjuror Roger North's *Examen*, published posthumously in 1740.[80] It was presented as a tract

[75] Discourse xxvii, 'Submission to Government', *Works*, vol. iii, pp. 387–9, 391–4.

[76] 'A Charge Intended to have been Delivered to the Clergy of Norwich, at the Primary Visitation of George, Lord Bishop of that Diocese' (1792), *Works*, vol. iv, pp. 528–9.

[77] Robert Lowth (1710–87). Winchester and New College, Oxford; Fellow; Bishop of St Davids 1766; Oxford, 1766; London, 1777.

[78] Robert Lowth, Bishop of Oxford, *A Sermon Preached before the Lords Spiritual and Temporal in the Abbey-Church, Westminster; on Friday, January 30, 1767* (London, 1767), pp. 7, 10.

[79] Cf. his *Works*, ed. W. Stevens (12 vols., London, 1801).

[80] Roger North (1653–1734). Jesus Coll., Camb. 1667; Middle Temple 1669; KC 1682; Solicitor General to the Duke of York, 1684; Attorney General to the Queen, 1686; MP 1685; Nonjuror after 1688; 1690 bought estate of Rougham, Norfolk; resided there till his death, writing on law and history.

providing people 'with a few rational principles concerning the nature of civil power', and showing

> ...that no plan can be made sense of, except that doctrine of allegiance against which they have been taught to clamour; and that *resistance to civil government*, asserted on principle, is nothing but the extravagance and nonsense of designing writers, who want to be resisting every thing for their own private ends...Every government ought to be upon its guard against such men, before they have intoxicated the lower order of the people with that enthusiastic notion of natural privilege against positive law, which leads directly to rebellion.[81]

So the Nonjuror doctrine was applied directly to George III, with no sense at all that any problem lay in the transference rather than the doctrine: 'If it be a truth that laws (however originated) bind a people, the people of England are bound not to resist with force the king, or those commissioned by him, in any case, or upon any pretence whatsoever.'[82]

Roger North had written from the standpoint of constitutional law. William Jones endorsed such doctrines in his preaching on the classic texts: I Peter 2:13–17; Romans 13; I Timothy 2:1–3; II Peter 2:9–10. Physical power was to be distinguished from the power of authority. The latter descended from God; 'they who derive it from beneath, must go as low as they can, even down to the father of all that tumultuous rage and disorder, which distinguishes the power of the people'. And if authority descended from above, 'the honour of the people is involved in that of their king. We must judge of states as we do of families'.[83]

Jones, like other Orthodox thinkers, had defined his position in response to 1760s radicalism, and to the events of the American Revolution, in such a way that the French Revolution, from its earliest stages, and even before its more sanguinary episodes, was identified at once as the most terrible threat, not merely to a particular political regime, but to Christian civilisation.

> We are fallen into times, when the doctrine of the divine authority of government is received by the multitude with such pride, and impatience, and mockery, that it is plain their reason is disordered upon the subject. When their opinions prevail, and they are permitted to assume to themselves that power which belongeth only to God, no greater calamity can happen to any nation.[84]

It was this insight which Burke shared, and which informed his equally swift reaction to the events in Paris.

---

[81] *A Discourse on the English Constitution; Extracted from a Late Eminent Writer, and Applicable to the Present Times* (London, 1776), Preface pp, 3–4, 6.

[82] *Ibid.*, text, p. 1.

[83] William Jones, *The Fear of God, and the Benefits of Civil Obedience. Two Sermons...June 21, 1778* (London, 1778), pp. 24, 26, 28, 32 and *passim*.

[84] William Jones, *Popular Commotions Considered as Signs of the Approaching End of the World. A Sermon Preached in the Metropolitical Church of Canterbury, on Sunday, September 20, 1789*, (London, 1789), p. 13.

The political idiom of Cambridge Whigs was different from that which prevailed at their sister university. Oxford theorising had usually concerned itself directly and principally with dynastic titles, monarchical allegiance, and divine sanctions, and had at times been equivocal about applying those principles to the Hanoverian regime. Cambridge theorising had more often addressed itself principally and directly to the Whig regime as such under the first two Georges, praising it as the perfect embodiment of constitutional liberty, and expounding the nature of the liberty enjoyed under it.

This traditional Cambridge emphasis persisted after 1760. It was given additional prominence through the patronage of radicals by Grafton and Shelburne, and, more importantly, through the patronage exercised by Lord North and William Pitt. One of its beneficiaries was Pitt's tutor at Pembroke, George Pretyman. Another was the 'Cambridge Blackstone', Dr Samuel Hallifax,[85] whose law lectures Pitt attended. He used his 30th January sermon before the Commons in 1769 for an eulogy of the political establishment. Since Christianity 'in its tendency...is calculated to oppose the pretensions of despotic power, as its genius is favourable to civil no less than religious freedom, it may with propriety be affirmed in this as well as other senses of the word, that we *have been called unto liberty* by the gospel'. Nevertheless, liberty was liable to abuse: 'It was liberty inflamed and blown up into licentiousness' which reduced the constitution to ruin in the 1640s. Charles I's early actions tended towards arbitrary power; but the present danger was from the contrary direction.

> We have nothing to apprehend from that amiable and illustrious prince, under whose mild and equal administration we now live; we have every assurance we can wish, that our privileges are safe in his hands; the danger, if there be any, is from our selves; lest our love of liberty degenerate into licentiousness, and our private vices and party quarrels defeat his endeavours, and counteract his designs for the public welfare...the reformation, for which some amongst us are so clamorous, may on enquiry be found to be only wanting in themselves.[86]

The voice of liberty was an indictment of the 'Present Discontents'.

Hallifax's reward was the Regius Chair of Civil Law from Lord North the following year. In 1769, his tone had been one of cool satisfaction: popular agitation was an insignificant danger. By 1772, Hallifax's defence of the establishment was urgent and agitated. What had sounded the alarm was the attack on Trinitarian Orthodoxy and on one of the bastions of the clerical intelligentsia, his own university, in the movement to abolish

---

[85] Samuel Hallifax (1733–90). Jesus Coll., Camb. 1749–; Fellow 1756–60; Fellow of Trinity Hall, 1760–5; law tutor; Regius Professor of Civil Law, 1770–82; livings; Bishop of Gloucester 1781; St Asaph 1789 – d. His enemies spread a rumour that he died a Roman Catholic.

[86] Samuel Hallifax, *A Sermon Preached before the Honourable House of Commons...on Monday, January 30, 1769* (Cambridge, 1769), pp. 2, 8–9, 13–14.

subscription. Hallifax rushed to its defence.[87] Particularly marked was the bitter tone in which he replied to what he saw as a recent but profoundly subversive attack. It was 'a disavowal of every moral principle, by an open and bare-faced naturalism'; its champions directed a 'particular virulence' towards the Church of England. What rankled most was that the attack had come not only from those 'who are by profession the enemies of our ecclesiastical administration', but also from within:

We can, in some sort, allow for the petulance of sectaries in this cause; who may think themselves obliged to reflect on the national worship, as necessary for a vindication of their own; but we are at a loss for arguments to exculpate those, who, after voluntarily devoting themselves to the service of the Establishment, and actually living on the wages they receive from it, can yet allow themselves to join, with our bitterest adversaries, in reviling its ordinances, and inveighing against its doctrines... what shall we say to those, who serve at the same altar, and are greedy to eat of the same sacrifices with us; who, in an affair where conscience and religion are essentially concerned, can deviate so wide from the strait path of Christian simplicity, as to conform to our liturgy and doctrines, and to impugn their truth.

Warburton, in *The Alliance between Church and State*, had found a formula to justify, in acceptable and neutral terms, the hegemony of the Church of England: because its establishment was expedient, not because its doctrine was true. But many churchmen could assent to the first without necessarily discarding the second; they were enabled to be reticent about the second by the numerical weakness of orthodox Dissent, and by the intellectual defeat of early-eighteenth-century Deism.

The revival of Socinianism in the late 1760s and early 1770s destroyed this convenient calm. Hallifax responded in a revealing way. Towards *orthodox* Dissent, Hallifax held out the hand of friendship. He cited Warburton's *Alliance* to show that,

If for reasons of prudence, and to secure the existence of the national church, we think ourselves justified, from the clearest principles of the law of nations, in excluding them from offices of profit and trust in the disposal of the magistrate; we have not so much as a wish to narrow the bounds of that free Toleration, which is at once an honour to our religion, and a security to them and to ourselves. We renounce all pretensions to coercive power, in matters of opinion, as a violation of the rights of human nature, and of civil society.

The *Alliance* would also, he claimed, have answered the objections of 'the present cavillers against the Establishment'. Nevertheless, Hallifax went into battle against *heterodox* Dissent – Priestley – not by expounding Warburton, but by asserting the *truth* of the Church's doctrines on the Trinity, the pre-existence of Christ, and the Atonement. It was to overthrow such fundamentals, he warned, that 'the first incroachment on our religious

[87] Samuel Hallifax, *Three Sermons Preached before the University of Cambridge, Occasioned by an Attempt to Abolish Subscription to the XXXIX Articles of Religion* (Cambridge, 1772).

constitution is to begin among ourselves...The very *being* of the national church may, perhaps, depend on your vigilance.'[88]

When Hallifax next preached a 30th January sermon before Parliament, as Bishop of Gloucester, to the Lords in 1788, this frenzied tone had subsided: the immediate threat had been beaten off. The establishment was again eulogised as the nearest approach to perfect liberty. Romans 13 is accepted, but glossed: it was not St Paul's intention

...to state and ascertain what are the bounds and limits of civil authority on one hand, or of civil subjection on the other: we are to look for the just measure of both these duties where we did before; we are to go to the law of nature, and learn what are the ends and purposes to be served by civil union, and from thence determine the different obligations of governors and governed.

Such a position led to an entirely normal exposition and endorsement of the Warburtonian doctrine of alliance. But the rider is now different: the magistrate will 'indulge a toleration' to 'other sects, whose opinions are harmless or merely absurd'. Such, it was implied, was not the case of the pernicious doctrines of Socinianism. Concessions over the Test law would 'expose us to the incursions of our most inveterate enemies', men comparable with those who wreaked havoc in the 1640s. We should, rather,

...guard our common Christian faith, of which the Church of England is at once the depositary and the bulwark, by *giving place by subjection, no not for an hour*, to those, who, with the most plausible appearances of respect for its discipline, are known to have no just regard to some of its most essential doctrines; and for the same reason too, which influenced the great Apostle to oppose the *false brethren* of his own times, *that the truth of the Gospel may continue with us.*[89]

William Pitt was sometimes accused by radicals of having preferred three reactionary intellectuals, above all, in the Church of England: Horne, Hallifax and Horsley. Samuel Horsley[90] was also a Cambridge man, friend of Samuel Johnson and sometime domestic chaplain to Lowth as Bishop of London. Horsley, like Hallifax, was drawn into politico-theological controversy by the doctrinal exchanges with Priestley which followed the Archdeacon's attack in his weighty *Charge* of 1783.[91] Elevation to the bench was his reward for what contemporary churchmen regarded as his victory over Priestley's arguments. Once in the Lords, he pursued his campaign

---

[88] *Ibid.*, pp. 3–4, 6–7, 18–20, 23.

[89] Samuel Hallifax, *A Sermon Preached before the Lords Spiritual and Temporal... January 30, 1788* (London, 1788), pp. 7, 13–14, 18–19 (quoting Galatians 2:4–5).

[90] Samuel Horsley (1733–1806). Son of clergyman; educated by his father; Trinity Hall, 1751–8; living 1759; FRS 1767; Prebendary of St Paul's 1777; chaplain to Lowth, Bp of London; Archdeacon of St Albans, 1781; livings; Prebendary of Gloucester, 1787; Bishop of St Davids, 1788; St Asaph, 1802 – d.

[91] Samuel Horsley, *A Charge, Delivered to the Clergy of the Archdeaconry of St Albans, at a Visitation Holden May 22nd 1783* (London, 1783) was largely taken up with a scholarly denunciation of the Unitarian doctrines of Priestley's *History of the Corruptions of Christianity* (1782).

vigorously in speeches, episcopal charges, and sermons. His position was overtly theoretical, believing as he did that 'The practice of religion will always thrive in proportion as its doctrines are generally understood and firmly received; and the practice will degenerate and decay in proportion as the doctrine is misunderstood and neglected.'

Accordingly, Horsley announced that he accepted the label 'High Churchman', but not in the illegitimate sense:

...one that is a bigot to the secular rights of the priesthood, – one who claims for the hierarchy, upon pretence of a right inherent in the sacred office, all those powers, honours, and emoluments, which they enjoy under an establishment; which are held indeed by no other tenure than at the will of the prince or by the law of the land...But in the language of our modern sectaries, every one is a high-churchman who is not unwilling to recognise so much as the spiritual authority of the priesthood, – every one who, denying what we ourselves disclaim, any thing of a divine right to temporalities, acknowledges, however, in the sacred character, somewhat more divine than may belong to the mere hired servants of the state or of the laity; and regards the service which we are thought to perform for our pay as something more than a part to be gravely played in the drama of human politics. My reverend brethren, we must be content to be high-churchmen according to this usage of the word, or we cannot be churchmen at all; for he who thinks of God's ministers as the mere servants of the state, is out of the church – severed from it by a kind of self-excommunication.

As antidotes, he recommended Archbishop Wake's translations of Clement and Ignatius; Hooker; 'the celebrated Charles Leslie'; and William Jones' *An Essay on the Church*.[92]

Horsley's intellectual eminence gave a particular significance to his delivery of the State sermon before the Lords on 30th January 1793. Events conspired to give it a heightened drama: he preached only days after the arrival of news of the execution of Louis XVI. Horsley began, however, with moderation. His insistence on the apostolic succession, and a 'high' view of the sacraments, did not, he said, entail that any one form of government was especially sanctioned by Providence. In traditional Cambridge fashion, he continued to maintain

...that the principles which I advance ascribe no greater sanctity to monarchy than to any other form of established government; nor do they at all involve that exploded notion, that all or any of the present sovereigns of the earth hold their sovereignty by virtue of such immediate or implied nomination on the part of God, of themselves personally, or of the stocks from which they are descended, as might confer an endless indefeasible right upon the posterity of the persons named...all the particular forms of government which now exist are the work of human policy, under the control of God's general over-ruling providence.

---

[92] 'The Charge of Samuel, Lord Bishop of St Davids, to the Clergy of his Diocese, Delivered at his Primary Visitation, in the Year 1790', in *The Theological Works of Samuel Horsley...Lord Bishop of St Asaph* (6 vols., London, 1845), vol. III, pp. 7, 29–32.

In Britain, the king entered into an 'explicit, patent and precise' contract with the nation, 'summarily expressed in the coronation oath' and in detail in Magna Carta, Habeas Corpus, the Bill of Rights and the Act of Settlement. Furthermore, the mechanism of the constitution ensured 'the monarch's performance of his engagements'. As in the familiar Cambridge Whig scheme, there was no danger to be expected – by definition – from a Whig sovereign. The force of Horsley's argument was not any limitations on the monarch which might be derived from it, but rather the doctrines which he therefore felt able to 'abominate and reject, as wicked and illegitimate, – namely, that "our kings are the servants of the people; and that it is the right of the people to cashier them for misconduct"'.

The divine legitimacy of government once established, Horsley argued from an account of the origins of the State which bore a strong likeness to Horne's. Like Horne, he insisted that 'Christians are possessed of authentic records of the first ages, and of the very beginning of mankind' which showed that man 'from the beginning never existed otherwise than in society and under government'. Like Horne, Horsley briefly reviewed and refuted the Lockeian arguments for a social contract: government historically did not originate, and logically could not have originated, in that manner. Political obligation arose not from contract, but from divine appointment: 'civil society, which always implies government, is the condition to which God originally destined man: whence, the obligation on the citizen to submit to government is an immediate result from that first principle of religious duty which requires that man conform himself, as far as in him lies, with the will and purpose of his Maker'.

Horsley's problem was to legitimate, in Whig fashion, changes of regime: in such cases,

> ...it is no just inference, that the obligation upon the private citizen to submit himself to the authority thus raised arises wholly from the act of the people conferring it, or from their compact with the person on whom it is conferred. In all these cases, the act of the people is only the means which Providence employs to advance the new sovereign to his station: the obligation to obedience proceeds secondarily only from the act of man, but primarily from the will of God.

One instance, in England, was the Act of Settlement. It

> ...is confessedly the sole foundation of the sovereign's title...Yet it is not merely by virtue of that act that the subject's allegiance is due to him whose claim is founded on it. It is easy to understand, that the principle of the private citizen's submission must be quite a distinct thing from the principle of the sovereign's public title; and for this plain reason, – the principle of submission, to bind the conscience of every individual, must be something universally known, and easy to be understood. The ground of the sovereign's public title, in governments in which the fabric of the constitution is in any degree complex and artificial, can be known only to the few who have leisure and ability and inclination for historical and political researches. In this country, how many thousands and ten thousands of the common people never

heard of the Act of Settlement? of those to whom the name may be familiar, how many have never taken the pains to acquire any accurate knowledge of its contents? Yet not one of these is absolved from his allegiance, by his ignorance of his sovereign's title. Where, then, shall we find that general principle that binds the duty of allegiance equally on all, read or unread in the statute-book and in the history of their country? Where shall we find it, but among those general rules of duty which proceed immediately from the will of the Creator, and have been impressed upon the conscience of every man by the original constitution of the world?

This 'divine right of the first magistrate in every polity to the citizen's obedience' was, even by 'the most zealous republicans acknowledged to be divine, in former times, before republican zeal had ventured to espouse the interests of atheism'.[93] Horsley's conclusion was an eulogy: 'Such is the British constitution, – its basis, religion; its end, liberty; its principal means and safeguard of liberty, the majesty of the sovereign.' He contrasted these blessings with recent events, in an emotional peroration: 'This foul murder, and these barbarities, have filled the measure of the guilt and infamy of France. O my country! read the horror of thy own deed in this recent heightened imitation! lament and weep that this black French treason should have found its example in the crime of thy unnatural sons!' Profoundly moved, as much by the occasion as the doctrine, the congregation in Westminster Abbey instinctively rose to its feet in approval.[94]

Horsley at once drew radical fire. Sheridan attacked him in the Commons for reviving the doctrines of passive obedience. The Whig lawyer Francis Plowden,[95] whose work on the constitution, *Jura Anglorum*, Horsley had criticised in an appendix to the published text of his sermon, claimed that Horsley's were the doctrines of Sacheverell. He quoted Burke, who had written in his *Appeal* that 'The solemn judgement of the House of Peers against Dr Sacheverell must in my opinion make it absolutely unlawful for any British subject in future openly to deny or disapprove of the Revolution principles, or publicly to maintain those, which are commonly called the *Tory* principles.' Now Plowden published extracts from Horsley's text in parallel columns with extracts from the articles of impeachment against Dr Sacheverell.[96]

Horsley was not deterred. He possessed a clearly structured political philosophy, and it was not an indiscreet outburst, but the epitome of a

---

[93] Horsley cited Hoadly's *Defence of Hooker*, and Calvin.
[94] 'Sermon XLIV. Preached before the Lords Spiritual and Temporal, January 30, 1793; Being the Anniversary of the Martyrdom of King Charles the First', in Horsley, *Works*, vol. II, pp. 228–46; Nichols, *Literary Anecdotes*, vol. II, p. 685.
[95] Francis Plowden (1749–1829). Ed. Jesuit College, St Omer; entered Society of Jesus; returned to civil life on its suppression, 1773; Middle Temple; conveyancer. Writer on law. DCL, Oxford, 1793 for his *Jura Anglorum* (1792). 1813 fled to France to avoid paying libel damages; lived there till his death.
[96] F. Plowden, *A Short History of the British Empire during the Last Twenty Months; viz. from May 1792 to the Close of the Year 1793* (London, 1794), pp. 205–10.

carefully considered position, which he delivered as his opinion in the House of Lords during debates on the Treason Bill in November 1795: that 'he did not know what the mass of the people in any country had to do with the laws but to obey them'.[97] Nor was Horsley alone in such sentiments. He echoed, for example, the views of another Cambridge Whig prelate, George Pretyman-Tomline, now Bishop of Lincoln: 'subordination of ranks, and the relation of magistrates and subjects, are indispensably necessary in that state of society for which our Creator has evidently intended the human species'; whoever weakens the social structure 'by his words or by his actions, weakens the particular form which is duly established and justly administered in the community of which he is a member, sins against the ordinance of God'.[98] He had spoken on 30th January 1789: an interesting conjunction of dates.

In response to the French Revolution especially, assertions about monarchical *allegiance*, still forcefully raised by the American Revolution, gave way to a different emphasis derived from the same premises: what was most defended now was monarchical *obedience*, social subordination. Just as, before 1688, inequalities of rank in society had been defended in patriarchal terms, resting overtly on a claim of divine design,[99] so in the later eighteenth century the end of the question of dynastic legitimacy broadened the issue to one of the existence of a divine sanction for the social hierarchy as a whole. This was roundly asserted by churchmen whose fathers, under the first two Georges, had been Tory if not Jacobite. One such was Lewis Bagot, son of Jacobite MP Sir Walter Bagot.[100] Not only had the events of the Civil War proved 'how essential monarchy is to the enjoyment of constitutional liberty'; but 'The self-same authority which enjoins us "To fear God and love the brotherhood", enjoins us also "To honour the King": our allegiance, therefore, cannot be dispensed with but at the expense of our religion and our charity.'[101] In response to the threat of atheist revolution, all clergy feared what H. R. Courtenay, son of the Tory MP,[102] called 'the

---

[97] *Parl Hist*, vol. XXXII, col. 258. His qualification was commonly overlooked: 'with the reserve of their undoubted right to petition against any particular law, as a grievance on a particular description of people'.

[98] Soloway, *Prelates and People*, p. 26.

[99] R. B. Schlatter, *The Social Ideas of Religious Leaders 1660–1688* (Oxford, 1940), esp. pp. 106–23.

[100] Lewis Bagot (1740–1802). Dean of Christ Church, 1777; Bishop of Bristol, 1782; Norwich, 1783; St Asaph, 1790 – d. Sir Walter Bagot had sat in the Commons 1724–54 and 1762–8; he and his other son, William Bagot, MP 1754–80, were stout champions of the Church of England: Namier & Brooke, vol. II, pp. 37–9.

[101] Lewis Bagot, Bishop of Bristol, *A Sermon Preached before the Lords Spiritual and Temporal, in the Abbey Church, Westminster, on Thursday, January 30, 1783* (London, 1783), pp. 10–11, 19.

[102] Henry Reginald Courtenay (1741–1803): Prebendary of Rochester 1773–4, 1783–97; Rector of St George, Hanover Square, 1774; Prebendary of Exeter, 1772–94; Bishop of Bristol, 1794; Exeter, 1797. Son of H. R. Courtenay (1714–63), Tory MP for Honiton 1741–7, 1754–63.

ruin of that establishment which it is our duty and our wish to support'.[103] The familiar moral was drawn by Henry Bathurst, son of Tory MP Benjamin Bathurst:[104] 'national prosperity, rightly understood, is, by the special direction of Providence, the effect of a just sense of religion among those who compose a nation'.[105]

IV. THE POLITICAL THEOLOGY OF METHODISM AND EVANGELICALISM, 1760–1832

A sign of the intellectual vitality and strength of Orthodox churchmanship in the eighteenth century was its capacity to put forth new branches: Methodism and Evangelicalism. Both drew on the parent stem for aspects of their devotional practice and theology, and distinguished themselves from their parent by different emphases on, or selections from, elements in the common tradition. But what establishes the similar parentage of both movements is, above all, the fact that they inherited almost intact the political theology of mainstream Anglicanism. The desire of the new movements to establish their respectability, to shield their innovations from criticism, often led them to emphasise this political orthodoxy, and even to represent themselves as more orthodox than the orthodox.

Especially is this true of Wesley, whose political views, as has been seen, were formed in the Oxford of the 1720s.[106] His political principles had been changed not so much in their nature as in their application, being aligned, from some point in the 1730s, behind the Hanoverian regime. Wesley was perhaps influenced by the argument of William Higden's *A View of the English Constitution*, which he read in 1733. Even so, his sermon before the university in June 1734 aroused charges that it expressed Jacobite

---

[103] H. R. Courtenay, *A Charge Delivered to the Clergy of the Diocese of Exeter* (Exeter, 1799), p. 6.

[104] Henry Bathurst (1744–1837): Canon of Christ Church, 1775; Prebendary of Durham, 1795; Bishop of Norwich, 1805 – d. He was 7th son of Hon. Benjamin Bathurst (1711–67; Tory MP Gloucestershire 1734–41, Cirencester 1754–61); nephew of Hon. Henry Bathurst (1714–94; MP Cirencester 1735–54, Solicitor General to the Prince of Wales 1745–8, Attorney General to P. of W. 1748–51, Attorney General to the Dowager Princess of Wales 1751–4, Justice of Common Pleas 1754–71, supporter of Lord North, Lord Chancellor 1771–8, Lord President of the Council 1779–82); grandson of Allen Bathurst (1684–1775; Tory MP Cirencester 1705–1711/12, cr. 1st Baron Bathurst Jan 1711/12, in minor office 1742–4 (dismissed), Treasurer to George, Prince of Wales 1757–60, pension from George III of £2,000 p.a., raised to Earldom 1772). The Bathurst family offers a classic example of the transition from early-eighteenth-century Toryism, with a Jacobite tinge, via Leicester House oppositions of Prince Frederick and Prince George, to office, wealth and power under George III, in Church as well as State.

[105] Henry Bathurst, *A Sermon Preached before the Honourable House of Commons . . . on Friday, February 28, 1794* (London, 1794), pp. 3–4.

[106] For his debt to Nonjuror theology, cf. J.B. Green, *John Wesley and William Law* (London, 1945).

doctrines,[107] and suspicion of Jacobite sympathies attached to Methodists during the '45. They responded, however, with loud and explicit professions of their Christian allegiance to the dynasty, views expressed also in Wesley's tract *A Word in Season: Or, Advice to an Englishman* of 1745.

Wesley was explicit about this transference. In June 1775 he wrote to Lord North to urge a negotiated settlement with the colonies, despite the fact that 'all my prejudices are against the Americans; for I am an High Churchman, the son of an High Churchman, bred up from my childhood in the highest notions of passive obedience and non-resistance'. Nevertheless, they were particularly relevant, he implied, because of a widespread disaffection among the people at large. In August that year he made the same point to the Secretary of State, the 2nd Earl of Dartmouth:

I aver that the people in general all over the nation are so far from being well satisfied that they are far more deeply dissatisfied than they appear to have been even a year or two before the Great Rebellion, and far more dangerously dissatisfied. The bulk of the people in every city, town, and village where I have been do not so much aim at the ministry, as they usually did in the last century, but at the king himself. He is the object of their anger, contempt, and malice. They heartily despise His Majesty and hate him with a perfect hatred. They wish to imbue their hands in his blood; they are full of the spirit of murder and rebellion; and I am persuaded, should any occasion offer, thousands would be ready to act what they now speak.[108]

Wesley had always practised the political virtue of non-resistance under the *de facto* Hanoverian regime. After he had come in the 1730s to acknowledge in it a divine right, he devised for it a defence in dynastic terms. His *Concise History of England* (1776; Vol. I, p. 189) announced that since the marriage in 1209 between King John and Isabella was not 'lawful', their children were illegitimate, and the Stuarts' title unfounded; King George I was 'lineally descended' from Matilda, who had a 'prior right'.[109] It seems likely that the dominant element in Wesley's thinking was not this somewhat fanciful genealogical discovery but the traditional teaching by many Anglicans which extended to *de facto* sovereigns the principle that 'the powers that be are ordained of God'; as Christ had said to Pilate, 'Thou

---

[107] Green, *The Young Mr Wesley*, pp. 78, 317. Wesley's friends included many Nonjurors and Jacobites, including John Byrom and Dr Thomas Deacon – *ibid.*, pp. 185–6, 202, 254.

[108] J. Telford (ed.), *The Letters of the Rev. John Wesley, AM* (8 vols., London, 1931), vol. VI, pp. 160, 175.

A recent scholar (Semmel, *Methodist Revolution*, p. 17) has written: 'It was a curious paradox that Wesley was a loyal churchman who leaned to the ritual and doctrine of the High Church, and who was a believer in the far-from-fashionable principle of the divine right of kings.' The paradox was created only by Professor Semmel's wish to see Methodism as 'essentially a liberal and "progressive"...ideology'; that Wesley's political doctrine was somehow an irrelevant gloss on 'a liberal and egalitarian Methodist religious doctrine', and that the political message of quiescence was illegitimately imposed on the movement (p. 5). The view of eighteenth-century dynastic political ideology advanced here sets these questions in a different light.

[109] Quoted Semmel, *Methodist Revolution*, p. 210.

couldest have no power at all against me, except it were given thee from above' (John 19:11). In 1785, John Wesley wrote to the *Gentleman's Magazine* to defend his deceased eldest brother, Samuel, from a charge of Jacobitism which had appeared in its pages:

Most of those who gave him this title did not distinguish between a Jacobite and a Tory; whereby I mean 'one that believes God, not the people, to be the origin of all civil power'. In this sense he was a Tory; so was my father; so am I. But I am no more a Jacobite than I am a Turk; neither was my brother. I have heard him over and over disclaim that character.[110]

Like Samuel Johnson, who produced *The False Alarm* (1770) and *The Patriot* (1774), John Wesley was first induced to deploy these attitudes in the political arena, during George III's reign, in response to the Wilkesite disturbances. Wesley was outraged that 'every cobbler, tinker, porter and hackney-coachman' took it upon himself to advise, or even censure, the king. George III's conduct was 'worthy of an Englishman, worthy of a Christian, and worthy of a king'. The fault lay with the radicals. If matters got out of hand, 'First the land will become a field of blood; many thousands of poor Englishmen will sheathe their swords in each others' bowels for the diversion of their good neighbours. Then either a commonwealth will ensue or else a second Cromwell. One must be; but it cannot be determined which, King Wilkes or King Mob.'[111]

From this specific and agitated reaction, he felt impelled to progress to more general statements of political principle. Wesley was reported to have offered his services to the government in response to the *Letters of Junius*,[112] but, as with Dr Johnson, his case needed no adapting for that purpose. *Thoughts upon Liberty* (1772) was a reiterated attack upon Wilkesite radicalism, and an assertion that Britons already enjoyed liberty in profusion: radical propaganda was 'poison', fed to the people with fatal effect. *Thoughts Concerning the Origin of Power* (1772) developed the standard Anglican case against the contractarian origin of government. Wesley was explicit that his Christian duty was not to take sides in a *party* quarrel,[113] but was drawn equally to side with government in the abstract and therefore with the British government in particular. By the mid 1770s, Wesley's journeys through England had awakened in him a vivid fear that the contagion of disaffection had taken root in his own country.[114] It was this which proved decisive for him, despite his opinion that the American case had, on a theoretical level, much to commend it.

[110] Wesley, *Letters*, vol. VII, p. 305.
[111] J. Wesley, *Free Thoughts on the Present State of Public Affairs* (1768) in *Letters*, vol. v, pp. 370–88.
[112] L. Tyerman, *The Life and Times of the Rev. John Wesley, M.A.* (3 vols., London, 1870–71), vol. III, p. 145.
[113] Wesley, *Letters*, vol. VI, pp. 142–3, 149–50.
[114] Cf. A. Raymond, '"I fear God and Honour the King": John Wesley and the American Revolution', *Church History* 45 (1976), 319.

Samuel Johnson's pamphlet *Taxation no Tyranny* was published on 8th March 1775.[115] Wesley used it as the basis of his *A Calm Address to our American Colonies*, borrowing large sections of Johnson's argument,[116] but giving it a new clarity and definition, and adding elements of his own. Johnson's argument had focussed on issues of constitutional law and precedent. Nevertheless, he had insisted that without a legal basis for government in America, 'the whole fabric of subordination is immediately destroyed, and the constitution sunk at once into a chaos: the society is dissolved into a tumult of individuals, without authority to command, or obligation to obey'. This was so, claimed Johnson in familiar Anglican fashion, since allegiance and subordination were natural, not contractual.

How any man can have consented to institutions established in distant ages, it will be difficult to explain. In the most favourite residence of liberty, the consent of individuals is merely passive, a tacit admission in every community of the terms which that community grants and requires. As all are born the subjects of some state or other, we may be said to have been all born consenting to some system of government. Other consent than this, the condition of civil life does not allow. It is the unmeaning clamour of the pedants of policy, the delirious dream of republican fanaticism.[117]

In Wesley's *Calm Address*, these elements are emphasised. Though he repeats Johnson's constitutional case, the heart of Wesley's argument is religious and dynastic:

My opinion is this. We have a few[118] men in England, who are determined enemies to monarchy. Whether they hate his present Majesty on any other ground, than because he is a king, I know not. But they cordially hate his office, and have for some years been undermining it with all diligence, in hopes of erecting their grand idol, their dear Commonwealth upon its ruins.

Such 'designing men' 'love neither England nor America, but play one against the other, in subserviency to their grand design, of overturning the English government'. The remedy was a return to Christian obedience: 'Let us put away our sins; the real ground of all our calamities! Which never will or can be thoroughly removed, till we fear God and honour the King.'[119]

Wesley gave Johnson's case a considerable vogue, and it was principally Wesley who attracted the protests of indignant radicals. Among them was

---

[115] D. J. Greene (ed.), *The Yale Edition of the Works of Samuel Johnson*, vol. x, 'Political Writings' (New Haven, 1977), p. 408.

[116] The borrowings are set out in [Augustus Toplady], *An Old Fox Tarr'd and Feather'd* (London, 1775), pp. 8–18.

[117] Johnson, *Taxation no Tyranny*, pp. 425, 428.

[118] The contemporary owner of Cambridge University Library's copy added a footnote: 'and many in America, particularly in New-England, the inhabitants of that Province being the descendants of the Republicans of the last century'.

[119] John Wesley, *A Calm Address to our American Colonies* (London, [1775]), pp. 13, 17–18. Wesley claimed 40,000 copies printed within three weeks, and up to 100,000 within a few months: Raymond, 'Wesley', p. 322.

the provincial radical and Baptist minister Caleb Evans, who claimed that Wesley had 'revived the good old Jacobite doctrines of *hereditary, indefeasible, divine right*, and of *passive obedience* and *non-resistance*'. It was this monarchical element, claimed Evans, which had ultimately reversed Wesley's initial sympathy for the colonial cause.[120] Other Dissenters voiced their objections to Wesley's doctrine in similar terms – that he had 'sworn to the creed of Archbishop Laud, and the doctrine of Sacheverell'; John Fletcher, defending his leader, was led to reply that Wesley adhered to a *via media*: that Sacheverell 'ran as fiercely in the *high-monarchical* extreme, as Dr Price does into the *high-republican* extreme'.[121]

In turn, Wesley's political views increasingly found expression in a critique of Dissent. His pamphlet *Some Observations on Liberty Occasioned by a Late Tract* (1776) was a swift reply to Richard Price's *Observations on the Nature of Civil Liberty* of the same year. Wesley's appeals for calm, order, loyalty and subordination at home continued with such tracts as *A Seasonable Address to the More Serious Part of the Inhabitants of Great Britain* (1776), *A Calm Address to the Inhabitants of England* (1777) and *A Serious Address to the People of England, with Regard to the State of the Nation* (1778). Subjection to the higher powers was the duty of Christians: and this, unequivocally, meant submission to the British government. With the entry of France into the war, Wesley turned also to an anti-Papist crusade, defending Protestant England against another threat which he interpreted in religious terms.[122]

Many contemporaries, opposition Whigs as well as radicals and Dissenters, viewed with surprise and resentment the full extent of the principled loyalism which Wilkesite disorder and American rebellion prompted Wesley to affirm. Burke complained of the Methodists in 1783 that 'It is nearly five years since Wesley carried over that set of men to the Court, and to all the slavish doctrines of Charles the 2ds reign in their utmost extent.'[123] The events of 1789 produced, of course, a profound change in Burke's position as he dropped earlier libertarian remarks like these; but Wesley's theological politics only came to seem even more urgently relevant. His preaching in defence of monarchy remained vivid into his last years – as at a meeting in 1790, where he 'concluded his eulogium with the following emphatic words, *That if the best of Kings – the most virtuous of Queens –* and the most *perfect constitution*, could make any nation happy, the people of this country had every reason to think themselves so'.[124] His political doctrine was kept in repair after his death in 1791. In 1792, the Methodist Conference replied

---

[120] [Caleb Evans], *A Letter to the Rev. Mr John Wesley Occasioned by His Calm Address to the American Colonies* (London, 1775), quoted Raymond, 'Wesley', p. 322.
[121] Semmel, *Methodist Revolution*, pp. 66–9.
[122] Raymond, 'Wesley', p. 327.
[123] Burke to Portland, 3rd Sept. 1780: quoted Semmel, *Methodist Revolution*, p. 242.
[124] *Leeds Intelligencer*, 4th May 1790: quoted R. F. Wearmouth, *Methodism and the Common People of the Eighteenth Century* (London, 1945), p. 257.

to the question 'What directions shall be given concerning our conduct to the civil government?' with the officially-promulgated answer: '1. None of us shall, either in writing or conversation, speak lightly or irreverently of the government under which he lives. 2. We are to observe, that the Oracles of God command to be faithful to the higher powers: and that honour to the king is there connected with the fear of God.'

Similar sentiments were reiterated at the Conferences of 1793, 1794, 1797, 1798, 1799 and on into the next century;[125] and as the radical implications of Methodist practice, and even of some Methodist preachers, became more apparent, such professions were increasingly made. Methodists themselves, anticipating Halévy, stood forward to claim the credit for England's avoidance of revolution: 'the sermons and writings of the Methodist preachers abound with effusions of loyalty and patriotic affection', boasted one of them in 1805.[126] A sympathetic Anglican was able correctly to diagnose this position as stemming from a rejection of the Lockeian doctrine of a right of resistance 'residing in the governed' – a doctrine which, 'if even *theoretically true*, would if reduced to practice, deprive all governments of stability'.[127]

At a local level, this message was often in direct competition with what preachers called 'political agitators', and, as in the distress of 1819, such men could win converts among Methodist ranks. Preachers confronted this threat directly with denunciations of Paineite radicalism and assertions of a rival set of political values, as in John Stephens's best-selling tract, *The Mutual Relations, Claims, and Duties of the Rich and the Poor* (Manchester, 1819),[128] or in the prominent Methodist Adam Clarke's *The Rights of God and Caesar: a Discourse on Matt. XXII. 15–21* (London, 1821), analysing a Biblical passage to document a warning against 'the common people' entering into speculation on 'abstract questions concerning civil rights and civil wrongs, party politics, reasons of state, financial blunders, royal prerogatives, Divine right of kings, &c. questions, on which a thousand things may be said *pro* and *con*'. The Christian was clearly obliged to render to Caesar 'Honour', 'Obedience', and 'Tribute'. Since '*power*, or civil magistracy, is *from God*, and is *arranged under Him*; it is, therefore, worthy of the *highest respect*, next to that which we owe to God Himself'.[129] For the scholarly argument, Clarke referred to his work *The Origin and End of Civil Government* (London, 1822). Though a Whig, Clarke gave expression to a position which could be assented to by such another leader of the Connection

---

[125] Wearmouth, *op. cit.*, pp. 260–2. Conference in 1797 ordered the expulsion of those members who 'maintain and propagate opinions inimical to the civil government and established religion of the country': A. Armstrong, *The Church of England, the Methodists and Society 1700–1850* (London, 1973), p. 87.

[126] Cf. Semmel, *Methodist Revolution*, pp. 127ff, 129.

[127] *Strictures on Methodism* (London, 1804), quoted *ibid.*, p. 130.

[128] Semmel, *Methodist Revolution*, p. 139.   [129] Clarke, *Rights of God and Caesar*, pp. 12, 20.

as Jabez Bunting, whose inclinations were to the ministry: that God was 'the very *fountain* of *magistracy* or *dominion*'; the people consider the King of England 'the grand agent between God and them; the viceroy, lieutenant, or deputy, of God; acting as it were in His place, and ruling in His name'. Godly governments, '*conscientiously administered*', were 'strangely protected and upheld by an especial Providence', as Britain's recent survival showed. So long as the king ruled 'according to the constitution, nothing can justify rebellion against his authority'.[130]

This was the doctrine in a Whig accent. But Jabez Bunting was saying essentially the same thing from a different political standpoint in his famous declaration of the identity between democracy and sin.[131] Horne, Horsley or Hallifax could have said no more.

Nor was it the case that such a political theology was in decline, intellectually or practically, in Methodist hands. On the contrary, its most cogent and systematic expression was given by Richard Watson, 'the principal ideological spokesman of the Wesleyan Connection from the early 1820s until his death in 1832', virtually 'the official theologian of Methodism'.[132] Watson's *Theological Institutes* provided a classic synthesis, and one which gave considerable attention to the political implications of Christianity. Radicalism was seen substantially in religious terms, as Antinomianism; and government was held justified in restraining men 'where political opinions are connected with religious notions'. The idea of human equality in this life was a religious error; evil practical consequences flowed from it. On the contrary, human inequality went with the origin of power from above: the social contract was a 'pure fiction'. The origin of government was 'paternal', though this did not entail that present monarchical governments were unrestrained by law. Watson, like Burke, nervously sought a way of justifying 1688 which would not act as a justification for any subsequent revolution. In defence of the Whig regime, Watson continued to invoke the arguments which Whig churchmen had advanced for more than a century: '*subjection* and *obedience*' not only for wrath but for conscience' sake. Only if the sovereign attempted to subvert the constitution, against the general sense of the public, and relying on mercenaries or a foreign power, was resistance justified as 'a deliberate national act' of the people 'under their natural guides and leaders, – the nobility and gentry of the land'.[133]

[130] Clarke, *Civil Government*, pp. 9, 24. Clarke offered a patriarchal account of the origin of government, p. 13.

[131] T. P. Bunting, *The Life of Jabez Bunting, DD* (2 vols., London, 1859–87), vol. II, p. 166 linked his father's being 'a firm Royalist' to being 'educated...in the principles of a Whig of the old school'.

[132] Semmel, *Methodist Revolution*, p. 172.

[133] Richard Watson, *Theological Institutes: or A View of the Evidences, Doctrines, Morals and Institutions of Christianity* (3 vols., London, 1823–9), quoted Semmel *loc. cit.*, pp. 172–8.

This conclusion was all the more remarkable in that Methodism was deliberately directed towards the poor. The nobility and gentry were the principal target of the Evangelical movement within the Church of England, seemingly anticipating later historians' insights into the workings of 'cultural hegemony'. Yet, despite this difference of aim, and despite the reputed Calvinism of many Evangelicals, the practical affinities between the two movements and their leaders were considerable. The famous Evangelical Charles Simeon found large areas of agreement with John Wesley, even on controversial doctrinal points, when they met in 1787;[134] and William Wilberforce similarly admired Wesley when they met in 1789.[135] But this need not surprise us if the common Anglican parentage of both movements is remembered. Even before 1800, 'the Evangelicals had come to think of themselves as the protectors of the Methodists, and the Methodist leadership was flattered by this attention'.[136]

This affinity was not only one of mood; it extended to, perhaps in large part stemmed from, the political theology which Wesleyans and Evangelicals shared. They shared it because they had derived it from the same source. It may be noticed that historians who have argued that 'The steadiness and loyalty of Methodist people in days of riot and revolution saved England from the calamity that fell upon France'[137] neglected an important fact. The linked Wesleyan doctrines of social subordination and political reverence were precisely the typical doctrines of the Church of England. Wesleyans preached them to a minority. Anglican clergymen preached them to far greater numbers, over a much wider area, for a longer period, and with access to all the scholarly and practical resources of an established intelligentsia.

The High Church origins of Anglican Evangelicalism are easily overlooked in the light of its Victorian political connotations.[138] Yet, even then, the emotional and doctrinal affinities were considerable. Manning, Newman, Hope-Scott and Gladstone all made the transition from an Evangelical background to a High-Church Anglican position by the 1830s. Subsequently, Orthodox clergy and laity were often drawn to co-operate with Evangelicals in protest against what both regarded as the Romanising tendencies of the Tractarians.[139] Nor, at the outset of the movement, is 'Evangelical' to be equated with 'Low Church'; Evangelicals, like Methodists, usually attracted the opposition of mid-eighteenth-century

[134] Tyerman, *Wesley*, vol. III, pp. 510–11.
[135] R. I. and S. Wilberforce, *The Life of William Wilberforce* (5 vols., London, 1838), vol. I, pp. 206, 248.
[136] Semmel, *Methodist Revolution*, p. 179.
[137] Quoted Wearmouth, *Methodism*, p. 265.
[138] Cf. L. E. Elliott-Binns, *The Early Evangelicals: A Religious and Social Study* (London, 1953), pp. 394–5, 421 and *passim*.
[139] Peter Toon, *Evangelical Theology 1833–1856* (London, 1979), pp. 3–4.

Latitudinarians. Their intellectual origins were often different. Sir William Dolben, 3rd Bt., MP for Oxford University (1768, 1780–1806) and Evangelical supporter, was the son of the Rev. Sir John Dolben, Vicar of Finedon, in whose library the young George Horne discovered the works of Charles Leslie. William Legge, 2nd Earl of Dartmouth (1731–1801), 'the leading Evangelical nobleman', whom Wesley addressed in 1775, was heir to an early-eighteenth-century Tory tradition. In Oxford, the distinction between 'Methodist' and 'Evangelical' is not easy to make, before the public dimension had forced a definition on the positions of those men who left the university.[140]

George Whitefield, as a second-year undergraduate in the 1730s, was set on the road to spiritual awakening by the Nonjuror William Law's *Serious Call* and *Christian Perfection*.[141] So was Cambridge graduate Henry Venn, as curate of Clapham, in about 1754.[142] The conversion of Rowland Hill to 'vital religion' was begun in 1762 by reading a sermon of the High Church Bishop Beveridge, a favourite author with many Methodists; and the religious rebirth of the future Evangelical patriarch Charles Simeon was provoked while an undergraduate in 1779 by the High Church manual *The Whole Duty of Man*, consulted in preparation for a compulsory communion service at King's College, Cambridge.[143]

Evangelicals soon distinguished themselves by marked anti-sacerdotalist views, but in this they were merely emphasising a mid- and late-eighteenth-century Anglican position: High Churchmanship had already been defined primarily in political rather than sacramental terms. And although Evangelicals were preoccupied with the pastoral aspect of their role,[144] producing in consequence no single original work of theology, this did not imply a doctrinal illiteracy. On the contrary, Evangelicalism 'comes before us on its theological side as a clear-cut scheme of doctrines which men were required to accept as the embodiment of a divine revelation; and its exponents are never tired of insisting that the fruits of practical religion will be found to exist just in proportion to the clarity of the doctrinal belief'. And although Evangelicals were preoccupied with the individual rather than with his place in the polity, 'the bond of fellowship in a visible, ordered,

---

[140] A marked feature of the years c. 1730–60 is the number of simultaneous, *independent* conversions to 'vital religion': William Romaine, Grimshaw of Haworth, Henry Venn, John Newton, Berridge of Everton, Whitefield, Wesley.

[141] J. S. Reynolds, *The Evangelicals at Oxford 1735–1871* (Abingdon, 1975), pp. 3, 8, 22 and *passim*.

[142] M. Hennell, *John Venn and the Clapham Sect* (London, 1958), pp. 17–18.

[143] Charles Smyth, *Simeon & Church Order. A Study of the Origins of the Evangelical Revival in Cambridge in the Eighteenth Century* (Cambridge, 1940), pp. 83, 120.

[144] Evangelicals' general lack of attention to politics is evidenced by J. H. Pratt (ed.), *The Thought of the Evangelical Leaders. Notes of the Discussions of the Eclectic Society, London During the Years 1798–1814* (London, 1856); though cf. pp. 236–7, 348.

historical society', they became, over the decades, 'more markedly Churchmen'.[145]

As with Wesley, it was rebellion, the threat of Satanic insurrection, which progressively emphasised the political element in the Evangelicals' mission. It is particularly apparent in their preaching following the French Revolution. On 8th August 1795 the *Cambridge Intelligencer* published an open letter to the Rev. Charles Simeon from the Baptist minister, Robert Hall. Simeon had preached a sermon against Nonconformists, especially Baptists, whose doctrines, he claimed, 'had a manifest tendency to make people factious, or disturbers of the public peace', and had minimised the Anglican clergy's differences from the French émigré clergy. Hall protested that 'I never introduced a political topic into the pulpit on any occasion', but that

> ...it is well known that you are the chief, perhaps the only political preacher in the place; and that you often entertain your hearers with more politics in one sermon, than most dissenting ministers have done during their whole lives. The doctrines of passive obedience and non-resistance, which in better times Sacheverell was disgraced for preaching, are familiar in your mouth.[146]

In 1808 a commentator observed of the Evangelicals:

> Of their loyalty, I can say, with great truth, that in this point they have not only remained uncorrupted, but have often availed themselves of their situation as ministers, to stem the tide of sedition. It deserves notice, that in the most threatening periods of *Revolutionary* mania, those men spoke out very decidedly from the pulpit, in defence of our enviable constitution.[147]

The Rev. John Venn, pillar of the 'Clapham Sect' and 'a violent Pittite', had even played a part in the formation of the 'Clapham Armed Association' in 1798.[148] A less warlike preacher was the Rev. C. E. de Coetlogon. He enjoyed something of a vogue, delivering the 30th January sermon before the Lord Mayor and Corporation of London in 1790. The right of resistance could be abused, he argued. To prevent such evils 'a civil and ecclesiastical constitution has been framed, in which the respective rights, of the sovereign, and of the people, are very nicely ascertained, and very suitably adjusted'. So well, indeed, that it would be wrong to plead against the Revolution Settlement such abstractions as the Rights of Man, the Rights of the Citizen, or the Rights of Conscience.

Is there any encouragement in [Christ's] example, either to persecute, or to be seditious? And, is it not sedition, to speak in disrespectful terms of the religion, of the constitution, or of the sovereign of our country? We have been accustomed to

---

145 V. F. Storr, *The Development of English Theology in the Nineteenth Century 1800–1860* (London, 1913), pp. 66–70; cf. S. C. Carpenter, *Eighteenth Century Church and People* (London, 1959), p. 219.

146 Smyth, *Simeon*, pp. 295–6.

147 [J. Bean], *Zeal without Innovation* (London, 1808), pp. 165–6; quoted Smyth, *Simeon*, p. 297.

148 Hennell, *John Venn*, p. 149.

think, by all the laws of nations and of God, that the person of the sovereign is to be treated as sacred, on account of his office. To insult the office, is an act of treason – treason, against the constitution! For, is it necessary to remind some wilful novices in the knowledge of our government, that it is a monarchy? and, that the king is an essential branch, not the 'servant', of the constitution![149]

Similar eulogies of the Glorious Revolution were a feature of his Restoration Day sermon before the same audience that year, *National Gratitude for Providential Goodness, Recommended*. As with so many others, defending 1688 was now a way of defending the monarchy and the Church. In 1793, the General Fast called forth his 'discourse', *The Patriot King, and Patriot People*, dedicated to 'The General Association in England, for suppressing Sedition, and promoting Peace'. He argued that

Whatever difference of opinion may obtain among us, as to the origin of civil policy, and the rights of kings – whether they be human, or whether they be divine – whether hereditary, or otherwise, all must unite in this sentiment

– that power was a trust, to be exercised for the national good; that 'the greatest earthly potentates are accountable for their regal character and authority to *The King of Kings*'; that 'though in their political capacity they are exalted to a supremacy among men, they are only the ministers of God, to promote, in the first place, the cause of God and religion'. The great enemy of the public good was 'irreligion, and licentiousness':

Regicide, and philosophical atheism are not to be mentioned, but with indignation and horror; nor should universal dissipation, and the practical contempt of the divine being, be treated with less...All irreligion, all immorality, though it may assume very different aspects, is atheism in disguise.

Neglect of divine law was 'even more injurious to society' than of human law; 'An irreligious member of the Commonwealth, is one of its greatest evils.' De Coetlogon demanded an Establishment both in Church and State that was efficient in promoting national piety and virtue; religious truth alone 'has the exclusive prerogative, of laying the axe to the very root of all evil'. Whig checks on government, though not abandoned, now paled into insignificance beside the overriding need for government to be vigorously and rightly exercised. He quoted Hannah More with approval:

The crimes and errors of the distracted people of France, are an awful illustration and warning to us, that, no degree of wit, and learning; no progress in commerce, no advances in the knowledge of nature, or in the embellishments of art, can ever thoroughly tame that savage, *the natural human heart*, without religion.[150]

[149] C. E. de Coetlogon, *Religion and Loyalty, the Grand Support of the British Empire: a Sermon, Delivered in the Cathedral Church of St Paul, on January 30, 1790*... (London, 1790), pp. 16, 20.
[150] C. E. de Coetlogon, *The Patriot King, and Patriot People: A Discourse Occasioned by the General Fast* (London, [1793]), pp. iii–iv, 6–7, 9–10, 18–19, 23, 38.

Hannah More (1745–1833), a literary celebrity of the 1770s and 80s, was now emerging as a champion of the established order. Though moving increasingly in Evangelical circles, her political and social doctrines were indistinguishable from Orthodox Anglicanism (in retirement after 1815, her two cats were named 'Passive Obedience' and 'Non Resistance'). Her *Village Politics* (1793) was written at the request of Beilby Porteus, Bishop of London, as an answer to Paine's *Rights of Man*. It has been aptly described as 'Burke for Beginners': Edmund Burke was another of her friends. As she wrote to Zachary Macaulay in 1795, 'Vulgar and indecent penny books were always common, but speculative infidelity brought down to the pockets and capacity of the poor forms a new era in our history.' It was to counter such a phenomenon that the publishing venture was undertaken which produced the series known as Cheap Repository Tracts – 114 titles in the years 1795–8, Hannah More contributing at least 50. By March 1796, two million tracts had been sold; they gave rise in 1799 to the Religious Tract Society, which continued the work.[151] The effect of such popular writings in offsetting radical propaganda would be as difficult to gauge as it would be rash to underestimate; and radical historians have, not without justification, always singled out Hannah More for special vituperation.[152]

Her critique of radicalism, though simply phrased, was wide-ranging:

Some of the Tracts dealt directly with 'the new pestilential philosophy'. *Tis All for the Best* was an answer to Voltaire's *Candide; The History of Mr Fanton* to Paine's *Age of Reason*. Her ballad *Turn the Carpet* vindicated the justice of God in the apparently irregular distribution of good in the world by pointing to another world. 'Here you have Bishop Butler's *Analogy* all for a halfpenny', wrote Porteus to her.[153]

The influence of Anglican social theory, even at a later date, was evidenced by Cobbett's *Monthly Religious Tracts*, launched in 1821, which 'set out to dissociate order and religion'. And, in the years after Waterloo, Hannah

---

[151] M. G. Jones, *Hannah More* (Cambridge, 1952), pp. 134, 138–42, 150, 219.

[152] E.g. Victor E. Neuburg, *Popular Literature. A History And Guide* (Harmondsworth, 1977), p. 256 (italics added):

> Views like these were *convenient* for those whose concern was with government – those who were able to dispense both charity and tracts to 'the meaner sort'. For the majority of the population they *could hardly have been* palatable, and the identification of *political repression* with the kind of Christianity *peddled* in tracts *must have* done a great deal to turn the minds of some working men to infidelity and atheism

(the suggestion is wholly unsubstantiated); cf. Roy Porter, *English Society in the Eighteenth Century*, pp. 191–3, 372–3: 'Cascades of cheap Anglican literature, from the *New Whole Duty of Man* to Hannah More's uplifting tracts, peddled religion to the poor' as 'soup-kitchen religion from above', etc. etc.

[153] Jones, *Hannah More*, p. 147; cf. Neuburg, *Popular Literature* p. 249:

> In these tracts the recipients were constantly counselled to accept with humility and gratitude long hours of work, low wages and poverty. These, their betters were at pains to point out, were ordained by God, who had called the poor to their humble station in society. *Unsatisfactory* as such a social doctrine was, it is *impossible not to be astonished* by the extraordinary resilience with which it was *peddled* over nearly two centuries.

(Italics added). Evidently Miss More was not behaving as an early feminist should.

More was once again turned to by the government, and contributed tracts and songs to the drive against Cobbettite radicalism after 1817. Her biographer suggests that 'Her tracts reveal...an inability to discriminate between agitation for reform and agitation for revolution, and between the revolutionary and constitutional modes employed, an inability which she shared with her Evangelical and Tory friends'; and in 1832 she cut her young friend T. B. Macaulay out of her will for voting in favour of parliamentary reform.[154] Yet Hannah More's position was not undiscriminating, for, like other Evangelicals, she saw that 'reform' was essentially concerned not with tinkering with the parliamentary representation, but with the fundamental principle of the link between Church and State. Even William Wilberforce, in his best-selling *Practical View*, had made a firm declaration in a book which, otherwise, sought to avoid politics: 'The very loss of our church establishment, though, as in all human institutions, some defects may be found in it, would in itself be attended with the most fatal consequences. No prudent man dares hastily pronounce how far its destruction might not greatly endanger our civil institutions.'[155]

V. BURKE AND THE ANGLICAN DEFENCE OF THE STATE

It is difficult to distinguish the propaganda impact of Methodists and Evangelicals, since their arguments were directed to ends often indistinguishable from those of Orthodox Anglicans. Nor is it to be supposed that the Church of England failed to engage in the ideological conflict with society's enemies at the end of the century.[156] Wilkesite disorder, the American rebellion, the French Revolution and postwar atheism called forth a succession of champions, whose sermons, tracts, books and charges still, for the most part, await their historian.[157] In this campaign, it was generally the High Churchmen who were the most effective spokesmen: they possessed the most intellectually powerful doctrine of the State, and its possession identified them as the champions of society against what soon emerged as its typical threats.

Among the most active entrepreneurs in the field of publicity was the Rev. William Jones, who organised a compendium of six tracts in 1780 under the title *The Scholar Armed*.[158] Crucially, it contained a defence of the powers

---

[154] Jones, *Hannah More*, pp. 148, 203–5, 219–21.

[155] William Wilberforce, *A Practical View of the Prevailing Religious System of Professed Christians, in the Higher and Middle Classes in this Country, Contrasted with Real Christianity* (London, 1797), pp. 411–12.

[156] Modern historians have written scores of books on obscure radicals and agitators; almost nothing has been published on the official justification, rationale or self-image of the State.

[157] For notable exceptions cf. E. R. Norman, *Church and Society* and R. A. Soloway, *Prelates and People*.

[158] *The Scholar Armed against the Errors of Infidelity, Enthusiasm, and Disloyalty; or A Collection of Tracts on the Principles of Religion, Government, and Ecclesiastical Polity* (London, 1780). It is a collection of pieces, separately paginated, and previously published separately.

of the priesthood by apostolic succession; the Church was 'not a mere *voluntary* society; but one whereof men are obliged to become members, as they value their everlasting happiness; for it is a society appointed by God with enforcements of rewards and punishments'. So ran *A Treatise on the Nature and Constitution of the Christian Church*, which was claimed to be 'extracted chiefly from Archbishop Potter's excellent Discourse concerning Church Government'. On the basis of this theory, the collection went on to include Jones' sermons *The Fear of God, and the Benefits of Civil Obedience* and his reprint from the writings of the Nonjuror Roger North, under the title *A Discourse on the English Constitution*. Jones introduced it with the appeal

...that the people should be better informed in due time, lest their ignorance make them a prey to those who labour so industriously to deceive them. To wean them from that patriotic froth, with which they have been so long treated, we must teach them how to examine things by the plain rules of common sense and positive law; and then they will see how they have been dancing after the unsubstantial delusions of oratory, and discover at last, that there is no liberty without law, no security without obedience.

And he summarised North's discourse:

That the government of England, or any part of it, is *not legally resistible with force*, is the position he lays down; and he proves it by considering the people's allegiance pursuant to the positive law of the land, and the rights of the English monarchy, as they are by law expressly and undoubtedly established.[159]

Jones addressed himself to 'the people' indirectly, via the clergy. So did many others. John Randolph,[160] then Regius Professor of Divinity at Oxford, produced in 1792 a students' compendium which included, as well as Bishop Gibson's four Pastoral Letters, Charles Leslie's *Short and Easy Method with the Deists*.[161] In 1795, William Jones followed it with a second compendium entitled *The Scholar Armed*, now expanded to two substantial volumes.[162] It included three tracts by Charles Leslie: *A Short and Easy Method with the Deists*, *The Truth of Christianity Demonstrated*, and *A Short and Easy Method with the Jews*; the Nonjuror William Law's classic *Three Letters to the Bishop of Bangor*, and Roger North's *Discourse* alongside works by George Horne – *A Discourse on the Origin of Civil Government* and *Some Considerations on Mr Locke's Scheme of Deriving Government from an Original Compact* – and William Jones, including *The Catholic Doctrine of a Trinity*. In 1804 the

[159] North, *Discourse*. Preface pp. 6–8.
[160] John Randolph (1749–1813). Third son of T. R., Pres. of Corpus Christi College, Oxford. Westminster and Christ Church. BA 1771; Tutor 1779–83; Professor of Poetry; Regius Professor of Greek; Professor of Moral Philosophy; 1783 Regius Professor of Divinity; Canon of Christ Church; Bp of Oxford 1799; Bangor 1807; London 1809.
[161] John Randolph (ed.), *Enchiridion Theologicum, or a Manual, for the Use of Students in Divinity* (5 vols., Oxford, 1792).
[162] *The Scholar Armed against the Errors of the Time; or, a Collection of Tracts on the Principles and Evidences of Christianity, the Constitution of the Church, and the Authority of Civil Government* (2 vols., London, 1795; 2nd edn 1800).

Orthodox Churchman's Magazine claimed that the works of the Nonjurors Hickes and Leslie 'are daily rising in value and are sought after with the greatest avidity';[163] and the significance of their continued currency was political as well as devotional. They helped to educate a generation.

William Van Mildert's Boyle Lectures of 1802–5 used as sources, with no evident need to justify their orthodoxy, the works of Hickes, Leslie, Jones of Nayland, Daubeny, Horne, Sherlock, Hallifax, Bagot, Whittaker, Waterland; Dr Thomas Patten's Hutchinsonian sermon at Oxford in 1755; Balguy; Hooker; Bishop Jeremy Taylor; Bishop Pretyman Tomline's *Elements of Theology*; Henry Stebbing; and Atterbury.[164] In retrospect, Anglican apologists appeared to close ranks and advance as a single, formidable, phalanx. By 1837, when the Master of Trinity published another collection of tracts for students, volume III, 'Principles of Society and Government, Civil and Ecclesiastical', could cite some more modern examples along with Hooker, Barrow and Bishop Butler's 30th January sermon to the House of Lords in 1741. Bishop Horsley's sermon on the same occasion in 1793 now stood beside long quotations from the works of Edmund Burke.[165]

The ideas of that author have often been explained as if they came from nowhere – as if they sprang, fully armed, from his unaided imagination. Burke, it has been supposed, had no precursors within a tradition dominated by Lockeian rationalism. A general unfamiliarity with late-eighteenth-century writing on the themes which preoccupied Burke[166] has led historians into a curiously inconclusive debate on 'textual' questions: whether his central meaning is best explained as proto-Utilitarianism, as proto-Hegelianism, as an exemplification of continental natural law theory, or as *ad hoc* borrowings from English neo-Harringtonian, 'Country' ideology. The search for a usable Burke has too often taken priority over the attempt to reconstruct the historical Burke. Scholars have in fact been unaware of the existence, let alone the importance, of the broad and sophisticated tradition of Anglican political theology outlined here. Within this setting, it is evident that Burke's achievement in his later works was to give eloquent but unoriginal expression to a theoretical position largely devised by Anglican churchmen, and which owed its most problematic and equivocal features to the way in which an early-eighteenth-century ecclesiastical and

---

[163] J. Wickham Legg, *English Church Life from the Restoration to the Tractarian Movement* (London, 1914), p. 17.

[164] William Van Mildert, *An Historical View of the Rise and Progress of Infidelity, with a Refutation of its Principles and Reasonings: in a Series of Sermons Preached for the Lecture Founded by the Hon. Robert Boyle...1802 to 1805*, 3rd edn (2 vols., London, 1820), vol. I, pp. 465–544; vol. II, pp. 467–562.

[165] Christopher Wordsworth (ed.), *Christian Institutes: a Series of Discourses and Tracts* (4 vols., London, 1837).

[166] A recent book on Burke's political philosophy succeeded in surveying it without citing any other single work of political theory written in Burke's lifetime.

political antagonism was reconciled and adapted in defence of the monarchy of George III.

Burke, like many other Anglican theorists, was prompted to deploy such ideas after the 'discontents' of the late 1760s and the radical movement within the Church which produced the Feathers Tavern petition in 1772. But it is important to emphasise that his starting point was self-consciously libertarian. In the 1760s, Burke stood within a Whig tradition professing itself against 'persecution for conscientious difference in opinion'. Until 1790, his relations with Dissenters were typically cordial. In 1772 he denied the arguments, associated with Oxford Anglicans like Newdigate and North, that *no* change was permissible in the outward forms of the Church's worship, and that such changes had been rendered impossible by the Act of Union.[167] Even in 1792, he gave his opinion that the Coronation Oath did not debar the king from consenting to any measure of Roman Catholic emancipation passed by Parliament, and that the Test Act itself might be removed or modified 'whenever the Dissenters cease by their conduct to give any alarm to the government, in Church and State'.[168] Nevertheless, Burke departed from his early radicalism to emerge, after the French Revolution, as a champion of the Anglican aristocratic-monarchical regime. By 1792, this position had been formulated as an explicit denial of Warburtonian doctrine:

An alliance between Church and State in a Christian commonwealth is, in my opinion, an idle and fanciful speculation. An alliance is between two things that are in their nature distinct and independent, such as between two sovereign states. But in a Christian commonwealth the Church and the State are one and the same thing, being different integral parts of the same whole... Religion is so far, in my opinion, from being out of the province or the duty of a Christian magistrate, that it is, and it ought to be, not only his care, but the principal thing in his care; because it is one of the great bonds of human society, and its object the supreme good, the ultimate end and object of man himself.[169]

The historian must, above all, confront this profound discontinuity: he must explain how Burke's thought changed. Paradoxically, this has seldom been attempted. Writers on political thought have generally turned to Burke as the spokesman for a late-eighteenth-century conservative position (they knew no others). Yet Burke wrote no systematic treatise on political theory, in the manner of Hobbes or Locke. Historians were therefore drawn into the unhistorical enterprise of writing one for him, from materials which Burke left. This process naturally made the chosen organising categories of

[167] *Speech on the Acts of Uniformity February 6, 1772* in Burke, *Works*, vol. VII, pp. 7–10.
[168] *A Letter to Sir Hercules Langrishe, Bart., MP, on the Subject of the Roman Catholics of Ireland* (1792), in Burke, *Works*, vol. IV, pp. 259, 264.
[169] *Speech on a Motion made in the House of Commons by the Right Hon. C. J. Fox, May 11, 1792, for Leave to Bring in a Bill to Repeal and Alter Certain Acts Respecting Religious Opinions, upon Occasion of a Petition of the Unitarian Society*, in Burke, *Works*, vol. VII, p. 43.

even more importance in Burke's case than in the case of any other political theorist. Usually, the result was a wholly unchronological account of a Burkeian system, presented as a homogeneous and undifferentiated whole. If, rarely, a principle of development is introduced, it is typically assumed that Burke's characteristic later ideas took shape around the issues of parliamentary reform, or, less obviously, party. There is an element of truth in both assumptions; but neither attends to the centrality of religion and the Church in Burke's vision of the 1790s, or explains how they came to occupy that place.

Burke's rejection of Warburton was worked out over two decades during which a succession of practical parliamentary conflicts over religious toleration forced themselves on his attention. If Anglican Christianity was established not merely because it was expedient but because it was true, the exact forms of its established doctrines and liturgy were of infinitely greater importance. Burke's speech against the Feathers Tavern petition in 1772 showed him in the process of admitting this illiberal idea. The petitioners suffered no hardship, he claimed; only

They want to receive the emoluments appropriated for teaching one set of doctrines, whilst they are teaching another... The hardship amounts to this, – that the people of England are not taxed two shillings in the pound to pay them for teaching, as divine truths, their own particular fancies... Dissent, not satisfied with toleration, is not conscience, but ambition... the complaint is not, that there is not toleration of diversity in opinion, but that diversity in opinion is not rewarded by bishoprics, rectories, and collegiate stalls.

What, then, was the theoretical basis for change?

... the ground for a legislative alteration of a legal establishment is this, and this only, – that you find the inclinations of the majority of the people, concurring with your own sense of the intolerable nature of the abuse, are in favour of a change.

This seems ambiguous between an establishment from expedience and an establishment championing truth. Burke nevertheless wished to reply to a Whig nostrum:

If the Church be, as Mr Locke defines it, a *voluntary society*, etc, then it is essential to this voluntary society to exclude from her voluntary society any member she thinks fit, or to oppose the entrance of any upon such conditions as she thinks proper.[170]

If the Church was a society which men were not free to join at will, not free to remain members of at their discretion, and not free to leave at will without perpetrating schism, then the whole idea of the Church as a *voluntary* society became profoundly ambiguous. The term 'voluntary' began to take on a new and quite different meaning in Burke's usage, just as 'social contract' was to do later.

[170] *Speech on the Acts of Uniformity*, pp. 10–11, 13, 15, 17.

Burke's understanding of the issues was evidently still imperfect. His speech on 6th February 1772 argued that the Feathers Tavern petitioners, if dissatisfied with the Church's doctrines, were free to worship outside it as Dissenters (they were not: as anti-Trinitarians, they were formally outside the provisions of the 'Toleration' Act). Similarly, in supporting an application on 3rd April 1772 by Dissenting ministers for relief from the obligation to subscribe most of the Thirty-Nine Articles in order to enjoy the benefits of the Toleration Act, Burke's speech seems to show no awareness that the applicants were a minority of Arians and Socinians; and the majority of Dissenters were indeed still doctrinally orthodox. It is possible that Burke's understanding of the fact that it was *heterodox* Dissent which lay at the root of the emerging radicalism of the 1770s and 1780s (the interpretation argued in chapter 5 below) came slowly. In March 1779, however, when the Protestant Dissenters' Relief Act was debated, Burke voted for North's amendment to impose a declaration of Protestant Christianity in place of subscription to the Thirty-Nine Articles – a move which North intended to exclude Deists, Arians and Socinians.

The French Revolution in turn had an activating effect on Burke's perception of the issues, as on many others'. No longer was the major option the distant and improbable one which Warburton had postulated: the Church of England losing its title to establishment through the growth to majority status of some rival church. The great conflict was no longer between Popery and Protestantism or Anglicanism and Dissent, but between Christianity and Jacobinism:

If ever the Church and constitution of England should fall in these islands, (and they will fall together), it is not Presbyterian discipline nor Popish hierarchy that will rise upon their ruins. It will not be the Church of Rome nor the Church of Scotland, not the Church of Luther nor the Church of Calvin. On the contrary, all these churches are menaced, and menaced alike. It is the new fanatical religion, now in the heat of its first ferment, of the Rights of Man, which rejects all establishments, all discipline, all ecclesiastical, and in truth all civil order, which will triumph, and which will lay prostrate your Church, which will destroy your distinctions, and which will put all your properties to auction, and disperse you over the earth.[171]

Yet Burke's system in the 1790s was not a defence of *all* religion. It was a defence of Trinitarian religion – the Church of England and (where it was established) the Roman Catholic Church – against heterodox Dissent. Burke's position is, of course, most commonly traced in his *Reflections on the Revolution in France*, published on 1st November 1790. But the opinions which the book contains took shape during its writing earlier that year. Crucially, they crystallised around an English issue. On 2nd March 1790 Burke intervened to vote against the Dissenters' third motion, proposed by Fox,

---

[171] *A Letter to Richard Burke, Esq. on Protestant Ascendancy in Ireland* (1793) in Burke, *Works*, vol. VI, p. 398.

to repeal the Test and Corporation Acts. Three bitterly fought contests in 1787, 1789 and 1790 made this the classic issue on which the Anglican doctrine of the State was attacked, analysed and defended. On the first two occasions Burke absented himself, professing indecision. On the third he attended, voted against, and delivered an important speech[172] which anticipated the characteristic doctrines of the *Reflections*: the impossibility of recurring to 'abstract principles of natural right'; the non-utilitarian nature of the State; its semi-religious function; its special relationship with the Church; the profoundly subversive nature of Dissenters' aims and propaganda.[173]

Once Burke had assimilated radical Dissent with Jacobinism, his *Reflections* also took as its starting point, as a rival statement of principle, the 'political sermon' of the Unitarian minister Richard Price on 4th November 1789. Price had sought to advance his cause by opening up the intellectual fissures in the Revolution Settlement. Burke was drawn to reply in kind, defending the monarchy of George III by expounding a view of the events of 1688–9. Price had claimed that 'the people' had acquired three rights by the Revolution: to choose their own governors; to cashier them for misconduct; and to frame a government for themselves. Burke denied all three. The first implied that the Crown had been made elective; but this, the Declaration of Rights did not assert, any more than did the Act of Settlement. William III represented only 'a small and temporary deviation from the strict order of a regular hereditary succession'; he was 'a prince who, though not next, was, however, very near in the line of succession'. 'The crown was carried somewhat out of the line in which it had before moved; but the new line was derived from the same stock. It was still a line of hereditary descent; still an hereditary descent in the same blood, though an hereditary descent qualified with Protestantism.' An exception, in a case of necessity, did not invalidate a general rule: 'It is far from impossible to reconcile, if we do not suffer ourselves to be entangled in the mazes of metaphysic sophistry, the use both of a fixed rule and an occasional deviation, – the sacredness of an hereditary principle of succession in our government with a power of change in its application in cases of extreme emergency.' Consequently, 'The princes who succeeded according to the act of Parliament which settled the crown on the Electress Sophia and on her descendants, being Protestants, came in as much by a title of inheritance as King James did.'

---

[172] *Parl Hist*, vol. XXVIII, cols. 432–43. It has usually escaped the attention of historians of political thought; perhaps only because it is not reprinted in the generally-used editions of Burke's *Works*.

[173] Burke said he spoke 'from information lately received': he cited 'two printed catechisms circulated by the Dissenters for the use of young non-conformists, written by Mr Robinson and Mr Palmer', Priestley, and Price's sermon on 4th November 1789. Burke had been preoccupied with the impeachment of Warren Hastings; his mind may have been made up relatively suddenly. Who put this material into his hands? Possibly his friend Horsley; but there is no evidence.

The logic of Burke's case had easily been exploded by Jacobites, but it was no longer true that a large sector of society had an interest in levelling that critique against a regime which, after 1760, all parties had rallied to defend. Burke's most effective points were the failure of radical Whig contractarianism to be clearly embodied in the Revolution Settlement, and the non-contractarian nature of allegiance to the Hanoverian monarchy: the Act of Settlement was therefore presentable as an Act which 'secures both an hereditary crown and an hereditary allegiance'. This had been the familiar position of early-eighteenth-century Whigs. But in order to defend it against 1790s radicalism, in order to present it as a moderate and sober position, Burke was drawn like many others to caricature and to vilify the alternative case, with which, as has been shown, the Whig case actually possessed a profound affinity. Burke's opponents, he wrote, commonly disputed

...as if they were in a conflict with some of those exploded fanatics of slavery who formerly maintained, what I believe no creature now maintains, 'that the crown is held by divine, hereditary, and indefeasible right'. These old fanatics of single arbitrary power dogmatised as if hereditary royalty was the only lawful government in the world, – just as our new fanatics of popular arbitrary power maintain that a popular election is the sole lawful source of authority. The old prerogative enthusiasts, it is true, did speculate foolishly, and perhaps impiously too, as if monarchy had more of a divine sanction than any other mode of government, – and as if a right to govern by inheritance were in strictness *indefeasible* in every person who should be found in the succession to a throne, and under every circumstance, which no civil or political right can be. But an absurd opinion concerning the king's hereditary right to the crown does not prejudice one that is rational, and bottomed upon solid principles of law and policy.

Secondly, therefore, the people acquired no right of cashiering their governors for misconduct. Burke quoted the Commons' resolution asserting James II's abdication (p. 128 above) and inferred that they had left the Crown, 'what in the eye and estimation of law it had ever been, perfectly irresponsible'. Thus, thirdly, the Revolution did not imply a new right of framing a government. The Declaration of Rights reasserted ancient right. Englishmen claimed their liberties as an inheritance, not as the 'Rights of Man'. Burke directly denied Price's claim that a representation in the legislature was the sole basis of legitimate government. Burke held out an alternative social ideal: 'We know, and, what is better, we feel inwardly, that religion is the basis of civil society, and the source of all good, and of all comfort.' The English

...do not consider their Church establishment as convenient, but as essential to their state: not as a thing heterogeneous and separable, – something added for accommodation, – what they may either keep or lay aside, according to their temporary ideas of convenience. They consider it as the foundation of their whole constitution, with which, and with every part of which, it holds an indissoluble union. Church and State are ideas inseparable in their minds, and scarcely is the one ever mentioned without mentioning the other.

Within this religious but anti-Warburtonian vision of politics, the Whig commonplace of a social contract took on a wholly different and lesser significance to that which Price or Priestley might claim for it. Burke was unwilling to abandon the phrase; but its meaning was changed out of recognition. Just as men like Jones of Nayland denied that the Church was a 'voluntary society', so Burke extended that insight to the Church's other aspect, the State:

Society is, indeed, a contract. Subordinate contracts for objects of mere occasional interest may be dissolved at pleasure; but the State ought not to be considered as nothing better than a partnership agreement in a trade of pepper and coffee, calico or tobacco, or some other such low concern, to be taken up for a little temporary interest, and to be dissolved by the fancy of the parties. It is to be looked on with other reverence; because it is not a partnership in things subservient only to the gross animal existence of a temporary and perishable nature. It is a partnership in all science, a partnership in all art, a partnership in every virtue and in all perfection. As the ends of such a partnership cannot be obtained in many generations, it becomes a partnership not only between those who are living, but between those who are living, those who are dead, and those who are to be born. Each contract of each particular state is but a clause in the great primeval contract of eternal society, linking the lower with the higher natures, connecting the visible and invisible world, according to a fixed compact sanctioned by the inviolable oath which holds all physical and all moral natures each in their appointed place. This law is not subject to the will of those who, by an obligation above them, and infinitely superior, are bound to submit their will to that law. The municipal corporations of that universal kingdom are not morally at liberty, at their pleasure, and on their speculations of a contingent improvement, wholly to separate and tear asunder the bands of their subordinate community, and to dissolve it into an unsocial, uncivil, unconnected chaos of elementary principles.[174]

Much has been written about Burke's doctrine of prescription; but only Providence made it acceptable, guaranteeing the moral status of the outcome.

Nor was this a mere flight of fancy, a rhetorical flourish: it was a central point in the argument to assert, as churchmen asserted, that allegiance was natural, and to assert, as Whigs asserted, that it had not been ruptured in 1688 or 1714. In 1791 he returned to the attack, justifying his argument in the *Reflections* by repeating, on the one hand, the constitutional case, illustrated now from the arguments advanced at the impeachment of Dr Sacheverell, and, on the other, an Anglican theory of political and social obligation. Burke cited Whigs' speeches at that trial 'positively affirming

---

[174] *Reflections on the Revolution in France* (1790) in Burke, *Works*, vol. III, pp. 251–4, 258–62, 265, 267, 271–4, 304, 331–2, 335, 350, 359–63.

the doctrine of non-resistance to government to be the general moral, religious and political rule for the subject' in even stronger terms than Burke himself had used. It was possible for him therefore to claim that 'the Whig managers for the Commons meant to preserve the government on a firm foundation, by asserting the perpetual validity of the settlement then made, and its coercive power upon posterity'.

The proof of this led Burke, again, to theology:

Duties are not voluntary. Duty and will are even contradictory terms. Now, though civil society might be at first a voluntary act, (which in many cases it undoubtedly was), its continuance is under a permanent standing covenant, coexisting with the society; and it attaches upon every individual of that society, without any formal act of his own. This is warranted by the general practice, arising out of the general sense of mankind. Men without their choice derive benefits from that association; without their choice they are subjected to duties in consequence of these benefits; and without their choice they enter into a virtual obligation as binding as any that is actual. Look through the whole of life and the whole system of duties. Much the strongest moral obligations are such as were never the results of our option... Taking it for granted that I do not write to the disciples of the Parisian philosophy, I may assume that the awful Author of our being is the Author of our place in the order of existence, – and that, having disposed and marshalled us by a divine tactic, not according to our will, but according to His, He has in and by that disposition virtually subjected us to act the part which belongs to the place assigned us. We have obligations to mankind at large, which are not in consequence of any special voluntary pact. They arise from the relation of man to man, and the relation of man to God, which relations are not matters of choice. On the contrary, the force of all the pacts which we enter into with any particular person or number of persons amongst mankind depends upon those prior obligations. In some cases the subordinate relations are voluntary, in others they are necessary, – but the duties are all compulsive. When we marry, the choice is voluntary, but the duties are not matters of choice: they are dictated by the nature of the situation. Dark and inscrutable are the ways by which we come into the world. The instincts which give rise to this mysterious process of nature are not of our making. But out of physical causes, unknown to us, perhaps unknowable, arise moral duties, which, as we are able perfectly to comprehend, we are bound indispensably to perform. Parents may not be consenting to their moral relation; but, consenting or not, they are bound to a long train of burdensome duties towards those with whom they have never made a convention of any sort. Children are not consenting to their relation; but their relation, without their actual consent, binds them to its duties, – or rather it implies their consent, because the presumed consent of every rational creature is in unison with the predisposed order of things. Men come in that manner into a community with the social state of their parents, endowed with all the benefits, loaded with all the duties of their situation. If the social ties and ligaments, spun out of those physical relations which are the elements of the commonwealth, in most cases begin, and always continue, independently of our will, so, without any stipulation on our own part, we are bound by that relation called our country, which comprehends (as it has been well said) 'all the charities of all'.[175]

[175] *An Appeal from the New to the Old Whigs* in Burke, *Works*, vol. IV, pp. 125–6, 133, 165–7.

This view of the role of religion in Burke's thought is, therefore, entirely at odds with the superficial view of eighteenth-century ideology which supposed that Locke's 'great achievement...had been to free political thought from theological authority and bring it into the more reasonable realm of secularity and individual responsibility'; 'surely never has a secular writer obtained such universal recognition or been received with such unquestioning faith as Locke'; an unquestioning faith which meant that the influence of 'religious ideas' in Burke was a 'new thing', because, until the 1790s, 'The spirit of that age was secular and rationalist, tolerant of the amiable weaknesses of religious men, but scarcely approving them, frightened above all of "enthusiasm". Outward conformity for the sake of setting a good example to the lower orders was combined with real spiritual indifference.'[176] Readers will by now be familiar with the combination of ignorance and modern commitment which once produced polemic of this sort. It can easily be set aside.

The extent to which the Church–State alliance sustained a non-secular understanding of the State was an eighteenth-century commonplace as well as a carefully-articulated tenet of Whig ideology. This is not to suggest that Anglican political theology was the *only* element in Burke's conservatism, though it is to question the view that 'in order to explain his traditionalism, regarded simply as an isolated factor, there is no need to suppose more than his continued employment and highly developed understanding of certain concepts which came from the common law'.[177] Rather, the stress on political theology accounts far more fully for the anti-utilitarian, anti-contractarian, 'irrational' component of Burke's account of political action and motivation – not as a sudden wild reaction to 1789 but as a considered and long-standing component of the Whig defence of 1688 in the first half of the eighteenth century.

It was not strictly justified, therefore, but not without an element of truth, that a 'liberal' like the Rev. Christopher Wyvill could stigmatise Burke as 'our modern Filmer'.[178] Establishment thinkers explicitly rejected Filmer (and so, too, the label 'Tory'). That is, they rejected what they knew to be the key element in his theory: divine hereditary *indefeasible* right. The

---

[176] Alfred Cobban, *Edmund Burke and the Revolt against the Eighteenth Century*, 2nd edn (London, 1960), pp. 16, 96, 233. The 'spiritual indifference' is all too plainly that of the modern left-liberal intelligentsia.

[177] J. G. A. Pocock, 'Burke and the Ancient Constitution: A Problem in the History of Ideas', in *Politics, Language and Time* (London, 1972), p. 232. I entirely accept, however, Professor Pocock's insight (pp. 203, 227) that Burke is not to be understood as a lone reaction against a Lockeian political rationalism which had 'conditioned all political thinking before [Burke's] time and some special explanation [were] needed to be found of his breaking with it'.

[178] Rev. C. Wyvill, *A Defence of Dr Price, and the Reformers of England*, 2nd edn (London, 1792), p. 87.

divinely sanctioned, hereditary, hierarchical state which the late-eighteenth-century intelligentsia defended, identifying 'rights' with the privileges conceded by positive law, derived its form – especially the theoretical independence of aristocracy and gentry – from the rejection of 'indefeasible'. Having rejected it, having renounced Filmer, they retained most of the rest of his theory, applied to a Whig dynasty.[179] In that intellectual strategy they were entirely at one with orthodox Whigs under George I and George II.

VI. CHURCH-AND-STATE: ANGLICANS VERSUS RADICALS, 1789–1815

It was not only Establishment thinkers who used or responded to the idiom of Anglican political theology. Their radical critics recognised its existence, and implicitly conceded its force, by reacting to it as the official ideology of the State. In reacting against it, they naturally parodied it. Nevertheless, their attacks can sometimes bring the essential features of the system into sharp focus. In 1792, the lapsed Anglican Gilbert Wakefield[180] wrote (though with a retrospective colouring) of his relief at not having been sent to Oxford: 'Their powers of invention are unexerted, their ambition is at rest...Orthodox theology, high church politics, and passive obedience to the powers that be, sit enthroned there; and spread their stupefying influence through the atmosphere around them.'[181] Later, a French visitor, who seems to have moved in radical circles associated with Sir Francis Burdett, distinguished between the ideologies of ministry and opposition: 'The doctrine of passive obedience and non-resistance, and its contrary, constitute the most material difference between Whigs and Tories.'[182]

The most systematic enquiry into the Establishment position is to be found in a substantial tract by the Unitarian barrister Samuel Heywood.[183] *High Church Politics* was more than an attack on Horsley and Burke, however. Heywood accepted that their doctrines represented the current position of the Church, but argued, first, that the Church since the Reformation had

---

[179] The process was largely independent of any reading of Filmer. Whigs read Whig authors. But if they *did* read Filmer, they were surprised at the extent to which they agreed with him: cf. the case of John Reeves, below, pp. 263–5.

[180] Gilbert Wakefield (1756–1801). Son of clergyman. Jesus Coll., Camb.; BA 1776; Fellow; deacon 1778 (never took priest's orders); curacies; adopted unitarian views and resigned curacy. Vacated Fellowship on marriage, 1779. Classical tutor, Warrington Academy, 1779–83; then private tutor; 1790 tutor at Hackney Academy; resigned 1791. Pacifist, violent critic of Pitt, engaged in seditious pamphleteering in 1790s. Imprisoned 1799–1801, for seditious libel.

[181] *Memoirs of the Life of Gilbert Wakefield...Written by Himself* (London, 1792), p. 60.

[182] [L. Simond], *Journal of a Tour and Residence in Great Britain, During the Years 1810 and 1811* (2 vols., Edinburgh, 1815), Vol. I, p. 81. The author's reason for reviving the label 'Tory' for Spencer Perceval's ministry should be noted.

[183] [Samuel Heywood], *High Church Politics: Being a Seasonable Appeal to the Friends of the British Constitution, Against the Practices and Principles of High Churchmen; as Exemplified in the Late Opposition to the Repeal of the Test Laws, and in the Riots at Birmingham* (London, 1792).

always preached such divine right, anti-libertarian doctrines, 1688 making no difference; and, second, that the Church was at odds with the State in these respects, for the State since 1688 had been built on the principles of Locke and Hoadly.

Anglican clergy, Heywood contended, could be divided into 'High' and 'Low', but the former held sway: 'passive obedience and non-resistance are still the avowed principles of the Church'. Horsley made his claim to be a High Churchman 'as enjoying a *spiritual* commission for the administration of our Lord's proper kingdom'. Heywood, as a Dissenter, at once attacked this central point, citing Bishop Warburton, who 'has admitted that the apostolical succession was lost in the English Church at the revolution'. The Nonjuror Dr Hickes, too, was quoted, totally disavowing the spiritual validity of the post-revolution Church. Heywood seized on Warburton's central argument: 'I am not inclined to object to the State's giving a preference to that religion which is approved of by the majority of the people': but its title, in that case, would only be a civil one, ascending from the people rather than descending from God: 'if the divine right to the supremacy was lost at the revolution, with the divine right of kings, and the apostolical succession of bishops, it must now stand, as they do, merely on the authority of the State, and be a delegation of power *from the people*'. If Horsley accepted 'the *jure divino* right of episcopacy', why was not the Nonjuring Church the true Church of England?

Warburton's doctrine of an alliance was 'the sheet anchor of modern High Churchmen', but Heywood went on to challenge it in turn. An apostolical succession, 'if traced from the apostles, must be through *the pope and his bishops*, or, if from Christ, through *a race of jure divino kings*': neither of which, he claimed, Horsley would dare concede. 'Church and King' was a 'Jacobitical cry' since Jacobites 'believed that both Church and King had a *jure divino* original, and that, as to the *Lords* and *Commons*, they were only the trappings of royalty. But there seems to be no natural connection between a Church existing under a *divine* commission, and a King deriving power from *the people*', as he does since 1688. In reality, argued Heywood, the Church of England could not form an alliance with the State, for it had no separate existence from it, no divine commission. Henry VIII 'actually made a church of his own' as a prop to royal absolutism, and it had preached divine right ever since.

Heywood cited *The Institution of a Christian Man*, the Thirty-Nine Articles, the Homilies (especially those against rebellion), Bishop Overall's Convocation Book, the Canons of 1640, the forms of prayer for State services like those of 30th January and 29th May, the University of Oxford's resolutions and book-burnings in 1683 and similar definitions of Anglican doctrine. State services, he argued, were particularly influential. The Homilies against rebellion read, or the '*political* sermons' preached, on 5th November, 30th January and 29th May, were effective and dangerous in 'inculcating principles hostile to public liberty'. "Twice at least in every year, for more than a century, from nearly ten thousand pulpits (supposing all the clergy to be obedient to the law) have the doctrines of passive obedience and non-resistance been preached to the gaping multitude'; and it still went on.

Since the revolution no alterations have been made in the articles, canons, or homilies; they are now in force, and subscribed, as before that glorious aera, and the rubric remains unreformed, and in daily use, so that in direct opposition to the genius of the British monarchy, passive obedience and non-resistance are *still* the doctrines of the Church.

Here Heywood had to be both highly selective and undiscriminating in proving his case, ignoring the ways in which Anglican political theology *had* adapted itself to a new dynasty. He cited Dr Binckes' sermon to the Lower House of Convocation on 30th January 1701/2, Dr Sacheverell's sermon on 5th November 1709, and Dr Nowell's sermon on 30th January 1772, all of which had attracted some form of official censure, as if no distinction needed to be drawn between them.

But even in our own time, during the American war, my readers may recollect how violent many of the clergy of the establishment were against the colonists, and that sermons were preached, even by the highest dignitaries, couched in the most abject terms of courtly servility, and inculcating doctrines equally subversive of liberty on both sides of the Atlantic.

But these he did not cite, since he wished to suggest not only that their doctrines were identical with Filmer's or Sacheverell's, but also that they were *not* official: that the State disowned them, and that the contrast could be expressed in a table:

Principles of the State

I. That all kingly governments originate in a solemn compact made between the king and the people.

II. That kings are trustees for their subjects, and invested with power only for their advantage.

III. That the people may resist a king, who *endeavours* to subvert and extirpate their religion, laws, and liberties.

And that distant colonies may resist a parent country, which manifests a hostile mind against them, *by endeavouring to tax them without their own consent.*

IV. That the crown of England, and the descent, limitation, and *inheritance* thereof may be limited and bound by Act of Parliament.

Principles of the Church

I. That all kingly governments originate from God.

II. That kings, holding their crowns by divine right, and being the Lord's anointed, are accountable to God only.

III. That the people may not, in any case, even that of religion, resist their king; but must peaceably submit to all his measures, however oppressive or wicked.

IV. That the crown of England, descending by divine, hereditary, indefeasible right, neither it, nor the descent, limitation, or inheritance thereof, can be limited or bound by any human authority whatsoever.

Heywood had taken a radical contractarian case for his 'State' doctrine, and a caricature of Anglican political theology for his 'Church' doctrine. The former, as has been argued above, had failed unequivocally to be entrenched in the constitution in 1688. Heywood was therefore obliged to imply its official status negatively, by denying the cogency of Burke's account of the Glorious Revolution in his *Reflections on the Revolution in France* and *An Appeal from the New to the Old Whigs*. Burke had fallen into error, claimed Heywood, in arguing like Sacheverell that the Church was an *essential* part of the constitution. Such a position, if admitted, would make Heywood's caricature of Church doctrine in some sense the official State doctrine also. But the 'Old Whigs', he claimed, held no such doctrine:

Where, for example, in the works of the Whig *Bishops*, for such there were in those days, will he find that the Church is *essential to the State*, or that our *whole constitution is founded* upon it? The Bishops Burnet and Hoadly taught a different doctrine, and found it difficult enough to reconcile them at all with each other.

And Heywood was able roundly to endorse Price's claim that the people of England had a right 'to cashier their kings for *misconduct*'. It was the doctrine of Locke, and of Burke himself in 1770, in relation to America.

Indeed the systems of Dr Price and Mr Burke (as he states his own in 1790) differ little from each other, when fairly contrasted. Dr Price says, a king may be deposed for *misconduct*; Mr Burke says, No! *every* misconduct will not justify resistance, but there must be a grave and over-ruling necessity accompanying it

– of which, in Burke's terms, the people are the judge, as in 1688 or 1776.[184]

Heywood, among other of Burke's critics, had succeeded in identifying the flaws in Burke's constitutional defence of the Revolution. Yet the flaws were not inadequacies in Burke's reasoning, but the equivocations and ambiguities of the Revolution Settlement itself; and Heywood did little more than reiterate, from a different standpoint, the case which Jacobites and Nonjurors had deployed against the early Hanoverians. As in the early part of the century, so in the 1790s, the strongest element in the official case was not the constitutional one – the attempt to argue that the principles which justified 1688 would *not* justify a future revolution – but the religious element, the assertion of the centrality of the Church, its validation of the Hanoverian dynasty, and its political message of subordination, loyalty and obedience. Churchmen and committed Anglican laymen were therefore prominent in the propaganda war in defence of the State during the French Revolutionary and Napoleonic conflicts.[185]

[184] [Heywood], *High Church Politics*, pp. 4–9, 61–2, 73–103, 113–19, 181, 184–7.
[185] Works treating of the necessity of religion to society were numerous: cf. Edward Ryan, *The History of the Effects of Religion on Mankind* (London, 1788); Rev. David Scurlock, *Thoughts on the Influence of Religion in Civil Government* (London, 1792); Rev. Thomas Rennell, *Principles of French Republicanism* (Winton, 1793); Thomas Somerville, DD, *Effects of the French Revolution* (Edinburgh, 1793); John Erskine, DD, *The Fatal Consequences, and the General*

Clergy included such figures as William Coxe,[186] historian of the Whig ascendancy under Walpole and the Pelhams, who inveighed against Price for failing to praise the Revolution as a Whig should: 'No language can be too warm, no expressions too strong, no panegyric too animated, in commemorating that glorious aera.' But after a brief compliment, Price had dwelt on its imperfections: 'What I had long considered as a most glorious work, you look upon as imperfect; what I held to be a free constitution, you estimate as little better than slavery.' The British constitution, Coxe insisted, was as good as was consistent with the corruption of human nature in mankind's fallen condition. He recommended Paley's defence of the State in his *The Principles of Moral and Political Philosophy* of five years previously.[187] Paley himself soon re-entered the fray, justifying inequalities of rank and fortune in utilitarian terms, drawing attention to the sources of happiness of which mankind could partake in common, and saving till last his trump card: 'If in comparing the different conditions of social life we bring religion into the account, the argument is still easier. Religion smooths all inequalities, because it unfolds a prospect which makes all earthly distinctions nothing.'[188] Once again, Paley's gift for presenting a case produced a classic and lasting formulation of the Anglican argument for the rule of law and social subordination in an inegalitarian, Christian society. It remained in circulation, and the argument remained current. As late as 14th August 1819, the *British Volunteer and Manchester Weekly Express* reprinted Paley's text as an antidote to postwar disorder.[189]

As the immediate threat of a Jacobin revolution passed, emphasis often shifted to a vigorous inspiration of national martial resolution. The Rev. Johnson Grant, preaching on *Christian Patriotism* in 1809, rehearsed all the classic texts – I Peter 2:14; Romans 13; Titus 3:1; I Timothy 2:1–2; but had to emphasise: 'Military service, however, occupies a very limited and subordinate place amongst the methods by which the love of our country

---

Sources of Anarchy (Edinburgh, 1793); Rev. Dr Thomas Clarke, *The Benefits of Christianity Contrasted with the Pernicious Influence of Modern Philosophy upon Civil Society* (London, 1796); Rev. Jonathan Boucher, *A View of the Causes and Consequences of the American Revolution* (London, 1797); William Playfair, *The History of Jacobinism* (London, 1798); William Reid, *The Rise and Dissolution of the Infidel Societies in this Metropolis* (London, 1800); Robert Hall, *Modern Infidelity Considered in Respect to its Influence on Society* (Cambridge, 1800). Cf. Cobban, *Edmund Burke*, p. 156: 'Had thinking on politics, we are compelled to ask, ceased outside utilitarian circles? One did not expect it from orthodox Whigs and Tories', etc. etc.

[186] William Coxe (1747–1828). Son of royal physician. Eton; King's Coll., Camb.; Fellow 1768; curacy 1771; travelling tutor; living 1786; Rector of Bemerton 1788 – d.; Prebendary of Salisbury 1791; Archdeacon of Wiltshire 1804; historian.

[187] William Coxe, *A Letter to the Rev. Richard Price*... (London, 1790), pp. 5–6, 39, 43.

[188] William Paley, *Reasons for Contentment; Addressed to the Labouring Part of the British Public* (London, 1793), pp. 20–1 and *passim*. Radical historians are given to holding up such texts to derision; consequently we lack scholarly studies of them.

[189] Quoted in F. K. Donnelly, 'Ideology and Early English Working-Class History: Edward Thompson and His Critics', *Social History* 2 (1976), 231–2. Dr Donnelly did not identify the author, and instead drew an analogy with 'structural-functionalists' among modern sociologists.

may be signalized.'[190] The conservative and Anglican defence of the State in wartime was many-sided. Radical theory, social disorder, the claims of the Church or the secular organisation of the State could all provide the immediate material for discussion. Anglican laymen active in defence of the Establishment included the barrister John Bowles, who rushed to attack Paine in 1792 with a claim that 'Monarchy in this country is the principle which gives activity and energy to the whole system', hereditary but not indefeasible, linked in the traditional tripartite system of checks and balances with the Commons and with the Lords. 'As the direct way to demolish any building is, Sampson-like, to pull down the pillars by which it is supported; in order to abolish monarchy it is found expedient to attack the aristocratical branch of government.'[191] Circumstances had led churchmen to defend aristocracy and monarchy as outworks of the Church itself.

Sometimes this effusion of loyalty led men into doubtful phraseology. One such was another articulate Anglican, John Reeves,[192] founder in 1792 of the Association for the Preservation of Liberty and Property against Republicans and Levellers,[193] who led a respectable and officially-sanctioned campaign against Jacobin subversion in the early 1790s. Reeves' Association was hugely successful, propagating some two thousand local branches, and crystallising the formulation of loyalist opinion. It quickly aroused the hostility of radicals: Fox attacked it in his reply to the King's Speech at the opening of the parliamentary session in December 1792, 'and quoted the doctrines published and circulated by this learned chairman, that inculcated the *jure divino* right of kings, and which would have been treasonable in the years 1715 and 1745'. The publication in 1793 by the Association of its collected papers played on the fears of the Whig lawyer Francis Plowden that there existed 'a concerted league to introduce or revive in this country a spirit and principle disavowed since the aera of our Revolution';

As to the doctrine of Thomas Bull,[194] which these leaguers revive adopt and inculcate, if it mean any thing, means in the common and accepted terms of the English language, that the King of Great Britain reigns over his people *jure divino*,

---

[190] Rev. Johnson Grant, *Christian Patriotism. A Fast Sermon Preached in the Parish Church of St Pancras...February 17, 1808* (London, 1809), p. 12.

[191] [John Bowles], *A Protest against T. Paine's 'Rights of Man'* (London, 1792), pp. 14, 17, 22.

[192] John Reeves (?1752–1829). Eton; Merton Coll., Oxford 1771–; Fellow of Queen's Coll. 1778–; Commissioner of Bankruptcy 1780; 1791–2 Chief Justice of Newfoundland; various government appointments; writer on law and theology.

[193] For the Association, cf. C. B. Cone, *The English Jacobins* (New York, 1968), chapter 7; A. Mitchell, 'The Association Movement of 1792–3', *HJ* 4 (1961), 56–77; D.E. Ginter, 'The Loyalist Association Movement of 1792–3 and British Public Opinion', *HJ* 9 (1966), 179–60; E. C. Black, *The Association. British Extraparliamentary Political Organisation 1769–1793* (Cambridge, Mass., 1963), chapter 7.

[194] The Rev. William Jones published anonymously *A Letter from Thomas Bull to His Brother John* (1792), *One Penny-worth of Truth from Thomas Bull to His Brother John* (1792), *One Penny-worth More, or, a Second letter from Thomas Bull to His Brother John* (1792), *A Letter to John Bull, Esq...* (1793).

or that he is immediately appointed king by *God* and not by the people: and which of the eighteen members of the committee [of the Association] will stand forth like Sir Robert Filmer the avowed champion of this doctrine, and rashly attempt to *Un Locke* those revolution principles upon which alone the constitution stands?[195]

In 1795 Reeves himself stood forward to do the second with his tract *Thoughts on the English Government...Letter the First.* That November a radical seized on it in a Commons debate, as a way of attacking both Reeves and the work of the Association by presenting him as an extremist. Charles Sturt, MP, quoted the following passage (pp. 12–13):

With the exception, therefore, of the advice and consent of the Two Houses of Parliament, and the interposition of Juries; the Government, and the administration of it in all its parts, may be said to rest wholly and solely on the King, and those appointed by him. Those two adjuncts of *Parliament* and *Juries* are subsidiary and occasional; but the King's Power is a substantive one, always visible and active. By his Officers, and in his name, every thing is transacted that relates to the peace of the Realm and the protection of the Subject. The Subject feels this, and acknowledges with thankfulness a superintending sovereignty, which alone is congenial with the sentiments and temper of Englishmen. In fine, the Government of England is *a Monarchy*; the Monarch is the ancient stock from which have sprung those goodly branches of the Legislature, the Lords and Commons, that at the same time give ornament to the Tree, and afford shelter to those who seek protection under it. But these are still only branches, and derive their origin and their nutriment from their common parent; they may be lopped off, and the Tree is a Tree still; shorn indeed of its honours, but not, like them, cast into the fire. The Kingly Government may go on, in all its functions, without Lords or Commons: it has heretofore done so for years together, and in our times it does so during every recess of Parliament; but without the King *his* Parliament is no more. The King, therefore, alone it is who necessarily subsists, without change or diminution; and from *him* alone we unceasingly derive the protection of Law and Government.

It was a vulnerable target. Many opposition MPs rallied to denounce it in proceedings which extended over several days. Sheridan was particularly eloquent, recalling the terms of the motion against Sacheverell, and claiming: 'he considered this as part of a system of a set of men who, to screen themselves from punishment, clung to the throne, which they wished to strengthen by any and all means in their power'. The works of Soame Jenyns, the Rev. John Whitaker, and Arthur Young, he complained, were 'openly recommended and circulated' by Reeves' Association. Sylvester Douglas, too, saw that 'this was not a single pamphlet, but one of a number founded upon the same principles; as a proof of which he referred to particular passages in some letters from Thomas Bull to John Bull in which the same doctrine was held.' John Courtenay called it 'evidently a production from the school of Filmer'.[196] Fox reminded the House of the

[195] Francis Plowden, *A Short History of the British Empire...* (London, 1794), pp. 183, 295–6, 303.

[196] Not William Pitt, wrongly credited with the remark in A. Goodwin, *The Friends of Liberty: The English Democratic Movement in the Age of the French Revolution* (London, 1979), p. 393.

fate of the work entitled *Droit le Roy*. The ministry was put in a difficult
position: William Windham tried to deny that this was the meaning of the
passage, but Pitt preferred to defend the traditional Whig conception of
a tripartite constitution – King, Lords and Commons – and allowed the
House to refer the tract to the Attorney General for prosecution on a charge
of seditious libel.

Reeves was duly acquitted,[197] but not before a hornet's nest of controversy
had been aroused. The Rev. FitzJohn Brand stepped into the arena to justify
Reeves' arguments as good law and good history, citing Reeves' *Thoughts*
and Blackstone's *Commentaries* in parallel columns and calling too on Hume's
History, Burke, and Sir John Dalrymple.[198] Nor was Reeves himself at a loss.
As befitted the scholarly author of the standard *History of the English Law*,[199]
he published in 1799 a 196-page justification of his doctrine under the title
Thoughts on the English Government...Letter the Second. He had not, he wrote,
seen Filmer's *Patriarcha* when he published his first *Letter*; but, on examination, he found it a perfectly sound account of the constitution, up to the
point where Filmer credits the sovereign with a dispensing power. 'This is
the only part of the work brought into question by Locke and others, the
rest is founded upon records and history, and is clear of all exceptions, as
appeared to me.' Though Locke was Filmer's chief critic, 'it is worthy of
examining, whether, in his Chapter on Prerogative, there may not be found
almost as much latitude for arbitrary power, as in Sir Robert himself.'
Locke 'seems... amidst the reasons he adduces for overturning a government
which he disliked, to have at hand some very sound principles, for
supporting, in all its vigour, the one which he approved'[200]. Reeves offered
a detailed defence of the wording of his *Letter*, an examination of constitutional authorities, and a statement of his own constitutional creed. It
was scrupulously Whig: the English constitution was a *via media* between
the absolutism of an individual and of the mob (he ended by quoting
Hooker). Nevertheless, he was entirely at one with Burke in his historical
perspective on 1688: 'to my understanding, the principles most discernible
in the conductors of the Revolution, are those of preserving the ancient
hereditary monarchy of this realm, with its laws and government. Those
I think, are true *Revolution Principles*.'[201]

---

[197] *Parl Hist*, vol. XXXII, cols. 608–87; *State Trials*, vol. XXVI, col. 530. Burke intervened with
the ministry on Reeves's behalf, claiming 'As to the doctrine in the part complained of – it
is neither more nor less than the law of the land.' Burke to W. Windham, [25] Nov. 1795:
Burke, *Correspondence*, vol. VIII, p. 345.

[198] J. Brand, *A Defence of the Pamphlet ascribed to John Reeves, Esq. and Entitled, 'Thoughts on the
English Government'* (London, 1796).

[199] Cf. Holdsworth, vol. XII, pp. 412–15.

[200] Reeves here remarkably anticipates some of the arguments of John Dunn, *The Political
Thought of John Locke*.

[201] Reeves, *Thoughts...Letter the Second*, pp. 52, 161–3. Reeves gives a better account of the
conservative case than Burke's *Appeal;* his neglect is regrettable.

The effort to counter Jacobinism went on. Bowles gave implicit support to Reeves in his panegyric of George III, a prince

who has, at once, displayed a most ardent and steady attachment to the Constitution, and exhibited a most exemplary pattern of religious and moral excellence – a Prince whose piety, and whose virtues, combined with a manly firmness and consistency of character, have been for years the grand bulwark, not only of this country, but of the whole civilized world. If at such a time the British throne had been deficient in any one of the qualities by which it has been so eminently distinguished, it is more than probable that every religious and social establishment would, ere now, have been laid in the dust, and that an atheistical band of sanguinary anarchists, would, at this moment, have been triumphing upon the ruins of civil society.

He quoted with approval Blackstone (*Commentaries*, vol. iv, p. 432) 'that the constitution of England had arrived to its full vigour, and the true balance between liberty and prerogative was happily established by *law*, in the reign of King Charles the second'. The preservation of religion and law against James II were 'inestimable blessings'; but the 'best friends of lawful government'

...reflect, with heartfelt concern, on the very high price which was paid for these blessings; and it even lessens, in their estimation, the value of the high privileges which were thus procured, to know that they were purchased by a violation of the most sacred of all temporal duties – the duty of allegiance. They also most strenuously protest against every attempt to transform into a precedent an anomalous transaction, which was contrary to all law, and which nothing could even palliate, but the imperious and irresistible necessity of self-preservation.

Fox was 'generally supposed' to think otherwise; but it was his duty, insisted Bowles,

...to warn his countrymen, against the insidious endeavour of some persons, to convert the Revolution into an authority for the Anarchical and Jacobinical doctrine, that the people have a right to choose and to change their government, and to depose and elect their governors...The Revolution, far from affording any sanction to such a doctrine, had for its avowed object the preservation of the entire constitution in Church and State, the fundamental principle of which is *hereditary* monarchy.[202]

Bowles was as eloquent on the crime of the French nation as generations of preachers had been against the English regicides. The French crime, he wrote, was even worse: Louis XVI had offered no resistance.

The unutterable woes which the French people have since experienced – the inexpressible degradation to which they are now reduced, afford an awful proof of the Moral Government of that Supreme Ruler, who is sure to punish the crimes of States, as well as those of individuals. What sufferings they may still be doomed to endure, who can pretend to know? But the experience of all ages, and the immutable

---

[202] John Bowles, *Reflections on the Political and Moral State of Society, at the Close of the Eighteenth Century* (London, 1800), pp. 53–5.

principles of justice, warrant the conclusion, that they will continue to be objects of Divine vengeance, until they expiate, as far as is yet possible, their foul treason, by placing the Crown on the head which is entitled to wear it.

This was not, he warned, the policy of the English government. National unity in the war effort had been obtained at the price of a profession that England sought to impose no particular form of government on France.[203]

The restoration of *ancien régime* monarchies in 1815 seemed not to confirm this fear. Yet few Englishmen, by that date, were willing to hail the reinstatement of those governments as proof of the vindication of the doctrines of Joseph de Maistre, Louis de Bonald or any other counter-revolutionary theorists whose currency was due to emphasising a case as different as possible from the Jacobin one. Nor, once the Jacobin menace was over, did Englishmen continue so loudly to defend their own monarchy as such. With the elimination of that threat to the dynasty, men were often less preoccupied by its idealisable virtues under George III than with its practical failings under George IV. An institution for which, as men could suppose, such sacrifices had been made, was increasingly appraised in utilitarian terms. Whereas the dynasty had been hailed in the early part of the eighteenth century as the deliverer of a Protestant Church, it now seemed that the Church was taking credit for the survival of the monarchy (and many other things).

It was the Church, moreover, which was the more directly challenged by radicals, and the Church whose doctrines had emerged as the unifying principles of social and political order. The monarchy in the 1820s was consequently in the background of political debate, except in so far as George IV's Coronation Oath might or might not prevent him from yielding to Roman Catholic emancipation. Edward Harcourt's coronation sermon was an almost open reproof of that monarch's immorality by its ironic comparisons with the virtues of his royal father. 'We have seen a religious reign, during more than half a century, improving the morals of society. We have seen the throne of England established by righteousness, amidst the wreck of surrounding thrones, and while other governments, shaken almost to dissolution, were crumbling to pieces on every side.' But if 'those who surround the throne, and ought to reflect its lustre, if those whose station makes them at once objects of envy and imitation, if such men are worthless or wicked, the influence of their example will extend itself in every direction, and profligacy, originating in this source, will be rapidly diffused through all the gradations of society.'[204]

If the monarchy occupied a less central place in the argument after 1815,

---

[203] John Bowles, *Reflections at the Conclusion of the War* (London, 1801), pp. 18–21.
[204] Edward Harcourt, Archbishop of York, *A Sermon Preached at the Coronation of King George IV*... (London, 1821), pp. 11, 16.

the Church assumed even greater significance, in two senses: as a guarantee of social order, and as a constitutional entity. First, it had learned a lesson from 1790s radicalism and turned it into a central tenet. The comparison of the English and French Revolutions, 1688 and 1789, showed that society's advance, in a secular sense, was no safeguard against the horrors which no-one, for half a century, could forget. 'Civilization, then, is not a sufficient security. Other restraints are necessary to avert criminal excesses in great national convulsions', namely 'the due cultivation and reception of that Almighty assistance, which is alone sufficient to effect such wondrous things, and at the same time to still "the madness of the people"'. The blessings of 1688 'must be attributed to the influence of our mild religion in its purer and reformed state, under the divine protection of that influence; and we do not assume too much in claiming it as a conspicuous effect of calm Protestant principle.'[205] As a layman put it: 'We, who live in the present age, have had the most awful and instructive lessons presented to our experience, written in blood and heightened by every human misery. We have seen that law, science and civilization, – liberty, wealth, and order, may all sink under the want of religious and moral principle.'[206] Clergymen frequently claimed that their teaching and example had been vital in quelling disaffection in the 1790s:

If the evils under which Europe has so long groaned be traced to their source, the great predisposing cause will be found in the machinations of philosophy, falsely so called: by this, men were taught to treat with ridicule and scorn the fundamental truths of the Christian faith; by this, the sacred bands of religious and moral obligations were gradually loosened and dissolved; nor did Revolution triumph but by the aid of atheism and infidelity...but let us not forget how much also was effected by the active and zealous co-operation of the established clergy of this kingdom; who most strenuously and successfully exerted themselves in exposing the mischievous tendency of those revolutionary notions, which were so industriously propagated throughout this country...it is still incumbent upon you to follow their example. The storm has not yet subsided...Hence arises the necessity of inculcating the true principles of moral and civil obligation; a duty which is peculiarly incumbent upon the established clergy. Be it then your care to impress upon your hearers the duty of subordination; to establish loyalty upon its only sure foundation, religion.[207]

Far from subsiding, the storm broke out again with renewed violence in the wave of radicalism which followed 1815. Churchmen recalled the 1790s: 'upon that occasion the clergy, to their honour be it remembered, exerted

[205] James Cornwallis, Bishop of Lichfield, *A Sermon Preached before the Lords Spiritual and Temporal...March 20, 1811, Being the Day Appointed for a General Fast* (London, 1811), pp. 13–14.
[206] Rev. Richard Yates, *The Church in Danger* (London, 1815), p. 88.
[207] Bowyer Sparke, Bishop of Ely, *A Charge Delivered to the Clergy of the Diocese of Ely, at the Primary Visitation of that Diocese in the Year 1813* (London, 1813), pp. 6–7.

themselves most strenuously and successfully in stemming the torrent of sedition and disloyalty. – It is now your duty, my reverend brethren, to follow their example', declared the Bishop of Ely: 'seditious publications' had produced 'a spirit of insubordination and disaffection'. Radicals knew what they did: seeing that their doctrines would not be accepted

...while any sense of religion was remaining, infinite pains have been taken to eradicate every religious principle, to familiarize the minds of the people to the insult and mockery of every thing sacred, by circulating publications of the most impious and blasphemous description; thus preparing them for scenes of violence and tumult. The means were indeed well adapted to the end: the transition from infidelity to disloyalty is but too easy; they who do not fear God will not long honour the king.[208]

The same analysis was advanced by William Van Mildert,[209] the new Bishop of Llandaff: from the beginning of the French Revolution,

...which, in its desolating progress, uprooted every principle, every sentiment of religion, of loyalty, and of social order, – an extensive and formidable party in *this* country has been, either openly or covertly, endeavouring to effect among us a similar catastrophe. This disposition has been manifested, even with increased malignity and virulence, since the cessation of continental warfare. As if rendered desperate by that blow, which the return of peace and the restoration of legitimate sovereigns to their thrones had inflicted upon them, the disaffected among us appear to have been doubly impatient to involve their country in all the evils of popular licentiousness and revolutionary phrenzy. Experience, moreover, had taught them, that to such nefarious projects the *religion* of their country presented an insuperable obstacle. So thoroughly have they found it to be interwoven with all our civil institutions; so manifestly, have they perceived, is the entire fabric of our constitution, our laws, and our government, upholden by its influence on the public mind; that no reasonable hope could be entertained of subverting the one, without undermining the other. Hence it is, that infidelity and disloyalty, scepticism and sedition, blasphemy and treason, have so invariably coalesced and cooperated in the labours of these infatuated disturbers of mankind.

Even by the time Van Mildert wrote, however, clergymen had begun to credit themselves with repeating what they saw in retrospect as their success of the 1790s; for the radical storm was beginning to pass over. Only a short time ago, continued Van Mildert,

...there was, indeed, great reason to apprehend that this infection was spreading to a most formidable extent. Disloyalty, contempt of public justice, deliberate insults heaped upon the laws and the religion of the country, threatenings, loud and unreserved, of the overthrow of our most venerable institutions in Church and State...Happily, however, much of this disheartening scene is gone by: and that

---

208 Bowyer Sparke, Bishop of Ely, *A Charge Delivered to the Clergy of the Diocese of Ely, at the Second Quadrennial Visitation of that Diocese, in the Year MDCCCXVII* (London, 1817), pp. 7–8.
209 William Van Mildert (1765–1836). Son of distiller. Merchant Taylors'; Queen's Coll., Oxford 1784–; curacy 1790; rectory 1795; 1813 Regius Professor of Divinity, Oxford; 1819 Bishop of Llandaff, 1820 Dean of St Paul's; 1826 Bishop of Durham.

good sense, that plain, unsophisticated moral feeling, which has been considered as eminently characteristic of our fellow-countrymen, has so far, at least, recovered its tone, as to give good hopes that the disease is not irremediable.[210]

By the early 1820s, then, the Church had lost none of its sense that it was essential to the preservation of social order. If anything, events had served only to strengthen that conviction.

This contributed, in turn, to the second mode in which the Church achieved greater political prominence after 1815. Its constitutional position had been repeatedly challenged. On the other hand, it had been repeatedly and ably defended, and the activities of its defenders left as a legacy a great body of newly-formulated political theory focussing on the Church's role and importance. Partly this was the effect of Whig party politicians like Burke, covering the cracks in the secular side of the Revolution Settlement by emphasising the degree to which the modern State was still a Church-State. Partly it was the effect of the new relevance and currency given by events to the anti-Lockeian thought of traditional churchmen like Horne and Jones. Partly, too, it was the contribution of a new generation of High Churchmen like Archdeacon Daubeny,[211] theorising on the nature of the Church *per se* in ways which intimate Tractarian doctrines.

Daubeny's first major work, *A Guide to the Church*, appeared in 1798. The heart of its political message was a denunciation of schism from 'the Church' as represented, in England, by the Anglican Church. Since 'the Church' had been founded by Christ, 'no man can take upon himself to form a Church'; the 'hackneyed subjects' of '*liberty of conscience, toleration,* and *the right of private judgement* in religious matters' were 'vulgar phrases' to which 'vulgar errors of some magnitude have been attached'. Daubeny set out to detach them by an examination of the constitutional position of the Church, and the arguments of its minimalist defenders. Even in a secular sense, dissent was not a *right*:

By the Act of Uniformity, every person is required to conform to the mode of worship established in this country...the Act of Toleration, as it is called, *tolerates nothing*; if by toleration is to be understood a justification of practices, against which temporal penalties had been heretofore denounced. A suspension of those penalties, is all that it pretends to. But suspension of penalties, whilst the law to which they have been annexed continues unrepealed, as it has been already observed, does not lessen the obligation of that law, though it may destroy its effect.

This was justified, since 'the obligation to church unity, is not derived from the authority of the *civil*, but from that of the *divine* law'.

---

[210] William Van Mildert, Bishop of Llandaff, *A Charge Delivered to the Clergy of the Diocese of Llandaff, at the Primary Visitation in August MDCCCXXI* (Oxford, 1821) pp. 13–14, 17.

[211] Charles Daubeny (1745–1827). Son of a merchant. Winchester and New College, Oxford. Fellow; living; 1784 Prebendary of Salisbury; at Versailles in 1789; 1804 Archdeacon of Salisbury; 'a kind of High Church Paley' (S.C. Carpenter).

To say therefore that man has a right to worship God in the way he thinks proper, in other words, to make a religion for himself; is to place all religions upon the same level as to the divine favour, and to render an appeal to revelation wholly unnecessary; by leading him to conclude that he is at liberty to set up a standard of right and wrong for himself in this case, instead of accepting with humility that divine standard which has in wisdom been set up for him.

Obedience in sacred matters naturally pointed the way to obedience in secular matters. Other writers, Daubeny insisted, were equally mistaken in setting up 'the majesty of the people' as the origin of power in the State, and the 'mistaken plea of Protestantism as a sanction for divisions in the Church'.[212]

According to these writers, who either do not understand, or purposely misrepresent, the principle of protestantism; the right of judgement in religious matters, which the Church of England pleads in justification of her secession from the Church of Rome, is to be pleaded, by every individual Christian, for his separation from the Church of England; as if by *protestantism* was chiefly meant, a right of separation from the Church; without regard to the cause of it.

Daubeny and Burke thus addressed themselves to a similar problem. Burke, in *Reflections on the Revolution in France* and *An Appeal from the New to the Old Whigs*, tried to defend the Revolution Settlement of 1688 in its constitutional aspect from the claim that the principles which Whigs supposed had justified resistance then, would justify resistance now. He did so not least by appealing to the Church for evidence of the non-contractual nature of allegiance. Daubeny tried to defend the Revolution Settlement in its Church aspect from the claim that the principles which justified the Reformation and resistance to the threat of Popish tyranny under James II, and which identified the Whig Church, not the Nonjuring Church, as the rightful Church of England, did not also justify 'the extravagancies of the wildest sectary' in the 1790s. Again like Burke, he did so by appealing to the State for evidence that toleration in the sense of a *right* had never been legally conceded.

Consequently, Daubeny sought to link together the theories of three Whig churchmen as equally minimalist and equally inadequate:

It is not, indeed, to be wondered at, that the opinions of the modern clergy should become less settled upon Church matters, than they have been; since the authority of a *Hooker*, a *Hickes*, and a *Leslie*, is by many considered to be in a manner superseded by that of an *Hoadly*, a *Warburton*, and a *Paley*...were I a dissenter from the Church, I should seek for no argument to justify my separation, which might not be fairly drawn from their respective writings.

---

[212] Daubeny's *Vindiciae Ecclesiae Anglicanae* (London, 1803) was a weighty argument to prove that the Thirty-Nine Articles of the Church of England were not to be interpreted in a Calvinist sense.

Hoadly and Warburton in particular, Daubeny argued, were saying essentially the same thing:

Warburton acknowledges the church to be a society; that 'from the command of its Founder, obedience is due to it as such; and that authority without obedience and submission is a mockery'. At the same time he tells his readers, that this obedience and submission are to depend entirely upon the will and opinion of the party intended to be governed...So that conscience, in such case, not being governed by the *law laid down*, but by the judgement from time to time formed upon it, enjoining obedience or justifying disobedience, according to the different disposition of the judging party; it follows, that church communion, instead of being a matter of Christian obligation, dwindles down into a matter of mere private opinion.

This was the position, claimed Daubeny, which the Nonjuror William Law had refuted in his classic *Three Letters to the Bishop of Bangor* of 1717, directed against Hoadly's formulation of the case. It was only tenable on the assumption that the Church (and therefore, by implication, the State) was of merely human foundation. Hoadly and Warburton were quoted, arguing to justify the separation from Rome on grounds of 'Christian liberty'; Daubeny cited Bishop Jewell against them to show that 'the corruption of the Church of Rome...was the ground upon which our separation from it was built'. Anti-Romanism was a marked feature of pre-Tractarian High Churchmanship for this reason: Anglicanism was justified not on principles of private judgement, or of the expediency of *any* establishment, but, ultimately, because its doctrine was *true*.

Paley had argued differently: that Christ had given no instructions concerning the form of Church government, and that 'the authority of a church-establishment is founded in its utility'.[213] But because no instructions were on record, replied Daubeny, it did not follow that none had been given; it would be reasonable to assume that they had, and that Christ's wishes could be inferred in this respect from the practice of the early Church, and the teaching of SS. Clement and Ignatius. Paley's position, that the form of Church establishment was only temporary, to be altered as civil circumstances required, 'appears to be a position irreconcilable with the independence of the Christian church; and calculated only to corrupt it'.

Already, in Daubeny, as later in the Tractarians, a 'High' view of the Church began to draw it away from a Church–State alliance in which the State did not live up to its obligations. If the civil authorities deserted the Church, wrote Daubeny, its temporal position was weakened, but its 'establishment...as a *spiritual society*' was untouched. Paley's position would give scope to an 'innovating spirit'. Again 'the celebrated Mr Law' was called on, in defence of the Apostolical succession; and against Paley, Daubeny appealed to Ignatius, Clement and Cyprian; Andrewes, Hooker,

[213] Paley, *Works*, vol. II, pp. 443 ff.

Hammond, Hickes and Leslie. That disestablishment might be one implication of the High Church position was still a threat rather than a programme, a warning against national apostasy rather than a reaction to its consequences.

Daubeny deployed his arguments to support the position outlined by the American loyalist the Rev. Jonathan Boucher:

There is indeed, we are sorry to think, a wild sectarian spirit growing up in this country, which, if not properly counteracted, will work to the utter subversion of its constitution. For (as it has been excellently observed by a late writer, whose opinion I am proud to think perfectly corresponds with my own on this subject) 'sects in religion and parties in the state originate in general from similar principles. A sect is, in fact, a revolt against the authority of the church, just as a faction is against the authority of the state; or, in other words, a sect is a faction in the church, as a faction is a sect in the state: and the spirit which refuses obedience to the one, is equally ready to resist the other.' A position which will not be controverted, but by those who feel themselves indisposed to admit the regular establishment of authority in either case.[214]

It was an appropriate quotation. Boucher,[215] now Vicar of Epsom, had published his book *A View of the Causes and Consequences of the American Revolution* in 1797. It consisted of a lengthy reworking as 'Discourses' of his surviving notes of thirteen sermons, many of them political, preached by him in the American colonies between 1763 and 1775, together with a substantial introduction on the history of the rebellion and its causes.[216] The new currency of Lockeian contractarianism and revivalist Calvinism in the colonies in the 1760s and 70s not only prompted Boucher to analyse rebellion in terms of religious dissent, as Daubeny saw, but also to produce a direct critique of radical Whig doctrine worthy of comparison with Horne or Horsley.[217] It was for this reason that Filmer was brought forward as the most effective critic of the Lockeian position, though without Filmer's reverence for the semi-divine nature of the king or the *indefeasible* nature of

[214] Charles Daubeny, *A Guide to the Church, in Several Discourses* (London, 1798), pp. 16, 120, 136–8, 146–7, 399–403, 406–7, 412–24, 448, 456.

[215] Jonathan Boucher (1738–1804). Born Cumberland; ordained 1762; living in Virginia; from 1770 living in Maryland; MA of King's College, New York, 1774; initially sided with American case over Stamp Act, but increasingly loyalist; defended Anglican Church in colonies; forced to leave America, 1775; lived in poverty; Vicar of Epsom, Surrey, 1785 – d.

[216] Cf. M. D. Clark, 'Jonathan Boucher: The Mirror of Reaction', *HLQ* 33 (1969), 19–32; A. Y. Zimmer and A. H. Kelly, 'Jonathan Boucher: Constitutional Conservative', *Journal of American History*, 58 (1972), 897–922. Neither of these useful studies place Boucher in his appropriate context, and consequently both label his thought 'reactionary', 'out-moded', 'medieval', 'archaic', etc.

[217] Bernard Bailyn, *The Ideological Origins of the American Revolution* (Cambridge, Mass., 1967), pp. 310–19, similarly dismisses the ideology of Isaac Hunt, Samuel Seabury, Thomas Chandler, Daniel Leonard and Boucher as 'nostalgia for ancient certainties', a 'moribund philosophy' responsible for the 'extremism of their reaction'. In view of the now-evident currency of such doctrines in England at that time, and for long afterwards, we might be more cautious about dismissing them so briskly as 'anachronistic' in the colonies.

his hereditary title. Boucher, like Burke or Horne,[218] was concerned to emphasise the patriarchal, not the contractual, origin of the State, to deny a right of resistance, and to insist that obedience for conscience' sake in a Christian commonwealth extended only as far as the doctrine of passive obedience. Boucher referred his own understanding of liberty under law to Bishop Butler's 30th January sermon to the Lords in 1740/1: 'Civil liberty is a severe and restrained thing: implies, in the notion of it, authority, settled subordinations, and obedience.'[219]

Boucher has been introduced both as a powerful analogy to, and possible source of Daubeny's opinions, and as a classic instance of the form which late-eighteenth-century divine right doctrine could take in response to current problems, once it had dropped the Jacobite emphasis on 'the sacredness of kings'. Back in England, Boucher instinctively associated with High Churchmen, including John Bowles, Charles Daubeny, Joshua Watson and John Bowdler. English lay theorists, in return, came to rely less on the dynasty as the keystone of their argument and more on the Church. One effect of this was to make the theoretical structure of the Church–State far more rigid: it was defended against reform as if any innovation would be tantamount to sacrilege, and as if any change in the intellectual formulation of the Anglican hegemony would shatter the thing itself (it is no coincidence that Lord Eldon's spell as Lord Chancellor saw a renewed wave of prosecution for blasphemous libel).

A second, contradictory, effect was to encourage men to begin to distance the Church from the State, to withdraw the Church from the intimacy of Bishop Gibson's Church–Whig alliance. Both these effects, echoing Daubeny, can be found in the writings of John Bowles. In 1815, he wrote that the civil establishment

...has an indefeasible title to duty and submission from every subject of the realm. Disaffection towards this part of the constitution, when manifested by outward acts, is a crime punishable by the severest penalties of the law. In return for the protection afforded by civil government the obligation of allegiance is contracted; by an obligation which nothing can discharge, but the payment of the great debt of nature – which cannot be superseded by change of residence, or by the formation of new engagements – and which binds every one to whom it attaches, without exception, to submission, fidelity, and even to active exertion whenever his exertions are wanted for the protection of his lawful government, or the security of his native soil. In a word, allegiance to the civil government is the positive and the permanent duty of every person, whom birth has placed in a state of subjection to that government.

[218] Zimmer and Kelly argue convincingly that Boucher's views developed in a more English idiom after his exile from America. What is at issue here is principally his significance for his English public.

[219] Boucher, 'Discourse XII. On Civil Liberty, Passive Obedience, and Non-Resistance' in *A View of the Causes and Consequences of the American Revolution* (London, 1797), pp. 495–560 contains a formidable demolition of Locke on conventional Anglican lines even before Filmer is brought in as an ally. It is likely (cf. pp. 527ff) that Boucher's knowledge of Filmer was acquired after his return to England in 1775.

Bowles had also insisted that   1815

> The constitution of this country is composed of two distinct establishments, the one civil, the other ecclesiastical, which are so closely interwoven together, that the destruction of either must prove alike fatal to both.

But the just claims of the Church, he went on, were not temporal. Considered as a national establishment, its claims were merely those of Warburton's Church. The basis of the Church's claims was different:

> It is in this character, that is to say, as a *Church*, and not as an *Establishment*, that she offers herself as a guide to faith and worship; claiming, for that purpose, the authority of a spiritual commission from Christ himself.[220]

Nevertheless, in the short run, this might only strengthen the claims of the Church to a central, indeed a paramount, role. How the Anglican state, despite this body of theory, was overtaken and destroyed by Dissent, Roman Catholicism and parliamentary reform in the 1820s is the subject of chapter 6.

Between the seventeenth century and the twentieth, the principle of 'divine right' has been slowly secularised. From ascribing a semi-divine or semi-priestly quality to the person of the sovereign, the same principle in the later eighteenth century asserted a divine sanction for the political and social hierarchy as a whole. In our own day it survives as the fully secularised doctrine that 'the law must be obeyed until it is changed': that there is no right of resistance. This residual element was always present, as in Dr Johnson's claim in the 1770s that every State must contain an absolute principle of sovereignty in order to be a State. But the specific implications of the doctrine of sovereignty which every State must employ were determined, in the eighteenth century, by the Christian elements which were added to this residual one.

They were determined also by the political configurations within which such additions, for political purposes, were made. In contrast to the first decade of George III's reign, the 1770s witnessed a rallying behind North's ministry, especially of country gentlemen, many of them from ex-Tory families. The parliamentary opposition sometimes attributed this not to a change in the attitude of the gentry, but to the Court's conversion to Stuart attitudes.[221] This polemical fiction cannot be accepted as it stands. What the early years of George III's reign did see was a confluence of Whig and Tory positions. Lip service could still be paid to the social contract; but establishment ideology was increasingly ambiguous as political exigencies drew together intellectual components which were logically inconsistent. The inconsistency was resolved, in general, by a greater emphasis on the

---

[220] [John Bowles], *The Claims of the Established Church, Considered as an Apostolical Institution* (London, 1815), pp. 1–5.
[221] Langford, 'Old Whigs, Old Tories', p. 124.

Church. Yet the Orthodox theory of men such as Horne fitted so easily into place because, from different premises, it arrived at the same conclusions as Warburtonian doctrine. The High Church 'Toryism' of the 1790s,[222] therefore, is to be seen as a highlighting of the conservative aspect of the Whig tradition: not a literal revival of Filmer, but a confirmation of the extent to which the official Whig position under the first two Georges shared its main features with the Tory position, and, from 1760 on, absorbed its rival. The only possible effective criticism of this united front was a much more extreme radical case. Its emergence must now be investigated.

[222] It cannot be too clearly stressed that no public figure at that date accepted the title 'Tory', and that they had the best reasons for denying its appropriateness: cf. Christie, *Wars and Revolutions*, pp. 282–3.

5 ✓

The Ideological Origins of English Radicalism, 1688–1800

I. INTRODUCTION

In previous chapters it has been shown that the Church must occupy a large place in any picture of eighteenth-century English society; that it demands analysis not merely in secular terms, as an established corporation, drawing its revenues and playing a role defined by constitutional law, but also as an agency of religion. This view of priorities in social ideology has an important corollary: all forms of radicalism in early-modern England had a religious origin. This was true both doctrinally and practically. Doctrinally, the problem for the disaffected within a Christian-monarchical polity was precisely that of rejecting Trinitarian orthodoxy, the intellectual under-pinning of Church, King and Parliament. It could not be ignored or disregarded; the difficulty was to find an intellectual strategy which would permit escape from a political theology whose theoretical power and widespread reception walled in the dissident.

Practically, the subversive's target was similar. The agency of the State which confronted him in his everyday life was not Parliament, reaching out as a machinery of representative democracy: elections were infrequent, contests less frequent still, the franchise restricted, and access to MPs minimal for most electors. The ubiquitous agency of the State was the Church, quartering the land not into a few hundred constituencies but into ten thousand parishes, impinging on the daily concerns of the great majority, supporting its black-coated army of a clerical intelligentsia, bidding for a monopoly of education, piety and political acceptability. Consequently, the chief target for radical attack was not the representative machinery. Contemporaries were often willing to identify anomalies and imperfections in the unreformed electoral system, even though not widely subscribing to abstract doctrines of equal individual entitlement to the franchise. Such reservations and criticisms were not acted on for so long not because people could not find fault in this respect, but because the

277

representative machinery itself was seen as being of relatively minor importance within the overall framework of the Church-State. Attention was occupied elsewhere. The radical impetus was not generally aimed against a body of doctrine defending the allocation of seats or the extent of the franchise: such doctrine there was, but it was minimal in extent and achieved even a modest prominence only at the end of the eighteenth century. The radical critique was aimed mostly against what society saw as its fundamental political ideology: Trinitarian Christianity, as interpreted by the Church of England. Consequently, the main impetus of attack was against the Church's established status, and against its official commitment to the key articles of its creed.

Parliamentary reform cannot, therefore, be written about in isolation, as modern secular historians have too often done: it must be integrated into, and take its place within, the story of reform in all its varieties. Such a story, it will be argued, refutes any image of later-early-modern England as somnolently basking in 'pudding time', complacently enjoying the fruits of oligarchic dominance, thoughtlessly excluding 'the people' from rightful participation. Direct participation in the Church-State was exercised, for most people who participated at all, via the Church, not via Parliament; and the position of the Church raised the most profound theoretical questions.

The period between the Restoration and the Reform Bill is obviously marked by its conservatism. Historians sympathising with 'the' radical cause have reconstructed 'it' in such a way as to create a paradox: why, formulated so early, did it achieve significant victories so late, in 1828–32? This chapter and the next offer an outline of an answer by reformulating the radical case as initially and chiefly a religious, not a secular phenomenon, and by tracing its successive failures through to the decades in which the progressive 'weakening' of the Church presaged the swift 'collapse' of the State, as their theoretical structures were formulated by their defenders. In ideological terms, then, there was no 'oasis of tranquillity between two agitated epochs', as Basil Williams once put it: only historians' narrow focus on the secular interests of later radicals revealed the general absence of conflict on *those* issues before the 'era of reform'. It was on other territory that the ideological and practical battle was fought in earlier decades, as the Church defended itself, with a large measure of success, against a series of onslaughts. These phenomena are well known to ecclesiastical historians; an object of this chapter is to retrieve them from their position as a specialist study and to attempt to reintegrate them into the received account of 'radicalism' which the secular historical mind has entailed upon us. The relation of theological heterodoxy to political 'radicalism' is well known, too, to historians of the Civil War and to students of Algernon Sidney and his circle. The analysis presented here could only be strengthened by carrying it back to the 1640s or beyond. Yet every historian is tempted by this prospectively limitless regression, and distinctive developments in and after the 1680s offer some justification, at least, for taking up an endless thread at the time of the Revolution.

II. DEISM, ARIANISM, SOCINIANISM: THE OFFICIAL REACTION

It has been generally supposed that after the Glorious Revolution, and the publication of Locke's *Essay Concerning Human Understanding* and *Two Treatises of Government* in 1690, a Whig consensus was established across the board. Tories, if they existed at all, were supposed to have existed within it. Jacobites, who stood outside the consensus, were therefore a tiny minority of fanatics and extremists. The problem then became: how and why did the Whigs abandon their 1680s libertarian ideology and degenerate into the corrupt, complacent oligarchy of Walpole and the Pelhams? The picture offered in this book is very different. Tories and Jacobites before 1760, far from being a tiny fringe of fanatics, were a large sector of society. They possessed a powerful and credible ideology; as groups, they shaded ambiguously and equivocally into each other. Most Whigs, far from being secular, bourgeois, capitalist and contractarian in their outlook, shared the chief elements of this dynastic political theology, directing it instead to the monarchy of William III, Anne and the Georges. It was the radical Whigs – the 'Commonwealthmen' on whom modern scholarship has so unduly focussed – who were the anomaly, a tiny minority of 'freethinkers' in a Christian mental universe. The problem is therefore not how Walpolian Whigs betrayed libertarian origins (their indebtedness to Whig radicals was small), but how radical extremists arose and how they were able to sustain their intellectual position within a society still poring over the Caroline divines.

It is necessary at the outset to distinguish between a number of different doctrinal objections to orthodoxy.[1] 'Deism', though used to cover almost as many different positions as 'socialism' two centuries later, may be approximately identified as a reliance on 'natural religion', an attempt fundamentally to simplify traditional theology, distinguishing the major items of belief held in common between all religions and deriving a flexible and vague piety from the evidence of creation rather than from specific disclosures to mankind in revelation.[2] Revealed religion once rejected, Deists

---

[1] This attempt clearly to distinguish Deist and Arian-Socinian arguments simplifies a complex situation in which the two positions might overlap, and the appropriateness and meaning of the two labels was the subject of controversy. For a study which attends to these difficulties, cf. R. E. Sullivan, *John Toland and the Deist Controversy* (Cambridge, Mass., 1982).

[2] For Deism, cf. especially Stephen, *English Thought*, vol. 1. But Stephen inherited Victorian assumptions about the sharp separation of the spheres of politics and religion, and failed to appreciate the wider significance of the theological debates he described.

gave themselves considerable scope as to their other tenets (or lack of them); belief in a future life, and in rewards and punishments, were all called in question. In general, God was conceived as a Creator or First Cause who subsequently stood aside from his creation to allow it to run according to its own rules. Belief in Divine Providence was a major casualty, and rejection of it strengthened with time among Deists.

The assault on revelation took different forms in the seventeenth century. In the form familiar to early-eighteenth-century Deists, it seemed from their perspective to have begun with Charles Blount[3] in the 1680s, but Deism was launched as a self-conscious movement in the mid 1690s. Powerful indirect support was given by such works as Locke's *Essay*[4] of 1690 and *The Reasonableness of Christianity as Delivered in the Scriptures* (1695), which elevated reason into a criterion for assessing revelation. Locke's significance for the eighteenth century was not chiefly in introducing contractarianism into political theory, but heterodox theology into religious speculation. Contemporaries appreciated this: some argued that he was a Deist, others that he 'may pass for the Socinus of his age', or that he was 'Socinianized all over'.[5] His writings in fact helped both schools. Prudently, however, he denied these charges, and the Deist movement found its chief spokesman in John Toland,[6] beginning with his *Christianity not Mysterious*. Published anonymously in 1696, it demoted revelation to the level of 'a means of information'. He was seconded by other writers including Collins[7] and Tindal.[8] As a theological movement, Deism attracted trenchant attacks culminating in Butler's *Analogy* of 1736, which argued that natural religion was of the same status as an object of belief as was revelation. By the 1740s,

[3] Charles Blount (1654–93). Gentry background. Disciple of Hobbes. Wrote attacking priesthood, first with *Great is Diana of the Ephesians, or the Origin of Idolatry* (1680); *Religio Laici* (1682); Whig political tracts. Suicide.

[4] On reason and revelation, cf. Locke, *Essay*, BOOK IV, CH. 18, s. 8 and BOOK IV, CH. 19, s. 4.

[5] Quoted in H. McLachlan, *Socinianism in Seventeenth-Century England* (Oxford, 1951), pp. 325, 327.

[6] John Toland (1670–1722). Irish Roman Catholic; converted to Protestantism aet. 16; Glasgow, Edinburgh and Leyden universities; at Oxford 1694–5; fled to England 1697 after the condemnation of his *Christianity not Mysterious* by the Irish House of Commons. Precarious living by journalism; pensioner of Lord Shaftesbury. In 1701 defended Act of Settlement in *Anglia Libera*, seeking favour of the Hanoverian court. Travelled abroad; after 1710 engaged in polemic against Orthodox Anglicans and Jacobites, also amplifying his Deistic writings.

[7] Anthony Collins (1676–1729). Eton and King's, Camb. Deputy Lieutenant of Essex, 1715. Author of many works inc. *Essay Concerning the Use of Reason* (1707), *Priestcraft in Perfection* (1709), *A Discourse of Freethinking* (1713), *Philosophical Inquiry Concerning Human Liberty* (1715), *Discourse of the Grounds and Reasons of the Christian Religion* (1724). Friend of Locke.

[8] Matthew Tindal (1657–1733). Lincoln and Exeter Colls., Oxf.; Fellow of All Souls, 1678 – d. Briefly converted to Roman Catholicism under James II. Author of *The Rights of the Christian Church Asserted Against the Romish and All Other Priests who Claim an Independent Power Over It* (1706), which provoked his prosecution; *A Defence of the Rights of the Christian Church* (1709), burned by the common hangman on the orders of H. of Commons; *Christianity as Old as the Creation, or the Gospel a Republication of the Religion of Nature* (1730).

Deism was a spent force, and its later influence was chiefly due to its reimportation via Voltaire and other French thinkers rather than to a lasting native school.[9] In the early part of the eighteenth century, however, its impact was considerable. The rejection of revelation was a way of asserting that human reason could of itself attain access to all necessary religious truth; by inference, man would be self-sufficient, too, in the lesser sphere of politics. The sanction of tradition, and, more important, divine sanctions via revelation for any particular regime were all called in doubt. Deism was the most generalised intellectual solvent of its time.

Arianism and Socinianism had far older origins, and enjoyed a longer influence in eighteenth-century England.[10] Both were heretical doctrines concerning the Trinity. Arianism held that the Son, though divine, was not a co-equal person of the Deity but was created by the Father, and thus a subordinate, not an eternal, being. The doctrine of Arius (c. 250–c. 336) was carried further by Faustus Socinus (1539–1604) to a denial of the divinity of Christ, demoting Him to the status of a moral exemplar. Where Deism had a broad and diffuse weakening effect, the focus of Arianism and Socinianism was more restricted, and sharper. Their theology was much more complex, and more traditional, except in one vital respect. If Christ were not a person of the Trinity, the Catholic doctrine of the Atonement, held Socinians, was meaningless; if man was not in need of redemption, original sin did not descend by inheritance, and man must be assumed to be both fundamentally benevolent and capable of ordering his own affairs in all respects. Arians largely shared these dispositions, and were regarded as occupying a position on the way to outright Socinianism. A consequence of a denial that Christ exercised divine authority was that He could not institute a priesthood descending by apostolic succession and exercising its mediatory powers by virtue of that divine right: the Anglican clergy were thus on a par, in point of authority, with Dissenting clergy (or even with the private individual). If even the Church could not claim divine institution, the State was still more obviously secular. 'No bishop, no king' was once more a relevant challenge, if mankind was free to amend or reject its ecclesiastical and political hierarchy in the name of reason, conscience or utility.

Memories of Milton's republican politics and Arian theology[11] could easily be re-awakened by the political and theological writings of Locke.

---

[9] N. L. Torrey, *Voltaire and the English Deists* (New Haven, Conn., 1930).

[10] J. Hay Colligan, *The Arian Movement in England* (Manchester, 1913); E. M. Wilbur, *A History of Unitarianism* (Cambridge, Mass., 1952); John Hunt, *Religious Thought in England* (3 vols., London, 1870–3), vol. II, pp. 194–278.

[11] J. Redwood, *Reason, Ridicule and Religion. The Age of Enlightenment in England 1660–1750* (London, 1976), p. 162; H. McLachlan, *The Religious Opinions of Milton, Locke and Newton* (Manchester, 1941). For the links between Newtonian science and anti-Trinitarian theology, and the High Church critique, cf. L. Stewart, 'Samuel Clarke, Newtonianism and the Factions of Post-Revolutionary England', *JHI* 42 (1981), 53–72.

Attacks on anti-Trinitarians therefore came not least from Nonjurors and Jacobites. Charles Leslie, among politico-theological controversialists, was marked out not only as one of the most able intellects in the Stuart cause, but as a vigilant and trenchant opponent of doctrinal error in the Church. He was particularly concerned to detect the enemy within the gates in the person of Archbishop Tillotson, and pursued his attack on Socinians into the next decade.[12] Bishop Stillingfleet attacked Locke's *Essay*, similarly, as did other controversialists, for containing doctrines which led to Socinianism, and which therefore lent support to Toland's position in *Christianity not Mysterious*.[13] Similarly, in the midst of the Bangorian controversy, William Law charged Bishop Hoadly with anti-Trinitarianism:[14] to the Orthodox, it was a principal source of all other error.

The reticence of Arians and Socinians in the face of penalties avoidable by reticence led to much suspicion of worse evils hiding under a cloak of moderation. Latitudinarian bishops like Tillotson gave reason for such fears,[15] and Burnet too was stung by the charge that 'the orthodox Latitudinarians were concealed Socinians; and that they acquiesced in Trinitarian formulas for the sake of lucre or reputation'.[16] It was difficult to deny that the Latitudinarians' complacent reliance on the reasonableness of Christianity at least played into the hands of the Deists: Toland illustrated the title page of his *Christianity not Mysterious* with a quotation from Tillotson. But what in the hands of Latitudinarians might be claimed as an eirenic doctrine became, for Blount, Collins and Toland, a theoretical justification for a profoundly subversive and bitter attack on what they identified as 'priestcraft and tyranny'. Throughout the eighteenth century, it continued to be those, whether churchmen or Dissenters, who fell away from Trinitarian orthodoxy who provided by far the greater part both of the radical intelligentsia and its rank and file. And the reverse was true even among the 'disadvantaged': the Roman Catholic community, firmly Trinitarian as it was, made almost no contribution to radical ideology (unless Jacobitism is included in this category), and a contribution to radical practice only later, in the very different context of renascent Irish nationalism.

If contemporaries saw a connection between heterodoxy and politics, they had a more concrete and personal reason for objecting to it. The most immediate and shocking consequence of Deism or Socinianism was not a challenge to any specific social institution but rather, in a Christian society,

[12] Charles Leslie, *The Charge of Socinianism against Dr Tillotson Considered* (London, 1695); *idem*, *The Socinian Controversy Discuss'd* (London, 1708).

[13] Redwood, *Reason, Ridicule and Religion*, p. 162; Edward Stillingfleet, *A Discourse in Vindication of the Doctrine of the Trinity* (London, 1697).

[14] W. Law, *A Second Letter to the Bishop of Bangor* (London, 1717), p. 67.

[15] Tillotson told Burnet that 'I wish we were well rid of' the Athanasian creed: quoted McLachlan, *Socinianism*, p. 335.

[16] Quoted G. R. Cragg, *From Puritanism to the Age of Reason* (Cambridge, 1950), p. 76.

their apparent denial of Arminian Anglicanism's offer of salvation to every individual. Socinianism was, consequently, proscribed by the the the Act of 1 W & M c 18, inappropriately nicknamed the Toleration Act. In confining its benefits to Trinitarian Protestant Dissenters only, it left the doctrinally heterodox open to all the old penalties of Elizabethan and Caroline legislation, especially 5 Eliz. c 1 and 13 Car. II st. ii, c 1. Socinianism was proscribed because it was loathed; as the popular preacher the Rev. Robert South (1634–1716) tangily put it, 'The Socinians are impious blasphemers, whose infamous pedigree runs back (from wretch to wretch) in a direct line to the devil himself; and who are fitter to be crushed by the civil magistrate, as destructive to government and society, than to be confuted as merely heretics in religion.'[17] This applied also to others whose orthodoxy was in doubt. Thomas Woolston, while a prisoner within the Rules of the King's Bench in the early 1730s, was several times assaulted by members of the public, strangers to him, who were outraged by his writings against the miracles of Christ.[18] Even despite their Trinitarian orthodoxy, Methodist preachers and worshippers from the 1730s to the end of the century had to contend with repeated outbreaks of violence on the part of mobs which inarticulately but savagely reacted against what they perceived to be threats to the social and moral order of which they were part.[19] From the Sacheverell riots in 1710 to the Jew Bill affair in 1753 and the Gordon Riots in 1780, it was religious issues above all which were capable of evoking a mass response on a theoretical question. As 'late' as 1791, popular Anglican revulsion played a part in the Birmingham riots against local Dissenters, especially Unitarians, and above all the arch-theorist Joseph Priestley.[20]

Deist and Arian positions can be more sharply distinguished in principle than in the writings of some individuals, veiled as their thought often was by prudent equivocation. Hostile critics, however, often 'treated Unitarianism and Deism as interdependent phenomena'.[21] One such was the unfriendly biographer of Thomas Chubb, who recorded that his subject 'set out an Arian only, but ended a Deist, I had almost said, Atheist...he has given up the Trinity to the Arians and Mahometans, the pre-existence of the Son to the Socinians, and the authority of the Scriptures to the Deists'.[22]

If the orthodox tended to treat as essentially similar all forms of

---

[17] *Ibid*, p. 76. South's denunciation was long remembered: Fox quoted it in the Commons debate on the Unitarian application for toleration, 11th May 1792 (*infra*).

[18] *The Life of Mr Woolston* (London, 1733), pp. 26–7.

[19] M. R. Watts, *The Dissenters* (Oxford, 1978), vol. i, pp. 405–6.

[20] R. B. Rose, 'The Priestley Riots of 1791', *P&P* 18 (1960), 68–84, largely ignores popular religious motivation and treats the riots principally as class action against 'the social and political vanguard of the Birmingham bourgeoisie', 'an explosion of latent class hatred'. 'Consider the fury of religious mobs', said Hans Stanley in the Commons in 1772. 'Political mobs are in comparison of them harmless as doves': *Parl Hist*, vol. xvii, col. 261.

[21] Sullivan, *Toland*, p. 105.

[22] *Memoirs of Mr Thomas Chubb, Late of Salisbury...in a Letter from Another Gentleman of that City to His Friend in London* (London, 1747), pp. 27, 33.

heterodoxy, their opponents did not concur in this analysis. One problem for the heterodox was a profound antagonism within their own ranks. Deists and Arians, whatever the similarities in the origins of their beliefs, or the logical consequences of their views for society, were often at odds in theological controversy. Sometimes it was decorous: in 1711 the Arians Whiston and Clarke held conferences with the Deists Collins and Tindal in an attempt to convert them to Arian Christianity, though without success.[23] Usually the hostility was more open. The Deist Toland regarded Clarke as one of his chief antagonists,[24] and Clarke's Boyle Lectures of 1704–5 were equally directed against Deism and atheism: most forms of the first, he argued, led to the second. Clarke, too, attacked Collins' Deist theories as ending in determinism,[25] and the Arian camp in the early eighteenth century produced a series of champions of revelation explicitly writing against the Deists, culminating in Dissent's most distinguished scholar, Nathaniel Lardner.[26] Only the eclipse of Deism stayed their hands; but its recrudescence at the end of the century produced the same reaction, and Gilbert Wakefield found himself condemning Tom Paine's Deist attack on all revealed religion, *The Age of Reason*. Arians, like the orthodox in general, stigmatised the Deists as mere libertines, determined to throw over every moral and political restraint. As John Leland, Deism's first historian, put it, in what was almost the obituary of his subject, when one saw the Deists

...under pretence of disbelieving the doctrines, discarding the morals of the gospel; when with Christianity they seem to throw off the fear of God, and give themselves up to a boundless licentiousness; there is too just reason to apprehend, that the true cause of their dislike to the Christian revelation, is not so much their being dissatisfied with the evidences produced for it, as because they cannot bear the restraints it lays upon their corrupt lusts and passions.[27]

In general, the Arians contributed powerfully to the destruction of early-eighteenth-century Deism.

Despite the lapsing of the Licensing Act in 1695, radicals were obliged to be circumspect or elliptical in the expression of their views. Even in 1697 an Edinburgh student, Thomas Aikenhead, was convicted on charges of

[23] M. C. Jacob, *The Newtonians and the English Revolution 1689–1720* (Hassocks, 1976), p. 227; J. O'Higgins, *Anthony Collins* (The Hague, 1970), p. 77.

[24] Jacob, *Newtonians*, p. 208.

[25] Clarke attacked Collins's *Philosophical Enquiry*: Redwood, *Reason, Ridicule and Religion*, pp. 208–9.

[26] Wilbur, *Unitarianism*, pp. 251–2. The crusade of Arians against Deists is, it might be suggested, the real theme of the debates reconstructed in Jacob, *Newtonians*.

[27] J. Leland, *A View of the Principal Deistical Writers that have Appeared in England in the Last and Present Century* (2 vols., London, 1754–5), vol I, p. 404. Tindal dealt with the problem simply by denying its existence: ''Twould be impertinent to examine into the reasons given for the late excessive growth of irreligion, when I do not allow there is any such growth': [Tindal], *The Nation Vindicated, from the Aspersions Cast on it in a Late Pamphlet* (London, 1711), p. 8.

ridiculing the Scriptures, declaring Moses and Christ impostors and the doctrine of the Trinity self-contradictory; despite recanting, he was hanged.[28] Penalties in Scotland were far more severe, but the situation in England was not wholly dissimilar. Newton himself refused to publish his Arian writings or openly to commit himself on the subject, and, short of criminal penalties, careers continued to be destroyed on grounds of doctrinal unorthodoxy. Especially was this true of the Arian William Whiston,[29] Newton's successor at Cambridge in the Lucasian chair of mathematics; yet after his expulsion from it, even Newton distanced himself from his former friend. At Oxford, Arthur Bury was deprived of the Rectorship of Exeter College in 1694 for his book *The Naked Gospel*, intended to conciliate the Socinians. And Dr Samuel Clarke, among the most outstanding of Anglican theologians, was blocked from promotion to a bishopric on grounds of entertaining a similar Arian heresy.[30]

Beyond this, four formal routes were open for the reproof or punishment of religious radicalism: a motion in Parliament; a prosecution in the civil courts; a prosecution in the Church courts; or a motion in Convocation.[31] The penalties which Parliament could impose were strictly limited. It could order the imprisonment of an offender during the remainder of the session, but this penalty was seldom used. A motion of censure on a work, an order that it be burnt by the common hangman, and a direction to the Attorney General to prosecute was the common formula; but it had no weight with the civil courts in any subsequent trial. Such action was taken by the Commons in 1704 against William Coward's *Second Thoughts Concerning the Human Soul* and in 1710 against Tindal's *The Rights of the Christian Church Asserted* and *A Defence of the Rights of the Christian Church*, while the Lords could and did act independently, as in 1720 when they condemned Joseph Hall's anti-Trinitarian *A Sober Reply*. But infrequent Parliamentary censures had, at most, a symbolic effect.[32]

[28] *State Trials*, vol. XIII, cols. 918–40. Toland took his Edinburgh MA in 1690.
[29] William Whiston (1667–1752). Son of ex-Presbyterian rector. Clare Hall, 1686–; Fellow 1691–; deacon 1693. Scruples about taking oaths to William and Mary. 1701 deputy to Newton as Lucasian Professor; 1703 succeeded him. Boyle lectures 1707. Growing reputation as an Arian, which he did not conceal. Deprived of chair, 1710. Published *Primitive Christianity Revived* 1711. Joined Baptists 1747.
[30] Samuel Clarke (1675–1729). Caius Coll. 1691–; chaplain to Bp of Ely 1698–1710. Boyle lecturer 1704–5. Rector of St James' Westminster 1709, and Royal Chaplain. 1712 published *Scripture Doctrine of the Trinity*. Received no other preferment apart from Mastership of Wigston's hospital, 1718, despite friendship with Q. Caroline. Elevation to the bench did not require subscription to Thirty-Nine Articles; Clarke refused lesser offices in the Church, which did. Friend of Newton, Hoadly and Whiston.
[31] Research is still needed on the subject of the prosecution of religious and political heterodoxy in this period.
[32] C. R. Gillett, *Burned Books* (2 vols., New York, 1932); L. Hanson, *Government and the Press 1695–1763* (Oxford, 1936).

The criminal law, however, seemed to provide a remedy. In an attempt to counter the wave of radical writing of the 1690s, the Blasphemy Act of 1697 barred from office all those, educated as Christians, who denied the doctrine of the Trinity, the truth of Christianity, or the divine authority of the Bible; a second offence might incur penalties of inability to hold land, to bring an action at law, to receive a legacy, and imprisonment for up to three years. Despite this, complained Wake in 1720, 'men go on every day to oppose our Lord's divinity; and no prosecution is made of this crime, though confessed to be within the laws in force'.[33] Successive ministries were reluctant to act, except in flagrant and notorious cases.

There was a handful of prosecutions by the civil power, however, generally for the common-law offence of blasphemous libel, when action was unavoidable. In 1703 Thomas Emlyn, a Dublin Presbyterian minister, was convicted and imprisoned for two years for the Arian doctrines contained in his *An Humble Inquiry into the Scripture Account of Jesus Christ*.[34] Prosecution also overtook Edward Elwell, author of *A True Testimony for God and His Sacred Law*, in 1724. Thomas Woolston, for his *Six Discourses*, published in 1727–9, was convicted of blasphemy in March 1729, and, unwilling to give sureties against offending again, remained technically imprisoned within the Rules of the King's Bench prison until his death in 1733. It was a celebrated case, and produced an outcry, but prosecutions continued: the Deist Peter Annet was imprisoned for blasphemous libel in 1763.[35] Local Grand Juries, too, sometimes presented works as public nuisances; the Grand Jury of Middlesex so presented Toland's *Christianity not Mysterious* in 1699, Mandeville's *Fable of the Bees* in 1723, and Bolingbroke's collected *Works*, publishing for the first time his Deistic writings, in 1754. But action seldom went further.

In April 1721 the Dean of Windsor, Lord Willoughby de Broke, introduced a Bill in the Lords, along the lines of one drafted by Wake, to suppress atheism, profaneness and blasphemy. Its chief provision was a penalty of three months' imprisonment for speaking or writing against the existence of God, the divinity of Christ, the doctrine of the Trinity, the truth of revelation, or the divine inspiration of scripture, as defined in the Thirty-Nine Articles.[36] Wake spoke for it: it did not constitute persecution for opinion or an infringement of the Toleration Act, he maintained; that

[33] Sykes, *Wake*, vol. ii, p. 165.

[34] Watts, *Dissenters*, vol. i, p. 372.

[35] Peter Annet (1693–1769). Liverpudlian schoolmaster; lost job in consequence of published attack on Bp Sherlock and others, 1743–4. In 1761 published nine numbers of *The Free Enquirer*, attacking Old Testament history; for which he was tried, 1763.

[36] It would also: (a) deprive Dissenting preachers of the benefits of the Toleration Act if they denied 'any of the fundamental articles of the Christian religion'; (b) give the archbishops and bishops power to require any clergyman to subscribe a declaration of orthodoxy, on pain of dismissal; (c) give JPs at Quarter Sessions a similar power to require a declaration from Dissenting ministers, on pain of forfeiting the benefits of the Toleration Act.

Act protected only orthodox Dissent, and the new Bill aimed to restrain not men's opinions but the propagation of error. But the ministers appeared against it, to Wake's surprise, and it was lost by a large majority. Unwilling to upset the legal formulation of the Revolution settlement, the ministry had tried to meet the problem with a royal proclamation for the suppression of blasphemous clubs, and royal letters were now sent to the archbishops and bishops urging the enforcement of existing laws in defence of orthodox religion.[37]

It was far more effective if the civil power could intervene before the publication of objectionable writings. In 1723 Wake received information that an edition of the Socinian Servetus' works was being printed in London; 'I got the Secretary [of State]'s warrant to seize the whole impression', he boasted, 'and the printer is now under a legal prosecution for his attempt.'[38] Newcastle protested to Wake: 'You have never complained of any such writings but prosecutions have been immediately ordered against the offenders; and have in some instances been carried on with so much vigour that your Grace has been pleased to express to those unhappy people themselves a charitable commiseration of their sufferings.'[39]

The Church was thus not wholly without the assistance of the State in formal proceedings against ideological subversion. How effective the Church courts were, or might have been, in a similar cause is not clear. After the Revolution their powers to enforce Sunday church attendance on those not worshipping as Dissenters (powers still formally reiterated in the 'Toleration' Act) became unenforceable. Numbers of communicants declined sharply. Occasional conformity flourished among Trinitarian Dissenters as a way of avoiding the provisions of the Test and Corporation Acts. Without support at the centre, the ability of the Church courts to enforce local moral discipline similarly declined. Some of the prosecutions which were conducted were even dropped for political reasons, after minist rial intervention;[40] and in 1689, 1694 and 1708 'Whig administrations secured the passing of Acts of General Pardon which at a stroke brought proceedings in the church courts to a standstill and annulled the temporal penalties of excommunication.'[41]

Whether they were more effective in acting against heterodox theology is equally doubtful. A few cases are known, but the general pattern of the courts' business remains to be investigated. Robert Clayton, Irish Bishop of Clogher, was about to be prosecuted in 1757 for his attacks on the Trinity;

---

[37] Sykes, *Wake*, vol. II, pp. 135–8; *Parl Hist*, vol. VII, cols. 893–5. Five bishops voted in the minority of thirty-one, including Wake; eight in the majority of sixty, including Gibson.

[38] Sykes, *Wake*, vol. II, p. 161.

[39] Sykes, *Wake*, vol. II, p. 172.

[40] R. B. Barlow, *Citizenship and Conscience* (Philadelphia, 1962), pp. 59–60.

[41] G. V. Bennett, *The Tory Crisis in Church and State 1688–1730. The Career of Francis Atterbury Bishop of Rochester* (Oxford, 1975), pp. 11–15.

but his death frustrated (or transferred) his punishment.[42] In 1808 the Rev. Francis Stone, Rector of Cold Norton, Essex, was convicted of blasphemy and heresy in the Church courts after preaching and publishing a Socinian sermon openly denying the divinity of Christ, and deprived of his living.[43] Whether these were isolated instances is unclear.

Convocation

It was not the Church courts but Convocation, however, to which most churchmen looked for leadership; and here the Church's powers of independent action were first frustrated, then shackled. In 1701 the Tory majority in the Lower House of Convocation made an attempt to prosecute Toland's *Christianity not Mysterious*: they were frustrated by Archbishop Tenison's politically-motivated insistence that their House had no legal power to act,[44] and another attempt to condemn Bishop Burnet's *Exposition of the Thirty-Nine Articles* was frustrated by the Upper House by procedural delays and a similar legal claim.[45] The bishops likewise failed to act on their clergy's complaint that Hoadly's sermon of 29th September 1705 contained 'positions contrary to the doctrine of the Church, expressed in the first and second parts of the Homily against disobedience or wilful rebellion'.[46] In 1711, despite similar objections that Convocation had no legal power to punish for heresy, both Houses passed a motion of censure on the Arian doctrine of Whiston's *Primitive Christianity Revived*; but the Queen took no action to sign the document, and it remained formally inoperative.[47] In 1714 the Upper House of Convocation blocked the Lower House's prosecution of Dr Samuel Clarke for his *Scripture Doctrine of the Trinity*.[48]

The position, even during the Tory ascendancy, was one of stalemate; but the accession of George I wrought a profound change. Hoadly, who had remained silent during the Tory triumph of the last four years of Queen Anne, went over to the offensive. In 1716 appeared his *A Preservative against the Principles and Practices of the Nonjurors both in Church and State*. On 31st March 1717 he preached his infamous sermon before the king, *The Nature of the*

---

[42] Robert Clayton (1695–1758). Westminster and TCD, Fellow 1714. Friend of Samuel Clarke and supporter of his doctrines. Clarke secured him an Irish bishopric via Q. Caroline, 1730. Translated twice. Various publications, inc. *Essay on Spirit*, 1751. Duke of Dorset, Lord Lieutenant, refused to translate him to Archbishopric of Tuam. Proposed in Irish House of Lords, 2nd Feb. 1756, the removal of the Athanasian and Nicene creeds from the liturgy of the Church of Ireland. 1757 published 3rd part of *Vindication of...the Old and New Testament*, attacking Trinity; for which a prosecution was ordered.

[43] Wilbur, *Unitarianism*, p. 277.

[44] E. Cardwell, *Synodalia* (2 vols., Oxford, 1842), pp. 701–5; Bennet, *Tory Crisis*, pp. 58–9; E. Carpenter, *Thomas Tenison* (London, 1948), pp. 253ff.

[45] T. Lathbury, *A History of the Convocation of the Church of England*, 2nd edn (London, 1853), pp. 354ff.

[46] Lathbury, *Convocation*, p. 401; Cardwell, *Synodalia*, p. 723.

[47] Lathbury, *Convocation*, pp. 410–15; Cardwell, *Synodalia*, pp. 753–69; *Bishop Burnet's History of His Own Time* (1 vol., London, 1838), pp. 867–9; Sykes, *Sheldon to Secker*, pp. 58ff.

[48] J. P. Ferguson, *An Eighteenth Century Heretic: Dr Samuel Clarke* (Kineton, 1976), pp. 83–97; Cardwell, *Synodalia*, pp. 785–93.

Kingdom or Church of Christ. The Lower House of Convocation reacted to both works as intended

First, to subvert all government and discipline in the Church of Christ, and to reduce his kingdom to a state of anarchy and confusion.

Secondly, to impugn and impeach the regal supremacy in causes ecclesiastical, and the authority of the legislature to enforce obedience in matters of religion by civil sanctions.

The ministry intervened at once. Convocation was quickly prorogued; henceforth, until the 1850s, its existence was merely formal.[49]

III. HETERODOXY, CONVOCATION AND PARLIAMENTARY REPRESENTATION

Religious radicalism, then, was not systematically suppressed; neither did it escape without penalty. The numbers of men involved were, however, small. From the Revolution into the eighteenth century, freethinkers formed a fairly closely knit group, 'related by a bewildering series of marriages',[50] sometimes acting in secret, and all closely associated with radical or even republican politics. Into the 1730s and 40s, orthodox Whigs continued to voice fears of republican elements and sentiments within the camp of the Whig opposition, and republican imagery was still sometimes the idiom adopted by proletarian discontent. Republicanism was, however, the limit of the Commonwealthmens' political dissent. The members of the 'Grecian Tavern set', including such figures as Anthony Collins, Robert Molesworth, Walter Moyle, Henry Neville and James Tyrrell, were frequently of lesser-gentry status[51] or aspired to move in such circles; they envisaged only a world made even safer for members of their own order by the elimination of what they defined as priestly and monarchical tyranny. Some of them were perfectly frank in exploiting fears of the threat which the former might pose to gentry hegemony in society. Laud's alleged ambitions were recalled with contempt:

This upstart, plebeian priest, hoped to see the time, when ne'er a Jack Gentleman in England would dare to stand before a parson with his hat on. A fine scene truly! to see a gentleman of fortune and breeding, stand stooping, and bare-headed, to a small, ill-nurtured vicar; who had, perhaps, formerly cleaned his shoes, and lived upon the crumbs that came from his table![52]

---

[49] Cardwell, *Synodalia*, pp. 828–45; Lathbury, *Convocation*, pp. 451–61. Sherlock and Snape, Hoadly's two earliest opponents, were dismissed from their royal chaplaincies.
[50] Robbins, *Commonwealthman*, p. 381.
[51] John Toland and Thomas Gordon are important exceptions.
[52] T. Gordon, *The Character of an Independent Whig* (1720) in *A Collection of Tracts. By the Late John Trenchard, Esq.; and Thomas Gordon, Esq.* (2 vols., London, 1751), vol. 1, pp. 313–14.

Historians continue to see as problematic the question whether the Commonwealthmen should rank as radicals at all.[53] Their concern with the separation and balance of powers, the position of Parliament, the threat of military force versus the claims of a militia, and the independence of subordinate legislatures like those in Dublin or the American colonies, seems in no case to echo the preoccupation of later radicals with social engineering and economic redistribution. Even the reform of legislative institutions occupied a strictly subordinate place in their thought. Trenchard, in *Cato's Letters* (13th January 1721), bravely denying rumours of Whig plans to continue the first septennial Parliament's life still further, advocated frequent elections and a rotation of offices to guard against the arrogation of power by MPs, but never challenged the incidence of the franchise. Molesworth and his circle similarly laid stress on the exclusion of office-holders from Parliament without embracing a democratic conception of popular representation. Where some have sought to argue that the 'condition of the representative system and the question of parliamentary reform is...at the very heart of modern British history',[54] even radicals in the late seventeenth and early eighteenth centuries ignored it or mentioned it only briefly and in the context of other aims. Almost never was it looked to as a counter to what concerned them most, absolute monarchy. Proposals for franchise reform, made occasionally in the pamphlet press, were seldom taken up by the radical intelligentsia between the Restoration and the 1760s. Such constitutional adjustments as were advocated or made, were mostly concerned with the relative balance of Crown and Parliament, not electorate and Parliament. A series of Commons decisions in favour of narrower franchises in contested returns; legislation against bribery; place Bills; the introduction of a property qualification for MPs in 1711: all were aimed at buttressing the independence of the Commons from the executive, and all markedly failed to evoke a loud radical appeal to any significant countervailing body of democratic theory.[55]

Commentators from all parts of the political spectrum, from Defoe to Swift, could occasionally point to the parliamentary representation of depopulated boroughs as an amusing anomaly, an interesting absurdity; but intellectuals sustained no body of theory on political representation which these observations could activate. There was no means of turning an

---

[53] Cf. Robbins, *Commonwealthman*, p. 16: 'On the whole, the Real Whig was not egalitarian although he might emphasise to an embarrassing degree the equality of man before God, or in a state of nature. A ruling class and an uneducated and unrepresented majority were for a long time taken for granted.'

[54] Cannon, *Parliamentary Reform*, p. xi. Professor Cannon's evidence in fact reveals the striking *unimportance* of his theme from 1660 to the 1760s, if not until the 1820s.

[55] A few proposals in the pamphlet press are noted in Dickinson, *Liberty and Property*, pp. 116–18, 188–92. The elimination of illegitimate (though not legitimate) influence was the aim which led to proposals to *restrict* the franchise or to transfer seats from rotten boroughs to populous towns or counties.

absurdity into an affront. Trenchard indeed condemned the Presbyterians for the democratic element in their polity which supported a claim of their church's independence of the civil power (*Cato's Letters*, no. 81, 16th June 1722) – the same claim as that made by the Nonjurors.

It is a principle of historical enquiry that 'Clio abhors a vacuum'. The absence, in the period c. 1660–1760, of parliamentary reform in the idiom of the 1860s should not lead us to infer that there was a complete theoretical void.[56] It is more likely that what has been sought with a *question mal posée* was going on in a slightly different form, under another label, and directed to other ends. That is the case here, for, in that age of controversies, the place later filled by a debate over parliamentary reform was taken by the Convocation Controversy. Until the suspension of Convocation in 1717, the history, powers and claims of its two Houses[57] were a chief subject of theologico-political debate, producing a great volume of argument – sophisticated, theoretically articulate, bitter, and of immediate practical relevance.[58] What was most at issue both in theory and in practical conflict was not the democratic representation of 'the people' via the Members of the House of Commons, but their spiritual representation via the bishops and clergy assembled in Convocation. Once assembled, the targets of the orthodox – as in Atterbury's *A Letter to a Convocation Man* of 1697 – were not radical plans concerning parliamentary representation, but heterodox theology; not democracy, but heresy.[59]

Why the political nation in the early eighteenth century did not turn to parliamentary reform as 'an obvious remedy' to the Whig ascendancy has been proposed as a major paradox.[60] It is true that Tories and others occasionally did so; but far more significant is that they did so only rarely and with only superficial commitment. The framework of Tory thought was dynastic, not populist; and a dynastic solution was not only a goal in itself, but sufficiently often a practical possibility to make distant hopes of parliamentary reform appear of marginal relevance. Among opposition

---

[56] The only practical exception was the Tory search for a way of breaking the Whig stranglehold on the electoral machine betwen 1714 and the 1750s. It led Tories to toy with populist ideas and eventually to make stipulations about a free general election as part of the condition for a parliamentary alliance with Frederick, Prince of Wales, in 1747. Apart from the tactical prospects of Tory victories, such hopes had always at their back the belief that a majority of the political nation would have favoured a peaceful restoration of the Stuarts; democracy was not a goal in itself.

[57] Strictly, there were two Convocations: one at Canterbury (with two Houses), the other at York (with one House). The latter was politically quiescent.

[58] Cf. Sykes, *Gibson*, pp. 25–53; *idem*, *Church and State in England in the XVIIIth Century*, pp. 297–315; *idem*, *Wake*, vol. I, pp. 80–156; *idem*, *From Sheldon to Secker*, pp. 36–67; G. Every, *The High Church Party 1688–1718* (London, 1956), pp. 75–104.

[59] Bennett, *Tory Crisis*, pp. 48ff.

[60] P. Langford, *The Excise Crisis* (Oxford, 1975), p. 163: 'out of doors opinion scarcely appeared to resent its impotence', even when strongly incensed against the ministry, as at the time of the Sacheverell trial or excise crisis.

Whigs, a major reason for lack of interest in the franchise must be the absence within radical theory of an explicitly democratic component which could give political practicality to schemes otherwise conceived within a merely utopian framework, looking back to Harrington. The absence of such a component is to be explained not least by the success of orthodox theology: the populist implications of Deism and Arianism were checked and contained.

Seen from the establishment Whig perspective, the English Trinity of King, Lords and Commons was perceived in the first half of the century as treading a *via media* between Rome and Geneva, each claiming a deposing power – between a Stuart restoration and a republic. The dangers of these alternatives, which could be represented for political advantage as unacceptable extremes, were held to justify electoral practices which produced the 'right answer'. As the Foxite journal *The Test* observed in 1757, 'if a ministry should really look on with perfect indifference upon the fate of elections all over England, we might have a Parliament of Jacobites'. The Pittite journal *The Con-Test* (5th February 1757) was indignant: that would no longer be the result, it argued, since few Jacobites now remained. If, however, that outcome were to be

...a necessary consequence, the authors of the *Contest* would not blush to recommend corruption, as one of those intermediate acts, which, though not *immediately* moral, yet if it went no further than to exclude them, would nevertheless be *ultimately* consistent with the rules of morality, as it would contribute to the success of political virtue, and in that case, eventually promote the good of the whole community.

From mid-century, parliamentary reform became an opposition Whig option: there was now no danger of a pro-Stuart electorate registering its preference. Previously, that danger had been before the eyes of every Whig, in or out of office. Commonwealth intellectuals at the Grecian Tavern soon saw the advantages of the Septennial Act.[61] *The Craftsman* of 27th July 1734, which appeared just after a general election in which the ministry maintained its position despite the outcry over the excise, rightly pointed out that a redistribution of seats on the basis of land-tax contributions would give a very different result. Yet even in the face of such a telling analysis, parliamentary reform was not advocated:

I am very far from designing to propose any such alteration at present, when the power of the people is not in their own hands, and the very attempt might give our enemies an advantage over us. It would now be called a design to remove foundations, to subvert the constitution, and introduce a new form of government.[62]

The Stuarts might have secured widespread support in a referendum; but it was massively obvious to Deists, Arians, Socinians and republicans that they themselves would not.

[61] Kenyon, *Revolution Principles*, p. 183.   [62] Quoted Langford, *Excise Crisis*, p. 165.

The Commonwealthmen did not, then, seek to destroy gentry hegemony; nor were they democrats. Their thought does, however, deserve the title 'radical' in a loose sense, since it attacked the major features of the theoretical structure of the State: monarchy and the Church.[63] It has been suggested that neo-Harringtonian, Country ideology was that which arose when 'the *communitas* needed a new vision of itself in radically secular terms'.[64] In fact, Commonwealth theorists were preoccupied with religion. It formed the central core of their ideological position. A contemporary in 1707 appropriately hailed the Grecian Tavern set as 'that glorious club of heroes whose name will be held in honour by all who abhor Christianity'.[65] This had the most direct political application. The theological basis of monarchical claims meant that republicanism and anticlericalism were logically linked, as was widely realised.[66] It is this theme which will now be traced.

In the face of a danger of a Stuart restoration, radicals, especially in the 1690s and after 1714, often denied republican leanings and made fulsome professions of attachment to monarchs who provided the only realistic political alternative to what the radicals feared as an infinitely worse regime.[67] Monarchical loyalty of this sort was merely prudential, and radicals propounded the most secular and contractarian interpretation of post-1688 sovereigns' titles. In other respects such radicals' thought was not dissimilar to that of radical republicans. Avowed republicans like Moyle were equally explicit in blaming the clergy for divine right doctrines, identified as the chief threat to government by law.[68] Where sectaries of the 1640s, however, had usually sought a more organised and disciplined worship along their own lines, Commonwealthmen of the early eighteenth century were 'freethinkers', seeking to undermine the claims of all religion

---

[63] Professor Robbins' influential study established the received view that the Commonwealthmen's irreligion was essentially incidental to their secular radical purposes: 'In a complacent age this bickering, these fears of pope and bishops, these disputations about dogma averted stagnation, maintained freedom of opinion and thus encouraged sentiments *later* favourable to reforms.' Consequently, Dr Robbins defined action against Dissenters as unjustified oppression:

> The extent of levelling and republican ideas among nonconformists was much exaggerated by their oppressors and opponents. That there was something popular in the churches of Baptists and Independents from the beginning was true, but that there was much that was *revolutionary or subversive of property* in the ideas of most of them before the late eighteenth century was quite false.

(*Commonwealthman*, pp. 117, 228; italics added.) The argument here is that religious heterodoxy was *conceptually basic* to radicalism in the ancien-regime sense.
[64] J. G. A. Pocock, 'Machiavelli, Harrington and English Political Ideologies in the Eighteenth Century', in *Politics, Language and Time* (London, 1972), p. 128.
[65] Quoted O'Higgins, *Collins*, p. 77.
[66] Cf. Caroline Robbins (ed.), *Two English Republican Tracts* (Cambridge, 1969), p. 17.
[67] Cf. Gordon's apology for his late partner Trenchard, that he was neither a leveller nor a republican: *Cato's Letters*, 3rd edn (4 vols., London 1733), vol. I, pp. liii–lv.
[68] Robbins (ed.), *Republican Tracts*, pp. 30–1.

to secular authority. It was to break the professed theocratic unity and homogeneity of their society that Commonwealthmen were friends both to schemes for a general naturalisation of Protestant immigrants,[69] and also to far-reaching plans for religious toleration, which, as with Molesworth and Toland, 'included in its scope Jews, Atheists, Unitarians, Mohammedans, and even well-behaved Catholics',[70] though, in general, European Roman Catholic states provided radicals with their favourite examples of the mutual support of ecclesiastical and monarchical absolutism.

As we now know, the Arian Locke was far too radical to be taken up in debate by the vast majority of his contemporaries, anxious as they were to prevent 1688 leading to events like those of the 1640s. William Molyneux and Walter Moyle were, however, among the few authors who did openly rely on Locke, where even Hoadly avoided acknowledging a debt.[71] In so far as Locke had currency as a radical writer, it was mainly through the *First Treatise* with its attack on Filmer's monarchical doctrine. In the 1690s, an attack on such positions could be a chief purpose of the Deist Blount's ironic defence of William III:

Now then, for what end was government instituted? It must be for a wise and a gracious end, if God be the author of it; as, I suppose, they that refuse the Oath, believe he was. Was it then that God had such a particular kindness for the comparatively very few regal families, that are in the world; or rather to the very few particular men that are kings, that he is resolved to maintain their greatness, although at the expense of other men's lives and fortunes, that are their subjects? Is this an end becoming infinite wisdom and goodness? to make the welfare and happiness of millions subservient to, and at every turn give way to the greatness of one man? Certainly no man will say this. This is the end that tyrants aim at; but it was never intended by him that made and governs the world. What then? Is the good of the community, the principal end of government? I hope no man in his wits will deny it.[72]

John Trenchard went as far as anyone, claiming in 1698 that 'A government is a mere piece of clockwork, and having such springs and wheels must act after such a manner; and therefore the art is to constitute it so that it must move to the public advantage.'[73] The association of radical contractarian and even republican politics with religious heterodoxy had been profoundly strenghthened by Locke's *Reasonableness of Christianity* (1695) and Toland's *Christianity not Mysterious* (1696). Toland went on to draw the moral as openly as he dared with his *Life of Milton* (1699) and new edition of Harrington's *Oceana* (1700), the latter with Toland's introduction which

---

[69] Whigs after 1689 sponsored a series of Bills for a general naturalisation; one finally passed, at a moment of Whig strength, in 1709. It was repealed in 1711, after the Whig collapse.
[70] Robbins, *Commonwealthman*, p. 11.
[71] Kenyon, *Revolution Principles*, p. 19.
[72] [C. Blount], *King William and Queen Mary Conquerors* (London, 1693), pp. 40–1.
[73] J. Trenchard, *A Short History of Standing Armies*, quoted in Kenyon, *Revolution Principles*, p. 40.

not unreasonably anticipated a hostile charge that 'there's a pernicious design on foot of speedily introducing a republican form of government into the Britannic islands'.[74]

In his tracts of the 1690s, the Deist Tindal extended this utilitarian appraisal to the Church. On the one hand, religion was defined as a matter between the individual and God alone, removing from the Church any institutional role. On the other, the priesthood down the ages was credited with every variety of evil:

In a word, it has been the pride, ambition, and covetousness of the priests, and the force and violence which by their means and instigation the persecuting magistrates have used on the people to make 'em pay a blind submission to the decrees of the clergy, which has been the cause, not only of all the mischiefs and miserys which have happened in Christendom on account of religion, but of the great corruption of religion; which being a thing so plain and easy in itself, and suited to the capacity of the people, would never have been so much and so universally depraved, had there been an entire liberty of conscience.

The mutually corrupting effect of priestly obscurantism in alliance with civil tyranny was a theme which Tindal endlessly reiterated. 'Error', 'ignorance' and 'superstition' were the concepts running through his work; 'prejudice', 'priestcraft', 'idolatry', 'slavery', 'blind submission', 'despotism', 'persecution', 'cruelty', 'imposition' comprised his critical vocabulary. Nor was it directed only against Roman Catholics.

Nay, have not the Protestant clergy been every jot as much, if not more zealous and industrious than the Popish, to enslave the people, and promote arbitrary power, and have preached up absolute passive obedience even as much as faith in Christ; as knowing that the only way to secure tyranny in the Church, was first to get it established in the State; because tyranny, by bringing the generality to poverty and slavery, must depress their minds, and debase their thoughts, and make 'em ready blindly to submit to the determinations of the clergy?[75]

The theme of the effect of England's asserted identity of Church and State was taken up by John Toland. 'Absolute' equalled 'arbitrary', he insisted; and

...the will of an arbitrary monarch is not to be disputed. He has religion prepared to justify, and force to maintain him in whatsoever he does, all his subjects entirely depending on his pleasure, in their wealth and the endowments of their mind, as well as in the use and drudgery of their bodies.

---

[74] *Ibid.* pp. 50–1. Toland may have been responsible for the publication of the regicide Edmund Ludlow's *Memoirs*, and for an edition of the republican Algernon Sidney's *Discourses Concerning Government*, both in 1698.

[75] [M. Tindal], *Four Discourses on the Following Subjects: viz. I. Of Obedience to the Supreme Powers, and the Duty of Subjects in all Revolutions* [1694]. *II. Of the Laws of Nations, and the Rights of Sovereigns* [1694]. *III. Of the Power of the Magistrate, and the Rights of Mankind, in Matters of Religion* [1697]. *IV. Of the Liberty of the Press* [1698] (London, 1709), pp. 130–1, 215–16, 249.

The succession to the English throne since William the Conqueror was reviewed to demonstrate that hereditary right was not indefeasible. The alternative, therefore, was the radical contractarian case. The people should conclude

John Toland

> ...that no king can ever be so good as one of their own making; as there is no title equal to their approbation, which is the only divine right of all magistracy, for *the voice of the people is the voice of God*.[76]

Like other radicals, Toland argued to place as extensive an interpretation as possible on the Revolution. All should rally to support it, he demanded, on the basis of a radical, contractarian consensus. Party divisions were the legacy of Stuart artifice. William III sought to 'receive the good men of all parties into equal favour'; but some views were simply inconsistent with the Revolution. The king could not have 'designed to employ any who continued still a Tory; that is, who retained his old notions of passive obedience, unlimited prerogative, the divine right of monarchy, or who was averse to liberty of conscience'.[77] Church authority and monarchical allegiance were both destroyed by the Revolution, he insisted, or ought to have been. Remaining restrictions on freedom of expression in 'divine matters' were the illegitimate contrivances of a party in the Church.[78] Royalist ideology was a clericalist fiction:

> The doctrine of indefeasible right was set up at first by a few aspiring clergymen, to ingratiate themselves with weak princes, who had designs inconsistent with the laws: and therefore those Court-parasites represented to the said princes all true lovers of the constitution as enemies to their power, and as republicans, or Commonwealths-men, by which they meant men of levelling and democratical principles.[79]

Toland rightly denied this charge. Yet, in fact, his enemies principally and correctly charged him not with being a democrat but with being a Deist; with being a republican not because he was a leveller but because he was an anticleric. All the Whigs, protested Toland,

> ...as well Dissenters as Churchmen, without excepting one that ever appeared, have continued inviolably true to the allies and confederates, zealous for the legal constitution and monarchy, as well as unmoveably stanch for the Protestant interest and the Hanoverian succession: which last consideration ought to absolve 'em with all equitable judges, from being antimonarchical or popular republicans.[80]

---

[76] J. Toland, *Anglia Libera: or the Limitation and Succession of the Crown of England Explain'd and Asserted* (London, 1701), pp. 6, 9, 26, 110–32.

[77] [J. Toland], *The Art of Governing by Partys: Particularly, in Religion, in Politics, in Parliament, on the Bench, and in the Ministry* (London, 1701), pp. 8, 31, 44.

[78] John Toland, *Christianity not Mysterious*, 3rd edn (London, 1702), p. iv.

[79] [J. Toland], *The State-Anatomy of Great Britain* (London, 1717) p. 11.

[80] *Ibid.*, p. 17.

That it did not was due to the continued centrality of the theological component of Commonwealth ideology. Basic to Toland's position was a theory of the Church which dissolved its political authority:

I do not admit the Church itself to be a society under a certain form of government and officers; or that there is in the world at present, and that there has continued for 1704 years past, any constant system of doctrine and discipline maintained by such a society, deserving the title of the Catholick Church, to which all particular churches ought to conform or submit, and with which all private persons are obliged to hold communion. Much less do I believe that there was instituted in the Church a particular order of priests (tho' Christian priests I do allow) no priests, I say, whose office it is to instruct the people alone, and successively to appoint those of their own function, whether by the hands of one presiding Bishop, or of several equal presbyters, pastors, ministers or priests of any degree or denomination. And least of all will I grant, that either princes or priests may justly damnify any person in his reputation, property, liberty, or life, on account of his religious profession; nor lay him under any incapacities for not conforming to the national manner of worship, provided he neither professes nor practices anything repugnant to human society, or the civil government where he lives.[81]

This was, of course, the element of the radicals' case which provided the largest single target for their opponents. Charles Leslie seized on it. Radicals, he rightly observed, 'think Episcopacy an indifferent thing, and only a state point amongst us'. The Church held to the Apostolic succession; 'and the first who broached the contrary, Arrius an ambitious Presbyter in the fourth century, was condemned as a heretick, whose heresy is now received among us'. He took as an example Tindal's *The Rights of the Christian Church Asserted* (London, 1706): 'That the Church has no authority but from the State, nor the State but from the people, this is the whole scope and drift of this book.' The origin of the attack was theological:

...the cry of these men against the Church, is carried on by Deists, Socinians, and all our libertines who make use of their artillery; and wage war with the Church and all instituted religion upon their very principles, of not being tied to any church or communion, but to change at mere will and pleasure: that there is nothing essential in church government, or any authority of divine appointment in her governors: That she is no otherwise a society, than as the people please to make her: But only a sect of such and such opinions, which are free without hazard, for every man to take up, or lay down as he pleases... And from hence they argue the no necessity of any conformity or communion at all, further than to keep our selves safe from the hands of the law.

These were, Leslie argued, 'the principles of forty one'.

[81] John Toland, *The Primitive Constitution of the Christian Church, with An Account of the Principal Controversies about Church–Government, which at Present Divide the Christian World* (1704) in *The Miscellaneous Works of Mr John Toland* (2 vols., London, 1747), vol. II, pp. 122–3.

A Whig is a state enthusiast, as a Dissenter is an ecclesiastical:[82] they will be tied to no rules or government but of their own framing, and alterable at their pleasure.

The analogy was not coincidental: there was a common factor.

Rev. Charles Leslie

...without the belief of a divine authority, lodged in the character of bishops and kings, it is impossible for any to be a sound church-man, or a loyal subject: such are not, they cannot be faithful upon a principle, but merely to serve their own turns.

Leslie offered a rival theory of political association, which made the extent of his disagreement plain:

It is government alone, that can form men into society; without it they are but a loose company of people, be they never so many, like a flock of sheep, or a company of birds flying in the air. And as there can be no society without government, so there can be no government without governors, and those governors cannot be appointed by any but by him, who has authority over the people to be governed: for how else could he place a governor over them? Or how would they be bound to obey? And the people cannot appoint a governor over themselves, for then he must act by their authority, and would be accountable to them; and no man can govern me by an authority derived from myself,[83] for then I should still be judge over him; dispute his administration, and depose him from his power when I thought fit...thus none but Christ can appoint governors over the Church, and it is plain that he appointed his Apostles as such, and they, others under them, to rule and to govern.[84]

Such arguments were not confined to academic debate. They formed a staple of Leslie's periodical *The Rehearsal* (1704–9), a tri-weekly undertaken to reply to the radical doctrines of journals like John Tutchin's *Observator* (1702–12) and Defoe's *Review* (1704–13).[85] The currency of orthodox theologico-political doctrine was very wide. Leslie's *A Short and Easie Method with the Deists* (1698) was frequently reprinted, hailed as a polemical classic, and finally given the accolade of inclusion in both versions of *The Scholar Armed* (1780; 1795, 1800), the orthodox compendium of political conservatism. Leslie had claimed:

So closely is religion and government linked together, that the one supports the other, and corruption in a Christian government cannot come in, but by the corruption of religion, and overthrowing those principles which it teaches.

---

82 His opponent shared a similar analysis: 'parties in the state, are just of the same nature with heresies in the church': Toland, *State-Anatomy*, p. ii.

83 Tindal adopted an identical analysis, but the contrary conclusion. A right to command must derive from 'a commission either from God or men: but there's no person who can pretend to have an immediate commission from God; therefore they who lay the foundation of any magistrate's power, not on a human, but a divine right, destroy all obligation of obedience to him'. Tindal, *Four Discourses*, p. 131.

84 [C. Leslie], *The Second Part of the Wolf Stript of his Shepherds Cloathing...Wherein the Designs of the Atheists, Deists, Whigs, Commonwealths-men, &c. and All Sorts of Sectarists against the Church, are Plainly Laid Open and Expos'd* (London, 1707), pp. 1, 3–5, 26, 66–7.

85 For Tutchin's 'unacknowledged debt to the Levellers' and the 'Jacobin tinge' of Defoe's *Review*, cf. Kenyon, *Revolution Principles*, pp. 106–11, 122–3.

Hence we see the method and endeavours of the Whigs to depreciate religion, and to fall foul upon the holy scriptures themselves; knowing well, that while they are retained as lively oracles amongst us, the principles of Whiggism can never prevail, of taking off all reverence to kings and governors, of deposing and murdering them; of paying no obedience to them for conscience sake, as having no higher authority than the deputies and servants of the people, and accountable to them.[86]

For polemical effect, Leslie misrepresented the extreme Whig position as mainstream Whiggism. But it continued to be a fair assessment of the Commonwealthmen of the school of Trenchard and Gordon.

The survival of the dynastic issue, and its continued theological involvement, had the effect of confining radicalism for many decades to the idiom of the 1690s. There is much truth in the suggestion that a single generation of radicals extended from Robert Molesworth's *Account of Denmark* (1693) to Trenchard and Gordon's *Cato's Letters* (1720–3) and the collected edition of Walter Moyle's *Works* (1726–7).[87] Proliferating controversy, especially that surrounding the Sacheverell trial, raised the temperature of debate without changing its idiom. The threat of a restoration gave point to an ever-sharper identification of Nonjurors with Jacobites. High Churchmen too, complained Toland, were still preaching absolutist theories; and 'the doctrines of passive obedience are not more inconsistent with the principles of the revolution, than the powers they claim over the consciences of the people are with the principles of the Reformation'.[88] The Deist Collins joined in the same hunt: if the Church of England was justified in separating from Rome, then Anglican Protestants were justified in relying on the scriptures alone, not the authority and forgeries of priests.[89] Jacobitism was to be firmly associated with Popery; orthodox Anglicanism was to be implicated by pointing to the logical consequences of its traditional political teaching.

The Deist attack was sustained through the 1720s by works like Collins' *Discourse of the Grounds and Reasons of the Christian Religion* (1724) and *Scheme of Literal Prophecy Considered* (1727), Thomas Woolston's six *Discourses on the Miracles of Our Saviour* (1727–9), and Matthew Tindal's *Christianity as Old as the Creation* (1730). Its practical impact must now be examined.

IV. THE IMPACT OF HETERODOXY, 1714–1754

For radical theorists, the Hanoverian accession could be represented as a great triumph. Nonjurors, and Jacobites who nevertheless took the oaths,

---

[86] *The Rehearsal*, 12th October 1706.   [87] Robbins, *Commonwealthman*, p. 6.
[88] [J. Toland], *The Jacobitism, Perjury and Popery of High-Church Priests* (London, 1710), p. 12; cf. [Toland], *High Church Display'd: Being a Compleat History of the Affair of Dr Sacheverell* (London, 1711).
[89] [A. Collins], *Priestcraft in Perfection...* (London, 1710); [A Collins], *A Discourse of Free-Thinking* (London, 1713).

were henceforth to be hounded.[90] So were Orthodox churchmen. Great play has recently been made with the notion of political stability as something which England swiftly and silently achieved after 1714, ushering in what George Saintsbury called in 1915 *The Peace of the Augustans*, and what others have since termed the 'Venetian Oligarchy', or, more simply, 'Pudding Time'. In fact, one consequence of the Hanoverian accession was to open the floodgates for an attack on the Church in all its aspects – an attack which, though less in intensity, was unparalleled between the 1640s and the 1830s, except for the similar difficulties of the 1690s.[91]

One aspect of this was Toland's call for 'a firmer friendship between the Low-Churchmen and Dissenters'.[92] Its implications were fully explored in the Bangorian controversy – the outcry which followed Bishop Hoadly's sermon on 31st March 1717, *The Nature of the Kingdom or Church of Christ*. His position had been fully anticipated in Deists' denials of the essential difference between churchman and Dissenter, once the doctrine of 'the divine right of bishops' was rejected as a papist delusion.[93] A logical consequence was an attack on the Test and Corporation Acts: ''Tis a notion therefore as false in itself, as common among shallow politicians, that *tis necessary for a government to have but one religion*... they who would confine all civil employments to one sect, must be of opinion (if they have any real opinion in the matter beyond a selfish fetch) that *Dominion is founded in Grace*.'[94] Or, as the Deist Chubb succinctly put it, 'positive religious institutions cannot possibly lay men under any reasonable restraint, which natural religion does not lay them under', so that civil governors have 'no authority in matters of religion'.[95] Yet, in fact, the demand from within the ranks of the Dissenters as a whole to abolish the Test and Corporation Acts was belated and feeble during the reigns of the first two Georges. Most Dissenters were still orthodox in their doctrine of the Trinity; and they seemingly accepted with gratitude their privileged position within an Anglican State. The attack on the Church came principally from another source: not from Dissenters in response to 'oppression', but from the heterodox in response to priestly orthodoxy.

A second aspect of the campaign was the extension and intensification of the vilification of the clergy, familiar from the 1690s. After 1714 this was particularly associated with the Commonwealthmen John Trenchard[96] and

---

[90] Cf. [Toland], *State-Anatomy*, p. iv.
[91] Cf. Bennett, *Tory Crisis*, pp. 213ff.
[92] [Toland], *State-Anatomy*, p. 16.
[93] *Ibid.*, p. 24.
[94] *Ibid.*, pp. 29, 32.
[95] Thomas Chubb, *Some Short Reflections on the Grounds and Extent of Authority and Liberty, with Respect to Civil Government: Wherein the Authority of Civil Governors, in Matters of Religion, is Particularly Considered* (London, 1728), pp. 8, 24.
[96] John Trenchard (1662–1723). Gentry background; private means. TCD. Political writer. 1719 began co-operation with Gordon: *Independent Whig*, *Cato's Letters* etc. MP for Taunton 1722–3.

Thomas Gordon,[97] who specialised in works of an anticlerical nature. Among the most notorious was their periodical *The Independent Whig* (20th January 1720 – 11th January 1721), later republished in several collected editions with ever-lengthening accretions of other occasional pieces; it became a classic of early-eighteenth-century invective against 'Popery' and 'priestcraft'. Rome or 'the Bishop of Bangor's scheme' was the choice it offered Protestants. It was a message echoed in a spate of tracts from both authors in the 1720s and 30s, filling two substantial volumes in the collected edition of 1751. Gordon was at pains to deny the truth of the cry 'no bishop, no king':

Had it not been for Dissenters, I question whether we should now have had either this constitution, this king, or this religion. It is well known that a great majority of our churchmen have got claims and principles utterly irreconcilable to either. The most mischievous tenets of Popery are adopted and maintained, and the ground upon which our security and succession stand, is boldly undermined. It is dreadful, and incredible what a reprobate spirit reigns amongst the High clergy.

High Churchmen, in particular, had politicised their faith: 'Politics are now become an universal theme, and we hear more of them from the pulpit than soul-saving doctrine: no man is reckoned orthodox, who does not dabble in state-affairs'; consequently, 'Independency at Court is a heresy in politics'; the independent Whig 'scorns all implicit faith in the State, as well as the Church'.[98]

The same doctrines, applied to secular political issues, informed Trenchard and Gordon's 'Cato's Letters' (5th November 1720 – 27th July 1723), which appeared weekly in the *London Journal* and *British Journal* successively, and were later republished in four collected editions as a handbook of early-eighteenth-century radical Whiggery. It was these theorists who provided a justification for radical action. As a scarcely impartial foreign observer commented,

It is entirely owing to the enterprising genii of this age that we have seen religion besieged openly from every quarter; its mysteries are turned into ridicule by the ingenious Mr Toland; its clergy are become contemptible to many since they have read that smart piece, 'The Independent Whig'; which having effectually cleared the way and given assault to religious outworks, its very foundations were afterwards violently shaken by the celebrated performances of Mr Collins; and finally, down tumbled the whole edifice by means of those inimitable masterpieces of Mr Woolston.[99]

[97] Thomas Gordon (d. 1750). Origins obscure. Possibly practised at Scottish bar. Became Trenchard's amanuensis; married his widow. Walpole bought him off; he held the post of first commissioner of wine licences until his death.

[98] T. Gordon, *The Character of an Independent Whig* (1720) and *Priestianity: or, A View of the Disparity between the Apostles and the Modern Inferior Clergy* in *A Collection of Tracts. By the Late John Trenchard, Esq.; and Thomas Gordon, Esq.* (2 vols., London, 1751), vol. I, pp. 311, 317; vol. II, pp. 400–1.

[99] Count Albert de Passaran, *A Succinct History of the Priesthood, Ancient and Modern* (London, 1737), quoted in Sykes, *Gibson*, p. 258.

Although the great majority of politically active Whigs were not extremists, the radicals' campaign, sustained as it was over several decades, had a profound impact in changing the climate of debate. Mainstream Whigs imbibed not democracy or republicanism but a measure of anticlericalism. In 1744 Bishop Gibson complained that 'For some years past the excess of Church power has been the great subject of conversation and writing',[100] and even the Whigs' legal oracle, Lord Hardwicke, explicitly set himself against the extensive view of Church powers set out in Gibson's classic *Codex Juris Ecclesiastici Anglicani* of 1713.

Such anticlerical doctrine led the Commonwealthmen to their closest involvement with practical affairs. Molesworth took a leading part in the campaign that led to the abolition of the Schism and Occasional Conformity Acts in 1718.[101] Their repeal was only one episode in a series of moves against Anglican social hegemony. The Close Vestries Bill, introduced in the Lords in May 1716, aimed at a major reduction in the role of the clergy in parish government; Archbishop Wake threw his weight against it, and it was lost.[102] The favour shown to Hoadly since the accession of George I gave an implication of official status to his sermon before the king in 1717, on the text 'My kingdom is not of this world.' Christ, he argued, had 'left behind him no visible, human authority; no vicegerents who can be said properly to supply his place; no interpreters, upon whom his subjects are absolutely to depend; no judges over the consciences or religion of his people'. It was the most profoundly radical doctrine, implying as it did the fraudulent nature of the Church of England's claims to authority. Neither that Church nor any other, it suggested, could validly frame a doctrinal test of orthodoxy; require subscription to it; punish heresy, so defined; or exclude from civil offices or rewards any who adhered to another doctrine. It was not Lockeian contractarianism but Hoadleian latitudinarianism which provoked the most bitter domestic ideological conflict of the century.[103]

If all the prerogatives of the Church of England were in question, an attempt to repeal the Test and Corporation Acts was to be expected. Deist, Arian, even Socinian objections to subscription had received a powerful boost; Church authority was now made a central target of political attack, as the Commonwealthmen had sought. In the spring of 1717 a ministerial Bill was drafted to control disaffection in the Universities by vesting the nomination to all offices, masterships, fellowships and scholarships in the Crown for seven years; but it was progressively postponed, to await the outcome first of the attempt to repeal the Test and Corporation Acts, then of the Peerage Bill. In the autumn of 1719, Sunderland reported the king's

---

[100] Quoted Sykes, *Sheldon to Secker*, p. 202. [101] Robbins, *Commonwealthman*, p. 115.
[102] Sykes, *Wake*, vol. II, pp. 112–14.
[103] So extensive is the literature of the Bangorian controversy that historians have been deterred from tackling it, and no full study of the subject exists.

determination to force through the Peerage Bill, the Universities Bill, and a repeal of the Septennial Act (so removing the need for periodic general elections);[104] but the defeat of the first meant the abandonment of the others.

The other part of the programme went forward. In December 1718 the Stanhope–Sunderland ministry introduced the widest conceivable measure aimed against Anglican hegemony: a Bill repealing the Occasional Conformity and Schism Acts, and providing a way of avoiding the reception of the sacrament required by the Test and Corporation Acts.[105] Episcopal resistance, unexpectedly led by the new Whig Archbishop, Wake, removed from the Bill in committee the last provision; but the two Anglican triumphs of Anne's last years were reversed.[106] The Act for Quieting and Establishing Corporations of 1719 indemnified local office-holders without a sacramental qualification if they were unchallenged for six months: temporarily the issue was suspended, and the way opened for a series of local compromises. Other legislative action continued. The Quakers' Affirmation Bill, introduced in the Commons in January 1722, outraged Bishop Atterbury and many clergy as an attack on the principle of Christian oaths and, indirectly, on their entitlement to tithes, secured by law and testimony under oath. The Bill, as a clerical petition objected, 'seems to imply, that justice may be duly administered, and government supported without the intervention of any solemn appeal to God as a witness of the truth of what is said'. Both Archbishops found themselves aligned with Atterbury against the Bill, but the bench was divided, and the measure passed with substantial majorities.[107]

became law

The Parliament of 1727–33 'recalled the Reformation Parliament of Henry VIII in its zeal to attack the stronghold of clerical privilege and abuse'.[108] In 1730, unsuccessful attempts were made in the Commons to undermine the power of the clergy to collect tithes, and to prevent the translation of bishops from see to see. In 1733 a Bill attacking the jurisdiction of ecclesiastical courts passed the Commons and was only rejected in the

---

[104] B. Williams, *Stanhope* (Oxford, 1932), pp. 410, 456–63.

[105] The occasion produced a classic defence from Thomas Sherlock, *A Vindication of the Corporation and Test Acts* (London, 1718).

[106] *Parl Hist*, vol. VII, cols. 567–89; Sykes, *Sheldon to Secker*, pp. 101–2; *Wake*, vol. II, pp. 122ff. Even so, eleven bishops voted for the Bill, fifteen against (including the Archbishops and the Bishops of London, Durham and Winchester). Gibson voted in favour, allegedly swayed by hopes of a legacy from a rich Presbyterian uncle. In the Commons, where the Bill passed its second reading by 243 to 202, 'It was observed, that the majority was mainly owing to the Scotch members, for of 37 of them that were in the House, 34 voted for the Bill, and only 3 against it.' Boyer, *Political State*, quoted in *Parl Hist*, vol. VII, col. 585. How far the Anglican hegemony was always qualified, and in 1828–32 finally destroyed, by the Celtic fringe deserves consideration.

[107] *Parl Hist*, vol. VII, cols. 937–48. The Lords' Protest, signed by the Archbishop of York, the Bishops of Rochester and Chester, and eight lay peers, was a ringing declaration of the principle of a homogeneous Christian society, enforced and defined by oaths.

[108] Sykes, *Gibson*, p. 149.

Lords. The same session, the Church Rates Bill, which would have vested powers to levy rates for church repairs in JPs, was with difficulty defeated on its third reading in the lower House. Lord Chancellor Talbot's nomination of the Arian Rundle to the vacant bishopric of Salisbury in January 1734 produced a major crisis in which Bishop Gibson was able only with extreme difficulty to have the appointment set aside.[109]

Dissenting congregations had established a joint body for united action in 1727; stimulated by an application from Irish Presbyterians for an end to the sacramental test,[110] it belatedly moved into a cautious and reticent campaign for a repeal of the Test and Corporation Acts in the 1730s. At this point many even of those bishops most in sympathy with the regime drew the line. Episcopal unanimity was marked. Gibson, who had voted for the repeal of the Occasional Conformity and Schism Acts, produced the classic defence of the Acts now challenged.[111] The Church–Whig alliance held: Walpole warned the Dissenters not to pursue their claims, and when they persisted he arranged the defeat of their petition in the Commons on 12th March 1736 by 251 to 123.[112]

After thus defending constitutional orthodoxy in its most essential respect, Walpole may have made a tactical error in not foreseeing the outcry raised by two other measures that session. On 10th March 1736 the Master of the Rolls introduced the government-backed Mortmain Bill in the Commons, preventing deathbed bequests to charitable (mainly Church) causes. An amendment to include Queen Anne's Bounty among the exceptions was lost in the Commons, and Hardwicke openly attacked Gibson's theory of the Church in the Lords debate. The Bishop of London found himself fighting side by side with Sherlock, acknowledged leader of the Tory clergy, but in both Houses Gibson could only call on Tory votes, and the Bill passed the Lords on 13th May.[113] The same alignment was provoked by the Quakers' Tithe Bill, similarly introduced in the Commons with ministerial approval on 17th March, which sought to restrict actions for tithe to the jurisdiction of JPs.[114] Ministerial majorities drove it through the Commons despite a

 Bishop

---

[109] Sykes, *Gibson*, pp. 157–9. Talbot employed Thomas Gordon to write for Rundle and to vilify Gibson: T. J. F. Kendrick, 'Sir Robert Walpole, the Old Whigs and the Bishops, 1733–1736', *HJ* 11 (1968), 427.

[110] Barlow, *Citizenship and Conscience*, p. 78.

[111] Sykes, *Sheldon to Secker*, pp. 102–3. E. Gibson, *The Dispute Adjusted, About the Proper Time of Applying for a Repeal of the Corporation and Test Acts: by Shewing that No Time is Proper* (London, 1732); cf. T. Sherlock, *The History of the Test Act* (London, 1732).

[112] *Parl Hist*, vol. IX, cols. 1046–59.

[113] Sykes, *Gibson*, pp. 161–4; *Parl Hist*, vol. IX, cols. 1110–56.

[114] Quakers were otherwise open to expensive actions in Church or Exchequer courts. But it was essentially a matter of principle, not numbers. Quakers were, in the 1730s, 'grossly exaggerating the extent of the persecution they suffered... It is a tribute to the strength of the Friends as a propaganda machine that so many distinguished historians have been misled' into accepting their claims at face value: N. C. Hunt, *Two Early Political Associations. The Quakers and the Dissenting Deputies in the Age of Sir Robert Walpole* (Oxford, 1961), pp. 64–5.

clerical outcry and a wave of petitions against it. The Tories, again, aligned themselves as the Church party.[115] But if Walpole had split Whigs from Tories in the opposition, he had aligned the bishops against him with dangerous unanimity. The Church–Whig alliance itself seemed at risk. Accordingly, the Bill's second reading in the Lords on 12th May saw a ministerial retreat. The Lord Chancellor and Lord Hardwicke spoke against, and the Bill was lost with fifteen bishops in the majority.[116]

This did not exhaust sources of principled conflict. In November 1736, in the case of Middleton *v.* Croft, Hardwicke as Chief Justice of the King's Bench held that post-Reformation Canons of the Church and enactments of Convocation were binding on the laity only in so far as they had been specifically confirmed by statute[117] – a doctrine which Gibson cogently but unavailingly denied. Even more momentously, Gibson, Sherlock, Butler and Secker championed plans for the establishment of the Anglican episcopate in the American colonies – plans which Whig politicians from the 1720s to the 1770s consistently frustrated.[118]

Gibson's stand against the Quakers' Tithe Bill had averted the measure, but at the price of the loss of his position as Walpole's chief ecclesiastical adviser. Hanoverian prelates henceforth occupied a markedly more subordinate political position in relation to the civil power and to Church appointments. The radical campaigns of the early part of the century had not been without results. The institutional structure of the Church was largely intact, but it was open to argument that Gibson's Whig High Churchmanship had been unseated as the received, official interpretation of the State's theoretical status. Significantly, 1736 saw the publication of Warburton's minimalist *Alliance between Church and State*, a work which achieved its currency, it might be argued, in the vacuum left by Gibson's *Codex* and Potter's *Discourse of Church Government*. Hardwicke's ascendancy in Whig counsels in the 1740s and 50s might equally be seen as symbolic.

Yet this argument should not be carried too far. Warburton's *Alliance*, as has been shown, was not an Erastian work. Wake was succeeded at Canterbury in 1737 by the High Churchman Potter; when his relations with

---

[115] Gibson thought 'the ministry had unwarily espoused the Bill', not anticipating the scale of the reaction against it: Sykes, *Gibson*, p. 168. These two Bills of 1736 have been explained as Walpolian attempts to split Tories and opposition Whigs by exploiting their ideological differences: S. Taylor, 'Sir Robert Walpole, the Church of England, and the Quakers Tithe Bill of 1736', *HJ* 28 (1985), pp. 51–77.

[116] Six deposited proxies; four were absent; none voted against. The bench was not split: Taylor, *op. cit.* p. 67; *Parl Hist*, vol. IX, cols. 1156–220.

[117] Yorke, *Hardwicke*, vol. I, pp. 121–4.

[118] Even in 1771, the Anglican clergy of New York and New Jersey warned Lord Hillsborough, Secretary of State for the American colonies, that 'Independency in religion will naturally produce Republicanism in the State'; Hillsborough replied to an English Dissenting representative that the ministers 'from political principles could not adopt such a measure': J. M. Sosin, 'The Proposal in the Pre-Revolutionary Decade for Establishing Anglican Bishops in the Colonies', *Journal of Ecclesiastical History* 13 (1962), 83–4.

ministers and sovereign turned sour, Gibson was approached once more, and even offered Canterbury on Potter's death in 1747. The 1730s saw an important anti-latitudinarian initiative in the writings of Berkeley, Butler, Law and Wesley. A disaffected Anglican like Francis Blackburne could observe that Secker, Archbishop of Canterbury 1758–68, was 'animated with the spirit of Laud, Gibson and others of that stamp, as appears plainly by many passages in his charges, and particularly in his *Oratio Synodalis* delivered in Convocation 1761, and was consequently attached, in his judgement, to the *old posture of defence*' current before Warburton's *Alliance*.[119] Paradoxically, too, the fall from favour of Gibson opened the way to the advance of Sherlock and the beginning of the reconciliation of the Tory clergy to the regime, promoted by Newcastle in the 1750s and cemented in the 1760s. The fortuitous eclipse of Gibson's regal Alliance was the prelude to the reassertion, by men like George Horne, of something which Gibson might have regarded as much more extreme. When the State again called on the theoretical support of the Church, from the late 1760s, it was to such neo-Nonjuror doctrine that it turned.

Gibson believed that, in general, 'there was no feeling against the Church Establishment, nor was non-conformity as a theory ever less in favour': the real problem was the challenge to doctrine posed by Deists and anti-Trinitarians.[120] In this he was correct: the attack of Dissenters on the Corporation and Test Acts had been easily beaten off, and was not renewed for many decades. By the 1740s, too, it seemed that doctrinal orthodoxy had weathered the Arian and Deist storms. After the publication of Butler's *Analogy* in 1736, the flow of Deist theology and Commonwealth radicalism alike dried up. A belated echo of past conflicts was produced by Bolingbroke's collected *Works*, published posthumously in 1754. They included, for the first time, his theological writings. These caused far more shock and indignation than ever his political chicanery had done. In the light of them, it was evident that his critique of Walpolian England had not been purely secular. Walpole's 'greatest iniquity', he had declared in the *Patriot King*, had been to 'corrupt the morals of men', a theme which he frequently reiterated. Even in that work, which nevertheless attained considerable popularity in George III's reign, he had attacked the theological dimension of the State: 'the notions concerning the divine institution and right of kings, as well as the absolute power belonging to their office, have no foundation in fact or reason, but have arisen from an old alliance between ecclesiastical and civil policy. The characters of king and priest have been sometimes blended together', Bolingbroke maintained, but falsely (his Deism was now

---

119   *The Works, Theological and Miscellaneous...of Francis Blackburne* (7 vols., Cambridge, 1804), vol. I, p. xxxvi.

120   E. Gibson, 'Positions, touching the Rights of ye Civil Power in Matters of Religion', quoted in Sykes, *Gibson*, p. 259.

seen to demand their separation).[121] Yet this was a charge which could apply as well to Stuart sovereigns as to Hanoverian upholders of Warburton's *Alliance*. As contemporaries sensed, Bolingbroke's cynical irreligion was as damaging to his allies as to his opponents.

Bolingbroke's tactical predicament after 1714 meant that his religious heterodoxy had to be muzzled; it could not be allowed to unleash the profoundly radical implications of contract theory. For Bolingbroke's allies, however, 1754 was too late. Henry St John's irreligion, encased in the five volumes of Mallet's edition, had a strictly limited impact; the new developments of the late 1760s owed virtually nothing to him.

V. RADICAL THEORY C. 1745–1765: WILKES AND THE REVIVAL OF SOCINIANISM IN THE CHURCH OF ENGLAND

In the early eighteenth century, the Commonwealthmen were hopelessly upstaged. As has been seen in chapter 3, the most 'radical', as well as the most politically practicable, alternative to the Hanoverian regime was a Stuart one. Whether in intellectual force or in sheer volume, most 'radical' propaganda was Jacobite. The millenarian impulse, which was to fuel radicalism to such effect in the latter part of the eighteenth century, was largely enlisted behind Jacobitism in the reigns of the first two Georges. After that doctrine lost impetus and fell away in the years 1745 – c. 1750, there was an hiatus. Whig opposition publicists searched in vain for a new idiom in which a basic (but anti-Jacobite) critique of the Whig establishment could be couched. In general, they found only the vocabulary of moral condemnation: luxury, effeminacy, cowardice, faction, decadence and vice were the themes on which pundits dwelt, whether in response to the incompetent and half-hearted attempts to repel Charles Edward in 1745, to the minor London earthquakes of 1750, to the devastating Lisbon earthquake of 1755, or to the series of military defeats at the start of the Seven Years' War.

The first was typified by James Burgh's tract *Britain's Remembrancer* (1746),[122] which pointed to national misfortunes as acts of God, 'for no other end than the punishment of guilt, and the moral improvement of mankind'. 'LUXURY and IRRELIGION' were 'the characteristic vices of the age'. They called for moral (not parliamentary) reform.[123] The same prescription

---

[121] Bolingbroke, *The Idea of a Patriot King*, in *Works*, vol. II, pp. 373, 377.

[122] James Burgh (1714–75). Born Perthshire, son of Presbyterian minister. Educated at St Andrews for the ministry, but abandoned the idea. Failed in business. Various jobs in London. 1746 *Britain's Remembrancer*. 1747 set up a school at Stoke Newington; ran it till 1771.

[123] Pp. 4, 8. He diagnosed the characteristic objects of consumer indulgence as clothes, china, silver, wine and coaches (p. 15). Burgh aptly represents the petty radicalism of the Dissenting schoolmaster or shopkeeper.

Socianism – sect which denied the divinity of Christ.

was applied to England by the observers of the sudden destruction of Lisbon.[124] And when the loss of Minorca seemed to bear out this analysis, it was given classic and hugely popular expression in the Rev. Dr John Brown's *An Estimate of the Manners and Principles of the Times*.[125] Its appositeness was short-lived, however. A spectacular series of military victories from the *annus mirabilis* of 1759 could seem a crushing refutation of any merely moral critique of the social order. The debate took a different course; Brown's life, overshadowed by insanity, ended in suicide.

There seems, indeed, something self-consciously futile and mannered in the radicalism of the decade and a half following the '45. A more purposive mode might have been devised by the literary hack James Ralph, used by the Prince of Wales' opposition to produce its paper *The Remembrancer* (1748–51) and, after Frederick's death, by the Duke of Bedford to write *The Protester* (2nd June–10th November 1753); but the ministry bought him off with a pension.[126] Thomas Hollis' radical activities 'affected both his health and his mental balance',[127] a judgement which would be an understatement for the erratic psychological history of his closest associate at Westminster, William Pitt. Most symptomatic was the sad case of Alexander Cruden 'the Corrector', self-appointed moral pundit of the 1750s and itinerant reformer, who moved in a grey area between the reformation of manners, evangelism and insanity, but whose egregious newsworthiness perhaps did as much as anything to highlight the ultimate foolishness of a certain radical idiom.

One source of this futility was the frustration and final dissolution of the largest element of the opposition, the Tory party. Its commitment to parliamentary reform had been opportunistic, fitful and doctrinally super-ficial, so that no intellectual tradition sustained the issue as a vital and immediate one after the party was no more. The Tories' orthodox Anglicanism, with which they made so much play, checked the reception of a populist doctrine that authority ascended from below, while many Tory eyes were directed instead towards the millenarian hopes of social regeneration which the possibility of a Stuart restoration could awaken. It was this millenarianism, as we have seen, which Bolingbroke's image of the 'Patriot King' was used to exploit in the late 1740s in order to promote a Tory alignment behind a Hanoverian Prince of Wales. The echo of these hopes which the accession of George III produced, and the disintegration of the traditional Tory party, took much of this charismatic idealism into the sphere of establishment ideology from 1760. Opposition ideology from

---

[124] T. D. Kendrick, *The Lisbon Earthquake* (London, 1956).

[125] (2 vols., London, 1757–8). The approval of Thomas Hollis was qualified. Parliamentary reform was the solution to the problem, he noted in the copy of the *Estimate* he donated to Harvard. Robbins, *Commonwealthman*, p. 309.

[126] R. W. Kenny, 'James Ralph: An Eighteenth Century Philadelphian in Grub Street', *Pennsylvania Magazine of History and Biography* 64 (1940), 218–42.

[127] Robbins, *Commonwealthman*, p. 264.

that date drew on both Whig and Tory antecedents; but it was now cast in a more utilitarian idiom. Opposition personnel similarly drew on those who had been unambiguously Whig or Tory before 1760: Wilkes, in particular, was often supported by men whose disaffection had previously been enlisted behind the Tory party. The symbolic significance of the number 45 in Wilkesite propaganda aimed at the mob was a particularly open reference to a populist rebellion against a corrupt establishment.

It was ironic that Wilkes should make this use of an older symbol. Beginning his political career under Newcastle's wing and with all the traditional arts of electoral bribery, Wilkes' journal, *The North Briton*, exploited recent memories of the Jacobite nexus by levelling the Stuart slur against Bute and his allies. A series of papers in 1763 dwelt on the Tories' past associations. On 8th January he assailed the members of the Cocoa Tree:

The infinite number of writings you formerly published to recommend passive obedience, non-resistance, and indefeasible right, were a disgrace to the free government under which you lived; and your slavish maxims led a former unhappy prince, James the Second, to attempt the reducing into practice what you had for some years inculcated through the nation as the clear right of the Crown. You have now rather softened the terms, and you only talk of the independence and prerogative of the Crown; but your meaning clearly remains the same. These were the universal doctrines; and characteristics of a Tory. All your friends at your headquarters in the capital loudly proclaimed these tenets of slavery, and your favourite country residence of Oxford echoed them through the nation.

Was it conceivable that Tories of this opinion had completely abandoned their deepest beliefs, honestly taking the oaths to qualify themselves for office? If so, could they be trusted not to re-adopt their old principles? If they took the oaths disingenuously, again, was not the constitution in danger?[128]

The early Wilkes was steeped in a radical tradition which was the reverse of forward-looking. Although outwardly conforming to the Church of England in order to participate in public life, Wilkes came from a Dissenting family and had been educated at Dissenting academies; from 1739, at a school run by a Presbyterian minister who was soon forced to abandon his school when his Arian opinions became known.[129] It was licence that almost destroyed Wilkes' career, the House of Lords in 1763 voting his poem *An Essay on Woman* and the *Veni Creator*,[130] as well as a breach of privilege, 'a most scandalous, obscene, and impious libel; a gross profanation of many parts of the Holy Scriptures; and a most wicked and blasphemous attempt

---

[128] G. Nobbe, *The North Briton. A Study in Political Propaganda* (New York, 1939), pp. 149–54.
[129] *Ibid.*, pp. 4–9; F. Bleackley, *Life of John Wilkes* (London, 1917), pp. 8–9, 54–5, 259–60.
[130] As well as the infamous *Essay*, Wilkes had written obscene parodies of the *Veni Creator* and Pope's *Universal Prayer* – one of which, it seems, had amused William Pitt in 1754: Bleackley, *Wilkes*, pp. 440–1.

to ridicule and vilify the person of our blessed Saviour'.[131] With blasphemy went obscenity put to political use: the poem contained attacks on the Earl of Bute and on the clerical dictator of Ireland, George Stone, Archbishop of Armagh, the latter accused of sodomy with Lord George Sackville.[132] Wilkes' defence was that he had printed but not published the work; and that

In my own closet I had a right to examine and even try by the keen edge of ridicule any opinions I pleased. If I have laughed pretty freely at the glaring absurdities of the most monstrous creed which was ever attempted to be imposed on the credulity of Christians, a creed which our great Tillotson wished the Church of England was fairly rid of, it was in private I laughed. I am not the first good Protestant who has amused himself with the egregious nonsense... of that strange, perplexed and perplexing mortal... Athanasius.[133]

Nevertheless, the *Essay on Woman* as much as issue 45 of the *North Briton* forced him into four years' self-imposed exile in Paris, and earned him imprisonment on his return – twelve months for the first, on a charge of blasphemous libel; ten months for the seditious libel of the second.

Wilkes' resort to obscenity was nothing new, as any student of eighteenth-century political caricature will appreciate. What put him beyond the pale in the 1760s was his linking obscenity to blasphemy and heterodoxy. Yet he had found ready to hand a tradition of freethinking antinomianism which excused an easy equation of liberty and licence. In the edition of Thomas Gordon's tracts, *A Cordial for Low-Spirits*, a copy of which Wilkes owned, he could read the anticlerical invective of the 1720s and 30s directed to present uses by the republican editor, Richard Baron. Socinianism led him to the assertion that 'scarcely one point of faith, as professed and taught in any national church, is to be found in the scriptures, but every thing is distorted and misrepresented: to say nothing of the hierarchy, prelacy, and church power, with their appurtenances and tackle, all of them as contrary to Christianity, as sodomy is to nature'. Already, Wilkes' combination of obscenity and blasphemy as a weapon against the political establishment was anticipated from a theological root. 'Therefore, I say,' said Baron, 'let the hierarchy be demolished, and the Trinity be kicked out of doors.'[134] Freethinking parodies of the Liturgy duly took their place in Wilkesite propaganda, some of it reprinted in the American colonies:

I believe in Wilkes, the firm patriot, maker of number 45. Who was born for our good. Suffered under arbitrary power. Was banished and imprisoned. He ascended

---

[131] *Lords Journals* 30, p. 415.
[132] The text may be read with supporting documents in A. Hamilton (ed.), *The Infamous Essay on Woman* (London, 1972). I refrain from quotation.
[133] Quoted Bleackley, *Wilkes*, p. 438. Wilkes' closest friends were 'spoiled Anglicans': Thomas Potter, *roué* son of the Archbishop; the Rev. John Horne; and the Rev. Charles Churchill, 'drunkard as well as debauchee' (Bleackley).
[134] R. Baron (ed.), *A Cordial for Low-Spirits*, 3rd edn (3 vols., London, 1763), vol. i, preface, pp. x, xv. Wilkes' copy is in Cambridge University Library.

into purgatory, and returned some time after. He ascended here with honour and sitteth amidst the great assembly of the people, where he shall judge both the favourite and his creatures. I believe in the spirit of his abilities, that they will prove to the good of our country. In the resurrection of liberty, and the life of universal freedom forever. Amen.[135]

If these considerations lay behind Wilkes' disposition to decry authority, he translated them into no other body of radical theory. Complaints of the high-handed power of the executive were familiar within the Commonwealth tradition (and outside it). The urban disorder which Wilkes both exploited and fostered scarcely went beyond a popular cry for the restitution of traditional 'rights' which people were brought to believe themselves robbed of: Wilkesite rioters were not proto-democrats. 'Wilkism', therefore, was a phenomenon which was as intellectually shallow as it was evanescent, a 'movement which, for all its astonishing vigour and resilience, did not long outlast Wilkes' election as Lord Mayor of London' in 1774.[136] Wilkes may have been an unusually populist symptom of a Commonwealth anticlerical, anti-establishment tradition; but he founded no tradition of mass action (he dropped the mob entirely after securing the sinecure post of Chamberlain to the City of London, worth £1,500 p.a., in 1779) and left no intellectual legacy.

For the origins of radical doctrine we must look elsewhere. Defeated though Arianism may have been within Anglican theology by the brilliant polemics of Daniel Waterland in the 1720s, the Church found no way of excluding from its ranks those who sought to enjoy the material rewards of establishment, or the title of priest, while teaching doctrines antithetical to orthodoxy. The State's refusal to support the Church over the 1721 Bill meant that some men were able to dissemble their views sufficiently to maintain positions from which to undermine the Church from within. The cause of heterodox theology and the abolition of subscription within the Church was associated, above all, with Newcastle's henchman in Cambridge university politics, Edmund Law.[137] Master of Peterhouse from 1754, he obtained the bishopric of Carlisle from old Petrean and Unitarian the Duke of Grafton in 1768, but remained in residence in the Lodge. Earlier in his Cambridge career, the thesis he defended in public disputation for his DD

---

[135] *A New Form of Prayer, and Thanksgiving for the Happy Deliverance of John Wilkes, Esq.* (London, 1768), republished in Boston as *Britannia's Intercession for the Deliverance of John Wilkes, Esq.*; quoted in Pauline Maier, 'John Wilkes and American Disillusionment with Britain', *WMQ* 20 (1963), 373. For the trial in 1817 of the radical William Hone on a charge of publishing this and similar blasphemous libels, see chapter 6 below, pp. 381–2.

[136] G. Rudé, *Wilkes and Liberty* (Oxford, 1962), p. 172.

[137] Edmund Law (1703–87). Yeoman family of Lancashire. St John's Coll., Camb.; BA 1723; Fellow of Christ's Coll.; living, 1737; 1743–54 Archdeacon. 1754 Master of Peterhouse; 1764 Knightbridge Professor of Moral Philosophy (a Peterhouse foundation); 1768 Bishop of Carlisle. 1774 published anonymously *Considerations on the Propriety of Requiring Subscriptions to Articles of Faith*; 1777 edited Locke's *Works*.

in 1749 was objected to by some Doctors as Socinian;[138] he obtained the degree with some difficulty, but, once back in Cambridge, he propagated Socinian doctrines to a growing circle of acolytes.

Peterhouse, during Law's mastership, produced a remarkable string of graduates whose radicalism had its roots in religious heterodoxy, including Jebb,[139] Disney[140] and Lofft.[141] Immediately before Law's arrival, the fellows who elected him taught three undergraduates later to play prominent roles as politicians on the anti-subscription side: Lord John Cavendish;[142] Augustus Fitzroy, 3rd Duke of Grafton;[143] and Sir James Lowther, later 1st Earl of Lonsdale.[144] They were followed by Whig politicians James Adair[145] and George 'Citizen' Tierney.[146] In the university

[138] Archbishop Herring approved; but the idea that Law obtained the degree only after pressure from Herring, 'always liberal and appreciative of good Christians' (Robbins, *Commonwealthman*, p. 304) seems to rest on a misreading of Nichols, *Literary Anecdotes*, vol. II, p. 70. Professor Robbins conceived of Unitarians as 'supporters of undogmatical Christianity' (p. 325), which is rather like calling a Trotskyite a supporter of undogmatical capitalism.

[139] John Jebb (1736–86). Son of Dean of Cashel. TCD 1753; Peterhouse, 1754; fellow 1761–4; deacon 1762, priest 1763, living 1764. Continued to lecture in the university on mathematics; and from 1768 on the Greek Testament, displaying Unitarian views: some colleges forbad attendance. Took part in Feathers Tavern petition; 1775 resigned all livings. Lindsey wished to recruit him to the Essex Street chapel, but he took up medicine, practising in London from 1778.

[140] John Disney (1746–1816). Peterhouse 1764–; ordained 1768, and at once appointed chaplain to Bp Law. 1768 wrote in defence of Blackburne's *Confessional*. 1769 presented to two livings in Lincolnshire. 1771 involved in anti-subscription movement; henceforth omitted Athanasian and Nicene creeds; resigned livings 1782, joining Lindsey at Essex Street; succeeded as sole minister on Lindsey's retirement, 1793; resigned 1805 after receiving a large inheritance.

[141] Capel Lofft (1751–1824) Eton; Peterhouse 1769–70; Lincoln's Inn; called to bar 1775. Independent means 1775; inherited family estates 1781. Founder member of Society for Constitutional Information. Admirer of Fox and Napoleon. Writer on law and politics.

[142] Lord John Cavendish (1732–96). 4th son of 3rd Duke of Devonshire. Peterhouse; MA 1753. MP 1754; Lord of the Treasury under Rockingham, 1765; refused place in Chatham–Grafton ministry. Chancellor of Exchequer in Rockingham's 2nd ministry. Opposed expulsion of Wilkes; voted for Feathers Tavern petition; supported Burke on economical reform.

[143] Augustus Henry Fitzroy, 3rd Duke of Grafton (1735–1811). Succeeded 1757. Westminster and Peterhouse; MA 1753. MP 1756–7. In opposition to Bute. Secretary of State, Northern Department in Rockingham ministry 1765; resigned 1766; took Treasury in alliance with Chatham, 1766; resigned 1770. Privy Seal under North 1771–5; under Rockingham 1782–3. Elected Chancellor of Cambridge University 1768; declined customary degree of LLD in order not to subscribe the Thirty-Nine Articles. Regular attender at Essex Street. Wrote tracts for the revision of the liturgy in 1789 and 1797.

[144] Sir James Lowther (1736–1802). Peterhouse 1752–; MP 1757–; 1761 married Bute's eldest daughter. In opposition during North's ministry; acted with Lord John Cavendish. Brought William Pitt into Commons for a pocket borough, 1781. Earldom, 1784.

[145] James Adair (?1743–98). ?Eton; Peterhouse; BA 1764. Lincoln's Inn; called to bar. MP 1775–80, 1793–9. Wilkesite lawyer; opposed North's ministry; pro-American, anti-subscription, pro-Dissenter.

[146] George Tierney (1761–1830). Eton; Peterhouse 1778–; called to bar 1784; MP 1789–90, 1796 – d. Treasurer of the Society of Friends of the People; leading figure in the Whig opposition under Grey; fought Pitt in duel, 1798.

at large, Law was the patriarch of a heterodox interest, and numbered among his associates and admirers William Paley (who was, in turn, the tutor of the Unitarian radical William Frend[147]), Richard Watson and Gilbert Wakefield. Wakefield was taught at Jesus by a Mr Mounsey, lately elected from Peterhouse to a sympathetically radical society; was briefly taught mathematics by Jebb; and was a friend of Tyrwhitt. He was present at Law's famous sermon in Great St Mary's on 5th November 1773, of which Jebb wrote that Law

...showed, that the spirit of popery was not peculiar to popish countries; that spiritual tyranny consisted in imposing other articles, as terms of communion, than what Christ had given; that religious liberty was too valuable a right to be complimented away; and that every effort to oppress conscience should be opposed. In short no *petitioner* would have wished him to say more.[148]

Edmund Law represented the survival of Samuel Clarke's doctrines among the grandly beneficed of the Anglican intelligentsia. They survived also among obscure clergymen. One such was John Jones (1700–70), author of the anonymous *Free and Candid Disquisitions* (1749) – a work which attracted little attention at the time, but which later gave encouragement to his friend (and Law's) Archdeacon Francis Blackburne[149] to voice similar ideas. He in turn had a small circle of admirers, chief among them Theophilus Lindsey,[150] who were to demonstrate their solidarity by their secession from the Church in the 1770s.

Blackburne had been disappointed of his ambition for a foundation-fellowship at St Catharine's Hall, Cambridge, where he was briefly chaplain in 1728, as he wrote:

...the majority of the fellows being high royalists on the principle of hereditary right, and [Blackburne] having by the conversation of some liberal minded friends, and

---

147 William Frend (1757–1841). King's School Canterbury and Christ's Coll., Camb. 1775–; BA 1780; fellow of Jesus 1781–; deacon 1780, priest 1783. 1787 converted to Unitarianism; supported Grace of 11th Dec. 1787 for abolishing subscription on taking MA. Removed from tutorship. 1793 published *Peace and Union* and, *inter alia* condemning liturgy of C. of E. Expelled from the university, but remained a Fellow of Jesus, drawing his income, until he resigned his Fellowship by marriage, 1808. Lived in London associating with radicals, including Burdett and Horne Tooke.

148 *Memoirs of the Life of Gilbert Wakefield...Written by Himself*, ed. J. T. Rutt and A. Wainewright, 2nd edn (2 vols., London, 1804), vol. 1, pp. 88, 93, 113. Wakefield defended Mounsey: 'On his *abilities* his numerous acquaintance will reflect with more pleasure than on his *life*; but his virtues were disinterestedly benevolent, and his vices chiefly prejudicial to himself.'

149 Francis Blackburne (1705–87). Born Richmond, Yorks. St Catharine's Hall, Camb., 1722–8. College friend of Edmund Law. Deacon 1728; lived with an uncle in Yorkshire till 1739; ordained priest, rector of Richmond 1739 – d. Archdeacon 1750; refused again to subscribe Thirty-Nine Articles. 1750 defended Jones's *Free and Candid Disquisitions*; 1751 attacked Bp Butler in an anonymous piece, published with his name in Baron (ed.), *Pillars of Priestcraft and Orthodoxy Shaken* (1767).

150 Theophilus Lindsey (1723–1808). Born Middlewich, Cheshire. Ed. Leeds and St John's Coll., Camb. 1741–; fellow, 1747. Ordained; livings; 1763 took rectory of Catterick to be near Blackburne. Signed Feathers Tavern petition; resigned living on its rejection.

the reading of Locke, Hoadly, &c. acquired a strong attachment to the principles of ecclesiastical and civil liberty, he became an obnoxious candidate to the society; and having disclosed his sentiments too freely, in a public speech, on the 5th of November, immediately preceding the time of his taking his degree, he was rejected, though otherwise the only qualified candidate.[151]

Left to rot in his native Yorkshire, Blackburne took his revenge in *The Confessional*, published anonymously in 1766 at the prompting of the republican Hollis. It achieved what Hoadly had failed to do: a major campaign within the Church for the abolition of subscription and the modification of the Thirty-Nine Articles to conform with 'modern' opinions. Blackburne had already written in favour of Jewish naturalisation and against an Anglican episcopate in the American colonies; now, his critique went deeper. He was widely regarded as a Socinian, like his friends who left the Church; and though, after Lindsey's apostasy, he wrote a short paper, 'An Answer to the Question, Why are you not a Socinian?', he left it unpublished.[152] His sympathies were hardly in doubt. His daughter, stepdaughter and granddaughter married Unitarians (Disney, Lindsey and Frend respectively); from Blackburne's circle emerged the 'Feathers Tavern' petition of 1772, demanding the abolition of subscription for Anglican clergymen. In some circles, especially in certain radical Cambridge colleges, it enjoyed a minor vogue. 'The Master of Jesus College, Cambridge, and every resident Fellow has signed the petition', boasted Lindsey; 'The Bishop of Carlisle highly approved.'[153] Jebb believed that 'It is now well known, that a majority of the thinking clergy are disposed to embrace the hypothesis of Arius or Socinus, with regard to the person of Jesus. And that the opinion of Athanasius, though sanctified by the acts of uniformity, is now exploded by almost every reader of the Bible.'[154] Perhaps he exaggerated. Despite the untiring efforts of the organisers, the petition attracted the signatures of only some two hundred out of twelve thousand clergy. The Methodists were strongly opposed. In the Commons debate, the Member for Oxford University, Sir Roger Newdigate, warned that 'Civil and religious establishments are so linked and incorporated together that when the latter falls the former cannot stand'; Lord North and Edmund

[151] Blackburne, *Works*, vol. 1, p. iv.

[152] Blackburne, *Works*, vol. 1, pp. lxi–lxii, cxx–cxxvi.

[153] H. McLachlan (ed.), *Letters of Theophilus Lindsey* (Manchester, 1920), p. 43. Hans Stanley, MP, was not impressed by 'the example of a college in Cambridge': as he wrote to Lindsey (*Parl Hist*, vol. xvii, col. 259):

> I have quite accidentally heard somewhat of the secret history which has passed within those walls; if I am not deceived, that signature has been chiefly promoted by a factious abettor of those senseless seditious disputes which have divided us upon political subjects, and which are already enough envenomed without your throwing in the fresh corrosive of religious controversy.

[154] J. Disney (ed.), *The Works...of John Jebb* (3 vols., London, 1787), vol. iii, p. 67 (28th May 1772).

Burke repeated a similar doctrine. The petition was lost by 217 to 71.[155] A second attempt in May 1774 was abandoned for lack of support without a division being forced. Defeat was total.

The rejection of the petition, and the exodus of the tiny band of its articulate proponents, was decisive: the late-Georgian Church, despite the presence within it of a few men like Bishops Law, Watson and Shipley, was increasingly committed to monarchical and theological orthodoxy.

VI. DISSENT AND ITS AIMS, 1714–1775

The rejection of the Feathers Tavern petition provoked the departure from the Church of England, one by one, of a series of self-acknowledged Unitarians, following the precedent of William Robertson:[156] Lindsey in 1773, Jebb in 1775, Tyrwhitt in 1777,[157] Wakefield[158] in c. 1779, Disney in 1782, Palmer in 1783.[159] They entered the ranks of Dissent, where the spread of heterodoxy had prepared a natural home for them. It is to the position of Dissent that we must now turn.

The social position of doctrinally orthodox Dissent was an increasingly weak one in the early and mid-eighteenth century. On the one hand, numbers were subject to a steady and serious decline in the face of the attractive alternative provided by a powerful Church establishment. On the other, the Stuart threat committed them to a subservient, even adulatory, attitude towards the Hanoverian regime. By 1717, in the wake of an almost-successful Jacobite rising, even the rabid John Toland was denying that there were any republicans in the kingdom; announcing that kingship was 'essential to our constitution, and is the very first of our three Estates'; and claiming that

...the Whigs are no democratic Commonwealthsmen, but zealous supporters of the ancient constitution under King, Lords and Commons: and tho' they are avowedly for resisting of tyrants by arms on behalf of the laws, they are also as ready to expose

---

[155] *Parl Hist*, vol. XVII, cols. 245–97 (6th February 1772). Chatham's nephew Thomas Pitt seconded the motion. Thomas Townshend spoke for it who, after its defeat, took a leading part in the campaign against Dr Nowell (see above).

[156] William Robertson (1705–83). Deacon 1728, priest 1729, livings in Ireland. 1759 read *Free and Candid Disquisitions*; decided he could no longer subscribe. Refused preferment; omitted Athanasian creed; resigned livings 1764. Lindsey wrote of him as 'the father of unitarian nonconformity'. 1778 agreed to become Lindsey's colleague at Essex St, but never left Warrington, where he was master of the grammar school from 1768.

[157] Robert Tyrwhitt (1735–1817). Grandson of Gibson, son of canon of St Paul's. Jesus Coll., Camb. 1753–; fellow 1759. Influenced by Clarke. Took part in 1772 anti-subscription campaign; resigned fellowship 1777, though he continued to reside in Jesus until his death.

[158] For whom, see p. 258 n. 180.

[159] Thomas Fysshe Palmer (1747–1802). Eton and Queens' Coll., Camb. 1765–; fellow 1781–; curacy. Converted to Unitarianism by Priestley's writings. Unitarian minister in Scotland 1783–. Became involved in Dundee radicalism 1793; sentenced to seven years transportation. Died in Pacific.

their lives and fortunes in defence of the honour and persons of good princes, no less than for the preservation of monarchy itself.[160]

Such sentiments were a measure of the anguish with which radicals perceived the Jacobite threat.

Those fears continued for a decade and a half after the '45. Thomas Hollis, the Commonwealth propagandist, reflected in his diary on 25th October 1760 on the death of George II, a king 'under whose reign I have passed the principal part and flower of my life in peace and full security and happiness'; and he wished George III well.[161] Richard Price, Dissenting minister at Stoke Newington, preached on 29th November 1759 a sermon in uncritical eulogy of the liberty and prosperity enjoyed under the establishment: 'our religious liberty', he maintained, 'is the crown of all our national advantages'. 'All sects enjoy the benefits of toleration, and may worship God in whatever way they think most acceptable to him; and nothing exposes any person to civil penalties or censures, but overt acts inconsistent with the peace and security of society.' It was republished by a critic in 1791 as evidence of how far the Dissenting position had moved.[162]

Secondly, Dissenters' reception by the establishment grew progressively less chilly during the reigns of the first two Georges. Almost annual Indemnity Acts from 1727 generally suspended the effect of their legal disqualifications: some Dissenters became MPs, more exercised local power, many profited from the 'spoils system' of unreformed politics.[163] Three developments broke this stalemate. First, after the accession of George III the Stuart option was seen to have disintegrated; with the disappearance of what they saw as a much more hostile alternative, forces disaffected to the Anglican hegemony realised in the 1760s that they had inherited a much wider scope. Soon, the Whig monarchy, hitherto identified as a central pillar of English liberties, was being described in the language hitherto reserved for Stuart 'despotism'. The Nonjuror insistence on the independence of the Church from the civil power became, after 1760, an equally radical claim on behalf of Dissent, in the hands of men like Priestley.[164] From 1760, Dissenting aims subtly shifted from a defence of the toleration they enjoyed under the Revolution settlement to a destruction of the Church–State alliance. 'Toleration' became an offensive rather than a defensive creed.

---

[160] [Toland], *State-Anatomy*, p. 14.
[161] [F. Blackburne] (ed.), *Memoirs of Thomas Hollis, Esq.* (2 vols., London, 1780), vol. i, p. 98.
[162] Richard Price, *Britain's Happiness, and Its Full Possession of Civil and Religious Liberty, Briefly Stated and Proved* (London, 1791), pp. 14, 17.
[163] Watts, *Dissenters*, vol. i, p. 483; J. E. Bradley, 'Whigs and Nonconformists. "Slumbering Radicalism" in English Politics, 1739–89', *ECS* 9 (1975), 1–27. Dr Bradley also notes the importance of the Act for Quieting and Establishing Corporations (5 Geo. I c 6) in allowing the Dissenters to hold local office. For a different interpretation, cf. K. R. M. Short, 'The English Indemnity Acts 1726–1867', *Church History* 42 (1973), 366–76.
[164] Cf. Priestley, quoted in Robbins, *Commonwealthman*, pp. 227–8.

This had, indeed, always been implicit in the Dissenters' position; but political realities under the first two Georges had enforced quiescence.

Secondly, the detailed objections of orthodox Dissent to the Church of England had become ritualised, losing their vitality. Many intelligent and respectable Dissenters returned to the Church, including figures of such calibre as Joseph Butler and Thomas Secker (both of whom became bishops). The residual identity of Dissent therefore became much more political: 'Dissent had become in one sense an end in itself, in that the Dissenters rejected conformity because they stood for liberty in matters of conscience. They Dissented to proclaim their right to dissent. Yet in that affirmation Dissent was once again made instrumental – not now to the kingdom of God but to the cause of liberty.'[165] It was hardly surprising, wrote Dr Johnson, that the Wilkesite disturbances had been supported by 'the sectaries, the constant fomenters of sedition, and never-failing confederates of the rabble, of whose religion little now remains but hatred of establishments'.[166]

Thirdly, this shibboleth of 'liberty', no longer necessarily invoked in favour of the Hanoverian regime, was given new virulence from the late 1760s by the re-emergence of Socinianism. Although the Church of England largely fought off the subversive challenge posed by Clarke and Hoadly, the orthodox Dissenters, lacking the resources of the establishment, did not. The Salters' Hall assembly in March 1719 revealed London Dissenting ministers equally divided. The meeting voted narrowly against requiring subscription to a creed from Dissenting ministers; each congregation was henceforth free to pursue its own doctrinal course. Presbyterians and General Baptists, in particular, slid down a slippery slope from Arianism to Socinianism.[167] The short run consequence, in the mid-eighteenth century, was greatly to weaken Dissent, both in numbers and vigour.[168] The long run consequence, evident from the late 1760s, was to leave Dissenters as a highly politicised radical rump, freed now both from the political imperative which tied them to a Hanoverian monarch, and from the Trinitarian imperative which restricted their dissent from the Church to a few points of form and ceremonial. It is a measure of the strength of the Trinitarian-dynastic nexus that it held in check for several decades the radical possibilities of growing Dissenting heterodoxy.

In the early part of the century Dissenting Arians and Socinians produced almost no political theory of any calibre, though they included in their ranks

---

[165] R. E. Richey, 'The Origins of British Radicalism: The Changing Rationale for Dissent', *ECS* 7 (1973–4), 179–92.

[166] Dr Johnson, *The False Alarm* (London, 1770) in D. J. Greene (ed.), *Samuel Johnson. Political Writings* (New Haven, Conn., 1977), p. 344.

[167] Watts, *Dissenters*, vol. I, pp. 374ff; Wilbur, *Unitarianism*, pp. 252ff.

[168] D. Bogue and J. Bennett, *History of the Dissenters, from the Revolution in* 1688, *to the year* 1808 (4 vols., London, 1808), vol. III, pp. 319ff; 386ff.

men like the patriarch of Dissenting scholarship, Nathaniel Lardner.[169] All Dissenters were still busy defending the existing order against the perceived threats of Jacobites and papists. Within a few years of 1760, however, this changed totally. Dissenting propagandists, like the Socinian Fleming,[170] now assailed the Church with the charge, always latent in the Dissenting case, of 'priestcraft and oppression'.[171] This was a portent of things to come. In the late 1760s the radical position took a decisive lurch 'leftwards' with the reassertion of Arian and, more importantly, Socinian doctrines by a new generation both of hereditary Dissenters and of eager converts. Historians have described how the late 1760s saw a proliferation of radical activity and theory, yet it has been suggested that 'No very satisfactory explanation of this development has ever been offered'.[172] Traditional accounts pointed to industrialisation, urbanisation, or the 'rise of the middle class', in the familiar economic-reductionist framework.[173] Yet, on the contrary, the new political ideologies moved from property to persons as the demanded basis of representation, and nothing in the economic trends commonly appealed to accounted for a transition occurring when it did, or as suddenly as it did. For it was a transition in the world of ideas, not of economic circumstances; and a transition confined to a small circle of largely metropolitan intellectuals. They had one thing in common: heterodox theological opinions.[174] This has, indeed, sometimes been noticed in passing, as a coincident fact, another manifestation (though a less important one) of these men's commitment to 'liberty'. As has been seen, however, theological questions

---

[169] Nathaniel Lardner (1684–1768). Son of Dissenting minister, Kent. Dissenting academy; univs. of Utrecht and Leyden. Dissenting minister and tutor in London, 1703–. A non-subscriber at Salters' Hall, 1719. Friend of Priestley, Kippis, Thomas Hollis. Initially Trinitarian; came to accept Clarke's Arianism in 1720s; from 1740s, a Socinian.

[170] Caleb Fleming (1698–1779). Son of Calvinist hosier, Nottingham. Trained for ministry; gave up. Socinian. 1738 became Dissenting minister; from 1740, in London. Prolific author against Jacobites, popery, Deists etc.

[171] Barlow, *Citizenship and Conscience*, pp. 134–5.

[172] Brewer, *Party Ideology*, p. 19. Professor Brewer added a new suggestion, but still within the old context of economic reductionism: 'the American debate about taxation and its relationship to representation', he wrote, 'was crucial'. Important, secondly, were the 'skilled marketing techniques' with which Wilkes 'commercialised politics' (pp. 20–1). The radical thrust was 'predominantly bourgeois and characteristically commercial'; Wilkesites' 'conception of social and political relations was entrepreneurial rather than deferential. They had a vested interest in opening up politics, just as they were concerned to open up new markets for their products' (pp. 267–8). Such ideas may be allowed to take their place within the historiographical tradition of which they are part.

[173] For an equally materialist interpretation, cf. J. Brewer, 'English Radicalism in the Age of George III' in J. G. A. Pocock (ed.) *Three British Revolutions: 1641, 1688, 1776* (Princeton, 1980).

[174] Exceptions to this rule were rare, and provoked comment. In 1786 the American Ambassador, John Adams, was astonished to meet an Anglican Trinitarian reformer – Granville Sharp, grandson of the Archbishop: 'as zealously attached to episcopacy and the Athanasian Creed as he is to civil and religious liberty – a mixture which in this country is not common'. C. Bonwick, *English Radicals and the American Revolution* (Chapel Hill, N. Carolina, 1977), p. 7.

provided (as they had always provided) both the theoretical formulation of, and the occasion for, manifestations of radicalism in the civil sphere. American issues certainly injected tactical problems into English politics; but it should not be forgotten that the conflict in the colonies, superficially about the details of taxation, expressed also the most profound issues of allegiance and religion.[175] Since the seventeenth century, colonial Dissenters had defined threats to their liberties chiefly in terms of the rival claims and possible advance of the Anglican church; what was new in the 1760s was that colonists came to perceive the English ministry as being similarly aligned with the Church as part of a wider, but long-familiar, conspiracy; and that growing American heterodox anticlericalism found a nationwide political target.[176]

In England, Dissenters claimed a similar 'rightwards' shift in the position of the Establishment. From 1714, wrote the Dissenters' historians, 'the majority' of the Anglican clergy had been 'disaffected to the House of Hanover, and cherished in their bosoms the exiled family of Stewart as the legitimate claimants to the British throne'. Despairing at last of success, about 1760 they transferred their allegiance to the Hanoverians and were 'received with open arms'.

Into this new state of favour they brought with them all their former principles. Like their predecessors, they entertained the most exalted ideas of the powers and prerogatives of kings, and an aversion to all who were without the pale of the establishment, whom they designated by the title of schismatics and fanatics. These sentiments, to which the moderate dignitaries of the two former reigns were strangers, began to echo from the pulpits, and were insinuated into the ears of the court.

Dissenters, they argued, merely reacted to this development.[177] Yet just as historians have failed to discover any political plot against English liberties behind the ministerial instability at the outset of George III's reign, so too no evidence has emerged of a conspiracy to undo 'the Toleration'. Bogue

---

[175] 'The long-standing antipathy on the part of historians, bitten by the bug of economic determinism, to giving religion any consideration in any part of our history is too well known to need comment': W. W. Sweet, 'The Role of Anglicans in the American Revolution', *HLQ* 11 (1947–8), 51–70.

[176] W. M. Hogue, 'The Religious Conspiracy Theory of the American Revolution: Anglican Motive', *Church History* 45 (1976), 277–92, points to the rapid growth of the American episcopal church after independence as evidence of its potential threat in the decades before the revolution. The long and articulate rivalry of Church and Dissent in the colonies, rather than any sudden American psychosis, probably lies behind the prevalence of conspiracy theories in the revolution. For the recent debate, and another explanation, Gordon S. Wood, 'Conspiracy and the Paranoid Style: Causality and Deceit in the Eighteenth Century', *WMQ* 39 (1982), 401–41. Cf. also C. Bridenbaugh, *Mitre and Sceptre. Transatlantic Faiths, Ideas, Personalities and Politics 1689–1775* (New York, 1962); A. Heimert, *Religion and the American Mind from the Great Awakening to the Revolution* (Cambridge, Mass., 1966); S. Lynd, *Intellectual Origins of the American Revolution* (London, 1969).

[177] Bogue and Bennett, *History of the Dissenters*, vol. IV, p. 147.

and Bennett, though themselves theologically orthodox and deploring the havoc wrought within Dissent by the recrudescence of Arianism and Socinianism, failed to see the political significance of those doctrinal developments. Even orthodox Dissenters, after all, had sought a repeal of the Test and Corporation Acts: in one way, Price and Priestley merely inherited the old objectives. Yet what is most striking about the Dissenters under George I and George II is their adulation of a regime which, from the 1760s, they came to denounce as tyrannical. For the orthodox Dissenter, the sacramental test which defended Anglican hegemony had posed no basic problem: occasional communion in the Church had long been practised among some Dissenting congregations as a gesture of fellowship with other Protestants. Only with the advance of militant heterodoxy did the Test and Corporation Acts strike a new generation of Dissenting intellectuals as blasphemous and sacrilegious.

Just as a salient fact of the 1790s was the emergence, as a social force, of open and unpunished atheism, so a salient fact of the late 1760s and 1770s was the advent of open and unpunished Socinianism. The numbers of those involved were never large; but they included a galaxy of talented figures, Dissenters who were both fired with a prophetic zeal, and given an institutionalised framework by their religious denomination. Churches, not parties, organised ordinary men in late-eighteenth-century England; radicals found their way into public life in a sectarian context.

Radical intellectuals in the 1760s and 1770s were few enough to be contained within a single London coffee-house. They gravitated to the 'Club of Honest Whigs', the great majority of whose members were Dissenting schoolmasters and ministers, most of them identifiably Arian or Socinian: James Burgh, Philip Furneaux, Andrew Kippis, Richard Price, Joseph Priestley, and the Americans Benjamin Franklin and Josiah Quincy, Jr.[178] A devotional focus was provided by the Unitarian chapel which Lindsey opened, at first illegally, in Essex Street,[179] its services based on Samuel Clarke's revised Prayer Book. It also enjoyed the support of those who stopped short of full Unitarianism, like the Arian Price, and its congregation included at different times a wide range of radicals and reformers, including Benjamin Franklin, the 3rd Duke of Grafton and the 3rd Duke of Richmond.[180] With these Unitarian radicals were associated three great causes: the attack on religious tests; American independence; and parliamentary reform.

When opposition Whigs returned to the issue of parliamentary reform from the mid 1750s, as in Richard Beckford's City weekly *The Monitor*, it was still within a Harringtonian context: measures against bribery and placemen, a repeal of the Septennial Act and a redistribution of seats to offset

[178] V. W. Crane, 'The Club of Honest Whigs', *WMQ* 23 (1966), 210–33.
[179] Whether its close proximity to the Grecian Tavern was coincidence is unclear.
[180] Robbins, *Commonwealthman*, pp. 329–30.

ministerial influence over small boroughs. No democratic impetus was evident: property qualifications for MPs were strongly urged as a guarantee of their independence, the extension of the county franchise to copyholders resisted, a proposal floated to raise the freeholder franchise to £40, and an easy endorsement offered of the variegated franchises of the boroughs.[181] Plans for parliamentary reform were, in general, launched in the 1760s from quarters preserving a link with earlier heterodoxy. The Dissenting minister, Socinian and republican Richard Baron,[182] friend of Gordon and admirer of Collins, published a scheme in the London newspapers in 1765 calling for an increase in county members as a remedy for corruption. His friend Thomas Hollis backed it; Archdeacon Blackburne thought it did not go far enough.[183] Such plans evoked little reaction either at Westminster or in the country at large. But for radicals of the 1760s they performed a great service. They gave the vacuous and sometimes hysterical moralising rhetoric of the 1750s a specific, concrete and apparently realistic application.

Plans for parliamentary reform were, therefore, persisted in for half a century during which they had no prospect of success. They related to no sense of widespread concrete grievance, and they appealed to no social strata identified in their own perception by material self-interest.[184] In the 1760s, before the acceptance of the idea of a class-based society, pro- and anti-ministerial candidates were supported at the polls by voters whose occupational and social composition was generally indistinguishable.[185] Until this changed, Burke's analysis had great force:

On what grounds do we go to restore our constitution to what it has been at some given period, or to reform and reconstruct it upon principles more conformable to a sound theory of government? A prescriptive government, such as ours, never was the work of any legislator, never was made upon any foregone theory. It seems to me a preposterous way of reasoning, and a perfect confusion of ideas, to take the theories which learned and speculative men have made from that government, and then, supposing it made on those theories which were made from it, to accuse the government as not corresponding with them.[186]

---

[181] M. Peters, 'The "Monitor" on the Constitution, 1755–1765: New Light on the Ideological Origins of English Radicalism', *EHR* 86 (1971), 706–27.

[182] Richard Baron (d. 1766). Born Leeds; Glasgow univ. 1737–40; became Dissenting minister 1753 in London. Friend of Thomas Gordon; edited his tracts as *A Cordial for Low-Spirits* 1751; ed. *The Pillars of Priestcraft and Orthodoxy Shaken* (1752, 1767); Sidney's *Discourse Concerning Government*, 1751; Milton's prose works, 1753; Ludlow's *Memoirs* 1751; Nedham's *Excellencie of a Free State*, 1767.

[183] Robbins, *Commonwealthman*, p. 261; *Hollis Memoirs*, vol. I, 321–2.

[184] The attempt to identify an objective social base for 'reform' from the 1760s in the rise of the middle class, in possible alliance with 'the country gentlemen, pining for their old seventeenth-century pre-eminence' (Cannon, *Parliamentary Reform*, p. 52) is completely unproven.

[185] J. A. Phillips, *Electoral Behaviour in Unreformed England* (Princeton, 1982), p. 268.

[186] 'Speech on a Motion made in the House of Commons, May 7, 1782. For a Committee to Inquire into the State of the Representation of the Commons in Parliament', in Burke, *Works*, vol. VII, pp. 96–7. The passage is sometimes quoted by 'Whig' historians of parliamentary reform; but they never allow it to revise the explanatory framework which they bring to the subject.

There was no 'objective' case for reform, and the economic structure of society did not – could not – provide one. Burke was right in seeing that the unreformed parliamentary system was not open to criticism in the light of its own principles; it could only be criticised effectively by the application to it of new principles, and these the Dissenters supplied from theological roots.

In so doing, they evoked from the outset ancient but still vivid fears. The political elite had learned a bitter lesson from the populism of the 1640s. When the Stamp Act raised the question of American taxation in 1765–6, the logical alternative to 'virtual representation' was at once in the public mind: 'This doctrine of universal representation', as a correspondent put it in the *Public Advertiser* of 3rd February 1766, 'utterly overthrows the present happy constitution of Great Britain, destroys all order, degree and subordination in the state, and makes the fabric of society a ruin and a heap of rubbish.'[187] If such were, on the establishment side, the perceived consequences, it followed that men would need a powerful incentive to embrace the principle of universal suffrage. This the American crisis of itself failed to provide. Instead, from the 1770s it prompted a closing of the ranks on the part of the nobility and gentry, and American independence in due course actually removed from debate an example by comparison with which the franchise in Britain might be held to be anomalous.[188] Englishmen predisposed to a radical position on reform questions took a predictably pro-American stance; but the intellectual origins of their radicalism were self-sufficiently English. Thus it was that parliamentary reforming schemes were formulated in the late 1760s by radical intellectuals in the circle of Archdeacon Blackburne – Jebb, Luther, Fleming, Lindsey – and reissued in 1774 as *A Collection of Letters and Essays in Favour of Public Liberty*.[189]

The definitive statement of the reforming case was, however, provided by a Dissenter: the schoolmaster James Burgh. His *Political Disquisitions* appeared in three volumes in 1774–5, the fruit of years of laborious compilation. Much of it was the reverse of original, consisting of extracts from authors of the previous century, mostly in the Commonwealth tradition,[190] in favour of public liberty. It stood at the end of a tradition,

---

[187] Quoted in Brewer, *Party Ideology*, p. 211.

[188] Professor Brewer (*Party Ideology*, pp. 201–16) argued that a process of 'ideological contamination' explains the English adoption of reforming ideas from America at this time, and that the Americans thus 'acted as an ideological midwife, bringing into the political world a qualitatively different sort of reform'. But Englishmen thus contaminated have not yet been identified, and figures like Burgh must be placed within their proper context of Dissenting political ideology. Schemes of parliamentary reform had been discussed for many decades; what was new at this point was a Dissenting emphasis on personality as the proper basis of entitlement to the franchise, and this did not derive from an American example.   [189] Robbins, *Commonwealthman*, pp. 327–8.

[190] He included a few Tories. Just as late-eighteenth-century conservatives assimilated Nonjurors into their rationale for the defence of the State, so radicals enlisted Walpole's Tory critics into their radical pantheon.

and summed it up. Burgh looked back over early-eighteenth-century political corruption and 'a succession of pretended patriots', lamenting the progress of national degeneracy and looking to constitutional re-arrangements for a check both to executive tyranny and the corruption of manners. He wrote, he claimed, 'in the spirit of a true independent Whig', which Gordon had defined; he sought only the restoration of the constitution. Burgh's prophecies of the 1740s about the enervating effects of luxury, which the triumphs of the Seven Years' War had stilled, were brought forward once more in a warning of impending national disaster (soon, fortuitously, given substance). But the theology of his associates Price and Priestley now produced a new element. The early-eighteenth-century Dissenting doctrine that authority ascends from below began to take on democratic overtones.

All lawful authority, legislative, and executive, originates from the people. Power in the people is like light in the sun, native, original, inherent and unlimited by any thing human. In governors, it may be compared to the reflected light of the moon; for it is only borrowed, delegated, and limited by the intention of the people, whose it is, and to whom governors are to consider themselves as responsible, while the people are answerable only to God; themselves being the losers, if they pursue a false scheme of politics.

Consequently, 'I assert, that, saving the laws of prudence, and of morality, the people's mere absolute, sovereign will and pleasure, is a sufficient reason for their making any alteration in their form of government.'

This high theory began to have a practical application. Emerging through and out of older views about the representation of property was a new stress on the need for a wider franchise. Since almost all paid taxes; since even the poor owned some property and had material interests, claimed Burgh, they contributed to government and stood to lose by its actions. 'The people', an undefined concept, should be included within the electorate and defended from corrupt influences by secret ballot. Most of Burgh's attention was still focussed, within a tripartite constitution of King, Lords and Commons, on schemes for shorter parliaments, eliminating placemen, and the redistribution of seats to reflect wealth and taxation; but without clearly enunciating the doctrine of universal manhood suffrage, his ideas pointed in that direction, and did so in the context of a Trenchard-and-Gordon-like assault on the hereditary rulers of society.[191] Already, Dissenting intellectuals had formulated a theory of reform too extreme for the political nation.

The Pitt–Temple–Beckford group took up the issue of parliamentary reform in the 1768 general election as a stick to beat the government, but evoked no popular response.[192] William Beckford used the Wilkes affair in

---

[191] J. Burgh, *Political Disquisitions: or, An Enquiry into Public Errors, Defects, and Abuses* (3 vols., London, 1774–5), vol. I, pp. v, xii, xvi, 3–4, 37–9, 82, 130, 178, 403; vol. III, p. 278; cf. Ian R. Christie, *Wilkes, Wyvill and Reform* (London, 1962), pp. 53–7.

[192] Christie, *Wilkes, Wyvill and Reform*, pp. 18–24; Cannon, *Parliamentary Reform*, pp. 53ff.

1769 as the vehicle for the continued agitation of the issue, but failed to enlist other opposition groups in its support – the Rockinghams and Grenvilles. Politicians in general were reluctant to involve themselves with so extreme a body as the Society of Supporters of the Bill of Rights, or its dubious activists, especially its chief founder, the Rev. John Horne, whose Anglican orders seemed ever more anomalous.[193] The SSBR split in 1771, and Chatham's declaration in favour of triennial parliaments that year was ineffectual. The base of radicalism in the 1774 general election was revealed as limited to London.[194] And the American war had a profound effect on the course of radicalism, revealing the ultimate aim of Dissenting heterodoxy as an assault on the Anglican-monarchical principle. It can best be illustrated through an examination of the works of Tom Paine.

VII. TOM PAINE AND WILLIAM GODWIN

The Seven Years' War had a strikingly similar effect on political ideologies on both sides of the Atlantic. In England, the Stuart option was definitively removed, and an ancient ideological polarity finally disintegrated. In the American colonies, the threat posed by the divine-right monarchies of France to the north and Spain to the south was eliminated. Americans, like British radicals, were released from a strategic imperative which had made them such vociferous loyalists to the Hanoverian regime. Colonists could now safely – indeed profitably – begin to demand the restitution of traditional 'rights' that had been supposedly infringed by English ministries, and Commonwealth rhetoric, especially about the independence of subordinate legislatures, was given new scope. But it was not until relatively late that this traditional idiom was transformed into a new, virulently radical, one. The demand for 'no taxation without representation' was, initially, a demand for 'no taxation', not a claim for seats at Westminster, still less an assertion of American independence. Yet the American question was undoubtedly converted from a debate over 'ways and means' to a question of high principle. The route taken by the debate was mapped out for Americans first and foremost by Tom Paine.

The case for the specifically Christian character of political obligation, and for the divine sanction of monarchical government, commanded a powerful following into the 1770s. Paine recognised this in devoting the greater part of his tract *Common Sense* (1776) to an attack on the ideology of monarchical legitimism. The heart of the pamphlet is not an exposition

---

[193] 'It is true I have suffered the infectious hand of a bishop to be waved over me; whose imposition, like the sop given to Judas, is only a signal for the devil to enter...but I hope I have escaped the contagion': Rev. John Horne to Wilkes, 3rd Jan. 1766: Alexander Stephens, *Memoirs of John Horne Tooke* (2 vols., London, 1813), vol. i, p. 76.

[194] Ian R. Christie, 'The Wilkites and the General Election of 1774', in *Myth and Reality*, pp. 244–60.

either of republicanism or of democracy as such, for his acquaintance with both was largely academic. Nor did he give an account of colonial grievances. Rather Paine sought to justify independence by arguing against the non-contractual nature of monarchical allegiance. This was necessary, he believed, since 'the government of England is nearly as monarchical as that of France or Spain': the Crown was the 'overbearing part in the English constitution...though we have been wise enough to shut and lock a door against absolute monarchy, we at the same time have been foolish enough to put the Crown in possession of the key':

> ...the *will* of the king is as much the *law* of the land in Britain as in France, with this difference, that instead of proceeding directly from his mouth, it is handed to the people under the most formidable shape of an act of parliament. For the fate of Charles the First, hath only made kings more subtle – not more just.

Paine accepted, too, the moral basis of the State: 'Government, like dress, is the badge of lost innocence'; hence 'the necessity, of establishing some form of government to supply the defect of moral virtue'. Educated as a Quaker, he was committed to a view of the individual's direct access to the Deity: 'But where says some is the King of America? I'll tell you Friend, he reigns above'. Paine therefore professed to condemn 'the idolatrous homage which is paid to the persons of kings' as an invasion of 'the prerogative of heaven'.

How then did kingly government arise? If by lot, argued Paine, as in the case of Saul, then that 'establishes a precedent for the next, which excludes hereditary succession'. Nor could it arise by a social contract, for the contractors could not bind their successors in future ages:

> ...for to say, that the *right* of all future generations is taken away, by the act of the first electors, in their choice not only of a king, but of a family of kings forever, hath no parallel in or out of scripture but the doctrine of original sin, which supposes the free will of all men lost in Adam; and from such comparison, and it will admit of no other, hereditary succession can derive no glory. For as in Adam all sinned, and as in the first electors all men obeyed; as in the one all mankind were subjected to Satan, and in the other to sovereignty; as our innocence was lost in the first, and our authority in the last; and as both disable us from re-assuming some former state and privilege, it unanswerably follows that original sin and hereditary succession are parallels. Dishonourable rank! Inglorious connexion! Yet the most subtle sophist cannot produce a juster simile.

It was a penetrating insight, but it went far to destroy Paine's case among those of his readers who entertained the doctrine of original sin. In order to maintain, as he wished to do in the rest of his pamphlet, that monarchy was undesirable in a utilitarian sense, Paine had therefore to argue directly that kingship was not of divine institution. The second section of the work, 'Of Monarchy and Hereditary Succession', occupies a crucial place in the argument; and the idiom was an ancient one. It might have been written fifty years earlier. For although Paine advanced in a perfunctory way the argument that the division of mankind into kings and subjects 'cannot be justified on the equal rights of nature', the bulk of the section is an argument from scriptural texts in the ancient manner of politico-theological controversy. Against Matthew 22:21, with all that it implied, Paine advanced Judges 8 – Gideon refusing to be elected king – and I Samuel 8 and 13 – the nation of Israel asking Samuel to appoint a king despite God's explicit warnings.[195]

These portions of scripture are direct and positive. They admit of no equivocal construction. That the Almighty hath here entered his protest against monarchical government is true, or the scripture is false. And a man hath good reason to believe that there is as much of king-craft, as priest-craft in withholding the scripture from the public in Popish countries. For monarchy in every instance is the Popery of government.

Paine's positive prescription was once again the weak point in his argument, for Gideon and Samuel had contended for a theocracy, not a democracy, whereas Paine contended that 'As to religion, I hold it to be the indispensable duty of all government, to protect all conscientious professors thereof, and I know of no other business which government hath to do therewith.' But this flaw was unimportant, since what was effective in *Common Sense* was its negative aspect. Breaking the tie of monarchical allegiance was the crucial step in the intellectual viability of the idea of American independence.[196]

It was the monarchy, too, which was the direct object of attack in America, and, where George III insisted that he was fighting Parliament's battle, the American critique focussed on the person of the sovereign. If the presence of the Anglican Church in many states was minimal, the Orthodox doctrine of Church-and-State as a divinely sanctioned, non-contractual body was seen in a stark light when applied to the monarchy alone. There seems little doubt that Paine's polemic was effective, in colonial minds, and perceived as directed against kingship itself. William Jones gave, as one cause of the American rebellion, the failure of the British government to introduce bishops into the colonies.[197] It is not necessary to suppose that such a step in the 1760s would have averted what occurred in order to recognise the force of the analysis.

---

[195] For a reply to this argument, cf. Rev. John Whitaker, *The Real Origin of Government* (London, 1795), pp. 27–8.

[196] T. Paine, *Common Sense* (Philadelphia, 1776; ed. I Kramnick, Harmondsworth, 1976), pp. 66–7, 70–81, 98, 108–9. The account given here, emphasising religion, is at odds with Professor Kramnick's Introduction. There Paine appears, like Adam Smith, primarily as the spokesman of the material interests of the rising middle class, the proponent of 'liberal bourgeois values'. 'Nowadays', Professor Kramnick assures us, 'Tom Paine societies abound in America and England.'

[197] W. Jones, 'An Address to the British Government on a Subject of Present Concern. 1776' in *The Theological and Miscellaneous Works of the Rev. William Jones* (6 vols., London, 1810), vol. VI, pp. 268–74; quoted Wilde, 'Hutchinsonianism', p. 10.

By 1791–2, when Paine published the two parts of *Rights of Man* (seen through the press by the Unitarian Lindsey), the target was different.[198] No longer was the critique levelled so specifically against the monarchy, but rather against a system of government which had, in Paine's eyes, been wholly permeated by the principles of monarchy. Burke was accused of building a 'political church' on 'parliamentary clauses', the wording of the Acts and declarations of the Revolution settlement. To establish the continuity of monarchical legitimacy in 1688–9, Burke had cited the Lords' and Commons' address to William and Mary: that, in the name of the people of England, they 'most humbly and faithfully submit themselves, their heirs and posterities, for ever'. This, claimed Paine, amounted to an absolutism no less complete than that of James II. It amounted to 'governing beyond the grave...the most ridiculous and insolent of all tyrannies. Man has no property in man.'

Mr Burke talks about what he calls an hereditary crown, as if it were some production of nature; or as if, like time, it had a power to operate, not only independently, but in spite of man; or as if it were a thing or a subject universally consented to. Alas! it has none of those properties, but is the reverse of them all.

The 'offence for which James II was expelled, that of setting up power by *assumption*', was repeated by William III's first Parliament, and, by implication, by the English State in the 1790s also. It was as if Paine wrote against the Nonjurors.

Despite its title, Paine's book contained only the most elementary theory of natural rights. Although its author displayed a detailed knowledge of recent American and French history, and of public finance, he did not obviously draw on the long natural rights tradition. Talk of 'rights' was merely the new idiom in which Paine made some old points about the origin of legitimate government, derived from the origin of man. Burke's arguments from precedent, he challenged, must be carried back 'all the way, till we come to the divine origin of the rights of man at the creation'. Men were created equal; therefore, in all ages, 'men are born equal, and with equal natural right'. Kings, parliaments, magistrates, priests, nobility, all lauded by Burke, were described as 'barriers' between man and 'his Maker'. Such institutions arose initially as 'a government of priestcraft' in which 'a set of artful men pretended, through the medium of oracles, to hold intercourse with the Deity'.

After these a race of conquerors arose, whose government, like that of William the Conqueror, was founded in power, and the sword assumed the name of a sceptre. Governments thus established, last as long as the power to support them lasts; but that they might avail themselves of every engine in their favour, they united fraud to force, and set up an idol which they called *Divine Right*, and which, in imitation

---

[198] T. Paine, *Rights of Man* (London, 1791–2; ed. H. Collins, Harmondsworth, 1969).

of the Pope, who affects to be spiritual and temporal, and in contradiction to the Founder of the Christian religion, twisted itself afterwards into an idol of another shape, called *Church and State*. The key of St Peter, and the key of the Treasury, became quartered on one another, and the wondering cheated multitude worshipped the invention.

It was blasphemy as well as tyranny: 'We can all see the absurdity of worshipping Aaron's molten calf, or Nebuchadnezzar's golden image; but why do men continue to practise themselves the absurdities they despise in others?' A rational constitution, newly established by social contract, was the answer.

Even in *Rights of Man*, the great bulk of the volume, and the heart of the argument, is taken up not with an exposition of the theory or practice of democracy, but with a denunciation of the two central features of ancien regime governments, including England's: the hereditary principle, underpinning monarchy and aristocracy,[199] and 'priestcraft', offering a divine sanction for authority and hierarchy. Hence the importance of Voltaire, whose 'forte lay in exposing and ridiculing the superstitions which priestcraft united with statecraft had interwoven with governments'. Paine's debts to an English intellectual tradition were contracted in great part via Voltaire, with the English Deist onslaught on the Church in the 1720s and 30s.[200] As Paine committed himself more and more bitterly against European regimes which defined themselves ever more clearly in religious terms, the element of theological heterodoxy assumed an even greater prominence in his work. The restrained and sceptical view of human nature professed in *Common Sense* gave way to a militant secularism. Not Christ, but world revolution, would produce 'a Regeneration of man'.[201]

Such views led Paine on to *The Age of Reason*, which was to become a classic for nineteenth-century atheists. For although it did not explicitly reject belief in a Deity, it poured scorn on all the doctrines which gave Him a familiar and accessible form. All churches were 'human inventions set up to terrify and enslave mankind, and monopolize power and profit'. All revealed religion was rejected, together with the doctrines of Christianity. The Incarnation was denied. Christ was merely 'a virtuous and an amiable man', a 'virtuous reformer and revolutionist'. The doctrines of the Resurrection and the Atonement fell similarly. The Bible was not of divine authority, he claimed. All its apparent flaws and inconsistencies were

---

[199] For sections of the work read in court at the trial of Hardy in 1794, cf. H. Twiss, *The Public and Private Life of Lord Chancellor Eldon*, 2nd edn (3 vols., London, 1844), vol. 1, pp. 245–6: 'A general revolution in the principle and constitution of governments is necessary...All hereditary government is in its nature tyranny', etc.

[200] Paine later wrote that he 'never read Locke nor ever had the work in my hand': quoted Introduction, p. 13.

[201] *Rights of Man* pp. 62–5, 87–9, 91–2, 99, 116, 136, 144. The editor observed that interest in Paine had 'powerfully revived' during the 1960s (p. 46).

savagely exposed: it was 'the stupid Bible of the church, that teaches man nothing'; 'the grovelling tales and doctrines of the Bible and Testament are fit only to excite contempt'. God existed, but only as an abstract First Cause. Addison was quoted with approval. The only honourable religion was Deism.

It must have been the first and will probably be the last that man believes. But pure and simple Deism does not answer the purpose of despotic governments. They cannot lay hold of religion as an engine but by mixing it with human inventions, and making their own authority a part; neither does it answer the avarice of priests, but by incorporating themselves and their functions with it, and becoming, like the government, a party in the system. It is this that forms the otherwise mysterious connection of Church and State; the Church human, and the State tyrannic.[202]

A pious-sounding attempt to sever the union of Church and State in *Common Sense* was one thing; a sneering assault on revealed religion itself was quite another. Back in America from 1802 to his death in 1809, Paine was ostracised.

In early-eighteenth-century England, Arians and Socinians had been in the forefront of the attack on radical Deists. This had faded with the decline of Deism itself after c. 1740, and 'rational Christians' had increasingly professed a wish to make common cause. Now, Priestley, Lindsey and Wakefield, among others, joined in the denunciation of Paine's *Age of Reason*.[203] It was too late: heterodox nostrums of 'all one struggle' had been too widely taken at their word. In England in the 1790s, Paine's creed was not without effect. As Leslie Stephen summarised it: 'kings, like priests, are cheats and impostors. The dawn of the "Age of Reason" implies the disappearance of loyalty from politics as of superstition from religion. Democracy corresponds in one sphere to Deism in the other.'[204] In 1790, Burke had noted that atheist and infidel writers 'who made some noise in their day...repose in lasting oblivion'.

Who, born within the last forty years, has read one word of Collins, and Toland, and Tindal, and Chubb, and Morgan, and that whole race who called themselves freethinkers? Who now reads Bolingbroke? Who ever read him through? Ask the booksellers of London what is become of all these lights of the world.[205]

This was true; but his dismissal of radical Deism was premature. It reawoke with Paine, in whom 'Democracy and infidelity have embraced',[206] and reached its logical conclusion with Godwin in atheism and anarchism.

[202] T. Paine, *The Age of Reason. Being an Investigation of True and Fabulous Theology* (part 1, Paris, 1794; part 2, London, 1795), ed. M. D. Conway, (London, 1896), pp. 22, 26, 28, 32–3, 42–3, 47–8, 184–95.
[203] J. E. Cookson, *The Friends of Peace. Anti-War Liberalism in England, 1793–1815* (Cambridge, 1982), p. 35.
[204] Stephen, *English Thought*, vol. II, p. 222.
[205] Burke, *Reflections on the Revolution in France*, in *Works*, vol. III, p. 349.
[206] Stephen, *English Thought*, vol. I, p. 387.

Outright atheism had been a rare phenomenon in the eighteenth century. Dr Johnson, in 1775, reported as credible a Quaker friend's opinion that there were not more than two hundred 'infidels' in England;[207] and such men typically kept their opinions to themselves. Deism was the most advanced position that could be admitted to, or that it was considered possible to argue for. In the 1790s, this changed profoundly. Under the impact of French ideas and example, Deism declined to something indistinguishable from infidelity; and self-confessed atheism arose as a philosophical position. William Godwin,[208] educated at the Dissenting Academy at Hoxton under the Socinian Kippis, took heterodoxy to its final conclusion. With Godwin, atheism and materialism meant that political speculation revolving around metaphysical 'rights' was wholly superseded by utilitarian calculations. Seen from such a perspective, previous rationales for government resolved themselves into three: intellectual or physical force; *jure divino*, by divine institution; and the social contract. Godwin rejected them all. The majority vote of individuals, acting through their representatives, was the only true guide to public utility.[209]

VIII. RICHARD PRICE AND JOSEPH PRIESTLEY

The political theory of militant Deism, descending to atheism, has been illustrated from the writings of Paine and Godwin. The downward progress of Arianism into Socinianism can equally be illustrated in the persons of Price and Priestley.

Unlike Trinitarian Anglicans, the Arian Price's political philosophy was not built around an account of the origin of the State, but derived from a moral theory of the autonomy of the individual. Original sin was rejected as inconsistent with free will. Restraint on the individual conscience was thus a definition of arbitrary power. Free will was identified as good by the individual's obligation to pursue his religion as his private judgement led him: a concept of natural *rights* thus filled the vacuum created by the disappearance of Christian *obligation*.[210] Civil liberty in general seemed to follow from Price's preoccupation with religious liberty. Authority was not acquired by inheritance or divine right. The independence, in this sense, of the individual meant the equality of all individuals; hence the familiar Whig nostrums about the English Parliament acquired a new and vivid

---

[207] Boswell, *Life of Johnson*, p. 623.

[208] W. Godwin (1756–1836). Son and grandson of Dissenting ministers; ed. at Hoxton Academy 1775–8; 1778 became Dissenting minister in Herts. 1783 left ministry. Atheist by 1787. Present at Price's sermon, 4th Nov. 1789. *Enquiry Concerning the Principles of Political Justice* 1793; *Caleb Williams* 1794; received sinecure from Grey's government, 1833.

[209] W. Godwin, *Enquiry Concerning Political Justice* (ed. I. Kramnick, Harmondsworth, 1976), pp. 209–35.

[210] Richard Price, *A Review of the Principal Questions and Difficulties in Morals* (London, 1758).

significance. The representation of 'the people' meant the representation of individuals; the Lower House, removed from its old context within the English Trinity of King, Lords and Commons, was suddenly revealed as having one function: as a system of representative democracy. A state will be free, he announced, 'in proportion as it is more or less fairly and adequately represented'. Such an opinion, he wrote in 1776, would be 'very absurd' if authority had a divine origin, independent of popular choice: but Locke had refuted those theories.[211]

If that was his belief, Price must have been horrified to find his *Observations* attacked on just such grounds. 'Mankind', he replied in 1777, were created with a God-given right to 'equality or independence'; governments

...which are not free, are totally inconsistent with it. They imply, that there are some of mankind who are born with an inherent right of dominion; and that the rest are born under an obligation to subjection; and that civil government, instead of being founded on any compact, is nothing but the exercise of this right. Some such sentiments seem to be now reviving in this country, and even to be growing fashionable. Most of the writers against the *Observations on Civil Liberty* argue on the supposition of a right in the *few* to govern the *many*, independently of their own choice. Some of these writers have gone so far as to assert, in plain language, that civil governors derive their power immediately from the Deity, and are *his* agents or representatives, accountable to him only.

Price was incredulous with radical indignation: 'Must we embrace Sir Robert Filmer's Patriarchal scheme? One would have thought, that Mr Locke has said more than enough to expose this stupid scheme.' Its principles were 'absurd' and 'pernicious'. 'I say, pernicious; for they imply, that King James the Second was deposed at the Revolution unlawfully and impiously; that the present king is an usurper; and that the present government, being derived from rebellion and treason, has no right to our allegiance.'[212] Divine right once rejected, the basis of legitimate government became far more literally contractarian; and the relation of Westminster to subordinate legislatures became fraught with difficulty. Colonial independence was justified by reference to the Commonwealthman William Molyneux (1656–98) and his classic *The Case of Ireland's Being Bound by Acts of Parliament in England Stated* of 1698. Price thus hailed America as a 'rising empire, extended over an immense continent, without BISHOPS, – without NOBLES, – and without KINGS'.[213]

---

[211] R. Price, *Observations on the Nature of Civil Liberty, the Principles of Government, and the Justice and Policy of the War with America* (London, 1776), pp. 10, 16. The *Anti-Jacobin* later recalled that it was this tract which 'contributed very much to the spreading among the Dissenters (the Socinians at least) of those democratic principles to which Socinians are so prone': quoted in Anthony Lincoln, *Some Political & Social Ideas of English Dissent 1763–1800* (Cambridge, 1938), p. 48.

[212] R. Price, *Additional Observations on the Nature and Value of Civil Liberty, and the War with America* (London, 1777), pp. 22–3, 25–6. He returned to the theme in the introduction to his republication of these two works, *Two Tracts on Civil Liberty* (London, 1778).

[213] C. B. Cone, *Torchbearer of Freedom. The Influence of Richard Price on Eighteenth Century Thought* (Lexington, 1952), p. 87.

The 1780s thus reactivated the issues of the 1680s. A contractarian right of resistance, from 1689 to 1760, was scarcely a disruptive doctrine: only Jacobites were likely to overthrow the regime, and they rarely resorted to Whig arguments to attack it. After 1760, the Hanoverian monarchy itself began to be threatened by this claim of right, both by American rebellion and domestic radicalism. This was especially evident in the propaganda of the Society for Commemorating the Revolution in Great Britain. The Dissenters and radicals who delivered addresses on its chosen festival, the birthday of William III, said nothing new. But a reactivated religious dynamic gave a new radical impetus to conventional formulae about the rights of Englishmen, particularly the right of resistance and the Protestant right of private judgement in matters of religion, levelled against 'priestcraft' and 'tyranny' by Arians like Towers and Socinians like Kippis.[214] The apogee in this minor art form was reached by Price himself, whose flights of oratory on 4th November 1789 led him to associate the aims and means of 1688 with those of the revolutionaries in France. It was this revolutionary re-interpretation of the Whig tradition which led Price to draw a practical conclusion from his platitudes: an assertion of the 'right to chuse our governors; to cashier them for misconduct; and to frame a government for ourselves'.

Price found an even more effective way of arguing the inadequacy of the Revolution settlement, and which, if remedied, pointed towards his asserted right of cashiering:

But the most important instance of the imperfect state in which the Revolution left our constitution, is the INEQUALITY OF OUR REPRESENTATION. I think, indeed, this defect in our constitution so gross and so palpable, as to make it excellent chiefly in form and theory. You should remember that a representation in the legislature of a kingdom is the *basis* of constitutional liberty in it, and of all legitimate government; and that without it a government is nothing but an usurpation.

The example of the French revolution was a tempting one to atheist and Dissenter alike. Parliamentary reform, from being a means of promoting civic virtue, had become a means of launching a radical assault on Church and King, the Anglican-aristocratic hegemony.

The spectacle of France persuaded Price of 'a general amendment beginning in human affairs; the dominion of kings changed for the dominion of laws, and the dominion of priests giving way to the dominion of reason and conscience'.[215] Such language brought him close to the position of the aggressive Socinian, Priestley. Born, like Price, of Calvinist parents, Priestley

---

[214] Cf. Andrew Kippis, *A Sermon Preached at the Old Jewry, on the Fourth of November, 1788* (London, 1788); Joseph Towers, *An Oration Delivered at the London Tavern, on the Fourth of November 1788* (London, 1788).

[215] R. Price, *A Discourse on the Love of Our Country, Delivered on Nov. 4, 1789, at the Meeting-House in the Old Jewry* (London, 1789), pp. 34, 39, 50. He printed as an appendix the French National Assembly's *Declaration of the Rights of Men and of Citizens*.

was educated in that tradition; embraced Arianism at the age of 20, in 1753, and Socinianism 'soon' after moving to Leeds, as a Dissenting minister, in 1767. This second conversion he attributed to reading Nathaniel Lardner's *Letter...Concerning...the Logos* (1758), and 'I was greatly confirmed in this doctrine after I was fully satisfied that man is of an uniform composition, and wholly mortal; and that the doctrine of a separate immaterial soul, capable of sensation and action when the body is in the grave, is a notion borrowed from Heathen philosophy, and unknown to the Scriptures.' Hartley's *Observations on Man* (1749) 'established me in the belief of the doctrine of necessity, which I first learned from Collins' – hence Priestley's republication of the Deist Collins's *Philosophical Inquiry Concerning Human Liberty* in 1790. Physics and theology went together. Priestley's materialism led to an identification of mind, soul and brain. Destroyed at death, resurrection meant its physical reassembly by Divine power. There was no sense, therefore, in the idea of the pre-existence of two of the three Persons of the Trinity: 'that man is wholly material is eminently subservient to the doctrine of the proper, or mere humanity of Christ...it is my firm persuasion, that the three doctrines of materialism, of what is commonly called Socinianism, and of philosophical necessity, are equally parts of one system'.[216]

Priestley thus re-opened questions that Hutchinson had raised, and a controversy with George Horne was one result. Another was an attack on monarchical politics, anticipating the arguments expressed with greater crudity and violence in Paine's *Common Sense*, in Priestley's *An Essay on the First Principles of Government, and on the Nature of Political, Civil and Religious Liberty*, published at the time of his conversion to Socinianism. Although Priestley there made a brief gesture to the Lockeian account of the origins of the State by contract among unconnected individuals in a state of nature, it filled no important place in the argument, which displayed both a preoccupation with religion, and a marked millenarian impulse: 'whatever was the beginning of this world, the end will be glorious and *paradisiacal*, beyond what our imaginations can now conceive'.[217] Most of the tract concerned the Church, and Priestley organised his analysis of liberty around that preoccupation. 'The most important question concerning the extent of civil government', he claimed, 'is, whether the civil magistrate ought to extend his authority to matters of religion.'[218] A complete severing of Warburton's *Alliance* was demanded. The target was divine right:

I can conceive no method whatever, in which the civil magistrate can be invested with ecclesiastical power, or ecclesiastics with civil power, so that a conscientious

---

[216] J. T. Rutt (ed.), *The Theological and Miscellaneous Works of Joseph Priestley* (25 vols., London, [1817–31]), vol. I, part 1, pp. 24, 69; vol. XVIII, pp. 40–1; vol. III, p. 220.
[217] J. Priestley, *An Essay on the First Principles of Government, and on the Nature of Political, Civil and Religious Liberty* (London, 1768) in *Works*, vol. XXII, pp. 9, 10.   [218] *Ibid.*, p. 54.

Christian shall consider himself as under any obligation to yield them obedience in their new character.[219]

Priestley claimed to be incredulous that anyone could still think in these terms:

Nothing can more justly excite the indignation of an honest and oppressed citizen, than to hear a prelate, who enjoys a considerable benefice, under a corrupt government, pleading for its support by those abominable perversions of scripture, which have been too common on this occasion; as by urging in its favour that passage of St Paul, 'The powers that be, are ordained of God', and others of a similar import. It is a sufficient answer to such an absurd quotation as this, that, for the same reason, the powers which *will be* will be ordained of God also.

Such doctrines might once have served a useful purpose against 'wild enthusiasts',

...but to maintain the same absurd principles at this day, when the danger from which they served to shelter us is over, and the heat of controversy is abated, shows the strongest and most blameable prepossession. Writers in defence of them do not deserve a serious answer.[220]

Rather than deal directly with establishment orthodoxy, Priestley wisely took his stand on the purely negative case entailed by Socinianism. Civil officers thus became merely servants of the public, and open to dismissal and punishment by 'the people'; an 'injured and insulted people' might assert their 'natural rights' and alter 'the whole form of their government' if they wished.[221] Once theology had identified the Anglican hegemony as a perversion, Priestley's prescriptions for reform were pushed further to be little short of calls for rebellion. If a '*good* government' is

...one in which sufficient provision is made for the happiness of the subjects of it. If it fail in this essential character, respecting the true end and object of all civil government, no other property or title, with which it may be dignified, ought to shelter it from the generous attack of the noble and daring patriot.[222]

Parliamentary inadequacies were not so much an object of constructive reform as an occasion for revolt:

Whenever the House of Commons shall be so abandonedly corrupt, as to join with the court in abolishing any of the essential forms of the constitution, or effectually defeating the great purposes of it, let every Englishman, before it be too late, re-peruse the history of his country, and do what Englishmen are renowned for having formerly done in the same circumstances.[223]

Yet even the nominal forms of the constitution, argued Priestley, failed to answer their purpose in one essential respect:

The toleration in England, notwithstanding our boasted liberty, is far from being complete. Our present laws do not tolerate those more rational Dissenters, whom

[219] *Ibid.*, p. 85.   [220] *Ibid.*, pp. 19–21.   [221] *Ibid.*, pp. 18–19.
[222] *Ibid.*, pp. 23–4.   [223] *Ibid.*, p. 37.

the Bishop of Gloucester looks upon as brethren. It is known to every body, that if the Toleration Act was strictly put in execution, it would silence all those Dissenting ministers who are held in any degree of esteem by the church; in the same manner as a truly conscientious subscription to the Thirty-nine articles would silence almost all that are rational, and free from enthusiasm, among themselves. It is not the law, but the mildness of the administration, and the spirit of the times, to which we are indebted for our present liberties.[224]

Hence the significance, within a heterodox theological context, of the Feathers Tavern and Dissenters' applications to Parliament. They stood for far more than just a modest constitutional adjustment. A whole millenarian impulse, fuelled by Arianism and Socinianism, lay behind them. As Priestley wrote to Lindsey on 23rd August 1771:

To me every thing looks like the approach of that dismal catastrophe described, I may say predicted, by Dr Hartley, in the conclusion of his Essay, and I shall be looking for the downfall of Church and State together. I am really expecting some very calamitous, but finally glorious, events.[225]

For these he had to wait some time. Eventually, however, the destruction of Europe's most powerful and prestigious regime seemed sufficient confirmation. Priestley met the occasion with *The Present State of Europe Compared with Antient Prophecies* (1794): 'The Declaration of Rights in one hand, and the Book of Revelation in the other, Priestley awaited the imminent fall of the Papacy and the Ottoman Empire and the return of the Jews to Judea.'[226] Even these events, he thought, were merely preliminaries to the Second Coming.[227] The radical chiliasm normally associated only with the French Revolution and its impact in England had a quite different chronological origin: it can be traced to certain developments in English radical theology in the mid and late 1760s.

IX. THE IMPACT OF HETERODOXY, 1772–1800

If the vision of the most influential radicals was increasingly frenzied, the initial reaction of politicians within the establishment was cool. In the debates on the Feathers Tavern petition, North, Fox and Burke reinforced their insistence on doctrinal orthodoxy within the Church by professions of the widest toleration for those outside it. The old laws against anti-Trinitarians were now, in practice, not enforced. This could be a reason for their abrogation, as Burke saw. George III, on the other hand, advanced it as a reason for not agreeing to a Dissenting petition which was evoked in April 1772 by the Anglican one: 'there is no shadow for this petition as

[224] *Ibid.*, p. 96.   [225] *Works*, vol. 1, part 1, p. 146.
[226] Lincoln, *Political & Social Ideas*, p. 173.
[227] Clarke Garrett, 'Joseph Priestley, the Millennium, and the French Revolution', *JHI* 34 (1973), 51–66.

the Crown regularly grants a noli prosequi if any over nice Justice of Peace encourages prosecutions'.[228] With the prospect of a general election making MPs reluctant to offend the Dissenting vote, a Bill to that purpose passed the Commons. In the Lords, Shute Barrington, Bishop of Llandaff, quoted passages from Priestley's writings to show the subversive nature of his doctrines; Richard Terrick, Bishop of London, spoke on behalf of orthodox Dissenters who wished to retain subscription as a defence against Unitarianism. The Bill was lost by 102 to 29.[229] A repeat performance in February and March 1773 found even fewer MPs willing to vote against, with the election still closer; but once more it was defeated in the Lords with only one bishop in favour.

These petitions, Dissenting and Anglican, had clarified the grounds on which the establishment defended itself. It had reacted to radical claims not as a demand for civil liberties *tout court*, not for 'freedom *from*' but for 'freedom *to*' – as a demand impelled by religious heterodoxy. The Bishop of Bristol saw that, if the request were granted,

There would be nothing then that can hinder the revival of all the fanaticism and enthusiasm, of all the heresies and blasphemies which were broached in the last century, and terminated in the ruin of the constitution both in Church and State…It is…improperly entitled a Bill for the relief of Protestant Dissenters. It is more justly and truly a Bill for the public preaching of Arianism, Socinianism, any schism, any heresy that any fanatic or incendiary may advance.[230]

Such defenders of the establishment were taken at their word. Dissenting champions only raised the bidding. Priestley and Price, Williams and Toulmin began to call for the repeal of *all* laws which distinguished between religions. Such demands had to be phrased, therefore, in terms of an appeal by Dissenters not 'as Christians' but 'in the character of men':[231] natural rights became the label under which a Dissenting, democratic, anti-Trinitarian attack was to be launched on the Church-State. Wilkes, moving on 21st March 1776 for leave to bring in a Bill 'for a just and equal representation of the people of England in Parliament', commended Cromwell's reforms together with Dr Price's calculations, and echoed almost exactly the words of James Burgh in defending the personal right of the 'meanest mechanic, the poorest peasant and day labourer' to be 'comprehended in a fair majority' by virtue of having *some* interest in property and liberty, the protection of the individual, and his 'wife, sister or daughter

---

[228] George III to Lord North, 2nd April 1772: Sir John Fortescue (ed.) *The Correspondence of King George the Third* (6 vols., London, 1927–8), vol. II, p. 334.

[229] *Parl Hist*, vol. XVII, cols. 431–46. The Bill was supported by Chatham, Lyttelton, Shelburne and Richmond: oppposition Whigs of the 1730s joined hands with Unitarian reformers of the 1770s.

[230] Thomas Newton, *A Speech Designed for the House of Lords*, quoted in Barlow, *Citizenship and Conscience*, pp. 180–1; *Parl Hist*, vol. XVII, cols. 442–6.

[231] Barlow, *Citizenship and Conscience*, pp. 193–200.

against violence and brutal lust'. North replied, presuming Wilkes was 'not serious', and leave was refused without a division.[232] But new principles were emerging as the basis of reforming claims.

The analogy with the American rebellion was inescapable, and Anglicans did not hesitate to point it out. Roman Catholics, too, seized the occasion of France's recognition of the American republic for a (Trinitarian) declaration of loyalty to George III, and received as a reward the Catholic Relief Act of May 1778.[233] The immediate result was a massive backlash of anti-papist sentiment, originating in Scotland and quickly spreading south of the Border. With the approval of the bench of bishops, the ministry's reaction in March 1779 was a Bill making similar concessions to Protestant Dissenters. Only a handful of MPs opposed, until Lord North, on behalf of Oxford University, proposed the insertion of a declaration of Protestant Christianity as a condition of toleration. Wilkes had commended the Bill, as first introduced, in a way which many Dissenters would have resented: there was no danger of the spread of atheism as a result: 'Deism indeed, Sir, sound pure Deism, has made a rapid progress, not only in this island, but in every part of the continent. It is almost become the religion of Europe. Atheism is certainly not the prevailing, fashionable error of this enlightened age or country, but every year adds to the number of disciples of Deism.' He took the opportunity for a denunciation of the Athanasian creed. Persecution, not Deism, he claimed, caused civil disorder (Sir Roger Newdigate pointed to the stream of Anglican clergy exiled from the colonies as living refutation). Trenchard and Gordon found in John Wilkes their most effective parliamentary spokesman. He now also opposed North's amendment, in a long, theologically well-informed speech echoing the arguments of the Commonwealthmen. 'I deny that the civil magistrate has the least concern with the salvation of souls, or that any power of that nature is delegated to him', he announced. He sang the praises of those 'wise and virtuous citizens... the doctors Price, Priestley and Kippis', over whom 'the iron rod of persecution hangs...by a single thread', but in vain. The amendment passed. North announced: 'As to Deists, and persons denying the Trinity, or professing other singular religious opinions, not being either Christians or Protestants, the Bill had nothing to do with them. But certainly the State had a right to guard against authorizing men, by authority of parliament, to be teachers of their notions.'[234]

By comparison with what the most radical Dissenters were demanding by 1780, the concession of what had been resisted in such principled terms

---

[232] *Parl Hist*, vol. xviii, cols. 1286–98; cf. Burgh, *Political Disquisitions*, vol. i, pp. 37–8. Perhaps Wilkes' eye was caught by Burgh's curious remarks about 'the chastity of their wives and daughters, &c.'; though exactly what threat undemocratic government posed to female virtue was left unclear.

[233] *Parl Hist*, vol. xix, cols. 1137–45.

[234] *Parl Hist*, vol. xx, cols. 239–48, 305–22.

in 1772–3 might have been held to be insignificant, a prudent attempt to disarm orthodox Dissenters. If so, it was less than fully effective, for the running was being made by Dissenting extremists. Kippis encouraged his coreligionists not to subscribe even the minimal declaration required by the Act, and it seems that it was in practice ignored.[235] For the moment, however, the political classes could believe that one aspect of the problem had been solved. Attention swung instead to a form of radicalism which could be adopted within the Anglican nexus by the official Whig opposition.

'Economical reform', the invention of the Rockinghams, represented the ideas of men who had been half persuaded by the Commonwealth tradition: they took from that tradition only what suited their needs. 'Arbitrary power' was proved by George III's exclusion of the Rockinghams from office. The remedy was the minimum necessary to reverse this result: a reduction in monarchical power by the reduction of the numbers of placemen and pensioners in the Commons, and the disfranchisement of revenue officers in the constituencies. Rockingham, Burke and most others in the party were still explicitly opposed to parliamentary reform.[236] As a simple call for economy and honesty in government, economical reform, by contrast, might evoke wide support; but it raised no basic issues. Its counterpart, the Association movement, which began in a familiar Commonwealth idiom,[237] finally did, when the Unitarian Jebb added to its purposes the claim that a national association, composed of delegates of county associations, might dissolve the House of Commons and act in its place as the sovereign body.[238] That authority ascended from below was, of course, the Dissenting reply to the early-eighteenth-century monarchical establishment. The increasing disaffection of Dissent revitalised this position, producing a populist critique of Authority before democracy existed as an ideology in its own right.

Although it took a far more radical direction under the influence of acknowledged Socinians, the Association movement was the brainchild of the Rev. Christopher Wyvill, a 'liberal' Anglican who abandoned his parochial ministry as soon as he married into landed wealth, an admirer of Clarke, Hoadly, John Jones, Jortin, Blackburne and Edmund Law, and a signatory of the Feathers Tavern petition.[239] Radical intellectuals in the

---

[235] Barlow, *Citizenship and Conscience*, pp. 209–10.

[236] Christie, *Wilkes, Wyvill and Reform*, p. 100.

[237] The Yorkshire Association was founded in March 1780 pledged to a triple programme of economical reform, triennial parliaments, and the addition of one hundred county MPs: Ian R. Christie, 'The Yorkshire Association, 1780–4: A Study in Political Organization', in *Myth and Reality*, pp. 261–83.

[238] Herbert Butterfield, *George III, Lord North and the People*, p. 192; J. Disney (ed.), *The Works...of John Jebb* (3 vols., London, 1787), vol. III, pp. 285–9.

[239] C. Wyvill, *A Defence of Dr Price, and the Reformers of England*, 2nd edn (London, 1792), pp. 49ff. He defended the Arian Price, but stopped short of Paine's *Rights of Man*. Wyvill's Unitarian proclivities were pointed out in Christie, *Wilkes, Wyvill and Reform*, p. 71.

circle of Jebb and Cartwright soon stood forward to exploit a promising development. They took a leading part in the debates at the St Albans Tavern at the first national meeting of deputies in March 1780 which attempted to swing the Association movement behind parliamentary reform, though only a minority of the counties endorsed the full programme then drawn up. The way was nevertheless open for the Westminster Association to pursue an even more radical line of its own, proposals appearing under its aegis for annual parliaments elected by manhood suffrage in numerically equal constituencies, demanding the secret ballot and the payment of MPs, and casting doubt on the sanctity of property. Such ideas, propagated from 1780 by Jebb, Cartwright and Lofft through the Society for Constitutional Information, now began to evoke the serious attention of the political classes. Instead of forwarding them, it revealed only the massive extent of opposition. Fox now joined Burke in opposing Sawbridge's yearly motion for annual parliaments, and Richmond's reform Bill, embodying the Westminster Committee proposals for universal manhood suffrage, introduced into the Lords at the singularly inappropriate moment of the Gordon riots in June 1780, was thrown out without a division.[240] Merely theoretical questions of democratic representation were still swamped by religious controversies, and the massive public response they could suddenly evoke.

The failure of Richmond's Bill was to Unitarian–democratic parliamentary reform what the rejection of the Feathers Tavern petition was to Unitarian Church reform. The campaigns had served only to define the proposals as those of an extremist fringe, and they were rejected as such. The doctrines remained within the public arena, but not as practical politics. Political practicality was represented first by economical reform, implemented by the second Rockingham administration in the wake of North's defeat, and aimed at increasing the independence of the Commons from the executive;[241] and, secondly, by the shape which moves for parliamentary reform *did* take in the late 1780s. Associated above all with William Pitt the younger, it represented the last effort of the 'Commonwealth' tradition. The views of his father had been formed as an opposition Whig in the 1730s. Chatham's friend and theoretical mentor Thomas Hollis in turn singled out the young William Pitt for attention in the 1770s, and it was Hollis' tradition to which the younger Pitt was heir. Nor was Chatham wholly out of touch with recent developments: it was Price, via Shelburne, who had induced Chatham to speak in favour of the Dissenters' Bill to abolish subscription on 19th May 1772, accusing the Church of

---

[240] Cannon, *Parliamentary Reform*, pp. 80–4; Christie, *Wilkes, Wyvill and Reform*, pp. 107–15; Jebb, *Works*, vol. III, pp. 403ff.
[241] Ian R. Christie, 'Economical Reform and "The Influence of the Crown", 1780', in *Myth and Reality*, pp. 296–310.

England of possessing 'a Calvinistic creed, a Popish liturgy, and an Arminian clergy'.[242]

William Pitt, an MP at 22, Prime Minister at 24, had little time to progress beyond a 'stock of ideas' which was 'largely inherited' from his father, or drawn from bookish studies of the Whig classics at Cambridge. Thus equipped, however, he had nothing to do with the new form of radicalism represented by the Westminster Association and the Society for Constitutional Information.[243] Pitt's moves for reform were still within the context of Commonwealth ideas of the ancient constitution, repairing defects by restoring a former mythical purity. Even so, his unspecific motion for a committee of enquiry on 7th May 1782 failed to avoid arousing fears of something more fundamental: followers of North and Rockingham voted it down by 161 to 141. On 7th May 1783 Pitt tried again, with specific proposals. He denied a wish to 'innovate', or countenance 'visionary and impracticable ideas'; universal suffrage was explicitly rejected. Rotten boroughs were not to be removed, but their influence offset by the addition of a large number of county MPs. It was an academic gambit, a merely theoretical response. There was no widespread sense of practical grievance which such a scheme might redress. The new industrial towns were silent. Cheap government was enough. Lord North, the defender of the Church in the 1770s, shot down Pitt's scheme, and it failed by 293 to 149. Wyvill, with massive understatement, recognised that the Westminster Association's demand for universal suffrage had been 'a disadvantage to the cause'.[244] On 18th April 1785 Pitt, now leading the ministry, made his last attempt. Lord North, speaking for a majority now sensitised to the far more radical principles to which a Commonwealth scheme might lead, repeated his success: the plan was lost by 248 to 174. Wyvill's Yorkshire Association had already ceased to meet. Commonwealth reform was seemingly at an end.

The implications of the defeat were not immediately apparent. Dissenters took heart from the sight of a Prime Minister willing to promote at least one sort of reform, and voted heavily Pittite in the 1784 general election. Such expectations produced a renewed appeal for the abolition of the Test and Corporation Acts, and an outburst of propaganda to that end.[245] A Bill was introduced on 28th March 1787. Lord North appeared, again, as a chief opponent, arguing that the exclusion from civil office of any category of men

---

[242] W. S. Taylor and J. H. Pringle (eds.), *Correspondence of William Pitt, Earl of Chatham* (4 vols., London, 1838–40), vol. IV, pp. 217–20, 268–70, 273–4, 286–7.

[243] Ehrman, *Pitt*, vol. I, pp. 57, 67, 70.

[244] Quoted Cannon, *Parliamentary Reform*, p. 90.

[245] [J. Disney], *An Arranged Catalogue of the Several Publications which have Appeared Relating to the Enlargement of the Toleration of Protestant Dissenting Ministers and the Repeal of the Corporation and Test Acts* (London, 1790).

was within the State's competence and could not be classed as persecution for conscience' sake:

> If Dissenters claim it as their undoubted, their natural right, to be rendered capable of enjoying offices, and that plea be admitted, the argument may run to all men. The vote of a freeholder for a representative to parliament is confined to those who possess a freehold of 40s. or upwards; and those not possessing that qualification, may call it an usurpation of their right, by preventing them from voting also.

To the Dissenters' dismay, the same argument was used by Pitt, who spoke against. 'Is a man...to be considered as marked with infamy, because he does not vote for a city, a county or a borough?' The existing Acts, he maintained, did not impose a penalty for religious beliefs. They were also necessary, since it was 'impossible to separate the ecclesiastical and political liberties of this country'. It was a matter of expediency, not of the overriding claims of any right.

> The Church and State are united upon principles of expediency; and it concerns those to whom the well-being of the State is intrusted, to take care that the Church should not be rashly demolished...no means can be devised of admitting the moderate part of the Dissenters, and excluding the more violent: the bulwark must be kept against all.

How violent were they? Sir William Dolben now produced evidence from Priestley's writings, especially *The Importance of Free Inquiry in Matters of Religion* (1785) which described the Dissenters as 'wisely placing, as it were, grain by grain, a train of gunpowder, to which the match would, one day, be laid to blow up that fabric which never could be again raised upon the same foundation'. It was sufficient: the Bill failed by 176 to 98.[246]

   More significant even than its defeat was Pitt's disengagement from the reforming cause. Lindsey believed that Pitt and 'all his young friends' had been 'swayed entirely' by the arguments of Bishop Sherlock's classic tract of 1718, *A Vindication of the Corporation and Test Acts*, republished in 1787[247] and 'read over' to Pitt by his former Cambridge tutor Dr Pretyman, recently elevated by his former pupil to the see of Lincoln.[248] Its new edition was dedicated to Pitt himself: 'You have had the singular felicity, Sir, to obtain at once the favour of Prince and People. Take Sherlock for your counsellor, and you will long preserve it. Let the Throne support the Church, the Church support the Throne, and God will support both.'

---

[246] *Parl Hist*, vol. xxvi, cols. 780–832. Burke again reminded the House of Priestley's 'train of gunpowder' in the debate on 2nd March 1790 – *infra*, p. 343.

[247] Under the title *Bishop Sherlock's Arguments against a Repeal of the Corporation and Test Acts* (London, 1787; again reprinted, 1790 and 1827). It seems possible that Pretyman was responsible for its publication.

[248] H. McLachlan (ed.), *Letters of Theophilus Lindsey* (Manchester, 1920), p. 64. If so, few pamphlets in the whole century can have had so decisive a result.

Sherlock had written explicitly against Hoadly; but it was the High Churchman, not the Latitudinarian, to whom the establishment now turned,[249] and Pitt's denial that the sacramental test imposed a penalty for religious belief, or prostituted a religious observance, was at the heart of Sherlock's argument. Moreover, Sherlock had written before the repeal of the Occasional Conformity Act, and his assumptions about a sharp distinction between Church and Dissent, and the political danger of nonconformity, were stronger than those which Dissenters had come to take for granted.

Priestley launched at once into bitter invective in *A Letter to the Right Honourable William Pitt*. The Dissenters, he said, would certainly want more than repeal in order to achieve 'a complete toleration'. His list was described by the *Gentleman's Magazine* as a plan to eliminate 'all New Testament Christianity' from the Church and replace it by

...that of the author of *The History of the Corruptions of Christianity*, by letting Unitarians avow their principles...by abolishing subscriptions in the *stagnant pools* called universities, by turning the bishops out of the House of Lords...and by abolishing tithes and leaving the clergy as much at the mercy of their congregations as the dissenting ministry are.[250]

The defeat of the Bill, and the approach of the anniversary of the Glorious Revolution, raised Dissenting indignation to new heights. This, not a rational calculation of political practicality, led to a second application to the Commons on 8th May 1789. The personalities, the arguments, the results were as before. It was rejected by 122 to 102. Something of the heat had, perhaps, gone out of the issue as the American crisis receded. Had not Oxford High Churchmanship in the person of Lord North been joined in opposing the application by the heir to the Commonwealth tradition, William Pitt, the result might have been different. Dissenters were nevertheless still optimistic about the onward march of 'reason'. In fact, the crucial moment had been missed. Events in France henceforth moved with an increasing pace. The expropriation and destruction of the Roman Catholic establishment appalled Anglicans and was hailed by Dissenters. As the latter moved blithely forward towards yet another demand for the repeal of Test and Corporation Acts, a wave of Anglican meetings in January and February 1790 petitioned for their retention.[251] A loyalist, anti-Jacobin viewpoint crystallised at such a moment that the Acts became embedded in the received account of the structure of the State, as essential guarantors of its stability. When Fox, with disastrous timing, gave notice of a repeal Bill, Pitt replied with a call of the House, and the application

---

[249] The Dissenters replied with a republication of Hoadly's *The Common Rights of Subjects, Defended* (London, 1719), the turgid prose turned into modern English.

[250] *Gentleman's Magazine*, May 1787, quoted in Barlow, *Citizenship and Conscience*, p. 240.

[251] Barlow, *Citizenship and Conscience*, pp. 257–60.

was massively voted down on 2nd March 1790 by 294 to 105. It served no other purpose than to provide a platform for speeches by Pitt and Burke, the latter in particular intervening on the question for the first time to denounce 'abstract principles of natural right – which the Dissenters rested on, as their strong hold' as 'the most idle, because the most useless and the most dangerous to resort to. They superseded society, and broke asunder all those bonds which had formed the happiness of mankind for ages.'[252]

Flood, moving for leave to bring in a reform of Parliament two days later, on 4th March, tried to turn Sherlock against the establishment:

In his treatise on the test and corporation laws, he says, 'That though the dissenters were but a twentieth part of the people, yet if they got into corporations, the petty boroughs being so numerous, they might by them obtain a majority in the House of Commons against the whole nation.' In a word, it is undeniable that a great majority of the House of Commons are under another influence than that of the people.

It was an ironic anticipation of the Ultra response to the events of 1828–9; but, for the moment, the prospect seemed remote. Flood's motion was lost without a division.[253] Debate became even more vitriolic. Burke's *Reflections* chose Price as its spokesman for the radical case. Price's defenders included Paine and Priestley. The latter did little more than reiterate in 1791 the principles which his Socinianism had generated in 1768. He had now, however, a famous opponent.

If the principles that Mr Burke now advances (though it is by no means with perfect consistency) be admitted, mankind are always to be governed as they have been governed, without any inquiry into the nature, or origin, of their governments. The choice of the people is not to be considered, and though their happiness is awkwardly enough made by him the end of government; yet, having no choice, they are not to be the judges of what is for their good. On these principles, the church, or the state, once established, must for ever remain the same. This is evidently the real scope of Mr Burke's pamphlet, the principles of it being, in fact, no other than those of passive obedience and non-resistance, peculiar to the Tories and the friends of arbitrary power, such as were echoed from the pulpits of all the high-church party, in the reigns of the Stuarts, and of Queen Anne.

The alternative was, again, his millenarian vision of love and truth: 'Together with the general prevalence of the true principles of civil government, we may expect to see the extinction of all national prejudice and enmity, and the establishment of universal peace and good will among all nations.'[254] Having thus framed the alternatives, radicals were aghast to see events choosing between them.

---

[252] *Parl Hist*, vol. xxviii, cols. 387–452. Fox foolishly admitted that 'The object of the test-laws, at first, had been to exclude anti-monarchical men from civil offices.'

[253] *Parl Hist*, vol. xxviii, cols. 452–79.

[254] J. Priestley, *Letters to the Right Honourable Edmund Burke, Occasioned by His Reflections on the Revolution in France* (Birmingham, 1791) in *Works*, vol. xxii, pp. 149–238.

At the same time, the other term in an ancient equation was suddenly removed. The radical assault on the Church in France now unequivocally identified the English Roman Catholics as defenders of a Trinitarian social order. Pitt and the bishops joined with Fox and the Dissenters to applaud the unopposed passage of a Roman Catholic Relief Bill in March 1791.[255] Some Dissenters now began to appreciate that a Trinitarian distinction lay at the heart of the establishment case. Priestley wrote to Lindsey from the thriving manufacturing town of Birmingham in June 1791, recognising that 'a majority' of Englishmen sympathised with the 'High Church Party', so that 'an attachment to high maxims of government gains ground here, and the love of liberty is on the decline'.[256] The mob's reaction to republican anticlerical sedition in that town was the famous riots of July 1791 in which Dissenting meeting houses, and Priestley's own house, were burned. Similar 'Church and King' activism was prominent also at Manchester,[257] where public life had a long tradition of Tory High Churchmanship in the early eighteenth century (industry did not necessarily lead to republicanism).

As if regardless of the extent and form of the opposition they had aroused, the logic of the Unitarians' creed drove them to make an application to Parliament for the abrogation of the penalties on anti-Trinitarians by a repeal of the Blasphemy Act of 1697. Fox, proposing it on 11th May 1792 on the grounds of 'the fundamental, unalienable rights of man', denouncing Hallifax and Horsley, merely provided Burke with another opportunity for identifying radicalism with heterodoxy. 'This faction (the authors of the petition)', he argued, 'are not confined to a theological sect, but are also a political faction.'

The principle of your petitioners is no passive conscientious dissent on account of an over-scrupulous habit of mind; the dissent on their part is fundamental, goes to the very root: and it is at issue not upon this rite or that ceremony, on this or that school opinion, but upon this one question of an establishment, as unchristian, unlawful, contrary to the Gospel, and to natural right, popish and idolatrous.

Pitt agreed, and the vote was lost in a thin House by 142 to 63.[258] It was a foregone conclusion. Not only was Pitt prepared to uphold the Toleration Act against the heterodox; he was willing to consider abridging it. Only with difficulty did William Wilberforce dissuade him from introducing a Bill to give JPs the power to prevent itinerant preaching.[259]

The Birmingham riots of 1791 were 'symbolic of the eclipse of rational Dissent'. A generation of Unitarian intellectuals died; no figures of equal

---

[255] Barlow, *Citizenship and Conscience*, pp. 282–3.
[256] Priestley, *Works*, vol. II, p. 114.
[257] F. Knight, *The Strange Case of Thomas Walker* (London, 1957).
[258] *Parl Hist*, vol. XXIX, cols. 1372–403.
[259] Barlow, *Citizenship and Conscience*, pp. 293–4; R. I. and S. Wilberforce, *Life of William Wilberforce* (London, 1838), vol. II, pp. 360–2.

calibre replaced them. The popular appeal of their creed was small. Already, 'the triumph of Evangelicalism over rational Dissent'[260] was evident, and this was a major reason for the weakness of the radical case into the 1820s. From c. 1790, Arianism went into a steep and rapid decline in numbers. Some Dissenting congregations returned to Trinitarian (often Calvinistic) orthodoxy; others progressed to outright Socinianism in the manner of Priestley.[261] Socinianism was often only a resting place on the road to unbelief. Paine's *Age of Reason*, the first popularised Deist tract, equally promoted atheism. As 'rational Christianity' degenerated from religion to ethics, it set the scene for the triumph of utilitarianism from the 1820s.

Among the 'respectable', radicalism after 1793 tended increasingly to find expression in opposition to war as such. It was a position which raised few theoretical issues in itself, though political agitation to that end was usually organised by Unitarians. Nevertheless, their commitment had political consequences. 'The anti-war liberals, more than any other group, challenged the oligarchical society in the late eighteenth and early nineteenth century. Their value orientation was primarily anti-aristocratic. It was this ideological position that mainly explains their opposition to the war.'[262] The self-indulgence of this small radical intelligentsia had almost nothing to do with what Chartists were to term 'knife and fork' questions: 'as ideologues and political activists, these intellectuals remained relatively indifferent to the hardships and degradation of the poor'.[263]

'The poor' therefore turned elsewhere, and a disaffected plebeian consciousness can be identified from the 1790s. Yet the politically articulate were drawn neither from the great army of rural labourers, nor from the relatively prosperous factory operatives in expanding industries, nor again from the unskilled, the desperately poor, the 'lumpenproletariat'. Leaders of sedition in the 1790s came usually from the ranks of intelligent artisans, tradesmen and shopkeepers; usually, too, men with backgrounds (like Thomas Gordon, John Toland and others before them) in Ireland, Scotland or America, remote from the Anglican cultural nexus.[264] Classic radical expositions like Paine's *Rights of Man* achieved a substantial circulation, but whether their influence extended far beyond the minor tradesman and the skilled worker may be doubted. It continued, therefore, to be a small cadre of extremists who drew up the political agenda: 'For a generation the cause of reform was inexorably linked with godless republicanism and the total overthrow of established society.'[265]

The theory that large masses of Englishmen were organised to rebel, and in fact poised on the brink of rebellion, at any time between 1793 and 1815

---

[260] Watts, *Dissenters*, vol. I, pp. 487–90.
[261] *Ibid.*, vol. I, pp. 477–8.
[262] Cookson, *Friends of Peace*, pp. 27, 33.
[263] *Ibid.*, p. 28.
[264] Goodwin, *Friends of Liberty*, p. 21.
[265] Cannon, *Parliamentary Reform*, p. 120.

has rightly been rejected. Yet if the facts of suffering, poverty and (what radical intellectuals never saw) the horrors of war failed to be widely translated into popular politics directed against the establishment, a major reason must be the activities of those theorists who, even before 1789, had defined their position in terms so extreme (in relation to society's ruling orthodoxy) that radicalism itself could easily be equated with the destruction of civilisation.[266] The Peterhouse radical Tierney's *Report on the State of Parliamentary Representation* appeared in 1793 immediately after the arrival of news of the execution of Louis XVI, and Charles Grey's untimely motion for reform on 6th May was lost by the eloquent margin of 282 to 41.[267]

If parliamentary reform was relatively unimportant in the country at large during the 1790s, one reason was that it was rendered insignificant by the far more extensive programme of the English Jacobins and their fellow-travellers. Millenarian revolution was both an end in itself, and a means; tinkering adjustments to the franchise or the distribution of seats were no longer the options presented by circumstances to the political nation. As in the early eighteenth century, when the periodic prospect of a Jacobite revolution lay behind the Tories' electoral populism, so in the 1790s universal suffrage was regarded as the banner of Jacobin revolution. English Jacobin intellectuals had one striking similarity with Common-wealth radicals of the early eighteenth century: they were markedly unconcerned with meliorist social reform, the poor law, public health, education, welfare or charity in any of its multifarious forms (this was, typically, the province of Anglicans). Jacobins and Commonwealthmen were primarily concerned to mount an attack on the State via its official theoretical structure. Outside the Commons, advocates of universal suffrage were therefore open to prosecution for seditious libel, seditious words, or even treason; and the trials of Frost, Gerrald, Hardy, Margarot, Muir, Skirving and their like, though some of them escaped conviction, effectively disposed of the reform movement of the 1790s.[268] When the new century opened, the work of parliamentary reform was still all to do.

X. CONCLUSION

It is paradoxical that historians of radicalism – since the great majority of them identified with their subject – seldom troubled to ask *why* radical

---

[266] The idea that radicals were 'primarily concerned to use parliamentary reform in order to rectify their social and economic grievances as victims of the industrial revolution' (Goodwin, *Friends of Liberty*, p. 23) does not survive the results presented above.

[267] Cannon, *Parliamentary Reform*, p. 125.

[268] It is noticeable how many of them, above the rank of artisan, were in holy orders: the Rev. John Horne Tooke, the Rev. Thomas Fysshe Palmer, the Rev. Gilbert Wakefield, the Rev. William Frend, the Roman Catholic Fr James O'Coigley, and a Dissenting minister – Winterbotham.

theory and commitment emerged. Radicalism has typically been explained in terms of itself: a radical critique of eighteenth-century society was obviously necessary, it was suggested, and men needed no other motive to adopt radical doctrine than its self-evident truth and morality. Thus fortified, historians have all too often reconstructed the radical case around those elements which seem self-evidently true to the modern mind. A consequence, of course, has been a compartmentalist approach: reform of one sort (say, of the franchise) is dealt with in one volume; of another sort, by a different historian; and the theological context by a third, usually regarded as a narrow specialist of no general interest. Specialisation has promoted compartmentalisation, and the very popularity of a subject can act to reinforce basic, but anachronistic, assumptions.

Yet historians have traditionally been preoccupied with radicals, for at least two reasons. First, radicals seemed to anticipate the future, so justifying the teleology of the 'Whig interpretation'. Secondly, the radical critique seemed to disclose the economic and power structure of the establishment, revealing its true workings, stripped of its excuses, as a system of exploitation. If the argument advanced above is correct, neither reason is tenable. The radicals were fighting old battles, not anticipating modern values; and the radical critique had its origins in theology, not economics.[269] Beside partisanship, there is a large element of truth in a Dissenter's claim that Unitarians 'have been leaders in most of those changes which have transformed the England of the eighteenth century into the England of the present day' [i.e. 1938].[270] But they did so by destroying 'the past', not by anticipating 'the future'.

The approach outlined here, then, offers a solution to the problem created by historians' materialism: why was there so little radical activity and ideology in eighteenth-century England which the nineteenth century would have recognised, and why was the radical impetus unsuccessful for so long? Professor Palmer, for example, in arguing that Europe and America were 'swept in the last four decades of the eighteenth century by a single revolutionary movement', had difficulty in defining it since, as he realised, it was 'not primarily' to do with universal suffrage.[271] Elsewhere, students are familiar with the argument that the Glorious Revolution substituted the

---

[269] This argument is also at odds with the reductionist claim that religious dissent 'was from the social point of view the sublimated form taken by vertical social antagonism...such resentment of the higher orders as existed was diverted into religion': Perkin, *English Society*, p. 36. The historian is under no requirement to explain religion in terms of something else; the concept of 'sublimation' is wholly unproven.

[270] R. V. Holt, *The Unitarian Contribution to Social Progress in England* (London, 1938; 2nd edn, 1952), p. 13.

[271] R. R. Palmer, *The Age of the Democratic Revolution* (2 vols., Princeton, 1959–64), vol. 1, pp. 4–5. He was puzzled that 'bourgeois radicalism' frequently turned against the Church, or 'ignorance and superstition', rather than addressing 'the essential class problem' (p. 79).

divine right of property owners for the divine right of kings, so that eighteenth-century England was, in a secular idiom, preoccupied with the oligarchical defence of property.[272] The assumption that the divine right of kings was extinguished in 1688 has been disposed of in previous chapters; the corollary that radicals drew the structure of their arguments primarily from a materialist analysis of society may be compared with the results set out in this chapter.

The use in this book of the term 'radical' has been, until now, a deliberate anachronism, and an explanation is due. Before c. 1815, 'liberal' as an adjective was current, meaning 'unrestrained', 'generous' or 'open', but the nouns 'liberal' and 'liberalism', with their later political meaning, were not. Equally absent were the nouns 'radical' and 'radicalism'.[273] The chief reason for this, it is here suggested, was that the political and social spheres were conceived to overlap with the religious to such an extent that the roots of reform lay in theology: Deist, Arian, Socinian, Dissenter, sectary were the appropriate and accurate labels. The use of 'radical' in this book to cover such positions is intended to indicate the form which a nineteenth-century genre took in an earlier period. Nor has it been thought proper to adopt that contemporary euphemism, 'rational Christianity': Unitarians like Priestley believed in reason and the right of private judgement only in so far as they led to their own doctrines. Dogmatism was a characteristic of all parties in a debate in which infidelity was taken as seriously as religion.

[272] Cf. Holmes (ed.), *Britain After the Glorious Revolution*, p. 54, and more generally in the work of Dickinson, Plumb, Porter, etc.

[273] Cookson, *Friends of Peace*, p. 2. 'Radical' as a noun achieved currency only after c. 1819: E. Halévy, *The Growth of Philosophic Radicalism* (London, 1928), p. 261.

6

The End of the Ancien Regime, 1800–1832

I. THE IDEOLOGY OF THE OLD SOCIETY

A Whig in 1823 correctly sensed that 'The Tory...feels a sort of religious abhorrence to touch what he calls the sacred fabric' of the constitution.[1] This attitude was nothing new; it was the Foxite Whigs' dogmatic insistence, from about the 1780s, on the separation of the spheres of religion and politics which made traditional attitudes worthy of remark, and which made the party of Grey and Holland increasingly revive the label 'Tory' to insult its Whig ministerial opponents. 'Church and King' loyalists nevertheless celebrated the birthday of William III, not James III. They disavowed what they called the doctrine

...that kings may rule by the dictates of their own will, that no action of the governor is to be inquired into by the governed, that the expressions of popular opinion are to be checked as dangerous or punished as seditious, in short, that unconditional authority is the privilege of the monarch, and unconditional obedience the duty of the subject

– that is, they repeated the traditional Whig misdescription of Stuart legitimism. Equally they disavowed populism: the idea that the king was 'merely the servant and instrument of the people...that the people have a right to alter the government at their will'. Monarchical loyalty could now be used as a barrier against universal suffrage, whether by a claim of the utility of the ancient constitution or a claim that 'men living in a state of civil society have no political rights at all, except those which the laws and regulations of that society allow them'.[2] Natural rights were surrendered by those entering the old society. It reflected the entrenched priority not of natural rights but of Christian (and, specifically, Anglican) political and social duties.

Social subordination and Anglican supremacy were still conceptually

---

[1] Quoted in A. Mitchell, *The Whigs in Opposition 1815–1830* (Oxford, 1967), p. 15.
[2] *An Address to His Fellow Countrymen: in a Letter from Verus* (London, 1820), pp. 5–6, 13–14.

indispensable to each other. Toleration and liberty (freedom *from*), society's professed ideals, found their expression within these larger assumptions (freedom *to*). Seen in this perspective, all Anglicans could be retrospectively assimilated in the defence of a social order. Southey excused the Nonjurors: 'their offence consisted only in adhering to the principle without which no government can be secure'.[3] Ironically, establishment theorists tried to join hands with ancient enemies to defend the existing regime: since 1688

...every British monarch must have known, that the constitution of this country was, by the collected voice of the people, declared to be essentially and *exclusively Protestant*. Every monarch of these realms must therefore have considered himself placed by divine Providence on the throne under the most solemn obligation to God and his country to preserve the constitution of it, so far as respected its fundamental principles of *Protestantism*, in the same state in which he found it.[4]

In the early nineteenth century, three explicit challenges were made to this interlocking system of beliefs and institutions: demands for the repeal of the Test and Corporation Acts, for the repeal of legislation against Roman Catholics, and for parliamentary reform (here termed 'Repeal', 'Emancipation' and 'Reform'). For most of the 1820s, establishment doctrine was levelled against what was perceived as the major threat, Emancipation; Repeal seemed a remoter danger. When it suddenly returned to the agenda in 1828, it provoked some hasty restatements. 'The country had almost hoped, from the long silence on the subject of the Corporation and Test Acts in Parliament', wrote one observer, 'that peoples' minds were at rest upon the matter.'[5] None of the petitions to Parliament in favour of Repeal, it was observed, came from (Trinitarian) Wesleyan Dissenters:[6] the object was not toleration, which Dissenters enjoyed already, but the destruction of Anglican ascendancy.[7] A minister of the Church of Scotland in London, Edward Irving, addressing the King as 'nursing father of the church', traced the demand not to orthodox Dissenters but to the 'Unitarians, and Deists, and Infidels, who are now multiplied to a mighty host within the realm, taking to themselves the name and banner of liberality, in order to entrap the unwary'.[8] The 'essential polity of the nation', insisted a Surrey country gentleman, was 'the indefeasible union of divine with human law...The principle of these restrictive statutes is clearly, that the nation and the church are one; and that the unity of the individual with the nation is to be attested by his unity with the church.'

---

[3] Robert Southey, *The Book of the Church* (2 vols., London, 1824), vol. II, p. 527.
[4] Charles Daubeny, *A Letter to the Right Honourable George Canning* (London, 1827), pp. 5–6.
[5] *The Necessity of the Corporation and Test Acts Maintained* (London, 1828), p. 4.
[6] Rev. R. Jermyn Cooper, *A Letter to the Rt Hon Lord John Russell* (London, [1828]), p. 27.
[7] G. I. T. Machin, 'Resistance to Repeal of the Test and Corporation Acts, 1828', *HJ* 22 (1979), 127.
[8] Rev E. Irving, *A Letter to the King, on the Repeal of the Test and Corporation Laws, as it Affects our Christian Monarchy* (London, 1828), pp. 8, 30.

The total and unqualified repeal, therefore, of all tests of Christianity in the office-bearers of the state implies, and does effect, the separation of the church from the state, and of religious from political duty; and thereby inculcates, that kingly government is a matter of human contrivance, and of human expediency, with which divine obligation has no concern. Hence, too, the false opinion is sanctioned, that the people, and not God, are the source of legitimate power; that power is delegated from the people to their rulers, and consequently may be resumed by the people, whenever the people shall deem such resumption to be for their benefit; whereas the true foundation of this, and of every Christian monarchy, rests upon the principle, that 'the powers which be, are ordained of God', and that, therefore, 'whosoever resisteth the power, resisteth the ordinance of God; for the king beareth not the sword in vain, because he is the minister of God, a revenger to execute wrath upon him that doeth evil': that the king is Christ's vicegerent, and delegate of Him, who is King of Kings, Lord of Lords, the ONLY ruler of princes, the representative of Him in His kingly office, even as the Church is the representative of Him in His priestly office.[9]

Democracy and Dissent were profoundly related, as Anglicans had long realised:

The very '*principium et fons*' of all dissent, where the communion that is left is not sinful (and no one could ever assert that ours is sinful) is nothing else than a satanic impatience of Godly discipline – a hatred of, and rebellion against, constituted authorities. He who impugns the hierarchy of the Church of England, and contends for the equality of all ministers of religion...he who advocates the right of the people to follow spiritual teachers with no ostensible commission, at the same time that they forsake those who are sent forth by Christ, cannot but be considered as deeply imbued with principles in their very nature and essence democratical. The principle is a principle of rebellion: and dissent or schism may not inaptly be termed spiritual republicanism...*he*, whose mind is so weak that he can see no sin in resisting the spiritual government established by the Deity, cannot be expected to see any sin in resisting civil government, and more especially as such an one fancies that civil government is an institution of man, forgetting '*whose* authority he hath' who is at the head of civil government. In short, whoever is hostile to the hierarchy, if only he be consistent with himself, cannot in reality, though he may appear to be, attached to the civil government.[10]

It has been rightly pointed out that the Ultras 'have probably received a worse press than any other party in the history of the English Church and State'.[11] This was not for lack of a coherent ideology, however. As Lord Eldon summarised it:

My opinion is that the Establishment is formed, not for the purpose of making the Church political, but for the purpose of making the State religious: that an

---

[9] [Henry Drummond], *A Letter to the King, against the Repeal of the Test Act. By a Tory of the Old School* (London, 1828), pp. 4, 6–7.

[10] Rev. Stephen Hyde Cassan, *Considerations on the Danger of any Legislative Alteration Respecting the Corporation and Test Acts; and of any Concession to Dissenters or Papists* (London, 1828), pp. 28–9.

[11] G. F. A. Best, 'The Protestant Constitution and its Supporters, 1800–1829', *TRHS* 5th ser., 8 (1958), 107–27.

Establishment, with an enlightened toleration, is as necessary to the peace of the State, as to the maintenance of religion, without which the State can have no solid peace: that our Establishment is founded upon the purest system of Christianity, and that which in its nature is most tolerant: that a Protestant Church and a Roman Catholic Church cannot co-exist upon equal terms: that one of them must be predominant: that if the Protestant is predominant, the Roman Catholic may have the full benefit of toleration – but that it cannot have political power, with any hope that it will allow a fair degree of toleration to the Protestant Church. Its principles are founded in ecclesiastical tyranny, and ecclesiastical tyranny must produce civil despotism.

I know not, moreover, how I can alter my conduct, without declaring the Revolution of 1688 to have been rebellion, and the throne to have been filled for a century by usurpers.[12]

As was shown in chapter 4, this was in its essentials the doctrine which had provided the defence of the State against the American and Dissenting challenges in the 1770s and the French challenge in the 1790s; and as Burke saw, it derived inescapably from the Whig defence of the Glorious Revolution in the decades immediately after that event. Because it was very widely current, because it was of long standing, the doctrine was not original, and did not generate a personality cult around its ideologues – Hallifax or Horsley, Reeves or Bowles. As a doctrine, it was as monarchical and anti-democratic in its implications as it was anti-Catholic or anti-Dissenter; but it was these last two aspects which were chiefly brought into prominence by the challenges to which the 'old society' was subject in the early nineteenth century.

The Anglican ascendancy justified itself on a principle of toleration – the toleration of other forms of Trinitarian Christian *worship*. It drew a sharp distinction between this and the admission of non-Anglicans to political *power*. Practice however fell short of principle, for the Test and Corporation Acts still allowed Dissenters to vote in parliamentary elections, and the same privilege was conceded to Irish Catholics in 1793. The equalisation of privilege therefore became a goal among the discontented. They were met by the rationale of a hierarchical society: Dissenters' objections that they were second-class citizens were not fully effective in a social order in which a great range of privilege and status was accepted and, indeed, justified as a Providential (i.e. Anglican) dispensation. The loudest objections to this view had always come not from those who merely occupied an inferior position on the social scale, but from those in particular who objected to Anglican Christianity on the grounds that it was untrue – that its theology was false and blasphemous, or (recently and more infrequently) that all religion was a fraud. After a succession of such challenges, Anglican theorists presumed a necessary connection: Roman Catholics must be demanding

---

[12] Eldon to Rev. Matthew Surtees, Feb. 1825: Horace Twiss, *The Public and Private Life of Lord Chancellor Eldon*, 2nd edn (3 vols., London, 1844), vol. II, pp. 537–8.

Emancipation on the basis of a claim that Catholicism was true and Protestantism false, and the granting of Emancipation must therefore lead the Roman Church to seek the suppression of heresy. Enough Dissenters could be found saying the same thing to make such inferences widely credible. Into this situation the Irish problem now intruded. From the rebellion of 1798, the 'Catholic Question' reappeared – not in the context of the post-Jacobite loyalty of English Catholics, a tiny minority, but in the context of the nationalist disaffection of the great majority of Irishmen to English rule.

Instead of the hundred additional county Members demanded by English reformers, there arrived at Westminster as a consequence of the Union in 1801 one hundred Irish MPs. Pitt's object had been to guard against a Catholic majority at Dublin by the immersion of Irish Members in the Anglican body at Westminster: he did not, perhaps, foresee that the Irish would come to hold the balance there. In fact, the strategic implications of this shift in the balance of power were not to become apparent for a quarter of a century. The immediate effect was quite different: parliamentary reformers, already despondent, now despaired. No support for Reform was expected from the Irish contingent.[13] In the 1780s, even the most extreme English advocates of universal manhood suffrage had drawn back rather than press for the extension of that principle to Irish Roman Catholics,[14] and the Volunteer Movement had not engineered a political alliance with those advanced thinkers. Irish Catholics had been given the vote on existing franchises (though not the right to sit in the Dublin Parliament) in 1793, not as the result of moves for franchise reform but when the overriding consideration was perceived as the unity of Christian civilisation against an atheist Jacobin menace. This arrangement was continued in 1801, for the franchise was deliberately left undisturbed in those of the Irish constituencies which now returned Members to Westminster.

The immediate result of the Union was not, therefore, the injection of a democratic impulse into Irish politics: the Anglo-Irish gentry still provided MPs for Westminster. The emerging problem was not that they were gentry, but that they were Protestants. In England, an anomaly had emerged: the 1791 Relief Act, though removing most sixteenth- and seventeenth-century disabilities, still left Catholics subject to exclusion under the Test and Corporation Acts, and debarred from voting or sitting in Parliament by Acts of 1678 and 1689 which imposed the Oath of Supremacy and a Declaration against Transubstantiation as conditions. Widespread English and Scottish anti-Catholicism meant that Emancipation could scarcely be promoted in those countries on a wave of popular reformist sentiment, and for three decades Emancipation produced political

[13] J. R. Dinwiddy, *Christopher Wyvill and Reform 1790–1820* (York, 1971), p. 12.
[14] Cannon, *Parliamentary Reform*, p. 103.

alignments which cut across alignments on the issue of the extension of the franchise. Irish Catholics had been encouraged to expect the abolition of all disabilities after the Union, and the failure of this to materialise, thanks to George III's resistance,[15] kept the issue alive as a grievance. So did the possibility, on which the politicians of the Protestant Ascendancy dwelt, of an armed rebellion, or of the peaceful disestablishment of the Church or Ireland and, logically, Protestant expropriation and Irish independence.[16] In England, the inviolability of the unreformed constitution was particularly challenged by what soon came once more to be depicted as the ancient and unchanging enemy, Rome. What made it theoretically so sensitive was that Orthodox Anglicans, who supplied the State's rationale, were (unlike Tractarians later) militantly anti-Papist. It was this spectacle of an Irish Catholic hierarchy, ready to fill the place of the Protestant Establishment in Ireland, which converted Bishop Horsley to vote against Emancipation in 1805.

For several reasons on both sides, therefore, the Emancipation debate was kept clear from involvement in the populist philosophy of Jebb, Price and Priestley; nor, in an issue so patently one of religion, did Bentham have much to do. The Catholic Question was instead argued as a classic issue of political theology. It was its Indian summer: in Eldon and Newcastle; Wordsworth, Southey and Coleridge; Phillpotts and Van Mildert, an ancient tradition found its last and not its least distinguished defenders.[17] Their defence of the Church-State, and their ultimate defeat, provided the definition and marked the dissolution of the ancien regime in England.

Religion, nationalism and allegiance were as inseparable in the Irish case as in the English. The Ascendancy politician Lord Redesdale wrote to Spencer Perceval in 1804 that

Those who resisted the authority of the legislature in establishing the Reformation were as guilty of treason, tho' they acted on opinions which they conceived to be right, as those who adhered to the Stuart family after their expulsion, believing the divine hereditary right to be in that family, indefeasibly by any act of man; and the legislature had, in point of conscience, as well as of expedience, as much right to enact laws against the rebel of one description as the rebel of the other.[18]

Seen in an English perspective, a Roman Catholic claim of superior spiritual allegiance could seem a natural concomitant of a claim to a right of rebellion. The events of 1798 seemed practical confirmation. The same

---

[15] Cannon, *ibid.*, p. 146 suggests that religious toleration, 'inextricably bound up with reform' in 1828, could have been separated in 1801 by the grant of Catholic Emancipation.

[16] U. Henriques, *Religious Toleration in England 1787–1833* (London, 1961), pp. 140–5.

[17] Among the best general statements of the position are the separate pieces collected in Robert Southey, *Essays, Moral and Political* (2 vols., London, 1832) and the Duke of Newcastle, *Thoughts in Times Past Tested by Subsequent Events* (London, 1837). See also G. C. B. Davies, *Henry Phillpotts Bishop of Exeter, 1778–1869* (London, 1954).

[18] Quoted Henriques, *Toleration*, p. 149.

principle could be held to be embodied in what Protestants claimed was the Roman maxim that 'No faith is to be kept with heretics': a standard complaint of Anglican apologists for centuries, kept alive now both in the Orthodox and Evangelical camps, and by Methodists referring to John Wesley's *Letter Concerning the Civil Principles of Roman Catholics* (1780). A society bound by Christian oaths could not, Anglicans maintained, accept those – whether atheists or Papists – who could not give guarantees of their behaviour; and the Roman doctrine of 'exclusive salvation' could be expected to make Catholics unreliable fellow citizens of, let alone legislators for, a Protestant society. The 'Alliance between Church and State' could thus be defended on the plausible grounds of the superiority of Anglican to Roman doctrine, rather than with dubious arguments about how the contract of alliance was to be understood. The claim of Catholic Emancipation was fought on ground most advantageous to the defenders.

In addition to theology, defenders of the Protestant constitution could link it to an issue which aligned with them all except a minority of Whigs: the royal prerogative.[19] Repeated Whig ejections and exclusions from ministerial office since the 1760s had induced in them a paranoia about royal power which, conveniently for generations of ministerialists, quite failed correctly to diagnose the reasons for their long sojourn in the wilderness. Ministerial insistence that the Coronation Oath Act of 1689 and the Act of Union of 1707 debarred sovereigns from assenting to any measure of Catholic Emancipation thus played on a major Whig weakness, since outright republicanism would be political suicide. Here as elsewhere, the reformers' problem was to find a measure which would be effective without committing them to something damagingly extreme as a logical corollary. From 1801, when Pitt resigned rather than force the measure on George III, Emancipation could be regarded as a move against the monarch in his twin capacity as head of the Church and of the State.

Defenders of the Oath could fall back, too, on the high view of kingship left untouched in the Revolution settlement and recently reiterated, to radicals' fury, by John Reeves. The Rev. Henry Phillpotts did exactly this in his famous polemics on the subject. He took as his starting point the claim that the Anglican Church, as the local branch of *the* Church, was 'an essential part of the British constitution', and proved it by reviewing English law since 702. The Coronation Oath prescribed by 1 W & M c 6 and interpreted as the oath required from the sovereign by the Act of Union, 5 Anne c 8, was an overriding obligation on him; it bound the monarch to maintain not merely Christianity, but 'the Protestant reformed religion established by law'. Those who framed it clearly believed that James II's religion was not incidental but basic to his attempt to erode English liberties. Subsequent sovereigns were not bound to comply with the advice of their

[19] Best, 'Protestant Constitution', pp. 115–20.

ministers in the interpretation which they placed on an oath which concerned them and God directly. Any measure of Emancipation or Repeal, insisted Phillpotts, 'must depend on' the sovereign's '*own personal conviction* of the tendency of such measures, in respect to the established Church and religion of the country'.

The Whig theory, as enunciated by Francis Jeffrey, editor of the *Edinburgh Review*, claimed that the sovereign was bound by the oath in his executive capacity, but not in his capacity as a branch of the legislature. The legislature, therefore, could determine what was that religion 'established by law' which the king as head of the executive was bound to defend. This did not, replied Phillpotts, entail that the legislature could do *anything*: 'That there are "fundamental laws", if not above the power, yet beyond the moral competence, of the whole legislature to rescind them, what Englishman will hesitate to affirm? what Prince, who has read the Bill of Rights, will refuse to acknowledge? None of the illustrious House of Brunswick, I am well assured.' To assert that would be tantamount to crediting the Hanoverian sovereign with a dispensing power. Jeffrey's doctrine was 'immediately borrowed from the very liberal school of Mr Thomas Paine and Dr Richard Price'. The law, however, did not treat the king as merely a branch of the legislature: law is the King's law, made with Parliament's advice and consent. England, in Coke's phrase, was 'an absolute monarchy' – that is, not 'without legal restrictions on the prerogative', but 'perfect in all that is necessary to a monarchy, wherein the king is not, in strictness of speech, a *branch* of the legislature, but rather he is the legislator, limited, indeed, and restrained, moved and advised, in the exercise of legislation' by Parliament. To say otherwise, suggested Phillpotts, would imply (like Jeffrey) that the King could 'attack the Church *by law*', could 'take away *by law* its rights, privileges and establishment': 'Such is the crowning achievement of modern liberality, as applied to the Royal Oath: it will, doubtless, in due time, be equally successful in accommodating the duty of subjects, and the "Oath of Allegiance", to its plans for the improvement of the social system.'[20]

Not all the Ultras had as highly developed an understanding of the law. They all thought the Crown much more important than the Whigs did, but expressed this insight in different ways. Even Sir Robert Inglis said, in the Commons in 1828, 'that the King of England is not, as some half-republicans call him, merely the first magistrate, but an original integral, essential part

[20] Henry Phillpotts, *A Letter to an English Layman on The Coronation Oath* (London, 1828), pp. 7–8, 52, 68, 72, 75, 83, 130. Cf. *idem*, *A Letter to the Right Honourable George Canning, on the Bill of 1825* (London, 1827) and *A Short Letter to the Right Honourable George Canning, etc.* (London, 1827). Henry Phillpotts (1778–1869). Son of an innkeeper. Corpus Christi College, Oxford, 1791–; Fellow of Magdalen 1795–1804. Protégé of Dr Routh. Deacon 1802, priest 1804. Married Lord Eldon's niece. Livings; Chaplain to Bp of Durham 1806; Prebend of Durham 1809–; Dean of Chichester 1828; Bishop of Exeter 1930–d.

of the legislature, and as much entitled to a deliberative voice in any measure as either House of Parliament'.[21] These differences, logically of immense importance, were practically largely ignored: attention focussed on the issue of the role in society of religion, more than of the monarchy.

The Whigs brought similar criteria to the appraisal of both, however. If there was nothing sacrosanct in the institution and establishment of any particular church, neither was there anything sacred about kingship. Whig doctrine 'could not exclude (though their political practice was careful to ignore) the possibility of abolishing the monarchy'.[22] Religious and political institutions were all judged as furthering or hindering Fox's religion of Tolerant Virtue,[23] and liberty was the natural route to a high-minded utilitarianism.

Both sides saw themselves as the heirs of early-eighteenth-century Whigs. When in 1798 the Duke of Norfolk was dismissed from his lord lieutenancy after toasting 'Our Sovereign, the People', Fox consoled him: he had been dismissed for 'an opinion which to have controverted in the times of the first two Georges would have been deemed a symptom of disaffection'.[24] The radical Sir Francis Burdett, standing, as he imagined, outside this Whig consensus, even saw himself in 1819 as the heir to the Toryism of Queen Anne's reign. His political principles, however, dispensed with natural rights theories in favour of the historic rights of Englishmen. In equally traditional fashion, he linked parliamentary reform not to a theoretical principle of universal suffrage but to redress of practical grievance – high taxation resulting from corruption, placemen and pensioners, in turn produced by a 'borough-mongering oligarchy'. Crippling wartime and postwar taxation, especially during economic recessions, rather than doctrines of personal representation, still created most of what political mileage there was in the issue of parliamentary reform.[25] Few even of the radicals were yet committed to anything as revolutionary as universal suffrage.[26]

It would be wrong to overlook the extent to which, on most issues, most gentlemen on both sides of the House of Commons shared similar attitudes. If there was a widespread acceptance of aristocratic ideals, there was an equally widespread rejection of extreme radical demands. Lord John Russell denied that each man possessed a *right* to the franchise: 'The right which a man possesses with respect to voting is an artificial right, and must be that which the laws allow him.' Universal suffrage 'is calculated to produce and

[21] Quoted Best, 'Protestant Constitution', p. 117.
[22] G. F. A. Best, 'The Whigs and the Church Establishment in the Age of Grey and Holland', *History* 45 (1960), 113.
[23] *Ibid*, p. 107.
[24] Fox to Norfolk, in G. M. Trevelyan, *Lord Grey of the Reform Bill* (London, 1920), p. 105.
[25] J. R. Dinwiddy, 'Sir Francis Burdett and Burdettite Radicalism', *History* 65 (1980), 17–31.
[26] J. R. Dinwiddy, '"The Patriotic Linen-Draper": Robert Waithman and the Revival of Radicalism in the City of London, 1795–1818', *BIHR* 46 (1973), 86.

nourish violent opinions and servile dependence'.[27] Whigs were consequently lukewarm on parliamentary reform before 1830: piecemeal, moderate measures were as far as they wished to go, and their interest in the subject was fitful. What marked them out were their views on the role of religion.

For the Whigs, Catholic Emancipation offered an issue of reform of a familiar type. Like all issues of conscience and civil liberty, it conferred a sense of political rectitude on its advocates while calling for little in the way of state-directed social engineering in the wake of its success. Few of them appreciated the nationalist impulses which lay behind Irish demands. Whigs saw the Anglican Church's Irish establishment as merely a more aggravated, more inappropriate version of its English establishment. Warburton's arguments about the status of the majority church could be taken at their word. Above all, the Orthodox insistence on the threat of Roman Catholicism and Dissent could have no meaning for Whigs, committed since the 1780s to a view of the total separation of religion and politics, and the wholly secular nature of the State. If natural rights theories had been discredited in the 1790s, an advancing secular viewpoint, and arguments from expediency, proved a more effective reply to Orthodox arguments couched in semi-sacred terms. Holland House's wit and *bon viveur* the Rev. Sydney Smith argued in 1807: 'I am as disgusted with the nonsense of the Roman Catholic religion as you can be...but what have I to do with the speculative nonsense of his theology, when the object is to elect the mayor of a county town, or to appoint a colonel of a marching regiment?'[28]

Whig aristocratic *hauteur* and religious indifference allowed them as little real knowledge of the practical connection of religion and politics in Ireland, and the party of Fox and Grey could as often dismiss Orthodox Anglican theology as 'speculative nonsense'. For radicals, all these antipathies were present in a more vivid form. Radicals were paradoxically closer to the Orthodox analysis in perceiving the essential unity of secular and sacred reforming issues. The radical Thomas Perronet Thompson wrote in 1829: 'The struggle for fairness of representation in Ireland, is only the cause of the people of England tried under Irish names; and they are waiting for the decision of this question, before they proceed to their own.'[29]

Many opposition Whigs, however, instinctively shared this understanding. As the Bishop of Oxford described their leaders: 'suppose a Whig ministry, who are they to be? Lord Holland, his wife an atheist, and himself not far from it. Lord Lansdowne, a confessed Unitarian, Brougham a Deist,

---

[27] Lord John Russell, *An Essay on the History of the English Government and Constitution, from the Reign of Henry VII to the Present Time*, 2nd edn (London, 1823), pp. 350–1. For the aristocratic character of Whig assumptions, cf. Leslie Mitchell, *Holland House* (London, 1980), pp. 63–87 and *passim*.

[28] *Peter Plymley's Letters* in *The Works of the Rev. Sydney Smith* (London, 1850), p. 488.

[29] 'The Catholic Question', *Westminster Review* Jan.–Apr. 1829: Henriques, *Toleration*, p. 166.

and others whom I could easily enumerate, of the same principles.'[30] In the 1820s, Whig politicians were increasingly drawn into venomous controversies with Anglican churchmen, which acted yet again, and now decisively, to identify the Church as a pillar of the whole social order which Whigs defined themselves against. It began in 1819 with opposition attacks on the Manchester magistrates (the most active of them a clergyman) at the time of the St Peter's Field incident, escalated with Henry Phillpotts' replies, and continued in 1820 on the new topic of George IV's treatment of Queen Caroline. Again Phillpotts opened fire, this time scoring hits on Earl Grey himself. The controversy raged on into 1822, Phillpotts exchanging blows with Francis Jeffrey. But if Church polemic was effective, Whig sensibilities had been thoroughly aroused, and the trial of the editor of the *Durham Chronicle* for libelling the local clergy turned into an inquisition on the Church itself, its politics and its practices.[31] Ecclesiastical 'abuses' returned to the political arena in a way not seen since the 1730s. Tithes, endowments and disestablishment were back on the the agenda. If the Whigs had slowly acquired a Dissenting psephological base in the last three decades of the eighteenth century, this did not at once commit them to policies systematically hostile to Anglican hegemony. But from the early 1820s anticlericalism reassumed a priority in the interests of Whig politicians and publicists which the events of 1828–32 revealed as programmatic.

II. BUSINESS AS USUAL, 1800–1815

In 1830, John Wilson Croker wrote: 'I will only here sum up what I have to say to those Tory gentlemen who belong to what are called Pitt Clubs, that the two most formidable objects of their apprehensions, Parliamentary Reform and Catholic Emancipation, were the measures of Mr Pitt.'[32] Nothing more clearly shows the inappropriateness of later generations' idolisation of Pitt than his legacy on the Catholic question. Every ministry after his death was divided on the issue, and many of his protégés inherited his commitment. On the ministerial bench under Liverpool were included, in favour of the measure, Canning, Castlereagh, Palmerston and Huskisson;[33] without the groups they represented, no administration was seemingly possible. Such men treated the issue strategically: the importance of conciliating Irish loyalties took priority over native English politico-theological demands, though all these ministerialists were engaged in the

---

[30] Charles Lloyd to Peel, 6th Jan. 1828: Best, 'Whigs and Church Establishment', p. 103. Peel was not obviously responsive to this abstract threat.

[31] G. F. A. Best, *Temporal Pillars* (Cambridge, 1964), pp. 245–50.

[32] L. J. Jennings (ed.), *The Correspondence and Diaries of the Late Right Honourable John Wilson Croker*, 2nd edn (3 vols., London, 1885), vol. II, p. 86.

[33] Lord Mahon and Edward Cardwell (eds.), *Memoirs by the Right Honourable Sir Robert Peel* (2 vols., London, 1856–7), vol. I, pp. 61–2.

confusing and finally futile search for 'securities', constitutional guarantees of Roman Catholic loyalties under a new dispensation.

By comparison, minor matters of electoral reform might seem of little consequence. Attempts to treat the whole political order as sacrosanct were not always successful. Eldon, Lord Chancellor in 1801–6 and 1807–27, began his systematic defence of the constitution by resisting in 1804 the Bill to extend the franchise of the borough of Aylesbury, where bribery had been proved and one Member returned in 1802 unseated on petition, to the three neighbouring hundreds. Eldon

> ...argued, that if the measure was fit at all, it ought to be adopted as one generally connected with the state of the representation. He saw no reason for picking and choosing particular boroughs, but if the principle of the Bill was to be countenanced, why not go over towns, counties, boroughs, with the application of the same regulations. Even then he should feel it his duty to oppose the measure as contrary to the best views of the constitution, and founded on idle and theoretical views of reform...It was no argument for the Bill that bribery and corruption had prevailed to a great degree in the borough of Aylesbury. The common law of the country provided a sufficient remedy for this evil, and independent of this, there were salutary regulations, fully adequate to the punishment of these offences.

The precedents for this sort of reform – New Shoreham in 1770, Cricklade in 1782 – had nothing to do with democracy and served only to increase the influence of the counties. Consequently even a conservative like Lord Grenville spoke for this Bill:

> He was astonished that the noble and learned lord should oppose a species of reform which he had often gloried in declaring arose out of the very essence of the British constitution. This reform was the power of correcting an existing evil without adopting any theoretical views of reform, started by men who acted on speculation rather than on experience.[34]

Aylesbury's illogical but seemingly practical treatment was not widely regarded as implying a commitment to Whig reform in general: Eldon mustered only seven votes against thirty-nine in the Lords division.

Yet Grenville, though opposed to systematic Reform, was inclined to Emancipation. On 13th May 1805 Eldon opposed Grenville's motion for a committee to consider the Roman Catholic petition. It was his first formal declaration of resistance:

> Those objects, he conceived, were inconsistent with our Protestant Constitution, which he felt it the duty of the House to transmit to their posterity as pure as they had received it from their ancestors...Whatever was required by the principle of religious toleration had been already conceded to the Roman Catholics. There was some check or some limitation in the case of almost every class of the people...The liberties of the country might be said to be sustained by a system of checks; and exclusions were applied against Protestants no less than against the present petitioners...The British constitution was not based upon the principle of equal

---

[34] *Parl Debs*, vol. II, cols. 513–18.

rights to all men indiscriminately, but of equal rights to all men conforming to, and complying with, the tests which that constitution required for its security. In order to give due effect to the principle of the Act of Settlement and of the Bill of Rights, the councils as well as the person of the sovereign should be Protestant.[35]

Grenville's motion was voted down in the Lords by 178 to 49; Fox's similar motion was lost in the Commons by 336 to 124. George III had a particular regard for Eldon: their constitutional principles coincided. Such articulate support can only have strengthened the king's resistance.

It was Grenville's support for Emancipation which made possible his alliance with Fox in the 'Ministry of All the Talents', installed after Pitt's death. It was an inauspicious beginning: 'Burdett, Cobbett and other reformers subsequently looked back on Fox's entry into office with Grenville in 1806 as the beginning of the Foxite Whig betrayal of reform.'[36] In fact, the Foxites took office without a specific reformist programme: it was the course of events which engineered their commitments to Emancipation and against the royal prerogative – commitments which were huge liabilities, and which could be turned into assets only by the destruction of the social order itself a quarter of a century later. In March 1807 George III took alarm at the Talents' evident intentions of concession to the Catholic claims, and demanded a written declaration from them that they would propose no more. The Foxite Whigs refused, were dismissed, and were out of office until 1830.

The new ministry obtained a dissolution; the general election of May 1807 was made to turn to a remarkable degree on a single clear-cut issue, Emancipation. Coupled with the traditional techniques of ministerial management, the successful cry of 'No Popery' took its toll: the Whigs lost over 50 Members and were reduced to a strength in the Commons of about 155. The road back would be a long one. Moreover, their sojourn in the wilderness was marked both by practical pusillanimity and theoretical weakness. Holland House

...could not make up in wit and learning for the fact that its host and hostess belonged to a beaten party with a barren future. Deserted by its ablest aides, high-whiggism, its courtier-like vocabulary progressively less relevant to the politics of an expanding commercial society, tended to withdraw from debate, to leave the protection of its interests to others, and to contract from a political party into an ethic of high-toned and scrupulous inaction.[37]

Inaction was all the more easy in that politicians generally perceived no groundswell of support for parliamentary reform. The events of the 1790s inclined even former radicals like Wyvill to believe that substantial franchise

[35] Twiss, *Eldon*, vol. I, pp. 492–3.
[36] A. D. Harvey, *Britain in the Early Nineteenth Century* (London, 1978), p. 170.
[37] W. E. S. Thomas, *The Philosophic Radicals. Nine Studies in Theory and Practice 1817–1841* (Oxford, 1979), pp. 54–5; Mitchell, *Holland House*, pp. 36–7, 44–5, 61.

extension would mean expropriation of property. County meetings, as in 1795 and 1803 in once-reformist Yorkshire, voiced overwhelmingly patriotic and anti-radical sentiments.[38] When the Foxites at last tasted office in 1806–7, an initiative on the issue would have split the temporary coalition on which the administration rested. After their expulsion, they were attracted to Reform for the ancient reason of reducing the influence of the Crown, but repelled from it for fear of unleashing Demos. If there was no zeal among Fox, Grey or Sheridan for the question, the aged Wyvill equally realised that there was a 'general apathy on all that concerns Liberty'.[39] Nor were Burdett, Cartwright or Cobbett able to make a public issue take fire until, fortuitously, a radical MP in 1809 accused the Duke of York's mistress of selling army commissions. Sinecures, corruption and waste were once more on the political agenda. This did not create a common front, however, and a reforming banquet organised by Cartwright in May 1809 only emphasised the gulf between the MPs present and new London radicals like Waithman.

Some opposition MPs were willing to pursue a campaign against ministerial 'influence', as when Castlereagh induced the Member for an Irish borough, who had purchased his seat from the Treasury, to resign it after he voted against the government; J. C. Curwen introduced a Bill in 1809 to penalise a money transaction or other *quid pro quo* in exchange for a seat. Though the Bill passed it was, as Lord John Russell said in 1821, 'totally inefficacious': influence was the common currency of the political system. There was a widespread recognition among politicians and others that property did, and should, command influence. William Windham defended 'influence' as a principle in the debate on Curwen's Bill: it has been maintained that the argument was actually strengthening at this time, turning a practice which had been universally denounced as 'corruption' in the early eighteenth century into an openly-acknowledged component of the existing order (conservative ideologies as well as radical ideologies were strengthening in the last decades of the ancien regime). Even a Whig like Francis Horner could accept a 'pocket' seat in 1812 on the familiar and honourable condition that the MP should resign it if his opinions came to differ fundamentally from his patron's.[40] Mainstream Whigs, too, tended to distinguish between legitimate and illegitimate influence; their parliamentary concern for electoral purity did not therefore extend to a campaign over the franchise, to the radicals' disgust.

Without the support of the bulk of the Whigs, Burdett's Bill for parliamentary reform, introduced on 15th June 1809, attracted only fifteen votes, and was voted down with derisory ease.[41] Cobbett's *Political Register*,

---

[38] Dinwiddy, *Wyvill*, pp. 4, 9, 12–13. [39] *Ibid.*, p. 16.
[40] Pole, *Political Representation*, pp. 460–2; Cannon, *Parliamentary Reform*, pp. 152–5; Harvey, *Britain*, pp. 220–50. [41] *Parl Debs*, vol. XIV, cols. 1041–71.

Leigh Hunt's *Examiner* and (in a cooler idiom) the *Edinburgh Review* continued to eulogise the irresistible rising tides of reform;[42] but as far as parliamentary reform was concerned, Whig MPs and peers failed to see them. Why they did not has puzzled historians. Some pointed to the divided leadership of the Whig party, and the pusillanimous inactivity of both leaders in the House of Lords, Grey and Grenville. The evidence does not, however, bear out the hypothesis that they were trying to engineer a commitment to Reform and weakly failing: Grenville was decidedly opposed to the idea on principle; Grey's tactical diffidence masked a principled commitment to an aristocratic social order.

Nevertheless, the Whigs, defining themselves against ministries defended by such hated men as Eldon, Castlereagh and Liverpool, could scarcely restrain themselves from voting for parliamentary reform measures which could be made to seem moderate. Thomas Brand's motion in May 1810 so qualified: Cartwright wrote of it as 'half reform'.[43] As such, it received 115 votes (234 voted it down). Lord Holland lectured the hot-headed Lord John Russell: Grey's restraint was tactically wise; Grey *had* spoken for Reform on the last occasion, in 1797 –

...in urging which he was very coldly supported by all and actually abandoned by some of those very men who are now so forward to accuse him of inconsistency [by his coolness on the issue]; and here allow me to observe that those who are most abusive of us for not doing more in the cause of freedom when in office and most clamorous against places and sinecures are precisely the persons who were most inclined to give up what little we did do at the smallest appearance of its risking our places, who blamed us most loudly for attempting those things by which we lost them, and who were so far from urging reform in sinecures and pensions, that they were the most clamorous against us for not bestowing them largely on our adherents and on them in particular.

In their attitudes to Reform, and to the *political* values of the 'old society', the two sides of the House were not far apart:

...the notion of a reform being a cure for all our evils has *always* appeared and does now appear to me to be a very foolish delusion, and that the only reason for which I wish for a reform is because the House of Commons has lost *its influence* with the people, not because I think a new mode of chusing them would make them either wiser, better or more independent than they are or than it did the only time it was tried in Cromwell's time. I have no interest in the borough system and if it depended on me I would get rid of the boroughs, but indeed, my dear John, I cannot concur in the vulgar and unjust abuse of *Borough Mongers*, nor do I think when you reflect on it that you will think any man a *worse* man for either representing or possessing a borough. The influence of property *must* exist, and I certainly think it is happy that it *must*, and if you were chosen for Bedfordshire you would be as much your father's Member as if you were chosen for Tavistock.[44]

[42] Cannon, *Parliamentary Reform*, pp. 151, 157.
[43] *Ibid.*, p. 160.
[44] Lord Holland to Russell, 13th Aug. 1810: R. Russell (ed.), *The Early Correspondence of Lord John Russell* (2 vols., London, 1913), vol. I, p. 131.

If moderate and extreme Reform could be separated, the issue might at last turn on Whig numbers, even if these were not a reflection of a nation-wide commitment to the issue. Yet the Catholic Question increasingly acted, in the eyes of some ministerialists, to make all reform seem alike a challenge to basic principle. On 6th June 1810 Lord Donoughmore presented the Lords with a further collection of Catholic petitions. Eldon opposed: 'He was too sensible of the blessings of the civil and religious liberty enjoyed in this country to risk them on a speculation of which the grounds were not distinctly laid.' The motion failed by 154 to 68.[45] Much the same happened on 18th June 1811. Donoughmore repeated his motion. The Bishop of Norwich and Lord Grenville urged the opinions of Pitt, Fox, Burke and Windham in favour of the Catholics; Hoadly and Locke were cited; Wake was represented as agreeing with them. Eldon replied: Pitt had never disclosed the 'securities and safeguards' which would have to accompany Emancipation.

When I look into the books which lay down the principles of our laws and constitution in Church and State, – the books of civil law, the books of canon law, nay, the Book of Common Prayer, which last, I think, ought to have its weight, and a conclusive weight, with a reverend prelate of our Church [the Bishop of Norwich, a Whig], – I cannot, especially as a lawyer, accept the opinion of Mr Fox, for whose name I have much respect, – nor those of Mr Pitt, Mr Burke, and Mr Windham, – as decisive on this subject. We are now told that the King's supremacy means nothing. I can hardly tell where I am – I could hardly think myself in a British House of Lords, when I heard some of the things uttered this night. I have read something of Archbishop Wake, having myself, in early life, been intended for the Church, and I can quote him, page by page, with other noble Lords; and I can quote Fénelon, too, on some of these subjects. Am I too rash in standing upon the Constitution of England and the principles of the Revolution, which united and knitted together a Protestant State and Constitution, and a Protestant Church Establishment, for the express purpose of handing them down together, with all their benefits, to our remotest posterity? Will your Lordships concur to alter the settlement of 1688, by consenting to a motion which can create only uneasiness and disappointment? There is no security to be heard of but the rejected Veto.[46] I may be called a bigot, ay, very likely, a monk; but in answer to such epithets I have still to say, Give me your distinct propositions – explain to me your safeguards and your securities – and then I will most anxiously consider and examine them on their own grounds, and see what can be done; but I will not consent to go into a Committee on any general statement of a petition.

The House agreed by 121 to 62.[47]

Nor were reforming moves all in one direction. Anglican politicians and prelates were concerned not only at the growth of itinerant preaching which the sectarian revival brought, but at the growing attempts to secure

---

[45] Twiss, *Eldon*, vol. II, p. 123.
[46] Lord Grenville had proposed as a safeguard a British veto on the appointment of Catholic bishops; Catholics had rejected the idea.
[47] Twiss, *Eldon*, vol. II, pp. 176–7.

exemption from military service by registering under the 'Toleration' Acts of 1689 and 1779 as a Dissenting minister. Sidmouth raised the problem in Parliament in June 1809 and June 1810, and, on reflection, ministerial emphasis shifted to a consideration of the threat posed by Dissenting itinerancy as such. Sidmouth's remedy was a Bill, introduced in May 1811, which would have greatly strengthened the powers of JPs in Quarter Sessions to refuse registration. But it produced a swift and massive nation-wide reaction in the form of a petitioning movement. Liverpool pointed to the priority of maintaining an anti-Catholic front, and warned of the danger of Dissenters and Catholics making common cause; Sidmouth prudently withdrew the Bill.[48] The contrast is great between the increasing political weight of various forms of non-Anglican religion, and the still shallow appeal and repeated failure at Westminster of abstract radical theories of representation. What was ultimately decisive was not the excited and noisy posturing of a handful of articulate London radicals, which only served to increase Whig caution, but the slow and profound shifts of allegiance in the country at large, and the use to which they were put by politicians.

The Whigs meanwhile, lukewarm on Reform, nailed their colours to the mast of Emancipation. In January 1812 the state of George III's health made it clear that authority was now permanently in the hands of the Prince Regent. He quickly began overtures to form a new ministry by the inclusion of some of the Whigs. Eldon at once refused to serve with Grey and Grenville,[49] chiefly on the issues of principle which the Catholic Question raised. Grey and Grenville made the issue a *sine qua non* and refused to join a coalition. So the Whigs' greatest chance of a reversal of their fortunes slipped away; their indignation soon soured relations with the Prince Regent and shut the door on further negotiations.

It was the improbable figure of Spencer Perceval who then narrowly succeeded in fashioning that alliance of conservative forces, soon inherited by Liverpool, which weathered the most desperate crises of European convulsion and domestic distress over the next decade, as the war reached its climax and disaffection at home took on its most revolutionary appearance. At Westminster, the challenge took a familiar form: once again Lord Donoughmore moved for a Committee on the Catholic claims, on 21st April 1812; once again Eldon delivered a formidable oration in reply in defence of the principles of 1688; the motion was lost by 174 to 102. The question of Reform was overshadowed. Brand's repeated motion on 8th May 1812 before 'empty benches', as he admitted, showed widespread indifference even within his own party; Grenvillites were even prominent in speaking against. Brand secured only 88 votes (against 215) out of a Whig

[48] R. W. Davis, *Dissent in Politics 1780–1830. The Political Life of William Smith, MP* (London, 1971), pp. 148–69, 171.
[49] Twiss, *Eldon*, vol. II, pp. 187–9.

maximum strength of some 164.[50] 'The flame of 1809 burned lower and lower, flickered, and went out.'[51]

The vital question was not Reform but Emancipation. Spencer Perceval's assassination on 11th May 1812 compelled a ministerial reshuffle. The Cabinet felt obliged to recruit Canning and Lord Wellesley to keep out Grey and Grenville; yet the two first would only serve in a government not committed against Emancipation. Liverpool's long ministry began with the issue an 'open question'. Wellesley, on behalf of the new recruits, moved on 1st July for taking the question into consideration: again Eldon's resistance was effective. The balance of forces, even under the new ministerial alignment, was shown to be decisively against such a measure. The 'open question' arrangement proved to be an excuse for inactivity. World events dominated the national agenda as the war moved to its climax.

III. DEMOCRACY, DEMOGRAPHY, DISSENT: THE EROSION OF THE OLD SOCIETY

Several issues overlapped in the post-1815 reform debates. There was a provincial protest against the metropolitan elite's affluence and corruption. There was a moving desire by the starving and the desperate to see in universal suffrage a remedy for their material distress, the elevation of 'Reform' into a shibboleth. There was a successful attempt by radical agitators to use such forces as a battering-ram against the ancien regime as a whole. There were the extreme doctrines of universal manhood suffrage, worked out by heterodox Dissenting intellectuals in the 1770s and 1780s, ideas still capable of alarming almost everyone, and now the property of an increasing number of those disaffected towards the Anglican establishment. And there was a Whig willingness to countenance moderate, piecemeal reform both for its own sake and to head off radical extremism. Moderate reform was, of these, the least effective. It was highly reticent about franchise extension: Brand's speech in support of his motion of 1810 explained a plan to give the vote in the counties to copyholders and in the boroughs to householders paying parish rates, a modest measure. Instead, central to the moderate case was the redistribution of seats from 'rotten' boroughs to new concentrations of population.

Yet the issue of redistribution failed to engage with a widespread sense of grievance. Discussion of the question has often revolved around an assumption that the new industrial towns were 'unrepresented'.[52] In fact,

---

[50] Cannon, *Parliamentary Reform*, p. 163; *Parl Debs*, vol. XXXIII, cols. 99–161: 'he confessed, that on such a subject, he expected a more full attendance of those members who usually voted on the same principles with himself'.

[51] Cannon, *Parliamentary Reform*, p. 164.

[52] Cannon, *Parliamentary Reform*, p. 31: 'The first census, in 1801, revealed that of the seven largest towns in England, four – Manchester, Birmingham, Leeds and Sheffield – were not represented at all.' Cf. p. 171: 'the unrepresented towns – Manchester, Birmingham...'

their residents almost always voted[53] in the elections for the county in which the town was situated, and did so on the relatively wide forty-shilling freeholder franchise which applied in all counties – a franchise much wider that that applying in many boroughs returning their own MPs. Any demand from the new towns for 'representation' was therefore a demand for a privilege additional to that enjoyed by all other county voters, including the citizens of many other small towns merged in the county electorate. It proved exceedingly difficult for reformers to induce the populations of industrial centres to demand what would initially appear as a privilege, not a right hitherto withheld. Local men indeed often pointed to the absence of political strife in such towns as a commercial advantage: a writer in the *Leeds Intelligencer* in 1792 observed that 'It is notorious that elections promote profligacy, immorality and indolence; it is also equally notorious that those manufacturing towns (such as ours and Manchester) which delegate no Members are in a more prosperous condition than those which elect their representatives.'[54] He echoed Burke:

When did you hear in Great Britain of any province suffering from the inequality of its representation? what district from having no representation at all?... The very inequality of representation, which is so foolishly complained of, is perhaps the very thing which prevents us from thinking or acting as members for districts. Cornwall elects as many members as all Scotland. But is Cornwall better taken care of than Scotland?[55]

The absence of separate representation for new centres of population, and narrow franchises in many existing parliamentary boroughs, were offset by the fact that the inhabitants of almost every place (including those boroughs) who could possess themselves of sufficient property to qualify as forty-shilling freeholders could *ipso facto* obtain votes, for their county MPs.[56] Poverty, not principle, set the hurdle; increasing prosperity helped ever greater numbers to surmount it; and this can only have acted to dissipate mass support for redistribution as such. The vital issue was the franchise, not redistribution; but the wide extension of the franchise could only be demanded on grounds of principle far more radical than any but a minority were prepared to entertain.

Nor, until the 1820s, was redistribution a useful ploy for securing a closer representation of population (in effect, a more democratic system) by asking for something else. Estimates differed of the population, its distribution and its growth or decline; reliable statistics were not available until the census

---

[53] The position was more complex in certain boroughs which had the status of county: cf. D. C. Moore, *The Politics of Deference. A Study of the Mid-nineteenth Century English Political System* (Hassocks, 1976), p. 459.

[54] Quoted in C. Emsley, *British Society and the French Wars 1793–1815* (London, 1979), p. 11.

[55] *Reflections on the Revolution in France* in Burke, *Works*, vol. III, p. 481.

[56] This perhaps explains the relative unimportance, and infrequent use, of the concept of 'virtual representation'.

of 1801, and trends were only established by comparison with subsequent censuses in 1811 and 1821. (A similar ignorance surrounded the facts of sectarian allegiance until the religious census of 1851.) The 1801 census revealed London's population as equal to that of the next *seventy* towns and cities combined:[57] the urban phenomenon still meant, overwhelmingly, London, and this was a fact to which politicians had attended for decades if not centuries. London was already highly politicised. The inhabitants of the conurbation, too, though not represented in proportion to their numbers, nevertheless voted in the election of ten MPs: four for the City of London itself, two each for Southwark, Westminster, and the County of Middlesex; and it is not clear that the capital's powerful continued growth made a significant difference in this period to its long-standing political literacy.

Nor did the most recent forces of economic change produce urbanisation alone: 'the industrial and population expansion of the eighteenth century was almost as great proportionally in the countryside as in the towns'.[58] Much industry grew up in small towns and villages, often in previously isolated and thinly populated areas: in 1801 places like Blackburn, Bolton, Bradford, Halifax, Huddersfield, Macclesfield, Oldham, Preston, Stockport, Swansea, Wakefield, Walsall, Wigan and Wolverhampton were no larger than ancient county towns and market towns like York, Exeter, Shrewsbury or Oxford. Even in 1831 the group first listed was still no larger than the flourishing ancien-regime resorts of Bath and Brighton, and still markedly smaller than the old commercial centres of Bristol and Norwich or the port and dockyard towns – Hull, Liverpool, Newcastle on Tyne, Plymouth, Portsmouth. Only four new industrial centres had moved into a higher league by 1831: Manchester, Birmingham, Leeds and Sheffield; and they still amounted to only 3.89 per cent of the total population of England and Wales.[59]

Moreover, although some new industrial centres were growing rapidly, the number of their voters was still modest compared to that of their surrounding counties. It is a measure of the social standing of the vast majority of industrial workers that the forty-shilling freeholder franchise produced only a small number of eligible electors in the new towns. In 1807, Leeds contributed only 627 voters and Sheffield 596 to Yorkshire's total of 23,007; in 1820 Birmingham contributed only 399 to Warwickshire's 3,122.[60] The contrast was great in this respect between the new towns and

---

[57] In 1801, the population of Greater London was 1,117,000; in 1831, 1,907,000: B. R. Mitchell and P. Deane, *Abstract of British Historical Statistics* (Cambridge, 1971), p. 19.

[58] J. Rule, *The Experience of Labour in Eighteenth-Century Industry* (London, 1981), p. 18.

[59] Mitchell and Deane, *Statistics*, pp. 24–6.

[60] The proportion was, however, rising in industrialising counties, and given added significance by the partisanship of urban voters: Moore, *Politics of Deference*, p. 458.

the effect of 'old money' in the capital, for London's overflow into Middlesex produced great numbers of freehold county voters.

Electorally, the nascent industrial centres were not *per se* a dynamic force before c. 1830. Areas of new industry were remarkably quiescent, in terms of parliamentary politics, during the first stage of the so-called 'Industrial Revolution'. Lancashire, Derbyshire and Staffordshire witnessed only 'token contests' in the years 1800–32; Cheshire was uncontested at general elections since 1734, Nottinghamshire since 1722. Yorkshire saw only one real, and one 'token' contest between 1734 and 1832; Warwickshire was contested only once after 1774. Lancashire's and Staffordshire's last real contests were in 1747, Derbyshire's in 1768. The inappropriateness of analysing even industrialising areas on assumptions drawn from modern practice is again clear.

Aside from the threat of revolution, the growing industrial centres of the northern counties markedly failed to generate much parliamentary 'pressure from without' on the part of a nascent manufacturing or working class interest: if contests provide an index, the manufacturing interest seems to have found expression within the old system, as the early careers of Peel and Gladstone, both from manufacturing families, also show. (For decades many growing commercial centres, like Liverpool, preferred aristocratic candidates as their MPs: their connections made them better parliamentary lobbyists, and they were impartial as between local economic interests.) The great majority of electors, with the franchise as it stood, still lived in the countryside, in villages and in small towns, voting for their county MPs. According to 'unreformed' political criteria, even the counties in which heavy industry was sited were not yet markedly more urbanised than the long-prosperous south.[61] Seen in *this* perspective, in the terms of the ancien régime, the industrial phenomenon was still of minor importance. Only in the light of extreme radical principles of personal representation did the mushrooming centres of population appear as a major and a real grievance; and those principles were entertained by only a few. Contemporaries within the traditional order did not therefore have nearly as sharp a perception of technological-industrial developments transforming an 'old society' as have most subsequent historians. The new was still viewed through the eyes of the old, and recognised as generically similar.

The elements of continuity were indeed still vastly greater than the dissimilarities. In many ways, industrial man fell short of his gleaming new social ideals. One reason for the remarkable tardiness with which Reform

---

[61] The above is based on the tables in Cannon, *Parliamentary Reform*, pp. 276–98. Figures for the percentage of the county vote made up by towns contributing over 100 voters give: Hampshire 1806, 34 per cent, Surrey 1826, 34 per cent, Durham 1820, 34 per cent, Cambridgeshire 1830, 33 per cent, Kent 1802, 32 per cent; but Yorkshire 1807, 22 per cent, Warwickshire 1820, 18 per cent. Once again, Professor Cannon's evidence gives reasons for the *unimportance* of parliamentary reform.

emerged as a major issue was that until the 1830s many even of committed reformers believed (probably correctly) that the vast majority of potential voters still subscribed to the political values of the old society – 'corruption', as later ages were to term them. As the Unitarian Smith reminded a meeting of reformers in 1816, 'You have against your course the whole body of corrupt electors in the kingdom: and in vain will Parliament be reformed, in vain will it be attempted to make choice for its members of men faithful and zealous in the discharge of their duties, unless the electors themselves be honest and incorrupt.' Widening the franchise would only let in more 'corrupt' voters;[62] and some historians have indeed suggested that the 1832 Act increased the incidence of bribery.[63] Whigs, too, realised this: the £10 householder franchise of the Reform Bill was deliberately intended to exclude the working man, and did have that effect.[64]

If the great majority of previous voters recognised this also, and acknowledged no democratic imperative to enfranchise the masses, why did the Whigs steadily grow in numbers after their schism in 1794? There was one consideration which was able to override Anglican, gentry influence and to promote consistent voting for the Whig opposition, even though many Whigs were committed to Reform, and despite the danger of a newly enfranchised multitude proving to be drunken and corruptible, or even xenophobic, anti-Jacobin monarchists. One consideration above all operated to create a powerful and principled voting bloc: religious affiliation. Pollbook analysis for the late eighteenth century[65] has revealed that even in urban constituencies, and whether or not the constituency had a record of political conflict and literacy, no significant and consistent differences of social status distinguished the voters supporting administration candidates from those voting for the opposition.[66] By 1802, the correlation with anti-ministerial voting was not of economically-determined social strata but of religious denomination, namely any subdivision of Protestant Dissent. This identification emerged with time. In the reigns of George I and George II, Dissenters were inescapably committed to Whig candidates. In 1761 some 70 per cent of a sample of Norwich Dissenters voted for administration

---

[62] Davis, *Smith*, p. 146. Only in 1823 did the Protestant Dissenting Deputies adopt a contrary view, looking to extra-parliamentary campaigning rather than high-political manoeuvre to achieve Repeal. In fact, no such campaign was organised. It was manoeuvre which secured Repeal in 1828.

[63] J. A. Phillips, *Electoral Behaviour in Unreformed England* (Princeton, 1982), pp. 77–8.

[64] Cannon, *Parliamentary Reform*, pp. 256–7.

[65] Phillips, *Electoral Behaviour*, pp. 253–305. Dr Phillips uses his figures for a critique of the class analysis adopted in the work of the Hammonds, the Webbs, Rudé, Hobsbawm, Douglas Hay, E. P. Thomson *et al.*

[66] Phillips conceded that Norwich voters in 1796 and 1802 were a 'possible exception' (p. 275). It may be that the largest cities, at the very end of the century, especially London, begin to witness slight effects of wealth in influencing voter preference: more work is needed here. But it is the tardiness and weakness of any such influence, and the few constituencies in which it was evident, which is remarkable.

candidates (marginally more than of Norwich voters as a whole); by 1768 this was down to a little over 60 per cent, and in Northampton to slightly more than 50 per cent. Ministerial loyalty then collapsed to under 5 per cent in Northampton in 1774, and to about 20 per cent in Norwich in 1780. Equally, Dissenting support of anti-administration candidates climbed steeply to reach almost 90 per cent of voting Dissenters in Norwich in 1802. There the decisive break, the point at which Dissenters diverged dramatically from all other voters, came between the elections of 1768 and 1780 (1774 seeing no contest); in Northampton the existence of a contest in 1774 highlights the dramatic conversion to opposition of Dissent since 1768. Dissenters provided the reliable, consistent psephological backbone of a reviving party. Whig numbers rose from about 150 in c. 1800–10 to slightly over 200 in c. 1820–30, plus a fringe of doubtfuls:[67] insufficient alone to capture power, but enough to hold office after the ministerial schism of 1829–30.

Parliamentary reform as such remained an abstract question of principle which manifestly failed to evoke a mass response. Even in Norwich, where political consciousness was unusually sophisticated and frequently exercised, the attempt to use the issue in the 1818 election produced 'no mass demonstration of popular support'. Radical agitation in Norwich still 'came from above, not from below... Norwich radicalism was led by Dissenters, mostly Unitarians.'[68] Major Cartwright's missionary tours of the midlands and north in 1812–13 similarly evoked little interest in Reform, except in so far as it was a subsidiary manifestation of something else.[69] When Henry Hunt appealed to the huge electorate of Westminster in 1818 on a platform of universal manhood suffrage, he received only eighty-four votes.

Nor was Emancipation a popular issue. Whig candidates found their party's commitment to Emancipation an embarrassment, and successfully played it down at the polls. It seems that their opponents in 1812, 1818 and 1820 neglected to challenge them on it, and anti-Catholicism was limited and unorganised even at the 1826 elections.[70] Not until mid 1828 was the Brunswick Club movement launched by the Ultras as an answer to O'Connell's Catholic Association.[71] By the mid 1820s, the 'condition of England question', the economy, the Corn Laws and parliamentary reform were powerful weights, usually in the scale against anti-Catholicism. In the 1826 elections, pro-Catholics often concealed their intentions from the

---

[67] Mitchell, *Whigs in Opposition*, pp. 60–1.
[68] Davis, *Smith*, p. 133.
[69] J. E. Cookson, *The Friends of Peace. Anti-war Liberalism in England 1793–1815* (Cambridge, 1982), p. 193.
[70] For the 1826 general election, G. I. T. Machin, *The Catholic Question in English Politics 1820 to 1830* (Oxford, 1964), pp. 63–87.
[71] *Ibid.*, pp. 131–56. One critic suggested they would more aptly be called 'Stuart Clubs': the House of Brunswick stood for religious liberty.

electors, and Liverpool's adherence to the principle of the 'open question' meant that the Treasury did not systematically back anti-Catholic candidates. In Ireland, the Catholic Association made significant popular gains, and seemed set to sweep the board in the future. In England, Wales and Scotland the balance tilted slightly, producing a net anti-Catholic gain of sixteen MPs in England, a net loss of three in Ireland.[72] Popular anti-Catholicism was widespread, but was not organised to a single end. People were given what was thought to be good for them: the evangelical rank-and-file, including Old Dissent, were largely anti-Catholic; but the majority of their representatives in Parliament voted for Emancipation.[73]

The indications are that the doctrine of the Protestant constitution, 'Church and State', remained convincing for those whom it convinced; but that they steadily diminished as a percentage of the population. To Anglicans, it could seem that the failure of the Church to extend her care to new centres of population, rather than the unacceptability of her teachings, was the cause of her decline: 'the increase of Methodism and sectarian disunion, ought to be considered a consequence rather than a cause of the present state of the established church'.[74] One aspect of the problem was geographical. As William Otter, later Bishop of Chichester, observed in 1820, the labourers were increasingly living 'in crowded and populous villages, in the neighbourhood of the towns, where they form as it were an isolated class, without that due admixture of ranks and orders, which in all other cases tends, by the infusion of benevolence, respect, and intelligence, to temper and soften the whole mass'.[75] Even in rural society, as Edmund Law's son, now Bishop of Bath and Wells, feared in 1831, 'the strong tie which had for ages bound together the clergyman and his parishoners, the landlord and his tenants, by a sense of benefits mutually conferred and received, appears now to be inauspiciously weakened, if not entirely rent and torn asunder'.[76]

Industrialisation in itself did not produce a rejection of Anglican doctrine by the labouring population. Nor, it seems, did urbanisation in itself, for rates of church attendance had already declined substantially in the countryside.[77] What changed was not the theoretical validity or potential success of Anglicanism in an urban or industrial society, but the emergence of that society very largely beyond the pale of the traditional Anglican

---

[72] *Ibid.*, pp. 85–6, 195.
[73] Cf. J. H. Hexter, 'The Protestant Revival and the Catholic Question in England, 1778–1829', *JMH* 8 (1936), 297–319.
[74] Rev. Richard Yates, *The Church in Danger* (London, 1815), p. 95.
[75] Rev. William Otter, *Reasons for Continuing the Education of the Poor at the Present Crisis: A Sermon, Preached...16th of March, 1820* (Shrewsbury, 1820), pp. 31–2.
[76] G. H. Law, Bishop of Bath and Wells, *A Charge...at the Visitation of the Diocese, in May, and June, 1831* (Wells, [1831]), pp. 18–19.
[77] E. R. Norman, *Church and Society in England 1770–1970* (Oxford, 1976), pp. 50–1.

parochial structure. First, new industrial centres were very often located in places which had never been within the nexus of squire and parson, and the Church did not act swiftly to extend her parochial ministrations to such areas. Secondly, English society in the early nineteenth century experienced unprecedentedly rapid demographic change. The estimated population of England grew from 8,664,490 in 1801 to 13,283,882 in 1831; and these gross figures conceal a still larger shift, 13,211,295 births and 8,191,762 deaths being estimated between these dates.[78] The death of one cohort of eighteenth-century Anglicans and the arrival of new, much larger cohorts posed a vast problem of education if these new masses of population were to be assimilated into the Anglican-aristocratic nexus. The Establishment eventually responded with impressive programmes of school and church building,[79] but it did so after the problem had become acute, and did so on an insufficient scale to prevent very many of these new cohorts either evading Anglican teaching altogether, or interpreting their religious indifference in terms both sectarian and political.

This process had little to do with the 'objective' pressure of any material 'reality'. Even radicals before 1789, including the most extreme men of the Society for Constitutional Information, had phrased their critique of the establishment in terms which owed almost nothing to an economic analysis of causes or solutions. For all their talk of 'the people', they had little practical sympathy for suffering humanity. When Paine tacked on schemes of social engineering to the critique of the ancien regime in *Rights of Man*, the radical intelligentsia responded least to his economic planning. The patrician Society of the Friends of the People embraced Reform without envisaging consequences of social reconstruction. Leading individuals, too, provided personal links with much older reforming idioms. Important among them was John Cartwright (1740–1824), whose *The Commonwealth in Danger* (1795) offered, in response to French stimuli, an echo of early-eighteenth-century Commonwealthmen's vision of a gentry-ruled, militia-defended republic.[80] Almost his last work, *The English Constitution Produced and Illustrated* of 1823, included the familiar condemnation of monarchical inequalities and a recommendation of Deism.[81] Cartwright's

---

[78] E. A. Wrigley and R. S. Schofield, *The Population History of England 1541–1871* (London, 1981), pp. 500–1, 528–9 (the figures exclude Monmouth). Some qualifications must be made. On one hand, many of the burials were of young people. On the other, making for the dilution of the old homogeneity, was the effect of the emigration of Anglican English and the immigration of Catholic Irish.

[79] Norman, *Church and Society*, pp. 52–61.

[80] J. W. Osborne, *John Cartwright* (Cambridge, 1972), pp. 47, 52–3: 'Some of the conservatives who rejected any suggestion of reform may have had a truer understanding of the possibilities of an extension of the suffrage than most advocates of change.'

[81] *Ibid.*, p. 147. Cartwright (aged 84) sent a copy to the American Deist, Thomas Jefferson (aged 81); it was not only the ancien regime which was about to die, but a particular cohort of its critics.

indefatigable efforts carried into the activity of the 1820s a radicalism largely devoid of explicit economic purpose. By 1820, most radicals still 'expressed themselves within the framework of that libertarian rhetoric...of constitutional rights... culled from the Saxons and Alfred; the barons and Magna Carta; and from Russell, Hampden, Sidney, and the Bill of Rights'. Far from taking a more forward-looking course, the campaigns of 1817–19 saw a revival of Deist- and infidel-inspired attacks on the Church and the 'Political Priestcraft' of the ancien regime.[82] So powerful was this complex legacy that, into the 1840s and long afterwards, English radicalism never wholly accommodated itself to Marxist precepts. The old anti-monarchical, anti-aristocratic, anticlerical ideal of cheap government was indeed inimical to any legislative programme which might be derived from Paine, and Cartwright did much to prevent economic goals being central to radicalism as most of the political classes saw it.[83]

The common man, less articulate, less intelligent, less informed than his artisan-radical leaders, was still slower to perceive and to leap aboard the industrial bandwaggon of class action. Sometimes even very much older mass allegiances surfaced from the folk memory, as in 1802 when an informer claimed knowledge of a plot to 'Ristore the throne Back from this present Royal Family, which Rob'd the Stuard Family of it.'[84] Mass bitterness and hatred, nocturnal gatherings, illegal oaths, drilling, anonymous threats, acts of violence, conspiracies – all were widely known about, even if accurate information was impossible for anyone to obtain; the Jacobin option obviously provided a perfectly viable successor to the Jacobite as the possible occasion for action. The apparent unavailability of vast areas of meliorist social reform later at the centre of populist radical attention meant that the common man was still presented with relatively simple options of obedience or revolt, and it would be wrong to underestimate the revolutionary possibilities of early-nineteenth-century Britain and Ireland.[85] Proletarian mass meetings, violence and threats were therefore still widely perceived as merely the first steps towards insurrection, as indeed they were in Ireland in 1798. Since economic fluctuations and postwar disruptions were largely beyond the power of the State to remedy, the natural solution to such dangers seemed a reassertion of traditional ideals of social order, and the presence or absence of revolution would be treated as an index of the effectiveness of those ideals. What finally made them untenable was not the scale of popular disorder, which declined sharply with

---

[82] J. Ann Hone, *For the Cause of Truth. Radicalism in London 1796–1821* (Oxford, 1982), pp. 322, 333–9.

[83] There were some exceptions among radical activists, including Thomas Spence and Robert Owen; but they were few, and their influence came later.

[84] Quoted in Harvey, *Britain*, p. 83.

[85] For a review of the evidence for 1797–1802, cf. Hone, *Radicalism*, pp. 41–82; for 1811–13, pp. 232–7; for 1817–20, pp. 270–319.

economic recovery in the 1820s, but the intellectual challenge offered to those ideals by the alternative ideals and practice of sectarianism and atheism, and the political articulation which they received.

In ancien-regime England, the mass of the population was organised, given an identity and a direction within the public arena (in so far as those things happened at all) not by political parties but by churches. Not until the 1830s did parties assume a psephological role that led to progressive bouts of franchise extension. Not until the 1850s did the Liberal party assume from Dissenting religion the role of intellectual and moral emancipator of small men from traditional ties, obligations and allegiances.[86] To understand traditional society, therefore, we must look not only at pollbooks but also at the Church and the sects.

What was evident in England in the half century after the American Revolution was not any massive conversion of the population to toleration (Repeal, Emancipation) or democracy (Reform), but the largely negative phenomenon of the steady erosion of Anglicanism, and the related growth of Protestant Dissent and unbelief. Except in the 1690s, the gradual, silent disengagement of many of the labouring people from formal Anglican affiliation failed to evoke much alarm or comment. Before 1789 their silence could still realistically be interpreted as assent. It was complained of by incumbents as apathy, not atheism. Anglicanism was a natural thing, almost universal; taken for granted; inherited; acquired like one's nationality:

The general notion appears to be, that, if born in a country of which Christianity is the established religion, we are born Christians. We do not therefore look out for positive evidence of being out of that number; but putting the *onus probandi* (if it may be so expressed) on the wrong side, we conceive ourselves such *of course*, except our title be disproved by positive evidence to the contrary.[87]

Wilberforce hardly found it necessary to say *Anglican* Christianity.

It was not silent absenteeism but organised, formal Dissent to which churchmen had normally addressed themselves, and, from the 1790s, Jacobin ideology added a new target. Within the public arena, as was suggested above, the Church's theoretical success was considerable. But this very success, in the circumstances which arose after 1789, cast the Church in a new role. From defending 'order' as such, she now seemed to increasing numbers to be defending a particular social order. To those outside the Anglican nexus, 'Church and State' doctrine seemed only an increasingly accurate description of aristocratic-monarchical hegemony. A one-class society, and a confessional State, could be made to seem a justification of only a part of society, dominating the rest by the mechanics of patronage and corruption.

[86] Cf. John Vincent, *The Formation of the Liberal Party 1857–1868* (London, 1966).
[87] William Wilberforce, *A Practical View of the Prevailing Religious System of Professed Christians, in the Higher and Middle Classes of this Country, Contrasted with Real Christianity* (London, 1797), p. 296.

The Church, time out of mind, had defended property and preached obedience to sovereigns and social superiors. These realities had not changed; what was new was the perspective in which this social role was increasingly cast by the existence of a growing bloc of society within the ranks of Dissent, religious indifference, and Jacobin atheism. In 1801, a pamphleteer appealed: 'Every kind of separation from the Established Church, by narrowing the ground on which that Church stands, tends to weaken the foundation on which the government of this country is built.'[88] This was not a controversial claim. In his episcopal *Charge* of 1799, Bishop Cleaver of Chester predicted that 'at no very distant period' the Anglican Church would 'lose its due weight and influence in the political constitution of these kingdoms' since 'an increasing majority of dissidents, however heterogeneous in the complexion and sentiment of the component parts' successfully united against it.[89]

It is difficult to quantify this claim; but it would be wrong to exaggerate it. Roman Catholics were a tiny minority in eighteenth-century Britain, rising to about 129,000 in 1800 as Irish immigration began to get under way. The total of Protestant Nonconformists has been estimated at 312,000 in Britain by 1810: they had not yet recovered the total of 355,000 estimated for England and Wales in 1715 (6.2 per cent of the population of England, 5.7 per cent of Wales). Of the 1810 figure the Methodists contributed by far the largest part: some 145,000 in 1810, they rose to about 315,000 in 1832 (of which the Wesleyans contributed about 256,000). Yet even the Wesleyans, at the 1831 census, constituted only 2.38 per cent of the population of Britain over the age of 15 (against 7.2 per cent for Anglican Easter communicants). Even this represented a substantial advance on the Wesleyans' very small numbers in the eighteenth century: 56,000 in 1791; still only 87,000 by 1801. Figures for other Dissenting congregations were lower still: in 1800, Congregationalists are estimated at 35,000; Particular Baptists at 24,000; General Baptists at 3,000.[90]

Growth rates among Dissenting groups were often high not least because their initial numbers were very low; preoccupation with the phenomenon of growth has distracted attention from the fact that Dissenting totals were

[88] *A Letter Humbly Addressed to the Most Rev. and Right Rev. the Archbishops and Bishops of the Church of England* (London, 1801), p. 15: A. D. Gilbert, 'Methodism, Dissent and Political Stability in Early Industrial England', *Journal of Religious History* 10 (1978–9), 389.

[89] Quoted in N. U. Murray, 'The Influence of the French Revolution on the Church of England and its Rivals, 1789–1802' (Oxford D.Phil. thesis, 1975), p. 391.

[90] The above figures are from R. Currie, A. Gilbert and L. Horsley, *Churches and Churchgoers. Patterns of Church Growth in the British Isles since 1700* (Oxford, 1977), pp. 23, 65, 154, 161; Watts, *The Dissenters*, vol. I, p. 270; A. D. Gilbert, *Religion and Society in Industrial England. Church, Chapel and Social Change, 1740–1914* (London, 1976), pp. 28, 31, 37. Dr John Walsh reminds me that the number of Methodist 'hearers' was considerably larger than the inner corps of ticket holders. Much the same, of course, is true of the Church of England also.

modest in 1800 and not dominant by 1830. Active religious involvement was still, as it had been since the Revolution of 1688, a minority affair; the question was the way in which committed minorities provided leadership and set the tone for the mass of society, residually Christian but less often churchgoing.

Against a pattern of Nonconformist collapse in the early eighteenth century and partial revival at the end must be set figures for a slow Anglican decline in absolute terms (even more in relative terms) throughout the century, and a substantial revival in absolute numbers beginning only after c. 1830. These figures need careful interpretation, however. A sample of Oxfordshire parishes showed a 25 per cent fall in Anglican communicants between 1738 and 1802.[91] Yet this reflects in part the fact that the reception of the sacraments was an increasingly infrequent and special aspect of eighteenth-century Anglican devotional practice, not the regular and frequent index of churchmanship which it became in the wake of the Tractarians. Even in 1851, as the religious census showed, a far smaller percentage of active Anglicans communicated than of any other denomination. Dissenting figures are thus likely to give an exaggerated impression of sectarian strength when set against figures for Anglican communicants. Secondly, the question was not only the extent but the significance of infrequent attendance: only after the 1790s in any area is it realistic to read this as a gauge of anti-Anglican sentiment, with the end of the 'Church and King' mob or anti-Methodist riot – both of which had 'reflected the existence of a conservative consensus which transcended the major barriers of social status in the traditional society'.[92] By the 1820s, Cobbett's *Rural Rides* (though with radical bias) not only recorded the relative absence of the labourer from Anglican services, but echoed the farmer's (and, by reflection, the common man's) widespread rejection of the moral authority of the Church. This rejection fed on the frictions generated in rural society by the operation of tithe, enclosure and poor law;[93] but popular disengagement from the Anglican nexus had already begun. Rural discontent was nothing new; but from about the 1790s, its expression was different. Discontent was often translated into disaffection by Dissent: men were persuaded of a group interest as a sect, against the Church; not yet as a class, against the employer.

Although 'respectable' Evangelicals within the Church preached Orthodox politico-theological doctrines, accepting rank, order and degree, the phenomenon at parish level was sometimes different: evangelical zeal could

---

[91] Gilbert, *Religion and Society*, p. 27.

[92] *Ibid.*, p. 79; John Walsh, 'Methodism and the Mob in the Eighteenth Century', in C. J. Cuming and D. Baker (eds.), *Popular Belief and Practice* (Cambridge, 1972), pp. 213–27.

[93] E. J. Evans, 'Some Reasons for the Growth of English Rural Anti-Clericalism c. 1750 – c. 1830', *P&P* 66 (1975), 84–109.

imply a condemnation of squire and parson as somnolent if not hypocritical. Itinerant Dissenting preachers, a growing problem from the 1790s, drew this moral in cruder terms: priests and establishments were now held up as a target for popular hostility, and Old Dissent – especially Baptists and Independents – caught the contagion as the evangelical mood spread. This emancipation was not unrelated to the Evangelicals' theology, since despite their emptily formal respect for the social hierarchy they lacked a sense of the Church as an indispensable, authoritative, divinely instituted body. Without this framework, deference to hierarchy as such proved an insufficient barrier against the antinomian implications of evangelical enthusiasm. Could one be both a Christian and a gentleman? No, implied the Evangelicals: the second of those ideals had to be profoundly modified to fit the first (it was so modified in Victorian England). Similarly, Evangelicals' zeal was seemingly for religion, not the Church: their attitude to the Establishment was therefore profoundly equivocal, as contemporaries realised.

Much the same was true of Methodism: official Wesleyan monarchical orthodoxy was sometimes at odds with the local impact of sectarian affiliation, withdrawing men from the Establishment's nexus and providing them with a doctrine which offered scope for a critique of their betters. Wesley's own preaching contained a profound contradiction between its political conservatism and its condemnation of the sinfulness (almost it seemed the *necessary* sinfulness) of the rich, the patrician, or the conventionally learned. The appeal to the poor now contained an explicit rejection of the ideal of the gentleman, as traditional society understood it.[94] For Methodists, and for other Dissenters, the majority of the population, still subscribing to traditional society's values, represented 'the world', a sink of corruption from which the elect must distance themselves in daily life and in allegiance. The Arian-Socinian position of the late 1760s that the Establishment was not merely malfunctioning, calling for piecemeal reform, but positively blasphemous and totally to be rejected was thus increasingly echoed in Methodist and Dissenting *practice*, despite any theological orthodoxy on the doctrine of the Trinity. The title 'Methodist', too, was often loosely applied to itinerants of various persuasions but largely radical politics. Even official Methodists aroused alarm by their very organisation: a nationwide, disciplined, obedient, centrally directed body was something new and alarming in the 'old society', and provoked Southey's observation in 1803 that the Methodists 'are, literally and precisely speaking, an Ecclesiastical Corresponding Society'. In many cases, action was taken to expel radicals from Methodist membership; nevertheless, many Methodists and ex-Methodists were involved with the Luddite and later with the Chartist

---

[94] Cf. John Walsh, 'Elie Halévy and the Birth of Methodism', *TRHS* 5th ser., 25 (1975), 17–19.

disturbances, especially men who seceded in 1811 to form the Primitive Methodists (Loveless, the ringleader of the Tolpuddle conspirators, was a Methodist local preacher).

It remained true both for radical intellectuals and for numbers of mute, inglorious parishioners that Dissent ultimately implied a gesture of defiance against the idea of a hierarchical, deferential Anglican society. The most explicit form of deviance was therefore provided by militant atheism, a largely urban phenomenon. Churchmen into the 1820s lost nothing of their realisation of the fundamental identity of disaffection and irreligion:

...the advocates of sedition...have specially endeavoured, in the pursuit of their nefarious plans, to supplant the Gospel in the minds of those whom they intended to ensnare...Accordingly we are informed, that among the deluded multitudes who were assembled under the various pretexts of Reform, blasphemous pamphlets were industriously circulated; and that the first step made in that revolutionary project, which seemed to threaten the existence of the Constitution itself, was to cast off the fear of God, and their allegiance to our Saviour...the union of disloyalty and irreligion may be traced to the remotest periods of history...But it was reserved for our own times to exhibit in their full maturity the bitter fruits of this foul connection...when we reflect upon the striking resemblance in the characters of the Demagogue and the Infidel, as presented to us in the scenes around us – the same arrogant pretensions to superior light, the same bold assumption of imaginary rights, the same vulgar contempt for every thing that is sacred in authority, or venerable in law, the same disregard of either public or private happiness, provided their own ends can be accomplished – when we consider further the sympathies excited towards each other, in their respective operations, and the mutual assistance and support rendered in each other's difficulties – above all, when we reflect upon the simultaneous movements of that moral volcano, which has scattered so much dismay over our fair cities and fruitful fields, bursting out into the flames of sedition in one place, and pouring forth the clouds and thick darkness of infidelity in another – diversified in the matter and in the form of its eruptions, but always pregnant with destruction to every thing that is peaceful and sacred in the institutions of mankind – the cry of 'there is no God' in one place, answered by the exclamation of 'let there be no king' in another – these are undoubted testimonies that the leaders of these parties are either actuated by the same spirit, and embarked in a common cause, or at least that they are attracted and united by a sense of mutual advantage in their separate pursuits.[95]

Like the law of allegiance, the law of blasphemous and seditious libel provided a definition of central elements in the 'old society'. The first three decades of the nineteenth century saw a wave of prosecutions as the old order sought to defend itself on both fronts. One apparent concession left the reality little changed. In 1813 the Unitarian Smith raised once more the claims last advanced in 1792. The Bill which he brought forward, after negotiations with the ministry, was broadly drawn to affirm a general freedom of religious expression; Lord Eldon shrewdly secured its replacement by a specific Bill repealing the Blasphemy Act of 1697 and equivalent

[95] Otter, *Reasons for Continuing the Education of the Poor*, pp. 15–18.

Scottish legislation. The common law offence of blasphemous libel therefore remained, and Unitarians soon discovered that attacks on Trinitarian Christianity could still be regarded by the courts as within the bounds of this offence. The epic Wolverhampton Chapel case, begun in 1816 and not settled until 1836, was Eldon's opportunity to insist that the 1813 Act had left Unitarianism punishable at common law.[96]

Warburtonian doctrine of an Alliance of Church and State could still be accepted as a minimalist account of a route to something much more positive. Hooker's, and eighteenth-century High Churchmens' views on the essential unity of the two spheres still found a powerful support in the attitude of the law to religion. A maxim of Lord Chief Justice Coke was periodically repeated by judges: in 1676 Sir Matthew Hale, Chief Justice of the King's Bench, in a regularly cited judgement, held that

...such kind of wicked and blasphemous words were not only an offence to God and religion, but a crime against the laws, State and Government, and therefore punishable in this Court; for to say 'Religion is a cheat' is *to dissolve all the obligations whereby the civil societies are preserved*, and *Christianity is parcel of the laws of England*, and, therefore, to reproach the Christian religion is to speak in subversion of law.[97]

In 1729, in the trial of Thomas Woolston, Raymond, CJ, said:

Christianity in general is parcel of the Common Law of England, and therefore to be protected by it. Now, whatever strikes at the very root of Christianity tends manifestly to a dissolution of the civil government; so that to say an attempt to subvert the established religion is not punishable by those laws upon which it is established is an absurdity.[98]

Even the anticlerical Sir Philip Yorke, later Lord Hardwicke, who as Attorney General prosecuted in the case, adhered to the same doctrine;[99] it was cited again at the trial of Carlile in 1819.

This being so, conflict was inevitable; for the period after 1790 marked the emergence as a political force not merely of Dissent, but of unbelief. In 1797, Wilberforce lamented the 'declension of Christianity into a mere system of ethics' and the recent advance of infidelity. The latter, however, was not the result of 'the reasonings of the infidel writers having been much studied':

The literary opposers of Christianity, from Herbert to Hume, have been seldom read. They made some stir in their day: during their span of existence they were noisy and noxious; but like the locusts of the east, which for a while obscure the air, and destroy the verdure, they were soon swept away and forgotten. Their very names would be scarcely found, if Leland had not preserved them from oblivion.

[96] Henriques, *Toleration*, p. 210.
[97] Quoted in W. H. Wickwar, *The Struggle for the Freedom of the Press, 1819–1832* (London, 1928), p. 25.
[98] *Ibid.*, pp. 25–6.
[99] Yorke, *Hardwicke*, vol. I, p. 81.

The cause, rather, was 'the progress of luxury, and the decay of morals'; so far as it was due to the attacks of infidels, it was not by argument but by the accumulating weight of sarcasm and ridicule on those who had merely taken their faith for granted.[100] As Wilberforce wrote to Lord Milton in 1819:

What your lordship and I saw amongst the papers of the Secret Committee, gave me but too much reason to fear that the enemies of our political constitution were also enemies to our religion...Heretofore they inveighed against the inequality of property, and used every artifice to alienate the people from the constitution of their country. But now they are sapping the foundations of the social edifice more effectually by attacking Christianity. The high and noble may be restrained by honour; but religion only is the law of the multitude.[101]

The advance of infidelity is, of course, impossible to quantify. It is, however, possible to follow the conflicts to which the expression of that position gave rise. Deism, and Deism as a euphemism for infidelity, were powerfully advanced by Paine's *Age of Reason*. As commentators realised, it made infidelity accessible to the masses for the first time. From the outset, publishers of the work risked prosecution on a charge of blasphemous libel. Thomas Williams, bookseller to the London Corresponding Society, was fined £1,000 and sentenced to a year's hard labour for publishing a cheap edition of the first part of that work in 1796; only by c. 1811–12 did a freethinking campaign revive on the scale of the 1790s. The Deist publisher Daniel Eaton, similarly jailed in 1803–5 for issuing part 2 of the same work in 1796, resumed his campaign and received eighteen months imprisonment in 1812 for publishing the third part. After the end of the war, infidel invective reached heights of bitterness and virulence exceeding even that of the 1720s.[102] A running battle began with both government and private societies[103] instituting a spate of prosecutions. Writers like Richard Carlile echoed Cobbett's denunciation of taxation, sinecures and bureaucratic corruption and from c. 1818 added to it, more importantly, Paine's assault on the religious basis of the State.

'Deism' now became a thinly disguised euphemism for militant atheism. It was so used, for example, by plebeian propagandists of the stamp of William Hone, whose satires and parodies, including *The Political Litany*, *The*

---

[100] Wilberforce, *Practical View*, pp. 379, 473–4.

[101] R. I. and S. Wilberforce, *The Life of William Wilberforce* (5 vols., London, 1838), vol. v, p. 40.

[102] Cf. Wickwar, *Freedom of the Press* and Joel H. Wiener, *Radicalism and Freethought in Nineteenth-Century Britain. The Life of Richard Carlile* (London, 1983). Those familiar with the works of Toland, Trenchard and Gordon (cf. chapter 5 above) will recognise the idiom; it would be superfluous to compile a catalogue of 1820s denunciations of priests, churches, scriptures and liturgy.

[103] Including the Society for the Suppression of Vice (founded 1802) and the Constitutional Association for Opposing the Progress of Disloyal and Seditious Principles (founded 1821). We need to know more about such bodies.

Sinecurist's Creed and *The Late John Wilkes' Catechism*, published in 1817, brought him to trial the same year. Carlile, detained for republishing Hone's libels, took up the same idiom of blasphemous parodies of the liturgy with *The Order for the Administration of the Loaves and Fishes, or, the Communion of Corruption's Host* (1817). Such ends were most effectively served by the systematic republication of the works of Paine, a task which Carlile now undertook. When he brought out *The Age of Reason* and Elihu Palmer's *Principles of Nature* in December 1818, the result was a conviction for blasphemous libel, and he remained in gaol (though refusing to associate with common prisoners) until 1825. As the appeal judge, Sir John Bayley, observed: 'If...an attack is to be made upon these bonds and rules which embrace together all our moral and social institutions in life, what can be expected as the consequences here and hereafter?'[104]

The arguments of the 1770s were still the most appropriate critique of the ancien regime into the 1820s; Carlile's irreligion was propagated in his paper (1819–25) appropriately titled *The Republican*.[105] Anonymity was still necessary for those not anxious for a confrontation. At this point Bentham joined the hunt, his writings on religion all appearing in a particular period: *Church of Englandism and its Catechism Examined* (1818), *Analysis of the Influence of Natural Religion* (1822) and *Not Paul but Jesus* (1823); but the reaction to the first encouraged him to publish the next two under pseudonyms. Following the 'Six Acts' of 1819, a renewed drive was mounted against the publications of Carlile, Hone and others which ran on through the 1820s, a saga of deliberate martyrdom and increasing extremism on the part of the disaffected, which meant that blasphemy and sedition were only forged more strongly into a radical tradition.[106] It looked back not only to Paine but to the French enemies of the old order – Voltaire, Rousseau, Volney, Diderot, d'Holbach – and beyond to the English Deists of the early eighteenth century. Carlile republished not only Paine and the French classics, but Peter Annet's *Free Enquirer* of 1761. In 1848 the Chartist Thomas Cooper appealed to an intellectual tradition embracing Blount, Toland, Tindal, Collins, Chubb and Bolingbroke.[107] Such men, in the 1820s as in the 1720s, were a small minority, the most extreme of the extreme. Their effectiveness as yet was on the climate of debate rather than on mass

---

[104] Hone, *Radicalism*, pp. 223–8, 336; Wiener, *Carlile*, p. 48.

[105] Ironically, Carlile added an historical theory to his perception of the tyranny and oppression of Hanoverian monarchs. The Glorious Revolution began the rot: William III was an usurper, James II the rightful king. By contrast, Carlile was 'a comparative moderate on social and economic questions', rejecting levelling ideas: Wiener, *Carlile*, pp. 104–5.

[106] Wickwar, *Freedom of the Press*, pp. 82ff.

[107] Edward Royle, *Radical Politics 1790–1900. Religion and Unbelief* (London, 1971), pp. 17–37; idem, *The Infidel Tradition from Paine to Bradlaugh* (London, 1976).

allegiance. Dissent, not Doubt, guided the conduct of the majority of those who rejected the old order.

Nevertheless, a qualification must be made to the impact of Nonconformity. Aggregate numbers alone are not a sufficient index: their geographical distribution is also important. Wesleyan and other forms of Methodism were numerically strongest where Anglicanism was numerically weakest: the effect of Methodism in undermining Anglicanism is qualified by the extent to which Methodism offered a substitute, in different areas. It was the New Dissent – Congregationalists, Baptists – which was strongest where Anglicanism was strongest, offering an alternative, a challenge deliberately hostile to the Established Church; but, as we have seen, these sects were as yet numerically insignificant compared with the Methodists.[108] Here again, the evidence points not so much to a subversion of the 'old society' by the 'new society', as to a growing up of 'the new' in other areas: the old society retained much of its force, in its traditional locations, until events at Westminster in 1828–32 symbolised a decisive confrontation and collision between 'the new' and 'the old' (not until the late 1970s did power swing back decisively to the old Anglican heartlands of the south, south midlands and south east).

Methodism, Dissent, the Evangelical movement both within and outside the Church: the main developments undermining the old society had two important similarities. They were not liberal, and they were not democratic. Liberalism did not yet exist as a concept, and the developments here discussed drew their emotional force from an increase in sectarian bigotry and commitment, not from any growing mood of relaxed, tolerant indifference. Similarly, democracy meant Jacobin-atheist insurrection: new or revitalised sects were often run in highly totalitarian, autocratic ways, and their quite different ends meant that they seldom elevated secular democratic ideals. Liberalism and democracy were Victorian shibboleths, but they had little to do with the hard realities of that society's daily life, and even less to do with how the old society actually ran, or how it was destroyed. The forces hostile to the traditional social order still fell far short of what was needed to overthrow it. There was nothing inevitable about the destruction of Anglican-aristocratic hegemony in 1828–32, and to explain it we must give priority to political events.

IV. THE DEFENCE OF THE PROTESTANT CONSTITUTION, 1815–1827

After 1815, as Lord Eldon's biographer put it, 'the dangerous dispositions which had for a time been absorbed or overlaid by foreign hostility, were

---

[108] Gilbert, *Religion and Society*, pp. 115–21.

again let loose upon the constitution of England'.[109] The strains of economic growth were compounded by the postwar slump, and the years 1815–20 witnessed unprecedented and widespread distress; agitators quickly stepped forward to place their own interpretations on the realities of human suffering. The political classes reacted in familiar fashion. Two parliamentary Committees, set up in 1817 to investigate the unrest after an alleged attempt on the life of the Prince Regent, had no doubt in identifying the commitment of so-called 'Hampden Clubs' to universal manhood suffrage and the secret ballot as a conspiracy to destroy the social order. They were particularly drawn to that conclusion by the blasphemous and anticlerical element which they perceived as basic to revolutionary propaganda. As the Lords' report described the clubs:

...the meetings are frequently terminated, particularly in London, by profane and seditious songs and parodies of parts of the liturgy, in which the responses are chanted by the whole company. By such means, and by the profession of open infidelity in which some of the members indulge in their speeches, the minds of those who attend their meetings are tainted and depraved; they are taught contempt for all decency, all law, all religion and morality, and are thus prepared for the most atrocious scenes of outrage and violence.

Amongst the most effectual means of furthering these dangerous designs, the committee think it their duty particularly to call the attention of the House to the unremitting activity which has been employed throughout the kingdom in circulating to an unprecedented extent, at the lowest prices or gratuitously, publications of the most seditious and inflammatory nature, marked with a peculiar character of irreligion and blasphemy, and tending not only to overturn the existing form of government and order of society, but to root out those principles upon which alone any government or any society can be supported.

The Commons' report added:

It seems, indeed, to be a part of the system adopted by these societies, to prepare the minds of the people for the destruction of the present frame of society, by undermining not only their habits of decent and regular subordination, but all the principles of morals and religion.[110]

The rabble-rousing activities of Henry Hunt, Samuel Bamford and their like gave all too much substance to these fears. The violence of such zealots was brought home to MPs by a petitioning movement orchestrated in early 1817 by Cartwright and (to a lesser extent) Burdett, but this only served to scare Grey and Brougham away from the issue, in common with many previously-sympathetic freeholders. Grey wrote to Wyvill in March 1817: 'I have now no hope of seeing a moderate and useful reform effected during my life, and we have to thank Major Cartwright Mr Cobbett & Co principally for it.'[111] The Whigs, too, were divided in opinion on Reform, many

---

[109] Twiss, *Eldon*, vol. 1, p. 19.
[110] *Parl Debs*, vol. xxxv, cols. 411–19, 438–47.
[111] Quoted Dinwiddy, *Wyvill*, p. 29.

senior figures, including the Grenvilles, being frankly opposed to it on Burkeian grounds. As Grey recognised,

...agreement upon that question is hopeless. It must be left, as it hitherto has been, for individuals to act upon according to their respective opinions. It may undoubtedly assume so much importance as to make this hereafter impossible; but for the present it must be set aside in any consideration of our party politics. To get any declaration in favour of it assented to by the party is obviously out of the question.

As the Benthamite radical John Arthur Roebuck later observed,

All the great Whig families had almost entirely seceded from the ranks of the reformers, and they looked with great jealousy and suspicion upon all who based their pretensions to popular favour upon views of parliamentary reform...the Cavendishes, with the Duke of Devonshire at their head – Lord Fitzwilliam, Lord Milton, Lord Carlisle, Lord Morpeth, Lord Holland, the Duke of Norfolk, together with the men of ability who formed their intellectual *condottieri* – such as Burke, Sheridan, Tierney, Romilly, and others, never adopted reform as the chief topic of their discourse, or made it the chief object of their labours, except when driven by party necessities to employ what always to them appeared a dangerous weapon of offence.[112]

Even the radicals were at odds in such an embittered climate: as Burdett revealingly observed, they 'acted towards each other with the hostility of different sects of religion'.[113] His motion for a Select Committee on Reform on 20th May 1817, the culmination of the campaign, was lost by 265 to 77. When, in June 1818, Burdett blithely introduced a whole compendium of extreme reforming measures, systematised by Bentham, he went down to defeat by 106 to nil.[114] The gap between Whigs and radicals could not have been more sharply revealed.

This did not apply to Emancipation, however. Burdett's Reform motion of 1817 had followed soon after Emancipation motions in both Houses: a brilliant display by Peel in defence of the Protestant constitution was needed to secure a victory in the Commons by 245 to 221.[115] Emancipation was the issue on which the opposition's whole strength could be relied on. They therefore recurred to it. Grattan in the Commons and Donoughmore in the Lords raised the Catholic question once more in May 1819. Eldon's

---

[112] Grey to Holland, 17th Jan. 1817, quoted in A. Mitchell, 'The Whigs and Parliamentary Reform before 1830', *Historical Studies Australia and New Zealand* 12 (1965–7), 24. J. A. Roebuck, *History of the Whig Ministry of 1830, to the Passing of the Reform Bill* (2 vols., London, 1852), vol. 1, p. 205.

[113] Quoted Cannon, *Parliamentary Reform*, p. 170–1. At last, petitions were suddenly procured from the new industrial centres, including Manchester, Birmingham, Sheffield, Leeds, Bradford, Bolton, Halifax, Wolverhampton, Blackburn – apart from the first three, all apparently petitioning for Reform for the first time. This striking coincidence can hardly have been lost on observers.

[114] Cannon, *Parliamentary Reform*, pp. 175–6. It combined annual parliaments, manhood suffrage, secret ballot and equal electoral districts.

[115] N. Gash, *Mr Secretary Peel* (London, 1961), pp. 204–10. Peel thus fully committed himself on the issue in the eyes of his party.

objections were if anything stronger than before: from 1660 to 1688 'the Roman Catholics had systematically pursued the accomplishment of their own objects and the destruction of our national Church, through every obstacle and through every difficulty; and there was no proof that any change had since occurred in their religious principles'; none of the securities proposed would be effective. The House agreed by 147 to 106.[116]

Of the three possibilities – Emancipation, Repeal and Reform – it was not yet the case that each forwarded the cause of the others. O'Connell in October 1819, for example, thought Emancipation best served by isolating it from other questions, especially Reform; English radicals committed to Reform were equally reluctant to make Emancipation a theoretical priority,[117] and it was generally advocated by Catholics on partisan grounds, not by radicals as a general civil right. Dissenters were naturally committed to Repeal, but were divided on Emancipation: Unitarians backed it on principle, but Trinitarian Dissenters influenced by evangelical fervour were very likely to express anti-Popery sentiments. Politically, this was a disastrous split, and prevented Dissenting leaders from whipping up the Dissenting rank and file in the 1820s; only skilful manoeuvre allowed the schism to be disguised to the point where Emancipation and Reform could go through in alliance.[118]

Attention was soon directed to 'corrupt' boroughs which could be made scapegoats under the provisions of Curwen's Act. The 1818 general election provided several. In December 1819 Castlereagh, on behalf of Liverpool's ministry, accepted the principle of such reform, perhaps in order to take the wind from the opposition's sails. Debate was drawn into technicalities, especially in the case of Grampound. It became the first English borough since the seventeenth century to be disenfranchised, its two seats being destined for Leeds by Lord John Russell but diverted to Yorkshire by Lord Liverpool during the Bill's passage through the Lords in May 1821. In retrospect it seemed an important breach of principle. At the time, the prospect of proletarian insurrection and the mass agitation which led to the tragedy of Peterloo in August 1819 served only to confirm the support of the majority for the established order. In January 1820 Earl Grey told his son-in-law that there was little prospect of Reform 'being carried during my life or even yours'.[119]

It was a little premature. Whig leaders soon began to notice that the agricultural interest, articulate enough to recognise the damage done to it by the ministry's Ricardian economic policies, was restive in a way not seen since the Association Movement of the 1780s. Then, as now, a 'Country'

[116] Twiss, *Eldon*, vol. II, pp. 330–5.   [117] Machin, *Catholic Question*, pp. 21, 48.
[118] Cf. R. W. Davis, 'The Strategy of "Dissent" in the Repeal Campaign, 1820–1828', *JMH* 38 (1966), 374–93.
[119] Quoted in M. G. Brock, *The Great Reform Act* (London, 1973), p. 15.

impetus in favour of Reform might indeed provide enough votes to bring the issue within reach of success. If an increase in county Members and a decrease in rotten boroughs could widely be seen as a solution to practical problems, then radical doctrines of representation need not be involved. Grey had fought the 1820 elections on a commitment to Emancipation, the measure most uncongenial to the shires; but in January 1821 he announced to a Northumberland county meeting his dedication to 'a complete and total change in the system of government' of which parliamentary reform would be a principal feature.[120]

The Whigs had abandoned moderation. Plunket's Bill for Roman Catholic relief passed the Commons and arrived in the Lords on 3rd April 1821; Eldon delivered a massive oration on the second reading on 17th, one of only two speeches which he published. It was a recapitulation of his arguments against concession, and a justification of the constitution in Church and State: 'He should ever assert that an established religion was a great benefit to a people – that the object of such an establishment was not to make the Church political, but to make the State religious.' The present Bill would logically lead to a repeal of the Test and Corporation Acts; its object was not to relieve Catholics from 'pains and penalties', but 'to give them *political power* in almost as great a degree, and to as large an extent, as it can possibly be conferred'. If passed, 'demand will follow from time to time upon demand' in an 'eternal struggle for power'.[121] The Bill failed by 159 to 120.

If reformers were depressed by the scanty votes they had been able to muster for parliamentary reform, conservatives were equally depressed by declining majorities against Emancipation. Liverpool was thought to be irresolute; George IV to be persuadable. The same pattern was repeated the following year. Attending to what he saw as the mood of county meetings, asking for some sort of reform but not specifying which (still less demanding universal suffrage), in April 1822 Lord John Russell brought forward a measure to remove one MP from each of the hundred smallest boroughs and redistribute them, sixty to the counties and forty to new towns. It was a plain echo of Pitt's schemes of the 1780s. Whigs were euphoric, and backed the measure with 164 votes – the largest Reform vote since 1785. At last the Whigs seemed united on a bold measure of principle. But 269 ministerialists voted it down;[122] and the realisation swiftly dawned that the gulf between 164 and 269 was wide. Wellington's confidante Mrs Arbuthnot noticed that

The Reformers have very much lowered their tune, they no longer insist on annual parliaments and universal suffrage, they do not even mention triennial parliaments,

[120] Mitchell, *Whigs in Opposition*, p. 155; for the party's conversion to Reform, Mitchell, 'Whigs and Parliamentary Reform', pp. 27–37.
[121] Reprinted in Twiss, *Eldon*, vol. III, pp. 498–512. [122] *Parl Debs* NS, vol. VII, cols. 51–141.

they chiefly turn their views to obtaining an encrease in the number of county members and disfranchising the rotten boroughs...the truth is, the Opposition feel that under the present system they have no chance of getting in [and] they would alter the constitution in any way which would enable them to turn their adversaries out.[123]

Any method, presumably, would do.

Others did not regard Reform as the Whigs' obvious option and most powerful ploy. In August 1822 Croker warned Peel: 'It is said that Lord Holland begins to talk of the propriety of making the Catholic question the touchstone of parties, and to insinuate that if you lead the government, Canning may lead the opposition, and may put that question on such grounds as to make it a pure stand-or-fall government question.' Croker was incredulous: how would the Whigs square their position on Reform with an alliance with Canning?[124] Yet exactly that was to happen in 1827: Emancipation had indeed emerged as the 'touchstone of parties'. In June 1822 Canning's Roman Catholic Peers' Bill had passed the Commons and had been halted at its second reading in the Lords, after another Eldonite oration, by 171 to 129.[125] The same month, in the Commons, Brougham's curiously atavistic repeat of Dunning's motion of 1780, 'the influence of the Crown has increased, is increasing, and ought to be diminished', failed by the comfortable margin of 216 to 101.[126] Religion, not representation, was shown to be the weak spot in the ministerial defences. Religion, not representation, increasingly emerged as the main object of popular demands for legislative social change.

Accelerating economic recovery in the 1820s produced the dramatic withering away of both rural and urban clamour for Reform, as its opponents had predicted that it would. The small extent of gentry commitment to the measure became clear. In 1823 Russell produced a motion similar to that of 1822, with a similar result. In 1824 and 1825 nothing was done. Russell's repeated motion on 27th April 1826 was lost by 247 to 124; he announced that he would not raise the issue in the Commons again. From 1824 to 1829 inclusive, no petitions on Reform were presented to the House;[127] the issue sank into oblivion. A few enthusiasts

---

123 F. Bamford and the Duke of Wellington (eds.), *The Journal of Mrs Arbuthnot 1820–1832* (2 vols., London, 1950), vol. I, pp. 159–60.

124 C. S. Parker, *Sir Robert Peel* (3 vols., London, 1891–9), vol. I, p. 329.

125 Twiss, *Eldon*, vol. II, pp. 452–8. It would have allowed Roman Catholic peers to take their seats in the House of Lords. A necessary consequence, insisted Eldon, was that Catholic commoners must be admitted to the Commons.

126 *Parl Debs* NS vol. VII, cols. 1265–319. He moved 'that the influence now possessed by the Crown is unnecessary for maintaining its constitutional prerogatives, destructive of the independence of Parliament, and inconsistent with the well government of the realm'.

127 As Croker pointed out in his speech of 4th March 1831 (*Parl Debs* 3rd ser., vol. III, col. 87). In 1821, there had been only 19 petitions; in 1822, 12; in 1823, 29; in 1830, 14. The demand for Reform, Croker argued, had been created by the Whigs themselves in the 1830 election campaign.

continued to announce that the tide of history made success inevitable. Nothing happened.

Protestant Dissenters were gloomy about their chances of securing a repeal of the Test and Corporation Acts. When in 1823 their Deputies once again resolved, after over thirty years' quiescence, to press for Repeal, the Unitarian Smith warned of the great difficulties, and that 'the apathy and indifference of the Dissenters under their grievances were not the least among them'.[128] He and many coreligionists realised correctly that Protestant Dissent, its principles and its political weight in the country, were insufficient to break down the old order; only the Catholic question could do that. After 1823, the Protestant campaign for Repeal was itself hamstrung by the refusal of many Dissenters to press for a reform which would logically lead to Catholic Emancipation. Despite the growing psephological strength of non-Anglicans, too, it was open to some to argue (like the radical Roebuck) that the Test and Corporation Acts were not a real burden on Dissenters:

At first the complaint did not excite much attention. In ten years not a dozen petitions were presented to Parliament on the subject. Party exigencies at length however produced the feeling which it professed to pity. By talking of this grievance people began at last to think it really was a thing much to be deplored and resented, – a cry was raised, the opposition were delighted, and gladly seized upon the occasion, since it gave them the means of annoying an administration deemed peculiarly intrusted with the mission of protecting the Church.[129]

This was, perhaps, excessively cynical; but it contained an important truth.

In 1823 a Bill passed the Commons to relieve English electors (in line with Irish) of the Williamite obligation to take the Oath of Supremacy before voting, so admitting the Catholics to the franchise while excluding them from office. It was rejected at its second reading in the Lords on 9th July by only 80 to 73. Eldon made use of an unexpected ally, arguing that 'it had been well observed by Bishop Hoadly, that the Reformation would have been no blessing without the Revolution, which, by giving a supreme head to the Church, had established the union between Church and State'.[130] But with both Peel and Liverpool supporting the Bill, the outlook was poor. The Archbishop of Canterbury himself supported a Bill in April 1824 to allow Unitarians to conduct their own marriage services. Eldon denied that the repeal of the Blasphemy Act of 1697 made anti-Trinitarian teaching legal; and if relief were granted to Unitarians, 'could it be denied to the Roman Catholics?'

It was said, that the persons calling themselves Unitarians had real scruples of conscience on the doctrine of the Trinity. So had deists, atheists, and others. If he understood the doctrines of the Church of England at all, it was impossible that there

[128] Davis, *Smith*, p. 217.   [129] *Ibid.*, p. 223. Roebuck, *Whig Ministry*, vol. I, p. 67.
[130] Twiss, *Eldon*, vol. II, p. 475; Gash, *Mr Secretary Peel*, p. 412.

could be a greater repugnance between any doctrines than there was between the doctrine of the Church of England and that of the Unitarians. The Unitarians must think the Church of England idolatry. What, therefore, would be the sort of comprehension that it would effect?[131]

The Bill was lost by 105 to 66. Lansdowne's two Catholic Relief Bills, introduced into the Lords that May, would have extended to them both the vote and the right to hold civil office. 'Securities' were again the stumbling block; Eldon objected that the Bills made no provision for requiring English Catholic voters to take the Oath of Supremacy. The Bills were lost on 24th May by majorities of thirty-eight and thirty-four votes.

Some were converted to the cause of Emancipation, others against it. The most notable of the latter was the heir presumptive to the throne, the Duke of York, who delivered a major statement of his position in presenting to the Lords on 25th April 1825 a petition from the Dean and Canons of Windsor against further concessions: 'thousands of copies of it, in gold letters, were framed and hung up in the houses of zealous Protestants'.[132] The Duke repeated standard Eldonite doctrine: 'political power and toleration are perfectly different'. The Coronation Oath, he added, was an insuperable barrier against the royal assent ever being given to Catholic Emancipation. It was rumoured that Eldon had composed the speech. In fact, the Duke of York was merely repeating a doctrine which was held, among its adherents, with remarkable uniformity. The effect of his announcement was, nevertheless, sensational. It produced what Eldon had long sought in vain, a stiffening of George IV's will to resist, and a popular Protestant backlash. Even Protestant Dissenters were divided on the question. Unitarians tended to treat Roman Catholic doctrine as immaterial, and to support Emancipation on the general, and secularised, ground of a right to civil liberties. The great majority of Dissenters were, however, Trinitarians in the wake of the evangelical movement, and Trinitarian Protestantism was now (as it had always been, except in the unusual circumstances of the 1790s) largely anti-Papist.[133] Tactically this was a disaster for the Dissenting cause, for the only arguments which might secure Repeal entailed Emancipation also.

Despite several Dissenting petitions against it, among a flood of some 400 hostile petitions,[134] the Commons again sent up a Catholic Relief Bill in May 1825. Fortified by the Duke of York's commitment, Eldon increased his majority; the Bill failed by 178 (including 3 archbishops, 18 bishops and

---

[131]   Twiss, *Eldon*, vol. ii, p. 514.
[132]   *Ibid.*, vol. ii, p. 542.
[133]   Davis, *Smith*, pp. 228–35. Many Trinitarians nevertheless supported the Catholic claims from tactical calculation, or 'liberal' opinion, especially in London.
[134]   Machin, *Catholic Question*, p. 54.

6 bishops' proxies) to 130 (including 1 bishop and 1 bishop's proxy). The anti-Catholics regarded it as a 'triumph', producing 'great elevation of spirits'.[135] Eldon's optimism was soon qualified. A Unitarian Bill in the Lords on 3rd June secured the backing of both Archbishops, and the Bishops of London, Bath and Wells, Exeter and Norwich. It failed by only 56 to 50; 'our good orthodox friends were absent', noted Eldon, 'most at Ascot – so that how a horse runs is much more important than how the Church fares'.[136] Others less committed might see a stalemate between pro- and anti-Catholic forces at Westminster. Prospects for Protestant Dissenters seemed no better after their petitions against Emancipation, and the Dissenting Deputies were advised by sympathetic MPs that the time was not ripe to apply for Repeal. Canning feared a Protestant landslide; in September 1825 he persuaded Liverpool to postpone the imminent general election until the following autumn, and persuaded the Whigs not to press for Emancipation before then. In 1826, the issue was not raised; the cry of 'No Popery' was avoided in most constituencies. The Dissenters, too, were inactive.[137]

The Duke of York's death on 5th January 1827 was seriously to weaken the 'Protestant' camp. Eldon later wrote that

His existence appeared to me to be essential to the effectively counteracting that influence, which soon after his death prevailed, to place at the head of the administration the great advocate in the House of Commons of the Roman Catholic claims [Canning], to whom the greatest aversion had been often expressed in the highest place, and to continue that advocate in that station, although it was found necessary to his support in it that he should have the aid of all those, whose principles, save with respect to that question, he had been combating in youth and in manhood, as an anti-jacobin, and an anti-radical; till, within a short period before his advancement, he had been, as some thought, obviously and apparently courting them in debates.[138]

This was not at once obvious. It is possible that the anti-Catholic coalition was gaining slightly in strength at this point, following the general election of 1826.[139] Burdett's motion on the Catholic question on 7th March 1827 was lost by 276 to 272, the first such defeat in the Commons since 1821.[140] The prosperity of the 1820s extended even to Ireland, and the level of 'outrage and violence' there steadily declined.[141] Would Emancipation become as empty an issue as Reform? Chance intervened to replace it at the centre of political attention.

---

[135] Twiss, *Eldon*, vol. II, p. 553; *Parl Debs* NS, vol. XIII, cols. 766–8.
[136] Twiss, *Eldon*, vol. II, p. 558.
[137] Davis, *Smith*, p. 235; Machin, *Catholic Question*, p. 66.
[138] Twiss, *Eldon*, vol. II, pp. 580–2.
[139] Machin, *Catholic Question*, pp. 63–87.   [140] Davis, *Smith*, p. 235.
[141] E. Halévy, *The Liberal Awakening 1815–1830* (London, 1949), pp. 218–21.

On 17th February, Liverpool suffered the stroke which put an end to his political career; in April, Canning succeeded him at the age of fifty-six, seemingly with years of office before him. Negotiations to form a ministry had revolved around the Catholic question, despite Peel's plea to remember all the issues (opposition to parliamentary reform included) on which Liverpool's colleagues had been united.[142] The anti-Catholics within the late ministry felt themselves unable to serve – Eldon, Wellington, Peel, Bathurst and Westmorland. Canning sought to keep the Catholic question an open one; but the tendency of his ministry was obvious. The Whigs saw their chance to achieve office by dropping Reform and shelving Repeal,[143] and took it. To the dismay of radicals, Canning lured a substantial segment of the Whig leadership, including Brougham and Tierney, into a coalition. It was an explicitly reformist ministry on many issues, with two minor exceptions. The new Whig ministers agreed not to bring forward a measure aimed against the Test and Corporation Acts. On parliamentary reform, Canning adhered to the position of his *Anti-Jacobin* days: the cabinet, and his new allies, were explicitly committed against it.

Astonishingly, the renegade Whigs found no difficulty in dropping the issue. Even Grey and Lord John Russell, who did not accept office, played down their ringing commitments of the early 1820s. Russell justified his change of tack in May 1827 by announcing that 'he found a great lukewarmness on the subject throughout the country'.[144] Grey, too, justified his colleagues: Reform was 'not a question to which they are pledged, nor on which the party to which they belong are agreed...The question of parliamentary reform is not so uniformly supported, nor has it at present the public opinion so strongly in its favour, as that it should be made a *sine qua non* in forming an administration.'[145] Brougham revealed the overriding intention of his colleagues: 'My principle is – *anything* to lock the door for ever on Eldon and Co.'[146]

At once, however, at the beginning of May, both Emancipation and Repeal were raised in Parliament. Eldon justified his resignation and the whole course of his conduct by reference to the Catholic question (the franchise was strikingly ignored).[147] Both measures were presumably imminent. Meanwhile, the Commons passed a Unitarians' Marriage Bill. In the Lords, Eldon repeated his former objections: 'Year after year, this Bill had been proposed to the House – the same objections had been urged

---

142 Twiss, *Eldon*, vol. II, p. 589.
143 Canning reiterated his past refusals to consider Repeal before Emancipation had been achieved.
144 Cannon, *Parliamentary Reform*, pp. 186–7.
145 Quoted J. R. M. Butler, *The Passing of the Great Reform Bill* (London, 1914), p. 45.
146 Brougham to Creevey, 21st April 1827: Sir H. Maxwell (ed.), *The Creevey Papers* (London, 1906), p. 456.
147 Twiss, *Eldon*, vol. II, pp. 596–600.

against it, and yet its authors continued to press the measure.' This time, on 26th June, the Bill passed by sixty-one to fifty-four.[148] The mood among the few reformers who thought parliamentary reform more important than Emancipation or Repeal was one of gloom. On 7th June, Lord John Russell withdrew his motion for Repeal; but he promised to bring it forward next session. The most likely result, under the existing ministry, seemed to be that the fate of Repeal and Emancipation would be decided by a confrontation with the Lords and the Crown, but that Reform would be shelved. But on 8th August 1827 the unforeseen happened: Canning died.

V. 'A REVOLUTION GRADUALLY ACCOMPLISHED', 1827–1832

He [Wellington] went on, in reference to the revolutionary aspect and prospect of the times, to say that, in the general state of disorganization and contempt of all authority which the ministers had excited and kept up to secure their party triumph, there was no doubt a danger that they might be suddenly overborne by the irregular power they had called into action; but the great body of the nation was sound enough, he thought, to prevent any immediate violence. As the revolutionists are now all with the ministry and enjoying a common triumph, I think this ferment will pass away; but its effects will remain, and grow gradually and quietly more and more destructive of our old constitution. First, all reverence for old authorities, even for the House of Commons itself, has received an irrecoverable shock, and then the composition of the new House of Commons, which will only change to become worse, will render government by royal authority impracticable. So it will go down step by step, quicker or faster, as temporary circumstances may direct, but the result will be that at last we shall have a revolution gradually accomplished *by due form of law!* (J. W. Croker, 21st September 1831: *Croker Papers*, vol. II, pp. 124–5.)

After an unsuccessful attempt to keep together Canning's coalition, a reversion to the Liverpool pattern was set up in January 1828 under Wellington as First Lord of the Treasury. Grey thought it meant 'an end to every hope and chance of carrying the Catholic question', and the Whigs used Repeal as the excuse for recovering their unity. The Ultras still had grounds for unease over Emancipation, however. Estimates of the ministry's composition varied: Eldon, on 25th January, counted seven anti-Catholics, six pro-Catholics;[149] but the figures were reversed if Aberdeen's sympathies lay with the other side. Eldon was astonished and apprehensive at being left out: it heralded, he thought, capitulation on the Catholic question, and he was right. Unknown to Eldon, Wellington had been willing to envisage a compromise on Emancipation in 1825, and he and Peel were now willing to do much to secure the alliance of the pro-Catholic Canningites. They were

---

[148] It was later abandoned. Twiss, *Eldon*, vol. III, p. 5.

[149] Pro: Dudley, Huskisson, Melville, Ellenborough, Grant, Palmerston. Anti: Wellington, Lyndhurst, Bathurst, Peel, Goulburn, Aberdeen, Herries, 'but some *very loose*': Twiss, *Eldon*, vol. III, p. 27; Machin, *Catholic Question*, p. 110.

certainly willing to distance themselves from the Ultras, whom they had come to regard as impracticably rigid.[150]

Peel had already convinced himself that change was inevitable. A close friend wrote in 1824: 'Peel considers a revolution at no great distance – not a bloody one and perhaps not one leading to a republic, but one utterly subversive of the aristocracy and of the present system of carrying on the government. He thinks we may get on quite as well after this change as before; but he considers it inevitable.'[151] Not all the Ultras were immoveable, however. Crucially, Wellington found an ecclesiastical adviser, initially 'unconvinced' by the case for Emancipation, who was ultimately willing to co-operate in concession. The Rev. Dr Henry Phillpotts had made his reputation as an anti-Catholic polemicist; now he wrote privately to the Duke with suggestions for ways of arranging a compromise. Phillpotts' letters to Wellington began in January, immediately after the Duke's ministry was formed. They accepted that sufficient securities could be exacted to safeguard the Church; that Catholics 'may, without any violence to their conscience, engage to maintain the civil rights and privileges of the Church of England'.[152] His *Letter... on the Coronation Oath* of that year (a copy of which he sent to the Duke) did not, he pointed out, shut the door on concession if 'real and adequate security for our Church' could be offered. As he also urged Eldon, 'the true principles of the British constitution require that concessions should *not* be made'; but circumstances 'make it certain that, ere it is very long, concessions *will* be made'.[153] It was advice which Wellington did, but Eldon did not, wish to hear.

If many of the ministers were more than half resigned to what they saw as the inevitability of Emancipation, they had few reasons for seriously contesting Repeal. Many professions, too, were made that Repeal did not entail Emancipation, and that the first was advocated on quite different grounds. That Repeal was brought forward so unexpectedly, and with anti-Catholic assurances, may explain the remarkable absence of a petitioning movement against it.[154] Ministerialists, however, knew better the connection of the two concessions. The situation of the 1780s was thus reversed: it was now the Dissenters who profited from the success of the Catholic claims. By comparison with the 'threat' of Rome, Protestant Dissent, including now the staunchly loyalist and anti-Catholic Methodists, could even be made to seem allies in the defence of the Protestant constitution.

[150] Peel, *Memoirs*, vol. I, pp. 16–18, 59.
[151] Denis Le Marchant, quoted in Brock, *Reform Act*, p. 15.
[152] *Despatches, Correspondence and Memoranda of Field Marshal Arthur Duke of Wellington, KG* (8 vols., London, 1867–80) vol. IV, pp. 229, 254, 317, 324, 486, 500, 549, 580, 635, 664, 675; vol. V, *passim.*
[153] Davies, *Phillpotts*, pp. 77–83.
[154] Machin, 'Resistance to Repeal', p. 119.

It could not be said that the episcopate was uninformed. Bishop Lloyd of Oxford, lately Peel's tutor at Christ Church, was exchanging opinions with his ex-pupil on the history of the subject, including Mansfield's judgement and Blackstone's exchange with Furneaux in 1770. 'I have now fourteen volumes lying before me on the subject of the Corporation and Test Acts, written in the years 1789 and 1790', he added, recommending the 1787 republications of Sherlock and Hoadly.[155] Lloyd's tepid defence of the Acts struck no chord in his old pupil, who expected Repeal to pass, and who claimed that the Commons could not be made to respond to Sherlock's principled rationale; expedience, moderation, tranquillity were the only grounds, he claimed, for defending the existing order.[156] They were, of course, insufficient grounds, and Lord John Russell's Bill for Repeal passed the Commons on 26th February by 237 to 193, with remarkable ease. The ministry hardly bothered to whip its supporters; the opposition strained every muscle. Thirty seven anti-Catholics voted for the Bill, believing that they thereby hindered Emancipation.[157] Peel made a token resistance, then bowed to what he chose to call the inevitable. Lord John Russell shrewdly observed that his opponent was 'a very pretty hand at hauling down his colours'.[158]

1828

Wellington wrote: 'I believe we could have thrown the Bill for the repeal of the Corporation and Test Acts out of the House of Lords', but did not attempt to do so. The bishops, he claimed, were in favour of the concession.[159] In fact, their support had been carefully orchestrated. In March 1828 Peel met the two Archbishops and the Bishops of London, Durham, Chester and Llandaff and secured their agreement to the passage of Repeal in the Lords, an agreement which a meeting of the whole bench then ratified.[160] Van Mildert, Bishop of Durham, had resisted; but the higher clergy in general had become irresolute in the face of government determination, and Dissenting arguments that the Acts profaned the sacrament; they no longer urged Sherlock's arguments (which had persuaded Pitt in 1787) that the sacrament was not itself the qualification, but the evidence of the qualification. Liberal sentiments, generosity, and open-handedness to Dissenters now characterised their mood, responsive as it was to the increasingly secular tone of their society. The mood of the 1820s had been one of growing confidence on the part of the Establishment, after the radical storms of

[155] Bishop of Oxford to Peel, 10th Feb. 1828: Peel, *Memoirs*, vol. 1, pp. 64–6.
[156] Letters between Peel and Charles Lloyd, *ibid.*, vol. 1, pp. 66–98.
[157] Machin, 'Resistance to Repeal', p. 124.
[158] 'It is really a gratifying thing to force the enemy to give up his first line, that none but churchmen are worthy to serve the state, and I trust we shall soon make him give up the second, that none but Protestants are.' Russell to Moore, 31st March 1828: *Early Correspondence of Lord John Russell*, vol. 1, p. 272.
[159] Wellington to Montrose, 30th April 1828: *Wellington Despatches*, vol. IV, p. 411.
[160] W. J. Copleston, *Memoir of Edward Copleston* (London, 1851), p. 123.

c. 1815–20 had been weathered: 'The immediate danger is now passed', announced the Bishop of London in 1822.[161] Concession seemed safe; Establishment still appeared unchallenged by a major threat.

Peel now backed the Bill on the ministry's behalf in return for the inclusion of a declaration on the Church as a condition of office.[162] Eldon wrote:

> ...the administration have – to their shame, be it said – got the Archbishops and most of the Bishops to support this revolutionary Bill. I voted as long ago as in the years, I think, 1787, 1789, and 1790, against a similar measure; Lord North and Pitt opposing it as destructive of the Church Establishment – Dr Priestley, a Dissenting minister, then asserting, that he had laid a train of gunpowder under the Church, which would blow it up; and Dr Price, another Dissenting minister, blessing God that he could depart in peace, as the revolution in France would lead here to the destruction of all union between Church and State. The young men and lads in the House of Commons are too young to remember these things. From 1790 to 1827, many and various have been the attempts to relieve the Catholics, but through those thirty-seven years nobody has thought, and evinced that thought, of proposing such a Bill as this in Parliament, as necessary, or fit, as between the Church and the Dissenters. Canning, last year, positively declared that he would oppose it altogether.[163]

Eldon despaired of success. No bishop opposed the Bill.[164] As it passed through the Lords, with Wellington's support, no division was forced on the principle of the measure; the defenders sought to modify the Bill by amendments. Again Eldon repeated the doctrine that 'the Church of England, combined with the State, formed together the constitution of Great Britain, and that the Test and Corporation Acts were necessary to the preservation of that constitution'; but the Ultras' wrecking amendments were lost by large margins.[165]

Lord Holland (displaying no premonition of the imminence of parliamentary reform) wrote:

> It is the greatest victory over the *principle* of persecution & exclusion yet obtained. Practically there have been greater such as the Toleration Act in W 3d's time & the Catholick bill of 1792. Practically too the Catholick Emancipation when it comes

[161] William Howley, quoted Norman, *Church and Society*, p. 49.
[162] 'I, A. B., do solemnly declare that I will never exercise any power, authority, or influence, which I may possess by virtue of the office of — to injure or weaken the Protestant Church as it is by law established within this realm, or to disturb it in the possession of any rights or privileges to which it is by law entitled.' Davis, *Smith*, p. 246.
[163] Eldon to Lady F. J. Bankes, April 1828: Twiss, *Eldon*, vol. III, p. 37.
[164] The division list in *Parl Debs*, vol. XIX, cols. 236–7 refers to the division on Eldon's amendment on 23rd, not the third reading on 28th: Cannon, in *The Whig Ascendancy*, p. 209.
[165] Bishop Copleston of Llandaff did secure the inclusion of the phrase 'upon the true faith of a Christian' in the declaration, despite Lord Holland's opposition. A religious test of a sort thus remained, until finally abolished in 1866; but it did not necessarily exclude Unitarians. Eldon failed to secure the inclusion of the words 'I am a Protestant.' Davis, *Smith*, p. 247; Machin, 'Resistance', p. 137.

will be a far more important measure, more immediate & more extensive in its effects – but *in principle* this is the greatest of them all as it explodes the real Tory doctrine *that Church & State are indivisible*.[166]

As soon as Repeal had passed through Parliament, Burdett in the Commons and Lansdowne in the Lords at once raised the Catholic question. Eldon expected the ministry to capitulate on that issue also even before the election of 'the great Irish agitator, O'Connell' at a by-election for County Clare in July 1828.[167]

Wellington was already labouring to reconcile the disenchanted Ultras, accepting Huskisson's resignation when he rashly offered it over a minor Reform issue in May and restoring the anti-Catholic majority in the Cabinet.[168] These were merely attempts to avert the split in the ministerial ranks which Wellington saw Emancipation would bring. Before Lansdowne's motion, Peel was already contemplating capitulation,[169] and in the Lords' debate on 10th June Wellington echoed Phillpotts' advice in rejecting the idea of a concordat with Rome: 'What we must do must be done by legislation...if it shall be deemed necessary, we shall do it fearlessly.'[170] In September, the Duke wrote to Peel that he had been 'moved' by the contests in Monaghan, Louth and Waterford in 1826 and the by-election in Clare in 1828, and that 'I see clearly that we have to suffer here all the consequences of a practical democratic reform in Parliament, if we do not do something to remedy the evils'[171] by a measure of Emancipation: if the Catholics were not let in as Catholics, they would have to be let in as democratic individuals. Emancipation would avert Reform. As a rationalisation of capitulation, it was potentially persuasive.

After the King's Speech on 5th February 1829, in effect announcing a Bill for Catholic Emancipation, the largest petitioning campaign yet known appealed against it: by the First Reading of the Bill on 5th March, 957 petitions had opposed (against 357 in favour, mostly from Ireland).[172] Proletarian anti-Catholic interference was most unwelcome to Whig grandees, however; Lord Holland stigmatised one Brunswick Club meeting as a 'manoeuvre' by the 'Kentish clodpolls and bigots',[173] and pro-Catholics

---

[166] Lord Holland to Henry Fox, 10th April 1828, quoted in Mitchell, *Holland House*, p. 105.
[167] Twiss, *Eldon*, vol. III, p. 54. As a Roman Catholic, O'Connell would be unable to take his seat. Burdett's motion passed in the Commons by a majority of 6; Lansdowne's failed in the Lords by 44.
[168] Machin, *Catholic Question*, p. 117.   [169] Peel, *Memoirs*, vol. I, pp. 28–33.
[170] *Parl Debs* NS, vol. XIX, col. 1291.
[171] Parker, *Peel*, vol. II, p. 64: Wellington to Peel, 12th Sept. 1828.
[172] B. Ward, *The Eve of Catholic Emancipation* (3 vols., London, 1911–12), vol. III, p. 248. The anti-Catholic periodical *John Bull* claimed over 2,000 petitions against the Bill by the end of March: Machin, *Catholic Question*, p. 148.
[173] Holland to Russell, Oct. 1828: *Early Correspondence of Lord John Russell*, vol. I, pp. 279–80. Holland relied on the Unitarians to beat the Brunswickers: 'one of that stamp [Unitarian] is generally in talent and always in stoutness a match for two of any other denomination'.

in their constituencies were decidedly worried by such populist, Anglican phenomena. Patrician Whigs attempted to ignore most manifestations of English democratic opinion. Politicians were certainly to be found in 1828–32 who committed themselves behind 'issues' marked out by their libertarian or loyalist viewpoints; but they did so only on their own terms, in their own time, and in ways which suited their convenience as politicians.

For Peel and Wellington Co. Clare was a lucky accident, for it allowed them to represent their capitulation as a prudent act of political expediency, to avoid civil war in Ireland. In retrospect, 'necessity' was Wellington's excuse for the events of 1828–30. The anti-Catholics believed that it was the ministry's pusillanimity which made its position untenable. General Gascoyne, in the Commons' debate on the Address, warned that 'The hon. gentlemen around him need no longer despair of obtaining universal suffrage and parliamentary reform: they had nothing to do but to get up an association, and straight the alarmed minister would come down to the House with a proposal to grant all they wanted.'[174] But the ministry went ahead. When Peel moved on 5th March for a Committee to consider the Catholic laws, 160 ministerialists voted against him.

Eldon's stand against the resulting Bill came on its second reading in the Lords on 2nd April:

> The people were justly attached to the constitution of 1688; they looked to it as the foundation and bulwark of their freedom. If a part were changed, there might be a change of the whole; and that change they dreaded. Perhaps the state of the opinions of the people might be more manifest to one who had risen from the people, and who had been long in communication with the people, the strength and ornament of the empire, than to most of their lordships, the proprietors of hereditary titles.[175]

But the Bill passed its second reading on 4th April by 217 to 112, and its third on 10th April by 213 to 109. The bench was divided: nine bishops (and one proxy) in favour; three archbishops, thirteen bishops (and three bishops' proxies on the second reading, four on the third) against.[176] Many of those in favour deferred reluctantly, like Lloyd of Oxford, to 'the progress and continuing course of public opinion throughout the country'.[177] Most, however, were shocked into a belated concern for the ancient constitution, conceived in Eldonite terms.

George IV complained to Eldon that he had been

> ...deserted by an aristocracy that had supported his father – that, instead of forty-five against the measure, there were twice that number of peers for it – that every thing

---

[174] *Parl Debs* NS, vol. xx, col. 96.

[175] Twiss, *Eldon*, vol. iii, p. 75. Two Ultra peers, Falmouth and Mansfield, thought it important to announce in this debate that their opposition to Emancipation did not imply a commitment to Reform: Machin, *Catholic Question*, p. 176.

[176] *Parl Debs* NS, vol. xxi, cols. 394–7, 694–7.   [177] *Ibid.*, vol. xxi, col. 77.

was revolutionary – every thing was tending to revolution – and the peers and the aristocracy were giving way to it...[Eldon] took the liberty to say that I agreed that matters were rapidly tending to revolution – that I had long thought that this measure of Catholic emancipation was meant to be and would certainly be a step towards producing it – that it was avowed as such with the Radicals in 1794, '5, and '6: – that many of the Catholic Association were understood to have been engaged in all the transactions in Ireland in 1798 – and what had they not been threatening to do if this measure was not carried, and even if it was carried?[178]

Eldon believed that if the King had taken an open, firm and resolute stand against Emancipation, 'it would have prevented a great deal of that ratting, which carried the measure'.[179] Now, he feared 'attempts at revolution under name of Reform':

...a renewal, of a more frightful kind than the prospects of 1791, 2, 3, 4, and 5. The occurrences of those days, involving the Crown as well as the Houses of Parliament, by express mention, in revolutionary projects – the language 'No King' – gave a treasonable character to the proceedings of that era, which enabled government to deal with it by law. This is now, in their resolutions, and declarations, and petitions, carefully avoided; and the proceedings of this day, therefore, are more difficult to be dealt with, because more difficult to be met by the existing laws. They are, of course, more dangerous.[180]

At last, after decades of unsuccessful efforts, local political organisations took root in certain new industrial towns, devoted to Reform as if it were a remedy for a concrete local grievance. As significant were the consequences of Emancipation: the belief that the sovereign would not resist massive constitutional change; and the profound schism which now rent the party of Wellington and Peel.

Indignation centred on those two ministers as the betrayers of the ancient constitution and of the Church. The Duchess of Richmond 'had a number of stuffed *rats* under glass cases on her drawing-room table, to which Her Grace affixed the names of all the apostates'; someone 'conveyed a live rat into the House of Lords and let him loose during one of the last debates', recorded Croker.[181] Peel felt obliged to offer himself for re-election to his constituents of Oxford University and was defeated, Keble, Newman and Froude campaigning for his anti-Catholic opponent. Phillpotts, who persisted in voting for Peel, became 'the great rat' to the Oxford Orthodox. An undergraduate stopped him in the street, holding out his hand: 'Rat it, Phillpotts, how are you?'[182] Wellington was forced by the Ultra Lord Winchelsea's vilification to issue a challenge, and a duel followed (Peel

---

[178] Twiss, *Eldon*, vol. III, pp. 83–7.   [179] *Ibid.*, vol. III, p. 88.
[180] *Ibid.*, vol. III, p. 107.
[181] *Croker Papers*, vol. II, p. 15.
[182] Davies, *Phillpotts*, pp. 86–7. His reward was the Bishopric of Exeter in the autumn of 1830, the last appointment of the ancien regime. Phillpotts' defence of his consistency is 'perhaps not wholly convincing', thinks his biographer (p. 88).

neglected to vindicate his honour against his equally savage critic, Sir Charles Wetherell).

Schism took a particular form. Crucially, a group of Ultras announced their conversion to Reform as the only way to defend what remained of the constitution against what they saw as the cynical manipulation of the Peels and Wellingtons, flying in the face of the demonstrable opinion of the vast majority of Englishmen. Historians have often been astonished at the Ultras' *renversement des alliances*; but, as has been shown above, it was the Church, not the rotten boroughs, that was at the heart of the conservative Whig conception of the social order. This was even more true in the country: if the number of ministerial converts to Reform was limited, county meetings suddenly began to affirm their support. Agricultural distress in the winter of 1829–30, added to anti-Catholic resentment, found a principled focus.

On 2nd June 1829 the Marquess of Blandford moved in the Commons two motions for the elimination of pocket boroughs: his object, he said, was to prevent the emergence of a specifically Catholic bloc of MPs by the purchase of seats. The Unitarian Smith was delighted: 'One effect, he was happy to find had been produced by the Roman Catholic Relief Bill – an effect which its best friends had not anticipated: it appeared to have transformed a number of the highest Tories in the land to something very nearly resembling radical reformers.'[183] Blandford attracted little support. The Ultras were not yet determined to bring down the ministry, but continued divided in their opinion; Wellington survived a vote on the King's Speech in the Commons on 4th February 1830 only by Whig support.[184] On the 18th, Blandford tried again, proposing in that House the most extensive and compendious measure of Reform, echoing the 'Country' schemes of the last century and a half.[185] Remarkably, it attracted only fifty-seven votes: there was no massive Whig commitment to Reform which the achievement of Emancipation unleashed, and the Whigs were slow in seizing on the issue: enough popular opinion was still Anglican and loyalist to make democracy a risk. But Ultra disaffection was real enough, and Wellington's government teetered on with unreliable majorities. It was the unrestrainable Lord John Russell who began to engineer his party's commitment with a motion, five days after Blandford's, for the much more limited objective of granting seats to Birmingham, Manchester and Leeds; But it was lost by 188 to 140, and an imprudent motion by O'Connell in May embodying the principle of manhood suffrage produced a revulsion, failing by 319 to 13.[186]

183 *Parl Debs* NS, vol. XXI, col. 1688; Machin, *Catholic Question*, p. 186.
184 Machin, *Catholic Question*, p. 187.
185 Cannon, *Parliamentary Reform*, pp. 193–4. It included a general scot and lot franchise (i.e. householders paying poor rates), not universal suffrage.
186 *Ibid.*, pp. 195–6.

Even at this date, Reform was not a foregone conclusion. But the general election which followed the death on 26th June of George IV further undermined Wellington's position. Crucially, even the counties began to slip away from the ministry: of seventeen new county MPs, fifteen were to vote with the opposition in the division of 15th November.[187] The rural distress which produced the 'Captain Swing' riots bore heavily on tenant farmers also. Many identified with their labourers sufficiently to blame 'the system': high taxation must be going to the support of placemen and pensioners, waste and corruption. Parliament had done nothing to deal with their economic plight: its reform could now, at last, seem a solution. And the channels of communication in the 'old society' faithfully transmitted the message to the landowners – many of them, in the 'Swing' counties of the south and east, Ultra politicians.

The Whigs, too, endeavoured to exploit the distress which all perceived. 'Among the most popular topics, as they unexpectedly found', noted the radical Roebuck, 'was that of reform in parliament.'

They evidently knew little of the popular feelings which they sought to lead, and little suspected the strength of the current to which they were about to commit themselves. Not aware of the highly excitable condition of the people, they, when they began the contest of the elections, employed language most inflammatory and unguarded, supposing that it would fall on the dull ears of ordinary constituencies. They were startled by the response they received, and began very quickly to be alarmed by their own success.

Even so, the Whigs' role was not yet fixed. When the parliamentary session opened in November 1830, although Brougham threatened to bring forward a Reform Bill in the Commons, Grey in the Lords debate on the King's Speech only spoke tepidly of Reform as desirable, as 'sooner or later' inevitable, but not as imminent or urgent. Roebuck was astonished:

That which was to be the great means of his party and ministerial victory was, at this moment mentioned in this slight and almost slighting manner, quickly dismissed as one of the necessary but tiresome subjects, one of the common-places of opposition rhetoric, obliged to be used as a sort of decoration in an opposition speech, but about which no one was really solicitous, because no one believed it to be of import to party success.[188]

Wellington was conscious of his crumbling position, however, and provoked to make a stand in an effort to retrieve it. The 'state of the representation', he announced in the same debate on 2nd November, was the best attainable: he would never introduce, and would always resist, parliamentary reform. In the light of the widespread public disorder which

---

[187] *Ibid*, p. 198.
[188] Brock, *Reform Act*, pp. 123–5; B. T. Bradfield, 'Sir Richard Vyvyan and the Country Gentlemen, 1830–1834', *EHR* 83 (1968), 729–43; Roebuck, *Whig Ministry*, vol. i, pp. 346–7, 367–8.

followed in 1831 and 1832, this has seemed an extreme statement and a commitment to an impossible position; but this was not evident at the time. Like the Duke of York's successful anti-Catholic speech of 25th April 1825, Wellington's announcement was merely the reaffirmation of a familiar position. Tactically, it was a realistic bid to win back Ultra support (some were indeed won back); but it failed wholly to close the split in his party which Emancipation had caused. On the contrary, it provoked a sudden and disastrous reaction on the part of men still bitter at the ministry's betrayal over the Catholic question.

On 15th November, the ministry was defeated in the Commons, the division being decided by the desertion of the Ultras and the English county Members.[189] Earl Grey took office at the head of a coalition of Whigs, Canningites and Ultras. Its shibboleth was, had to be, Reform: it was the only issue on which all were agreed. 'The logic of circumstances rather than any commitment to a *sine qua non* bound the Whigs to reform in 1830.'[190] Consequently they had no scheme prepared in advance of entering office. Most of Grey's cabinet were amateurs in politics, not bureaucrats or legislators by training or instinct. Reform proposals in the previous fifty years had been infrequent and disconnected. Almost no-one had foreseen as politically practicable a measure as comprehensive and sweeping as that which was brought forward in 1831. The 'Great Reform Bill' has usually been portrayed as the result of 'pressure from without', steadily mounting for half a century and finally irresistible; politicians by contrast were aware of no such tide of sentiment and were mostly astonished by the scale of the public reaction in 1831–2. Discontent there had been in the past, and public disorder had been a familiar phenomenon for decades, sometimes acute, often residual, seldom wholly absent. But it had not been widely perceived as focussing on Reform in particular before 1830, and radical agitators had not generally succeeded in placing that interpretation on the multifarious activities of mobs.[191]

Not all varieties of radicalism expressed a new, populist affirmation of rational individualism and the centrality of universal suffrage. Thomas Attwood, for example, possessed an organic vision of society and was responsible for a campaign in Birmingham which in many ways echoed the early-eighteenth-century Tory critique of establishment corruption.[192] From November 1830, however, the situation was transformed by the

---

[189] 'I never saw a man so delighted as Peel', wrote Mrs Arbuthnot; 'he was so delighted at having so good an opportunity for resigning.' *Arbuthnot Journal*, vol. II, p. 402. Perhaps it saved Peel from having to rat again.

[190] Mitchell, 'Whigs and Parliamentary Reform', p. 42.

[191] E. J. Hobsbawm and G. Rudé, *Captain Swing* (London, 1969), traced the rural riots of 1830 to economic distress, not to a demand for parliamentary reform or a response to urban radical leadership.

[192] D. J. Moss, 'A Study in Failure: Thomas Attwood, MP for Birmingham 1832–1839', *HJ* 21 (1978), 545–70.

existence of a ministry committed to Reform, and appealing to the country for an endorsement. In the familiar fashion of the 'old society', such an endorsement was given. Half a century of anti-establishment resentment was provided with a definitive issue on which to focus.

The alliance of patrician Whigs with patrician Ultras made Grey's ministry, to a striking degree, one of blue blood and great landowners. Ironically, the Reform Bill was framed and passed by those who had most to lose and who imagined they were acting wisely and liberally to preserve the social order which prevailed on their broad acres. The scheme which they adopted was, therefore, moderate: that is, moderate in principle (though sweeping, indeed shattering, in its extent). Grey and other colleagues disavowed the ballot, universal suffrage, equal electoral districts, annual parliaments, the payment of MPs. The extreme principles which such things expressed could not possibly secure a parliamentary majority. Even so, the remaining complexities of franchise and redistribution gave almost endless scope for negotiation, debate and resistance. Much of it was conducted in a fog of statistical ignorance and partial knowledge about the exact effects of various alternative schemes: Reform was not the culmination of a well-informed campaign of enquiry and planning, but the hurried and confused consequence of Emancipation.

On 1st March 1831 Lord John Russell announced the ministry's plan in the Commons. A well-kept secret, its extent and audacity now came as a bombshell. Grey was guilty of a disastrous miscalculation:[193] he believed he commanded a majority large and reliable enough to pass the Bill quickly through both Houses and produce a final solution to the problem. In reality, it required a lengthy campaign and an extra-parliamentary, democratic agitation which verged on revolution, which escaped from ministerial control, and which was soon expressed as a fundamental attack on both aristocracy and Church. The sheer fact of a popular, insurrectionary upheaval apparently focussed on the state of parliamentary representation did much to swamp the carefully aristocratic letter of the Bill. The events of 1831–2 set its formal provisions in a very different light.[194] One MP wrote:

The whole country took fire at once. The working people expected that they were to change places with their employers. The middle classes believed that by breaking

[193] Brock, *Reform Act*, pp. 152–6. Equally, Grey's

> ...whole notion that it might be passed without any popular upheaval was unrealistic. If it had become law in the summer of 1831 there would have been great pressure for household suffrage, triennial parliaments, and secret ballot. Inevitably the radicals would have concluded that the second stage of their programme need be no harder to achieve than the first.

Cf. M. I. Thomis and P. Holt, *Threats of Revolution in Britain 1789–1848* (London, 1977), pp. 85–97.

[194] Historians stressing the limited extent of Grey's reforming intentions have, perhaps, neglected a much more radical, and possibly more effective, element in Whiggism: cf. Ellis Wasson, 'The Spirit of Reform, 1832 and 1867', *Albion* 12 (1980), 164–74.

down the parliamentary influence of the peers, they should get the governing power of the State into their own hands. And the ministers, the contrivers of the design, persuaded themselves that the people, out of sheer gratitude, would make the rule of the Whigs perpetual. If, to all these interested hopes, we add the jealousy of the vulgar at all privileges not shared by themselves, – the resentment of the majority of the nation at the disregard of their sentiments respecting the Roman Catholic Bill – and the superficial notion that the direct representation of numbers is the principle of the elective franchise, – we shall have a tolerably correct conception of the motives of a revolution

which, in the 1840s, he continued to deplore.[195]

Petitions poured in to the Commons. But what did they mean? It was still by no means obvious that Reform was the main goal. Croker claimed that in the 'vast majority' of the petitions 'the most prominent demand of the petitioners is...for the abolition of tithes and taxes. The first object of the petitioners is, generally, reduction of taxation; the second is the suppression of tithes; and Reform occupies, most frequently, only the third place in the prayers of the petitioners.'[196] This was not the interpretation which the ministry wished to adopt, however, and the Bill was forced through. The division on the second reading, on 23rd March, the famous victory of 302 to 301, was decisive. Most of the Ultras, by now thoroughly frightened, divided with the opposition: of 140 identified by Professor Aspinall, only 28 voted for the Bill – though they were enough to turn the scale.[197] Analysed another way, the vote was carried by a combination of the Irish MPs, who backed the Bill by 51 to 36, and of English county Members, who similarly sided with Reform by 51 to 25 (the remaining English MPs being opposed by 205 to 174).[198] It was an insufficient majority to carry the Bill, but sufficient to persuade William IV to agree to a general election when the ministry was defeated in committee. It followed only a week after the snap dissolution, and voting took place in a semi-revolutionary mood of excitement and resentment against the Bill's opponents. With the king's name being cited in favour of Reform, the result was a landslide against the Ultras. Of English county Members, 76 were returned in favour of the Bill, 6 against. Now, at last, the extent of public commitment to the measure became evident.

Peel's opposition to Reform was henceforth increasingly 'measured', and ultimately marked by 'indifference'. He refused to align himself with the Ultras, with whom he was profoundly out of sympathy.[199] His instincts pointed to concession and compromise; but to 'rat' again would be political suicide. The ministry's majority was in any case sufficient to make his

195 Twiss, *Eldon*, vol. III, p. 123.
196 *Parl Debs* 3rd ser., vol. III, col. 88.
197 A. Aspinall (ed.), *Three Early Nineteenth Century Diaries* (London, 1952), p. xxix.
198 Brock, *Reform Act*, p. 178. Twenty-five MPs now voting for Reform had voted against Emancipation in 1829.
199 N. Gash, *Sir Robert Peel* (London, 1972), pp. 19–20.

irresolution irrelevant, and the second Bill passed by 367 to 231. It was, at last, a margin sufficient to coerce the upper House.

Or was it? After the landslide against them at the general election, anti-Reformers now proceeded to win nearly all the by-elections between then and October. Had the public mood been wrongly diagnosed? On 7th October 1831 Eldon, at the age of 80, gathered (as it seemed) his last strength to speak against the second reading of the second Bill in the Lords. It amounted, he said, to the sweeping away of a multiplicity of legal rights. The doctrine of the law was that boroughs were both political trusts, and property.

Is it possible for any man to have the boldness to say that property is secure, when we are sweeping away near one hundred boroughs, and almost all the corporations in the country, because we have a notion that those who are connected with them have not executed their trust properly?... This new doctrine... affects every species of property which any man possesses in this country... the Bill will be found, I fear from my soul, to go the length of introducing in its train, if passed, universal suffrage, annual Parliaments, and vote by ballot. It will unhinge the whole frame of society as now constituted... with this Bill in operation, the Monarchy cannot exist, and ...it is totally incompatible with the existence of the British constitution.[200]

The Bill was lost by 199 to 158. With the majority voted 21 bishops, who would have been just sufficient to turn the scale the other way (Blomfield prudently absented himself). Many of the Bill's opponents were friends to more moderate, non-partisan Reform, but were repelled by Grey's insistence that no amendments would be accepted in Committee. 'I dreaded the precedent of founding representation upon numbers, as likely to lead to a farther and to an indefinite extension', wrote the Bishop of Llandaff.[201]

The 1831 general election had not been marked by anticlericalism. Now, however, when it was too late, the Church had decisively declared itself on the side of the ancient constitution. Prelates thus incurred the twin inconveniences of vilification and defeat. Brougham had threatened in August 1831 that if the House of Lords rejected the Bill, 'the Bishops will be made to bear the blame'.[202] This was now the result. Disorder was widespread; popular organisations began to break free from moderate leaders. Plebeian fury vented itself not least against clergymen and Church property. Bishops were in physical danger; the Bishop's Palace at Bristol was burned down during three days of insurrection; that at Exeter was saved only by armed force. 'Such a proof of public antipathy towards the entire order', noted The Times, 'is without example in modern history, and is worth a whole library of comments.'[203] The non-payment of tithes and Church rates was threatened; Disestablishment became a widespread cry.

---

[200] Twiss, Eldon, vol. III, pp. 147–52.   [201] Copleston, Memoir, pp. 143–8.
[202] E. Hughes (ed.), 'The Bishops and Reform, 1831–3: Some Fresh Correspondence', EHR 56 (1941), 464.
[203] A. Blomfield (ed.), A Memoir of Charles James Blomfield (London, 1863), vol. I, p. 169.

A third Bill passed the Commons, and in January 1832 the ministry secured the king's promise of support, in the last resort, to force it through the Lords. The process of capitulation continued: the abolition of tithes in Ireland came before the Lords in February and March 1832. None of the bishops spoke against it. Eldon expected the next Reform Bill to pass: 'I attribute much to affright and fear of mobs.'[204] He nevertheless spoke against it on the second reading in the Lords, which extended from 9th to 13th April 1832:

For the sake of the higher, the middle, and the lower orders of society, – for all of whom, and more particularly for the last, he considered himself a trustee, – he was determined, as far as in him lay, to preserve the blessings of that constitution under which they had all been born and spent their lives, which had rendered them happier than any other people on God's earth, and which had given to their country a lustre and a glory that did not belong to any other nation in the world.[205]

The Bill passed by 184 to 175.

On the second reading sixteen bishops voted against the Bill, twelve in favour: a decisive swing. The key man in their conversion was Blomfield, Bishop of London, who was squared by Grey and who then lobbied his colleagues on the bench. He persuaded enough of them with his fears that 'a great political convulsion' would be the result of the Bill's rejection.[206] He therefore spoke of the Bill merely in terms of its renovation and restoration of a constitution which all valued, a language which others of his colleagues continued to think wholly inappropriate. Phillpotts called the Bill a measure designed 'to effect a complete and entire change in the whole representative system',[207] and his private willingness to compromise in the face of defeat did not alter his analysis. Lord George Murray, Bishop of Rochester, warned the Lords that they should not 'legislate on expediency upon a question involving the total subversion and annihilation of law and justice'.[208] Such extravagant language, in itself unpersuasive, reflected an accurate perception that what was at issue in 1828–32 was not a number of piecemeal adjustments, but a fundamental discontinuity in principles and values. But a belated defence of the last ditch was insufficient to avert such a change.

Despite the passage of the second reading, resistance to the Bill was still not at an end: Grey's majority evaporated in Committee, and the ministry resigned. The disorders known as the 'days of May' seemed to many to be the preliminaries to civil war. The only basis on which an alternative ministry was feasible was one of more moderate reform: yet Peel refused to

[204] Twiss, *Eldon*, vol. III, p. 171.
[205] *Ibid.*, vol. III, pp. 172–5; Davies, *Phillpotts*, pp. 130ff.
[206] Soloway, *Prelates and People*, p. 252; Blomfield, *Memoir*, vol. I, pp. 169–73.
[207] *Parl Debs* 3rd ser., vol. XII, col. 273 (11th April 1832).
[208] *Ibid.*, vol. XII, col. 400 (13th April 1832).

rat again, and Wellington's declaration against any Reform cast doubt on the Duke as the head of a reforming ministry. On 14th May, when a new ministerial team appeared in the Commons, the charge of ratting was once again levelled at Wellington, and the ministry disintegrated in a hostile House.[209] Formally Grey's ministry had never left office, and they merely resumed the reins. The opposition in the Lords largely stayed away: the third reading passed by 106 to 22, and the third Reform Bill received the royal assent on 7th June.

Blomfield, Bishop of London from 1829 to 1857, became the central figure of the Anglican Church in the new society. He was an excellent committee man. His diligence and bureaucratic vision caught the mood of much that was valued in the new order; but these strengths stemmed from the weaknesses of the old. Blomfield represented the ineffectual tone of the late-eighteenth-century episcopate. Educated in traditional political theology, ordained in wartime, he nevertheless worked with the tide of postwar reform in a mood of graceful concession and courteous capitulation. He spoke for the repeal of the Test and Corporation Acts, and clashed in Committee with Lord Eldon, their defender. Disraeli, sketching Blomfield in *Tancred*, diagnosed a 'great talent for action' together with 'very limited powers of thought': 'All his quandaries terminated in the same catastrophe, a compromise. Abstract principles with him ever ended in concrete expediency.'[210] Imperious and unaccommodating towards his clergy, he was on friendly terms with the Church's opponents. A distinguished career at Cambridge did not disguise a certain weakness: as his son wrote,

After the strain and stimulus of his undergraduate life, he began to feel the effects of his over exertions. One day, while walking in the gardens of St John's College, he was seized with violent spasms; and this attack left him for years with an impaired digestion, and so weakened his nervous system for the time, that he could not ride on horseback without having to dismount at the slightest alarm, and cling for support to a tree or railing, until the nervous tremor had passed off.[211]

Others traced their objections to Blomfield to his theology. Newman wrote of 1830:

there had been a Revolution in France; the Bourbons had been dismissed: and I believed that it was unchristian for nations to cast off their governors, and, much more, sovereigns who had the divine right of inheritance. Again, the great Reform agitation was going on around me as I wrote. The Whigs had come into power;

---

[209] Cannon, *Parliamentary Reform*, pp. 236–8 argues that Peel's refusal of office, not public opinion, prevented a viable ministry.

[210] Quoted in O. J. Brose, *Church and Parliament. The Reshaping of the Church of England 1828–1860* (Stanford, 1959), p. 74.

[211] Blomfield, *Memoir*, vol. 1, p. 10. Blomfield was widely accused of having abandoned his early commitment to Emancipation in order to obtain a bishopric; it was suggested that he 'became the servile courtier, the interested hunter after preferment, and the intolerant bigot' (*ibid.*, p. 130). His son denied the charges.

Lord Grey had told the Bishops to set their house in order, and some of the prelates had been insulted and threatened in the streets of London. The vital question was, how were we to keep the Church from being liberalized? there was such apathy on the subject in some quarters, such imbecile alarm in others; the true principles of churchmanship seemed so radically decayed, and there was such distraction in the councils of the clergy. Blomfield, the Bishop of London of the day, an active and open-hearted man, had been for years engaged in diluting the high orthodoxy of the Church by the introduction of members of the Evangelical body into places of influence and trust. He had deeply offended men who agreed in opinion with myself, by an off-hand saying (as it was reported) to the effect that belief in the Apostolical succession had gone out with the Nonjurors. 'We can count you', he said to some of the gravest and most venerated persons of the old school.[212]

Early-eighteenth-century prelates, of the stamp of Gibson, Potter, Waterland or Wake, were both formidable ideologues and theologians, and forceful, independent personalities. Such qualities persisted in clever meritocrats like Phillpotts and Van Mildert. But increasingly the bench submitted to a smooth, bland, and ultimately anti-intellectual norm which critics found merely obsequious. Blomfield, typically, owed his early advancement to the patronage of Lords Spencer and Bristol. Such prelates, even when scholars, did not entertain the sort of ideas which might put them at odds with the polite society in which they sought to move, or challenge them to lead, rather than respond to, social trends.

VI. CONSEQUENCES

In the light of the arguments developed earlier in this book, it is possible to understand the position of those men who so long and so successfully defended the 'Protestant constitution'. They have, indeed, had a very bad press. Yet it is now clear that the Ultras did not represent a reaction, an extreme movement away from a common ground, a retreat from the 'spirit of the age'. The later Burke, Reeves, Eldon, Phillpotts and the Ultras were defending a doctrine essentially similar to that which ministerial Whigs had held since the days of Burnet, Wake, Gibson and Potter. The State still found its most vocal ideologues in those in whom knowledge of religion and the law joined, like the frustrated clergyman Lord Eldon or the would-be barrister, Bishop Phillpotts. What made them seem extreme was, first, that an increasing number of Dissenters and men of no religion were ceasing to subscribe to a doctrine which its adherents found as persuasive as ever, and, second, that the Ultras committed the greatest historical crime: they lost. Where the regime which Wake, Gibson and Potter championed fought off the Stuart challenge, the political and ecclesiastical Establishment of Blomfield and Peel compromised with, and capitulated to, sectarianism and democracy. Eldon and his associates were stigmatised by their enemies as

---

[212] J. H. Newman, *Apologia Pro Vita Sua*, ed. W. Ward (Oxford, 1913), pp. 131–2.

blindly opposing all change; yet, as we have seen, they saw themselves opposing a certain sort of change – not piecemeal adjustments but the shattering of a whole social order, and its appropriate values and modes of behaviour. In that perception they still spoke for a clear majority of Englishmen, as the Catholic issue demonstrated.

The years 1800–32 witnessed, then, not so much the progressive advance of a liberal mood shared by all as the gradual numerical erosion of a social, religious and political hegemony from without, and a final and sudden betrayal from within. In that process, parliamentary reform played a subordinate part. That it was a shibboleth of Victorian society does not entail that it was a major social goal, or a major engine of change, in the English ancien regime. Interest in it as a political issue, never at a very high level, waxed and waned; in the 1820s it almost died away entirely. Relatively few men at any time had hailed it as the *obvious solution* to society's manifold problems. Throughout the first decades of the nineteenth century, Emancipation and Repeal took a great, and a growing, precedence over Reform: Catholic and Protestant Dissent counted for much, democracy for little. Far from Emancipation being 'an aspect of the reform question',[213] Reform was a consequence of the shattering of the old order by Emancipation.

That a whole social and political order had been destroyed by the events of 1828–32 was the reaction of its erstwhile defenders. The historian cannot accept or reject such a view in an objective sense; but he can endorse it in relation to the self-image of the old society which its defenders formulated, and which has been explored above. Modern parliamentary historians, by contrast, have usually seen no great discontinuity in 1832. A modest but not revolutionary number of men received the vote. Some towns received separate representation, but many small constituencies remained. With open voting and published pollbooks, the techniques of influence remained very relevant. Magnates continued to sway elections, and the sociological composition of the House of Commons was little changed, at least in the short run. Cabinets in the early and mid-nineteenth century were still largely composed of peers and their sons. Historians have attended to Grey's assurances that the Bill was a moderate, limited and final measure, designed to frustrate revolution by the conciliation of the middle classes. Armed revolution duly failed to materialise. Seen within the traditionally narrow, positivist terms of reference – the extent of the franchise and the distribution of seats – it is difficult to understand the scale of the crisis which the three Reform Bills of 1831–2 caused, the bitterness and tenacity with which the Bills were resisted, and the despair and triumph which accompanied the third Bill's final passage. To appreciate these things it is necessary to look

[213] 'That is being concerned with the qualifications of MPs and with the Irish franchise': Cannon, *Parliamentary Reform*, p. 245.

not merely at the literal provisions of the 1832 Act but at its wider consequences, and at the effects of Repeal and Emancipation also. The events of 1828–32 must be understood together if they are to be understood at all. The modern historian of Victorian and twentieth-century England sees in 1832 a classic crisis, but a viable social order in subsequent decades. The eighteenth-century historian by contrast sees in the events of 1828–32 a dissolution of the social order with which he is familiar.

The provisions of the 1832 Act were not in themselves intended to effect the triumph of Industry or Democracy. Whig ministers generally attempted not to act on radical principles of personal representation, and the Act did not provide for 'one man, one vote'. An attempt was made to preserve a balance between rural and urban interests: of 140 redistributed seats, 64 went to new boroughs, 62 to the counties. Boundary changes, the new borough seats, and the borough householder clause,[214] removed some urban voters from the counties in which they lay, so strengthening gentry influence[215]. Yet more significant than the *constructive* aspects of the Act were its *destructive* aspects. The removal of these 140 seats shattered the electoral basis on which the late-eighteenth-century Establishment had rested in the House of Commons. No longer could the King's chosen ministers present a seemingly impregnable, unchanging facade to the opposition. Henceforth the balance was far more evenly poised between two great parties, and their tenure of office quickly came to turn exclusively on the results of general elections.

Even the narrowly political consequences of Reform were seldom expressed in the provisions of the Act itself. The chief results were unforeseen. A two-party polarity was created with remarkable suddenness, Liberal and Conservative between them absorbing virtually every MP, the two parties alternating as ministry and opposition. This was completely new. Since the alterations were henceforth effected by general elections, and since the newly-coherent parties increasingly generated their own leaders, the ability of the sovereign to choose and sustain ministers at once went into a steep and irreversible decline: the power of the monarchy was very quickly a shadow of what it had been, even under George IV. The electorate had been appealed to, and its allegiances polarised, in respect of a single issue: this too was prophetic, and both the precedents of 1830–2 and the system then instituted meant that politics passed into a new age of manifestos, platforms, and ever-widening mass appeals. The *working* of the new party system came

---

[214] It provided that certain borough freeholders lost their county votes in certain circumstances.

[215] Cf. D. C. Moore, 'The Other Face of Reform', *Victorian Studies* 5 (1961–2), 31–2. It is not necessary to accept Professor Moore's early overstatement that 'In many counties most freeholders were urban' to concede that there is much force in this argument. For qualifications, cf. E. P. Hennock, 'The Sociological Premises of the First Reform Act: a Critical Note', *Victorian Studies* 14 (1971), 321–7.

to place a far more democratic interpretation on the Reform Act than most of its framers intended, and the question of the progressive widening of the franchise to reflect wealth and, ultimately, numbers could not now be avoided.

The House of Lords had been decisively defeated in 1828–32, and its power to resist future reform was dramatically reduced. Together with this, as was argued in chapter 2, the cultural hegemony of the aristocracy and gentry disintegrated with great rapidity in the 1830s and 40s; the repeal of the Corn Laws in 1846 was a last, symbolic, defeat. Aristocratic power was henceforth based on wealth and on political skill, and both these things, though considerable, provided only a stay of execution. 'Cultural hegemony', before 1828–32, is a phrase aptly describing the aristocracy's entrenched dominance in a unitary society, a confessional State; after 1832 the English elite, and the Anglican Church, fought for survival within a plural society. Their survival for so long was a remarkable achievement; but the rules of the game had been changed, and the elite had been deprived of a winning advantage. If the power of the monarchy and the House of Lords was decisively reduced, the eighteenth-century constitution, conceived as a system of checks and balances between monarchy, aristocracy and democracy, was at an end. To a large degree, Britain henceforth possessed a unicameral form of government, in fact if not in name; and it contained an inbuilt populist bias.

That the Bill would deal a decisive blow to the power of monarchy and aristocracy was the fear which preoccupied William IV. In October 1831 he quoted Bolingbroke's *Patriot King* to Grey to justify his attempt to slow down the avalanche, but without effect.[216] As the Bishop of Llandaff, a friend of moderate reform, also foresaw:

...the chief fear is, that the advocates for parliamentary reform will do too much at once. If the House of Commons is chosen entirely by the people, there is an end of monarchy and aristocracy, for in the House of Commons has long resided virtually, though not nominally, the whole power of the State. The only thing that has kept us from pure democracy has been the influence of the crown and the nobility, or great proprietors in the representative body. A few of those who see this danger, and who have no care for the church, may think to pacify the republicans by sacrificing the interests of the church. But this would be merely as a sop thrown to a surly dog. As soon as his appetite returned he would be more ravenous than before.[217]

Some nineteenth-century politicians fought a long rearguard action against such dangers. Their sophistication and skill has mesmerised historians; the duration of the breathing-space they won has made their political world seem almost stable, and distracted attention from the nature of the

---

[216] Henry, Earl Grey (ed.), *The Correspondence of the Late Earl Grey with His Majesty King William IV and with Sir Herbert Taylor* (2 vols., London, 1867), vol. I, pp. 381–2 and *passim*.
[217] Edward Copleston to W. J. Copleston, 26th Jan. 1831: Copleston, *Memoir*, p. 139.

discontinuity in 1828–32 which made the efforts of Gladstone, Disraeli, Salisbury and others, as they supposed, so necessary.

Such consequences were sometimes foreseen by those who framed the legislation, sometimes not. Often they thought the most that could be done was to avoid immediate revolution. Initially, more innocent ideals came into play. Men who voted for Repeal and Emancipation had no conception that the impact of those measures was about to be vastly magnified by Reform, especially a measure as extensive as that which passed in 1832. Taken together with Emancipation and Repeal, the electoral situation in Ireland, Scotland and Wales was transformed.[218] Many constituencies in Wales and Scotland made an abrupt transition from tiny electorates and management to significant electorates and political articulacy: a system was destroyed. In the eighteenth century, the community of four nations had been dominated by Anglican-aristocratic England; in the nineteenth century it was swayed increasingly by its anti-Anglican, proletarian, Celtic fringe. But for demographic disaster in the 1840s, Irish independence could scarcely have been so long delayed.

In England itself, the effect of the measures of 1828–32 was to open the floodgates to a deluge of Whig-radical reform aimed against the characteristic institutions of the ancien regime. Prime targets were the universities, the public schools, the professions, the armed forces, colonial administration, the civil establishment's patronage machine, the corporations, the old poor law, and the criminal law. A sacred constitution, taking seriously the thirty-seventh Article of Religion of the Anglican Church, had defended itself with the death penalty. After 1832, the number of capital convictions fell precipitously, and soon capital punishment was confined to a handful of murder cases.[219] The number of clergymen newly appointed to the magistrates' bench fell sharply, and clerical JPs tried dramatically fewer cases. Religion and law were no longer two aspects of the same thing.

Above all, Whig and radical attack focussed on the Church. A feature of Anglican reaction to the Reform Act was to assess it in quasi-religious terms. Two Fellows of Eton (their Fellowships destined soon to be 'reformed' out of recognition) stayed up all night to hear the result of a crucial division on the Bill, pacing the corridor above the cloisters. When a messenger brought the news, as dawn broke, one turned to the other and said 'This is the worst crime since the Crucifixion.'[220] (John Calcraft, MP, believing that his switching his vote in the division lost by 302 to 301 had been decisive, committed suicide in September 1831.) Gladstone wrote in

---

218 Cf. W. Ferguson, 'The Reform Act (Scotland) of 1832: Intention and Effect', *Scottish Historical Review* 45 (1966), 105–14. The best account of the electoral machinery in Scotland and Ireland before 1832 is the seldom-examined second volume of E. and A. G. Porritt, *The Unreformed House of Commons* (Cambridge, 1903).

219 Cf. the figures in Derek Beales, 'Peel, Russell and Reform', *HJ* 17 (1974), 879.

220 Richard Ollard, *An English Education. A Perspective of Eton* (London, 1982), p. 56.

retrospect: 'There was in my eyes a certain element of Antichrist in the Reform Act.'[221] Hurrell Froude believed that 'In 1832, the extinction of the Irish Protestant boroughs, and the great power accidentally given to Dissenters by the Reform Act, gave a concluding blow to the ancient system.'[222] Even Wellington wrote:

> The revolution is made, that is to say, that power is transferred from one class of society, the gentlemen of England, professing the faith of the Church of England, to another class of society, the shopkeepers, being Dissenters from the Church, many of them Socinians, others atheists.
>
> I don't think that the influence of property in this country is in the abstract diminished. That is to say, that the gentry have as many followers and influence as many voters at elections as ever they did.
>
> But a new democratic influence has been introduced into elections, the copy-holders and free-holders and lease-holders residing in towns which do not themselves return members to Parliament. These are all Dissenters from the Church, and are everywhere a formidably active party against the aristocratic influence of the landed gentry. But this is not all. There are Dissenters in every village in the country; they are the blacksmith, the carpenter, the mason, &c. &c. The new influence established in the towns has drawn these to their party; and it is curious to see to what degree it is a Dissenting interest.[223]

'The real question', he said in 1838, 'that now divides the country and which truly divides the House of Commons, is church or no church. People talk of the war in Spain, and the Canada question. But all that is of little moment. The real question is church or no church.'[224]

Contrary to Bishop Blomfield's naive prediction that the concession of Reform would soon bring 'the people' to 'look with reverence to their ancient institutions', 1832 inaugurated a 'bleak interlude of extreme unpopularity' for the Church. The expropriation of her property, or the subversion of her liturgy, were all feared by clergymen, with different degrees of realism.[225] The Church's identification with the old order turned her into a scapegoat; far from radical opinion being assuaged, the very scale and profundity of the revolution of 1828–32 meant that, for the Church, there was no forgiveness. Dissenters and others now had far fewer reasons for reticence in their attacks, and a wide prospect of future gains. Even the Whig Lord Melbourne soon declared: 'What all the wise men promised has not happened; and what all the damned fools said would happen has come to pass.'[226]

A Unitarian, Wade, had provided the most damaging attack by issuing a statistical account of the methods of the old society, now labelled Old

[221] John Morley, *The Life of William Ewart Gladstone* (3 vols., London, 1903), vol. I, p. 182.
[222] *Remains of the Late Reverend Richard Hurrell Froude* (4 vols., London, 1838–9), vol. III, p. 207.
[223] Wellington to Croker, 6th March 1833: *Croker Papers*, vol. II, p. 205.
[224] Morley, *Gladstone*, vol. I, p. 155.
[225] Norman, *Church and Society*, pp. 88ff.
[226] W. M. Torrens, *Memoirs of William Lamb, Second Viscount Melbourne* (London, 1890), p. 234.

Corruption, in *The Black Book; or, Corruption Unmasked!* (1820), updated in *The Extraordinary Black Book* (1831), as the title continued: *An Exposition of the United Church of England and Ireland; Civil List and Crown Revenues; Incomes, Privileges and Power, of the Aristocracy...Presenting a Complete View of the Expenditure, Patronage, Influence, and Abuses of the Government, in Church, State, Law and Representation.* It was the most explicit attack imaginable on the three interrelated institutions which characterised the ancien regime: monarchy, aristocracy, church. Many of his figures were inaccurate, but the damage was done nevertheless. The attack was increasingly now conducted in these terms, with an 'openness and savagery' that came as an 'unwelcome surprise' to many clergy and politicians,[227] even to Whigs who believed that concession and compromise were in the best interests of the Established Church.

For a decade, the Church was menaced with disestablishment, a fate which overtook the Irish Church in 1869.[228] A series of less sweeping measures amounted to 'gradual disestablishment' for the English Church. Liberal ministries of the early nineteenth century flooded the bench with Liberal clergymen (in so far as they could be found) chosen for their political acceptability in the new era: Grey and Melbourne nominated fifteen bishops between 1830 and 1841. From 1846 to 1852 Lord John Russell's choices sometimes caused 'consternation'. The aristocracy's hold on the episcopate, as on the boroughs, was broken.[229] In due course, this had its effect on the social status of the clergy as a whole. Between 1842 and 1862 the number of Oxbridge graduates being ordained was halved.[230] The ideal of the gentleman, and the ideal of the clergyman, were decisively diverging.

Some of this had been foreseen. The High Churchman Alexander Knox wrote in 1816:

It cannot be dissembled, that, in what concerns the Established Church, the House of Commons seems to feel no other principle, than that of vulgar policy. The old High Church race is worn out...So soon, therefore, as the majority of the active public (which, unfortunately, is a very different thing from that of the thinking public) are seen to desert the Church, the House of Commons will, I suspect, no longer shelter her. The crisis may be resisted, for a time, by the still remaining habits of the House of Lords; but it can be only for a time. And who can say to what political results, even such a temporary effort may lead? The House of Lords and the Established Church are specially united to each other. They fell together before; and it would be hard to imagine, how the one could long continue to exist, without the other. In truth, we actually see the reverence for both aristocracies (the ecclesiastical and the political), scarcely by slow, but certainly by sure, degrees, going down together; and, among other causes, this similar one has clearly operated in both, that the aristocratic character has been injured by a neutralising blendure; that is, by making men of low descent, peers, and by making men of low Church principles, bishops.

[227] G. F. A. Best, 'The Constitutional Revolution, 1828–32', *Theology* 62 (1959), 229–30.
[228] Brose, *Church and Parliament*, pp. 22ff.
[229] Soloway, *Prelates and People*, pp. 6, 11–12.   [230] Gilbert, *Religion and Society*, p. 133.

The first he dated to 1783, the second to 1714.[231] Henry Phillpotts reacted similarly, writing in May 1831:

If symmetry is to be adopted, the constitution is gone; it may last a few years in a degraded and shattered form; but its foundations will have been removed, and the superstructure must, ere it be very long, follow. I cannot see that Gatton has a weaker right to its franchise than Lord Durham (the miserable author of this miserable bill) to his privileges as a peer.[232]

Seen from the viewpoint of the clerical intelligentsia, Repeal, Emancipation, Reform and the seemingly imminent consequences of these things invalidated the Warburtonian conception of the Alliance. 'Erastianism' was now the excuse for the imposition of revolutionary liberalism upon the Church. Hurrell Froude wrote:

...in 1833, we have witnessed the assembling of a parliament in which few perhaps can detect the traces of a LAY SYNOD OF THE CHURCH OF ENGLAND...it does appear that, according to Hooker, our *civil* legislature is no longer qualified, as it formerly was, to be our *ecclesiastical* legislature; that the CONDITIONS on which our predecessors consented to *parliamentary interference in matters spiritual* are CANCELLED.[233]

This was one response: Froude, Newman, Keble and their allies henceforth generally sought to distance the Church from the State. In this they drew on a strand in Orthodox Anglican thinking which led back via Richard Whately's anonymous *Letters on the Church: by an Episcopalian* (1826), to Daubeny, and to the later Nonjurors like Brett and Dodwell. When the Whigs' Irish Church Act of 1833 abolished bishoprics and reallocated endowments by secular *fiat*, John Keble responded with his famous Assize Sermon on 'National Apostasy', and one branch of Oxford opinion aligned itself into a 'movement'. It was, of course, under way already, in response to events since 1828. The Tractarians' point of origin was more political than it was patristic or sacramental, and their realisation of the origin of their predicament was swift. In May 1831, Hook wrote: 'I refer our calamities to the repeal of the Test Act; for then the State *virtually* renounced every connexion with religion. It pronounced religion to be, so far as the State is concerned, a thing indifferent.'[234]

The Tractarians' was not the only reaction to the events of 1828–32. Traditional, pre-Tractarian High Churchmen still outnumbered the Oxford zealots, and sought merely to preserve as much as could be preserved of previous theology and practice. Van Mildert's contribution to the problems of the 1820s was to edit a ten-volume republication of the works

[231] *Remains of Alexander Knox Esq.* (4 vols., London, 1834–7), vol. I, pp. 49–50.
[232] Davies, *Phillpotts*, p. 103.
[233] Froude, *Remains*, vol. III, p. 207; cf. 198ff for Hooker's doctrine of Parliament as a synod of the laity.
[234] W. R. W. Stephens, *The Life and Letters of Walter Farquhar Hook* (2 vols., London, 1878), vol. I, p. 221.

of the Rev. Daniel Waterland (1683–1740), the greatest theologian of Gibson's Church–Whig alliance. Even among the Tractarians, many still tried to adhere to the older doctrine of the theocratic unity of Church and State. Especially was this true of John Keble, whose Accession Day sermon in 1836, 'Kings to be honoured for their office sake', proclaimed sovereigns to be the 'anointed of the Lord, a living type, of the supreme dominion of Jesus Christ'.[235] Phillpotts continued to fight a hopeless rearguard action on such principles long after 1832.

If 'old' High Churchmen continued to insist both on the apostolic authority of the Church and on a connection with the State that pointed to the inferior status of Dissenters, other schools of thought reverted to the equally ancient idea of comprehension. S. T. Coleridge's *On the Constitution of the Church and State According to the Idea of Each* (1830) brought to that plan an 'almost mystical doctrine of group personality',[236] and merged the clergy in an inclusive national intelligentsia reminiscently entitled the 'clerisy'. Thomas Arnold's *Principles of Church Reform* (1833) lacked these Germanic overtones and proposed to deal with Dissent merely by bringing all Trinitarian Protestants under the Anglican label, irrespective of other differences. By being all-inclusive, the Church in Arnold's plan lost its authority and definition as a separate, apostolically-appointed corporation. The objects of Church and State were the same: 'religious society is only civil society fully enlightened: the State in its highest perfection becomes the Church'.[237] But Whigs, radicals and Dissenters were still committed to the secularisation of politics, and such schemes lacked political practicality.

With Gladstone, the rival theories which the 'old society' had generated to justify and make effectual a confessional State received their obituary notice. Like so many young intellectuals in the early nineteenth century, he had found traditional Anglican social and political doctrine profoundly appealing. Gladstone's reading at Eton (1821–7) included Pretyman-Tomline's *Elements of Christian Theology*, Waterland, Beveridge and Charles Leslie,[238] and at Oxford (1828–31) Hooker, Jones of Nayland, Burke, Horsley and Van Mildert. He had a lifelong interest in Bishop Butler. Consequently, as even the agnostic Morley realised, 'the association of political and social change with theological revolution was the most remarkable of all the influences in the first twenty years of Mr Gladstone's public life':

Then rose once more into active prominence the supreme debate...the inquiry: what is a church? This opened the sluices and let out the floods. What is the Church

[235] P. B. Nockles, 'Continuity and Change in Anglican High Churchmanship in Britain, 1792–1850' (Oxford D.Phil. thesis, 1982), p. 6 and *passim*.

[236] Norman, *Church and Society*, p. 98.

[237] T. Arnold, *Principles of Church Reform*, ed. M. J. Jackson and J. Rogan (London, 1962), p. 163.

[238] It does not seem that Peel, at Whiggish Harrow (1800–5), read such works.

of England? To ask that question was to ask a hundred others. Creeds, dogmas, ordinances, hierarchy, parliamentary institution, judicial tribunals, historical tradition, the prayer-book, the Bible – all these enormous topics sacred and profane, with all their countless ramifications, were rapidly swept into a tornado of such controversy as had not been seen in England since the Revolution.[239]

It was an anti-democratic fervour which produced the apocalyptic note in Gladstone's famous speech at the Oxford Union against the Reform Bill, and, appropriately, he owed his first seat in Parliament to the Ultra Duke of Newcastle. In 1838 his first book, *The State in its Relations with the Church*, offered a critique of previous theories as a preliminary to his own case. The subservience of the Church to the State (Hobbes) or the State to the Church (Bellarmine) were rejected as extreme. From Hooker Gladstone took the view of the State as a moral person, 'having a conscience, cognizant of matters of religion'. This revealed the great '*moral* defect' of Warburton's utilitarian requirement that the State merely ally with the largest Church: 'In fact, Warburton appears to have adopted the views of Locke, and to have copied his representation of the alliance from the original compact, not himself objecting to the use that has been made of that arbitrary mode of stating the case, but, on the contrary, considering any derivation of political from patriarchal rule, as an absurdity.'

For similar utilitarian reasons, Paley's views 'of the office of the clergy, of the visible church, of creeds, of the method of weighing different forms of Christianity, and of the irrelevancy of religious distinctions to the discharge of civil duties, are full of the seeds of evil'.[240] Rather, Gladstone began with the Orthodox Anglican conception of the Church as a distinct, divinely instituted society and demanded that the State endorse the Church – the Anglican Church – as part of its moral duty to forward religious truth, requiring conformity to that religion as a precondition of civil office. It was a counter-revolutionary doctrine: it demanded in effect the reversal of the changes of 1828–9. Church and State, Gladstone admitted, were not congruent in Hooker's sense; but if the Church was essential to the State, the converse was not true. The Church was essential to the State since the State was not an artificial, human device: in his conception,

Political society was a natural institution, bound by fundamental laws fixed by the mandate of divine justice. Social obligation was therefore no mere matter of expediency. The relation of the members to the body was to be determined by a natural and ordained relation, like that of the members of a family to a father, 'and not as one originating in the choice and therefore shaped by the fancy of those who

[239] Morley, *Gladstone*, vol. I, pp. 33, 79–81, 155–7; Perry Butler, *Gladstone. Church, State and Tractarianism. A Study of His Religious Ideas and Attitudes, 1809–1859* (Oxford, 1982), pp. 17, 43; M. R. D. Foot (ed.), *The Gladstone Diaries*, vol. I, (Oxford, 1968), pp. 46, 59, 75, 93, 197, 258, 300, 376, 379, 396.

[240] W. E. Gladstone, *The State in its Relations with the Church* (London, 1838), pp. 4, 9, 12–13, 16, 21.

are comprehended in it'. Thus the view that the will either of the individual or of the majority was a rightful arbiter in matters of government should be denounced. The notion of *vox populi* was an absurdity.

Hereditary rule, primogeniture and religion were society's organising principles.[241]

In 1828, this might have seemed an orthodox statement of an Anglican politico-theological position. By 1838, it belonged to a lost world. Peel rejected his young backbencher's work with contempt: expediency and pragmatism, even scepticism, were henceforth the hallmarks of Conservatism (in time, it was forgotten that the regime before 1832 had been defended in highly principled, even dogmatic, terms). Macaulay seized on the book for a review now reasserting as obvious and accepted truths the Whig dogmas, from Charles James Fox to Grey, of the absolute separation of the spheres of religion and politics, and of the superiority of a plural to a unitary and confessional society. Gladstone had advanced conformity as a qualification for office; 'But why stop here?' answered Macaulay; 'Why not roast Dissenters at slow fires? All the general reasonings on which this theory rests evidently lead to sanguinary persecution.' Plurality of belief already existed, not only in society at large, but in the Anglican Church: few of its clergy, insisted Macaulay, shared Gladstone's tenets.[242]

Macaulay, as usual, perfectly caught the prevailing mood. As Gladstone himself admitted in 1868, 'Scarcely had my work issued from the press, when I became aware that there was no party, no section of a party, no individual person, probably, in the House of Commons, who was prepared to act upon it. I found myself the last man on a sinking ship.'[243] Unknowingly, Gladstone had written the swan song of the old society. This was so despite the fact that almost as many people were still Anglicans, and almost as many Anglicans as before were prepared to subscribe to Eldonite doctrine. Most voters, let alone non-voters, still behaved as if they subscribed to a hierarchical order. The aristocracy and gentry still held their estates, and the great majority of the Whig party in Parliament remained landed and Anglican. For this reason the widespread fears of the expropriation of property proved premature, though the events of 1848 across Europe warn against treating English security as a foregone conclusion. What had changed was that, relatively suddenly, a particular description of a social nexus had been unseated from its intellectual and constitutional hegemony.

This was a political phenomenon, and it was the Whig party which rightly claimed responsibility. What the Whigs did in 1828–32 was not a reluctant

---

[241] Butler, *Gladstone*, pp. 42–4.
[242] 'Gladstone on Church and State' (*Edinburgh Review*, April 1839) in Macaulay, *Works*, vol. IX, pp. 137, 169–70.
[243] Morley, *Gladstone*, vol. I, p. 179.

concession, nor was it an attempt to cure the salient political symptoms of their age. It was a deliberate attempt to aggravate those symptoms by the implementation of a programme. It was a programme with many components, and the Whig party, too, was diverse. Some Whigs were committed to some goals and not to others, but in the last resort it was the Whigs' unity and their opponents' schism which forced the legislation through. It is necessary to emphasise that Reform itself was a relatively unimportant component of that programme. Parliamentary reform did not arrive as the 'culmination of a long historical process' in which the state of the franchise and the distribution of seats were central, or widely seen to be central, to social and political change; it arrived by accident, in a hurry, as a consequence of something else. It was not an irrelevant consequence; on the contrary, Reform was intimately associated with Repeal and Emancipation. Nevertheless, Reform came third and last in the process by which the theoretical hegemony of the ancien regime was destroyed in 1828–32.

What mattered most – monarchy or Church? In 1688–9 the political classes ultimately chose the second; in 1828–9 they reversed that choice. Ironically, the later events echoed the earlier dilemma. In 1828, the Secretary of the Admiralty recorded his discussion of Catholic Emancipation – the Duke of Clarence 'observed on the inconsistency of the King's refusing in Ireland what he granted in Hanover. I said the cases were not quite the same. The King held Hanover by hereditary right, but England only by the Protestant Settlement.'[244] Now, as in 1688, the governing elite was divided. The Ultras chose the Church; others chose (as they thought) the monarchy – that is, the civil power. For many supporters of the governing coalition, the ministry's apostasy over the Catholic question abrogated their allegiance, and it was ministerial schism which allowed in Grey's ministry and led necessarily to Reform. It might even be argued that the period covered by this book was defined by two instances of betrayal: Englishmen's breach of their oath of allegiance to James II in 1688–9; and George IV's breach of his coronation oath in agreeing to Repeal and Emancipation in 1828–9. Whether it will be considered heretical to speak thus disrespectfully of these two inglorious revolutions is, perhaps, still a question.

It is of course unnecessary as well as inappropriate to venture a moral verdict on the basis of the analysis presented here. Contemporaries, however, did so, and with considerable realism. Hurrell Froude wrote a *Farewell to Toryism* (1833):

---

[244] *Croker Papers*, vol. 1, p. 412. Two years later Clarence succeeded to the throne as King William IV.

'Doubtless Thou art our Father, though Abraham be ignorant of us, and Israel acknowledge us not':

'Tis sad to watch Time's desolating hand
> Doom noblest things to premature decay:
> The Feudal court, the Patriarchal sway

Of kings, the cheerful homage of a land

Unskill'd in treason, every social band
> That taught to rule with sweetness, and obey
> With dignity, swept one by one away;

While proud Empirics rule in fell command.
> Yet, Christian! faint not at the sickning sight;

Nor vainly strive with that Supreme Decree.

Thou hast a treasure and an armoury
> Locked to the spoiler yet: Thy shafts are bright:
> Faint not: HEAVEN'S KEYS are more than sceptred might;

Their Guardians more than king or sire to thee.

Afterword

Evidence for (and against) one's hypotheses continues to accumulate even after one has laid down one's pen. A text, once finished, is only launched into the stream and carried on by the current, taking its place within an academic context of subsequent research and of older writings which one subsequently discovers. In the months between finishing this book and its publication, several studies appeared which it would have been wrong to ignore, but equally impossible at the last moment to integrate into my own work. Students of the issues discussed above can now pursue in several splendid books themes which I was able to deal with only in outline.

The aristocracy and gentry (if not the clerical intelligentsia) seem suddenly to be back on the agenda and even near the top of it. Professor John Cannon's 1982 Wiles Lectures, published as *Aristocratic Century. The Peerage of Eighteenth-Century England* (Cambridge, 1984), help take the sting out of my strictures on earlier historians for resolutely ignoring society's ruling elite, and Professor Cannon elegantly and profitably pioneers a trail for others to follow. The same can be said of a magnum opus by Professor Lawrence Stone and Jeanne C. Fawtier Stone, *An Open Elite? England 1540–1880* (Oxford, 1984). How powerful was the elite in the social structure of the ancien regime, and how 'open' was that elite to influence or entry by new men? Both works in their different ways give valuable evidence in support of the answers I, too, had given: more powerful, and less open, than we had thought. Yet, here too, we are left with the same unanswered question that was raised by *The World We Have Lost*: when did these characteristics of English society come to an end?

One sort of answer would be positivist, tracing declining estates and counting the declining proportions of peers in late-nineteenth-century Cabinets. Such calculations can, of course, be made for the century after 1832, and this is indeed part of the story. Yet if the traditional account used mobility into the landed elite as an explanation of long-term social stability and of prudent concession to inexorable but moderate and reasonable political change, I sought by contrast to question this major premise of Whig and Whiggish historiography. Though armed revolution on a large scale *was* avoided in Britain after 1760,[1] the events of 1828–32 and their aftermath must strike the eighteenth-century historian as among the most dramatic and profound changes ever effected in English society since the Reformation without recourse to widespread armed conflict.[2]

If so, the question becomes even more critical: what gave the old order such strength and tenacity in the half-century from c. 1780? Professor Christie and I were, independently, exploring similar issues; in his magisterial Ford Lectures of 1984, published as *Stress and Stability in Late Eighteenth Century Britain: Reflections on the British Avoidance of Revolution* (Oxford, 1984), he grasps a nettle which has deterred many historians, exploring the social, ideological and political structures, institutions and practices which underpinned a powerful and resilient regime. In pointing, *inter alia*, to the integral role of the Church within the established order, Professor Christie's analysis dovetailed also with Professor Gunn's work on the survival of legitimist, divine right, High Church ideas in *Beyond Liberty and Property: the Process of Self-Recognition in Eighteenth-Century Political Thought* (Kingston and Montreal, 1983). Professor Gunn's innovative and important book came to hand only after I had finished my own, and I was flattered to find that my approach had coincided even to a small degree with his. I had sought to go much further along some of these roads, however, and have stated my case in a different form. In particular, I feel that the idea that a Tory nexus of ideas survived only as a spectre at an essentially Whig feast fails adequately to diagnose either early-eighteenth-century Whiggism, or the united Whig establishment viewpoint which formed after the accession of George III.

Only after sending my book to the Press did I read Rhys Isaac's *The Transformation of Virginia 1740–1790* (Chapel Hill, N. Carolina, 1982). Isaac splendidly illustrates the impact at parochial level of some of the developments which I had sought to trace at metropolitan level, and in the realm of theory: where the Church of England was an integral part of a hierarchical social order, the effect of Dissent and of heterodoxy could only be destructive in

---

[1] It is, however, necessary to emphasise how many *small* outbreaks of armed rebellion occurred, like the Gordon riots, the Luddite disturbances, the Pentridge episode of 1817, the Swing riots or the Bristol disorders of 1831. If we recognise the duel as a symbol (if a specialised, profitless symbol) of patrician independence of the State, there seems little reason to refuse to extend that analysis to many outbreaks of proletarian civil disorder (other than a wish by some commentators to legitimise all such acts under a single category of 'riot').

[2] The long-standing domination of the last decades of the ancien regime by historians whose interests, expertise and sympathies lie in the century after 1832 continues to obscure and to understate the importance of these transitions.

the widest sense.[3] The theme of the divine sanction for civil authority, and the theological element in establishment ideology, can be further explored from the other side: Dr McCalman has well demonstrated the continuing close links of obscenity and blasphemy in the radical tradition for an even later period.[4] If such modern scholarly works encouraged me by seeming to support some of my own arguments, the equally discouraging process continues of recovering evidence which reminds one of the themes to which one has failed to do full justice. I recently bought for a small sum in a Cambridge bookshop a Nonjuring classic: the Rev. Richard Welton's *The Substance of Christian Faith and Practice: Represented in Eighteen Practical Discourses, Preached Some Time in the Parish-Church of S. Mary Whitechappel* (London, 1724). Welton's legitimist denunciations of rebellion, usurpation and schism are a powerful reminder of the vitality of High Churchmanship and of Jacobite ideology at a proletarian level – themes to which many historians will surely turn.

It sometimes seems that to write a wide-ranging book is only to multiply the number of major scholarly works which one has failed adequately to attend to. One such, not noticed in my text, is J. G. A. Pocock's fine book *The Machiavellian Moment* (Princeton, 1975). While admiring Professor Pocock's treatment of mediaeval and early modern Italian thought, however, I was not persuaded that England and its American colonies (let alone Wales, Ireland and Scotland) spoke with a 'humanist and Machiavellian vocabulary' after 1688, political issues increasingly revolving around the secular concepts of credit and commerce, virtue and corruption. Against such a picture, in which it seems that the terms of political debate are dictated to conservatives by radicals, I offered as an alternative a model of a society, preoccupied with religion, in which the terms of politico-theological debate were dictated to the heterodox by the orthodox, and in which theological heterodoxy provided the intellectual starting point for the formulation of radical doctrine. The problem of reconciling these two worlds of discourse, Professor Pocock's and my own, could not be tackled in so brief a book as this.

Moreover, the historiographical tradition into which the 'Commonwealthmen' have generally been fitted since the publication of Caroline Robbins' *The Eighteenth Century Commonwealthman* in 1959 yields, by extrapolation, an interpretation of late-eighteenth-century 'radicalism' which

---

[3] In particular, the effect in the colony in the early 1770s of two freethinkers, new arrivals at the College of William and Mary – the Rev. Thomas Gwatkin and the Rev. Samuel Henley (the latter a Socinian and a protégé of Dr John Jebb and Edmund Law, Bishop of Carlisle) – was very much what one would expect.

[4] Iain McCalman, 'Unrespectable Radicalism: Infidels and Pornography in Early Nineteenth-Century London', *P&P* 104 (1984), 74–110.

was perfectly captured by an article of Professor Kramnick's.[5] It might seem excessively combative, in these closing reflections, to pursue my objections to such a use of what I contend are the anachronistic concepts of 'Lockeian liberalism' or 'bourgeois radicalism', articulated by 'middle-class radicals' and expressed in 'the language of economic determinism'. None of these things are discoverable in England before c. 1820, if at any time, and I hope I have shown what then occupied the place within the mental universe of the ancien regime which 'liberalism' and 'radicalism', whether 'Lockeian' or 'bourgeois', later occupied.

Obviously, I have sought to give due attention not only to the social structure of a monarchical, aristocratic, Anglican regime, but also to the ideological formulations with which it was defended. In particular, I have emphasised deference and popular religion, especially Anglican religion. What would follow if full justice were done to such themes, in more extended studies than this? Certainly, we would see a social, religious and political system unseated in 1828–32; but we would see also the great residual power of its premises about human nature and conduct. We can already begin to question the quantitative importance, after the Reform Bill, of 'liberalism', 'bourgeois individualism', 'class', 'democracy' and so forth. We can even begin to ask: did their later devotees, in retrospect, wrongly diagnose the essence and origin of such phenomena? Indeed, in the terms of their familiar self-definitions, have they ever existed at all? At a moment in English history when the ideologies of both liberalism and socialism were being progressively scrutinised, it seemed possible that these questions might at last receive serious attention, and serious examination of the premises of such positions leads us inevitably back to the social, intellectual and religious experience of England's ancien regime.

[5] Isaac Kramnick, Religion and Radicalism. English Political Theory in the Age of Revolution', *Political Theory* 5 (1977), 505–34. A large part of the problem in this tradition, it seems, is the confusion of 'secular' with 'heterodox'. Although Professor Kramnick rightly senses the role of Dissenters in destroying the Anglican-aristocratic Establishment, he traces their significance to a 'progressive and innovative bourgeois nexus' rather than, what might seem obvious, to their *religion*.

Index

Aberdeen, George Hamilton-Gordon, 4th
  Earl of (1784–1860), 393
Acts: Corporation (1661) and Test (1673),
  140, 208, 230, 250–3, 258n, 287,
  300–4, 320, 340–2, 350–420 *passim*;
  Uniformity (1662), 270; 'Bill' of
  Rights (1689), 120n, 129, 134, 232,
  356, 361, 374; Coronation Oath
  (1689), 355; 'Toleration' (1689), 94,
  207, 208n, 252, 270, 283, 286–7, 335, 344,
  265; Licensing (lapsed 1695), 284;
  Blasphemy (1697), 207, 286, 344,
  379, 389; A. of Settlement (1701),
  134, 173, 178, 232, 280n, 361; Union
  (1707), 355; Occasional Conformity
  (1711) and Schism (1714), 302, 304,
  342; Septennial (1716), 15, 292, 303,
  320; Quieting and Establishing
  Corporations (1719), 303; Indemnity
  (from 1727), 316; Last Determinations
  (1729), 15; Witchcraft (repeal, 1736),
  169; Mortmain (1736), 304; Licensing
  (1737), 180; Gaming (1739), 108;
  Jewish Naturalisation (1753), 283;
  Gaming (1755), 108; Stamp (1765),
  322; Quebec (1774), 215; Catholic
  Relief (1778), 337; Protestant
  Dissenters Relief (1779), 252, 365;
  Catholic Relief (1791), 344, 353;
  Canada (1791), 216; 'Six Acts' (1819),
  382; Reform (1832), 15–6, 35–7, 75,
  92–3, 370, 402–20; Irish Church
  (1833), 415; Naturalisation (1870),
  191
Adair, James (?1743–98), 312
Adam, William (1751–1839), MP, 114
Adams, John (1735–1826), 318n
Addison, Joseph (1672–1719), 180, 329
Aiken, John, 67
Aikenhead, Thomas, 285

All Souls College, Oxford, 204, 280n
Allen, John (1771–1843), atheist, 210–12
Allestree, Rev. Richard (1619–81), 106n
d'Allonville, Comte, 97
Almack's, 108
American colonies: electorate in, 23–5;
  Locke in, 48–9; ideology of order, 79;
  gentry in, 99; divine right in, 149–50;
  Anglican episcopate and, 149, 216,
  305, 314, 326
American Revolution: and antipatriarchal
  ideology, 84–5; and English reaction,
  237ff, 322ff; and religion, 319
Andrewes, Lancelot (1555–1626), bishop,
  272
Andrews, J, 97n
Angelo, Domenico, 114n
Anne, Queen (1665–1714), and party
  politics, 12, 26; and electorate, 20; and
  ideology, 119ff, 288, 343; and
  succession, 129, 133n, 175; and King's
  Evil, 186
Annett, Peter (1693–1769), Deist, 286, 382
Arbuthnot, Mrs, 387, 402n
Archenholz, J. W. von, 98n
Arian(ism): xiii, 47, 218, 252ff, 279n,
  280–8, 292, 297, 306, 309, 311, 314,
  317–21, 329, 333, 335–6, 345, 378. *See
  also* Socinianism, Unitarianism
Arne, Thomas (1710–78), composer, 157
Arnold, Thomas (1795–1842), of Rugby,
  103n, 416
Arran, Charles Butler (1671–1758), 2nd
  Earl of, 154, 155n
Association for the Preservation of Liberty
  and Property against Republicans and
  Levellers, 263–4
Astell, Mary, feminist, 85
Athanasian Creed, 160, 282, 288n, 310,
  312n, 314, 315n

Atterbury, Francis (1662–1732), bishop,
    51, 144, 152, 175, 249, 291, 303
Attwood, Thomas (1765–1838), MP, 402
Augusta, Princess (1768–1840), doubts
    Hanoverian title, 161
Austria, 122
Aylesbury, 360

Bagot, Lewis (1740–1802), bishop, 234, 249
Bagot, Sir Walter, 5th Bt (1702–68), MP,
    Jacobite, 234
Balguy, Rev. Thomas (1716–95), 249
Ballantyne, George, 133
Balliol College, Oxford, 55n, 153, 156n
Bamford, Samuel, agitator, 384
Banks, T. C., 168n
Baron, Richard (d. 1766), Dissenting
    minister, Socinian, republican, 310,
    321
Barrington, Shute (1734–1826), bishop, 336
Barrow, Rev. Isaac (1630–77), 249
Barruel, Abbé, 122
Bathurst, Allen (1684–1775), 1st Baron
    Bathurst, 1st Earl Bathurst, 235
Bathurst, Benjamin (1711–67), MP, 235
Bathurst, Henry (1714–94), MP, 235
Bathurst, Henry (1744–1837), bishop, 235,
    364
Bathurst, Henry (1762–1834), 3rd Earl,
    392, 393n
Baxter, Dudley, statistician, 72
Bayley, Sir John (1763–1841), judge, 382
Bean, J., 244n
Beaufort, Charles Noel Somerset
    (1709–56), 4th Duke of, 154n, 160
Beaumont, John, 169n
Beckford, Richard (c. 1712–56), MP, 320
Beckford, William (1709–70), MP, 323
Bedford, John Russell (1710–71), 4th Duke
    of, 308
Bedford, John Russell (1766–1839), 6th
    Duke of, 115n
Bellamont, Charles Coote (1738–1800), 5th
    Earl of, 114n
Bellarmine, St. Robert (1542–1621), 417
Bentham, Edward (1707–76), Fellow of
    Oriel, 142n, 150–1, 154–5, 174n, 193n
Bentham, Jeremy (1748–1832), and
    monarchical legitimacy, 50–1, 195;
    and Jacobitism, 51, 155n;
    anti-Lockeian, 57; view of man,
    59–61; and Filmer, 75–6; and origins
    of State, 81; and coercive authority,
    90; destroys Blackstone, 209–10;
    ignored, 354; on religion, 382; and
    parliamentary reform, 385; mentioned,
    119n, 189

Bentley, Dr Richard (1662–1742), 160n
Berkeley, George (1685–1753), bishop, 58,
    152, 306
Berridge, Rev. John (1716–93), of Everton,
    243
Berryman, Rev. Dr, 160n
Beveridge, William (1637–1708), bishop,
    152, 175n, 243, 416
Binckes, Rev. Dr William, 175, 260
Birmingham, 258n; 1791 riots, and
    Anglicanism, 283, 344; and franchise
    reform, 368, 385, 400, 402
Blackall, Offspring (1654–1716), bishop, 58
Blackburne, Archdeacon Francis (1705–87),
    306, 312n, 313–14, 321–2, 338
Blackstone, Sir William (1723–80): Tory
    background, 59; adapts, 189; and
    Bute, 201; and *Commentaries*, 204–9,
    265–6, 395; mentioned, 180, 211
Blacow, Richard, 155n, 156n
Blandford, George Spencer-Churchill
    (1793–1857), 6th Marquess of, 400
blasphemous libel, 283–9, 309–10, 379–82
Blomfield, Charles James (1786–1857),
    bishop, 405–8, 413
Blount, Charles (1654–93), Deist, 280, 282,
    294, 382
Bolingbroke, Henry St John (1678–1751),
    1st Viscount, Deist: anti-Lockeian, 57;
    and *Patriot King*, 75, 179–85, 308, 411;
    on Jacobitism, 142; irreligion, 286,
    306–7, 329, 382
Bonald, Louis de (1754–1840), 123, 267
Boodle's, 108
Bosquett, A., 111
Bossuet, Jacques Bénigne (1627–1704),
    bishop, 121
Bostock, Bridget, 165
Boswell, J., 220n
Boswell, James (1740–95), biographer; on
    succession, 186–7
Boucher, Rev. Jonathan (1738–1804),
    loyalist, 150, 262n, 273–4
Boulainvilliers, Comte Henri de, 96, 100,
    106
Boulton, R., 169n
'bourgeois': term examined, 70–1, 76–7,
    95; historiographical model built on, 6,
    55, 197, 200, 318n, 424; middle class
    and, 105–6; religion and, 283n
Bowdler, John (1746–1823), 274
Bowles, John, 263, 266–7, 274, 352
Bradbury, Thomas (1677–1759), Dissenting
    minister, 159
Bradshaw, William (1671–1732), bishop,
    160n
Braithwaite, Richard, 106

Brand, Rev. Fitzjohn, 265
Brand, Thomas (1774–1851) MP, 363,
    365–6
Brasenose College, Oxford, 224
Brecknock, Timothy, 203
Brett, Thomas (1667–1744), Nonjuror
    bishop, 146, 415
Bristol, Frederick-William Hervey
    (1769–1859), 5th Earl and 1st
    Marquess of, 408
Brooke, Henry (1703–83), playwright, 179
Brooks's, 107–8
Brougham, Henry (1778–1868), 1st Baron,
    358, 384, 388, 392, 401, 405
Brown, Rev. Dr John (1715–66), 308
Browne, John (1642–1700), surgeon, 163n
Brunswick Clubs, 371, 397
Buckingham, Richard
    Temple-Nugent-Brydges-Chandos-
    Grenville (1776–1839), 1st Duke of,
    115n
Buckle, H. T., polemicist, 5
Bull, George (1634–1710), bishop,
    152
Bunting, Jabez (1779–1858),
    Methodist minister, 241
Burdett, Sir Francis, 5th Bt (1770–1844),
    MP, 114n, 258, 313n, 357, 361–2,
    384–5, 391, 397
Burgh, James (1714–75), Dissenter, 307,
    320, 322–3, 336
Burke, Edmund (1729–97), MP: and
    patriarchalism, 80; and gentility, 93;
    and French Revolution, 97–9, 120n,
    216, 227; and party, 195; and
    Blackstone, 205; and religion, 141,
    226, 315, 329, 335, 341–4, 364, 408;
    and Sacheverell, 233; and Methodists,
    239; political philosophy, 247–58, 271;
    attacked, 261, 327; and parliamentary
    reform, 321–2, 338–9, 367, 385;
    mentioned, 58, 189, 246, 265, 274,
    416
Burlamaqui, Jean-Jacques, jurist, 209
Burnet, Gilbert (1643–1715), bishop, 175,
    261, 282, 288, 408
Bury, Rev. Arthur (1624–1713), 285
Bute, John Stuart (1713–92), 3rd Earl of:
    34; and Johnson, 188; and Prince of
    Wales, 201–2; in 1760s, 309–10, 312n
Butler, Joseph (1692–1752), bishop, 193,
    220, 246, 249, 274, 280, 305–6, 313n,
    317, 416
Byrom, John (1692–1763), Nonjuror: and
    Locke, 46; and State sermons, 159;
    and King's Evil, 165; and Bolingbroke,
    182; and Wesley, 236n

Calcraft, John, MP, 412
Calvin(ism), 233n, 242, 271n, 273, 292,
    332, 340, 345
Calvin's Case, 191
Cambridge University, 112–13, 152–3,
    156–9, 214–15, 228–30, 312–13
Cameron, Dr Archibald (1707–53),
    Jacobite, 172
Canada, social policy in, 216, 413
Canning, George (1770–1827), MP, 114n,
    359, 366, 388, 391–3
Carlile, Richard (1790–1843), Deist, 380–2
Carlisle, Frederick Howard (1748–1825),
    8th Earl of, 385
Carlton Club, 108
Carnarvon, Henry Brydges (1708–71),
    Marquess of, later 2nd Duke of
    Chandos, 153
Caroline of Ansbach, Queen (1683–1737),
    138n, 142, 144, 285n, 288n
Carte, Rev. Thomas (1686–1754), Jacobite,
    106, 144–6, 160–1, 222
Cartwright, Major John (1740–1824),
    Deist, 339, 362–3, 371, 373–4, 384
Cassan, Rev. Stephen Hyde, 351
Castiglione, Baldassare, 106
Castlereagh, Robert Stewart (1769–1822),
    Viscount, MP, 114n, 359, 362–3, 386
Catholic Emancipation, 115, 250, 349–420
    passim
Cato's Letters, 169, 290–1, 299, 301
Cavendish family, 385
Cavendish, Lord John (1732–96), 312
Central Society of Education, 166
Chamberlayne, John, 134
Chamres, Rev. Mr, 160n
Chandler, Rev. Thomas, 273n
Charles I, King, 50, 121, 127, 148–9,
    158–9, 164, 175, 186, 206, 213, 221,
    228, 325
Charles II, King, 127, 162, 167, 188, 239,
    266
Charles Edward Stuart (1720–88), Prince
    of Wales, King Charles III in the
    Stuart succession from 1766; and
    Church of England, 136, 186; and '45,
    132, 143, 150, 171; visit in 1750, 186;
    popularity among undergraduates,
    154; at Cambridge, 157; death, 172n
Charles II of Spain, King, 122n
Charles X of France, King, 167
Chartism, 345, 378–9
Chateaubriand, François-René de, 58–9
Chatham, William, Pitt (1708–78), 1st Earl
    of, 154, 173, 197, 292, 308, 309n,
    323–4, 336n, 339
Cherry, Francis, 124

Chesterfield, Philip Dormer Stanhope
(1694–1773), 4th Earl of, 101, 106,
145, 163, 167
Christ Church, Oxford, 51, 154n, 234n,
235n, 248n, 395
Christ's College, Cambridge, 175n, 311n,
313n
Chubb, Thomas (1679–1747), Deist, 283,
300, 329, 382
Churchill, Rev. Charles (1731–64), 310
Clare, John (1793–1864), poet, 166
Clare Hall, Cambridge, 285
Clarence, H.R.H. Prince William Henry
(1765–1837), later King William IV,
419
Clarendon, Edward Hyde (1609–74), 1st
Earl of, 222n
claret, political effects of, 142
Clarke, Adam (?1762–1832), Methodist,
240–1
Clarke, Rev. Samuel (1675–1729), Arian,
152, 281, 284–5, 288, 313, 317, 318n,
320, 338
Clarke, Rev. Dr Thomas, 262n
class: other allegiances alternative to, 32,
86–8, 196, 347n, 377, 424; date of
emergence of idea, 61–4; and industry,
67–8, 70–3; middle, and franchise, 83;
absence of, in confessional State, 90–3,
352; and social mobility, 105; and
parliamentary reform, 92, 321, 374.
Clayton, Robert (1695–1758), bishop,
287–8
Cleaver, William (1742–1815), bishop, 376
Clement, St, 226, 231, 272
Clementina Sobieska, Queen, 186
Clonmel, folk customs of, 171
Club of Honest Whigs [sic.], 320
Club of 27, 142n
Coade, George, 160
Cobbett, William (1762–1835), MP, 61,
89–90, 246, 361–2, 377, 381, 384
Cocoa Tree, 108, 154n, 309
Coetlogon, Rev. C. E. de (?1746–1820),
244–5
Coke, Lord Chief Justice, 380
Cole, Rev. William (1714–82), Jacobite,
142n, 157
Colebrooke, Sir George (1729–1809), MP,
194
Coleridge, Samuel Taylor (1772–1834), 78,
354, 416
Colley, T., hanged, 170
Collier, Jeremy (1650–1726), Nonjuror
bishop, 146
Collier, Rev. Nathaniel, 160n
Collins, Anthony (1676–1729), Deist, 280,

282, 284, 289, 299, 301, 321, 329, 333,
382
Colquhoun, Patrick, statistician, 72–3
Commonwealthmen, 279, 306–7, 311, 315,
324, 337, 339–40, 373
Coningsby, Dr George, 159
Convocation, 285, 288–91, 305–6
Cooper, Rev. R. Jermyn, 350
Cooper, Thomas, 382
Copleston, Edward (1776–1849), bishop,
395–6, 405, 411
Cornbury Park, Oxfordshire, 143
Cornwallis, James (1742–1824), bishop,
268n
coronations, 135, 139, 166–8, 175, 177–8,
217, 267
Corporation of London v. Evans (1767), 208
Corpus Christi College, Cambridge, 156
Corpus Christi College, Oxford, 154, 219n,
224n, 248n, 356n
Cotton family, of Madingley, 156
Cotton, C., 107n
Courtenay, H. R., MP, 234
Courtenay, Henry (1741–1803), bishop,
234
Courtenay, John, MP, 264
Coward, William, 285
Coxe, Rev. William (1747–1828), 262
Cricklade, 360
Crockford's, 108
Croker, John Wilson (1780–1856), MP,
161, 195, 359, 388, 393, 399, 404, 419
Cromwell, Oliver (1599–1658), 237
Crown and Anchor Tavern, Strand, 186
Croxall, Rev. Samuel, 160
Cruden, Alexander, reformer, 308
Cumberland, Richard, 103n
Curwen, J. C., MP, 362, 386
Cycle of the White Rose, 142n
Cyprian, St., 226, 272

Dalrymple, Sir John, 4th Bt (1726–1810),
215, 265
Dartmouth, William Legge (1731–1801),
2nd Earl of, 236, 243
Daubeny, Archdeacon Charles
(1745–1827), 249, 270–4, 350n, 415
Davies, Rev. David, 75
Dawes, Jacobite undergraduate, 155
Deacon, Dr Thomas (1697–1753),
Nonjuror bishop, 236
Declaration of Rights, 129, 254
Defoe, Daniel (?1661–1731), 43–4, 105,
169n, 290, 298
Deism, 49, 126, 147–8, 169, 187, 229,
279–329, 337, 345, 350, 358, 373–4,
381, 389

Delany, Patrick, 85n
D'Esterre, Mr, 115n
Diderot, Denis (1713–84), 382
Disney, Rev. John (1746–1816), later a
    Unitarian, 312, 314–15
Disraeli, Benjamin (1804–81), MP, 407, 412
Dissent(ers): electoral behaviour, 38;
    geography of, 69; numbers, 137,
    366–77; weakness of, 139; legal
    position of, 207–8; in America, 216;
    Deism and Arianism within, 216–7,
    229; political attitudes of, 244, 250,
    252ff, 277–348 *passim*; and repeal
    campaign, 349–420 *passim*.
Dodwell, Henry (1641–1711), Nonjuror,
    146
Dodwell, Henry (d. 1784), 415
Dolben, Rev. Sir John, 2nd Bt
    (1684–1756), 147, 243
Dolben, Sir William, 3rd Bt (1727–1814),
    243, 341
Donoghmore, Richard Hely-Hutchinson
    (1756–1825), 1st Earl of, 364–5, 385
Dorset, Lionel Sackville (1688–1765), 10th
    Duke of, 288n
Douglas, Sylvester, MP, 264
Dowling, Matthew, 115n
Drennan, William, 115n
Droit le Roy (1764), 202, 265
duelling, 106–18
Drummond, Robert Hay (1711–76),
    archbishop, 217
Dudley, John Wood, 1st Earl of, 393n
Dupplin, Thomas Hay (1710–87),
    Viscount, 30
Durham, John Lambton (1792–1840), 1st
    Baron, 415
Durham Report (1839), 216

Earbery, Matthias (1690–1740), Nonjuror,
    144, 146
earthquakes, 49, 124, 171, 307
Eaton, Daniel (d. 1814), Deist, 381
Eclectic Society, 243n
Edinburgh Review, 112, 210, 356, 363
Egmont, Sir John Perceval (1683–1748), 1st
    Earl of, 160
Eikon Basilike, 222
Eldon, John Scott (1751–1838), 1st Earl of,
    274, 351–2, 354, 360, 363–6, 379–80,
    383, 385–99, 405–8, 418.
elections:
    general: (1701), 21; (1702–41), 132;
    (1774), 21; (1807), 361; (1812–26),
    371; (1818), 386; (1826–41), 38;
    (1826), 391; (1830), 21, 401; (1831),
    21, 404.

individual: Aylesbury (1802), 360;
    Cambridge (1741), 156;
    Cambridgeshire (1724, 1727), 156–7,
    (1747), 22, (1830), 369; Cambridge
    University (1727), 156; Cheshire
    (1734–1832), 369; Co. Clare (1828),
    397; Derbyshire (1768, 1806–32), 369;
    Durham (1820), 369; Hampshire
    (1710), 16, (1806), 369; Kent (1713,
    1715), 18, (1802), 369; Lancashire
    (1747, 1800–32), 369; Northampton
    (1768, 1774), 371; Norwich (1761,
    1768, 1780, 1796, 1802, 1818), 370;
    Nottinghamshire (1722–1832), 369;
    Oxford University (to 1768), 156;
    Oxfordshire (1754), 151n, 204;
    Staffordshire (1747, 1800–32), 369;
    Suffolk (1710), 16; Surrey (1826), 369;
    Warwickshire (1774–1832), 369,
    (1820), 368; Westminster (1818), 371;
    Yorkshire (1708), 17, (1734–1832),
    369, (1807), 368–9.
Ellenborough, Edward Law (1790–1871),
    2nd Baron, 393n
Elwell, Edward, 286
Emlyn, Thomas, Dissenting Minister,
    Arian, 286
Emmanuel College, Cambridge, 188
Emmett, Thomas, 115n
Erastianism, 136–41
Erskine, Dr John, 261n
Eton College, 51, 103, 114, 139n, 151–2,
    262n, 263n, 280n, 312n, 315n, 412,
    416
Evangelical movement, 242–7, 345
Evans, Caleb, Dissenting minister, 239
Exeter College, Oxford, 155n, 280n, 285

Falmouth, Edward Boscawen (1787–1841),
    2nd Earl of, 398n
The Family, Cambridge club, 142n, 157
Farmer, Richard, 188
Feathers Tavern Petition (1772), 212–13,
    250–2, 312n, 313n, 314–15, 335, 338
Fénelon, François (1651–1715), archbishop,
    100, 153n, 364
Fiddes, Richard, 152
Fielding, Henry (1707–54), novelist, 104,
    151n
Fifteen, rebellion of, 144, 172
Filmer, Sir Robert (d. 1653): and
    Bentham, 75–6; versus bourgeois
    culture, 79; and Adam Smith, 106; on
    kingship, 125–6; in America, 149–50;
    studied at Cambridge, 153; and
    Providential divine right, 175; out
    Filmer'd, 219; and Burke, 257;

Filmer, Sir Robert *cont.*
  survival of, 121, 123, 258, 273, 274n,
  276, 294, 331; identified with Whig
  regime by radicals, 82, 260, 264–5;
  underestimated by historians, 45, 84,
  120n
Fitzwilliam, William Fitzwilliam
  (1748–1833), 2nd Earl, 385
Fleetwood, William (1656–1723), bishop,
  213
Fleming, Caleb (1698–1779), Dissenting
  minister, Socinian, 131n, 318, 322
Fleming, Robert, 124n
Fletcher, Rev. John, of Madeley (1729–85),
  239
Flint, George, Jacobite, 145
Flood, Henry (c. 1732–91), MP, 343
Fortescue, Sir John (?1394–?1476), 161
Forty-five, rebellion of, 132, 143, 150, 172,
  186, 236, 307, 309
Fothergill, Rev. Thomas, 148–9, 160n
Fox, Charles James (1749–1806), MP:
  Fox–North coalition, 12; continuity of
  his party, 35; attacks Johnson, 188,
  and loyalists, 263; and Burke, 216,
  252; and religion, 283n, 335, 344, 349,
  357, 361, 364, 418; and parliamentary
  reform, 339, 342, 362; mentioned, 107,
  114, 250n, 264–6.
Fox, Henry (1705–74), MP, 1st Baron
  Holland, 153n, 154n, 212, 292
France: towns, 70; industry, 73–4; social
  elite, 95–101; popular culture, 166–7;
  Revolution, 96–7; British army in,
  110; government, 122ff
Franklin, Benjamin, 320
Frederick, Prince of Wales (1707–51), 156,
  179–80, 182, 235n, 291n, 308
'Freethinkers', 140, 289, 293
Freind, Dr Robert, 51
Frend, Rev. William (1757–1841), later a
  Unitarian, 313–14, 346n
Frost, John, Jacobin, 346
Froude, Rev. Richard Hurrell (1803–36),
  399, 413, 415, 419–20
Fullarton, Col. William (1754–1808), MP,
  114n
Furneaux, Philip (1726–1783), Dissenting
  minister, 207, 320, 395

gaming, 106–9
Gandy, Henry (1649–1734), Nonjuror
  bishop, 146
Gascoyne, Gen. Isaac (1770–1841), MP,
  398
General Warrants, 203
gentleman, ideal of, 55–6, 91–118, 289, 378,
  411, 414

Gentleman's Magazine, 106, 110n, 165, 170,
  237, 342
Georg Ludwig (1660–1727), Duke of
  Braunschweig-Lüneburg, Electoral
  Prince (from 1692) and Elector (from
  1698) of Hanover, from 1714 also
  styled King George I of Great Britain,
  20, 26–33, 119–98, 236, 288ff
Georg August (1683–1760), Duke of
  Braunschweig-Lüneburg, Elector of
  Hanover, from 1714 styled Prince of
  Wales and from 1727 King George II
  of Great Britain, 26–33, 119–98,
  201–2, 316.
George William Frederick (1738–1820),
  Duke of Braunschweig-Lüneburg,
  Elector and from 1814 King of
  Hanover, from 1751 Prince of Wales
  and from 1760 King George III of
  Great Britain in the Hanoverian
  succession; and Patriot idiom, 179–80;
  and 'Jacobite principles', 182–3;
  accession, 167n, 184, 217; and party,
  194; eulogised by Blackstone, 205, by
  Johnson, 188, by Nowell, 213, by
  Wesley, 237, by Bowles, 266; and
  religion, 158, 335–6, 354, 361;
  mentioned, 235n, 267, 275, 338, 365
George Augustus Frederick (1762–1830),
  King of Hanover, from 1820 King
  George IV of Great Britain in the
  Hanoverian succession, 167, 267, 359,
  365, 387, 390, 398, 401, 410, 419
Germain, Lord George, formerly Sackville
  (1716–85), 114, 310
Gerrald, Joseph, Jacobin, 346
Gibbon, Edward (1737–94), 189, 220n,
  224n
Gibson, Edmund (1669–1748), bishop,
  137–8, 148, 186, 248, 274, 302–6, 408,
  416
Gladstone, W. E. (1809–98), MP, 242, 369,
  412–3, 416–18
Glanvill, Joseph, 169n
Glorious Revolution, 36, 45–6, 48; and
  patriarchalism, 81ff; and the family,
  84–5; dispensing power and, 113;
  ideological consequences, 119–98
  passim; debate on, 233, 253ff, 261ff,
  352, 364, 416–17
Gloucester, Duke of (d. 1700), 130
Glover, Richard (1712–85), poet, 179
Godwin, William (1756–1836), atheist, 330
Goldsmith, Oliver (1728–74), 99
Gonville and Caius College, Cambridge,
  157, 285n
Gooch, Sir Thomas, 2nd Bt. (1674–1754),
  157

Goostree's, 108

Gordon, Dr John, 214–15

Gordon, Thomas (d. 1750),
Commonwealthman, 169, 289n, 293n,
301, 304n, 310, 321, 323, 337, 345,
381n

Gordon Riots, 283, 339

Goulburn, Henry (1784–1856), MP, 393n

Grafton, Augustus Henry Fitzroy
(1735–1811), 3rd Duke of, Unitarian,
228, 311–12, 320

Grampound, 386

Grant, Charles (1778–1866), MP, 393n

Grant, Rev. Johnson, 262

Grascome, Samuel (1641–1708), Nonjuror,
146, 185

Grattan, Henry (1746–1820), MP, 385

Greatrakes, Valentine, 165

Grenville, William Wyndham (1759–1834),
1st Baron, 216, 360–1, 363–6, 385

Grey, Charles (1764–1845), 2nd Earl, 330n,
346, 349, 359, 362–3, 365–6, 384–7,
392–3, 401–9, 411, 414, 418.

Grimshaw, Rev. William (1708–63), of
Haworth, 243

Gronow, Captain, 107, 110

Grosseteste, Robert (c. 1175–1253), 135

Grotius, Hugo (1583–1645), 153n, 209

Guyot, Pierre, 96n

Gwatkin, Rev. Thomas, 423n

Hale, Sir Matthew (1609–76), Chief
Justice, 380

Halifax, Charles Montagu (1661–1715), 1st
Earl of, 46

Hall, Joseph, 285

Hall, Robert (1764–1831), Dissenting
minister, 244, 262n

Hallifax, Samuel (1733–90), bishop, 193n,
220, 228–30, 249, 344, 352

Hamilton, James Hamilton (1724–58), 6th
Duke of, 155n

Hammond, Rev. Henry (1605–60),
theologian, 273

Hampden, John (1594–1643), MP, 374

Hampden Clubs, 384

Handel, George Frederick, (1685–1759),
composer, 178

Hanway, Jonas, 104n

Harbin, George (?1665–1744), Nonjuror,
146, 153

Harcourt, Edward (1757–1847),
archbishop, 267

Hardwicke, Philip Yorke (1690–1764), 1st
Earl of, 141, 142n, 157, 193, 302–5,
380

Hardy, Thomas (1752–1832), Jacobin,
328n, 346

Hare, Francis (1671–1740), bishop, 160n

Harley family, of Wimpole, 156

Harrington, James (1611–77), 292, 294, 320

Hartley, David (1705–57), 333, 335

Harvard University, 153n, 308n

Harvey, Bagenal, 115n

Hastings, Warren, 253

Hay, Dr George (1715–78), MP, 203

Hay, John, 154n

Hearne, Thomas (1678–1735), Jacobite
scholar: and Locke, 47; conversion,
124; on Wake and Gibson, 138; on
Nonjurors, 142; on party distinctions,
151; on State sermons, 160; and
King's Evil, 162

Henley, Rev. Samuel, Socinian, 423n

Henry II, King, 133

Henry III, King, 135

Henry VIII, King, 259, 303

Henry Stuart, Prince (1725–1807),
Cardinal York, from 1788 King Henry
IX in the Stuart succession, 155, 161

Herries, John Charles (1778–1855), MP,
393n

Herring, Thomas (1693–1757), archbishop,
141, 312n

Hervey, John, Lord (1696–1743), 114, 139

Heywood, Samuel, Unitarian, 258–61

Hickes, Dr George (1642–1715), Nonjuror
bishop, 122n, 146, 147n, 152, 167,
176n, 221, 249, 259, 271, 273

Higden, Rev. William (d. 1715), 152–3,
235

Hill, Rev. Rowland (1744–1833), 243

Hillsborough, Wills Hill (1718–93), 2nd
Viscount, 305

Hoadly, Benjamin (1676–1761), bishop,
137–40, 152–3, 160, 178n, 220, 233n,
259, 261, 271–2, 282, 285n, 288, 289n,
294, 301–2, 314, 317, 338, 342, 364,
389, 395

Hobart, Sir Henry, MP, 114n

Hobbes, Thomas (1588–1679), 153, 209,
280n, 417

Hoby, Sir Thomas, 106

d'Holbach, Paul-Henri, Baron, 382

Holland, Henry Fox (1773–1840), 3rd
Baron, 210, 349, 358, 361, 363, 385,
388, 396–7

Hollis, Thomas (1720–74), Dissenter and
republican, 308, 314, 316, 318n, 321,
339

Hone, William (1780–1842), atheist, 311n,
381–2

Honourable Board of Loyal Brotherhood,
142n

Hook, Rev. Walter Farquhar (1798–1875),
415

Hooker, Richard (c. 1554–1600),
    theologian, 141, 223, 226, 231, 249,
    265, 271–2, 380, 415n, 416–17
Hope, Sir William, 114n
Hope-Scott, James (1812–73), 242
Horne, George (1730–92), bishop, 147,
    155n, 219, 221–6, 230–2, 243, 248–9,
    270, 273–4, 276, 306, 333
Horne, later Horne Tooke, Rev. John
    (1736–1812), 310n, 313n, 324, 346n
Horner, Francis (1778–1817), MP, 362
Horsley, Samuel (1733–1806), bishop, 140,
    220, 230–4, 249, 253, 258–9, 273, 344,
    352, 354, 416
Howell, Rev. Lawrence (?1664–1720),
    Jacobite, 144
Howley, William (1766–1848), archbishop,
    395–6
Hume, David (1711–76): on dynastic
    questions, 51–5, 132, 189; on origin of
    the State, 57; his Whiggism, 51–2; on
    Locke, 192; used by Bentham, 209, by
    Horne, 222, by conservatives, 265;
    mentioned, 119n, 380.
Hunt, Henry (1773–1835), agitator, 371,
    384
Hunt, Isaac, 273n
Hunt, Leigh (1784–1859), 363
Hunt, Thomas, 126
Huskisson, William (1770–1830), MP, 359,
    393n, 397
Hutcheson, Francis (1694–1746), 57
Hutchinson, Francis (1660–1739), bishop,
    169
Hutchinson, John (1674–1737), 218–9, 221,
    333

Ignatius, St., 226, 231, 272
Independent Whig, The, 160
'Industrial Revolution': concept examined,
    65; and technology, 65–6; and work
    experience, 66–8; and units of
    production, 67–9; and urbanisation,
    69–70; and social mobility, 70–1; and
    income distribution, 71–3; in Europe,
    73–4
Inglis, Sir Robert, 2nd Bt (1786–1855),
    MP, 356
Ireland, 353ff, 358, 372, 374, 391, 397–9,
    406, 412
Irving, Rev. E., 350

Jackson, John, 152
Jacksonian democracy, 24
Jacobitism: 119–98 *passim,* 292–3, 299,
    315–16, 423; and Tory party, 30–3,
    182–4, 279; and hereditary right, 46;

and contract, 48, 50, 56; in London,
    50–1; and Hume, 52; and the army,
    117; and Nonjurors, 122n; and
    Methodism, 179, 235; and *Patriot King,*
    179; Johnson on, 187; alleged
    impossibility of, 190; and Bathurst
    family, 235n; and Wesleys, 237;
    alleged revival 1750s–70s, 203, 219,
    239, 259, 261, 319; in folk memory,
    374, 382
James I, King (1566–1625), 133
James II, King (1633–1701), 46, 119, 122,
    127, 131, 146, 158, 164, 167, 202, 208,
    215, 253–4, 266, 271, 280n, 309, 327,
    331, 355, 419
James Francis Edward Stuart (1688–1766),
    from 1701 King James III in the
    Stuart succession, 49, 127–8, 136n,
    144–5, 154n, 155, 160–1, 163, 171–2,
    186, 349
Jebb, Rev. John (1736–86), later a
    Unitarian, 312–15, 322, 338–9, 354,
    423n
Jefferson, Thomas, Deist, 373n
Jeffrey, Francis (1773–1850), editor, 356,
    359
Jenkin, Robert, Nonjuror, 146, 147n
Jenyns, Soame (1704–87), MP, 75, 264
Jesuits, 128, 191, 233n
Jesus College, Cambridge, 156, 226n, 228n,
    258, 313–14, 315n
Jesus College, Oxford, 154
Jewell, John (1522–71), bishop, 272
John, King, 133, 236
Johnson, Dr Samuel, (1709–84), Nonjuror,
    132, 186–9, 216, 224n, 230, 237–8,
    275, 317, 330
Johnson, Thomas, 152
Johnstone, George, 114n
Jones, Rev. John (1700–70), 313, 338
Jones, Thomas, 154
Jones, Rev. Thomas, 113
Jones, Rev. William (1726–1800) of
    Nayland, 147n, 218–21, 226, 231,
    247–9, 255, 263n, 270, 326, 416
Joseph II, Emperor, 122

Keble, Rev. John (1792–1866), 399, 415–16
Ken, Thomas (1637–1711), bishop,
    Nonjuror, 146, 147n, 152
Kennicott, Benjamin (1718–83), 155, 219
Kettlewell, Rev. John (1653–95), Nonjuror,
    143n, 146, 147n, 152, 196
King, Gregory (1648–1712), statistician, 15,
    72–3, 83
King, Dr William (1685–1763), Jacobite,
    145, 153, 155, 186, 201, 212

King's College, Cambridge, 243, 262n, 280n
King's Evil, 119, 148, 158n, 160–7, 171, 186
Kippis, Andrew (1725–95), Socinian, 318n, 330, 332, 337–8
Knox, Alexander (1757–1831), 414–15

Labat, M., 114
Lackington, James (1746–1815), 168
Lambert, Dr, 156
Lansdowne, Henry Petty-Fitzmaurice (1780–1863), 3rd Marquess of, 358, 390, 397
Lardner, Nathaniel (1684–1768), Dissenting minister, Socinian, 284, 318, 333
Laud, William (1573–1645), archbishop, 137, 239, 289, 306
Law, Edmund (1703–87), bishop, 311–315, 338, 423n
Law, George Henry (1761–1845), bishop, 372
Law, William (1686–1761), Nonjuror, 146, 147n, 220–1, 243, 248, 272, 282, 306
Lawson, George (d. 1678), 136
Le Blanc, Abbé, 98
Leeds, 367–8, 385–6, 400
Leicester House, 179, 182–4, 235n
Leland, John (1691–1766), Dissenting minister, 284, 380
Leman, Sir T., 131n
Lennox, Col. Lord George (1737–1805), 114n
Leonard, Daniel, 273n
Leslie, Rev. Charles (1650–1722), Nonjuror intellectual: in America, 49; and Gallican Church, 122n; and origin of State, 47, 136; and oath of allegiance, 143n; in exile, 144; and contemporaries, 146; and Wesley, 152; studied at Cambridge, 153; admired by Johnson, 187, by Horsley, 231, by Daubeny, 271–3, by Gladstone, 416; opponent of heterodoxy, 282, 297–9; late eighteenth-century influence of, 147, 220–1, 243, 248–9.
liberal(ism), absence of term, 348, 383, 424
Lichfield, George (1718–72), 3rd Earl, Jacobite, 155n, 182
Lincoln College, Oxford, 138n, 219n, 280n
Lindsay, John, 149n
Lindsey, Rev. Theophilus (1723–1808), later a Unitarian, 313–15, 322, 327, 329, 335, 341, 344
Liverpool, Robert Banks Jenkinson (1770–1828), 2nd Earl of, 359, 363, 365–6, 372, 386–7, 389, 391

Lloyd, Charles (1784–1829), bishop, 359, 395, 398
Lloyd, William (1637–1710), bishop, Nonjuror, 146
Locke, John (1632–1704), Arian: political theory of, 45–50, 56; denied by Hume, 53–4, 190–2, by others, 57–8, by Blackstone, 208, by Leslie, 221, by Horne, 222–3, by Whitaker, 224, by Horsley, 232, by Burke, 251, by Boucher, 274, by Stillingfleet, 282, by Wesley, 152, 240, by W. Jones, 220, by Gladstone, 417; fails to refute Filmer etc., 75–6, 82, 150, 163, 265; Lockeian individualism, 64; on education and the family, 85–6, 126; historians' misconceptions of, 120n, 200, 257, 279; argued against at Cambridge, 153; and innate ideas, 185; radicalism and heterodoxy, 259, 261, 273, 280–2, 294, 311n, 314, 328n, 331, 364
Lockhart, George (1673–1731), Jacobite, 124
Lofft, Capel (1751–1824), Unitarian, 312, 339
Logan, Rev. George, 131n
Lolme, J. L. de, 121
Long, Roger, 156–7
Lonsdale, Sir James Lowther (1736–1802), 1st Earl of, 312
Louis XIV, King, 122n, 127, 166, 167n, 188, 215
Louis XV, King, 161
Louis XVI, King, 121n, 166–7, 231, 266, 346
Loveless, George, agitator, 379
Lowth, Robert (1710–87), bishop, 215n, 226, 230
Lucas, T., 107n
Ludlow, Edmund, regicide, 295n, 321n
Luxmore, Jacobite undergraduate, 156
Lyndewode, William (?1375–1446), 135
Lyndhurst, John Copley (1772–1863), 1st Baron, 393n
Lyttelton, George (1709–73), 1st Baron, 179, 183, 203, 336n

Macaulay, Thomas Babington (1800–59), 63, 83, 247, 418
Macaulay, Zachary (1768–1838), 246
Macdonald, Aeneas, Jacobite, 191
Macgregor, clan, 142
Magdalen College, Oxford, 221n, 356n
Magdalene College, Cambridge, 152
Mainwaring, Roger (1590–1653), bishop, 185, 213

Maistre, Joseph de (1753–1821), 76n, 123, 267

Mallet, David (1705–65), playwright, 179, 307

Malthus, Rev. Thomas (1766–1834), 88

Manchester: industrial organisation, 67; Jacobitism in, 143; Paley's doctrines in, 262; loyal politics, 224n, 344; and franchise reform, 367–8, 385, 400

Mandeville, Bernard de (1670–1733), 286

manners, history of, 102–6

Manners-Sutton, Charles (1755–1828), archbishop, 389

Manning, Rev. Henry (1808–92), 242

Mansfield, David Murray (1777–1840), 3rd Earl of, 398

Mansfield, William Murray (1705–93), 1st Earl of, 140n, 154n, 204, 208, 395

Margarot, Maurice, Jacobin, 346

Maria Theresa, Empress, 122

Marlborough, John Churchill (1650–1722), 1st Duke of, 138n

marriage: and social mobility, 70–1; and the modern family, 84–5

Martin, Samuel, MP, 114n

Mary, Queen, 130, 202

Massie, Joseph, statistician, 72–3

Matilda, Princess, 133, 236

Matthews, John, Jacobite, 144

Mawson, Dr, 156

Mayhew, Jonathan, Dissenting minister, Arian, 149, 153n

Melbourne, William Lamb (1779–1848), 2nd Viscount, 413–14

Melville, Robert Dundas (1771–1851), 2nd Viscount, 393n

Menestrier, Claude François, 96

Menin, Nicolas, 168n

Merton College, Oxford, 263n

Methodism, 67, 179, 218, 235–47, 283, 314, 372–83

Middleton, Dr, 160n

Middleton, Dr Conyers (1683–1750), 157

Miège, Guy, 86

Milbourne, Rev. Luke (1649–1720), Nonjuror, 146, 159

Mill, James (1773–1836), 61–4, 81, 83, 92, 201

Mill, John Stuart (1806–73), 7

Milton, Charles Wentworth-Fitzwilliam (1786–1857) Viscount, MP, later 3rd Earl Fitzwilliam, 381, 385

Milton, John (1608–74), Arian, 153n, 158, 281, 294, 321n

Mist, Nathaniel (d. 1737), Jacobite, 145

Molesworth, Robert (1656–1725), 1st Viscount, 289, 294, 299, 302

Molyneux, William (1656–98), Commonwealthman, 294, 331

Monmouth, James Scott (1649–85), Duke of, 171

Montague, James (?1568–1618), bishop, 213

Montesquieu, Charles de Secondat, Baron de (1689–1755), 99–101

Moore, Charles, 106, 110–11, 113, 117

More, Hannah (1745–1833), moralist, 104, 171, 245–7

Morgan, Thomas (d. 1743), Dissenting minister, Deist, 329

Morpeth, George Howard (1773–1848), Viscount, later 9th Earl of Carlisle, 385

Moyle, Walter (1672–1721), republican, 289, 293–4, 299

Muir, Thomas, Jacobin, 346

Murray, Lord George (?1700–60), Jacobite, 132

Murray, Lord George (1784–1860), bishop, 406

Murray, James, 154n

Nedham, Marchamont (1620–78), 321n

Negus, Samuel, 145

Nelson, Robert (1656–1715), Nonjuror, 138, 147n, 152, 226

Neville, Henry (1620–94), 289

New College, Oxford, 226n, 270

New Shoreham, 360

Newcastle, Henry Pelham (1785–1851), 4th Duke of, 354, 417

Newcastle, Thomas Pelham-Holles (1693–1768), 1st Duke of, 156, 193, 204n, 287, 306, 309, 311

Newdigate, Sir Roger, 5th Bt (1719–1806), MP, 213, 250, 314, 337

Newman, Rev. J. H. (1801–90), 242, 399, 407–8, 415

Newton, Sir Isaac (1642–1727), Arian, 218, 281n, 285

Newton, Rev. John (1725–1807), 243

Newton, Thomas (1704–82), bishop, 336

Nicholl, Dr John, headmaster, 103

Nonjurors, 122n, 124, 127, 138–40, 142–3, 146–7, 156, 192, 224, 226–7, 235n, 248–9, 259, 261, 271, 281–2, 291, 322n, 350, 408, 423

Norfolk, Charles Howard (1746–1815), 11th Duke of, 357

Norfolk, Bernard Howard (1765–1842), 12th Duke of, 385

Norris, John (1657–1711), 152

North, Roger (1653–1734), Nonjuror, 226–7, 248

North, Frederick North (1732–92), Lord: Fox–North coalition, 12; and party, 34, 275; and Patriot idiom, 180; Whiggism of, 199; and Dr Nowell, 212; and Wesley, 236; and the Church, 250, 314, 335–7, 342, 396; mentioned, 228, 235n, 340
North Briton, 203
Norton, Fletcher, MP, 203
Nowell, Dr Thomas (1730–1801), 151n, 154n, 160, 186, 212–14, 260, 315n

Oak Society, 186
Oastler, Richard, 78
O'Coigley, Fr James, 346n
O'Connell, Daniel (1775–1847), MP, 63, 115n, 371, 386, 397, 400
O'Connor, Arthur (1763–1852), 115n
Oriel College, Oxford, 150, 151n, 154n, 212n
Ormonde, James Butler (1665–1745), 2nd Duke of, 154
Orrery, John Boyle (1707–62), 5th Earl of, 155n
Osborne, Ruth, 170
Otter, William (1768–1840), bishop, 87, 372
Overall, John (1560–1619), bishop, 259
Owen, Dr, 159
Owen, J., 131
Owen, Robert (1771–1858), socialist, 374n
Oxford University, 142ff, 148, 151–6, 159, 186, 218, 221, 228, 235, 243, 249, 258–9, 309, 337, 415–17

Paine, Tom (1737–1809), Deist: on war, 107; on hereditary right, 185; on nationality, 191; on religion, 284, 324–30, 343, 345, 381–2; mentioned, 215, 220n, 246, 263, 356, 373–4
Paley, Archdeacon William (1743–1805), 50, 57, 80, 86, 110, 115, 220, 262, 271–2, 313, 417
Palmer, Elihu, Deist, 382
Palmer, Rev. Thomas Fysshe (1747–1802), later a Unitarian, 315, 346n
Palmerston, Henry Temple (1784–1865), 3rd Viscount, MP, 359, 393n
Panting, Dr, Jacobite, 186
parliamentary reform, 277–8, 290–2, 308, 320–4, 336–46, 349–420 *passim*
Passaran, Count Albert de, 301
Paterson, James, 135
patriarchalism, 42–92, 178, 181–2, 208, 223–4, 227, 241n, 274, 372, 420
Patten, Rev. Thomas (1714–90), Methodist and Hutchinsonian, 219n, 249

Paull, James (1770–1808), 114n
Peacham, Henry, 106
Pearce, Zachary (1690–1774), bishop, 148, 160n
Pearson, John (1613–86), bishop, 126
Peel, Sir Robert, 2nd Bt (1788–1850), MP, 359n, 369, 385, 388–9, 392–8, 402n, 404, 406–8, 416n, 418
Peerage Bill (1719), 156, 303
Pelham, Hon. Henry (1696–1754), MP, 132, 262, 279
Pembroke College, Cambridge, 157, 228
Pembroke College, Oxford, 154n, 186, 204n
Perceval, Spencer (1762–1812), MP, 258n, 354, 365–6
Peterhouse, Cambridge, 311–13, 346
Phillips, Erasmus, 153n
Phillips, Sir John, 6th Bt (1700–64), MP, 154n
Phillpotts, Henry (1778–1869), bishop, 354–6, 359, 394, 397, 399, 406, 408, 415–16
Pickering, Rev. Dr Thomas, 160n
Pitt Clubs, 359
Pitt, William (1759–1806), MP, 104, 108, 114n, 118, 199, 216, 228, 230, 244, 264n, 265, 312n, 339–44, 359, 364, 387, 395–6
Playfair, William, 262
Plowden, Francis (1749–1829), SJ, 233, 263
Plumtree, Dr, 156n
Plunket, William Conyngham (1764–1854), 1st Baron, MP, 387
Pope, Alexander (1688–1744), 80
Porteus, Beilby (1731–1808), 246
Potter, John (?1674–1747), archbishop, 138, 140, 154n, 175n, 248, 305–6, 408
Potter, Thomas, 310n
Presbyterianism, 172, 285n, 291, 304, 307n, 309, 317
Pretyman (later Pretyman Tomline), Sir George (1750–1827), bishop, 228, 234, 249, 341, 416
Price, Sir John, Bt, 165
Price, Richard (1723–91), Dissenting minister, Arian, 239, 253, 261–2, 316, 320, 323, 330–7, 339, 343, 354, 356, 396
Priestley, Joseph (1733–1804), Dissenting minister, Socinian, 207, 220, 229–30, 253, 283, 315n, 316, 318n, 320, 323, 329, 330–7, 341–4, 354, 396
Price, Rev. Thomas, 176
Pufendorf, Samuel (1632–94), 153n
Pulteney, William (1684–1764), MP, 1st Earl of Bath, 114n

Quakers' Affirmation Bill (1722), 303
Quakers' Tithe Bill (1736), 304–5
Queens' College, Cambridge, 315n
Queen's College, Oxford, 51, 137n, 263n, 269
Quincy, Josiah, Jr. 320

Radcliffe Camera, opening (1749), 155
radical(ism), absence of term, 348
Raleigh, Sir Walter, 191
Ralph, James (?1705–62), 308
Ramsay, Andrew Michael (1686–1743), Jacobite, 153
Randolph, John (1749–1813), bishop, 248
Raymond, Sir Robert (1673–1733), 1st Baron, 380
Redesdale, John Mitford (1748–1830), 1st Baron, 354
Reeves, John (1752–1829), 204, 258n, 263–5, 352, 355, 408
Reform Club, 108
Regius chairs of history, purpose of, 153
Reid, William, 262n
Religious Tract Society, 246
Rennell, Rev. Thomas, 261
Ricardo, David (1772–1823), 61, 386
Richardson, Samuel (1689–1761), novelist, 151n
Richelieu, Cardinal (1585–1642), 121
Richmond, Charles Lennox (1735–1806), 3rd Duke of, 320, 336n, 339
Richmond, Caroline, 5th Duchess of, 399
Rimius, Henry, 168n
Ritson, Joseph (1752–1803), antiquary, 147
Robertson, Rev. William (1705–83), later a Unitarian, 315
Rockingham, Whigs, 13, 33–5, 195, 199, 312, 324, 338–40
Roebuck, John Arthur (1801–79), MP, 385, 389, 401
Rogers, John, 152
Romaine, Rev. William (1714–95), 243n
Roman Catholicism, 137, 172, 188, 252ff, 280n, 282, 294, 337, 349–420 *passim*
Romilly, Sir Samuel (1757–1818), 385
Roque, G. de la, 96
Rosewell, Rev. Samuel, 176
Rousseau, Jean-Jacques (1712–78), 76n, 382
Rowan, Hamilton, 115n
Royal Society, 151
Ruddiman, Thomas (1674–1757), Jacobite intellectual, 131n, 147
Rundle, Thomas (?1688–1743), Arian, 304
Russell, Lord John (1792–1878), 120, 210, 357, 362–3, 386–8, 392–3, 395, 400, 403, 414.

Russell, Lord William (1639–83), republican, 215, 374
Russia, dynastic politics in, 173
Ryan, Edward, 261n
Ryswick, treaty of, 122

Sacheverell, Rev. Dr Henry (1674–1724), 48, 123, 126n, 141, 144, 146, 153, 159, 163, 171, 185, 233, 239, 255–6, 260–1, 264, 283, 291, 299
Sackville, *see* Germain, Lord George
Sadler, Thomas, 78
St Catharine's Hall, Cambridge, 139n, 157, 313–14
St Clement Dane's church, 186
St Edmund Hall, Oxford, 212n
St John's College, Cambridge, 156, 311n, 313n, 407
St Mary Hall, Oxford, 155, 156n, 212
St Peter's Field, demonstration in, 359, 386
Saint-Simon, Louis de Rouvroy, Duc de, 100
Savage, Samuel Morton (1721–91), Dissenting minister, 121, 217
Sawbridge, John (1732–95), MP, 339
schools, public, 102–3
Scott, Sir Walter (1771–1832), 170n
Scurlock, Rev. David, 261n
Seabury, Samuel (1729–96), bishop, 273n
Secker, Thomas (1693–1768), archbishop, 176n, 305–6, 317
Seller, Abednego (?1646–1705), 123
servants: in husbandry, 67–8; domestic, 85–6, 104
Shaftesbury, Anthony Ashley Cooper (1671–1713), 3rd Earl of, 57
Sharp, Granville (1735–1813), 112, 318
Sharp, John (1645–1714), archbishop, 152, 159, 175
Sharp, Thomas, 218
Shebbeare, Dr John (1709–88), 188
Sheffield, 368, 385
Shelburne, William Petty (1737–1805), 2nd Earl of, 1st Marquess of Lansdowne, 108, 114, 228, 336n, 339
Shelley, P. B. (1792–1822), atheist, 14
Sheridan, Richard Brinsley (1751–1816), MP, 233, 264, 362, 385
Sherlock, Thomas (1678–1761), bishop, 121, 139–40, 151, 157, 171, 217, 249, 286n, 289n, 303n, 304–5, 341–3, 395
Sherlock, William (1641–1707), Dean of St Paul's, 58, 139n, 174n, 177
Shippen, William (1673–1743), MP, 193
Sibthorp, Rev. Robert (d. 1662), 213
Sidmouth, Henry Addington (1757–1844), 1st Viscount, 365

Sidney, Algernon (1622–83), republican, 126, 153n, 185, 215, 221, 278, 295, 321n, 374
Simeon, Rev. Charles (1759–1836), 242–4
Simond, Louis, 258n
Skirving, William, Jacobin, 346
Smalridge, George (1663–1719), bishop, 152
Smith, Adam (1723–90), 55–6, 78, 86, 102, 106, 189, 326
Smith, Rev. Sydney (1771–1845), 358
Smith, William (1756–1835), MP, Unitarian, 370, 379, 389, 400
Smollett, Tobias (1721–71), novelist, 151n, 218n
Snape, Dr Andrew (1675–1742), 151, 160n, 289n
Society for Commemorating the Revolution in Great Britain, 332
Society for Constitutional Information, 312n, 339–40, 373
Society of the Friends of the People, 312n, 373
Society of Sea Serjeants, 142n
Society of Supporters of the Bill of Rights, 324
Socinianism, xiii, 47, 139, 218, 229–30, 252ff, 279n, 280–8, 292, 297, 310, 312, 314, 317–20, 329, 331n, 332–8, 343, 345, 378, 413
Socrates, on passive obedience, 54
Somers, John Somers (1651–1716), 1st Baron, 46
Somerset, Charles Seymour (1662–1748), 6th Duke of, 156
Somerville, Dr Thomas, 261n
Sophia, Electress of Hanover, 46, 253
South, Rev. Robert (1634–1716), 283
Southey, Robert (1774–1843), 78, 350, 354, 378
Sparke, Bowyer (1759–1836), bishop, 268–9
Spence, Thomas, 374n
Spencer, George Spencer (1758–1834), 2nd Earl, 408
Spinckes, Nathaniel (1653–1727), Nonjuror bishop, 127, 146, 147n
Spock, Dr; cf. Locke, 85
Sprat, Thomas (1635–1713), bishop, 152
Stanhope, James (1673–1721), 1st Earl, 303
Stanley, Hans (1721–80), MP, 283, 314
State sermons, 49, 158–60, 175, 177, 193, 212, 215n, 219, 221, 226, 228, 230–1, 234, 244–5, 249, 259–60, 274, 416
Stebbing, Rev. Henry (1687–1763), 152, 249
Stephens, John, 240
Stillingfleet, Edward (1635–99), bishop, 282

Stone, Rev. Francis, 288
Stone, George (1708–64), archbishop, 310
Strange, James Smith Stanley (1717–71), Lord, 212
Sturt, Charles, MP, 264
suicide, 106
Sunderland, Charles Spencer (1674–1722), 3rd Earl of, 46, 302–3
Swift, Rev. Jonathan (1667–1745), 43, 107, 290
Swing, Captain, riots, 401

Talbot, Charles (1685–1737), 1st Baron, 304–5
Talbot, William (?1659–1730), bishop, 175–6
Tandy, Napper, 115n
Taylor, Arthur, 168n
Taylor, Jeremy (1613–67), bishop, 153n, 249
Taylor, John, 159
Temple, Richard Grenville-Temple (1711–79), 1st Earl, 323
Tenison, Thomas (1636–1715), archbishop, 137n, 138n, 288
Terrick, Richard (1710–77), bishop, 336
Thelwall, John, Jacobin, 171n
Thompson, Thomas Perronet, 358
Thomson, James (1700–48), poet, 179
Tierney, George 'Citizen' (1761–1830), 114n, 312, 346, 385, 392
Tillotson, John (1630–94), archbishop, 282, 310
Tindal, Matthew (1657–1733), Deist, 280, 284–5, 295, 297–9, 329, 382
Tocqueville, A. de, 100
Toland, John (1670–1722), Deist, 134, 280, 282, 284, 286, 288, 289n, 294–301, 315, 329, 345, 381n, 382
Tolpuddle conspirators, 379
Tone, Wolfe, 115n
Toplady, Augustus (1740–78), 238n
Tory party (1690s–1750s): alleged destruction in 1714–15, 27; and electoral system, 291–2; and hereditary right, 46; prevalence of Toryism, 79, 90; and Jacobitism, 30–3, 47, 182–4, 196–7, 237, 308–9; alliances in 1745–60, 182–3; Bute's view of, 201; reconciled with dynasty, 204; inappropriateness after 1760, 276; myth of revival under George III, 33–4; effect of dissolution, 194, 308, 322.
Toulmin, Joshua (1740–1815), Dissenter, 336
Towers, Joseph (1739–99), Arian, 332

Townshend, George (1724–1807), 4th
  Viscount and 1st Marquess, 114
Townshend, Hon. Thomas (1701–80), MP,
  188, 213, 315n
Tractarian movement, 242, 270, 272, 377,
  415ff
Trapp, Rev. Dr Joseph, 160n
Trenchard, John (1662–1723), Deist, 169,
  290–1, 293n, 294, 300, 337, 381
Trinity College, Cambridge, 46, 113, 249
Trinity College, Oxford, 154n
Trinity Hall, Cambridge, 228n, 230n
True Blue, The, Cambridge club, 157
Tudway, Mr, 156n
Tutchin, John (?1661–1707), 298
Tyrrell, James (1642–1718), 83, 126, 153,
  289
Tyrwhitt, Robert (1735–1817), Unitarian,
  313, 315

unenlightened despots, 122
Unitarianism, xiii, 230, 250, 283n, 312n,
  336, 339, 344–5, 347, 350, 358, 371,
  380, 386, 389–92, 396n, 397n, 413. See
  also Arian(ism), Socinianism.
University College, Oxford, 138n, 218n,
  219n, 221n
urbanisation, 69–70, 366–73
Ussher, James (1581–1656), archbishop, 81

Van Mildert, William (1765–1836), bishop,
  249, 269, 354, 395, 408, 415–16
Venn, Rev. Henry (1725–97), 243
Venn, Rev. John (1759–1813), 244
Volney, Constantin François de, Count,
  382
Voltaire, J. B. Arouet de (1694–1778), 100,
  150, 246, 281, 328, 382
Volunteer Movement, 353

Wade, John (1788–1875), Unitarian,
  413–14
Wagstaffe, Thomas (1692–1770), Nonjuror
  and Jacobite, 136, 146
Waithman, Robert (1764–1833), MP, 362
Wake, William (1657–1737), archbishop,
  126n, 138, 177, 231, 286–7, 302–3,
  305, 364, 408
Wakefield, Rev. Gilbert (1756–1801), later
  a Unitarian, 258, 284, 313, 315, 329,
  346n
Walpole, Horace (1717–97), 203, 212, 215
Walpole, Sir Robert (1676–1745), 51, 152,
  262, 279, 301, 304–6
Walsingham, Robert Boyle (1736–80), MP,
  212
Warburton, William (1698–1779), bishop,

139–41, 221–3, 226, 229, 250–2, 255,
  259, 271–2, 275, 305–7, 333, 335, 380,
  415, 417
Waterland, Rev. Daniel (1683–1740),
  theologian, 133, 152, 220, 249, 311,
  408, 416
Watson, Joshua, 274
Watson, Richard (1737–1816), bishop, 220,
  313, 315
Watson, Richard (1781–1833), Methodist
  theologian, 241
Webb, Philip, MP, 203
Webster, William, 131n
Wedderburn, Alexander, MP, 203
Wellesley, Richard (1760–1842), Marquess,
  366
Wellington, Arthur Wellesley (1769–1852),
  1st Duke of, 93, 387, 392–402, 407, 413
Wenham, Jane, 169n
Wesley, Rev. John (1703–91), 51, 133n,
  152, 159, 169, 179, 189, 219n, 235–47,
  306, 355, 378
Wesley, Rev. Samuel (1691–1739), 51, 237
Westminster School, 51, 103, 288n, 312n
Westmorland, John Fane (?1682–1762), 7th
  Earl of, 155n
Westmorland, John Fane (1759–1841),
  10th Earl of, 392
Wetherell, Sir Charles (1770–1846), MP,
  400
Wetherell, Rev. Nathan, 219
Wharton, Thomas (1648–1715), 1st
  Marquess of, 114n
Wharton, Philip (1698–1731), 1st Duke of,
  145
Whately, Richard (1787–1863), archbishop,
  415
Whig party (1690s–1750s): and
  republicans, 46, 56, 132–3; and right
  of resistance, 47–8, 52; and Locke, 50;
  effect of dissolution, 194; ideology of,
  279–323.
Whiston, Rev. William (1667–1752), Arian,
  138, 164, 284–5, 288
Whitaker, Rev. John (1735–1808), 220,
  224, 249, 264
White's, 107–8
Whitefield, Rev. George (1714–70), 243
Whitmore, Jacobite undergraduate, 156
Whole Duty of Man, The, 126, 166, 243
Whole Duty of Man, The New, 126–7, 246n
Wilberforce, William (1759–1833) 109, 242,
  247, 344, 375, 380
Wilkes, John (1727–97), Deist, 43, 114,
  142, 237, 309–11, 317, 323, 324n,
  336–7, 382
Willem of Orange Nassau, Prince

Willem *cont.*
(1650–1702), from 1689 styled King William III of Great Britain: and party, 12, 26; and 1688 Revolution, 46, 253; and title of in America, 84; and ideology, 119ff; and King's Evil, 163n, 164; Johnson on, 187; defended by Deists, 294, 296
William IV, King, 75, 404, 411
Williams, David, Dissenter, 336
Williams, Thomas, 381
Willoughby de Broke, Rev. George Verney (1661–1728), 12th Baron, 286
Willoughby de Broke, Richard Verney (1869–1923), 19th Baron, on Etonians, 103
Winchelsea, George Hatton (1791–1858), 10th Earl of, 115n, 399
Winchester College, 152, 226n, 270n
Windham, William (1750–1810), MP, 265, 362, 364

Winnington, Thomas (1696–1746), MP, 132
Winterbotham, William, Dissenting minister, 346
witchcraft, 142, 169–71
Wollaston, Rev. William (1660–1724), 152
Wollstonecraft, Mary, 85
Woolston, Thomas (1670–1733), Deist, 283, 286, 299, 301, 380
Wordsworth, Christopher (1774–1846), bishop, 249
Wyvill, Rev. Christopher (1740–1822), Arian, 257, 338, 361–2, 384

Yates, Rev. Richard (1769–1834), 268n, 372n
York, HRH Frederick (1763–1827), 11th Duke of, 114n, 362, 390–1, 402
Yorke, Philip (1720–90), MP, 22
Yorkshire Association, 338–40
Young, Arthur (1741–1820), 96, 264

Cambridge Studies in the History and Theory of Politics

Editors: Maurice Cowling, G. R. Elton and J. R. Pole

A series in two parts, studies and original texts. The studies are original works on political history and political philosophy while the texts are modern, critical editions of major texts in political thought. The titles include:

TEXTS

Vladimir Akimov on the Dilemmas of Russian Marxism 1895–1903. An English edition of 'A Short History of the Social Democratic Movement in Russia' and 'The Second Congress of the Russian Social Democratic Labour Party', with an introduction and notes by Jonathan Frankel

J. G. Herder on Social and Political Culture, translated, edited and with an introduction by F. M. Barnard

Kant's Political Writings, edited with an introduction and notes by Hans Reiss; translated by H. B. Nisbet

Karl Marx's Critique of Hegel's 'Philosophy of Right', edited with an introduction and notes by Joseph O'Malley; translated by Annette Jolin and Joseph O'Malley

The Political Writings of Leibniz, edited and translated by Patrick Riley

Turgot on Progress, Sociology and Economics: A Philosophical Review of the Successive Advances of the Human Mind. On Universal History. Reflections on the Formation and Distribution of Wealth, edited, translated and introduced by Ronald L. Meek

Georg Wilhelm Friedrich Hegel: Lectures on the Philosophy of World History: Reason in History, translated from the German edition of Johannes Hoffmeister by H. B. Nisbet and with an introduction by Duncan Forbes

A Machiavellian Treatise by Stephen Gardiner, edited and translated by Peter S. Donaldson

The Political Works of James Harrington, edited by J. G. A. Pocock

Selected Writings of August Cieszkowski, edited and translated with an introductory essay by André Liebich

De Republica Anglorum by Sir Thomas Smith, edited by Mary Dewar

Sister Peg: A Pamphlet Hitherto Unknown by David Hume, edited with an introduction and notes by David R. Raynor

1867: Disraeli, Gladstone and Revolution: The Passing of the Second Reform Bill, by Maurice Cowling

The Social and Political Thought of Karl Marx, by Shlomo Avineri

Idealism, Politics and History: Sources of Hegelian Thought, by George Armstrong Kelly

Alienation: Marx's Conception of Man in Capitalist Society, by Bertell Ollman

Hegel's Theory of the Modern State, by Shlomo Avineri

The Impact of Hitler: British Politics and British Policy 1933–1940, by Maurice Cowling

The Liberal Mind 1914–1929, by Michael Bentley

Revolution Principles: The Politics of Party 1689–1720, by J. P. Kenyon

John Locke and the Theory of Sovereignty: Mixed Monarchy and the Right of Resistance in the Political Thought of the English Revolution, by Julian H. Franklin

Adam Smith's Politics: An Essay in Historiographic Revision, by Donald Winch

Lloyd George's Secretariat, by John Turner

The Tragedy of Enlightenment: An Essay on the Frankfurt School, by Paul Connerton

Religion and Public Doctrine in Modern England, by Maurice Cowling

Bentham and Bureaucracy, by L. J. Hume

A Critique of Freedom and Equality, by John Charvet

The Dynamics of Change: The Crisis of the 1750s and English Party Systems, by J. C. D. Clark

Resistance and Compromise: The Political Thought of the Elizabethan Catholics, by P. J. Holmes

Nationalism, Positivism and Catholicism: The Politics of Charles Maurras and French Catholics, 1890–1914, by Michael Sutton

The Christian Polity of John Calvin, by Harro Höpfl

Sir John Davis and the Conquest of Ireland: A Study in Legal Imperialism, by Hans S. Pawlisch

Religion and Public Doctrine in Modern England, Volume 2: 'Assaults', by Maurice Cowling

English Society 1688–1832: Ideology, Social Structure and Political Practice during the Ancien Regime, by J. C. D. Clark

Democracy and Religion: Gladstone and the Liberal Party, 1867–1875, by J. P. Parry

A Protestant Vision: William Harrison and the Reformation of Elizabethan England, by G. J. R. Parry